P9-ECO-923

DISCOURSES OF BRIGHAM YOUNG

Brigham Young

DISCOURSES
OF
BRIGHAM YOUNG

SECOND PRESIDENT OF THE CHURCH
OF JESUS CHRIST
OF LATTER-DAY SAINTS

"I am called to preach the Gospel of Life and Salvation."

—*Journal of Discourses*, Vol. 8, p. 11

Selected and Arranged
By
JOHN A. WIDTSOE

EDITION OF 1951

DESERET BOOK COMPANY
Salt Lake City, Utah

PRINTED IN THE UNITED STATES OF AMERICA
BY THE DESERET NEWS PRESS

PREFACE

BRIGHAM YOUNG, second President of the Church of Jesus Christ of Latter-day Saints, and first Governor of Utah, was the founder and chief builder of the Great Intermountain West of the United States of America. He is recognized as one of the foremost colonizers and empire builders of all time. His unsurpassed methods of conquering for human use the Great American Desert have been adopted to some degree by all who, since his day, have been engaged in the reclamation and settlement of unoccupied lands, especially under a low rainfall. Statesmen, scholars and business men have acclaimed the leadership, organizing power and sound philosophy which brought social and economic happiness to the people who were led into the wilderness by Brigham Young. He not only brought contentment to the people, gathered from many lands, but he guided the Church over which he presided, until, at his death, it was larger in numbers and more firmly established than ever before.

The tremendous world significance of the labors of Brigham Young, and the universal applicability of his methods, under modern conditions, make it certain that the work he accomplished was not due, primarily, to the gigantic personality of the man. Rather, the success achieved must have been due to the possession of a life philosophy of sufficient depth and extent to meet varying human needs. Another man, of less dominant personality, armed with the same principles, would have won success. As he, himself, would say, it was the possession of the Gospel of Life and Salvation that enabled him and his associates to do the work so well. In fact, Brigham Young was first a spiritual teacher and secondly a material leader. The religion that he professed made him the man that he became; its principles were used in guiding the people in all their affairs.

Books enough to fill a library have been written about the history, character and accomplishments of Brigham Young. Few of these books attempt to analyze the system of doctrine and practice that brought unbounded success to the Latter-day Saints. Many display such extreme religious partisanship that even the sympathetic reader can place no reliance upon their statements. Something harsher might be said about the large number of books written about Brigham Young and his times that manifestly aim to secure popularity by appealing to the sensational and lurid, at the expense of truth. Even recently, when the years have given perspective, some writers have set up hypotheses concerning Brigham Young, and have proceeded to argue the case—as if that were history! It is amazing that intelligent people, knowing the high order of accomplishments of the Latter-day Saints, give credence to the weird and crude stories, appealing to the baser emotions of mankind, which fill the pages of anti-"Mormon" literature.

In this book Brigham Young is allowed to speak for himself. Excerpts have been made from his many discourses, and these have been arranged to show the coherent system of faith which he continuously taught his people and by which he was enabled to win success for his followers. The philosophy thus set forth is clear and unmistakable in its purpose. It reveals Brigham Young as a man who applied the simple principles of the Gospel of Jesus Christ to the everyday affairs of men; and who proved the efficacy in common life, among common men, of the Gospel of the Son of God.

This book was made possible because Brigham Young secured stenographic reports of his addresses. As he traveled among the people, reporters accompanied him. All that he said was recorded. Practically all of these discourses (from December 16, 1851, to August 19, 1877) were published in the *Journal of Discourses*, which was widely distributed. The public utterances of few great historical figures have been so faithfully and fully preserved. Clearly, this mass of material, covering nearly thirty years of incessant public speaking, could not be presented with any hope of serving the general reader, save in the form of selections of essential doctrines.

The discourses, from which this volume has been culled, were spoken extemporaneously. The state papers of Governor Brigham Young, and the epistles signed by him and his counselors in the Presidency of the Church, have not been used in this collection. The excerpts here presented came from his lips under the inspiration, at the moment, of the Power that guided his life. The corrections for the printer, as shown by existing manuscripts, were few and of minor consequence. The discourses are a remarkable self-revelation of the character and moving impulses of a man who accomplished huge tasks for his generation. It is marvelous that the enemies of Brigham Young, with this wealth of material before them, have found so little to use to his disadvantage. But, a dishonest or insincere man would not have had his public utterances reported and published all over the world. The consistency of the views presented, from the first to the last discourse, would be astounding, were it not for the fact that he clung constantly for interpretation to the Gospel of Jesus Christ as he had been taught it by the Prophet Joseph Smith. His devotion to his teacher and predecessor, the Prophet, is tenderly beautiful.

The school education of Brigham Young was very limited, but his discourses show a wide knowledge of men and affairs and an excellent power to use the English language clearly and forcefully. Often, his simple eloquence rises to great heights. Those who heard him speak have declared that they were held in tense attention, however long the address might be. His vivid imagination, dramatic power and unquestioned sincerity made him a natural orator. He seldom confined himself to one subject in his discourses. The needs of the day were the themes about which he wound his teachings.

No liberties have been taken, in this book, with the words of Brigham Young. In a few instances, errors in language or spelling, which should have been caught by the printer, have been corrected. All distinct sentiments, as expressed in the discourses, are represented by one or more quotations, except such as refer to conditions now no longer existing. The excerpts are confined to the principles of the Gospel. The mass of historical and autobiographical detail could not be included without making this volume too large for popular use. As it is, severe pruning and elimination have been employed to enable the inclusion of the message of each of the 363 addresses in the *Journal of Discourses*, and the many others printed in the *Deseret News*, the *Millennial Star* and other periodicals. The many summaries of Brigham Young's discourses, appearing in the *Deseret News*, have not been used. The excerpts contained in this volume are from verbatim reports. The figures at the end of each excerpt indicate the volume and page of the *Journal of Discourses*.

These discourses are Brigham Young's witness to the existence of God, the divine mission of Jesus the Christ, the restoration of the Gospel in its fulness by Joseph Smith, the Prophet, and the possibility of securing happiness here and hereafter by obedience to the requirements of the Gospel. This volume is but another testimony that the Lord continues to speak through his prophets.

PREFACE TO SECOND EDITION

The reception of this book far surpassed the hopes of the publishers. The first edition of fifteen thousand was soon exhausted. The second edition of ten thousand is the same as the first edition except for some minor letter corrections.

THE PUBLISHERS.

Feb. 15, 1926.

This 1941 Edition is the same as the previous edition, except as to size of type and the format.

THE PUBLISHERS.

Nov. 15, 1941.

CONTENTS

CHAPTER VIII
The Destiny of Man

CHAPTER IX
Dispensations of the Gospel

CHAPTER X
The Last Days

CHAPTER XI
The Scriptures

CHAPTER XII
The Priesthood

CHAPTER XIII
The First Principles of the Gospel

CHAPTER XIV
The Sabbath, Meetings, the Sacrament

CHAPTER XV
Tithing, the United Order

CHAPTER XVI
The Word of Wisdom

CHAPTER XVII
The Family

CHAPTER XVIII
Some Womanly Duties

CHAPTER XIX
Obedience

CHAPTER XX
Gratitude, Humility, Devotion, Liberality, Honesty

CHAPTER XXI
Happiness and Social Enjoyments

CHAPTER XXII
Education

CHAPTER XXIII
Self-Control

CHAPTER XXIV

Our Fellow-Men

CHAPTER XXV

Unity and Co-operation

CHAPTER XXVI

Thrift and Industry

CHAPTER XXVII

Wealth

CHAPTER XXVIII

Missionary Work

CHAPTER XXIX

Visions, Mysteries and Miracles

CHAPTER XXX

Trials and Persecution

CHAPTER XXXI

Political Government

CHAPTER XXXII

Death and Resurrection

CHAPTER XXXIII

The Spirit World

CHAPTER XXXIV

Eternal Judgment

CHAPTER XXXV

Salvation

CHAPTER XXXVI

Temples and Salvation for the Dead

CHAPTER XXXVII

MAN'S SEARCH FOR TRUTH AND SALVATION

CHAPTER XXXVIII

TESTIMONY OF THE TRUTH

CHAPTER XXXIX

THE CHURCH AND KINGDOM OF GOD ON EARTH

CHAPTER XL

SOME EFFECTS OF THE GOSPEL

CHAPTER XLI

JOSEPH SMITH THE PROPHET

CHAPTER XLII

THE SETTLEMENT IN THE WEST

DISCOURSES OF BRIGHAM YOUNG

CHAPTER I

THE GOSPEL DEFINED

Composed of Eternal Laws—The Gospel of the Son of God that has been revealed is a plan or system of laws and ordinances, by strict obedience to which the people who inhabit this earth are assured that they may return again into the presence of the Father and the Son. 13:233.*

The laws of the Gospel are neither more nor less than a few of the principles of eternity revealed to the people, by which they can return to heaven from whence they came. We delight in the heavenly law—in that law that will preserve us to all eternity. 8:208.

The laws and ordinances which the Lord has revealed in these latter days, are calculated to save all the sons and daughters of Adam and Eve who have not sinned against the Holy Ghost, for all will be saved in a kingdom of glory, though it may not be in the celestial kingdom, for there are many mansions. 15:122.

Our religion is nothing more nor less than the true order of heaven—the system of laws by which the gods and the angels are governed. Are they governed by law? Certainly. There is no being in all the eternities but what is governed by law. Who desires to have liberty and no law? They who are from beneath. 14:280.

Our religion, in common with everything of which God is the Author, is a system of law and order. He has instituted laws and ordinances for the government and benefit of the children of men, to see if they would obey them and prove themselves worthy of eternal life by the law of the celestial worlds. This holy Priesthood that we talk about is a perfect system of government. By obedience to these laws we expect to enter the celestial kingdom and to be exalted. 14:95.

The principles of truth and goodness, and of eternal lives and the power of God are from eternity to eternity. The principle of falsehood and wickedness, the power of the Devil and the power of death are also from eternity to eternity. These two powers have ever existed

*The numbers at the end of each excerpt refer to the volume and page of the *Journal of Discourses*. Where the excerpt occurs thus, 13:233, it means *Journal of Discourses*, Volume 13, page 233.

and always will exist in all the eternities that are yet to come. 11:234.

Embraces All Truth—Our religion measures, weighs, and circumscribes all the wisdom in the world—all that God has ever revealed to man. God has revealed all the truth that is now in the possession of the world, whether it be scientific or religious. The whole world are under obligation to him for what they know and enjoy; they are indebted to him for it all, and I acknowledge him in all things. 8:162.

I want to say to my friends that we believe in all good. If you can find a truth in heaven, earth or hell, it belongs to our doctrine. We believe it; it is ours; we claim it. 13:335.

In a word, if "Mormonism" is not my life, I do not know that I have any. I do not understand anything else, for it embraces everything that comes within the range of the understanding of man. If it does not circumscribe every thing that is in heaven and on earth, it is not what it purports to be. 2:123.

Our religion is simply the truth. It is all said in this one expression—it embraces all truth, wherever found, in all the works of God and man that are visible or invisible to mortal eye. 10:251.

The Gospel is simple, it is plain.

There is no mystery throughout the whole plan of salvation, only to those who do not understand. 3:367.

"Mormonism" embraces all truth that is revealed and that is unrevealed, whether religious, political, scientific, or philosophical. 9:149.

It comprehends all true science known by man, angels, and the gods. There is one true system and science of life; all else tends to death. That system emanates from the Fountain of life. 8:70.

True science, true art and true knowledge comprehend all that are in heaven or on the earth, or in all eternities. By these all beings exist, whether they be celestial, terrestrial, or telestial; or whether they are from beneath and dwell with the devils among the damned. All truth is ours. 14:281.

"Where is your code, your particular creed?" says one. It fills eternity; it is all truth in heaven, on earth or in hell. This is "Mormonism." It embraces every true science; all true philosophy. 14:280.

The philosophy of the heavens and the earth of the worlds that are, that were, and that are yet to come into existence, is all the Gospel that we have embraced. Every true philosopher, so far as he understands the principles of truth, has so much of the Gospel and so far he is a Latter-day Saint, whether he knows it or not. Our Father, the great God, is the author of the sciences, he is the great mechanic, he is the systematizer of all things, he plans and devises all things, and every particle of knowledge which man has in his possession is the gift of God, whether they consider it divine, or whether it is the wisdom of man; it belongs to God, and he has bestowed it upon us, his children, dwelling here upon the earth. 18:359.

A fact is a fact, all truth issues forth from the Fountain of truth, and the sciences are facts as far as men have proved them. 14:117.

"Mormonism," so-called, embraces every principle pertaining to life and salvation, for time and eternity. No matter who has it. If the infidel has got truth it belongs to "Mormonism." The truth and sound doctrine possessed by the sectarian world, and they have a great deal, all belong to this Church. As for their morality, many of them are, morally, just as good as we are. All that is good, lovely, and praiseworthy belongs to this Church and Kingdom. "Mormonism" includes all truth. There is no truth but what belongs to the Gospel. It is life, eternal life; it is bliss; it is the fulness of all things in the gods and in the eternities of the gods. 11:375.

We wish to frame, fashion and build after the pattern that God has revealed; and in doing so we take all the laws, rules, ordinances and regulations contained in the Scriptures and practice them as far as possible, and then keep learning and improving until we can live by every word that proceeds out of the mouth of God. 13:238.

The Lord reveals a little here and a little there, line upon line, and he will continue to do so until we can reach into eternity and embrace a fulness of his glory, excellency and power. 13:241.

Truth will endure for ever and for ever, and every man that preaches the Gospel of salvation may take the old text that some of us took in the commencement of the building up of the Kingdom of God upon the earth in the last days. I took truth for my text, salvation for my subject, and the whole world for my circuit, to go as far as I could and talk all I could about it. It takes every truth from every sect and party. What! in a civil capacity also? Yes. All law, all powers, all kingdoms, and all thrones,—in fine, all things are under the control of God. 7:148.

When the Gospel of the Son of God is introduced among the children of men, it comes with light and intelligence, with pure and holy principles. It embraces all mortality, all virtue, all light, all intelligence, all greatness, and all goodness. It introduces a system of laws and ordinances and a code of moral rectitude which, if obeyed by the human family, will lead them back to the presence of God. 11:235.

For me, the plan of salvation must be a system that is pure and holy in all its points; it must reveal things that no other church or kingdom can reveal; it must circumscribe the knowledge that is upon the face of the earth, or it is not from God. Such a plan incorporates every system of true doctrine on the earth, whether it be ecclesiastical, moral, philosophical, or civil; it incorporates all good laws that have been made from the days of Adam until now; it swallows up the laws of nations, for it exceeds them all in knowledge and purity; it circumscribes the doctrines of the day, and takes from the right and the left, and brings all truth together in one system, and leaves the chaff to be scattered hither and thither. That is the proof to me, and has been from the beginning, that the principles are pure and holy; and every person living to them will attain through them sanctification. 7:148.

I will tell you who the real fanatics are: they are they who adopt false principles and ideas as facts, and try to establish a superstructure upon a false foundation. They are the fanatics; and however ardent and zealous they may be, they may reason or argue on false premises till doomsday, and the result will be false. 13:271.

Increasing Knowledge of Gospel—I want to say that we are for the truth, the whole truth and nothing but the truth; we are pursuing the path of truth, and by and by we expect to possess a great deal more than we do now; but to say that we shall ever possess all truth, I pause; I do not know when. 14:196.

The laws that the Lord has given are not fully perfect, because the people could not receive them in their perfect fulness; but they can receive a little here and a little there, a little today and a little tomorrow, a little more next week, and a little more in advance of that next year, if they make a wise improvement upon every little they receive; if they do not, they are left in the shade, and the light which the Lord reveals will appear darkness to them, and the kingdom of heaven will travel on and leave them groping. Hence, if we wish to act upon the fulness of the knowledge that the Lord designs to reveal, little by little, to the inhabitants of the earth, we must improve upon every little as it is revealed. 2:314.

We know enough to damn us; and when we know enough for that, we know enough to save us, if that knowledge is improved upon. 6:198.

Holds Power of Priesthood—The Gospel which we preach is the Gospel of life and salvation. The Church which we represent is the Church and Kingdom of God, and possesses the only faith by which the children of men can be brought back into the presence of our Father and God. The Lord has set his hands to restore all things as in the beginning, and by the administration of his holy Priesthood, save all who can be saved, cleanse from the world the consequences of the Fall and give it to the hands of his Saints. 12:205.

The Gospel of salvation—the Priesthood of the Son of God—is so ordered and organized, in the very nature of it, being a portion of that law of heaven by which worlds are organized, that it is calculated to enlighten the children of men and give them power to save themselves. It is of the same nature as the further principles of eternal existence by which the worlds are and were, and by which they will endure; and these principles are pure in their nature, from the fact that they are of God, who is pure; but, without the revelation of the Spirit of God, no man can understand them. That is the peculiarity there is about this mysterious work. 7:54.

The power of all truth dwells in the bosom of our Father and God, which he dispenses to his children as he will, by the means of his eternal Priesthood. He is enthroned in the light, glory and power of truth. He has abided the truth, and is thereby exalted, and his power, light and glory are eternal. The Gospel and the Priesthood are the means he employs to save and exalt his obedient children to the possession with him of the same glory and power to be crowned with crowns of glory, immortality and eternal lives. 9:330.

Now, we say to the people of the nineteenth century, and we speak the truth and lie not, whosoever believes that Joseph Smith, Junior, was a Prophet sent of God, and was ordained by him to receive and hold the keys of the holy Priesthood, which is after the order of the Son of God, and power to build up the Kingdom of God upon the earth, to gather the House of Israel, to guide all who believe and obey to redemption, to restore that which has been lost through transgression—whosoever believes this, believing in the Lord, and obeying his commandments to the end of their lives, their names shall not be blotted out of the Lamb's book of life, and they shall receive crowns of glory, immortality, and eternal life. This is for the nineteenth century, for the generation of people now living. 12:101.

The Gospel of Life and Salvation—We have something more than morality alone to teach the people. What is it? It is how to redeem the human family. 19:47.

I will now say to my friends,—and I call you all, and all mankind, friends, until you have proved yourselves enemies,—you who do not belong to this Church, that we have got the Gospel of life and salvation. I do not say that we have a Gospel, but I say that we have the definite and only Gospel that ever was or ever will be that will save the children of men. 12:313 .

It Takes the Whole Man to Make a Saint—There are no exceptions in "Mormonism." Learn so to think and direct your acts in every transaction of life, that we may overcome the evil that is sown within us. Overcome the inward enemy; then we can overcome the Devil's kingdom. And while others choose evil principles and build upon a foundation which leads to destruction, let us build upon the principles of eternal salvation, as we have striven to do all the day long. 7:66.

The doctrines of salvation are the same now as they were in the days of Adam, or Elijah, or Jesus, when he was upon the earth. 5:229.

We have brought the doctrine of life and salvation to you, that you may exchange your low, narrow, contracted, selfish dispositions for the ennobling Spirit of the Lord, for the Spirit of the Gospel, which gives joy and peace. If you enjoy that, your food will be sweet to you, your sleep will be refreshing, and your days will pass away in usefulness. 3:119.

We have as good a right to adopt tenets in our religion as the Church of England, or the Methodists, or Baptists, or any other denomination have in theirs. Our doctrine is a Bible doctrine, a patriarchal doctrine, and is the doctrine of the gods of eternity, and of the heavens, and was revealed to our fathers on the earth, and will save the world at last. 2:187.

The revelations of the Lord Jesus Christ are sweeter than honey or the honeycomb. We can eat, and continue to eat; drink, and continue to drink. Is there durable satisfaction? Yes. I am in the height of my enjoyment. All the pleasure and all the joy that can be bestowed upon a finite being is in the Gospel of salvation, through the Spirit of revelation, upon the creature—upon the Saint of God—old or young, male or female. Not that this comparison fully conveys the idea; for the language of mortals fails to fully portray the joys of the Gospel of life everlasting. 8:139.

We have the Gospel of life and salvation, to make bad men good and good men better. We are to preach, exhort, expound, continue in our duty, be fervent in spirit, bearing and forbearing with our brethren, being filled with love and kindness. 8:130.

There is no freedom anywhere outside the Gospel of salvation. 5:52.

Offers Salvation to All—A few here and a few there will receive the truth, and the Lord will empty the earth of the wickedness that now dwells upon it. 8:195.

The Gospel of Jesus Christ is the opening avenue—the open gate in the road or way from earth to heaven, through which direct revelation comes to the children of men in their various capacities, according to their callings and standing in the society in which they live. The Gospel of salvation is a portion of the law that pertains to the kingdom where God resides; and the ordinances pertaining to the holy Priesthood are the means by which the children of men find access to the way of life, wherein they can extend their travels until they return to the presence of their Father and God. 8:159.

"But as many as received him, to them gave he power to continue to be the sons of God." Instead of receiving the Gospel to become the sons of God, my language would be—to receive the Gospel that we may continue to be the sons of God. Are we not all sons of God when we are born into this world? Old Pharaoh, King of Egypt, was just as much a son of God as Moses and Aaron were his sons, with this difference—he rejected the word of the Lord, the true light, and they received it. For "this is the condemnation, that light is come into the world, and men love darkness rather than light, because their deeds are evil." Then we receive not the Gospel that we may become the sons of God but that we may remain the sons of God without rebuke. Inasmuch as all had apostatized, they had to become the sons of God by adoption, still, originally, all were the sons of God. We receive the Gospel, not that we may have our names written in the Lamb's book of life, but that our names may not be blotted out of that book. "For," saith the Lord, "He that overcometh, the same shall be clothed in white raiment, and I will not blot out his name out of the book of life." Why? Because he had overcome through his faithfulness. My doctrine is—that there never was a son and daughter of Adam and Eve born on this earth whose names were not already written in the Lamb's book of life, and there they will remain until their conduct is such that the angel who keeps the record is authorized to blot them out and record them elsewhere. 12:100-101.

In conversation not long since with a visitor who was returning to the Eastern States, said he, "You, as a people consider that you are perfect?" "Oh no;" said I, "not by any means. Let me define to you. The doctrine that we have embraced is perfect; but when we come to the people, we have just as many imperfections as you can ask for. We are not perfect; but the Gospel that we preach is calculated to perfect the people so that they can obtain a glorious resurrection and enter into the presence of the Father and the Son." 11:304.

Our motive is to make every man and woman to know just as much as we do; this is the plan of the Gospel, and this is what I would like to do. I would like all the Latter-day Saints to come up to this standard, and know as much as I do, and then just as much more as they can learn, and if they can get ahead of me, all right. 19:96.

We declare it to all the inhabitants of the earth from the valleys in the tops of these mountains that we are the Church of Jesus Christ of Latter-day Saints—not a church but the Church—and we have the doctrine of life and salvation for all the honest-in-heart in all the world. 12:173.

This Gospel will save the whole human family; the blood of

Jesus will atone for our sins, if we accept the terms he has laid down, but we must accept those terms or else it will avail nothing in our behalf.

A Guide in Daily Life—I reduce the Gospel to the present time, circumstances and condition of the people. 10:1.

That system that brings present security and peace is the best to live by, and the best to die by; it is the best for doing business; it is the best for making farms, for building cities and temples, and that system is the law of God. But it requires strict obedience. The rule of right, and the line which God has drawn for the people to walk by insures peace, comfort, and happiness now and eternal glory and exaltation; but nothing short of strict obedience to God's law will do this. 13:241.

We do not allow ourselves to go into a field to plough without taking our religion with us; we do not go into an office, behind the counter to deal out goods, into a counting house with the books, or anywhere to attend to or transact any business without taking our religion with us. If we are railroading or on a pleasure trip our God and our religion must be with us. We are the most religious people in the world; but we are not so enthusiastic as some are. We have seen plenty of enthusiasm, but we do not care about it. Said I, "This shouting and singing one's self away to everlasting bliss, may be all very well in its place, but this alone is folly to me; my religion is to know the will of God and do it." 14:118.

With God, and also with those who understand the principles of life and salvation, the Priesthood, the oracles of truth and the gifts and callings of God to the children of men, there is no difference in spiritual and temporal labors—all are one. If I am in the line of my duty, I am doing the will of God, whether I am preaching; praying; laboring with my hands for an honorable support; whether I am in the field, mechanic's shop, or following mercantile business, or wherever duty calls, I am serving God as much in one place as another; and so it is with all, each in his place, turn and time. 13:260.

Our religion descends to the whole life of man, although some, sometimes, say, there is divine law, there is human law, and there are principles which pertain to our religion and there are principles which pertain to the philosophy of the world. But let me here say to you, that the philosophy of the religion of heaven incorporates every truth that there is in heaven, on earth, or in hell. 15:125.

My mission to the people is to teach them with regard to their every-day lives. I presume there are many here who have heard me say, years and years ago, that I cared very little about what will take place after the Millennium. Elders may preach long discourses concerning what took place in the days of Adam, what occurred before the creation, and what will take place thousands of years from now, talking of things which have occurred or that will occur yet, of which they are ignorant, feeding the people on wind; but that is not my method of teaching. My desire is to teach the people what they should do now, and let the Millennium take care of itself. To teach them to serve God and to build up his Kingdom is my mission. I have taught faith, repentance, baptism for the remission of sins, and the laying on of hands for the reception of the Holy Ghost. We are to be taught with regard to our every-day life in a temporal point of view. 12:228.

Our religion incorporates every act and word of man. No man should go to merchandising unless he does it in God; no man should go to farming or any other business unless he does it in the Lord. No man of council should sit to judge the people but what should judge in the Lord, that he may righteously and impartially discern between right and wrong, truth and error, light and darkness, justice and injustice. Should any legislature sit without the Lord? If it do, sooner or later it will fall to pieces. No nation ever did live that counseled and transacted its national affairs without the Lord, but what sooner or later went to pieces and came to naught. The same is true of all the nations that now live or ever will live. 13:60.

This Gospel is full of good sense, judgment, discretion and intelligence. 14:17.

No matter how true and beautiful truth is, you have to take the passions of the people and mould them to the law of God. 7:55.

A *Fountain of Truth*—The Gospel is a fountain of truth, and truth is what we are after. We have embraced the truth—namely, the Gospel of the Son of God. Its first principles are to believe in the Lord Jesus Christ, to repent of our sins, then go down into the waters of baptism for the remission of our sins, and have hands laid upon us for the reception of the Holy Ghost, which will lead us into all truth. 12:68.

Truth will abide when error passes away. Life will remain when they who have rejected the words of eternal life are swallowed up in death. I like the truth because it is true, because it is lovely and delightful, because it is so glorious in its nature, and so worthy the admiration, faith and consideration of all intelligent beings in heaven or on the earth. Should I be hated and my name cast out as evil because I love the truth? Yes, or the words of Jesus could not be fulfilled, for he said, "Ye shall be hated of all men for my name's sake." He told his disciples to rejoice evermore and to pray without ceasing when they were held in derision by their enemies, and to lift up their heads and rejoice when all men spoke evil of them, for "behold your redemption draweth nigh." 13:216.

To me it is more rational for an intelligent being to embrace truth, than it is to mix up a little truth with a great deal of error, or to embrace all error and undertake to follow a phantom. 13:235.

Some who call themselves Christians are very tenacious with regard to the Universalians, yet the latter possess many excellent ideas and good truths. Have the Catholics? Yes, a great many very excellent truths. Have the Protestants? Yes, from first to last. Has the infidel? Yes, he has a good deal of truth; and truth is all over the earth. The earth could not stand but for the light and truth it contains. The people could not abide were it not that truth holds them. It is the Fountain of truth that feeds, clothes, and gives light and intelligence to the inhabitants of the earth, no matter whether they are saints or sinners. Do you think there is any truth in hell? Yes, a great deal, and where truth is there we calculate the Lord has a right to be. You will not find the Lord where there is no truth. 12:70.

If you love the truth you can remember it. 3:358.

Again, what do you love truth for? Is it because you can discover a beauty in it, because it is congenial to you; or because you think it will make you a ruler, or a Lord? If you conceive that you will attain to power upon such a motive, you are much mistaken. It is a trick of the unseen power, that is abroad amongst the inhabitants of the earth, that leads them astray, binds their minds, and subverts their understanding.

Suppose that our Father in heaven, our Elder Brother, the risen Redeemer, the Savior of the world, or any of the gods of eternity should act upon this principle, to love truth, knowledge, and wisdom, because they are all powerful, and by the aid of this power they could send devils to hell, torment the people of the earth, exercise sovereignty over them, and make them miserable at their pleasure; they would cease to be Gods; and as fast as they adopted and acted upon such principles, they would become devils, and be thrust down in the twinkling of an eye; the extension of their kingdom would cease, and their Godhead come to an end. 1:117.

No man can disprove a truth. 8:132.

What do you know on natural principles? I do not say natural philosophy, because my religion is natural philosophy. You never heard me preach a doctrine but what has a natural system to it, and, when understood, is as easy to comprehend as that two and two equal four. All the revelations of the Lord Almighty to the children of men, and all revealed doctrines of salvation are upon natural principles, upon natural philosophy. When I use this term, I use it as synonymous with the plan of salvation; natural philosophy is the plan of salvation, and the plan of salvation is natural philosophy. 4:202.

Our doctrine and practice is, and I have made it mine through life—to receive truth no matter where it comes from. 14:160.

When we demonstrate a truth, we demonstrate a portion of the faith, law, or power by which all intelligent beings exist, whether in heaven or on earth, consequently when we have truth in our possession we have so much of the knowledge of God. I delight in this, because truth is calculated to sustain itself; it is based upon eternal facts and will endure, while all else will, sooner or later, perish. 14:115.

All truth is worthy and worth possessing. 19:39.

How easy it is to live by the truth. Did you ever think of it, my friends? Did you ever think of it, my brethren and sisters? In every circumstance of life, no matter whether among the humblest or lofty, truth is always the surest guide and the easiest to square our lives by. 14:76.

Be willing to receive the truth, let it come from whom it may; no difference, not a particle. Just as soon receive the Gospel from Joseph Smith as from Peter, who lived in the days of Jesus. Receive it from one man as soon as another. If God has called an individual and sent him to preach the Gospel that is enough for me to know; it is no matter who it is, all I want is to know the truth. 14:136.

All truth is for the salvation of the children of men—for the benefit and learning—for their furtherance in the principles of divine knowledge; and divine knowledge is any matter of fact—truth; and all truth pertains to divinity. 7:284.

We Need a Practical Religion—I am preaching to you practical religion. 13:155.

I am decidedly in favor of practical religion—of everyday useful life. And if I today attend to what devolves upon me to do, and then do that which presents itself tomorrow, and so on, when eternity comes I will be prepared to enter on the things of eternity. But I would not be prepared for that sphere of action, unless I could manage the things that are now within my reach. You must all learn to do this. 5:3.

I still feel to urge upon the Latter-day Saints the necessity of a close application of the principles of the Gospel in our lives, conduct and words and all that we do; and it requires the whole man, the whole life to be devoted to improvement in order to come to knowledge of the truth as it is in Jesus Christ. Herein is the fulness of perfection. It was couched in the character of our Savior; although but a scanty portion of it was made manifest to the people, in consequence of their not being able to receive it. All they were prepared to receive he gave them. All we are prepared to receive the Lord gives us; all that the nations of the earth are prepared to receive he imparts unto them. 12:255-256.

On reading carefully the Old and New Testaments we can discover that the majority of the revelations given to mankind anciently were in regard to their daily duties; we follow in the same path. The revelations contained in the Bible and the Book of Mormon are examples to us, and the book of Doctrine and Covenants contains direct revelation to this Church; they are a guide to us, and we do not wish to do them away; we do not want them to become obsolete and to set them aside. We wish to continue in the revelations of the Lord Jesus Christ day by day, and to have his Spirit with us continually. If we can do this, we shall no more walk in darkness but we shall walk in the light of life. 10:284.

If we wish to enjoy the Spirit of Zion, we must live for it. Our religion is not merely theory; it is a practical religion, to bring present enjoyment to every heart. 8:33.

At times when I think of addressing you, it occurs to me that strict sermonizing upon topics pertaining to the distant future, or reviewing the history of the past, will doubtless please and highly interest a portion of my hearers; but my judgment and the spirit of intelligence that is in me teach that, by taking such a course, the people could not be instructed pertaining to their every-day duties. For this reason, I do not feel impressed to instruct you on duties to be performed a hundred years hence, but rather to give those instructions pertaining to the present, to our daily walk and conversation, that we may know how to benefit ourselves under the passing time, and present privileges, and be able to lay a foundation for future happiness. 3:272.

The work of building up Zion is in every sense a practical work; it is not a mere theory. A theoretical religion amounts to very little real good or advantage to any person. To possess an inheritance in Zion or in Jerusalem only in theory—only in imagination—would be the same as having no inheritance at all. It is necessary to get a deed of it, to make an inheritance practical, substantial and profitable. Then let us not rest contented with a mere theoretical religion, but let it be practical, self-purifying, self-sustaining, keeping the love of God with us, walking by every precept, by every law, and by every word that is given to lead us. 9:284.

The religion of Jesus Christ is a matter-of-fact religion, and taketh hold of the every-day duties and realities of this life. 11:133.

I am in the hands of the Lord, and never trouble myself about my salvation, or what the Lord will do with me hereafter. It is for me to do the will of God today, and when tomorrow comes, to inquire what is his will concerning me; then do the will of my Father in the work he has appointed me to do, and that is enough for me. I am serving a God who will give me all I merit, when I come to receive my reward. This is what I have always thought; and if I still think so, it is enough for me. 6:276.

Temporal Labors are Necessary—In the mind of God there is no such a thing as dividing spiritual from temporal, or temporal from spiritual; for they are one in the Lord. 11:18.

The brethren have been talking about temporal things. We cannot talk about spiritual things without connecting with them temporal things, neither can we talk about temporal things without connecting spiritual things with them. They are inseparably connected. 10:329.

I cannot, however, define any difference between temporal and spiritual labors. I call it spiritual to accommodate my language to the ideas of the people. Anything that pertains to the building up of the Lord's kingdom on earth, whether it be in preaching the Gospel or building temples to his name, we have been taught to consider a spiritual work, though it evidently requires the strength of the natural body to perform it. 2:95.

Be wise: be as wise as the generations of this world. In the days of Jesus, those who received the kingdom and the spirit of the kingdom seemed to lose all sight of a temporal salvation; and Jesus said to his disciples, "The children of this world are wiser in their generations than the children of light." The children of light did not know how to sustain themselves; they did not understand how to preserve themselves and the kingdom with them. 4:343.

If you cannot provide for your natural lives, how can you expect to have wisdom to obtain eternal lives? God has given you your existence—your body and spirit, and has blest you with ability, and thereby laid the foundation of all knowledge, wisdom, and understanding, and all glory and eternal lives. If you have not attained ability to provide for your natural wants, and for a wife and a few children, what have you to do with heavenly things? 8:68.

We cannot even enter the temple when it is built, and perform those ordinances which lead to spiritual blessings, without performing a temporal labor. Temporal ordinances must be performed to secure the spiritual blessings the Great Supreme has in store for his faithful children. Every act is first a temporal act. The Apostle says, faith comes by hearing. What should be heard to produce faith? The preaching of the Word. For that we must have a preacher; and he is not an invisible spirit, but a temporal, ordinary man like ourselves, and subject to the same regulations and rules of life. To preach the Gospel is a temporal labor, and to believe on the Lord Jesus Christ is the result of a temporal labor. To be baptized is a temporal labor, both to the person administered to and the administrator. I am a living witness to the truth of this statement, for I have made my feet sore many a time, and tired myself out traveling and preaching, that by hearing the Gospel the people might have faith. The blessings we so earnestly desire will come to us by performing the manual labor required, and thus preparing all things necessary to receive the invisible blessings Jehovah has for his children. 9:240.

There is a natural body, and there is a spiritual body. All things are natural, and all are spiritual. Every duty of life, no matter what it is, every requirement necessary to sustain and exalt man, is incorporated in the Kingdom of God and in the ordinances of his house—in the duties God requires of his children. It is all in the Church and Kingdom of our God. "What! our labor?" Yes. I sometimes take the liberty of preaching upon economy to this people. Perhaps some are inclined to think that in so doing I transcend my own duties and obligations. I do not. I instruct the husbandman how to till his farm, because I know and understand the nature of the elements that produce grain better than he does. I know how he should prepare the elements for the seed to produce the increase which he desires in the things necessary to sustain himself and family. It is my duty to instruct my brethren, if I understand any branch of business better than they do. If I understand how to make myself comfortable—if I understand better than others do the organization of the elements God has given us ability to operate with for our benefit, it is my duty to instruct them. Here are the elements. They are not made in vain, but are made for the benefit, comfort, convenience, and happiness of God's children. 8:340.

The principles of eternity and eternal exaltation are of no use to us, unless they are brought down to our capacities so that we practice them in our lives. 4:28.

We Need a Present, Every-day Religion—My religion must be with me from one Monday morning to the next, the year around, or it will not answer me. 1:338.

The Gospel of Jesus Christ, as it is given in the Old and New Testaments, the Book of Mormon, the book of Doctrine and Covenants, and in the experience of every true Christian who has lived and still lives upon the earth, teaches that it is the privilege of every Saint so to live and walk before their God, as to enjoy the light of the spirit of truth from day to day, from week to week, and from year to year, through their whole lives. Without this privilege in the Gospel, connected with the gifts of the Holy Ghost, I should be inclined to believe that the religion that is taught in the Bible and in the Book of Mormon, would amount to nothing more than a mere phantom—an imaginary thing. It would be inadequate to satisfy, in any degree, the mind of man, as it is now organized. 1:233.

Were it not that our bodies have to be fed and clothed, I would propose that we tarry here a few months, to give all a chance to speak, to exhort, to pray, to prophesy, to sing, to speak in tongues, or to do whatsoever the Spirit should manifest unto them. But our work is a work of the present. The salvation we are seeking is for the present, and sought correctly, it can be obtained, and be continually enjoyed. If it continues to-day, it is upon the same principle that it will continue to-morrow, the next day, the next week, or the next year, and, we might say, the next eternity. 1:131.

It is present salvation and the present influence of the Holy Ghost that we need every day to keep us on saving ground. When an individual refuses to comply with the further requirements of Heaven, then the sins he had formerly committed return upon his head; his former righteousness departs from him, and is not accounted to him for righteousness; but if he had continued in righteousness and obedience to the requirements of Heaven, he is saved all the time, through baptism, the laying on of hands, and obeying the commandments of the Lord and all that is required of him by the heavens—the living oracles. He is saved now, next week, next year, and continually, and is prepared for the celestial kingdom of God whenever the time comes for him to inherit it. 8:124.

There is no life more precious than the present life which we enjoy; there is no life that is worth any more to us than this life is. It may be said that an eternal life is worth more. We are in eternity, and all that we have to do is to take the road that leads into the eternal lives. Eternal life is an inherent quality of the creature, and nothing but sin can put a termination to it. The elements in their nature are as eternal as are the gods. Let us learn, under the guidance and direction of Heaven, how to use these eternal elements for the building up, establishment and sending forth, of the Kingdom of God, gathering up the poor in heart to begin with, and the further things we will learn as we progress. 10:22.

I wish to urge upon the people the necessity of knowing what to do with their present life, which pertains more particularly to temporalities. The very object of our existence here is to handle the temporal elements of this world and subdue the earth, multiplying those organisms of plants and animals God has designed shall dwell upon it. When we have learned to live according to the full value of the life we now possess, we are prepared for eternal advancement in the scale of eternal progression—for a more glorious and exalted sphere. 9:168.

Tradition has taught us that the great purpose of religion is to prepare people to die; that when they have passed through a change of heart, become converted, then they are ready for glory at any moment and to dwell with the Father and the Son in the heavens to all eternity. This is a mistake; for they have to improve, become substantially changed from bad to good, from sin to holiness, here or somewhere else, before they are prepared for the society they anticipate enjoying. They would not be nearly so well prepared for the society of the sanctified in heaven as a person brought up in the lowest classes of society would be prepared to present properly and conduct himself among the highest and most polished grades of mankind. Those who are counted worthy to dwell with the Father and the Son have previously received an education fitting them for that society; they have been made fully acquainted with every pass-word, token and sign which has enabled them to pass by the porters through the doors into the celestial kingdom. 10:172.

I want present salvation. I preach, comparatively, but little about the eternities and Gods, and their wonderful works in eternity; and do not tell who first made them, nor how they were made; for I know nothing about that. Life is for us, and it is for us to receive it today, and not wait for the Millennium. Let us take a course to be saved today, and, when evening comes, review the acts of the day, repent of our sins, if we have any to repent of, and say our prayers; then we can lie down and sleep in peace until the morning, arise with gratitude to God, commence the labors of another day, and strive to live the whole day to God and nobody else. 8:124.

We Must Learn to Support Ourselves—I am under obligation to take a course which will sustain life within myself and others, on national principles, without any special manifestation from God. 14:111.

I have tried continually to get this people to pursue a course that will make them self-sustaining, taking care of their poor, the lame, the halt and the blind, lifting the ignorant from where they have no opportunity of observing the ways of the world, and of understanding the common knowledge possessed among the children of men, bringing them together from the four quarters of the world, and making of them an intelligent, thrifty and self-sustaining people. 12:195.

My warfare is, and has been for years, to get the people to understand that if they do not take care of themselves they will not be taken care of; that if we do not lay the foundation to feed and clothe and shelter ourselves we shall perish with hunger and with cold; we might also suffer in the summer season from the direct rays of the sun upon our naked and unprotected bodies. 10:200.

I see more and more that there are but very few men and women that are even capable of taking care of themselves temporally. 4:314.

Chapter II

THE GODHEAD

Our Father in Heaven—Let every person be the friend of God. 4:372.

Some believe or conceive the idea that to know God would lessen him in our estimation; but I can say that for me to understand any principle or being, on earth or in heaven, it does not lessen its true value to me, but on the contrary, it increases it; and the more I can know of God, the dearer and more precious he is to me, and the more exalted are my feelings toward him. 13:57.

There is a Power that has organized all things from the crude matter that floats in the immensity of space. He has given form, motion and life to this material world; has made the great and small lights that bespangle the firmament above; has allotted to them their times and their seasons, and has marked out their spheres. He has caused the air and the waters to teem with life, and covered the hills and plains with creeping things, and has made man to be a ruler over his creations. All these wonders are the works of the Almighty Ruler of the universe, in whom we believe and whom we worship. 11:120.

All the creations are his work, and they are for his glory and for the benefit of the children of men; and all things are put into the possession of man for his comfort, improvement and consolation, and for his health, wealth, beauty and excellency. 13:151.

He is a God of system, order, law, science, and art; a God of knowledge and of power. 13:309.

He is the Father, God, Savior, Maker, Preserver, and Redeemer of man. He holds in his hands the issue of all things and will judge every man according to his works. 3:259-260.

God is the source, the fountain of all intelligence, no matter who possess it, whether man upon the earth, the spirits in the spirit-world, the angels that dwell in the eternities of the Gods, or the most inferior intelligence among the devils in hell. All have derived what intelligence, light, power, and existence they have from God—from the same source from which we have received ours. 8:205.

Every good and perfect gift cometh from God. Every discovery in science and art, that is really true and useful to mankind has been given by direct revelation from God, though but few acknowledge it. It has been given with a view to prepare the way for the ultimate triumph of truth, and the redemption of the earth from the power of sin and Satan. We should take advantage of all these great discoveries, the accumulated wisdom of ages, and give to our children the benefit of every branch of useful knowledge, to prepare them to step forward and efficiently do their part in the great work. 9:369.

He is our Heavenly Father; he is also our God, and the Maker and upholder of all things in heaven and on earth. He sends forth his counsels and extends his providences to all living. He is the Supreme Controller of the universe. At his rebuke the sea is dried up, and the rivers become a wilderness. He measures the waters in the hollow of his hand, and meteth out heaven with a span, and comprehendeth the dust of the earth in a measure, and weigheth the mountains in scales, and the hills in a balance; the nations to him are as a drop in a bucket, and he taketh up the isles as a very little thing; the hairs of our heads are numbered by him, and not a sparrow falleth to the ground without our Father; and he knoweth every thought and intent of the hearts of all living, for he is everywhere present by the power of his Spirit—his minister, the Holy Ghost. He is the Father of all, is above all, through all, and in you all; he knoweth all things pertaining to this earth, and he knows all things pertaining to millions of earths like this. 11:41.

Whether they make good or bad use of it, all power is ordained of God and is in his hand. He sets up a kingdom here, and pulls down another there at his pleasure. He breaks the nations like a potter's vessel; he forms a nucleus, and around it builds up a kingdom or nation, permitting the people to act upon their own agency, that they may do right, or corrupt themselves, as did the Children of Israel; and after they have become ripe for destruction, they will be scattered to the four winds. If the people of God in ancient days had continued holy they would have continued in power and authority to this day. 7:148.

If there is anything that is great and good and wise among men, it cometh from God. If there are men who possess great ability as statesmen, or as philosophers, or who possess remarkable scientific knowledge and skill, the credit thereof belongs to God, for he dispenses it to his children whether they believe in him or not, or whether they sin against him or not; it makes no difference; but all will have to account to him for the way and manner in which they have used the talents committed unto them. If we believe the plain, broad statements of the Bible, we must believe that Jesus Christ is the light that lighteth every man that cometh into the world; none are exempt. 11:123.

The fulness of the heavens and the earth is the Lord's—the gold and the silver, the wheat, the fine flour, and the cattle upon a thousand hills; and when we fully understand his works, we shall know that he is in all the earth, and fulfils his will among the children of men, exalting and debasing them according to his pleasure, for the systems, creeds, thrones, and kingdoms of the world are all under his control. 1:49.

We believe that God is round about all things, above all things, in all things, and through all things. To tell about empty space is to tell of a space where God is not, and where the wicked might safely hide from his presence. There is not such a thing as empty space. 1:276.

He is compassionate to all the works of his hands, the plan of his redemption, and salvation, and mercy is stretched out over all; and his plans are to gather up, and bring together, and save all the inhabitants of the earth, with the exception of those who have received the Holy Ghost, and sinned against it. With this exception, all the world besides shall be saved. 3:92.

When the Lord fights the battles of the Saints, he does it so effectually that nobody gets nervous but the enemy. 8:325.

No person deceives the Lord. 16:163.

It is written that God knows all things and has all power. He has the rule and command of this earth, and is the Father of all the human beings that have lived, do live and will live upon it. If any of his children become heirs to all things, they in their turn can say, by-and-by, that they know all things, and they will be called Supreme, Almighty, King of kings, Lord of lords. All this and more that cannot enter into our hearts to conceive is promised to the faithful, and are but so many stages in that ceaseless progression of eternal lives. This will not detract anything from the glory and might of our Heavenly Father. For he will still remain our Father, and we shall still be subject to him, and as we progress in glory and power, the more it enhances the glory and power of our Heavenly Father. This principle holds good in either state, whether mortal or immortal. 10:5.

All that the Lord requires of us is a perfect submission in our hearts to his will. 18:238.

The Lord gives us little by little and is ever willing to give us more and more, even the fulness, when our hearts are prepared to receive all the truths of heaven. This is what the Lord desires, what he would delight in doing, for his children. 18:217.

Our Father in heaven wishes us to preserve that which he gives to us. 9:169.

He presides over the worlds on worlds that illuminate this little planet, and millions on millions of worlds that we cannot see; and yet he looks upon the minutest object of his creations; not one of these creatures escapes his notice; and there is not one of them but his wisdom and power has produced. 1:39.

I believe in a God who has power to exalt and glorify all who believe in him, and are faithful in serving him to the end of their lives, for this make them Gods, even the sons of God, and in this sense also there are Gods many, but to us there is but one God, and one Lord Jesus Christ—one Savior who came in the meridian of time to redeem the earth and the children of men from the original sin that was committed by our first parents, and bring to pass the restoration of all things through his death and suffering, open wide to all believers the gates of life and salvation and exaltation to the presence of the Father and the Son to dwell with them for evermore. 11:122.

As I said once to my brethren in the School of the Prophets, I have not asked you, I dare not ask you to fulfil almost the first requirement of the Kingdom of Heaven, almost the simplest principle, and one of the first things that should be observed. I have not asked the people to perform this great labor, I will say it is a great labor, and if I were to refer it to you, you would say the same. You may ask what it is? It is to love the Lord thy God with all thy heart, with all thy mind and with all thy strength, and thy neighbor as thyself. Now, is this not almost one of the first requirements that God has made of his people? And I have not yet required it of the people. Love the Lord thy God with all thy heart, and then speak evil of thy neighbor? No! No! Love the Lord thy God with all thy heart, and speak that which is not true? No, oh, no! Love the Lord thy God with all thy heart, and take that which is not thy own? No, no, no! Love the Lord thy God with all thy heart, and seek after riches of the world and forsake your religion? No! Love the Lord thy God with all thy heart and take his name in vain, curse and swear? No, never! If the love of God was really in the hearts of all who call themselves Latter-day Saints, there would be no more swearing, no more lying, no more deceiving, no more speaking evil of one another, no more running after the ungodly nor dealing with the enemies of Zion, no more running after the gold mines; nothing would be sought after, only to build up the Kingdom of God. This we have not yet asked. But we do ask some things. Let us forsake those sins that are so grievous, and let us try to do right before the Heavens and with each other. 12:229.

He has not committed the keys of the results of the acts of the nations of the earth to any man on the earth; but that power he retains to himself. 8:31.

What is commonly termed idolatry has arisen from a few sincere men, full of faith and having a little knowledge, urging upon a backsliding people to preserve some customs—to cling to some fashions or figures, to put them in mind of that God with whom their fathers were acquainted, without designing or wishing the people to worship an idol—to worship stocks, stones, beasts, and birds. Idols have been introduced, which are now worshiped, and have been for centuries and thousands of years; but they were not introduced at once. They were introduced to preserve among the people the idea of the true God. 6:194.

We are nothing, only what the Lord makes us. 5:343.

Cease bringing the names of God the Father and his Son Jesus Christ into disrespect and learn to reverence those names. 7:147.

The Lord operates upon the principles of continuing to organize, of adding to, gathering up, bringing forth, increasing and spreading abroad; while the opposite power does not. It shows the nature of his opposition to that peculiar trait of Christianity, based upon the principles of eternal duration, increase, power, glory, and exaltation; and points out the difference between the two adverse powers. 1:117.

Unless God blesses our exertions we shall have nothing. It is the Lord that gives the increase. 3:331.

The God that I serve is progressing eternally, and so are his children: they will increase to all eternity, if they are faithful. 11:286.

It is written, "Prove all things, hold fast that which is good." Refuse evil, choose good, hate iniquity, love truth. All this our fathers have done before us; I do not particularly mean Father Adam, or his Father; I do not particularly mean Abraham, or Moses, the Prophets, or Apostles, but I mean our fathers who have been exalted for millions of years previous to Adam's time. They have all passed through the same ordeals we are now passing through, and have searched all things, even to the depths of hell. 9:243.

The great architect, manager and superintendent, controller and dictator who guides this work is out of sight to our natural eyes. He lives on another world; he is in another state of existence; he has passed the ordeals we are now passing through; he has received an experience, has suffered and enjoyed, and knows all that we know regarding the toils, sufferings, life and death of this mortality, for he has passed through the whole of it, and has received his crown and exaltation and holds the keys and the power of this Kingdom; he sways his scepter, and does his will among the children of men, among Saints and among sinners, and brings forth results to suit his purpose among kingdoms and nations and empires, that all may redound to his glory and to the perfection of his work. 11:249.

How many Gods there are, I do not know. But there never was a time when there were not Gods and worlds, and when men were not passing through the same ordeals that we are now passing through. That course has been from all eternity, and it is and will be to all eternity. You cannot comprehend this, but when you can, it will be to you a matter of great consolation. 7:333.

Wherever the human family dwell upon the face of the earth, whether they are savage or civilized, there is a desire implanted within them to worship a great Supreme Ruler, and not knowing him they suppose that through offering worship and sacrifice to their idols they can conciliate his anger which they think they see manifested in the thunder, in the lightning, in the storm, in the floods, in the reverses of war, in the hand of death, etc. etc.; thus they try to woo his protection and his blessing for victory over their enemies, and at the termination of this life for a place in the heaven their imaginations have created, or tradition has handed down to them. I have much charity for this portion of the human family called heathens or idolators; they have made images to represent to their eyes a power which they cannot see, and desire to worship a Supreme Being through the figure which they have made. 11:120.

We believe in one God, one Mediator and one Holy Ghost. We cannot believe for a moment that God is destitute of body, parts, passions, or attributes. Attributes can be made manifest only through an organized personage. All attributes are couched in and are the results of organized existence. 10:192.

The Lord is perfectly independent. He has received his glory, he reigns supreme and omnipotent. He is not dependent upon you and me. If every one of us should apostatize and go down to hell, it would neither add to nor diminish from his glory. He would mourn at our folly in turning away from the holy commandments and suffering the wrath of the Almighty to come upon us; the heavens would weep over us, but still the Lord has his glory, and you and I are not laboring for his benefit. For whose benefit are we laboring? For our own. All my preaching, laboring and toils in this Kingdom have been for myself, to get into the Celestial Kingdom of God. I have been laboring for that and nothing else. 13:315.

Read the history of any kingdom or nation, and trace through all the channels from the history of nations and kingdoms to that of families and individuals who have not known God nor observed his commandments, and you will find that sorrow and disappointment have been intimately mingled in all the gaiety, luxuries, and pretended enjoyments of their mortal lives. They have found a bitter sting in their happiest moments and a deadly poison in their cups. 6:39.

There is no influence, truth, or righteousness in the world, only what flows from God our Father in the heavens. 5:78.

Personality and Fatherhood of God—Some would have us believe that God is present everywhere. It is not so. He is no more everywhere present in person than the Father and Son are one in person. 6:345.

God is considered to be everywhere present at the same moment; and the Psalmist says, "Whither shall I flee from thy presence?" He is present with all his creations through his influence, through his government, spirit and power, but he himself is a personage of tabernacle, and we are made after his likeness. 10:319.

Our God and Father in Heaven, is a being of tabernacle, or, in other words, he has a body, with parts the same as you and I have; and is capable of showing forth his works to organized beings, as for instance, in the world in which we live, it is the result of the knowledge and infinite wisdom that dwell in his organized body. His Son Jesus Christ has become a personage of tabernacle, and has a body like his Father. The Holy Ghost is the Spirit of the Lord, and issues forth from himself, and may properly be called God's minister to execute his will in immensity; being called to govern by his influence and power; but he is not a person of flesh as we are, and as our Father in Heaven and Jesus Christ are. 1:50.

The Kingdom of God on earth is a living, moving, effective institution, and is governed, controlled, dictated and led by the invisible God whom we serve who is an exalted, living being, possessing body, parts and passions, who listens to the prayers of his Saints, is a reasonable, merciful and intelligent being, who is filled with knowledge and wisdom, who is full of light and glory, and the foundations of whose throne are laid in eternal truth; whose personal form is perfect in proportion and beauty. He loves the good, and is angry with the wicked every day as it is written in the Scriptures. He hates the evil that is done by evildoers, and is merciful to the repenting sinner. He is beloved by all who know him for the attributes he possesses in and of himself, in common with all glorified beings who now dwell with him, and who will yet be glorified and crowned with crowns of glory, immortality and eternal lives. 11:251.

It must be that God knows something about temporal things, and has had a body and been on an earth. Were it not so, he would not know how to judge men righteously, according to the temptations and sin they have had to contend with. 4:271.

Our Father in Heaven begat all the spirits that ever were, or ever will be, upon this earth; and they were born spirits in the eternal world. Then the Lord by his power and wisdom organized the mortal tabernacle of man. We were made first spiritual, and afterwards temporal. 1:50.

He is our Father; he is our God, the Father of our spirits; he is the framer of our bodies, and set the machine in successful operation to bring forth these tabernacles that I now look upon in this building, and all that ever did or ever will live on the face of the whole earth. 13:250.

The Apostles and Prophets, when speaking of our relationship to God, say that we are flesh of his flesh and bone of his bone, God is our Father, and Jesus Christ is our Elder Brother, and both are our everlasting friends. 6:332.

The kingdoms he possesses and rules over are his own progeny. Every man who is faithful and gets a salvation and glory, and becomes a King of kings and Lord of lords, or a Father of fathers, it will be by the increase of his own progeny. Our Father and God rules over his own children. Wherever there is a God in all the eternities possessing a kingdom and glory and power it is by means of his own progeny. 11:262.

Many have tried to penetrate to the First Cause of all things; but it would be as easy for an ant to number the grains of sand on the earth. It is not for man, with his limited intelligence, to grasp eternity in his comprehension. There is an eternity of life, from which we were composed by the wisdom and skill of Superior Beings. It would be as easy for a gnat to trace the history of man back to his origin as for man to fathom the First Cause of all things, lift the veil of eternity, and reveal the mysteries that have been sought after by philosophers from the beginning. What then, should be the calling and duty of the children of men? Instead of inquiring after the origin of Gods—instead of trying to explore the depths of eternities that have been, that are, and that will be, instead of endeavoring to discover the boundaries of boundless space, let them seek to know the object of their present existence, and how to apply, in the most profitable manner for their mutual good and salvation, the intelligence they possess. Let them seek to know and thoroughly understand things within their reach, and to make themselves well acquainted with the object of their being here, by diligently seeking unto a super-power for information and by the careful study of the best books. 7:284-5.

God has given this great variety of intelligence. He has also given this great variety of forms—that eternal variety which we see upon this earth, not only among human beings, but in every class of all the creations of God; and they are all designed to be preserved to all eternity. None of them were made to be destroyed, except those that do not abide the law given them. 8:8.

I now see before me beings who are in the image of those heavenly personages who are enthroned in glory and crowned with eternal lives in the very image of those beings who organized the earth and its fulness, and who constitute the Godhead. 9:246.

The Son of God—Our faith is concentrated in the Son of God, and through him in the Father; and the Holy Ghost is their minister to bring truths to our remembrance, to reveal new truths to us, and teach, guide, and direct the course of every mind, until we become perfected and prepared to go home, where we can see and converse with our Father in Heaven. 6:98.

The Latter-day Saints believe in Jesus Christ, the only begotten Son of the Father, who came in the meridian of time, performed his work, suffered the penalty and paid the debt of man's original sin by offering up himself, was resurrected from the dead, and ascended to his Father; and as Jesus descended below all things, so he will ascend above all things. We believe that Jesus Christ will come again, as it is written of him: "And while they looked steadfastly toward heaven as he went up, behold two men stood by them in white apparel; which also said, Ye men of Galilee, why stand ye gazing up into heaven? this same Jesus which is taken from you into heaven, shall so come in like manner as ye have seen him go into heaven." 11:123.

Jesus is our captain and leader; Jesus, the Savior of the world—the Christ that we believe in. 14:118.

I testify that Jesus is the Christ, the Savior and Redeemer of the world; I have obeyed his sayings, and realized his promise, and the knowledge I have of him, the wisdom of this world cannot give neither can it take away. 18:233.

My faith is placed upon the Lord Jesus Christ, and my knowledge I have received from him. 3:155.

Our Lord Jesus Christ—the Savior, who has redeemed the world and all things pertaining to it, is the Only Begotten of the Father pertaining to the flesh. He is our Elder Brother, and the Heir of the family, and as such we worship him. He has tasted death for every man, and has paid the debt contracted by our first parents. 12:69.

None of them have power to produce themselves. Jesus Christ is the Heir of this vast family. He said that he had power to lay down his life and take it up again; but he had no more power to produce his life, in the beginning of his existence, than we have. Every human being is endowed, more or less, with eternal intelligence, with the germ of life everlasting, of glory immortal. 8:153.

He did nothing of himself. He wrought miracles and performed a good work on the earth; but of himself he did nothing. He said, "As I have seen my Father do, so do I." "I came not to do my will, but the will of him that sent me." We must come to the conclusion that the Son of God did not suggest, dictate, act, or produce any manifestation of his power, of his glory, or of his errand upon the earth, only as it came from the mind and will of his Father. 6:96.

The Lord has revealed to us a plan by which we may be saved both here and hereafter. God has done everything we could ask, and more than we could ask. The errand of Jesus to earth was to bring his brethren and sisters back into the presence of the Father; he has done his part of the work, and it remains for us to do ours. There is not one thing that the Lord could do for the salvation of the human family that he has neglected to do; and it remains for the children of men to receive the truth or reject it; all that can be accomplished for their salvation, independent of them, has been accomplished in and by the Savior. It has been justly remarked this afternoon that "Jesus paid the debt; he atoned for the original sin; he came and suffered and died on the cross." He is now King of kings and Lord of lords, and the time will come when every knee will bow and every tongue confess, to the glory of God the Father, that Jesus is the Christ. That very character that was looked upon, not as the Savior, but as an outcast, who was crucified between two thieves and treated with scorn and derision, will be greeted by all men as the only Being through whom they can obtain salvation. 13:59.

Jesus was appointed, from the beginning, to die for our redemption, and he suffered an excruciating death on the cross. 8:115.

He has died to redeem it, and he is the lawful heir pertaining to this earth. Jesus will continue to reign with his Father, and is dictated by his Father in all his acts and ruling and governing in the building up and overthrow of nations, to make the wrath of man praise him, until he brings all into subjection to his will and government. And when he has subdued all his enemies, destroyed death and him that hath the power of death, and perfected his work, he will deliver up the kingdom spotless to his Father. 7:144.

The character we have been hearing of is our Savior and Redeemer, the Savior of the whole world of mankind, and of all creatures pertaining to the earth, and the earth itself, for all will be redeemed by the blood of the Son of God. 14:130.

The moment the atonement of the Savior is done away, that moment, at one sweep, the hopes of salvation entertained by the Christian world are destroyed, the foundation of their faith is taken away, and there is nothing left for them to stand upon. When it is gone all the revelations God ever gave to the Jewish nation, to the Gentiles and to us are rendered valueless, and all hope is taken from us at on sweep. 14:41.

The knowledge of the character of the Only Begotten of the Father comes to us through the testimony, not of disinterested witnesses, but of his friends, those who were most especially and deeply interested for their own welfare, and the welfare of their brethren. We have no testimony concerning the Savior's character and works, only from those who were thus interested in his welfare and success, and in the building up of his kingdom. It has been often said, if a disinterested witness would testify that Joseph Smith is a prophet of God, many might believe his testimony; but no person could be believed, by any intelligent person, who would testify to a matter of such importance, and who would still view it as a thing in which he had no interest. But they who are interested, who know the worth of that man and understand the spirit and the power of his mission, and the character of the Being that sent and ordained him, are the proper persons to testify of the truth of his mission, and they are the most interested of any living upon the earth. So it was with those who bore witness of the Savior, and of his mission on the earth. 11:41.

The Latter-day Saints and every other person who is entitled to salvation, and all except those who have sinned against the Holy Ghost, may know that Jesus is the Christ in the same way that Peter knew it. Miracles do not give this knowledge to mankind, though they may serve as collateral evidence to strengthen the believer. The miracles of Jesus were known to the Jews, yet they suffered him to be put to death as a deceiver of mankind and one possessed of a devil. 10:193.

Who are the Saints? All those who believe in Jesus Christ and keep his commandments. And who may be Saints? All the inhabitants of the earth, for Jesus said, "Come unto me, all ye ends of the earth, and be ye saved." 10:305.

All the Lord has called us to do is to renovate our own hearts, then our families, extending the principle to neighborhoods, to the earth we occupy, and so continue until we drive the power of Satan from the earth and Satan to his own place. That is the work Jesus is engaged in, and we will be co-workers with him. 10:173.

"I and my Father are one," says Jesus; what, one body? No, it never entered the Savior's mind that such a rendering of this saying would ever enter into the minds of persons holding the least claim to good sense. They are no more one person than I and one of my sons are one person. If my son receives my teaching, will walk in the path I mark out for him to walk in, if his faith is the same as mine, his purpose is the same, and he does the work of his father as Jesus did the work of his Father, then is my son one with me in the scriptural sense. 10:192.

Inasmuch as the Father, Son and Holy Ghost are one, the desire of the Savior, as manifested in his sayings and teachings, is, that his people should also be one, even as he and his Father are one. 6:97.

All the works of mankind amount to but little, unless they are performed in the name of the Lord and under the direction of his Spirit. Let every man seek to learn the things of God by the revelaticns of Jesus Christ to himself. 10:1.

Jesus undertook to establish the Kingdom of God upon the earth. He introduced the laws and ordinances of the Kingdom. 15:125.

Jesus Christ will draw all men unto him, except those who contend against the power of God and against his Kingdom until they have sealed their own damnation. 11:238.

Jesus fulfilled the obligations he had entered into as the heir of all things pertaining to this earth. 8:115.

We, the Latter-day Saints, certainly believe that Christ will accomplish all that he undertook to do, but he never yet said he would save a sinner in his sins, but that he would save him from his sins. He has instituted laws and ordinances whereby this can be effected. The "Mormon" Elder says that he will save all who come to him, all who hearken to his word and keep his commandments, and Jesus has said, "If ye love me, keep my commandments." The "Mormon" says, "I love Jesus, and in proof of it I keep his commandments." 13:237.

Jesus will redeem the last and least of the sons of Adam, except the sons of perdition, who will be held in reserve for another time. They will become angels of the Devil. 8:154.

Christ will not cease his labors pertaining to this earth until it is redeemed and sanctified, ready to be presented spotless to the Father. 10:18.

We believe that Jesus Christ will descend from heaven to earth again even as he ascended into heaven. "Behold, he cometh with clouds, and every eye shall see him, and they also which pierced him: and all kindreds of the earth shall wail because of him." He will come to receive his own, and rule and reign king of nations as he does king of Saints; "For he must reign, till he hath put all enemies under his feet. The last enemy that shall be destroyed is death." He will banish sin from the earth and its dreadful consequences, tears shall be wiped from every eye and there shall be nothing to hurt or destroy in all God's holy mountain. 11:123.

The Savior has not finished his work, and cannot receive the fulness of his glory until the influence and power of the wicked are overcome and brought into subjection. When the wicked inhabitants of the earth, the beasts of the field, fowls of the air, fish of the sea, all mineral substances, and all else pertaining to this earth, are overcome, then he will take the kingdom, present it to the Father, and say, "Here is the work you gave me to do—you made the appointment —I have wrought faithfully, and here are my brethren and sisters who have wrought with me. We have wrought faithfully together; we have overcome the flesh, hell and the Devil. I have overcome, they have followed in my footsteps, and here are all thou hast given me; I have lost none, except the sons of perdition." 8:118.

When he again visits this earth, he will come to thoroughly purge his kingdom from wickedness, and, as ruler of the nations, to dictate and administer to them as the heir to the kingdom; and the Gentiles will be as much mistaken in regard to his second advent as the Jews were in relation to the first. 8:115.

Take a pride in acknowledging the Savior. Train and educate yourselves until you will take a pride in acknowledging God, the Author of all. Take a pride in the religion that makes you pure and holy, and that produces in the heart of every individual who embraces it a feeling to be truthful in every word he speaks, to be honest in every act he performs, in all his dealings with his neighbors. Take a pride in this and fear not the wicked. 12:326.

The Latter-day Saints believe in the Gospel of the Son of God, simply because it is true. They believe in baptism for the remission of sins, personal and by proxy; they believe that Jesus is the Savior of the world; they believe that all who attain to any glory whatever, in any kingdom, will do so because Jesus has purchased it by his atonement. 13:323.

The Holy Ghost—The Holy Ghost, we believe, is one of the characters that form the Trinity, or the Godhead. Not one person in three, nor three persons in one; but the Father, Son, and Holy Ghost are one in essence, as the hearts of three men who are united in all things. He is one of the three characters we believe in, whose office it is to administer to those of the human family who love the truth. I have stated that they are one, as the hearts of three men might be one. Lest you should mistake me, I will say that I do not wish you to understand that the Holy Ghost is a personage having a tabernacle, like the Father and the Son; but he is God's messenger that diffuses his influence through all the works of the Almighty. 6:95.

Not a desire, act, wish, or thought does the Holy Ghost indulge in contrary to that which is dictated by the Father. 6.95.

Now ask yourself whether you believe that the Holy Ghost ever commenced to produce a work or an effect before it was in the heart and mind of that Being we call our Heavenly Father. Do you think that the Holy Ghost ever thought of dictating that Being we call our God? This whole people have learned enough upon this subject to answer at once, that we do not believe that the Holy Ghost ever dictated, suggested, moved, or pretended to offer a plan, except that which the Eternal Father dictated. 6:95.

Though a man should say but a few words, and his sentences and words be ever so ungrammatical, if he speaks by the power of the Holy Ghost, he will do good. 8:120.

I have proven to my satisfaction, according to the best knowledge I can gather, that man can be deceived by the sight of the natural eye, he can be deceived by the hearing of the ear, and by the touch of the hand; that he can be deceived in all of what is called the natural senses. But there is one thing in which he cannot be deceived. What is that? It is the operations of the Holy Ghost, the Spirit and power of God upon the creature. It teaches him of heavenly things; it directs him in the way of life; it affords him the key by which he can test the devices of man, and which recommends the things of God. Not only the Saints who are present, and who gathered to Zion, but those of every nation, continent, or island who live the religion taught by our Savior and his Apostles, and also by Joseph Smith; they also bear the same testimony, their eyes have been quickened by the Spirit of God, and they see alike, their hearts have been quickened, and they feel and understand alike, and there are no disputations among them with regard to the doctrines of the Savior. 18:230.

Again it is asked:—"Is the Holy Ghost given in this age of the world?" Yes, but they could not send men to Joppa for Peter, for behold there was no Peter, or men possessing the holy Priesthood, to send for, neither has there been since the church lost the holy Priesthood, until it was restored through the Prophet Joseph Smith. Cornelius did not belong to the House of Israel, yet he received the Holy Ghost. Continue this history, and what does it give to us? It gives to us the key of knowledge with regard to receiving the Holy Ghost through the ordinances of the Gospel, that it is free to all, Jew and Gentile, as Peter exclaimed when Cornelius had related to him how he was instructed to send men to Joppa: "Of a truth I perceive that God is no respecter of persons; but in every nation, he that feareth him and worketh righteousness, is accepted of him." 10:322.

Without the power of the Holy Ghost a person is liable to go to the right or the left from the straight path of duty; they are liable to do things they are sorry for; they are liable to make mistakes; and when they try to do their best, behold they do that which they dislike. 10:289.

I want to see men and women breathe the Holy Ghost in every breath of their lives, living constantly in the light of God's countenance. 9:288-289.

Chapter III

THE COMMUNICATION BETWEEN GOD AND MAN

The Spirit of God—God is here: his influence fills immensity. He has his messengers throughout all the works of his hands. He watches every one of his creatures; their acts, their affections, and thoughts are all known to him; for his intelligence and power fill immensity. Not that his person does, but his Spirit does; and he is here teaching, guiding and directing the nations of the earth. 7:159.

The Spirit of the Lord enlightens every man that comes into the world. There is no one that lives upon the earth but what is, more or less, enlightened by the Spirit of the Lord Jesus. It is said of him, that he is the light of the world. He lighteth every man that comes into the world and every person, at times, has the light of the spirit of truth upon him. 14:201.

I do not believe for one moment that there has been a man or woman upon the face of the earth, from the days of Adam to this day, who has not been enlightened, instructed, and taught by the revelations of Jesus Christ. "What! the ignorant heathen?" Yes, every human being who has possessed a sane mind. I am far from believing that the children of men have been deprived of the privilege of receiving the Spirit of the Lord to teach them right from wrong. No matter what the traditions of their fathers were, those who were honest before the Lord, and acted uprightly, according to the best knowledge they had, will have an opportunity to go into the Kingdom of God. I believe this privilege belonged to the sons and daughters of Adam, and descended from him, and his children who were contemporary with him, throughout all generations. 2:139.

All who would understand the things of God must understand them by the Spirit of God. 8:115.

I will, in the commencement of my remarks, take up a subject upon which much has been said in the pulpit and in the chimney corner. It is regarding the Spirit of the Lord manifesting his will to his children. There is no doubt, if a person lives according to the revelations given to God's people, he may have the Spirit of the Lord to signify to him his will, and to guide and to direct him in the discharge of his duties, in his temporal as well as his spiritual exercises. I am satisfied, however, that in this respect, we live far beneath our privileges. If this is true, it is necessary that we become more fervent in the service of God—in living our religion—and more truthful and honest with one another, that we be not slack in the performance of any duty, but labor with a right good will for God and truth. If this people, called Latter-day Saints, live beneath their privileges in the holy Gospel of the Son of God, are they justified in every respect before him? They are not. If we do not live in the lively exercise of faith in the Lord Jesus, possessing his Spirit always, how can we know when he speaks to us through his servants whom he has placed to lead us? 12:104.

The light of the Spirit upon the hearts and understandings of some Latter-day Saints, is like the peeping of the stars through the broken shingles of the roof over our heads, when we are watching through the silent watches of the night and behold the glimmer of a twinkling star. 15:3.

No man can gain influence in this Kingdom, and maintain himself in it, magnify his calling without the power of God being with him. Persons must so live that they can enjoy the light of the Holy Spirit, or they will have no confidence in themselves, in their religion, or in their God, and will sooner or later turn from the faith. 8:65.

You need the Spirit of the Almighty to look through a man and discern what is in his heart, while his face smiles upon you and his words flow as smoothly as oil. 3:225.

Thrust a man into prison and bind him with chains, and then let him be filled with the comfort and with the glory of eternity, and that prison is a palace to him. Again, let a man be seated upon a throne with power and dominion in this world, ruling his millions and millions and without that peace which flows from the Lord of Hosts —without that contentment and joy that comes from heaven, his palace is a prison; his life is a burden to him; he lives in fear, in dread, and in sorrow. But when a person is filled with the peace and power of God, all is right with him. 5:1-2.

There are men of talent, of thought, of reflection, and knowledge in all cunning mechanism; they are expert in that, though they do not know from whence they receive their intelligence. The Spirit of the Lord has not yet entirely done striving with the people, offering them knowledge and intelligence; consequently, it reveals unto them, instructs them, teaches them, and guides them even in the way they like to travel. Men know how to construct railroads and all manner of machinery; they understand cunning workmanship, etc.; but that is all revealed to them by the Spirit of the Lord, though they know it not. 5:124.

I rejoice in the privilege of meeting with the Saints, in hearing them speak, and in enjoying the influence that is within and around them. That influence opens to my understanding the true position of those who are endeavoring to serve their God. I do not require to hear them speak to enable me to know their feelings. Is it not also your experience that, when you meet persons in the streets, in your houses, in your offices, or in your workshops, more or less of an influence attends them which conveys more than words can? By this the Father knows his children, Jesus knows his brethren, and the angels are acquainted with those who delight to associate with them and with those who hate them. This knowledge is obtained through that invisible influence which attends intelligent beings, and betrays the atmosphere in which they delight to live. 8:57.

Without the light of the Spirit of Christ, no person can truly enjoy life. 8:66.

Now, my friends, brethren and sisters, ladies and gentlemen, how do you know anything? Can you be deceived by the eye? You can, you have proved this; you all know that there are men who can deceive the sight of the eye, no matter how closely you observe their movements. Can you be deceived in hearing? Yes; you may hear sounds but not understand their import or whence they came. Can you be deceived by the touch of the fingers? You can. The nervous system will not detect everything. What will? The revelations of the Lord Jesus Christ, the spirit of truth will detect everything, and enable all who possess it to understand truth from error, light from darkness, the things of God from the things not of God. It is the only thing that will enable us to understand the Gospel of the Son of God, the will of God, and how we can be saved. Follow it, and it will lead to God, the Fountain of light, where the gate will be open, and the mind will be enlightened so that we shall see, know and understand things as they are. 13:336.

There is not a man upon the earth who can magnify even an earthly office, without the power and wisdom of God to aid him. 10:42.

The eloquence of angels never can convince any person that God lives and makes truth the habitation of his throne, independent of that eloquence being clothed with the power of the Holy Ghost; in the absence of this, it would be a combination of useless sounds. What is it that convinces man? It is the influence of the Almighty, enlightening his mind, giving instruction to the understanding, when that which inhabits this body, that which came from the regions of Glory, is enlightened by the influence, power and Spirit of the Father of light, it swallows up the organization which pertains to this world. 1:90.

Those who love righteousness and possess the Spirit of God, those who delight to do good can remember good. They can remember every good principle and every good act. 3:358.

What causes this people to do as they do? It is written, "But there is a spirit in man, and the inspiration of the Almighty giveth them understanding." It is a spirit that causes this people to do what they do—to leave their native countries, to leave their fathers and mothers, brethren and sisters, and take up their line of march and travel thousands of miles to this distant country; and then, when selected for missions, again to leave their fathers, mothers, and friends, and travel back to their native lands, or to some other place, wherever they are appointed to go. We cannot behold that spirit and influence with our natural eyes. The results alone are known. 8:174.

You hearken to that still small voice that whispers eternal truth, that opens the visions of eternity to you that you can discern, understand and follow, and the foul spirits that throng the air, and that fill our houses if we let them in, will not have power over you. 15:7.

Every individual that lives according to the laws that the Lord has given to his people, and has received the blessings that he has in store for the faithful, should be able to know the things of God from the things which are not of God, the light from the darkness, that which comes from heaven and that which comes from somewhere else. This is the satisfaction and the consolation that the Latter-day Saints enjoy by living their religion; this is the knowledge which every one who thus lives possesses. 16:163.

Now, I ask the wise, where did you get your wisdom? Was it taught you? Yes, I say it was taught you. By your professors in college? No, it was taught you by the influence of the spirit that is in man, and the inspiration of the Spirit of God giveth it understanding; and every creature can thus add intelligence to intelligence. 13:172.

Revelation—No person can receive a knowledge of this work, except by the power of revelation. 8:315.

The spirit of revelation, even the spirit of eternal life, is within that person who lives so as to bear properly the yoke of Jesus. The heavens are open to such persons, and they see and understand things that pertain to eternity, and also the things that pertain to this earth. 8:206.

The spirit of revelation attends the Gospel, and without that spirit no man can understand it. 8:130.

Many of the first revelations given to Joseph were of a temporal character, pertaining to a literal kingdom on the earth. And most of the revelations he received in the early part of his ministry pertained to what the few around him should do in this or in that case—when and how they should perform their duties; at the same time calling upon them to preach the Gospel and diffuse the spirit and principles of the Kingdom of God, that their eyes might be open to see and gather the people together that they might begin and organize a literal, temporal organization on the earth. 6:171.

How can you know the Latter-day work to be true? You can know it only by the spirit of revelation direct from heaven.

What proved this work true to you in England, Ireland, Scotland, Germany, France, the United States, etc.? Was it not the spirit of revelation that rested upon you? Then why should you lose the spirit? You should add to it day by day; you should add as the Lord gives—a little here and a little there, and treasure up truth in your faith and understanding, until you become perfect before the Lord and are prepared to receive the further things of the Kingdom of God. 7:159-160.

This principle we are in possession of, and it should be nourished and cherished by us; it is the principle of revelation, or if you like the term better, of foreseeing. There are those who possess foreknowledge, who do not believe as we believe with regard to establishment of the Kingdom of God on the earth. Take the statesman, for instance; he has a certain degree of knowledge with regard to the results of the measures which he may recommend, but does he know whence he derived that knowledge? No. He may say: "I foresee if we take this course we shall perpetuate our government and strengthen it, but if we take the opposite course we will destroy it." But can he tell whence he has received that wisdom and foreknowledge? He cannot. Yet that is the condition of the statesman in the nations of the earth. If the philosopher can gaze into the immensity of space, and understand how to fashion and make glasses that will magnify a million times, that knowledge comes from the Fountain of knowledge. A man of the world may say: "I can foresee, I can understand, I can frame an engine, make a track, and run that engine upon it bearing along a train of loaded cars at the rate of forty, fifty, or sixty miles an hour." Another may say: "I can take the lightning, convey it on wires, and speak to foreign nations." But where do they get this wisdom? From the same source where you and I get our wisdom and our knowledge of God and godliness. 12:112-113.

But we should all live so that the Spirit of revelation could dictate and write on the heart and tell us what we should do instead of the traditions of our parents and teachers. But to do this we must become like little children; and Jesus says if we do not we cannot enter the kingdom of heaven. How simple it is! Live free from envy, malice, wrath, strife, bitter feelings, and evil speaking in our families and about our neighbors and friends and all the inhabitants of the earth, wherever we meet them. Live so that our consciences are free, clean and clear. 14:161.

No man can know Jesus the Christ except it be revealed from heaven to him. 14:199.

No earthly argument, no earthly reasoning can open the minds of intelligent beings and show them heavenly things; that can only be done by the Spirit of revelation. 18:249.

When the Spirit of revelation from God inspires a man, his mind is opened to behold the beauty, order, and glory of the creation of this earth and its inhabitants, the object of its creation, and the purpose of its Creator in peopling it with his children. He can then clearly understand that our existence here is for the sole purpose of exaltation and restoration to the presence of our Father and God, where we may progress endlessly in the power of godliness. After the mind has thus been illuminated, the ignorance and blindness of the great mass of mankind are more apparent. Yet there is no son or daughter of Adam and Eve who has not incorporated in his organization the priceless gem of endless life, for the endless duration and endless lives which they are approaching. 9:256.

Without the revelations of God we know not who we are, whence we came, nor who formed the earth on which we live, move and have our being. Did I bring the particles of matter together and form the earth? No. Did you, Mr. Philosopher? No. Did you Mr. Infidel, or you Mr. Christian, Pagan or Jew? No, not any of us. We know that we are here, but who brought us here, or how we came are questions the solution of which depends upon a power superior to ours. The ideas of the inhabitants of the earth with regard to the destiny of the earth, are very crude and vague. But we must all acknowledge that some individual, being, power or influence superior to ourselves produced us and the earth and brought us forth and holds us in existence, and causes the revolutions of the earth and of the planetary system. These are facts that neither we nor all mankind can controvert; the whole Christian and even the heathen world will acknowledge all this; but what do they know about it? Who understands the modus operandi by which all this was brought about and continued? Who is able to leap forth into the immensity of thought, space, contemplation and research, and search out the principles by which we are here and by which we are sustained? The strangest phenomenon to the inhabitants of the earth today is that God, the maker and preserver of the earth and all it contains, should speak from heaven to his creatures, the works of his hands here. What would there be strange in the mechanician, after constructing the most beautiful and ingenious piece of mechanism it is possible to conceive of, speaking to it and admiring the beauty, regularity and order of its motions? Nothing whatever. Well, to me it is not at all strange that he who framed and fashioned this beautiful world and all the myriads and varieties of organizations it contains, should come and visit them; to me this is perfectly natural, and when we remember and compare the belief of this people with that of the rest of the world we need not be surprised at being considered "a strange people." 13:234.

How do we know that prophets wrote the word of the Lord? By revelation. How do we know that Joseph Smith was called of God to establish his Kingdom upon the earth? By revelation. How do we know that the leaders of this people teach the truth? By revelation. How do we know the doctrine of baptism for the remission of sins to be true? It is written in the Bible; but the Christian world deny it, because it is not manifested to them by the revelations of the Lord Jesus. 14:209.

Without revelation direct from heaven, it is impossible for any person to understand fully the plan of salvation. We often hear it said that the living oracles must be in the Church, in order that the Kingdom of God may be established and prosper on the earth. I will give another version of this sentiment. I say that the living oracles of God, or the Spirit of revelation must be in each and every individual, to know the plan of salvation and keep in the path that leads them to the presence of God. 9:279.

This people believe in revelation. This people did believe and do believe that the Lord has spoken from the heavens. They did believe and do believe that God has sent angels to proclaim the everlasting Gospel, according to the testimony of John. It was this that gave rise to the malice, hatred and vindictive feelings that have been so often made manifest against them. 12:282.

When a revelation is given to any people, they must walk according to it, or suffer the penalty which is the punishment of disobedience, but when the word is, "will you do thus and so?" "It is the mind and will of God that you perform such and such a duty"; the consequences of disobedience are not so dreadful, as they would be if the word of the Lord were to be written under the declaration, "Thus saith the Lord." 12:127.

Instead of considering that there is nothing known and understood, only as we know and understand things naturally, I take the other side of the question, and believe positively that there is nothing known except by the revelation of the Lord Jesus Christ, whether in theology, science, or art. 12:207.

It pleases me a little to think how anxious this people are for new revelation. I wish to ask you a question: Do this people know whether they have received any revelation since the death of Joseph, as a people? I can tell you that you receive them continually. 6:282.

All the revelations of God teach simply this—son, daughter, you are the workmanship of mine hands; walk and live before me in righteousness; let your conversations be chaste; let your daily deportment be according to my law; let your dealings one with another be in justice and equity; let my character be sacred in your mouth, and do not profane my holy name and trample upon my authority; do not despise any of my sayings, for I will not be disgraced. 6:284-85.

It has been observed that the people want revelation. This is a revelation; and were it written, it would then be written revelation, as truly as the revelations which are contained in the book of Doctrine and Covenants. I could give you revelation upon the subject of paying your tithing and building a temple to the name of the Lord; for the light is in me. I could put these revelations as straight to the line of truth in writing as any revelation you ever read. I could write the mind of the Lord, and you could put it in your pockets. But before we desire more written revelation, let us fulfil the revelations that are already written, and which we have scarcely begun to fulfil. 6:319.

In every part and portion of the revelations of God as given to the children of men, or to any individual in heaven or on earth, to understand them properly, a man needs the Spirit by which they were given—the Spirit that reveals such matters to the understanding, and makes them familiar to the mind. 8:27.

There are revelations, wisdom, knowledge, and understanding yet to be proclaimed. 8:59.

"Well, Brother Brigham, have you had visions?" Yes, I have. "Have you had revelations?" Yes, I have them all the time, I live constantly by the principle of revelation. I never received one iota of intelligence, from the letter A to what I now know, I mean that, from the very start of my life to this time, I have never received one particle of intelligence, only by revelation, no matter whether father or mother revealed it, or my sister, or neighbor.

No person received knowledge, only upon the principle of revelation, that is, by having something revealed to them. "Do you have the revelations of the Lord Jesus Christ?" I will leave that for others to judge. If the Lord requires anything of this people, and speaks through me, I will tell them of it; but if he does not, still we all live by the principle of revelation. Who reveals? Everybody around us; we learn of each other. I have something which you have not, and you have something which I have not; I reveal what I have to you, and you reveal what you have to me. I believe that we are revelators to each other. Are the heavens opened? Yes, to some at times, yet upon natural principles, upon the principle of natural philosophy. "Do you know the will and mind of the Lord?" Yes, concerning this people, and concerning myself. Does every one of my brethren and sisters know the will of the Lord? Let me say to the Latter-day Saints, if they will take up their cross and follow the Lord Jesus Christ in the regeneration, many of them will receive more, know more, and have more of the Spirit of revelation than they are aware of; but the revelations which I receive are all upon natural principles. 3:209.

I am so far from believing that any government upon this earth has constitutions and laws that are perfect, that I do not even believe that there is a single revelation, among the many God has given to the Church, that is perfect in its fulness. The revelations of God contain correct doctrine and principle, so far as they go; but it is impossible for the poor, weak, low, grovelling, sinful inhabitants of the earth to receive a revelation from the Almighty in all its perfections. He has to speak to us in a manner to meet the extent of our capacities, as we have to do with these benighted Lamanites; it would be of no benefit to talk to them as I am now speaking to you. Before you can enter into conversation with them, give them your ideas, you are under the necessity of condescending to their low estate, so far as communication is concerned, in order to exalt them. 2:314.

The construction of the electric telegraph and the method of using it enabling the people to send messages from one end of the earth to the other, is just as much a revelation from God as any ever given. The same is true with regard to making machinery, whether it be a steamboat, a carding machine, threshing machine, or anything else, it makes no difference—these things have existed from all eternity and will continue to all eternity, and the Lord has revealed them to his children. 13:305.

Many are pleading for revelations; do you suppose that Saints lack revelations? They have plenty of them, and they are stored in the archives of those who have understanding of the principles of the Priesthood, ready to be brought forth as the people need. 3:337.

Men who know nothing of the Priesthood receive revelation and prophecy, and yet these gifts belong to the Church, and those who are faithful in the Kingdom of God inherit them and are entitled to them; and all ought to live so as to enjoy the spirit of these gifts and callings continually. 11:325.

Should you receive a vision or revelation from the Almighty, one that the Lord gave you concerning yourselves, or this people, but which you are not to reveal on account of your not being the proper person, or because it ought not to be known by the people at present, you should shut it up and seal it as close, and lock it as tight as heaven is to you, and make it as secret as the grave. The Lord has no confidence in those who reveal secrets, for he cannot safely reveal himself to such persons. 4:288.

Take a course to open and keep a communication with your Elder Brother or file-leader—our Savior. Were I to draw a distinction in all the duties that are required of the children of men, from first to last, I would place first and foremost the duty of seeking unto the Lord our God until we open the path of communication from heaven to earth—from God to our own souls. Keep every avenue of your hearts clean and pure before him. 8:339.

That man who cannot know things without telling any other living being upon the earth, who cannot keep his secrets and those that God reveals to him, never can receive the voice of his Lord to dictate him and the people on this earth. 4:287.

It was asked me by a gentleman how I guided the people by revelation. I teach them to live so that the Spirit of revelation may make plain to them their duty day by day that they are able to guide themselves. To get this revelation it is necessary that the people live so that their spirits are as pure and clean as a piece of blank paper that lies on the desk before the inditer, ready to receive any mark the writer may make upon it. 11:240.

Yes, my brethren and sisters here, both men and women, have revelation, and I can say with Moses of old—"Would God that all the Lord's people were prophets." 1:242.

Angels—There is a difference of opinion as to getting the word of the Lord; but if you will read and cultivate the Spirit of God, you will understand how it is obtained. The Lord is not everywhere in person; but he has his agents speaking and acting for him. His angels, his messengers, his apostles and servants are appointed and authorized to act in his name. And his servants are authorized to counsel and dictate in the greatest and what might be deemed the most trifling matters, to instruct, direct and guide his Saints. 12:245.

The Lord is here with us, not in person, but his angels are around us, and he takes cognizance of every act of the children of men, as individuals and as nations. He is here ready by his agents, the angels, and by the power of his Holy Spirit and Priesthood, which he has restored in these last days, to bring most perfect and absolute deliverance unto all who put their trust in him, when they are ready to receive it. 11:14.

When an angel is appointed to perform a duty, to go to the earth, to preach the Gospel, or to do anything for the advancement of his Father's kingdom in any part of the great domain of heaven the vision of that angel is opened to see and understand the magnitude of the work that is expected of him to perform, and the grand results which will grow out of it. That is the reason why the angels are of one heart and of one mind, in their faithfulness and obedience to the requirements of their Father and God. They can desire and ask for nothing that will make them happy, good and great that is withheld from them; and life eternal is theirs. Why, then, should they not be of one heart and of one mind? They see alike, understand alike, and know alike, and all things are before them, and, as far as their knowledge and experience extend, they see the propriety of all the works of God, and the harmony and beauty thereof. 11:15.

What is the difference between Saints of God and an angel of God? One is clothed upon with mortality, the other has passed through mortality and has received the celestial glory of our Heavenly Father, and is free from the contaminating influences of sin that we have to contend with. 19:66.

There is much in my presence besides those who sit here, if we had eyes to see the heavenly beings that are in our presence. 8:207.

When the Lord commands those invisible beings, shall I say, those who have had their resurrection?—yes, millions and millions more than the inhabitants of this earth, they can fight your battles. 2:255.

Prayer—Let all persons be fervent in prayer, until they know the things of God for themselves and become certain that they are walking in the path that leads to everlasting life; then will envy, the child of ignorance, vanish and there will be no disposition in any man to place himself above another; for such a feeling meets no countenance in the order of heaven. Jesus Christ never wanted to be different from his Father. They were and are one. If a people are led by the revelations of Jesus Christ, and they are cognizant of the fact through their faithfulness, there is no fear but they will be one in Jesus Christ, and see eye to eye. 9:150.

If we draw near to him, he will draw near to us; if we seek him early, we shall find him; if we apply our minds faithfully and diligently day by day, to know and understand the mind and will of God, it is as easy as, yes, I will say easier than it is to know the minds of each other, for to know and understand ourselves and our own being is to know and understand God and his being. 13:312.

Practice your religion today, and say your prayers faithfully. 16:28.

The duty of the Latter-day Saints is to pray without ceasing, and in everything to give thanks, to acknowledge the hand of the Lord in all things, and to be subject to his requirements. 15:63.

Let every man and every woman call upon the name of the Lord, and that, too, from a pure heart, while they are at work as well as in their closet; while they are in public as well as while they are in private, asking the Father in the name of Jesus, to bless them, and to preserve and guide in, and to teach them, the way of life and salvation and to enable them so to live that they will obtain this eternal salvation that we are after. 15:63.

The Lord says, I will be sought unto by my people for the blessings that they need. And instead of our classing prayer among the duties devolving upon us as Latter-day Saints, we should live so as to deem it one of the greatest privileges accorded to us; for were it not for the efficacy of prayer what would have become of us both as a people and as individuals? 19:222.

You know that it is one peculiarity of our faith and religion never to ask the Lord to do a thing without being willing to help him all that we are able; and then the Lord will do the rest. 5:293.

I shall not ask the Lord to do what I am not willing to do. 8:143.

Do not ask God to give you knowledge, when you are confident that you will not keep and rightly improve upon that knowledge. 3:338.

I pray both for my friends and for my enemies, that, if they will not repent, the earth may be speedily emptied of the ungodly. 4:346.

If I ask him to give me wisdom concerning any requirement in life, or in regard to my own course, or that of my friends, my family, my children, or those that I preside over, and get no answer from him, and then do the very best that my judgment will teach me, he is bound to own and honor that transaction, and he will do so to all intents and purposes. 3:205.

When you approach the throne of grace and petition the Father, in the name of the Savior who has redeemed the world, do you use the name as the name of a stranger? If you understand your own religion, you petition that Personage as you would one of your brethren in the flesh. Is this strange to you? It should bring near to you things that pertain to eternity, give your reflections and views a more exalted cast, stamp your daily actions with truth and honesty, and cause you to be filled with the Spirit and power of God. 7:274-5.

Your prayers cannot prevail if there is disunion among you. 5:331.

I do not know any other way for the Latter-day Saints than for every breath to be virtually a prayer for God to guide and direct his people, and that he will never suffer us to possess anything that will be an injury to us. I am satisfied that this should be the feeling of every Latter-day Saint in the world. If you are making a bargain, if you are talking in the house, visiting in the social party, going forth in the dance, every breath should virtually be a prayer that God will preserve us from sin and from the effects of sin. 10:313.

Let us be humble, fervent, submissive, yielding ourselves to the will of the Lord, and there is no danger but that we shall have his Spirit to guide us. If we will open our lips and call upon our Heavenly Father, in the name of Jesus, we will have the spirit of prayer. I have proved this to be the best way. If we do everything in the season thereof, attending to our prayers and daily labors in their proper order and at the right time, all will go well. 13:155.

When you get up in the morning, before you suffer yourselves to eat one mouthful of food, call your wife and children together, bow down before the Lord, ask him to forgive your sins, and protect you through the day, to preserve you from temptation and all evil, to guide your steps aright, that you may do something that day that shall be beneficial to the Kingdom of God on the earth. Have you time to do this? Elders, sisters, have you time to pray? 15:36.

Say your prayers always before going to work. Never forget that. A father—the head of the family—should never miss calling his family together and dedicating himself and them to the Lord of Hosts, asking the guidance and direction of his Holy Spirit to lead them through the day—that very day. Lead us this day, guide us this day, preserve us this day, save us from sinning against thee or any being in heaven or on earth this day! If we do this every day, the last day we live we will be prepared to enjoy a higher glory. 12:261.

We may say that our work drives us and that we have not time to pray, hardly time to eat our breakfasts. Then let the breakfasts go, and pray; get down upon our knees and pray until we are filled with the spirit of peace. 10:174.

It matters not whether you or I feel like praying, when the time comes to pray, pray. If we do not feel like it, we should pray till we do. And if there is a heavy storm coming on and our hay is likely to be wet, let it come. You will find that those who wait till the Spirit bids them pray, will never pray much on this earth. Such people would come to meeting and look at each other and then when they had stayed as long as they felt inclined, address their brethren with—"Good-bye, I am going home," and then leave. But when the time comes to have prayers, let them be made, and there will be no danger. 13:155.

There are times and places when all should vocally repeat the words spoken, but in our prayer meetings and in our family circles let every heart be united with the one who takes the lead by being mouth before the Lord, and let every person mentally repeat the prayers, and all unite in whatever is asked for, and the Lord will not withhold, but will give to such persons the things which they ask for and rightly need. 3:53.

Some of the brethren come to me and say, "Brother Brigham, is it my duty to pray when I have not one particle of the spirit of prayer in me?" True, at times, men are perplexed and full of care and trouble, their ploughs and other implements are out of order, their animals have strayed and a thousand things perplex them; yet our judgment teaches us that it is our duty to pray, whether we are particularly in the spirit of praying or not. My doctrine is, it is your duty to pray; and when the time for prayer comes, John should say, "This is the place and this is the time to pray; knees bend down upon the floor, and do so at once." But John said, "I do not want to pray; I do not feel like it." Knees get down, I say; and down bend the knees, and he begins to think and reflect. Can you say anything? Can you not say, God have mercy on me a sinner? Yes, he can do this, if he can rise up and curse his neighbor for some ill deeds. Now, John, open your mouth and say, Lord, have mercy upon me. "But I do not feel the spirit of prayer." That does not excuse you, for you know what your duty is. You have a passion, a will, a temper to overcome. You are subject to temptation as other men; and when you are tempted, let the judgment which God has placed within you and the intelligence he has given you by the light of the Spirit be the master in this case.

If I could not master my mouth, I would my knees, and make them bend until my mouth would speak. "But the cattle are in the corn." Let them eat; you can attend to them when you have finished praying. Let the will of man be brought into subjection to the law of Christ—to all the ordinances of the house of God. What, in his darkness and depression? Yes; for that is the time to prove whether one is a friend of God, that the confidence of the Almighty may increase in his Son. We should so live that our confidence and faith may increase in him. We must even go further than that. Let us so live that the faith and confidence of our Heavenly Father may increase towards us, until he shall know that we will be true to him under any and all circumstances and at all times. When in our darkness and temptation we are found faithful to our duty, that increases the confidence of our God in us. He sees that we will be his servants. 7:164.

If the Devil says you cannot pray when you are angry, tell him it is none of his business, and pray until that species of insanity is dispelled and serenity is restored to the mind. 10:175.

Let every Saint, when he prays, ask God for the things he needs to enable him to promote righteousness on the earth. If you do not know what to ask for, let me tell you how to pray. When you pray in secret with your families, if you do not know anything to ask for, submit yourselves to your Father in Heaven and beseech him to guide you by the inspirations of the Holy Ghost, and to guide this people, and dictate the affairs of his Kingdom on the earth, and there leave it. Ask him to put you just where he wants you, and to tell you what he wants you to do, and feel that you are on hand to do it. 6:43.

When you have labored faithfully for years, you will learn this simple fact—that if your hearts are aright, and you still continue to be obedient, continue to serve God, continue to pray, the Spirit of revelation will be in you like a well of water springing up to everlasting life. Let no person give up prayer because he has not the spirit of prayer, neither let any earthly circumstance hurry you while in the performance of this important duty. By bowing down before the Lord to ask him to bless you, you will simply find this result—God will multiply blessings on you temporally and spiritually. Let a merchant, a farmer, a mechanic, any person in business, live his religion faithfully, and he need never lose one minute's sleep by thinking about his business; he need not worry in the least, but trust in God, go to sleep and rest. I say to this people—pray, and if you cannot do anything else, read a prayer aloud that your family may hear it, until you get a worshiping spirit, and are full of the riches of eternity, then you will be prepared at any time to lay hands on the sick, or to officiate in any of the ordinances of this religion. 12:103.

If I did not feel like praying, and asking my Father in Heaven to give me a morning blessing, and to preserve me and my family and the good upon the earth through the day, I should say, "Brigham, get down here on your knees, bow your body down before the throne of him who rules in the heavens, and stay there until you can feel to supplicate at that throne of grace erected for sinners." 16:28.

Chapter IV

PRE-EXISTENCE, THE PLAN OF SALVATION

Time—When was there a beginning? There never was one; if there was, there will be an end; but there never was a beginning, and hence there will never be an end; that looks like eternity. When we talk about the beginning of eternity, it is rather simple conversation, and goes far beyond the capacity of man. 2:307.

Here is time, where is eternity? It is here, just as much as anywhere in all the expanse of space; a measured space of time is only a part of eternity. 3:367.

Every mind that thinks deeply upon the things of time and eternity, sees that time, which we measure by our lives, is like the stream from the mountains which gushes forth, yet we cannot tell from whence it comes, nor do we know naturally where it goeth, only it passes again into the clouds; so our lives are here, and this we are certain of. We do know that we live and that we have the power of sight. We do know and can realize that we possess the faculty of hearing. We can discern between that which we like and that which we dislike. This life that you and I possess is for eternity. Contemplate the idea of beings endowed with all the powers and faculties which we possess, becoming annihilated, passing out of existence, ceasing to be, and then try to reconcile it with our feelings and with our present lives. No intelligent person can do it. Yet it is only by the Spirit of revelation that we can understand these things. By the revelations of the Lord Jesus we understand things as they were, that have been made known unto us; things that are in the life which we now enjoy, and things as they will be, not to the fullest extent, but all that the Lord designs that we should understand, to make it profitable to us, in order to give us the experience necessary in this life to prepare us to enjoy eternal life hereafter. 12:111-112.

The present is that portion of time that more particularly concerns us, and the greatest and most important labor we have to perform is to cultivate ourselves. That man may know his fellow creatures, it is necessary that he should first know himself. When he thoroughly knows himself, he measurably knows God, whom to know is eternal life. 10:2.

As far as we can compare eternal things with earthly things that lie within the scope of our understanding, so far we can understand them. 10:1.

As to the word annihilate, as we understand it, there is no such principle as to put a thing which exists, entirely out of existence, so that it does not exist in any form, shape, or place whatever. It would be as reasonable to say that endless, which is synonymous to the word eternity, has both a beginning and an end. 1:352.

The Organized Universe—The creations of God—the worlds that are and the worlds that have been,—who can grasp in the vision of his mind the truth that there never has been a time when there have not been worlds like this, and that there never will be a time when there will not be worlds organized and prepared for intelligent beings to dwell upon? 8:81.

There is an eternity of matter. Astronomers estimate that there is between us and the nearest fixed star matter enough from which to organize millions of earths like this. There is an eternity of matter, and it is all acted upon and filled with a portion of divinity. Matter is to exist; it cannot be annihilated. Eternity is without bounds, and is filled with matter; and there is no such place as empty space. And matter is capacitated to receive intelligence. 7:2.

Worlds are made of crude element which floats, without bounds in the eternities—in the immensity of space; an eternity of matter—no limits to it, in its natural crude state, and the power of the Almighty has this influence and wisdom—when he speaks he is obeyed, and matter comes together and is organized. 13:248.

According to all that the world has ever learned by the researches of philosophers and wise men, according to all the truths now revealed by science, philosophy and religion, qualities and attributes depend entirely upon their connection with organized matter for their development and visible manifestation. 11:121.

Man and Matter Eternal—Mankind are organized of element designed to endure to all eternity; it never had a beginning and never can have an end. There never was a time when this matter, of which you and I are composed, was not in existence, and there never can be a time when it will pass out of existence; it cannot be annihilated.

It is brought together, organized, and capacitated to receive knowledge and intelligence, to be enthroned in glory, to be made angels, Gods—beings who will hold control over the elements, and have power by their word to command the creation and redemption of worlds, or to extinguish suns by their breath, and disorganize worlds, hurling them back into their chaotic state. This is what you and I are created for. 3:356.

The elements with which we are surrounded are as eternal as we are, and are loaded with supplies of every kind for the comfort and happiness of the human race. 10:3.

Earthly things will be decomposed and their reorganization will be by the power of the resurrection; then we shall begin to understand the proper use of element. 7:65.

"Immaterial substance." It is like the center of a being everywhere and his circumference nowhere, or like being seated on the top of a topless throne. These are self-confounding expressions, and there is no meaning to any of them. 16:31.

If we could so understand true philosophy as to understand our own creation, and what it is for—what design and intent the Supreme Ruler had in organizing matter and bringing it forth in the capacity that I behold you here today, we could comprehend that matter cannot be destroyed—that it is subject to organization and disorganization; and could understand that matter can be organized and brought forth into intelligence, and to possess more intelligence and to continue to increase in that intelligence; and could learn those principles that organized matter into animals, vegetables, and into intelligent beings; and could discern the Divinity acting, operating, and diffusing principles into matter to produce intelligent beings and to exalt them—to what? Happiness. Will nothing short of that fully satisfy the spirits implanted within us? No. 7:2-3.

Gold and silver are composing, and so does every other kind of metal, the same as the hair upon my head, or the wheat in the field; they do not compose as fast, but they are all the time composing or decomposing. 1:219.

There never was a time when man did not exist, and there never will be a time when he will cease to exist. Eternity is without confines, and all things animate and inanimate have their existence in it. The Priesthood of God, that was given to the ancients and is given to men in the latter days, is co-equal in duration with eternity—is without beginning of days or end of life. It is unchangeable in its system of government and its Gospel of salvation. It gives to Gods and angels their supremacy and power, and offers wealth, influence, posterity, exaltations, power, glory, kingdoms and thrones, ceaseless in their duration, to all who will accept them on the terms upon which they are offered. 10:5

The life that is within us is a part of an eternity of life, and is organized spirit, which is clothed upon by tabernacles, thereby constituting our present being, which is designed for the attainment of further intelligence. The matter composing our bodies and spirits has been organized from the eternity of matter that fills immensity. 7:285.

Man is organized and brought forth as the king of the earth, to understand, to criticize, examine, improve, manufacture, arrange, and organize the crude matter, and honor and glorify the work of God's hands. This is a wide field for the operation of man, that reaches into eternity; and it is good for mortals to search out the things of this earth. 9:242.

Man the Offspring of God—No human being has had power to organize his own existence. Then there is a greater than we. Are we our own in our bodies? Are we our own in our spirits? We are not our own. We belong to our progenitors—to our Father and our God. 8:67.

Things were first created spiritually; the Father actually begat the spirits, and they were brought forth and lived with him. Then he commenced the work of creating earthly tabernacles, precisely as he had been created in this flesh himself, by partaking of the coarse material that was organized and composed this earth, until his system was charged with it, consequently the tabernacles of his children were organized from the coarse materials of this earth.

When the time came that his First-born, the Savior, should come into the world and take a tabernacle, the Father came himself and favored that Spirit with a tabernacle instead of letting any other man do it. The Savior was begotten by the Father and his Spirit, by the same Being who is the Father of our spirits, and that is all the organic difference between Jesus Christ and you and me. And a difference there is between our Father and us consists in that he has gained his exaltation, and has obtained eternal lives. The principle of eternal lives is an eternal existence, eternal duration, eternal exaltation. Endless are his kingdoms, endless his thrones and his dominions and endless are his posterity; they never will cease to multiply from this time henceforth and forever. 4:218.

I want to tell you, each and every one of you, that you are well acquainted with God our Heavenly Father, or the great Elohim. You are all well acquainted with him, for there is not a soul of you but what has lived in his house and dwelt with him year after year; and yet you are seeking to become acquainted with him, when the fact is, you have merely forgotten what you did know.

There is not a person here to-day but what is a son or a daughter of that Being. In the spirit world their spirits were first begotten and brought forth, and they lived there with their parents for ages before they came here. This, perhaps, is hard for many to believe, but it is the greatest nonsense in the world not to believe it. If you do not believe it, cease to call him Father; and when you pray, pray to some other character. 4:216.

We are the sons and daughters of celestial Beings, and the germ of the Deity dwells within us. When our spirits took possession of these tabernacles, they were as pure as the angels of God, wherefore total depravity cannot be a true doctrine. 10:192.

Our spirits once dwelt in the heavens and were as pure and holy as the angels; but angels have tabernacles and spirits have none; and they come to the meanest, lowest and humblest of the human race to obtain one rather than run any risk of not doing so. I have heard that the celebrated Mr. Beecher, of Brooklyn, once said that the greatest misfortune that could ever happen to man was to be born; but I say that the greatest good fortune that ever happened or can happen to human beings is to be born on this earth, for then life and salvation are before them; then they have the privilege of overcoming death, and of treading sin and iniquity under their feet, of incorporating into their daily lives every principle of life and salvation and of dwelling eternally with the Gods. 13:145.

When we look upon the human face we look upon the image of our Father and God; there is a divinity in each person, male and female; there is the heavenly, there is the divine and with this is amalgamated the human, the earthly, the weaker portions of our nature, and it is the human that shrinks in the presence of the divine, and this accounts for our man-fearing spirit, and it is all there is of it. 9:291.

The origin of thought was planted in our organization at the beginning of our being. This is not telling you how it came there, or who put it there. Thought originated with our individual being, which is organized to be as independent as any being in eternity. 2:135.

We were created upright, pure, and holy, in the image of our father and our mother, the image of our God.

Wherein do we differ? In the talents that are given us, and in our callings. We are made of the same materials; our spirits were begotten by the same parents; in the begetting of the flesh we are of the same first parents, and all the kindreds of the earth are made of one flesh; but we are different in regard to our calling. 3:365.

We have no true interest, only conjointly with our Father in Heaven. We are his children, his sons and daughters, and this should not be a mystery to this people, even though there are many who have been gathered with us but a short time. He is the God and Father of our spirits; he devised the plan that produced our tabernacles; the houses for our spirits to dwell in. 4:27.

The Spirit of Man—The spirits that live in these tabernacles were as pure as the heavens, when they entered them. They came to tabernacles that are contaminated, pertaining to the flesh, by the fall of man. The Psalmist says, "Behold, I was shapen in iniquity, and in sin did my mother conceive me." This Scripture has established in the minds of some the doctrine of total depravity—that it is impossible for them to have one good thought, that they are altogether sinful, that there is no good, no soundness, and no spiritual health in them. This is not correct, yet we have a warfare within us. We have to contend against evil passions, or the seeds of iniquity that are sown in the flesh through the fall. The pure spirits that occupy these tabernacles are operated upon, and it is the right of him that sent them into these tabernacles to hold the pre-eminence, and to always give the Spirit of truth to influence the spirits of men, that it may triumph and reign predominantly in our tabernacles, the God and Lord of every motion. We not only have this warfare continually, day by day, within ourselves, but we also have an outside influence or pressure to resist. Both the religious and the political world have influences to contend against that very much resemble each other; they are more or less exercised, governed and controlled by surrounding influences. We, Latter-day Saints, have an influence of this kind to contend against. 10:105.

We see life spring into existence all around us. Where is its fountain? And how is it originated? It exists for a day, a night, a year, or an age, and it is gone; and who can say where? Who can tell what has become of the life that dwelt in that tabernacle, causing it to think,—that lit up he eye with living fire, and caused the mouth to utter forth wisdom? Can mortal man tell? Not unless he is inspired by the Almighty, and understands eternal things. The origin of all things is in eternity. Like a cloud passing across a clear sky—like a bird that suddenly flits across our path—like a pure gushing stream from a hidden fountain, that soon sinks in some mountain chasm, so, apparently, life flashes into this mortal existence, and passes away. 7:173.

Intelligence is given unto us to improve upon. 8:81.

The origin of thought and reflection is in ourselves. We think, because we are, and are made susceptible of external influences, and to feel our relationship to external objects. Thus thoughts of revenge, and thoughts of blessing will arise in the same mind, as it is influenced by external circumstances. 2:135.

There is just as much difference in the spiritual organization, as you see in the temporal organization. You can see that eternal variety in both. 9:125.

I see a man grow up from the infant stage to be a scholar, and by and by he has an empire, and can give laws to the people, that can equalize them, and bring them to a state of happiness and excellency, and give them all the advantages that man can possess upon the earth, and make every man happy and comfortable. This is the work that we have upon our hands. Teach the people the faith of the Gospel. Teach them what God is, and what his work is, and that there never was a time such as many of our philosophers speak of, who drift back and back, and come to this theory and that theory, and go back, and back to the time when we were all reptiles. When was there a time when there was not a God? But, say they, there must have been a time. Then you declare to me, do you, that there was a time when there was no time? And this is the philosophy of a great many of the scientific in this day. They see the heavens stretched out, but they comprehend them not. And why do they not say, if there was a time when there was no time, there will be a time again when there will be no time. What a condition for man to be in! Can we look onward and upward through the immensity of space, and behold the worlds on worlds that we call stars, and imagine that they will be blotted out forever? What an ideal! 19:49.

Everything in heaven, on earth, and in hell is organized for the benefit, advantage, and exaltation of intelligent beings; therefore there is nothing that is out of the pale of our faith. There is nothing, I may say, good or bad, light or darkness, truth or error, but what is to be controlled by intelligent beings; and we should learn how to take into our possession every blessing and every privilege that God has put within our reach, and know how to use our time, our talents, and all our acts for the advancement of his Kingdom upon the earth. 6:145.

We are all his children. We are his sons and daughters naturally, and by the principles of eternal life. We are brethren and sisters. What is it that makes the distinctions we see in the classes of the children of men? We see the low and the degraded, like the aborigines of our country; what is the cause of their being in their present condition? It is because of the rejection by their fathers of the Gospel of the Son of God. The Gospel brings intelligence, happiness, and glory to all who obey it and live according to its precepts. It will give them intelligence that comes from God. Their minds will be open so as to understand things as they are; they will rejoice in being blessed themselves and in blessing their fellow beings, and in being prepared to re-enter the presence of the Father and the Son. This will be their delight. 13:178.

The Council in Heaven—The Council in heaven said, "Let there be an earth, and let there be a firmament above and beneath it," and it was so. They said, "Let there be heat and cold," and it was so. They said, "Let there be spring and summer, autumn and winter," and it was so. 9:254.

"Who will redeem the earth, who will go forth and make the

sacrifice for the earth and all things it contains?" The Eldest Son said: "Here am I"; and then he added, "Send me." But the second one, which was "Lucifer, Son of the Morning," said "Lord, here am I, send me, I will redeem every son and daughter of Adam and Eve that lives on the earth, or that ever goes on the earth." "But," says the Father, "that will not answer at all. I give each and every individual his agency; all must use that in order to gain exaltation in my kingdom; inasmuch as they have the power of choice they must exercise that power. They are my children; the attributes which you see in me are in my children and they must use their agency. If you undertake to save all, you must save them in unrighteousness and corruption. You will be the man that will say to the thief on the cross, to the murderer on the gallows, and to him who has killed his father, mother, brothers, and sisters and little ones, 'Now if you will say, I repent and believe on the Lord Jesus Christ, or on the Savior of the world, you shall be saved." This is what all the religious sects of the day are saying now, but Jesus did not say any such thing. 13:282.

When there was rebellion in heaven, judgment was laid to the line and righteousness to the plummet, and the evil were cast out. Yet there was a portion of grace allotted to those rebellious characters.

But they must go from heaven, they could not dwell there, they must be cast down to earth to try the sons of men, and to perform their labor in producing an opposite in all things, that the inhabitants of the earth might have the privilege of improving upon the intelligence given to them, the opportunity for overcoming evil, and for learning the principles which govern eternity, that they may be exalted therein. 3:256.

The Lord Almighty suffered this schism in heaven to see what his subjects would do preparatory to their coming to this earth. 14:93.

In regard to the battle in heaven, that Brother Truman O. Angell referred to, how much of a battle it was I have forgotten. I cannot relate the principal circumstances, it is so long since it happened; but I do not think it lasted very long; for when Lucifer, the Son of the Morning, claimed the privilege of having the control of this earth, and redeeming it, a contention arose; but I do not think it took long to cast down one-third of the hosts of heaven, as it is written in the Bible. But let me tell you that it was one-third part of the spirits who were prepared to take tabernacles upon this earth, and who rebelled against the other two-thirds of the heavenly host; and they were cast down to this world. It is written that they were cast down to the earth. They were cast down to this globe—to this terra firma that you and I walk upon, and whose atmosphere we breathe. One-third part of the spirits that were prepared for this earth rebelled against

Jesus Christ, and were cast down to the earth, and they have been opposed to him from that day to this, with Lucifer at their head. He is their general—Lucifer, the Son of the Morning. He was once a brilliant and influential character in heaven, and we will know more about him hereafter. 5:54-55.

From the spirit and tenor the ancient Scriptures and revelations which we have received, it is plainly set forth that there are men pre-appointed to perform certain works in their lifetime, and bring to pass certain ends and purposes in the economy of heaven. 11:253.

Do you think that the Lord has his eye upon a great many? There is a passage of Scripture that reads thus: "For whom he did foreknow, he also did predestinate to be conformed to the image of his Son, that he might be the firstborn among many brethren," etc. Whom did he not foreknow? I do not think there is anybody now on the earth, that has lived before us, or that will come after us, but what he knew. He knew who would be his anointed; he had his eye upon them all the time, as he had upon Moses, Pharaoh, Abraham, Melchizedek, and Noah, who was a chosen vessel to build the ark and save a remnant from the flood. 8:229.

It is a mistaken idea that God has decreed all things whatsoever that come to pass, for the volition of the creature is as free as air. You may inquire whether we believe in foreordination; we do, as strongly as any people in the world. We believe that Jesus was foreordained before the foundations of the world were built, and his mission was appointed him in eternity to be the Savior of the world, yet when he came in the flesh he was left free to choose or refuse to obey his Father. Had he refused to obey his Father, he would have become a son of perdition. We also are free to choose or refuse the principles of eternal life. God has decreed and foreordained many things that have come to pass, and he will continue to do so; but when he decrees great blessings upon a nation or upon an individual they are decreed upon certain conditions. When he decrees great plagues and overwhelming destructions upon nations or people, those decrees come to pass because those nations and people will not forsake their wickedness and turn unto the Lord. It was decreed that Nineveh should be destroyed in forty days, but the decree was stayed on the repentance of the inhabitants of Nineveh. God rules and reigns, and has made all his children as free as himself, to choose the right or the wrong, and we shall then be judged according to our works. 10:324.

You cannot give any persons their exaltation unless they know what evil is, what sin, sorrow, and misery are, for no person could comprehend, appreciate and enjoy an exaltation upon any other principle. The Devil with one-third part of the spirits of our Father's

Kingdom got here before us, and we tarried there with our friends, until the time came for us to come to the earth and take tabernacles, but those spirits that revolted were forbidden ever to have tabernacles of their own. You can now comprehend how it is that they are always trying to get possession of the bodies of human beings; you read of a man's being possessed of a legion, and Mary Magdalene had seven. 3:369.

Foreordination, for instance, and free grace are both true doctrines; but they must be properly coupled together and correctly classified, so as to produce harmony between these two apparently opposite doctrines. 6:291.

The Plan of Salvation—The great plan called the plan of salvation—the system of doctrine, ideas, and practices that pertain to all the intelligence that exists in eternity. 8:32.

Elevation, exaltation and glory are the objects of the Father in peopling this earth with his progeny. 10:191.

This is the plan of salvation. Jesus will never cease his work until all are brought up to the enjoyment of a kingdom in the mansions of his Father, where there are many kingdoms and many glories, to suit the works and faithfulness of all men that have lived on the earth. Some will obey the celestial law and receive of its glory, some will abide the terrestrial and some the telestial, and others will receive no glory. 13:76.

When you understand the Gospel plan, you will comprehend that it is the most reasonable way of dealing with the human family. You will discern that purity, holiness, justice, perfection, and all that adorns the character of the Deity are contributing to the salvation of men. 8:115.

Our mortal existence is a school of experience. 9:29.

Our mortal bodies are all important to us; without them we never can be glorified in the eternities that will be. We are in this state of being for the express purpose of obtaining habitations for our spirits to dwell in, that they may become personages of tabernacle. 9:286.

Our bodies are all important to us, though they may be old and withered, emaciated with toil, pain, and sickness, and our limbs bent with rheumatism, all uniting to hasten dissolution, for death is sown in our mortal bodies. The food and drink we partake of are contaminated with the seeds of death, yet we partake of them to extend our lives until our allotted work is finished, when our tabernacles, in a state of ripeness, are sown in the earth to produce immortal fruit. Yet, if we live our holy religion and let the spirit reign, it will not become dull and stupid, but as the body approaches dissolution the spirit takes a firmer hold on that enduring substance behind the veil, drawing from the depths of that eternal Fountain of Light sparkling gems of intelligence which surround the frail and sinking tabernacle with a halo of immortal wisdom. 9:288.

Until the last spirit that has been designed to come here and take a tabernacle has come upon the earth, the winding-up scene cannot come. 8:352.

Can you save all? Yes, you can save all that will be saved. If people are not saved, it is because they are not disposed to be saved. They act for themselves, and act from choice. 9:125.

The whole object of the creation of this world is to exalt the intelligences that are placed upon it, that they may live, endure, and increase for ever and ever. We are not here to quarrel and contend about the things of this world, but we are here to subdue and beautify it. Let every man and woman worship their God with all their heart. Let them pay their devotions and sacrifices to him, the Supreme, and the Author of their existence. Do all the good you can to your fellow-creatures. You are flesh of my flesh and bone of my bone. God has created of one blood all the nations and kingdoms of men that dwell upon all the face of the earth: black, white, copper-colored, or whatever their color, customs, or religion, they have all sprung from the same origin; the blood of all is from the same element. 7:290.

The Lord created you and me for the purpose of becoming Gods like himself; when we have been proved in our present capacity, and have been faithful with all things he puts into our possession.

How many will become thus privileged? Those who honor the Father and the Son; those who receive the Holy Ghost, and magnify their calling, and are found pure and holy; they shall be crowned in the presence of the Father and the Son. 3:93.

The great and grand secret of salvation, which we should continually seek to understand through our faithfulness, is the continuation of the lives. 18:260.

We are all the children of our common Father, who has placed us on the earth to prove ourselves, to govern, control, educate and sanctify ourselves, body and spirit, unto him, according to his will and pleasure. When all that class of spirits designed to take bodies upon this earth have done so, then will come the winding-up scene of this particular department of the works of God on this earth. It is his will that we should prepare ourselves to build up his Kingdom, gather the House of Israel, redeem and build up Zion and Jerusalem, revolutionize the world, and bring back that which has been lost through the fall. 10:2.

The Lord has given the earth to the children of men, that by the union of mind and matter, inspired and directed by the power of eternal Priesthood, all may be made subject to the Great Supreme Ruler of the universe. 9:255.

The very laws which govern eternity are planned to sustain an eternal growth, gathering together and increasing; so that the true servant of God cannot possibly suffer loss, but will reap eternal gain though he, for the cause of truth, is poor and needy through the whole of this short life. He has made truth his theme; and what is it? I will say it is that which endures; it is eternity, and its power is to grow, increase, and expand, adding life to life, and power to power, worlds without end. 2:129.

You may ask, "What is meted out to us?" I answer the ordinances, the sacraments that the Lord Jesus Christ instituted for the salvation of the Jews, for all the House of Israel, and then for the Gentiles. This is the Gospel—the plan of salvation the Lord has given to us. This is the Kingdom the Lord has presented to us; the same he presented to the Apostles in the days of Jesus. 3.90.

It is the wish of our Heavenly Father to bring all his children back into his presence. The spirits of all the human family dwelt with him before they took tabernacles of flesh and became subject to the fall and to sin. He is their spiritual Father, and has sent them here to be clothed with flesh, and to be subject, with their tabernacles, to the ills that afflict fallen humanity. When they have proved themselves faithful in all things, and worthy before him, they can then have the privilege of returning again to his presence, with their bodies, to dwell in the abodes of the blessed. If man could have been made perfect in his double capacity of body and spirit, without passing through the ordeals of mortality, there would have been no necessity of our coming into this state of trial and suffering. Could the Lord have glorified his children in spirit, without a body like his own, he no doubt would have done so. 11:43.

We had an existence before we came into the world. Our spirits came here pure to take these tabernacles; they came to occupy them as habitations, with the understanding that all that had passed previously to our coming here should be taken away from us, that we should not know anything about it. 3:367.

The plan by which God works is rational, and meets the capacity of his children. This earth is the home he has prepared for us, and we are to prepare ourselves and our habitations for the celestial glory in store for the faithful. None will be destroyed except those who receive the oracles of truth and reject them. None are condemned except those who have the privilege of receiving the words of eternal life and refuse to receive them. 8:294.

He governs by law. He has also provided means and, in connection with the attributes he has implanted within us, has instituted ordinances which, if we will receive and improve upon, will enable us to return back into his presence. 13:171.

Is there a debt contracted between the Father and his children? There is. Our first parents transgressed the law that was given them in the garden; their eyes were opened. This created the debt. What is the nature of this debt? It is a divine debt. What will pay it? I ask, Is there anything short of a divine sacrifice that can pay this debt? No, there is not.

A divine debt has been contracted by the children, and the Father demands recompense. He says to his children on this earth, who are in sin and transgression, it is impossible for you to pay this debt; I have prepared a sacrifice; I will send my Only Begotten Son to pay this divine debt. Was it necessary then that Jesus should die? Do we understand why he should sacrifice his life? The idea that the Son of God, who never committed sin, should sacrifice his life is unquestionably preposterous to the minds of many in the Christian world. But the fact exists that the Father, the Divine Father, whom we serve, the God of the Universe, the God and Father of our Lord Jesus Christ, and the Father of our spirits, provided this sacrifice and sent his Son to die for us; and it is also a great fact that the Son came to do the will of the Father, and that he has paid the debt, in fulfilment of the Scripture which says, "He was the Lamb slain from the foundation of the world."

Is this easy to understand? It is perfectly easy to me; and my advice to those who have queries and doubts on this subject is, when they reason and philosophize upon it, not to plant their position in falsehood or argue hypothetically, but upon the facts as they exist, and they will come to the conclusion that unless God provides a Savior to pay this debt it can never be paid. Can all the wisdom of the world devise means by which we can be redeemed, and return to the presence of our Father and Elder Brother, and dwell with holy angels and celestial beings? No; it is beyond the power and wisdom of the inhabitants of the earth that now live, or that ever did or ever will live, to prepare or create a sacrifice that will pay this divine debt. But God provided it, and his Son has paid it, and we, each and every one, can now receive the truth and be saved in the Kingdom of God. Is it clear and plain? It is to me, and if you have the Spirit of God, it is as plain to you as anything else in the world. 14:71.

Has the Lord cast an obstacle in the way of any individual, to deprive him of the privilege of being exalted? No, not one; but every thing that could be done has been done, every provision that could be made has been made, every law that could be instituted to encourage and elevate the people, to increase their faith, their knowledge, their understanding, and to lead them to life and salvation, the Lord has brought to this people. 4:196.

The world is before us, eternity is before us, and an inexhaustible fountain of intelligence for us to obtain. 8:8.

It seems to be absolutely necessary in the providence of him who created us, and who organized and fashioned all things according to his wisdom, that man must descend below all things. It is written of the Savior in the Bible that he descended below all things that he might ascend above all. Is is not so with every man? Certainly it is. It is fit, then, that we should descend below all things and come up gradually, and learn a little now and again, receive "line upon line, precept upon precept, here a little and there a little." 15:3.

We know the design of our Father in Heaven in creating the earth and in peopling it, and bringing forth the myriads of organizations which dwell upon it. We know that all this is for his glory—to swell the eternities that are before him with intelligent beings who are capable of enjoying the height of glory. But, before we can come in possession of this, we need large experience, and its acquisition is a slow process. Our lives here are for the purpose of acquiring this, and the longer we live the greater it should be. 14:229.

It has also been decreed by the Almighty that spirits, upon taking bodies, shall forget all they had known previously, or they could not have a day of trial—could not have an opportunity for proving themselves in darkness and temptation, in unbelief and wickedness, to prove themselves worthy of eternal existence. 6:333.

Recollect the saying of one of the Apostles, when speaking about getting into the kingdom of heaven, that "if the righteous scarcely be saved, where shall the ungodly and the sinner appear?" The best man that ever lived on this earth only just made out to save himself through the grace of God. The best woman that ever lived on the earth has only made her escape from this world to a better one, with a full assurance of enjoying the first resurrection. It requires all the atonement of Christ, the mercy of the Father, the pity of angels and the grace of the Lord Jesus Christ to be with us always, and then to do the very best we possibly can, to get rid of this sin within us, so that we may escape from this world into the celestial kingdom. 11:301.

Millions of them have passed away, both in the Christian and in the heathen worlds, just as honest, virtuous and upright as any now living. The Christian world say they are lost; but the Lord will save them, or at least, all who will receive the Gospel. The plan of salvation which Jesus has revealed, and which we preach, reaches to the lowest and most degraded of Adam's lost race. Is he going to save all in the same glory and bring all the same state of felicity? Will they who refuse to obey the Gospel of the Son of God be saved and exalted in the same kingdom and glory as they who have obeyed? No, never, never! It is impossible. 13:323.

Darkness and sin were permitted to come on this earth. Man partook of the forbidden fruit in accordance with a plan devised from eternity, that mankind might be brought in contact with the principles and powers of darkness, that they might know the bitter and the sweet, the good and the evil, and be able to discern between light and darkness, to enable them to receive light continually. 7:158.

The greatest desire in the bosom of our Father Adam, or of his faithful children who are co-workers with God, our Father in Heaven, is to save the inhabitants of the earth. 8:174.

CHAPTER V

FREE AGENCY

All rational beings have an agency of their own; and according to their own choice they will be saved or damned. 6:97.

The volition of the creature is free; this is a law of their existence and the Lord cannot violate his own law; were he to do that, he would cease to be God. He has placed life and death before his children, and it is for them to choose. If they choose life, they receive the blessing of life; if they choose death, they must abide the penalty. This is a law which has always existed from all eternity, and will continue to exist throughout all the eternities to come. Every intelligent being must have the power of choice, and God brings forth the results of the acts of his creatures to promote his Kingdom and subserve his purposes in the salvation and exaltation of his children. 11:272.

My independence is sacred to me—it is a portion of that same Deity that rules in the heavens. There is not a being upon the face of the earth who is made in the image of God, who stands erect and is organized as God is, that would be deprived of the free exercise of his agency so far as he does not infringe upon other's rights, save by good advice and a good example. 10:191.

When the Lord made man, he made him an agent accountable to his God, with liberty to act and to do as he pleases to a certain extent in order to prove himself. There is a law that governs man thus far; but the law of the celestial kingdom, as I have frequently told you, is, and always will be, the same to all the children of Adam. 2:139.

He has given them the privilege of choosing for themselves, whether it be good or evil; but the result of our choice is still in his hand. All his children have the right of making a path for themselves of walking to the right or to the left, of telling the truth or that which is not true. This right God has given to all people who dwell on the earth, and they can legislate and act as they please; but God holds them in his hands, and he will bring forth the results of his glory, and for the benefit of those who love and serve him, and he will make the wrath of men to praise him. All of us are in the hands of that God. 13:178.

We possess no ability, only that which is given us of God. He has endowed us with glorious faculties, with God-like attributes like those which are incorporated in his own nature, and he has placed us upon this earth to honor them, and to sanctify ourselves and the earth preparatory to enjoying it in its celestial state. We are not, in anything, independent of God. We inherit what we possess from him. Yet it is so ordained, in the fathomless wisdom of God, that we should be agents to ourselves to choose the good or the evil, and thereby save and exalt our existence, or lose it. 10:265.

Our Father controls the results of our acts at his own pleasure, and we cannot prevent it. Man can produce and control his own acts, but he has no control over their results. God causes even the wrath of man to praise him, to redound to his glory and the salvation of his children. 8:18.

The Lord has not established laws by which I am compelled to have my shoes made in a certain style. He has never given a law to determine whether I shall have a square-toed boot or a peaked-toe boot; whether I shall have a coat with the waist just under my arms, and the skirts down to my heels; or whether I shall have a coat like the one I have on. Intelligence, to a certain extent, was bestowed both upon Saint and sinner, to use independently, aside from whether they have the law of the Priesthood or not, or whether they have ever heard of it or not. 2:139.

We cannot all do as we please, because a great many times we want to and cannot, and that is what produces misery, which is called hell. 13:33.

How far does our agency extend? There are certain bounds to it. What we have witnessed in thirty years' experience teaches us that man can appoint, but God can disappoint. Man can load his gun to shoot his neighbor, but he cannot make the ball hit him, if the Lord Almighty sees fit to turn it away. He can draw the sword to hew down his fellow-man; but instead of that, he may fall upon it himself. 8:31.

There are limits to agency, and to all things and to all beings, and our agency must not infringe upon that law. A man must choose life or death, and if he chooses death he will find himself abridged, and that the agency which is given to him is so bound up that he cannot exercise it in opposition to the law, without laying himself liable to be corrected and punished by the Almighty.

A man can dispose of his agency or of his birthright, as did Esau of old, but when disposed of, he cannot again obtain it; consequently, it behooves us to be careful, and not forfeit that agency that is given to us. The difference between the righteous and the sinner, eternal life or death, happiness or misery, is this, to those who are exalted there are no bounds or limits to their privileges, their blessings have a continuation, and to their kingdoms, thrones, and dominions, principalities, and powers there is no end, but they increase through all eternity; whereas, those who reject the offer, who despise the proffered mercies of the Lord, and prepare themselves to be banished from his presence, and to become companions of the devils, have their agency abridged immediately, and bounds and limits are put to their operations. 3:267.

The Lord does not compel any person to embrace the Gospel, and I do not think he will compel them to live it after they have embraced it. 10:282.

Our religion will not permit us to command or force any man or woman to obey the Gospel we have embraced. And we are under no obligation to do this, for every creature has as good a right, according to his organization, to choose for himself as the Gods. 14:94.

Not that the diverse creeds are right but the agency of the believers therein demands protection for them, as well as for us. 3:257.

Do you suppose that the Lord would have ever given a king to Israel, if they had not required one of his hands? No, he would have been their king and ruler, and there would have been a prophet to guide them, had it not been for their rebellion. They made choice of a king, and God gave them one in his anger.

Their rebellion against the law, the agency given to them allowing their free choice, induced them to ask for a king, and God gave them one. 3:257.

When I contemplate the endless variety in the dispositions, understandings, temperaments, countenances, and organizations of people, I am not surprised that there are those who do not understand things as I do. I expect people to have their own peculiar views, forms, principles, and notions. In consequence of this great variety, we should not be astonished if all do not believe the Gospel —do not love the truth. 8:131.

It is as much my right to differ from other men, as it is theirs to differ from me, in points of doctrine and principle, when our minds cannot at once arrive at the same conclusion. I feel it sometimes very difficult indeed to word my thoughts as they exist in my own mind, which I presume, is the grand cause of many apparent differences in sentiment which may exist among the Saints. 2:123.

I am not going to drive a man or woman to heaven. A great many think that they will be able to flog people into heaven, but this can never be done, for the intelligence in us is as independent as the Gods. People are not to be driven and you can put into a gnat's eye all the souls of the children of men that are driven into heaven by preaching hell-fire. 9:124.

When misuse of power has reached a certain stage, the divinity that is within the people asserts its right and they free themselves from the power of despotism. 10:101.

When the people do all they can, the Lord is bound to do the rest. 3:154.

Many are disposed through their own wickedness "to do as I damned please," and they are damned. 11:254.

When a truth is presented to an intelligent person he ought to grasp it and receive it in his faith. 8:59.

You may know whether you are led right or wrong, as well as you know the way home; for every principle God has revealed carries its own convictions of its truth to the human mind, and there is no calling of God to man on earth but what brings with it the evidence of its authenticity. 9:149.

You cannot break nor destroy the will. It is influenced and controlled, more or less, by the evil that is sown in the flesh, but not in the spirit, until the body has grown to years of accountability; then evil, when listened to, begins to rule and overrule the spirit God has placed within man. 6:332.

Men should not be permitted to do as they please in all things; for there are rules regulating all good societies and the business intercourse of men with each other, which are just and righteous in themselves, the violation of which cannot be countenanced either by civil or religious usages. It is not the privilege of any man to waste the time of his employer under any pretense whatever, and the cause of religion, good government, and humanity is not in the least degree advanced by the practice, but the contrary is really the case. Men should be abridged in doing wrong; they should not be free to sin against God or against man without suffering such penalties as their sins deserve. 12:153.

Does it follow that a man is deprived of his rights, because he lists in his heart to do the will of God? Must a man swear to prove that he has an agency? I contend there is no necessity for that, nor for stealing nor for doing any wrong. I can manifest to the heavens and to the inhabitants of the earth that I am free-born, and have my liberty before God, angels and men, when I kneel down to pray, certainly as much as if I were to go out and swear. I have the right to call my family together at certain hours for prayer, and I believe that this course proves that I am a free agent, as much as if I were to steal, swear, lie, and get drunk. 10:323.

We would not make everybody bow down to our religion, if we had the power, for this would not be Godlike. 14:94.

The eternal laws by which he and all others exist in the eternities of the Gods decree that the consent of the creature must be obtained before the Creator can rule perfectly. 15:134.

The Lord has a school upon the earth, and we are his scholars.

and the Devil also has a school attended by a great number of scholars. While we have been learning how to sustain the Kingdom of God upon the earth, the Devil and his pupils have been learning how to sustain the kingdom of darkness. From the very nature of the two kingdoms upon one planet, the crisis must come when there will be a literal open warfare, just as much as there now is a warfare within us against evil; and if we, as individuals and as a community, have gained the victory over our passions to such a degree that our Father knows that we are capable of actually sustaining the Kingdom of God upon the earth, just so true we shall be a kingdom by ourselves. If we are not yet capable of maintaining and rightly managing that kingdom, it will not at present be given to us in the fulness thereof; but the time will come when it will be given and established in its perfect organization on the earth. 5:328.

The law of liberty, is the law of right in every particular. 12:152.

There is not, has not been, and never can be any method, scheme, or plan devised by any being in this world for intelligence to exist eternally and obtain an exaltation, without knowing the good and the evil—without tasting the bitter and the sweet. Can the people understand that it is actually necessary for opposite principles to be placed before them, or this state of being would be no probation, and we should have no opportunity for exercising the agency given us? Can they understand that we cannot obtain eternal life unless we actually know and comprehend by our experience the principle of good and the principle of evil, the light and the darkness, truth, virtue, and holiness,—also vice, wickedness, and corruption? We must discern and acknowledge that the provinces of the Lord are over all the works of his hands—that when he produces intelligent beings he watches over them for their good. He has given human beings an intelligence designed to become eternal, self-existent, independent, and as Godlike as any human being in the heavens.

To answer such design, we are given our agency—the control of our belief, and must know the darkness from the light and the light from the darkness, and must taste the bitter as well as the sweet. 7:237-238.

What would we know about heaven or happiness were it not for their opposite? 3:321.

Let the Kingdom alone, the Lord steadies the ark; and if it does jostle, and appear to need steadying, if the way is a little sideling sometimes, and to all appearance threatens its overthrow, be careful how you stretch forth your hand to steady it; let us not be too officious in meddling with that which does not concern us; let it alone, it is the Lord's work. 11:252.

Every person who will examine his own experience—who will watch closely the leading of his own desires—will learn that the very great majority prefer to do good rather than to do evil, and would pursue a correct course, were it not for the evil power that subjects them to its sway. In wrongdoing, their own consciences condemn them. 6:330-331.

Shall we deny the existence of that which we do not understand? If we do, we would want to keep an iron bedstead to measure every person according to our own measurements and dimensions; and if persons were too long we would cut them off, and if too short draw them out. But we should discard this principle, and our motto should be, we will let every one believe as he pleases and follow out the convictions of his own mind, for all are free to choose or refuse; they are free to serve God or deny him. We have the Scriptures of divine truth, and we are free to believe or deny them. But we shall be brought to judgment before God for all these things, and shall have to give an account to him who has the right to call us to an account for the deeds done in the body. 14:131.

There is not an individual upon the earth but what has within himself ability to save or to destroy himself; and such is the case with nations. 5:53.

Chapter VI

THE POWER OF EVIL

Lucifer—There was a devil in heaven, and he strove to possess the birthright of the Savior. He was a liar from the beginning, and loves those who love and make lies, as do his imps and followers here on the earth. 8:279-280.

The spirits that were cast out of heaven, which you know are recorded to have been one-third part, were thrust down to this earth, and have been here all the time, with Lucifer, the Son of the Morning, at their head. 4:133.

The spirits of devils have been deprived of bodies, and that constitutes their curse, that is to say, speaking after the manner of men, you shall be wanderers on the earth, you have got to live out of doors all the time you live.

That is the situation of the spirits that were sent to the earth, when the revolt took place in heaven, when Lucifer, the Son of the Morning, was cast out. Where did he go? He came here, and one-third part of the spirits in heaven came with him. Do you suppose that one-third part of all beings that existed in eternity came with him? No, but one-third part of the spirits that were begotten and organized and brought forth to become tenants of fleshly bodies to dwell upon this earth. They forsook Jesus Christ, the rightful heir, and joined with Lucifer, the Son of the Morning, and came to this earth; they got here first. As soon as Mother Eve made her appearance in the garden of Eden, the Devil was on hand. 3:368-369.

As it has always been, and will be yet for some time, when the sons of God assemble together Satan will be on hand as an accuser of the brethren, to find fault with those who are trying to do good. 11:141.

The power of the Devil is limited; the power of God is unlimited. 3:267.

Who owns this earth? Does the Devil? No, he does not, he pretended to own it when the Savior was here, and promised it all to him if he would fall down and worship him; but he did not own a foot of land, he only had possession of it. He was an intruder, and is still; this earth belongs to him that framed and organized it, and it is expressly for his glory and the possession of those who love and serve him and keep his commandments, but the enemy has possession of it. 15:5.

If true principles are revealed from heaven to men, and if there are angels, and there is a possibility of their communicating to the human family, always look for an opposite power, an evil power, to give manifestations also; look out for the counterfeit. 240.

I frequently think of the difference between the power of God and the power of the Devil. To illustrate, here is a structure in which we can be seated comfortably, protected from the heat of summer or the cold of winter. Now, it required labor, mechanical skill and ingenuity and faithfulness and diligence to erect this building, but any poor, miserable fool or devil can set fire to it and destroy it. That is just what the Devil can do, but he never can build anything. The difference between God and the Devil is that God creates and organizes, while the whole study of the Devil is to destroy. Every one that follows the evil inclinations of his own natural evil heart is going to destruction, and sooner or later he will be no more. I pray you Latter-day Saints to live your religion. 13:4.

What, then, is the mission of Satan, that common foe of all the children of men? It is to destroy and make desolate. 11:240.

The Devil delights in the work of destruction—to burn and lay waste and destroy the whole earth. He delights to convulse and throw into confusion the affairs of men, politically, religiously and morally, introducing war with its long train of dreadful consequences. It is evil which causeth all these miseries and all deformity to come upon the inhabitants of the earth. But that which is of God is pure, lovely, holy and full of all excellency and truth, no matter where it is found, in hell, in heaven, upon the earth, or in the planets. 11:240.

Every providence and dispensation of God to his earthly children tends directly to life and salvation, while the influences and powers exerted by the enemy upon mankind and every suggestion of our corrupt natures tends to death. 10:221.

The adversary presents his principles and arguments in the most approved style, and in the most winning tone, attended with the most graceful attitudes; and he is very careful to ingratiate himself into the favor of the powerful and influential of mankind, uniting himself with popular parties, floating into offices of trust and emolument by pandering to popular feeling, though it should seriously wrong and oppress the innocent. 11:238.

Show me one principle that has originated by the power of the Devil. You cannot do it. I call evil inverted good, or a correct principle made an evil use of. 3:157.

The Devil's forces are particularly marshalled against us. 5:353.

You are aware that many think that the Devil has rule and power over both body and spirit. Now, I want to tell you that he does not hold any power over man, only so far as the body overcomes the spirit that is in a man, through yielding to the spirit of evil. The spirit that the Lord puts into a tabernacle of flesh, is under the dictation of the Lord Almighty; but the spirit and body are united in order that the spirit may have a tabernacle, and be exalted; and the spirit is influenced by the body, and the body by the spirit.

In the first place the spirit is pure, and under the special control and influence of the Lord, but the body is of the earth, and is subject to the power of the Devil, and is under the mighty influence of that fallen nature that is of the earth. If the spirit yields to the body, the Devil then has power to overcome the body and spirit of that man, and he loses both.

Recollect, brethren and sisters, every one of you, that when evil is suggested to you, when it arises in your hearts, it is through the temporal organization. When you are tempted, buffeted, and step out of the way inadvertently; when you are overtaken in a fault, or commit an overt act unthinkingly; when you are full of evil passion, and wish to yield to it, then stop and let the spirit, which God has put into your tabernacles, take the lead. If you do that, I will promise that you will overcome all evil, and obtain eternal lives. But many, very many, let the spirit yield to the body, and are overcome and destroyed. 2:255.

Evil is with us, it is that influence which tempts to sin, and which has been permitted to come into the world for the express purpose of giving us an opportunity of proving ourselves before God, before Jesus Christ, our Elder Brother, before the holy angels, and before all good men, that we are determined to overcome the evil, and cleave to the good, for the Lord has given us the ability to do so. Consequently, when the evil is present with me, I have a little fighting to do, I must turn and combat it until it is eradicated from my affections, as well as from my actions, that I may have power to do all the good I wish to perform. Every person is capable of this, all can bridle their tongues, and cease from every evil act from this time henceforth and forever, and do good instead. 1:91.

There are but two parties on the earth, one for God and the other for the world or the evil one. No matter how many names the Christian or heathen world bear, or how many sects and creeds may exist, there are but two parties, one for heaven and God, and the other will go to some other kingdom than the celestial kingdom of God. 14:73.

Do not imagine that I am in the least finding fault with the Devil. I would not bring a railing accusation against him, for he is fulfilling his office and calling manfully; he is more faithful in his calling than are many of the people. God is not yet going to destroy wickedness from the earth. How frequently we hear it reiterated from the pulpit that he is going to destroy all wickedness. No such thing. He will destroy the power of sin. The work the Savior has on hand is to reduce the power of the Devil to perfect subjection; and when he has destroyed death and him that has the power of it, pertaining to this world, then he will deliver up the kingdom spotless to the Father. 9:108.

Cease to mingle with the wicked. Many of our Elders seem to believe that Christ and Baal can yet be made friends. How many times Elders of Israel try to make me fellowship the Devil, or his imps, or his servants; also try to make you fellowship your enemies, to amalgamate the feelings of the Saints and the ungodly! It cannot be done; it never was done, and never can be accomplished. Christ and Baal never can be friends. One or the other must reign triumphantly on the earth, and I say that Jesus Christ shall reign, and I will help him; and Baal shall not reign here much longer—the Devil shall not have power much longer upon the land of Joseph. 8:325-326.

Who is the enemy of mankind? He who wishes to change truth for error and light for darkness; he who wishes to take peace from a family, city, state or nation and give the sword in return. He is my enemy, he is your enemy and the enemy of mankind. Who is the friend of mankind? He who makes peace between those who are at enmity, who brings together those who, perhaps, through some misunderstanding, have been at variance with and lost friendship and fellowship for each other, and shows them that their ill-will is without foundation and existed simply because they did not understand each other. 16:24.

Who is your enemy and mine? He that teaches language that is unbecoming, that presents falsehood for truth, that furnishes false premises to build upon instead of true, or that is full of anger and mischief to his fellow beings. I call no other enemies. 16:24.

Can error live? No, it is the very plant of destruction, it destroys itself; it withers, it fades, it falls and decays and returns to its native element. Every untruth, all error, everything that is unholy, unlike God, will, in its time, perish. 14:93.

You need have no fear but the fear to offend God. 4:369.

Who are the evildoers? Those who have had the light presented to them, and rejected it. 8:357.

If we live so as to enjoy the spirit of the faith that we embraced there is no danger of our being deceived. 14:157.

The wicked cannot do anything against the truth. Every move they make to crush the Kingdom of God will be attended with the signal blessings of the Almighty for its further extension and ultimate triumph. All their efforts will result in the overthrow of sin and iniquity, and the increase of righteousness and the Kingdom of God upon the earth. 8:175.

False Spirits—There are many spirits gone out into the world, and the false spirits are giving revelations as well as the Spirit of the Lord. 3:44.

There are myriads of disembodied evil spirits—those who have long ago laid down their bodies here and in the regions round about, among and around us; and they are trying to make us and our children sick, and are trying to destroy us and to tempt us to evil. They will try every possible means they are masters of to draw us aside from the path of righteousness. 6:73-4.

The children of men give heed to the deceiving spirits that are abroad, and that is the cause of the ten thousand errors, wrongs, sins and divisions which are in the world, and for this reason the multitude are unable to distinguish between the voice of the Good Shepherd and the voice of the stranger. 16:75.

It was revealed to me in the commencement of this Church, that the Church would spread, prosper, grow and extend, and that in proportion to the spread of the Gospel among the nations of the earth, so would the power of Satan rise. It was told you here that Brother Joseph warned the Elders of Israel against false spirits. It was revealed to me that if the people did not receive the spirit of revelation that God had sent for the salvation of the world, they would receive false spirits and would have revelation. Men would have revelation, women would have revelation, the priest in the pulpit and the deacon under the pulpit would have revelation, and the people would have revelation enough to damn the whole nation, and nations of them, unless they would hearken to the voice of God. It was not only revealed to Joseph but to your humble servant, that false spirits would be as prevalent and as common among the inhabitants of the earth as we now see them. 13:280.

No man gets power from God to raise disturbance in any Branch of the Church. Such power is obtained from an evil source. 9:93.

We may be within the pale of the Kingdom of God on earth, yet we are liable to be overcome of evil. There are many spirits who have gone abroad in the world, and men are overcome by false spirits, and led astray from the path of truth. They will begin by doing some evil thing out of sight, and say, "O, it is nothing, it is a mere trifle, and the Lord is merciful and forgiveth sin." The sins which are considered trifles lay the foundation for greater evils, and expose men to be tempted, and buffeted by Satan, and they will be overcome little by little, until by and by they are overtaken in a fault which is more aggravating in the sight of justice, which lays the foundation for another trial more severe, and to be buffeted more by the Devil, for they lay themselves more liable to his power. 2:121.

Suppose I were to teach you a false doctrine, how are you to know it if you do not possess the Spirit of God? As it is written, "The things of God knoweth no man but by the Spirit of God." 18:72.

Our doctrine is right—there is no deception in it. It requires no argument, for it is a self-evident fact. Still, when we meddle with that which we know nothing about, we are apt to fall into error and differ; but we have so much which we do know, and think about and talk about, that we have no time to speculate about that which we do not know. We know that God lives. 10:327.

What is called spirit-rapping, spirit-knocking, and so forth, is produced by the spirits that the Lord has suffered to communicate to people on the earth, and make them believe in revelation. 7:239.

When we go into the world we find quite a portion of the people who belong to a class called Spiritualists. They would like to have it considered that "Mormonism" is nothing but Spiritualism. A great many want to know the difference between the two. I will give one feature of the difference, and then set the whole scientific world to work to see if they can ever bring to bear the same feature in Spiritualism. Take all who are called Spiritualists and see if they can produce the order that is in the midst of this people. Here are system, order, organization, law, rule, and facts. Now see if they can produce any one of these features. They cannot. Why? Because their system is from beneath, while ours is perfect and is from above; one is from God, the other is from the Devil, that is all the difference. 13:266.

Spiritualism is a mass of confusion, it is a body without parts and passions, principle or power. 13:266.

There is evil in the world, and there is also good. Was there ever a counterfeit without a true coin? No. Is there communication from God? Yes. From holy angels? Yes; and we have been proclaiming these facts during nearly thirty years. Are there any communications from evil spirits? Yes; and the Devil is making the people believe very strongly in revelations from the spirit world. This is called Spiritualism, and it is said that thousands of spirits declare that "Mormonism" is true; but what do that class of spirits know more than mortals? Perhaps a little more in some particulars than is known here, but it is only a little more. They are subject in the spirit world to the same powers they were subject to here. 7:240.

Mesmerism is an inverted truth; it originated in holy, good and righteous principles, which have been inverted by the power of the Devil. 3:156.

The principle of animal magnetism is true, but wicked men use it to an evil purpose. Speaking is a true gift, but I can speak to the glory of God, or to the injury of his cause and to my condemnation, as I please; and still the gift is of God. The gift of animal magnetism is a gift of God, but wicked men use it to promote the cause of the Devil, and that is precisely the difference. 3:370.

I know of many whom mesmerism has led out of this Church; they would see the sick healed, and attribute it to the power of God; would fall under its influence, embrace and practice it, and thus give the Devil power over them to lead them out of the Kingdom of God. They could not tell whether it was the power of God or the power of the Devil. What is the reason? They had not the light of revelation within them; they had not the knowledge of God. Are you not aware how easily we may be deceived? 3:156.

There are many Elders in this house who, if I had the power to mesmerize that vase and make it dance on that table, would say that it was done by the power of God. Who could tell whether it was done by the power of God or by the power of the Devil? No person, unless he had the revelations of Jesus Christ within him. I suppose you are ready to ask Brother Brigham if he thinks the power of the Devil could make the vase dance. Yes, and could take it up and carry it out doors, just as easy as to turn up a table and move it here and there, or to cause a rap, rap, rap, or to bake and pass around pancakes, or get hold of a person's hand, and make him write in every style you can think of, imitating George Washington's, Benjamin Franklin's, Joseph Smith's, and other autographs. Can you tell whether that is by the power of God or by the power of the Devil? No, unless you have the revelations of Jesus Christ. 3:157.

I have seen the effects of animal magnetism, or some anomalous sleep, or whatever it may be called, many a time in my youth. I have seen persons lie on the benches, on the floor of the meetinghouse, or on the ground at their camp meetings, for ten, twenty, and thirty minutes, and I do not know but an hour, and not a particle of pulse about them. That was the effect of what I call animal magnetism; they called it the power of God, but no matter what it was, I used to think that I should like to ask such persons what they had seen in their trance or vision; and when I got old enough and dared ask them, I did so. I have said to such persons: "Brother, what have you experienced?" "Nothing." "What do you know more than before you had this; what do you call it—trance, sleep or dream? Do you know any more now than before you fell to the earth?" "Nothing more." "Have you seen any person?" "No." "Then what is the use or utility of your falling down here in the dirt?" I could not see it, and consequently I was an infidel to this. But I said then as I say now—"Show me a church that God has organized, and you will find apostles to rule, govern, control, dictate, and give counsel. You will find prophets, evangelists, pastors, teachers, governments, helps, and diversities of tongues. When the Church and Kingdom of God is upon the earth you will find all these things and you will also hear prophesying therein. 14:113.

Many people in this city do not know whether astrology is true or not, whether it is of God or the Devil; hence they are liable to be deceived, as is every person unless they have the power of revelation within themselves. If there are any brethren here who have been studying astrology, and they were called upon to speak, would they not say that they believed it to be a true science? They would; they testify that they know it to be true. But what does it do for them? It leads them into thousands of errors. Does God ever lead you into error? Is he mistaken when he reveals? No; when he sets you to make calculations and figures, I will assure you that every sum will prove and come out precisely right. The Lord does not deceive people, but astrology and mesmerism do lead them astray. How many deceptions are there in the world? Millions, for a great many spirits have gone forth into the world to deceive the people. Spirit rappings are of the same class. 3:156.

Priestcraft—The priests are angry because they are afraid that their religion is nothing but a sandy foundation fabric; and whenever they meditate upon the subject and humble themselves, and the Spirit of the Lord finds its way to their hearts and convicts them, the truth then is made manifest before them, and they begin to learn the falsity of their systems; and when that spirit leaves them, they become angry. "Mormonism" is declared to be true by hosts of witnesses, and this makes the priests angry; for this Gospel bears its own weight and testimony, and they know not how to gainsay it. True, I have aimed to point out their errors; but it is not you or me that they are opposed to, although they throw their darts at us; but it is the spirit of conviction that goes with the report of this work; for wherever it goes it strikes conviction to the heart, and that is what disturbs the priests and the people. 5:4-5.

Go to the United States, into Europe, or wherever you can come across men who have been in the midst of this people, and one will tell you that we are a poor, ignorant, deluded people; the next will tell you that we are the most industrious and intelligent people on the earth, and are destined to rise to eminence as a nation, and spread, and continue to spread, until we revolutionize the whole earth. If you pass on to the third man, and inquire what he thinks of the "Mormons," he will say they are fools, duped and led astray by Joe Smith, who was a knave, and a false prophet, and a money digger. Why is all this? It is because there is a spirit in man. And when the Gospel of Jesus Christ is preached on the earth, and the Kingdom of God is established, there is also a spirit in these things, and an almighty spirit too. When these two spirits come in contact one with the other, the spirit of the Gospel reflects light upon the spirit which God has placed in man, and wakes him up to a consciousness of his true state, which makes him afraid he will be condemned, for he perceives at once that "Mormonism" is true. "Our craft is in danger," is the first thought that strikes the wicked and dishonest of mankind, when the light of truth shines upon them. Say they, "If these people called Latter-day Saints are correct in their views, the whole world must be wrong, and what will become of our time-honored institutions, and of our influence, which we have swayed successfully over the minds of the people for ages? This Mormonism must be put down." So priestcraft presents a bold and extended front against the truth. 1:188.

It is not in my being called a Quaker, a Methodist or a "Mormon" that is the true cause of contention between these two great powers —Christ and Belial; but it is in the fact that God has established his Kingdom upon the earth and restored the holy Priesthood which gives men authority and power to administer in his name. 11:238.

Instead of seeking unto the Lord for wisdom, they seek unto vain philosophy and the deceit and traditions of men, which are after the rudiments of the world and not after Christ. They are led by their own imaginations and by the dictates of their selfish will, which will lead them in the end to miss the object of their pursuit. 10:209.

Sin and Wickedness—God permits sin, or it could not be here. 13:151.

The law is for the transgressor. 15:161.

All evil is from beneath, while all that is good is from God. 13:267.

Aside from the revelations in our day, there is not knowledge enough to tell you why God suffered sin to come into the world. You have been told the reason why—that all intelligence must prove facts by their opposite. 6:144.

I wish you to understand that sin is not an attribute in the nature of man, but it is an inversion of the attributes God has placed in him. Righteousness tends to an eternal duration of organized intelligence, while sin bringeth to pass their dissolution. 10:251.

Sin has come into the world, and death by sin. I frequently ask myself the question: Was there any necessity for sin to enter the world? Most assuredly there was, according to my understanding and reasoning powers. Did I not know the evil I could never know the good; had I not seen the light I should never be able to comprehend what darkness is. Had I never tried to see and behold a thing in darkness I could not understand the beauty and glory of the light. If I had never tasted the bitter or the sour how could I define or describe the sweet? 13:59.

The annoyances, difficulties, errors, perplexities, sorrows, and troubles of this life, from first to last, are in consequence of sin being in the world. For me to say it is not right for sin to be in the world, or if we, as intelligent beings, come to the conclusion that sin entered the world by chance, through some mistake, and it was contrary to the design of him who created us, we should err. 14:98.

Let a Saint diverge from the path of truth and rectitude, in the least, no matter in what, it may be in a deal with his neighbor, in lusting after that which is not in his possession, in neglecting his duty, in having an over-anxiety for something he should not be anxious about, in being a little distrustful with regard to the providences of God, in entertaining a misgiving in his heart and feeling with regard to the hand of the Lord towards him, and his mind will begin to be darkened. 3:222.

The law of God is pointed against sin and iniquity, and where they appear it is unbending in its nature and must, sooner or later, hold sovereign rule against them, or righteousness could never prevail. 3:256.

Paul asks, "Shall we sin that righteousness may abound?" No, there is plenty of sin without your sinning. We can have all the experience we need, without sinning ourselves, therefore we will not sin that good may come, we will not transgress the law of God that we may know the opposite. There is no necessity for such a course, for the world is full of transgression, and this people need not mingle up with it. 3:224.

It is as manly and as praiseworthy for an individual to make the choice to do good, work righteousness and love and serve God—it is more noble, than to choose the downward road. One or the other will be the choice of every individual. Do not trifle with evil, or you will be overcome by it before you know. 12:231.

Many imbibe the idea that they are capable of leading out in teaching principles that never have been taught. They are not aware that the moment they give way to this hallucination the Devil has power over them to lead them onto unholy ground; though this is a lesson which they ought to have learned long ago, yet it is one that was learned by but few in the days of Joseph. 3:318.

It is far better to die doing good than to live doing evil. 11:134.

Sin is in the world, but it is not necessary that we should sin, because sin is in the world; but, to the contrary, it is necessary that we should resist sin, and for this purpose is sin necessary. Sin exists in all the eternities. Sin is co-eternal with righteousness, for it must needs be that there is an opposition in all things. 10:2.

Look at ourselves—run over our own experience, and we shall discover that ourselves, our neighbors, our friends, our acquaintances, and all people do not always know when they are happy. In other words, if you could crowd an individual or a community into heaven without experience, it would be no enjoyment to them. They must know the opposite; they must know how to contrast, in order to prize and appreciate the comfort and happiness, the joy and the bliss they are actually in possession of. 5:294.

There is a clear distinction made between the sinner and the ungodly. A person to be ungodly must have known godliness, and must have a knowledge of what the Lord requires concerning him. There are many in the midst of this people who believe the Gospel with all their hearts, but yet do wickedly; this makes them ungodly.

I would not associate with those who blaspheme the name of God, nor would I let my family associate with them. By this you may know whether you are in the path that leads to life and salvation. If you can hear the name of the Deity lightly spoken of and blasphemed, and not be shocked at it, you may know that you are not in the path. 12:219-220.

Improvement belong to the spirit and plan of the heavens. To improve in our minds, to increase in wisdom, knowledge and understanding, to gather every item of knowledge that we can in mechanism and in science of every description, respecting the earth, the object of the organization of the earth, the heavens, the heavenly bodies—all this is of Heaven, it is from God; but when a person or a people begin to dwindle, to lessen and to take the downward course, they are going from heaven and heavenly things. 16:65.

Many of us have been taught the doctrine of total depravity—that man is not naturally inclined to do good. I am satisfied that he is more inclined to do right than to do wrong. There is a greater power within him to shun evil and perform good, than to do the opposite. 9:247.

The wickedness of the children of men is what influences them to fear. They are not afraid of their own laws, because they originated from themselves; they can manage them and blot them out of existence whenever they wish. But when that which is said to be the Kingdom of God, or the theocracy of heaven, is upon the earth, many of the inhabitants thereof tremble, and fear that it is not correct. 7:148.

How much does it take to prepare a man, or woman, or any being, to become angels to the Devil, to suffer with him to all eternity? Just as much as it does to prepare a man to go into the celestial kingdom, into the presence of the Father and the Son, and to be made an heir to his Kingdom, and all his glory, and be crowned with crowns of glory, immortality, and eternal lives. 3:93.

Let not your feelings be afflicted or in anywise troubled by the sayings and doings of the wicked, for they are in the hands of the Almighty, and he will dispose of individuals and nations as seemeth him good. He must give them an opportunity to receive the truth and prepare themselves to dwell eternally with him, or to reject it and prepare themselves to be cut down as cumberers of the ground, suffer the wrath of the Almighty, and perish and be wasted away until they will be known no more. Seek for that which will endure. 7:270.

It is not right, I will say, for people to know the truth and live in disobedience to it; it is not right for them to understand the ways and providences of God as they are dealt out to the people on the earth, when they live and are determined to live in violation of every commandment and law of God; and because they do so live, ignorance covers them as with a mantle, shuts out the light of truth from them, and keeps them in darkness; and if the light were to shine upon them, as it does now and as it did in the days of the Apostles, would they receive it? No, they would not. Light has come into the world, but the wicked choose darkness rather than light. Why? It was told in days of old that their deeds were evil. That is the fact today—"They choose darkness rather than light, because their deeds are evil," and their hearts are fully set in them to do evil. 15:64.

Let the wicked say what they please, for their breath is in their nostrils, and all their glory is like the grass and the flower of the grass that passeth away. They are here but for a moment, and soon those who know them now will know them no more for ever. They will soon be as though they had not been upon the earth. 7:270.

The hand of the Almighty is over the wicked, and he handles them according to his good pleasure, as he does the Saints. His hand is over us, and his hand is over them. But there is a thick mist cast before their eyes, so they do not discern the truth of "Mormonism." Do you wonder that they are mad, when they see the progress of truth? I do not. 4:38.

I never believed that the righteous have ever suffered as much as the wicked. 11:274.

The wicked do not know how to enjoy life, but the closer we live to God the better we know and understand how to enjoy it. Live so that you can enjoy the Spirit of the Lord continually. 10:336.

Temptation—I am happy, brethren, for the privilege of having temptation. A great many people have thought that in my life I was not tempted like other men. I tell them if I am it is none of their business; it is nothing to them. Some say, "Brother Brigham, you slide along and the Devil lets you alone." If I have battles with him, I can overcome him single-handed quicker than to call in my neighbors to help me. If I am tempted to speak an evil word, I will keep my lips locked together. Says one, "I do not know about that, that would be smothering up bad feelings, I am wonderfully tried about my neighbor, he has done wrong, he has abused me and I feel dreadful bad about it. Had I not better let it out than to keep it rankling within me?" No. I will keep bad feelings under and actually smother them to death, then they are gone. But as sure as I let them out they will live and afflict me. If I smother them in myself, if I actually choke them to death, destroy the life, the power, and vigor thereof, they will pass off and leave me clear of fault, and pure, so far as that is concerned; and no man or woman on earth knows that I have ever been tempted to indulge in wicked feelings. Keep them to yourselves.

If you feel evil, keep it to yourselves until you overcome that evil principle. This is what I call resisting the Devil, and he flees from me. I strive not to speak evil, not to feel evil, and if I do, to keep it to myself until it is gone from me, and not let it pass my lips. 3:195.

Thousands of temptations assail, and you make a miss here and a slip there, and say that you have not lived up to all the knowledge you have. True; but often it is a marvel to me that you have lived up to so much as you have, considering the power of the enemy upon the earth. Few that have ever lived have fully understood that power. I do not fully comprehend the awful power and influence Satan has upon the earth, but I understand enough to know that it is a marvel that the Latter-day Saints are as good as they are. 8:285.

It is necessary in the very nature of things, in the economy of heaven, that we should be tried and tempted in all things, in order to prove ourselves and prepare ourselves to enjoy that eternal life that is prepared for the just. The time will be when people will not be tempted as they now are—when there will be no Tempter upon the earth. The knowledge and intelligence that will be diffused among the people will enable them to live a time and a season without the

Tempter. But we live in a day when the power and rule of that evil principle is more excessive upon the earth than it ever has been. 7:268.

When we neglect any one of these duties, the enemy says, "I have made so much ground." If the Devil can induce an Elder to drink a little, he is not satisfied with this triumph, but says to him, "Your wife and children know it, don't pray tonight." The Elder says to his family, "I feel tired tonight, we won't have prayers." The enemy says, "I have gained another point." You indulge still further, and you will find other excuses. Your head is not right, your heart is not right, your conscience is not right, and you retire again without praying. By and by, you begin to doubt something the Lord has revealed to us, and it is not long before such a one is led away captive of the Devil. 18:216.

When you are tempted to do wrong, do not stop one moment to argue, but tell Mr. Devil to walk out of your barn. 3:359.

When the Devil cannot overcome an individual through temptation to commit wickedness, when he sees that a person is determined to walk in the line and travel straight forward into the celestial kingdom, he will adopt a course of flattery, will strive to exercise a pleasing influence and move along smoothly with him, and when he sees an opportunity he will try to turn him out of the way, if it is only to the extent of a hair's breadth. 3:318.

Do not suppose that we shall ever in the flesh be free from temptations to sin. Some suppose that they can in the flesh be sanctified, body and spirit, and become so pure that they will never again feel the effects of the power of the adversary of truth. Were it possible for a person to attain to this degree of perfection in the flesh, he could not die, neither remain in a world where sin predominates. Sin has entered into the world, and death by sin. I think we shall more or less feel the effects of sin so long as we live, and finally have to pass the ordeals of death. Do not understand that in the flesh we shall ever overcome the power of sin to such a degree that we shall never taste death. I do not look for any such thing, though what we call death, or laying down this body, is only the door to a higher state of life for the faithful. If we live our religion it will enable us to so overcome sin that it will not reign in our mortal bodies but will become subject to us, and the world and its fulness will become our servant instead of our master. 10:173.

As soon as a man hears the Gospel preached and becomes convinced of its truthfulness, he is tempted of the Devil, who, whenever there is an opportunity, suggests doubt for his reflection. If he entertains these doubting influences it is not long before what he believed true becomes a matter of conjecture. Another may receive the Gospel, travel and preach it faithfully, feeling in his heart to exclaim, "Glory to God in the highest," having no other motive than to do good to his fellow beings. By and by he perhaps is left to himself, saying—"I wonder if I really was right?" This single doubt is perhaps the beginning of his apostasy from the Church. 18:215.

Serve God according to the best knowledge you have, and lay down and sleep quietly; and when the Devil comes along and says, "You are not a very good Saint, you might enjoy greater blessings and more of the power of God, and have the vision of your mind opened, if you would live up to your privileges," tell him to leave; that you have long ago forsaken his ranks and enlisted in the army of Jesus, who is your captain, and that you want no more of the Devil. 4:270.

When temptations come to you, be humble and faithful, and determined that you will overcome, and you will receive a deliverance, and continue faithful, having the promise of receiving blessings. 16:164

Apostasy—It is most astonishing to every principle of intelligence that any man or woman will close their eyes upon eternal things after they have been made acquainted with them, and let the gay things of this world, the lusts of the eye, and the lusts of the flesh, entangle their minds and draw them one hair's breadth from the principles of life. 4:59.

If the candle of the Almighty does not shine from this place, you need not seek for light anywhere else. 4:93.

To know the truth of my testimony he must have the visions and revelations of God for himself. And when he gets them, and turns aside becoming a traitor to the cause of righteousness, the wrath of God will beat upon him, and the vengeance of the Almighty will be heavy upon him. 2:140.

It was said here this morning that no person ever apostatized, without actual transgression. Omission of duty leads to commission. We want to live so as to have the Spirit every day, every hour of the day, every minute of the day, and every Latter-day Saint is entitled to the Spirit of God, to the power of the Holy Ghost, to lead him in his individual duties. 10:296.

He will make false prophecies, yet he will do it by the spirit of prophecy; he will feel that he is a prophet and can prophesy, but he does it by another spirit and power than that which was given him of the Lord. He uses the gift as much as you and I use ours. 3:364.

Let a man or woman who has received much of the power of God, visions and revelations, turn away from the holy commandments of the Lord, and it seems that their senses are taken from them, their understanding and judgment in righteousness are taken away, they go into darkness, and become like a blind person who gropes by the wall. 2:301.

The person that forsakes the faith of our Lord Jesus Christ will find himself ruined for time and eternity. How are they looked upon who have received the Spirit of the Gospel and forsaken it? With a few exceptions, they are despised by the good and wise among men, by the noble and ignoble; all despise them, and they are in a most miserable condition. 7:146.

Whenever there is a disposition manifested in any of the members of this Church to question the right of the President of the whole Church to direct in all things, you see manifested evidences of apostasy—of a spirit which, if encouraged, will lead to a separation from the Church and to final destruction; whenever there is a disposition to operate against any legally appointed officer of this Kingdom, no matter in what capacity he is called to act, if persisted in, it will be followed by the same results; they will "walk after the flesh in the lust of uncleanness, and despise government. Presumptuous are they, self-willed; they are not afraid to speak evil of dignities." 11:136.

When a man begins to find fault, inquiring in regard to this, that, and the other, saying, "Does this or that look as though the Lord dictated it?" you may know that that person has more or less of the spirit of apostasy. Every man in this Kingdom, or upon the face of the earth, who is seeking with all his heart to save himself, has as much to do as he can conveniently attend to, without calling in question that which does not belong to him. If he succeeds in saving himself, it has well occupied his time and attention. See to it that you are right yourselves; see that sins and folly do not manifest themselves with the rising sun. I repeat that it is as much as any one can well do to take care of himself by performing every duty that pertains to his temporal and eternal welfare. 8:12.

What is that which turns people away from this Church? Very trifling affairs are generally the commencement of their divergence from the right path. If we follow a compass, the needle of which does not point correctly, a very slight deviation in the beginning will lead us, when we have traveled some distance, far to one side of the true point for which we are aiming. 12:125.

When men lose the spirit of the work in which we are engaged, they become infidel in their feelings. They say that they do not know whether the Bible is true, whether the Book of Mormon is true, nor about new revelations, nor whether there is a God or not. When they lose the spirit of this work, they lose the knowledge of the things of God in time and in eternity; all is lost to them. 8:316.

Those who leave the Church are like a feather blown to and fro in the air. They do not know whither they are going; they do not understand anything about their own existence; their faith, judgment and the operation of their minds are as unstable as the movements of the feather floating in the air. We have not anything to cling to, only faith in the Gospel. 15:136.

If the people would live their religion, there would be no apostasy and we would hear no complaining or fault-finding. If the people were hungry for the words of eternal life, and their whole souls even centered on the building up of the Kingdom of God, every heart and hand would be ready and willing and the work would move forward mightily and we would advance as we should do. 13:153.

Men begin to apostatize by taking to themselves strength, by hearkening to the whisperings of the enemy who leads them astray little by little, until they gather to themselves that which they call the wisdom of man; then they begin to depart from God, and their minds become confused. 18:231.

You have known men who, while in the Church, were active, quick and full of intelligence; but after they have left the Church they have become contracted in their understandings, they have become darkened in their minds and everything has become a mystery to them, and in regard to the things of God, they have become like the rest of the world, who think, hope and pray that such and such things may be so, but they do not know the least about it. This is precisely the position of those who leave this Church; they go into the dark, they are not able to judge, conceive or comprehend things as they are. They are like the drunken man—he thinks that everybody is the worse for liquor but himself, and he is the only sober man in the neighborhood. The apostates think that everybody is wrong but themselves. 16:65.

You hear many say, "I am a Latter-day Saint, and I never will apostatize;" "I am a Latter-day Saint, and shall be to the day of my death." I never make such declarations, and never shall. I think I have learned that of myself I have no power, but my system is organized to increase in wisdom, knowledge, and power, getting a little here and a little there. But when I am left to myself, I have no power, and my wisdom is foolishness; then I cling close to the Lord, and I have power in his name. I think I have learned the Gospel so as to know, that in and of myself I am nothing. 1:337.

If you want to see the principle of devilism to perfection, hunt among those who have once enjoyed the faith of the holy Gospel and then forsaken their religion. We have the best and the worst. Why the worst? Because the Devil prompts men and women of the meanest and lowest grade to embrace the Gospel and get a foothold in the Kingdom of God to destroy it. 7:145.

People do, however, leave this Church, but they leave it because they get into darkness, and the very day they conclude that there should be a democratic vote, or in other words, that we should have two candidates for the presiding Priesthood in the midst of the Latter-day Saints, they conclude to be apostates. There is no such thing as confusion, division, strife, animosity, hatred, malice, or two sides to the question in the house of God; there is but one side to the question there. 14:92.

If the Saints neglect to pray, and violate the day that is set apart for the worship of God, they will lose his Spirit. If a man shall suffer himself to be overcome with anger, and curse and swear, taking the name of the Deity in vain, he cannot retain the Holy Spirit. In short, if a man shall do anything which he knows to be wrong, and repenteth not, he cannot enjoy the Holy Spirit, but will walk in darkness and ultimately deny the faith. 11:134.

What have the Latter-day Saints got to apostatize from? Everything that there is good, pure, holy, God-like, exalting, ennobling, extending the ideas, the capacities of the intelligent beings that our Heavenly Father has brought forth upon this earth. What will they receive in exchange? I can comprehend it in a very few words. These would be the words that I should use: death, hell and the grave. That is what they will get in exchange. We may go into the particulars of that which they experience. They experience darkness, ignorance, doubt, pain, sorrow, grief, mourning, unhappiness; no person to condole with in the hour of trouble, no arm to lean upon in the day of calamity, no eye to pity when they are forlorn and cast down; and I comprehend it by saying death, hell and the grave. This is what they will get in exchange for their apostasy from the Gospel of the Son of God. 16:160.

Why do people apostatize? You know we are on the "Old Ship Zion." We are in the midst of the ocean. A storm comes on, and, as sailors say, she labors very hard. "I am not going to stay here," says one; "I don't believe this is the 'Ship Zion.'" "But we are in the midst of the ocean." "I don't care, I am not going to stay here." Off goes the coat, and he jumps overboard. Will he not be drowned? Yes. So with those who leave this Church. It is the "Old Ship Zion," let us stay in it. 10:295.

Will there still be apostasy? Yes, brethren and sisters, you may expect that people will come into the Church and then apostatize.

You may expect that some people will run well for a season, and then fall out by the way. 2:250.

Many receive the Gospel because they know it is true, they are convinced in their judgment that it is true; strong argument overpowers them, and they are rationally compelled to admit the Gospel to be true upon fair reasoning. They yield to it, and obey its first principles, but never seek to be enlightened by the power of the Holy Ghost; such ones frequently step out of the way. 2:250.

What has already become of those who, during our short existence as a Church, have come out against us, politically, judicially, or otherwise, those who have raised their puny arms to destroy the Kingdom of God from the earth! They have become powerless, like the dew before the rising sun; they have vanished away, their names are almost forgotten; and if this is not the case with all, it will be. 18:232.

One of the first steps to apostasy is to find fault with your Bishop; and when that is done, unless repented of a second step is soon taken, and by and by the person is cut off from the Church, and that is the end of it. Will you allow yourselves to find fault with your Bishop? No; but come to me, go to the High Council, or to the President of the Stake, and ascertain whether your Bishop is doing wrong, before you find fault and suffer yourselves to speak against a presiding officer. 9:141.

God is at the helm of this great ship, and that makes me feel good. When I think about the world, and the enemies of the cause of God, I care no more about them than I do for a parcel of mosquitoes. All hell may howl, and they may run up and down the earth and seek whom they may destroy, but they cannot move the faithful and pure in heart. Let those apostatize who wish to, but God will save all who are determined to be saved. 4:111.

Chapter VII

THE LAW OF ETERNAL PROGRESSION

Object of Mortal Life—This life is worth as much to us as any life in the eternities of the Gods. 9:170.

The object of this existence is to learn, which we can only do a little at a time. 9:167.

What are we here for? To learn to enjoy more, and to increase in knowledge and in experience. 14:228.

The whole mortal existence of man is neither more nor less than a preparatory state given to finite beings, a space wherein they may improve themselves for a higher state of being. 1:334.

We are placed on this earth to prove whether we are worthy to go into the celestial world, the terrestrial, or the telestial or to hell, or to any other kingdom, or place, and we have enough of life given to us to do this. 4:269.

This is a world in which we are to prove ourselves. The lifetime of man is a day of trial, wherein we may prove to God, in our darkness, in our weakness, and where the enemy reigns, that we are our Father's friends, and that we receive light from him and are worthy to be leaders of our children—to become lords of lords, and kings of kings—to have perfect dominion over that portion of our families that will be crowned in the celestial kingdom with glory, immortality, and eternal lives. 8:61.

The first great principle that ought to occupy the attention of mankind, that should be understood by the child and the adult, and which is the main spring of all action, whether people understand it or not, is the principle of improvement. The principle of increase, of exaltation, of adding to that we already possess, is the grand moving principle and cause of the actions of the children of men. No matter what their pursuits are, in what nation they were born, with what people they have been associated, what religion they profess, or what politics they hold, this is the main spring of the actions of the people, embracing all the powers necessary in performing the duties of life. 2:91.

Man to Endure Forever—Hear it, all ye Latter-day Saints! Will you spend the time of your probation for naught, and fool away your existence and being? You were organized, and brought into being, for the purpose of enduring forever, if you fulfil the measure of your creation, pursue the right path, observe the requirements of the celestial law, and obey the commandments of our God. 1:113.

We are urged by the Spirit to refrain from articles which tend to death, to preserve this life, which is the most precious life given to mortal beings preparatory to an immortal life. It is our business to prepare to live here to do good. Instead of crying to the people, prepare to die, our cry is, prepare to live forever. These mortal houses will drop off sometime, and when they are cleansed and purified, sanctified and glorified, we shall inherit them again forever and ever. Let all the Saints pursue a course to live. 12:209.

Mankind, in general, do not stop to reflect, they are pressing headlong to grasp the whole world if possible; each individual is for himself, and he is ignorant of the design the Almighty had in his creation and existence in this life. To obtain a knowledge of this design is a duty obligatory upon all the sons and daughters of Adam. 1:334.

The Business of Life—The only business that we have on hand is to build up the Kingdom of God and prepare the way of the Son of Man. 5:230.

We are here to live, to spread intelligence and knowledge among the people. I am here to school my brethren, to teach my family the way of life, to propagate my species, and to live, if in my power, until sin, iniquity, corruption, hell, and the Devil, and all classes and grades of abominations are driven from the earth. That is my religion and the object of my existence. We are not here merely to prepare to die, and then die; but we are here to live and build up the kingdom of God on the earth—to promote the Priesthood, overcome the powers of Satan, and teach the children of man what they are created for—that in them is concealed the germ of all intelligence. Here is the starting-point—the foundation that is laid in the organization of man for receiving a fulness of eternal knowledge and glory. Are we to go yonder to obtain it? No; we are to promote it on this earth. 8:282.

Human beings are expected by their Creator to be actively employed in doing good every day of their lives, either in improving their own mental and physical condition or that of their neighbors. 9:190.

The purpose of our life should be to build up the Zion of our God, to gather the House of Israel, bring in the fulness of the Gentiles, restore and bless the earth with our ability and make it as the Garden of Eden, store up treasures of knowledge and wisdom in our own understandings, purify our own hearts and prepare a people to meet the Lord when he comes. 10:222.

Some say that "this is a miserable world, I do not care how soon I get through." Well, go and destroy yourselves, if you choose; you have all the opportunity that you can desire, there is plenty of arsenic, calomel, and other means, within your reach. But I would not give a cent for such persons; I do not delight in such characters, and I do not believe that the Lord delights in people who wish to die before they have accomplished the work that he designed for them to do. 2:270-271.

The Latter-day Saints throughout the valleys in these mountains and throughout the world ought to be learning what they are on this earth for. They are here to increase and multiply, to enlarge, to gather the House of Israel, redeem Zion, build up the Zion of our God, and to promote that eternal intelligence that dwells with the Gods, and begin to plant it in this earth, and make it take root downward and bring forth fruit upward to the glory of God, until every obnoxious principle in the hearts of men is destroyed, and the earth returns to its paradisiacal state, and the Lord comes and dwells with this people, and walks and talks with them as he did with Father Adam. That is our business, and not to suffer all our energies to be expended in merely preparing to die. 8:282.

It may appear strange to some of you, and it certainly does to the world, to say it is possible for a man or woman to become perfect on this earth. It is written, "Be ye therefore perfect, even as your Father which is in heaven is perfect." Again, "If any man offend not in word, the same is a perfect man, and able also to bridle the whole body." This is perfectly consistent to the person who understands what perfection really is.

If the first passage I have quoted is not worded to our understanding, we can alter the phraseology of the sentence, and say, "Be ye as perfect as ye can," for that is all we can do, though it is written, be ye perfect as your Father who is in heaven is perfect. He cannot be any more perfect than he knows how, any more than we. When we are doing as well as we know how in the sphere and station which we occupy here, we are justified in the justice, righteousness, mercy, and judgment that go before the Lord of heaven and earth. We are as justified as the angels who are before the throne of God. The sin that will cleave to all the posterity of Adam and Eve is, that they have not done as well as they knew how. 2:129.

When we use the term perfection, it applies to man in his present condition, as well as to heavenly beings. We are now, or may be, as perfect in our sphere as God and angels are in theirs, but the greatest intelligence in existence can continually ascend to greater heights of perfection. 1:93.

Prepare to Live—Instead of preparing to die, prepare to live in the midst of all the exaltations of the Gods. 9:291.

We are organized for the express purpose of controlling the elements, of organizing and disorganizing, of ruling over kingdoms, principalities, and powers, and yet our affections are often too highly placed upon paltry, perishable objects. We love houses, gold, silver, and various kinds of property, and all who unduly prize any object there is beneath the celestial world are idolaters. 3:257.

But so long as we willingly hold fellowship with that which tends to death and destruction, we cannot progress as we should in the work of perfection in ourselves, nor in the building up and beautifying Zion. 9:284.

It is our privilege to say, every day in our lives, "That is the best day I ever lived." Never let a day so pass that you will have cause to say, "I will live better tomorrow," and I will promise you, in the name of the Lord Jesus, that your lives will be as a well of water springing up to everlasting life. You will have his Spirit to dwell in you continually, and your eyes will be open to see, your ears to hear, and your understandings to comprehend. 8:140.

He gives a little to his humble followers today, and if they improve upon it, tomorrow he will give them a little more, and the next day a little more. He does not add to that which they do not improve upon, but they are required to continually improve upon the knowledge they already possess, and thus obtain a store of wisdom. It is plain, then, that we may receive the truth, and know, through every portion of the soul, that the Gospel is the power of God unto salvation; that it is the way to life eternal; still there may be added to this, more power, wisdom, knowledge, and understanding. 2:2.

Eternal Increase—This people must go forward, or they will go backward. 16:165.

This work is a progressive work, this doctrine that is taught the Latter-day Saints in its nature is exalting, increasing, expanding and extending broader and broader until we can know as we are known, see as we are seen. 16:165.

Unless this work is in progress as a whole, it is not complete—we are found wanting, and not prepared to do the work we are called and sent to do. 6:267.

Ignorant? Yes, we are ignorant; but we are on the high road to that eternal knowledge that fills the bosoms of the Gods in eternity. 7:4.

We can still improve, we are made for that purpose, our capacities are organized to expand until we can receive into our comprehension celestial knowledge and wisdom, and to continue, worlds without end. 1:92.

Shall we ever be learning and never be able to come to a knowledge of the truth? No, I say we shall not; but we shall come to the knowledge of the truth. This is my hope and anticipation, and this is my joy. 18:237.

We are in the school and keep learning, and we do not expect to cease learning while we live on earth; and when we pass through the veil, we expect still to continue to learn and increase our fund of information. That may appear a strange idea to some, but it is for the plain and simple reason that we are not capacitated to receive all knowledge at once. We must therefore receive a little here and a little there. 6:286.

We have the principle within us, and so has every being on this earth, to increase and to continue to increase, to enlarge and receive and treasure up truth, until we become perfect. It is wisdom for us to be the friends of God; and unless we are filled with integrity and preserve ourselves in our integrity before our God, we actually lay the foundation for our destruction. 5:54.

If we are saved, we are happy, we are filled with light, glory, intelligence, and we pursue a course to enjoy the blessings that the Lord has in store for us. If we continue to pursue that course, it produces just the thing we want, that is, to be saved forever and forever, which will amount to an eternal salvation. 1:131.

Can mortal beings live so that they are worthy of the society of angels? I can answer the question for myself—I believe that they can; I am sure that they can. But in doing this, they must subdue the sin that is within themselves, correct every influence that arises within their own hearts that is opposed to the sanctifying influences of the grace of God, and purify themselves by their faith and by their conduct, so that they are worthy. Then they are prepared for the society of angels. To be Saints indeed requires every wrong influence that is within them, as individuals, to be subdued, until every evil desire is eradicated, and every feeling of their hearts is brought into subjection to the will of Christ. 19:66.

We ought not to speak lightly of and undervalue the life we now enjoy, but so dispose of each passing day that the hours and minutes are spent in doing good, or at least doing no harm, in making ourselves useful, in improving our talents and abilities to do more good, cultivating the principle of kindness to every being pertaining to our earthly sphere, learning their uses and how to apply them to produce the greatest possible amount of good; learning to conduct ourselves towards our families and friends in a way to win the love and confidence of the good, and overcome every ungovernable passion by a constant practice of cool judgment and deliberate thoughts. 9:291.

Because of the weakness of human nature, it must crumble to the dust. But in all the revolutions and changes in the existence of men, in the eternal world which they inhabit, and in the knowledge they have obtained as people on the earth, there is no such thing as principle, power, wisdom, knowledge, life, position, or anything that can be imagined, that remains stationary — they must increase or decrease. 1:350.

Take the history of this Church from the commencement, and we have proved that we cannot receive all the Lord has for us. We have proved to the heavens and to one another that we are not yet capacitated to receive all the Lord has for us, and that we have not yet a disposition to receive all he has for us. Can you understand that there is a time you can receive, and there is a time you cannot receive, a time when there is no place in the heart to receive? The heart of man will be closed up, the will will be set against this and that, that we have opportunity to receive. There is an abundance the Lord has for the people, if they would receive it. 10:291.

To me, life is increase; death is the opposite. 1:350.

Do you think that we are always going to remain the same size? I am not a stereotyped Latter-day Saint, and do not believe in the doctrine. Every year the Elders of Israel are improving and learning and have more power, more influence with the Heavens, more power over the elements, and over diseases, and over the power of Satan, who has ruled this earth from the days of the fall until now. We have to gain power until we break the chain of the enemy. Are we going to stand still? Away with stereotyped "Mormons!" I have more power than I had last year. I feel much stronger than ever before, and that too in the power of God; and I feel as though I could take the people and bring them into the presence of God, if they only hearken to counsel. Do you think that I am improving? "Yes." Keep up, then; keep your places, and follow in the track. 8:185.

We are privileged, in a spiritual point of view, precisely as we are in a temporal point of view. We have the privilege of learning and adding to the knowledge we have already obtained. We have a knowledge, for instance, of the rudiments of the English language. If we continue in our studies—in our exertions to acquire information, we obtain more knowledge; and if we continue still to persevere, we add still more to that, until we are perfect masters of the language.

Again, with regard to mechanism, in a certain sense, the same principle will hold good. We have the privilege of learning the arts and sciences that the learned among the Gentile nations understand;

we have the privilege of becoming classical scholars—of commencing with the rudiments of all knowledge—of entering into the academies, we might say, of perfection. We might study, and add knowledge to knowledge, from the time that we are capable of knowing anything until we go down to the grave. If we enjoyed healthy bodies, so as not to wear upon the functions of the mind, there is no end to a man's learning. This compares precisely with our situation pertaining to heavenly things. 6:283-284.

But simply to take the path pointed out in the Gospel by those who have given us the plan of salvation, is to take the path that leads to life, to eternal increase; it is to pursue that course wherein we shall never, never lose what we obtain, but continue to collect, to gather together, to increase, to spread abroad, and extend to an endless duration. Those persons who strive to gain eternal life, gain that which will produce the increase their hearts will be satisfied with. Nothing less than the privilege of increasing eternally, in every sense of the word, can satisfy the immortal spirit. If the endless stream of knowledge from the eternal fountain could all be drunk in by organized intelligences, so sure immortality would come to an end, and all eternity be thrown upon the retrograde path. 1:350.

There is one principle that I wish the people would understand and lay to heart. Just as fast as you will prove before your God that you are worthy to receive the mysteries, if you please to call them so, of the Kingdom of heaven—that you are full of confidence in God—that you will never betray a thing that God tells you—that you will never reveal to your neighbor that which ought not to be revealed, as quick as you prepare to be entrusted with the things of God, there is an eternity of them to bestow upon you. Instead of pleading with the Lord to bestow more upon you, plead with yourselves to have confidence in yourselves, to have integrity in yourselves, and know when to speak and what to speak, what to reveal, and how to carry yourselves and walk before the Lord. And just as fast as you prove to him that you will preserve everything secret that ought to be—that you will deal out to your neighbors all which you ought, and no more, and learn how to dispense your knowledge to your families, friends, neighbors, and brethren, the Lord will bestow upon you, and give to you, and bestow upon you, until finally he will say to you, "You shall never fall; your salvation is sealed unto you; you are sealed up unto eternal life and salvation, through your integrity." 4:371.

Life is an accumulation of every property and principle that is calculated to enrich, to ennoble, to enlarge, and to increase, in every particular, the dominion of individual man. To me, life would signify an extension. I have the privilege of spreading abroad, of enlarging my borders, of increasing in endless knowledge, wisdom, and power, and in every gift of God. To live as I am, without progress, is not life, in fact we may say that is impossible. There is no such principle in existence, neither can there be. You may explore all the eternities that have been, were it possible, then come to that which we now understand according to the principles of natural philosophy, and where is there an element, an individual living thing, an organized body, of whatever nature, that continues as it is? It cannot be found. All things that have come within the bounds of man's limited knowledge — the things he naturally understands, teach him that there is no period, in all the eternities, wherein organized existence will become stationary, that it cannot advanve in knowledge, wisdom, power, and glory.

If a man could ever arrive at the point that would put an end to the accumulation of life—the point at which he could increase no more, and advance no further, we should naturally say he commenced to decrease at the same point. Again, when he has gained the zenith of knowledge, wisdom, and power, it is the point at which he begins to retrograde; his natural abilities will begin to contract, and so he will continue to decrease, until all he knew is lost in the chaos of forgetfulness. As we understand naturally, this is the conclusion we must come to, if a termination to the increase of life and the acquisition of knowledge is true. 1:349.

The knowledge we now have in our possession is sufficient to guide and direct us step by step, day by day, until we are made perfect before the Lord our Father. 8:167.

Can you not live it for one hour? Begin at a small point; can you not live to the Lord for one minute? Yes. Then can we not multiply that by sixty and make an hour, and live that hour to the Lord? Yes; and then for a day, a week, a month, and a year? Then, when the year is past, it has been spent most satisfactorily. 8:59-60.

There are great and glorious things yet to be revealed. We are but babes and sucklings in the knowledge of God and godliness. With all we know and understand by the Priesthood here in the midst of this people, we are mere infants before the angels in heaven. 8:203.

I will apply my heart to wisdom, and ask the Lord to impart it to me; and if I know but little, I will improve upon it, that to-morrow I may have more, and thus grow from day to day, in the knowledge of the truth, as Jesus Christ grew in stature and knowledge from a babe to manhood. 1:313.

This principle is inherent in the organization of all intelligent beings, so that we are capable of receiving, and receiving and receiving from the inexhaustible fountain of knowledge and truth. 3:354.

It is enough for me to know that mankind are made to improve themselves. All creation, visible and invisible, is the workmanship of our God, the supreme Architect and Ruler of the whole, who organized the world, and created every living thing upon it, to act in its sphere and order. To this end has he ordained all things to increase and multiply. The Lord God Almighty has decreed this principle to be the great, governing law of existence, and for that purpose are we formed. Furthermore, if men can understand and receive it, mankind are organized to receive intelligence until they become perfect in the sphere they are appointed to fill, which is far ahead of us at present. 1:92.

A time when there was no God, no eternity! It cannot be possible, and the philosopher who tries to establish such a doctrine cannot possess any correct ideas of his own being. Will there ever be such a time? No. But forever onward and upward. 19:50.

Knowledge increases among this people; they know more of the things of the Kingdom of God to-day than they did in the days of Joseph Smith. 10:222.

If a person suffers his feelings to rise above the natural level of his capacity, they will sink in the same ratio. 8:32.

Blessings are Proportioned to Our Capacity—We are prepared for some things, and we receive just as fast as we prepare ourselves. 15:4.

The heart of man is incapable of fully comprehending the blessings that God has in store for the faithful, unless he has revealed those blessings to them by the revelations of his Spirit. The natural man is contracted in his feelings, in his views, faith and desires, and so are the Saints, unless they live their religion. 8:188.

Some might suppose that it would be a great blessing to be taken and carried directly into heaven and there set down, but in reality that would be no blessing to such persons; they could not reap a full reward, could not enjoy the glory of the kingdom, and could not comprehend and abide the light thereof, but it would be to them a hell intolerable and I suppose would consume them much quicker than would hell-fire. It would be no blessing to you to be carried into the celestial kingdom, and obliged to stay therein, unless you were prepared to dwell there. 3:221.

A man who has had his mind opened to the operation of the Priesthood of the Son of God—who understands anything of the government of heaven, must understand that finite beings are not capable of receiving and abiding the celestial law in its fulness. When can you abide a celestial law? When you become a celestial being, and never until then. 7:143.

Chapter VIII

THE DESTINY OF MAN

The Gift of Eternal Life—This is the greatest gift that can be conferred on intelligent beings, to live forever and never be destroyed. 8:261.

It is written that the greatest gift God can bestow upon man is the gift of eternal life. The greatest attainment that we can reach is to preserve our identity to an eternal duration in the midst of the heavenly host. We have the words of eternal life given to us through the Gospel, which, if we obey, will secure unto us that precious gift. 8:7.

Suppose it possible that you have the privilege of securing to yourselves eternal life—to live and enjoy these blessings forever; you will say this is the greatest blessing that can be bestowed upon you, to live forever and enjoy the society of wives, children, and children's children, to a thousand generations, and forever; and also the society of brethren, sisters, neighbors, and associates, and to possess all you can ask for to make you happy and comfortable. What blessing is equal to this? What blessing is equal to the continuation of life—to the continuation of our organization? 8:63.

The intelligence that is in me to cease to exist is a horrid thought; it is past enduring. This intelligence must exist; it must dwell somewhere. If I take the right course and preserve it in its organization, I will preserve to myself eternal life. 5:53.

Never serve God because you are afraid of hell; but live your religion, because it is calculated to give you eternal life. It points to that existence that never ends, while the other course leads to destruction. 5:340.

I am for life everlasting. I have a being and a life here; and this life is very valuable; it is a most excellent life! I have a future! I am living for another existence that is far above this sinful world, wherein I will be free from this darkness, sin, error, ignorance and unbelief. I am looking forward to a world filled with light and intelligence, where men and women will live in the knowledge and light of God. 13:220.

I tell you that if we strive with all our powers, by-and-by the time will come that we will be Saints indeed. I have not said that we are Saints. We are trying to be, and we profess to have the keys that will lead us in the path of eternal life. 6:4.

Understand eternity? There is not and never was a man in finite flesh who understands it. Enoch has been referred to in this matter. How many of the Gods and kingdoms he saw when the vision of his mind was opened, matters not. If he had seen more than he could have enumerated throughout his long life, and more than all the men on earth could multiply from the time his vision opened until now, he would not have attained to the comprehension of eternity. How much Enoch saw, how many worlds he saw, has nothing to do with the case. This is a matter that wise men know nothing about. 8:17.

We are going to have the Kingdom of God in the fulness thereof, and all the heights and depths of glory, power, and knowledge; and we shall have fathers and mothers, and wives and children. 8:178.

Eternal Increase—Whenever we get into the Kingdom of Heaven, where God and Christ dwell, we shall find something more to do than to "sit and sing ourselves away to everlasting bliss." The mind of man is active, and we must have exercise and amusement for the mind as well as the body. 12:313.

Now understand, to choose life is to choose principles that will lead you to an eternal increase, and nothing short of them will produce life in the resurrection for the faithful. Those that choose death, make choice of the path which leads to the end of their organization. The one leads to endless increase and progression, the other to the destruction. 1:352.

If men are faithful, the time will come when they will possess the power and the knowledge to obtain, organize, bring into existence, and own. "What, of themselves, independent of their Creator?" No. But they and their Creator will always be one, they will always be of one heart and of one mind, working and operating together; for whatsoever the Father doeth so doeth the Son, and so they continue throughout all their operations to all eternity. 2:304.

The Lord has blessed us with the ability to enjoy an eternal life with the Gods, and this is pronounced the greatest gift of God. The gift of eternal life, without a posterity, to become an angel, is one of the greatest gifts that can be bestowed; yet the Lord has bestowed on us the privilege of becoming fathers of lives. What is a father of lives as mentioned in the Scriptures? A man who has a posterity to an eternal continuance. That is the blessing Abraham received, and it perfectly satisfied his soul. He obtained the promise that he should be the father of lives. 8:63.

I expect, if I am faithful, with yourselves, that I shall see the time, with yourselves, that we shall know how to prepare to organize an earth like this—know how to people that earth, how to redeem it, how to sanctify it, and how to glorify it, with those who live upon it who hearken to our counsels. 6:274-5.

The faithful will become gods, even the sons of God; but this does not overthrow the idea that we have a father. 6:275.

After men have got their exaltations and their crowns—have become gods, even the sons of God—are made kings of kings and lords of lords, they have the power then of propagating their species in spirit. Power is then given to them to organize the elements, and then commence the organization of tabernacles. 6:275.

The Father and the Son have attained to this point already; I am on the way, and so are you, and every faithful servant of God. 6:275.

The Celestial World—If we keep the celestial law when our spirits go to God who gave them, we shall find that we are acquainted there and distinctly realize that we know all about that world. 4:218.

When you are qualified and purified, so that you can endure the glory of eternity, so that you can see your Father, and your friends who have gone behind the veil, you will fall upon their necks and kiss them, as we do an earthly friend that has been long absent from us, and that we have been anxiously desiring to see. 4:55.

When you see celestial beings, you will see men and women, but you will see those beings clothed upon with robes of celestial purity. We cannot bear the presence of our Father now; and we are placed at a distance to prove whether we will honor these tabernacles, whether we will be obedient and prepare ourselves to live in the glory of the light, privileges, and blessings of celestial beings. We could not have the glory and the light without first knowing the contrast. Do you comprehend that we could have no exaltation, without first learning by contrast? 4:54.

Opposition to Death—We are striving for eternal life, and are opposed to those who love and have the power of death. We have the influence and the power of life, and that necessarily brings us in opposition to those who prefer the principles of death. 7:56.

We are not in opposition to anything in earth or hell, except the principle of death. God has introduced life, and it is the principle of life that we are after. The power of the enemy is all the time trying to destroy this life, and I am opposed to that power. 7:56.

The principle opposite to that of eternal increase is that the person decreases, loses his knowledge, tact, talent, and ultimately, in a short period of time, is lost; but where, Oh! where is his spirit? I will not now take the time to follow his destiny; but here, strong language could be used, for when the Lord Jesus Christ shall be revealed, after the termination of the thousand years' rest, he will summon the armies of heaven for the conflict, he will come forth in flaming fire, he will descend to execute the mandates of an incensed God, and, amid the thunderings of the wrath of Omnipotence, roll up the heavens as a scroll, and destroy death, and him that has the power of it. 1:118.

Mankind have forfeited the right they once possessed to the friendship of their Heavenly Father, and through sin have exposed themselves to misery and wretchedness. Who is to bring back to the sin-stained millions of earth that which they have lost through disobedience? Who is to plant smiling peace and plenty where war and desolation reign? Who is to remove the curse and its consequences from earth—the homestead of mankind? Who shall say to the raging and contending elements, "Peace, be still," and extract the poison from the reptile's tooth, and the savage and destructive nature from beast and creeping thing?

Who placed the dark stain of sin upon this fair creation? Man. Who but man shall remove the foul blot, and restore all things to their primeval purity and innocence? But can he do this independent of heavenly aid? He can not. To aid him in this work heavenly grace is here; heavenly wisdom, power, and help are here, and God's laws and ordinances are here; the angels and spirits of just men made perfect are here; Jesus Christ, our Great High Priest, with Prophets, Apostles, and Saints, ancient and modern, are here to help man in the great work of sanctifying himself and the earth for final glorification in its paradisiacal state. All this will be accomplished through the law of the holy Priesthood. 10:301.

Chapter IX

DISPENSATIONS OF THE GOSPEL

The Earth—The world and all its various grades of organized denizens, from the lowest forms of vegetable or animal life, up to man, the lord of creation, were framed and made, or they would not have been here. 14:41.

It is said in this book (the Bible) that God made the earth in six days. This is a mere term, but it matters not whether it took six days, six months, six years, or six thousand years. The creation occupied certain periods of time. We are not authorized to say what the duration of these days was, whether Moses penned these words as we have them, or whether the translators of the Bible have given the words their intended meaning. However, God created the world. God brought forth material out of which he formed this little terra firma upon which we roam. How long had this material been in existence? Forever and forever, in some shape, in some condition. We need not refer to all of those who were with God, and who assisted him in his work. The elements form and develop, and continue to do so until they mature, and then they commence to decay and become disorganized. The mountains around us were formed in this way. By and by, when they shall have reached their maturity, the work of disintegration and decay will commence. It has been so from all eternity, and will continue to be so until they are made celestial. 18:231.

This earth is brought together and organized from native elements as we now behold it, our tabernacles included. The matter of which all animate and inanimate existence is formed is from all eternity, and it must remain to all eternity, without beginning and without end. There are certain portions of this native element that will be refined and prepared to enter into the celestial kingdom—into the celestial family of the celestial world. If the spirit honors the body and the body honors the spirit while they are here united, the particles of matter that compose the mortal tabernacle will be resurrected and brought forth to immortality and eternal life; but it cannot be brought forth and made immortal, except it undergoes a change, for "dust thou art, and unto dust shalt thou return." What for? To prepare the body to be made immortal and fitted to dwell in the presence of the Gods. 8:27.

We shall go and come; and when we are in the eternity, we shall be on this earth, which will be brought into the immediate presence of the Father and the Son. We shall inhabit different mansions, and worlds will continue to be made, formed, and organized, and messengers from this earth will be sent to others. This earth will become a celestial body—be like a sea of glass, or like a Urim and Thummim; and when you wish to know anything, you can look in this earth and see all the eternities of God. We shall make our home here, and go on our missions as we do now, but at greater than railroad speed. 8:200.

We are for the Kingdom of God, and not going to the moon, nor to any other planet pertaining to this solar system; but are determined to have a heaven here, and are going to make it ourselves, by the help of God and his angels. We have been traditionated that when we were prepared to be saved, we ought then to pass from this stage of existence, and that then we never would have anything more to do with this earth; for all our connections and associations with it, as pertaining to this life, also passed away, and we should see and know nothing about it in the future. This is not according to the design, as we believe, of God and his providences and works. It is not the work of the Lord to organize an earth and destroy it. That is not the system he has devised. His plan is to organize an earth, people it with intelligent beings, present to them the principles of eternal life, and bestow upon them the keys thereof, that they may be able to prepare themselves to dwell to all eternity, and to bring forth their increase to dwell with them. This is our belief. 8:293.

The animal, vegetable, and mineral kingdoms abide the law of their Creator; the whole earth and all things pertaining to it, except man, abide the law of their creation. 9:246.

The earth is organized for a glorious resurrection. 1:274.

But the earth will not be utterly destroyed; the elements of which it is composed will not be annihilated, but they will be changed. Neither shall those be consumed who can abide the day of the Lord Almighty, and stand in his presence. The earth in that great day will be renovated—cleansed from wickedness—purified from dross, sanctified, and prepared for the habitation of the Saints of the Most High. 2:124.

The earth is very good in and of itself, and has abided a celestial law, consequently we should not despise it, nor desire to leave it, but rather desire and strive to obey the same law that the earth abides, and abide it as honorably as does the earth. 2:302-303.

The earth will abide its creation, and will be counted worthy of receiving the blessings designed for it, and will ultimately roll back into the presence of God who formed it and established its mineral, vegetable, and animal kingdoms. These will all be retained upon the earth, come forth in the resurrection, and abide for ever and for ever. 8:8.

This earth in its present condition and situation, is not a fit habitation for the sanctified; but it abides the law of its creation, has been baptized with water, will be baptized by fire and the Holy Ghost, and by-and-by will be prepared for the faithful to dwell upon. 8:83.

Adam and Eve—Mankind is composed of two distinct elements; the first is a spiritual organization in eternity, the second is a natural organization on this earth, formed out of the material of which this earth is composed. Man is first spiritual, then temporal.

These spirits I shall leave for the present, and refer to our first parents, Adam and Eve, who were found in the Garden of Eden, tempted and overcome by the power of evil, and consequently subject to evil and sin, which was the penalty of their transgression. They were now prepared, as we are, to form bodies or tabernacles for the reception of pure and holy spirits. 18:257.

When Father Adam came to assist in organizing the earth out of the crude material that was found, an earth was made upon which the children of men could live. After the earth was prepared Father Adam came and stayed here, and there was a woman brought to him. There was a certain woman brought to Father Adam whose name was Eve, because she was the first woman, and she was given to him to be his wife. 16:167.

When Moses wrote and said that man was formed precisely in the image of God he wrote the truth. We are the children of our Father—his offspring, of the same family; we belong to him by birthright, and we are his children and Jesus is our brother. Does the Bible tell all this? Just as plain as words can tell anything. 14:280.

In the beginning, after this earth was prepared for man, the Lord commenced his work upon what is now called the American continent, where the Garden of Eden was made. In the days of Noah, in the days of the floating of the ark, he took the people to another part of the earth; the earth was divided, and there he set up his kingdom. 8:195.

The human family are formed after the image of our Father and God. After the earth was organized the Lord placed his children upon it, gave them possession of it, and told them that it was their home—the place of their habitation from thenceforth; he told them to till the ground and subdue it; he gave it to them for their inheritance, and to do their will upon it. Then Satan steps in and overcomes them through the weakness there was in the children of the Father when they were sent to the earth, and sin was brought in, and thus we are subjected to sin. 10:300.

Some may regret that our first parents sinned. This is nonsense. If we had been there, and they had not sinned, we should have sinned. I will not blame Adam or Eve. Why? Because it was necessary that sin should enter into the world; no man could ever understand the principle of exaltation without its opposite; no one could ever receive an exaltation without being acquainted with its opposite. How did Adam and Eve sin? Did they come out in direct opposition to God and to his government? No. But they transgressed a command of the Lord, and through that transgression sin came into the world. The Lord knew they would do this, and he had designed that they should. Then came the curse upon the fruit, upon the vegetables, and upon our mother earth; and it came upon the creeping things, upon the grain in the field, the fish in the sea, and upon all things pertaining to this earth, through man's transgression. 10:312.

Mother Eve partook of the forbidden fruit. We should not have been here to-day if she had not; we could never have possessed wisdom and intelligence if she had not done it. It was all in the economy of heaven, and we need not talk about it; it is all right. We should never blame Mother Eve, not the least. I am thankful to God that I know good from evil, the bitter from the sweet, the things of God from the things not of God. When I look at the economy of heaven my heart leaps for joy, and if I had the tongue of an angel, or the tongues of the whole human family combined, I would praise God in the highest for his great wisdom and condescension in suffering the children of men to fall into the very sin into which they had fallen, for he did it that they, like Jesus, might descend below all things and then press forward and rise above all. 13:145.

The Devil had truth in his mouth as well as lies when he came to Mother Eve. Said he, "If you will eat of the fruit of the tree of knowledge of good and evil, you will see as the Gods see." That was just as true as anything that ever was spoken on the face of the earth. She did eat, her eyes were opened, and she saw good and evil. She gave of the fruit to her husband, and he ate, too. What would have been the consequence if he had not done so? They would have been separated, and where would we have been? I am glad he did eat. 12:70.

We are safe in saying that from the day that Adam was created and placed in the Garden of Eden to this day, the plan of salvation and the revelations of the will of God to man are unchanged, although mankind have not for many ages been favored therewith, in consequence of apostasy and wickedness. There is no evidence to be found in the Bible that the Gospel should be one thing in the days of the Israelites, another in the days of Christ and his Apostles, and another in the 19th century, but, on the contrary, we are instructed that God is the same in every age, and that his plan of saving his children is the same. The plan of salvation is one, from the beginning of the world to the end thereof. 10:324.

I wish you all to understand "Mormonism" as it is. We embraced it in different parts of the world, because we considered it the best religion we could find. Can we tell how much better "Mormonism" is than other religions and isms of the present day? More or less truth may be found in them all, both in civilized and barbarous nations. How has it transpired that theological truth is thus so widely disseminated? It is because God was once known on the earth among his children of mankind, as we know one another. Adam was as conversant with his Father who placed him upon this earth as we are conversant with our earthly parents. The Father frequently came to visit his son Adam, and talked and walked with him; and the children of Adam were more or less acquainted with him, and the things that pertain to God and to heaven were as familiar among mankind in the first ages of their existence on the earth, as these mountains are to our mountain boys, as our gardens are to our wives and children, or as the road to the Western Ocean is to the experienced traveler. From this source mankind have received their religious traditions. 9:148.

The Gospel was among the children of men from the days of Adam until the coming of the Messiah; this Gospel of Christ is from the beginning to the end. Then why was the law of Moses given? In consequence of the disobedience of the Children of Israel, the elect of God; the very seed that he had selected to be his people, and upon whom he said he would place his name. This seed of Abraham so rebelled against him and his commands that the Lord said to Moses, "I will give you a law which shall be a schoolmaster to bring them to Christ." But this law is grievous; it is a law of carnal commandments. 13:269.

Cain conversed with his God every day, and knew all about the plan for creating this earth, for his father told him. But, for the want of humility, and through jealousy, and an anxiety to possess the kingdom, and to have the whole of it under his own control, and not allow anybody else the right to say one word, what did he do? He killed his brother. Then the Lord put a mark on him. 2:142-143.

Here let me state to all philosophers of every class upon the earth. when you tell me that Father Adam was made as we make adobes from the earth, you tell me what I deem an idle tale. When you tell me that the beasts of the field were produced in that manner, you are speaking idle words devoid of meaning. There is no such thing in all the eternities where the Gods dwell. Mankind are here because they are the offspring of parents who were first brought here from another planet, and power was given them to propagate their species, and they were commanded to multiply and replenish the earth. 7:285-286.

We all belong to the races which have sprung from Father Adam and Mother Eve; and every son and daughter of that God we serve, who organized this earth and millions of others, and who holds them in existence by law. 14:111.

There are no persons without evil passions to embitter their lives. Mankind are revengeful, passionate, hateful, and devilish in their dispositions. This we inherit through the fall, and the grace of God is designed to enable us to overcome it. The grace of God is bestowed upon all, and the Kingdom of God is planted on the earth expressly to enable mankind to overcome the evil that is in them, and to save all. 8:160.

It is true mankind have wandered and have fallen from that which they might have attained through the redemption made by Jesus Christ; but there is one point in connection with this statement on which I differ from the orthodox divines of the day. They say that man is naturally prone to evil. In some respects this is true, where by the force of example and wrong tradition has become ingrained, but if man had always been permitted to follow the instincts of his nature, had he always followed the great and holy principles of his organism, they would have led him into the path of life everlasting, which the whole human family are constantly trying to find. 10:189.

Enoch to Moses—The Lord sent forth his Gospel to the people; he said, I will give it to my son Adam, from whom Methuselah received it; and Noah received from Methuselah; and Melchizedek administered to Abraham. 3:94.

Enoch possessed intelligence and wisdom from God that few men ever enjoyed, walking and talking with God for many years; yet, according to the history written by Moses, he was a great length of time in establishing his kingdom among men. The few that followed him enjoyed the fulness of the Gospel, and the rest of the world rejected it. Enoch and his party were taken from the earth, and the world continued to ripen in iniquity until they were overthrown by the great flood in the days of Noah; and, "as it was in the days of Noah, so shall it be in the days of the coming of the Son of Man." 9:365.

Enoch had to talk with and teach his people during a period of three hundred and sixty years, before he could get them prepared to enter into their rest, and then he obtained power to translate himself and his people, with the region they inhabited, their houses, gardens, fields, cattle and all their possessions. 3:320.

Abraham was faithful to the true God; he overthrew the idols of his father and obtained the Priesthood after the order of Melchizedek, which is after the order of the Son of God, and a promise that of the increase of his seed there should be no end; when you obtain the holy Priesthood, which is after the order of Melchizedek, sealed upon you, and the promise that your seed shall be numerous as the stars in the firmament, or as the sands upon the seashore, and of your increase there shall be no end, you have then got the promise of Abraham, Isaac, and Jacob, and all the blessings that were conferred upon them. 11:118.

If they had been sanctified and holy, the Children of Israel would not have traveled one year with Moses before they would have received their endowments and the Melchizedek Priesthood. 6:100.

Mankind have degenerated; they have lost the physical and mental power they once possessed. In many points pertaining to mechanism, men have in modern times been instructed by revelation to them, and this mechanical knowledge causes them almost to boast against their Creator, and to set themselves up as competitors with the Lord Almighty, notwithstanding they have produced nothing but what has been revealed to them. In the knowledge of astronomical and other philosophical truths, which our modern great men are searching after and pride themselves in, they are but babes, compared with the ancient fathers. Do the wise men of modern ages understand the laws which govern the worlds that are, that were, and that are to come? They cannot fathom this matter. They have grown weaker when they ought to have grown stronger and wiser. 8:61.

Jesus on Earth—It was necessary for Jesus Christ to open the heavens to certain individuals that they might be witnesses of his personage, death, sufferings, and resurrection; those men were witnesses. But as Jesus appeared to the two brethren going out of Jerusalem, he was made known to them in the breaking of bread. Now suppose he had eaten that bread, and gone out without opening their eyes, how could they have known that he was the Savior who had been crucified on Mount Calvary? They could not; but in the breaking of bread the vision of their minds was opened. This was necessary in order to constitute safe witnesses, and they returned to Jerusalem and told the brethren what they had seen. 3:208.

When we come to discriminate between the former and the Latter-day Saints we shall find there was a little difference in their callings and duties, and in many points that we may say pertain to our temporal lives. Not in the doctrine of baptism, the laying on of hands for the reception of the Holy Ghost, nor in the gifts of the

Gospel. There is no difference in these things, but there is a difference in regard to the temporal duties devolving upon us. 12:67.

The Apostasy—In the early days of the Christian Church we understand that there was a good deal of speculation among its members with regard to their belief and practice, and the propagation of these speculative ideas created divisions and schisms. Even in the days of the Apostles there was evidently considerable division, for we read that some were for Paul, some for Apollos, and others for Cephas. The people in those days had their favorites, who taught them peculiar doctrines not generally received and promulgated. 12:64.

Why have they wandered so far from the path of truth and rectitude? Because they left the Priesthood and have had no guide, no leader, no means of finding out what is true and what is not true. It is said the Priesthood was taken from the Church, but it is not so, the Church went from the Priesthood and continued to travel in the wilderness, turned from the commandments of the Lord, and instituted other ordinances. 12:69.

You can read the account given of our first parents. Along came a certain character and said to Eve, you know women are of tender heart, and he could operate on this tender heart, "The Lord knows that in the day thou eatest thereof thou shalt not surely die, but if thou wilt take of this fruit and eat thereof thine eyes will be opened and thou wilt see as the Gods see"; and he worked upon the tender heart of Mother Eve until she partook of the fruit, and her eyes were opened. He told the truth. And they say now, "Do this that your eyes may be opened, that you may see; do this that you may know thus and so." In the days of Jesus and his Apostles the same power was operating, and, actuated by that men hunted them until the last one was banished from human society, and until the Christian religion was so perverted that the people received it with open hands, arms, mouth and heart. It was adulterated until it was congenial to the wicked heart, and they received the Gospel as they supposed. But that was the time they commenced little by little to transgress the laws, change the ordinances, and break the everlasting covenant, and the Gospel of the kingdom that Jesus undertook to establish in his day and the Priesthood were taken from the earth. 15:126.

The land of Judea has fallen into disrepute, and it has become a desert, just through the apostasy of those who once inhabited it, who had the oracles of God among them. 16:66.

The Restoration—Generations have come and gone without the privilege of hearing the sound of the Gospel, which has come to you through Joseph Smith—that was revealed to him from heaven by angels and visions. We have the Gospel and the keys of the holy Priesthood. 7:173.

We are a people whose rise and progress from the beginning, has been the work of God our Heavenly Father, which in his wisdom he has seen proper to commence for the re-establishment of his Kingdom upon the earth. 2:170.

Do you think the Lord Almighty will reveal the great improvements in the arts and sciences which are being constantly made known and will not revive a pure religion? If any man imagines that with the mighty strides which the sciences have been making for a few years past, there will be no improvement in religion, that man is vain in his imagination. God will improve the religion of the nations of the earth in proportion to the improvement made in the sciences. This is true whether you believe it or not. The Lord has commenced the work, and it is a marvelous one. 12:325.

It was decreed in the counsels of eternity, long before the foundations of the earth were laid, that he, Joseph Smith, should be the man, in the last dispensation of this world, to bring forth the word of God to the people, and receive the fulness of the keys and power of the Priesthood of the Son of God. The Lord had his eyes upon him, and upon his father, and upon his father's father, and upon their progenitors clear back to Abraham, and from Abraham to the flood, from the flood to Enoch, and from Enoch to Adam. He has watched that family and that blood as it has circulated from its fountain to the birth of that man. He was fore-ordained in eternity to preside over this last dispensation. 7:289.

But as it was in the days of our Savior, so was it in the advent of this new dispensation. It was not in accordance with the notions, traditions, and pre-conceived ideas of the American people. The messenger did not come to an eminent divine of any of the so-called orthodoxy, he did not adopt their interpretation of the Holy Scriptures. The Lord did not come with the armies of heaven in power and great glory, nor send his messengers panoplied with aught else than the truth of heaven, to communicate to the meek, the lowly, the youth of humble origin, the sincere enquirer after the knowledge of God. But he did send his angel to this same obscure person, Joseph Smith, Jr., who afterwards became a Prophet, Seer and Revelator, and informed him that he should not join any of the religious sects of the day, for they were all wrong; that they were following the precepts of men instead of the Lord Jesus; that he had a work for him to perform, inasmuch as he should prove faithful before him.

No sooner was this made known, and published abroad, and

people began to listen and obey the heavenly summons, than opposition began to rage, and the people, even in this favored land, began to persecute their neighbors and friends for entertaining religious opinions differing from their own. 2:171.

You may remember it and lay it to heart, and if you wish, write it in your journals that some of the best spirits that have ever been sent to earth are coming at the present time. 11:117.

The beginning of this dispensation of the fulness of times may well be compared to the commencement of a temple, the material of which it is to be built being still scattered, unshaped and unpolished, in a state of nature. I am thankful that the way is being prepared, and that we have the privilege of erecting a spiritual and moral super-structure—a temple of God. 12:161.

The Book of Mormon—There is not another nation under heaven, in whose midst the Book of Mormon could have been brought forth. The Lord has been operating for centuries to prepare the way for the coming forth of the contents of that Book from the bowels of the earth, to be published to the world, to show to the inhabitants thereof that he still lives, and that he will, in the latter days, gather his elect from the four corners of the earth. It was the Lord who directed the discovery of this land to the nations of the Old World, and its settlement, and the war for independence, and the final victory of the colonies, and the unprecedented prosperity of the American nation, up to the calling of Joseph the Prophet. The Lord has dictated and directed the whole of this, for the bringing forth, and establishing of his Kingdom in the last days. 11:17.

Here is the Book of Mormon. We believe it contains the history of the aborigines of our continent, just as the Old Testament contains the history of the Jewish nation. In that book we learn that Jesus visited this continent, delivered his Gospel and ordained Twelve Apostles. We believe all this, but we do not ask you to believe it. What we do ask is that you will believe what is recorded in the Holy Bible concerning God and his revelations to the children of men. Do this in all honesty and sincerity, then you will know that the Book of Mormon is true. Your minds will be opened and you will know by the vision of the Spirit of God that we teach the truth. 13:335.

I was somewhat acquainted with the coming forth of the Book of Mormon, not only through what I read in the newspapers, but I also heard a great many stories and reports which were circulated as quick as the Book of Mormon was printed, and began to be scattered abroad. Then the spirit of persecution, the spirit of death, the spirit of destruction immediately seemed to enter the hearts of the pious priests more particularly than any other portion of the people; they could not bear it. 2:249.

What did Oliver Cowdery (one of the three witnesses to the Book of Mormon) say, after he had been away from the Church years and years? He saw and conversed with the angels, who showed him the plates, and he handled them. He left the Church because he lost the love of truth; and after he had traveled alone for years, a gentleman walked into his law office and said to him, "Mr. Cowdery, what do you think of the Book of Mormon now? Do you believe that it is true?" He replied, "No, sir, I do not!" "Well," said the gentleman, "I thought as much; for I concluded that you had seen the folly of your ways and had resolved to renounce what you once declared to be true." "Sir, you mistake me; I do not believe that the Book of Mormon is true; I am past belief on that point, for I know that it is true, as well as I know that you now sit before me." "Do you still testify that you saw an angel?" "Yes, as much as I see you now; and I know the Book of Mormon to be true." Yet he forsook it. Every honest person who has fairly heard it knows that "Mormonism" is true, if they have had the testimony of it; but to practice it in our lives is another thing. 7:55.

Chapter X

THE LAST DAYS

Confusion of the Last Days—The time is coming when a good man will be more precious than fine gold. 10:295.

The sinner will slay the sinner, the wicked will fall upon the wicked, until there is an utter overthrow and consumption upon the face of the whole earth, until God reigns, whose right it is. 2:190.

The world is drunk, but not with wine or strong drink; and our country is the most drunken of all. They are deluding themselves; they are drunk with party fanaticism; they are high-minded, heady, and senseless, and are fast going to destruction.

Thinking men, inquiring minds, ask whether it is really necessary for the Government of God to be on the earth at the present day; I answer, most assuredly; there never was a time when it was more needed than it is now. Why? Because men do not know how to govern themselves without it. Would it be considered treason of any Christian government in our day to profess to believe in the Lord Jesus Christ, and in the efficacy of his death and resurrection for the salvation of man, and to profess and declare that it is his inalienable, indisputable right and prerogative to reign over men, the earth and all things upon it? 10:320.

If we live, we shall see the nations of the earth arrayed against this people; for that time must come, in fulfilment of prophecy. Tell about war commencing! Bitter and relentless war waged against Joseph Smith before he had received the plates of the Book of Mormon; and from that time till now the wicked have only fallen back at times to gain strength and learn how to attack the Kingdom of God. 5:339.

All we have yet heard and we have experienced is scarcely a preface to the sermon that is going to be preached. When the testimony of the Elders ceases to be given, and the Lord says to them, "Come home; I will preach my own sermons to the nations of the earth," all you now know can scarely be called a preface to the sermon that will be preached with fire and sword, tempests, earthquakes, hail, rain, thunders and lightnings, and fearful destruction. What matters the destruction of a few railway cars? You will hear of magnificent cities, now idolized by the people, sinking in the earth, entombing the inhabitants. The sea will heave itself beyond its bounds, engulfing mighty cities. Famine will spread over the nations and nation will rise up against nation, kingdom against kingdom and states against states, in our own country and in foreign lands; and they will destroy each other, caring not for the blood and lives of their neighbors, of their families, or for their own lives. 8:123.

There never has been a day for ages and ages, not since the true church was destroyed after the days of the Apostles, that required the faith and the energy of godly men and godly women, and the skill, wisdom and power of the Almighty to be with them, so much as this people require it at the present time. There never was that necessity; there never has been a time on the face of the earth, from the time that the church went to destruction, and the Priesthood was taken from the earth, that the powers of darkness and the powers of earth and hell were so embittered, and enraged, and incensed against God and Godliness on the earth, as they are at the present. And when the spirit of persecution, the spirit of hatred, of wrath, and malice ceases in the world against this people, it will be the time that this people have apostatized and joined hands with the wicked, and never until then; which I pray may never come. 4:326.

The Devil is just as much opposed to Jesus now as he was when the revolt took place in heaven. And as the Devil increases his numbers by getting the people to be wicked, so Jesus Christ increases his numbers and strength by getting the people to be humble and righteous. The human family are going to the polls by and by, and they wish to know which party is going to carry the day. 4:38.

Ultimate Triumph of Righteousness—I most assuredly expect that the time will come when every tongue shall confess, and every knee shall bow to the Savior, though the people may believe what they will with regard to religion. 2:189.

The Savior will dictate his Kingdom, through his Apostles and Prophets, until all the heathen nations are virtually redeemed by the ordinances that effect redemption, that they may inherit the kingdom that is prepared for them. 8:83.

This is a day of days, a time of times; this is the fulness of times, in which all things that are in Christ are to be gathered in one. This is a momentous period. 10:308.

I expect to see the time when the inhabitants of the earth will pride themselves in doing good. 8:363.

The time will come when every knee will bow, and every tongue confess to and acknowledge him, and when they who have lived upon the earth and have spurned the idea of a Supreme Being and of revelations from him, will fall with shamefacedness and humble themselves before him, exclaiming, "There is a God! O God, we once rejected thee and disbelieved thy word and set at naught thy counsels, but now we bow down in shame and we do acknowledge that there is a God, and that Jesus is the Christ." This time will come, most assuredly. We have the faith of the Gospel of the Lord Jesus. 13:306.

What will they do? They will hear of the wisdom of Zion and the kings and potentates of the nations will come up to Zion to inquire after the ways of the Lord, and seek out the great knowledge, wisdom and understanding manifested through the Saints of the Most High. They will inform the people of God that they belong to such and such a church, and do not wish to change their religion.

They will be drawn to Zion by the great wisdom displayed there, and will attribute it to the cunning and craftiness of men. It will be asked, "What do you want to do, ye strangers from afar?" "We want to live our own religion." "Will you bow the knee before God with us?" "O yes, we would as soon do it as not;" and at that time every knee shall bow, and every tongue acknowledge that God who is the framer and maker of all things, the governor and controller of the universe. They will have to bow the knee and confess that he is God, and that Jesus Christ, who suffered for the sins of the world, is actually its Redeemer; that by the shedding of his blood he has redeemed men, women, children, beasts, birds, fish, the earth itself, and everything that John saw and heard praising in heaven. 2:316-317.

By and by the world will be overturned according to the words of the prophet, and we will see the reign of righteousness enter in, and sin and iniquity will have to walk off. But the power and principles of evil, if they can be called principles, will never yield one particle to the righteous march of the Savior, only as they are beaten back inch by inch, and we have got to take the ground by force. Yes, by the mental force of faith, and by good works, the march forth of the Gospel will increase, spread, grow and prosper, until the nations of the earth will feel that Jesus has the right to rule King of nations as he does King of Saints. 14:226.

Return to Jackson County—When are we going back to Jackson County? Not until the Lord commands his people; and it is just as much as you and I can do to get ready to go when he does command us. 6:269.

If that is back to Jackson County, do not be scared, for as the Lord lives this people will go back and build a great temple there. This people will surely go back to Jackson County. How soon that may be, or when it may be, I do not care; but that is not now the gathering place for this people. 3:278.

Where is the center Stake of Zion? In Jackson County, Missouri. 8:198.

There has been considerable said this afternoon with regard to redeeming and building up Zion, the Order of Enoch, etc. I see men and women in this congregation—only a few of them—who were driven from the central Stake of Zion. Ask them if they had any sorrow or trouble; then let them look at the beautiful land that the Lord would have given them if all had been faithful in keeping his commandments, and had walked before him as they should; and then ask them with regard to the blessings they would have received. If they tell you the sentiments of their minds, they will tell you that the yoke of Jesus would have been easy and his burden would have been light, and that it would have been a delightful task to have walked in obedience to his commandments and to have been of one heart and one mind; but through the selfishness of some, which is idolatry, through their covetousness, which is the same, and the lustful desire of their minds, they were cast out and driven from their homes. We have been driven many times; but each time, if they who professed to be the servants of God had served him with an undivided heart, they would have had the privilege of living in their houses, possessing their lands, attending their meetings, and spreading abroad on the right and the left, lengthening the cords of Zion, and strengthening her stakes until the land had been dedicated to the Gospel of the Son of God. Well, I have been with the rest and I exepect I have been covetous like them, and probably I am now; but if I am, I wish somebody would tell me wherein. 13:1.

Counting of Christ—Do you know that it is the eleventh hour of the reign of Satan on the earth? Jesus is coming to reign, and all you who fear and tremble because of your enemies, cease to fear them, and learn to fear to offend God, fear to transgress his laws, fear to do any evil to your brother, or to any being upon the earth, and do not fear Satan and his power, nor those who have only power to slay the body, for God will preserve his people. 10:250.

In the progress of the age in which we live, we discern the fulfilment of prophecy, and the preparation for the second coming of our Lord and Savior to dwell upon the earth. We expect that the refuge of lies will be swept away, and that city, nation, government, or kingdom which serves not God, and gives no heed to the principles of truth and religion, will be utterly wasted away and destroyed. 2:178.

Jesus has been upon the earth a great many more times than you are aware of. When Jesus makes his next appearance upon the earth, but few of this Church will be prepared to receive him and see him face to face and converse with him; but he will come to his temple. Will he remain and dwell upon the earth a thousand years, without returning? He will come here, and return to his mansions, where he dwells with his Father, and come again to the earth, and again return to his Father, according to my understanding.

Then angels will come and begin to resurrect the dead, and the Savior will also raise the dead, and they will receive the keys of the resurrection, and will begin to assist in that work. Will the wicked know of it? They will know just as much about that as they now know about "Mormonism," and no more. 7:142.

When your eyes are open, you will see that this earth has fallen from the glory and presence of the Father, to pass through certain ordeals, together with the people upon it. And by and by, when Jesus reigns and rules, King of nations, he will say to his Father, "Here is my work! Here are my brethren! Here is my redemption—the fruit of my labor! I have ceased not to contend with the Enemy until I have put him under my feet. I have destroyed death, and him that has the power of death." 8:297.

At times I may to many of the brethren appear to be severe. I sometimes chasten them; but it is because I wish them to live so that the power of God, like a flame of fire, will dwell within them and be around about them. These are my feelings and desires. I wish to see this people take a course to bring back the days, years, and intelligence that have been lost through transgression. This cannot be performed in a day. Zion will not be redeemed and built up in a day. Israel will not be brought back to the fold of Christ and redeemed in a day. 8:62.

The Millennium—The Millennium consists in this—every heart in the Church and Kingdom of God being united in one; the Kingdom increasing to the overcoming of everything opposed to the economy of heaven, and Satan being bound, and having a seal set upon him. All things else will be as they are now, we shall eat, drink, and wear clothing. 1:203.

When all nations are so subdued to Jesus that every knee shall bow and every tongue shall confess, there will still be millions on the earth who will not believe in him; but they will be obliged to acknowledge his kingly government. 7:142.

Let the people be holy, and the earth under their feet will be holy. Let the people be holy, and filled with peace; the soil of the earth will bring forth in its strength, and the fruits thereof will be meat for man. The more purity that exists, the less is the strife; the more kind we are to our animals, the more will peace increase, and the savage nature of the brute creation vanish away. If the people will not serve the Devil another moment whilst they live, if this congregation is possessed of that spirit and resolution, here in this house is the Millennium. Let the inhabitants of this city be possessed of that spirit, let the people of the territory be possessed of that spirit, and here is the Millennium, and so will it spread over all the world. 1:203.

In the Millennium, when the Kingdom of God is established on the earth in power, glory and perfection, and the reign of wickedness that has so long prevailed is subdued, the Saints of God will have the privileges of building their temples, and of entering into them, becoming, as it were, pillars in the temples of God, and they will officiate for their dead. Then we will see our friends come up, and perhaps some that we have been acquainted with here. If we ask who will stand at the head of the resurrection in this last dispensation, the answer is—Joseph Smith, Junior, the Prophet of God. He is the man who will be resurrected and receive the keys of the resurrection, and he will seal this authority upon others, and they will hunt up their friends and resurrect them when they shall have been officiated for, and bring them up. And we will have revelations to know our forefathers clear back to Father Adam and Mother Eve, and we will enter into the temples of God and officiate for them. Then man will be sealed to man until the chain is made perfect back to Adam, so that there will be a perfect chain of Priesthood from Adam to the winding-up scene.

This will be the work of the Latter-day Saints in the Millennium. 15:138.

When Jesus comes to rule and reign, King of nations, as he now does, King of Saints, the veil of the covering will be taken from all nations, that all flesh may see his glory together, but that will not make them all Saints. Seeing the Lord does not make a man a Saint; seeing an angel does not make a man a Saint by any means. A man may see the finger of the Lord, and not thereby become a Saint; the veil of the covering may be taken from before the nations, and all flesh see his glory together, and at the same time declare they will not serve him. 2:316.

Rapid Movements in the Last Days—Do you understand that what the Lord will perform in the latter days will be done quicker than in the former days? He suffered Noah to occupy one hundred and twenty years in building the ark. Were he to command us to build an ark, he would not allow so long a time for completing it. 8:134.

If I live as long as Enoch lived, who walked with the Lord three hundred and sixty-five years, can I then see a people prepared to enter at once in the celestial world? No. Many may think that Enoch and his whole city were taken from the earth directly into the presence of God. That is a mistaken idea. If, within three hundred and sixty-five years, I can see a people capable of surmounting every sin, of overcoming every evil and effect of sin to such a degree as to be separated in the flesh from the sinful portion of the world and from all the effects of the fall—a great people as pure and holy as were the people of Enoch, I should not complain, and, perhaps have no cause to. Yet, in the latter days, God will cut short his work in righteousness. 8:134.

According to my definition of the word, there is not a strictly and fully civilized community now upon the earth. Is there murder by wholesale to be found in a strictly civilized community? Will a community of civilized nations rise up one against another, nation against nation, and kingdom against kingdom, using against each other every destructive invention that can be brought to bear in their wars? When will they be civilized? When the Lord shall judge among the nations, and shall rebuke many people; and they shall beat their swords into ploughshares, and their spears into pruninghooks; when nations shall not lift up sword against nation, neither learn war any more. When the world is in a state of true civilization, man will have ceased to contend against his fellow-man, either as individuals, parties, communities, sects, or nations. This state of civilization will be brought about by the holy Priesthood of the Son of God; and men, with full purpose of heart, will seek unto him who is pure and holy, even our great Creator—our Father and God; and he will give them a law that is pure—a government and plan of society possessed by holy beings in heaven. Then there will be no more war, no more bloodshed, no more evil-speaking and evil-doing; but all will be contented to follow in the path of truth, which alone is calculated to exalt and dignify the whole man, mentally and physically, in all his operations, labors, and purposes. Short of this, mankind cannot be said to be truly civilized. 8:6-7.

Then, do not be too anxious for the Lord to hasten his work. Let our anxiety be centered upon one thing, the sanctification of our own hearts, the purifying of our own affections, the preparing of ourselves for the approach of the events that are hastening upon us. This should be our concern, this should be our study, this should be our daily prayer, and not to be in a hurry to see the overthrow of the wicked. 9:3.

Whether the world is going to be burned up within a year, or within a thousand years, does not matter a groat to you and me. We have the words of eternal life, we have the privilege of obtaining glory, immortality, and eternal lives, now will you obtain these blessings? 4:53.

This is the day in which we are to learn and to increase in our knowledge. 4:204.

The Lord's time is not for me to know; but he is kind, long-suffering, and patient, and his wrath endureth silently, and will until mercy is completely exhausted, and then judgment will take the reins. I do not know how, neither do I at present wish to know. It is enough for us to know how to serve our God and live our religion, and thus we will increase in the favor of God. 4:371.

It is too late in the day for this people ever to be cast off and disowned by the Lord. The work the Lord promised to do is too nigh accomplished, and he has promised to make a short work on the earth. This work has some time since commenced; and if any of the people will not serve their God and do the work he has given them to do, they will be removed out of the way, and that speedily. It is too late in the day for this people to apostatize and the Priesthood to be taken again from the earth; so there is not much ground for fears even in this respect. 6:267.

Zion—Where is Zion? Where the organization of the Church of God is. And may it dwell spiritually in every heart; and may we so live as to enjoy the spirit of Zion always! 8:205.

Do we realize that if we enjoy a Zion in time or in eternity we must make it for ourselves? That all, who have a Zion in the eternities of the Gods, organized, framed, consolidated, and perfected it themselves, and consequently are entitled to enjoy it? 9:282.

This is the Gospel; this is the plan of salvation; this is the Kingdom of God; this is the Zion that has been spoken and written of by all the Prophets since the world began. This is the work of Zion which the Lord has promised to bring forth. 12:172.

When we conclude to make a Zion we will make it, and this work commences in the heart of each person. When the father of a family wishes to make a Zion in his own house, he must take the lead in this good work, which it is impossible for him to do unless he himself possesses the spirit of Zion. Before he can produce the work of sanctification in his family, he must sanctify himself, and by this means God can help him to sanctify his family. 9:283.

There is not one thing wanting in all the works of God's hands to make a Zion upon the earth when the people conclude to make it. We can make a Zion of God on earth at our pleasure, upon the same principle that we can raise a field of wheat, or build and inhabit. There has been no time when the material has not been here from which to produce corn, wheat, etc., and by the judicious management and arrangement of this ever-existing material a Zion of God can always be built on the earth. 9:283.

Let me say a few words with regard to Zion. We profess to be Zion. If we are the pure in heart we are so, for "Zion is the pure in heart." Now when Zion is built up and reigns, the question may arise with some, will all be Latter-day Saints? No. Will there be this variety of classes and faiths that we now behold? I do not know whether there will be as many, or whether there will be more. But be that as it may, Jesus has gone to prepare mansions for every creature. Who will go down as "sons of perdition" and receive the reward of the damned? None but those who have sinned against the Holy Ghost. All others will be gathered into kingdoms where there will be a certain amount of peace and glory. Will the Methodists have their heaven? I will venture to say that John Wesley, if he never hears the Gospel preached in the world of spirits, will enjoy all the happiness and glory that he ever thought of. And so it will be with others; I mention him merely because he is a noted character. In all those kingdoms the people will be as varied as they are here. In the Millennium men will have the privilege of their own belief, but they will not have the privilege of treating the name and character of Deity as they have done heretofore. No, but every knee shall bow and every tongue confess to the glory of God the Father that Jesus is the Christ. 12:274.

My spiritual enjoyment must be obtained by my own life, but it would add much to the comfort of the community, and to my happiness, as one with them, if every man and woman would live their religion, and enjoy the light and glory of the Gospel for themselves, be passive, humble and faithful; rejoice continually before the Lord, attend to the business they are called to do, and be sure never to do anything wrong.

All would then be peace, joy, and tranquility, in our streets and in our houses. Litigation would cease, there would be no difficulties before the High Council and Bishops' Courts, and courts, turmoil, and strife would not be known.

Then we would have Zion, for all would be pure in heart. 3:255.

The Land of Zion—This is the land of Zion. West of us is a body of water that we call the Pacific, and to the east there is another large body of water which we call the Atlantic, and to the north is where they have tried to discover a northwest passage; these waters surround the land of Zion. 4:301.

And what is Zion? In one sense Zion is the pure in heart. But is there a land that ever will be called Zion? Yes, brethren. What land is it? It is the land that the Lord gave to Jacob, who bequeathed it to his son Joseph, and his posterity, and they inhabit it, and that land is North and South America. That is Zion, as to land, as to territory, and location. The children of Zion have not yet much in their possession, but their territory is North and South America to begin with. As to the spirit of Zion, it is in the hearts of the

Saints of those who love and serve the Lord with all their might, mind and strength. 2:253.

This American continent will be Zion; for it is so spoken of by the prophets. Jerusalem will be rebuilt and will be the place of gathering, and the tribe of Judah will gather there; but this continent of America is the land of Zion. 5:4.

This is the land of Zion—this is the continent whereon the Lord has commenced his work for the last time, and whereon Jesus will make his appearance the second time, when he comes to gather and save the House of Israel. 8:81-2.

Zion will extend, eventually, all over this earth. There will be no nook or corner upon the earth but what will be in Zion. It will all be Zion. 9:138.

The City of Zion—We look forward to the day when the Lord will prepare for the building of the New Jerusalem, preparatory to the City of Enoch's going to be joined with it when it is built upon this earth. We are anticipating to enjoy that day, whether we sleep in death previous to that, or not. We look forward, with all the anticipation and confidence that children can possess in a parent, that we shall be there when Jesus comes; and if we are not there, we will come with him: in either case we shall be there when he comes. 8:342.

We want all the Latter-day Saints to understand how to build up Zion. The City of Zion, in beauty and magnificence, will outstrip anything that is now known upon the earth. The curse will be taken from the earth and sin and corruption will be swept from its face. Who will do this great work? Is the Lord going to convince the people that he will redeem the center Stake of Zion, beautify it and then place them there without an exertion on their part? No. He will not come here to build a Temple, a Tabernacle, a Bowery, or to set out fruit trees, make aprons of fig leaves or coats of skins, or work in brass and iron, for we already know how to do these things. He will not come here to teach us how to raise and manufacture cotton, how to make hand cards, how to card, how to make spinning machines, looms, etc., etc. We have to build up Zion, if we do our duty. 10:172.

I have many times asked the questions, "Where is the man that knows how to lay the first rock for the wall that is to surround the New Jerusalem or the Zion of God on the earth? Where is the man who knows how to construct the first gate of the city? Where is the man who understands how to build up the Kingdom of God in its purity and to prepare for Zion to come down to meet it?" "Well," says one, "I thought the Lord was going to do this." So he is if we will let him. This is what we want: we want the people to be willing for the Lord to do it. But he will do it by means. He will not send his angels to gather up the rock to build up the New Jerusalem. He will not send his angels from the heavens to go to the mountains to cut the timber and make it into lumber to adorn the City of Zion. He has called upon us to do this work; and if we will let him work by, through, and with us, he can accomplish it; otherwise we shall fall short, and shall never have the honor of building up Zion on the earth. 13:313.

Purpose of Gathering—A remnant of the people of Israel are to be saved, and they will yet be gathered together.16:109.

Ephraim has become mixed with all the nations of the earth, and it is Ephraim that is gathering together. 2:268.

We are gathering the people as fast as we can. We are gathering them to make Saints of them and of ourselves. 9:137-138.

We have been gathered to the valleys of these mountains for the express purpose of purifying ourselves, that we may become polished stones in the temple of God. We are here for the purpose of establishing the Kingdom of God on the earth. To be prepared for this work it has been necessary to gather us out from the nations and countries of the world, for if we had remained in those lands we could not have received the ordinances of the holy Priesthood of the Son of God, which are necessary for the perfection of the Saints preparatory to his coming. 12:161.

The Jews and Jerusalem—Jerusalem is not to be redeemed by our going there and preaching to the inhabitants. It will be redeemed by the high hand of the Almighty. It will be given into the possession of the ancient Israelites by the power of God, and by the pouring out of his judgments. 2:141.

Jerusalem is not to be redeemed by the soft, still voice of the preacher of the Gospel of peace. Why? Because they were once the blessed of the Lord, the chosen of the Lord, the promised seed. They were the people from among whom should spring the Messiah; and salvation could be found only through that people. The Messiah came through them, and they killed him; and they will be the last of all the seed of Abraham to have the privilege of receiving the New and Everlasting Covenant. You may hand out to them gold, you may feed and clothe them, but it is impossible to convert the Jews, until the Lord God Almighty does it. 2:142.

By and by the Jews will be gathered to the land of their fathers, and the ten tribes, who wandered into the north, will be gathered home, and the blood of Ephraim, the second son of Joseph, who was sold into Egypt, which is to be found in every kingdom and nation under heaven, will be gathered from among the Gentiles, and the

Gentiles who will receive and adhere to the principles of the Gospel will be adopted and initiated into the family of Father Abraham, and Jesus will reign over his own and Satan will reign over his own. 12:38.

We have a great desire for their welfare, and are looking for the time soon to come when they will gather at Jerusalem, build up the city and the land of Palestine, and prepare for the coming of the Messiah. When he comes again, he will not come as he did when the Jews rejected him; neither will he appear first at Jerusalem when he makes his second appearance on the earth; but he will appear first on the land where he commenced his work in the beginning, and planted the Garden of Eden, and that was done in the land of America.

When the Savior visits Jerusalem, and the Jews look upon him, and see the wounds in his hands and in his side and in his feet, they will then know that they have persecuted and put to death the true Messiah, and then they will acknowledge him, but not till then. They have confounded his first and second coming, expecting his first coming to be as a mighty prince instead of a servant. They will go back by and by to Jerusalem and own their Lord and Master. We have no feelings against them. 11:279.

The Indians or Lamanites—The Lamanites or Indians are just as much the children of our Father and God as we are. So also are the Africans. But we are also the children of adoption through obedience to the Gospel of his Son. 11:272.

I spoke a harsh word yesterday with regard to a man who professes to be a Latter-day Saint who has been guilty of killing an innocent Indian. I say today that he is just as much a murderer through killing that Indian, as he would have been had he shot down a white man. To slay an innocent person is murder according to the law of Moses. 11:263.

We could circumscribe their camps and kill every man, woman and child of them. This is what others have done, and if we were to do it, what better are we than the wicked and the ungodly? It is our duty to be better than they in our administrations of justice and our general conduct toward the Lamanites. It is not our duty to kill them; but it is our duty to save their lives and the lives of their children. 11:264.

There is a curse on these aborigines of our country who roam the plains, and are so wild that you cannot tame them. They are of the House of Israel; they once had the Gospel delivered to them, they had the oracles of truth; Jesus came and administered to them after his resurrection, and they received and delighted in the Gospel until the fourth generation when they turned away and became so wicked that God cursed them with this dark and benighted and loathsome condition. 14:86.

As we have here an assemblage of the people from other settlements, I wish to impress them with the necessity of treating the Indians with kindness, and to refrain from harboring that revengeful, vindictive feeling that many indulge in. I am convinced that as long as we harbor in us such feelings toward them, so long they will be our enemies, and the Lord will suffer them to afflict us. I certainly believe that the present affliction, which has come upon us from the Indians, is a consequence of the wickedness which dwells in the hearts of some of our brethren. If the Elders of Israel had always treated the Lamanites as they should, I do not believe that we should have had any difficulty with them at all. This is my firm conviction, and my conclusion according to the light that is in me. I believe that the Lord permits them to chasten us at the present time to convince us that we have to overcome the vindictive feelings which we have harbored towards that poor, downtrodden branch of the House of Israel. 11:263.

Do we wish to do right? You answer, yes. Then let the Lamanites come back to their homes, where they were born and brought up. This is the land that they and their fathers have walked over and called their own; and they have just as good a right to call it theirs today as any people have to call any land their own. They have buried their fathers and mothers and children here; this is their home, and we have taken possession of it; and occupy the land where they used to hunt the rabbit, and, not a great while since, the buffalo, and the antelope were in these valleys in large herds when we first came here.

When we came here, they could catch fish in great abundance in the lake in the season thereof, and live upon them pretty much through the summer. But now their game has gone, and they are left to starve. It is our duty to feed them. The Lord has given us ability to cultivate the ground and reap bountiful harvests. We have an abundance of food for ourselves and for the stranger. It is our duty to feed these poor ignorant Indians; we are living on their possessions and at their homes. 11:264.

Chapter XI

THE SCRIPTURES

The Bible—In the Bible are the words of life and salvation 13:214.

We are believers in the Bible, and to our unshaken faith in its precepts, doctrine, and prophecy, may be attributed "the strangeness of our course," and the unwarrantable conduct of many towards this people. 1:237.

But I want to know if we agree with the teachings of the Bible, in our belief and practice. The Latter-day Saints believe in doing just what the Lord has told them to do in this book. 1:239.

We believe the New Testament, and consequently, to be consistent, we must believe in new revelation, visions, angels, in all the gifts of the Holy Ghost, and all the promises contained in these books, and believe it about as it reads. 1:242.

We have a holy reverence for and a belief in the Bible. 14:113.

The Bible is true. It may not all have been translated aright, and many precious things may have been rejected in the compilation and translation of the Bible; but we understand, from the writing of one of the Apostles, that if all the sayings and doings of the Savior had been written, the world could not contain them. I will say that the world could not understand them. They do not understand what we have on record, nor the character of the Savior, as delineated in the Scriptures; and yet it is one of the simplest things in the world, and the Bible, when it is understood, is one of the simplest books in the world, for, as far as it is translated correctly, it is nothing but truth, and in truth there is no mystery save to the ignorant. The revelations of the Lord to his creatures are adapted to the lowest capacity, and they bring life and salvation to all who are willing to receive them. 14:135.

Take the Bible just as it reads; and if it be translated incorrectly and there is a scholar on the earth who professes to be a Christian, and he can translate it any better than King James translators did it, he is under obligation to do so. If I understood Greek and Hebrew as some may profess to do, and I knew the Bible was not correctly translated, I should feel myself bound by the law of justice to the inhabitants of the earth to translate that which is incorrect and give it just as it was spoken anciently. Is that proper? Yes, I would be under obligation to do it. But I think it is translated just as correctly as the scholars could get it, although it is not correct in a great many instances. But it is no matter about that. Read it and observe it and it will not hurt any person in the world. 14:226.

By reading the Bible we find that the Gospel is contained not only in the New Testament, but also in the Old. Moses and the Prophets saw and predicted the apostasy of the Church. They saw that the Lord would strive with the children of men from time to time, that he would deliver to them the truth and the Priesthood; they also saw that through the wickedness of the people, they would change his ordinances, break the covenants, and transgress his laws, until the Priesthood would be taken from the earth, and its inhabitants be left in apostasy and darkness. 16:74.

I have heard ministers of the Gospel declare that they believed every word in the Bible was the word of God. I have said to them, "You believe more than I do." I believe the words of God are there; I believe the words of the Devil are there; I believe that the words of men and the words of angels are there; and that is not all,—I believe that the words of a dumb brute are there. I recollect one of the prophets riding, and prophesying against Israel, and the animal he rode rebuked his madness. 14:280.

I believe the words of the Bible are just what they are; but aside from that I believe the doctrines concerning salvation contained in that book are true, and that their observance will elevate any people, nation or family that dwells on the face of the earth. The doctrines contained in the Bible will lift to a superior condition all who observe them; they will impart to them knowledge, wisdom, charity, fill them with compassion and cause them to feel after the wants of those who are in distress, or in painful or degraded circumstances. They who observe the precepts contained in the Scriptures will be just and true and virtuous and peaceable at home and abroad. Follow out the doctrines of the Bible, and men will make splendid husbands, women excellent wives, and children will be obedient; they will make families happy and the nations wealthy and happy and lifted up above the things of this life. 13:175.

We take this book, the Bible, which I expect to see voted out of the so-called Christian world very soon, they are coming to it as fast as possible, I say we take this book for our guide, for our rule of action; we take it as the foundation of our faith. It points the way to salvation like a fingerboard pointing to a city, or a map which designates the locality of mountains, rivers, or the latitude and longitude of any place on the surface of the earth that we desire to find, and we have no better sense than to believe it; hence, I say that the Latter-day Saints have the most natural faith and belief of any people on the face of the earth. 13:236.

We as Latter-day Saints have confessed before Heaven, before the heavenly hosts, and before the inhabitants of the earth, that we really believe the Scriptures as they are given to us, according to the best understanding and knowledge that we have of the translation, and the spirit and meaning of the Old and New Testaments. 12:227.

Take up the Bible, compare the religion of the Latter-day Saints with it, and see if it will stand the test. 17:46.

This Book, which is the Old and New Testament, preaches but one sermon from Genesis to Revelation. 6:284.

The doctrine that we preach is the doctrine of the Bible, it is the doctrine the Lord has revealed for the salvation of the children of God, and when men, who have once obeyed it, deny it, they deny it with their eyes wide open, and knowing that they deny the truth and set at naught the counsels of the Almighty. 14:200.

I ask you, brother B, how I must believe the Bible, and how shall you and every other follower of the Lord Jesus Christ believe it? "Brother Mormon, how do you believe it?" I believe it just as it is. I do not believe in putting any man's interpretation upon it whatever, unless it should be directed by the Lord himself in some way. I do not believe we need interpreters and expounders of the Scriptures, to wrest them from their literal, plain, simple meaning. 1:237.

There is one idea entertained by the "Mormons" which is somewhat of a stumbling-block to the people, and apostates handle it to suit their purpose. It is, that we consider the Bible merely as a guide or fingerboard, pointing to a certain destination. This is a true doctrine, which we boldly advance. If you will follow the doctrines, and be guided by the precepts of that book, it will direct you where you may see as you are seen, where you may converse with Jesus Christ, have the visitation of angels, have dreams, visions, and revelations, and understand and know God for yourselves. Is it not a stay and a staff to you? Yes; it will prove to you that you are following in the footsteps of the ancients. You can see what they saw, understand what they enjoyed. 1:243.

The Standard Church Works—With us the Bible is the first book, the Book of Mormon comes next, then the revelations in the book of Doctrine and Covenants, then the teachings of the living oracles, yet you will find, in the end, that the living oracles of God have to take all things of heaven and earth, above and beneath, and bring them together and devote them to God, and sanctify and purify them and prepare them to enter into the Kingdom of heaven. 9:297.

There is no clash in the principles revealed in the Bible, the Book of Mormon, and the Doctrine and Covenants; and there would be no clash between any of the doctrines taught by Joseph the Prophet and by the brethren now, if all would live in a way to be governed by the Spirit of the Lord. All do not live so as to have the Spirit of the Lord with them all the time, and the result is that some get out of the way. 5:329.

We have learned much from the Bible. We have also learned much from the Book of Mormon and the book of Doctrine and Covenants; but all the salvation you can obtain by means of those books alone is comparatively of little value. They contain a history of what other men have done, show the path they walked in, and the way in which they obtained the words of eternal life for themselves; but all the Scriptures from the days of Adam until now cannot, alone, save one individual. Were they all committed to memory so perfectly that they could be recited with the greatest ease, that alone would not save one of the smallest of God's creatures, nor bring any person nearer the gate of the celestial kingdom. In visiting a foreign nation, an understanding of its language, geography, manners, customs, and laws is very agreeable and beneficial. So the reading of the Bible gives comfort and happiness to the traveler to eternity, and points out to him in part the character and attributes of the Being whom to know is life eternal. We have not yet attained to that knowledge, and the mere reading of the Scriptures can never put us in possession of it. 7:332.

It is your privilege and duty to live so as to be able to understand the things of God. There are the Old and New Testaments, the Book of Mormon, and the book of Doctrine and Covenants, which Joseph has given us, and they are of great worth to a person wandering in darkness. They are like a lighthouse in the ocean, or a finger-post which points out the road we should travel. Where do they point? To the Fountain of light. 8:129.

What do the infidel world say about the Bible? They say that the Bible is nothing better than last year's almanac; it is nothing but a fable of priestcraft, and it is good for nothing. The Book of Mormon, however, declares that the Bible is true, and it proves it; and the two prove each other true. The Old and New Testaments are the stick of Judah. You recollect that the tribe of Judah tarried in Jerusalem and the Lord blessed Judah, and the result was the writings of the Old and New Testaments. But where is the stick of Joseph? Can you tell where it is? Yes. It was the children of Joseph who came across the waters to this continent, and this land was filled with people, and the Book of Mormon or the stick of Joseph contains their writings, and they are in the hands of Ephraim. Where are the Ephraimites? They are mixed through all the nations of the earth. God is calling upon them to gather out, and he is uniting them, and they are giving the Gospel to all the world. Is there any harm or any false doctrine in that? A great many say there is. If there is, it is all in the Bible. 13:174.

The Christian world profess to believe the Old and New Testaments; the Jews say they believe the Old Testament. We believe both, and that is not all, we believe in the Book of Mormon, and the Doctrine and Covenants given by the Lord to Joseph Smith and by him to the Church. We also believe if we were destitute of the Spirit of the Lord, and our eyes were closed so that we could not see and understand things as they are by the spirit of revelation, we might say farewell to all these books, no matter how numerous. If we had all the revelation given since the days of Adam and were without the spirit of revelation to be and abide in the midst of the people, it would be impossible for us to be saved in the celestial kingdom of God. 12:259-260.

The book of Doctrine and Covenants is given for the Latter-day Saints expressly for their everyday walk and actions. 16:188.

The Use of the Scriptures—Do you read the Scriptures, my brethren and sisters, as though you were writing them a thousand, two thousand, or five thousand years ago? Do you read them as though you stood in the place of the men who wrote them? If you do not feel thus, it is your privilege to do so, that you may be as familiar with the spirit and meaning of the written word of God as you are with your daily walk and conversation, or as you are with your workmen or with your households. 7:333.

The people on every hand are inquiring, "What does this scripture mean, and how shall we understand this or that passage?" Now I wish, my brethren and sisters, for us to understand things precisely as they are, and not as the flitting, changing imagination of the human mind may frame them.

The Bible is just as plain and easy of comprehension as the revelation which I have just read to you, if you understand the Spirit of God—the Spirit of Revelation, and know how the Gospel of salvation is adapted to the capacity of weak man. 3:336.

We are not in the same attitude that the people were a few thousand years ago—they were depending on the Prophet or Prophets, or on having immediate revelation for themselves to know the will of the Lord, without the record of their predecessors, while we have the records of those who have lived before us, also the testimony of the Holy Spirit; and, to the satisfaction of all who desire a testimony, we can turn to this book and read that which we believe, learn the object of our pursuit, the end that we expect to accomplish—the end of the race as far as mortality is concerned—and the fulness of the glory that is beyond this vale of tears; consequently we have the advantage of those who lived before us. We are in pursuit of knowledge; and when you meet together, if you have a word of prophecy, a dream, a vision, or a word of wisdom, impart the same to the people. 15:35.

Is there anything in the Bible that should not be read by the scholars in schools? If there be, leave out such parts, or rather replace the language there used, with phraseology more in accordance with modern usage, so that the principles contained in the Bible may be taught in your catechisms or other books. I know that there is some plain talk in the Bible, plainer than I heard this morning; but that plain talk was the custom of the ancients. The mere phraseology there used is not of much consequence, it is the true principle which that book teaches which renders it so valuable. If any of you, ladies and gentlemen, were to step on a steamboat and cross over to Liverpool, you would hear language and see customs that you never heard or saw in Yankee land. It is the same with regard to the Bible, the phraseology is that which was customary centuries ago; but no matter what the language is, that is merely custom. But I will say that the doctrines taught in the Old and New Testaments concerning the will of God towards his children here on the earth; the history of what he has done for their salvation; the ordinances which he has instituted for their redemption; the gift of his Son and his atonement—all these are true, and we, the Latter-day Saints, believe in them. 13:174.

I am a witness, so far as this is concerned, that the persons whose names are mentioned, and many others of the first Elders of the Church, were looked upon almost as angels. They were looked upon by the young members as being so filled with the Spirit and power of God that we were hardly worthy to converse with them. You hear the names of Bishop Partridge, of Brother W. W. Phelps, who is now sitting on this stand, of Parley P. Pratt, of David Whitmer, of Oliver Cowdery, and the names of many others of the first Elders who had been up to Zion, and I declare to you that brethren in other parts of the land, those who had not seen the persons named, felt that should they come into their presence they would have to pull off their shoes, as the ground would be so holy upon which they trod.

Do you know what distance and age accomplish? They produce in people the most reverential awe that can be imagined.

When we reflect and rightly understand, we learn how easy of comprehension the Gospel is, how plain it is in its plan, in every part and principle fitted perfectly to the capacity of mankind, insomuch that when it is introduced among the lovers of truth it appears very easy and very plain, and how very ready the honest are to receive it.

But send it abroad and give it antiquity, and it is at once clothed with mystery. This is the case with all the ancient revelations. Those which were received and understood by the ancients are shrouded in mystery and uncertainty to this generation, and men are employed to reveal the meaning of the ancient Scriptures. 3:335-336.

Chapter XII

THE PRIESTHOOD

The Priesthood—All ye inhabitants of the earth, hearken and hear! God has, in our day, spoken from the heavens; he has bestowed his holy Priesthood on the children of men; he has called upon all people to repent. 8:136.

Let us submit to him, that we may share in this invisible, almighty, God-like power, which is the everlasting Priesthood. 3:259.

The Priesthood of the Son of God, which we have in our midst, is a perfect order and system of government, and this alone can deliver the human family from all the evils which now afflict its members, and insure them happiness and felicity hereafter. 13:242.

If anybody wants to know what the Priesthood of the Son of God is, it is the law by which the worlds are, were, and will continue for ever and ever. It is that system which brings worlds into existence and peoples them, gives them their revolutions—their days, weeks, months, years, their seasons and times and by which they are rolled up as a scroll, as it were, and go into a higher state of existence. 15:127.

When we talk of the celestial law which is revealed from heaven, that is, the Priesthood, we are talking about the principle of salvation, a perfect system of government, of laws and ordinances, by which we can be prepared to pass from one gate to another, and from one sentinel to another, until we go into the presence of our Father and God. This law has not always been upon the earth; and in its absence, other laws have been given to the children of men for their improvement, for their education, for their government, and to prove what they would do when left to control themselves; and what we now call tradition has grown out of these circumstances. 2:139.

The Priesthood of the Son of God in its operations comprises the Kingdom of God. 11:249.

Some of the brightest spirits who dwell in the bosom of the Father are making their appearance among this people, of whom the Lord will make a Royal Priesthood, a peculiar nation that he can own and bless; talk with, and associate with. 11:132.

Men who are vessels of the holy Priesthood, who are charged with words of eternal life to the world, should strive continually in their words and actions and daily deportment to do honor to the great dignity of their calling and office as ministers and representatives of the Most High. 11:216.

The Gospel has brought to us the Holy Priesthood, which is

again restored to the children of men. The keys of that Priesthood are here; we have them in our possession; we can unlock, and we can shut up. We can obtain salvation, and we can administer it. 4:299.

This Priesthood has been on the earth at various times. Adam had it, Seth had it, Enoch had it, Noah had it, Abraham and Lot had it, and it was handed down to the days of the Prophets, long after the days of the ancients. This High Priesthood rules, directs, governs, and controls all the Priesthoods, because it is the highest of all. 9:87.

But the Lord has so ordained that no man shall receive the benefits of the everlasting Priesthood without humbling himself before him, and giving him the glory for teaching him, that he may be able to witness to every man of the truth, and not depend upon the words of any individual on the earth, but know for himself, live "by every word that proceedeth out of the mouth of God," love the Lord Jesus Christ and the institutions of his Kingdom, and finally enter into his glory. Every man and woman may be a revelator, and have the testimony of Jesus, which is the spirit of prophecy, and foresee the mind and will of God concerning them, eschew evil, and choose that which is good. 2:189.

The Priesthood is given to the people and the keys thereof, and, when properly understood, they may actually unlock the treasury of the Lord, and receive to their fullest satisfaction. But through our own weaknesses, through the frailty of human nature, we are not capable of doing so. 3:191-192.

The Priesthood does not wait for ignorance; it instructs those who have not wisdom, and are desirous of learning correct principles. 7:64.

It is the business, duty, and power of the eternal Priesthood to commence laying the foundation to bring back the days, years, and intelligence that have been lost through transgression. I intend to pursue this course so long as I possibly can. I trust that I shall not commit an act that will annoy my feelings when I meet my Savior. I pray for this every day and every moment. 8:62.

The Lord Almighty will not suffer his Priesthood to be again driven from the earth. 2:183-184.

But mark it well, if we live according to the holy Priesthood bestowed upon us, while God bears rule in the midst of these mountains, I promise you, in the name of Israel's God, that he will give us seed-time and harvest. We must forfeit our right to the Priesthood, before the blessings of the heavens cease to come upon us. Let us live our religion and hearken to the counsel given to us. 10:292.

Much has been said about the power of the Latter-day Saints.

Is it the people called Latter-day Saints that have this power, or is it the Priesthood? It is the Priesthood; and if they live according to that Priesthood, they can commence their work here and gain many victories, and be prepared to receive glory, immortality, and eternal life, that when they go into the spirit-world, their work will far surpass that of any other man or being that has not been blessed with the keys of the Priesthood here. 7:288-289.

There is not a despot upon the earth whose power has not originally sprung from the Priesthood, and there is not a law in the Priesthood but what is founded on the revelations of Jesus Christ. These are the laws upon which all governments were originally based. Truth will endure forever, and every person that cannot abide truth will fail in obtaining eternal life. Truth is what we have. Let us live to it, and we shall abide for ever and no power can prevent it. 7:149.

When the faithful Elders, holding this Priesthood, go into the spirit world they carry with them the same power and Priesthood that they had while in the mortal tabernacle. 3:371.

When the holy Priesthood is upon the earth, and the fulness of the Kingdom of God has come to the people, it requires a strict obedience to every point of law and doctrine and to every ordinance which the Lord reveals. 10:286.

Were your faith concentrated upon the proper object, your confidence unshaken, your lives pure and holy, every one fulfilling the duties of his or her calling according to the Priesthood and capacity bestowed upon you, you would be filled with the Holy Ghost, and it would be as impossible for any man to deceive and lead you to destruction as for a feather to remain unconsumed in the midst of intense heat. 7:277.

An individual who holds a share in the Priesthood, and continues faithful to his calling, who delights himself continually in doing the things God requires at his hands, and continues through life in the performance of every duty will secure to himself not only the privilege of receiving, but the knowledge how to receive the things of God, that he may know the mind of God continually; and he will be enabled to discern between right and wrong, between the things of God and the things that are not of God. And the Priesthood—the Spirit that is within him, will continue to increase until it becomes like a fountain of living water; until it is like the tree of life; until it is one continued source of intelligence and instruction to that individual. 3:192.

It is the privilege of every person who is faithful to the Priesthood, who can overcome the enemy, thwart the design of death, or him that hath the power of it, to live upon the earth until their appointed time;

and they may know, see, and understand, by revelation, the things of God just as naturally as we understand natural things that are around us. 3:192-193.

All the acts we perform should be governed by the guidance of the Priesthood. 7:64.

There is no act of a Latter-day Saint—no duty required—no time given, exclusive and independent of the Priesthood. Everything is subject to it, whether preaching, business, or any other act pertaining to the proper conduct of this life. 7:66.

Until a selfish, individual interest is banished from our minds, and we become interested in the general welfare, we shall never be able to magnify our holy Priesthood as we should. 11:115.

No man will gain influence in this Kingdom, save what he gains by the influence and power of the Holy One that has called him to truth, holiness, and virtue. That is all the influence I have, and I pray God that I may never have any different influence. 7:140.

Let me say to the brethren and sisters, when you are chastened by any of your leaders, never consider that the enemy does it, but receive it always as a kindness from the hand of a friend and not as from an enemy. If your presidents were your enemies they would let you alone in your faults. If you are beloved of the Lord you will be chastened; receive it with joy. 10:174.

In trying all matters of doctrine, to make a decision valid, it is necessary to obtain a unanimous voice, faith and decision. In the capacity of a Quorum, the three First Presidents must be one in their voice; the Twelve Apostles must be unanimous in their voice, to obtain a righteous decision upon any matter that may come before them, as you may read in the Doctrine and Covenants. Whenever you see these Quorums unanimous in their declaration, you may set it down as true. Let the Elders get together, being faithful and true; and when they agree upon any point, you may know that it is true. 9:91-92.

I would like to see the High Council and Bishops and all Judges filled with the power of the Holy Ghost, that when a person comes before them they can read and understand that person, and be able to decide a case quickly and justly. When men have a just appreciation of right and wrong, their decision can be made as well the first minute after hearing a statement of the case, as to waste hours and days to make it. I would like the Bishops and other officers to have sufficient power and wisdom from God to make them fully aware of the true nature of every case that may come before them. But there are some of our great men who are so ignorant that a personal favor will so bias their minds that they will twist the truth and sustain a person in evil. Some, with a trifling consideration, can so prejudice the mind of a High Councilor, a High Priest, a Bishop, or an Apostle, that he will lean to the individual instead of the truth. I despise a man that would offer me money to buy me to his favor. 10:42.

In all High Councils, in Bishop's Courts, and in all other departments for transacting our business, the Church and Kingdom of God with the Lord Almighty at the head, will cause every man to exhibit the feeling of his heart, for you recollect it is written that in the last days the Lord will reveal the secrets of the hearts of the children of men. 3:47.

When I am brought to the test to fight for my religion, which I trust I never will be, I will call men who are full of the power of God for such an emergency. 7:143.

I relate these circumstances to show you that a person who is ordained to the office of an Elder in this Kingdom has the same Priesthood that the High Priests, that the Twelve Apostles, that the Seventies, and that the First Presidency hold; but all are not called to be one of the Twelve Apostles nor are all called to be one of the First Presidency; nor to be one of the First Presidents of all the Seventies, nor to be one of the Presidents of a Quorum of Seventies, nor to preside over the High Priests' Quorum; but every man in his order and place, possessing a portion of the same Priesthood, according to the gifts and callings to each. Does not this clear up the subject? This will explain it to you so that you can understand it. When we find where our callings and positions are in the midst of the people of God, and every person willing to act in the discharge of his duty, there is enough for us all to do. All persons can have all they desire to do to promote the Kingdom of God on the earth; they can exercise themselves in all that God has granted to them to prove themselves worthy before God and the people. 9:89.

Did they destroy it when they took the life of Joseph? No. "Mormonism" is here, the Priesthood is here, the keys of the Kingdom are here on the earth; and when Joseph went, they did not go. And if the wicked should succeed in taking my life, the keys of the Kingdom will remain with the Church. 5:76-77.

If I find a man, as I do once in a while, who thinks that he ought to be sustained in a higher position than he occupies, that proves to me that he does not understand his true position, and is not capable of magnifying it. Has he not already the privilege of exhibiting all the talents he has—of doing all the good he is capable of in this Kingdom? Is he curtailed in the least, in anywise or place, in bringing forth his wisdom and powers, and exhibiting them before the community and leading out? No, not in the least. Are any of you infringed upon or abridged in the least? Is there a sister who has not the privilege of exhibiting all the talent and power she will, or is capable of, for the benefit of her sisters and her children? Are the sisters deprived of any liberty in displaying their taste and talent to improve the community?

When I hear persons say that they ought to occupy a station more exalted than they do, and hide the talents they are in possession of, they have not the true wisdom they ought to have. There is a lack in them, or they would improve upon the talents given. 7:161-162.

I am more afraid that this people have so much confidence in their leaders that they will not inquire for themselves of God whether they are led by him. I am fearful they settle down in a state of blind self-security, trusting their eternal destiny in the hands of their leaders with a reckless confidence that in itself would thwart the purposes of God in their salvation, and weaken that influence they could give to their leaders, did they know for themselves, by the revelations of Jesus, that they are led in the right way. Let every man and woman know, by the whispering of the Spirit of God to themselves, whether their leaders are walking in the path the Lord dictates, or not. 9:150.

You may take the Quorums in this Church—the First Presidency, the Twelve, the Presidents of the High Priests, the High Councilors, and the Presidents of the Seventies; and a person may go to each of those Quorums for counsel upon any subject, and he will invariably receive the same counsel. Why is this the case? Because they are all actuated by the same spirit. 5:328-329.

Adam, Seth, Enoch, Noah, all the Patriarchs and Prophets, Jesus and the Apostles, and every man that has ever written the word of the Lord, have written the same doctrine upon the same subject; and you never can find that Prophets and Apostles clashed in their doctrines in ancient days; neither will they now, if all would at all times be led by the Spirit of salvation. 5:329.

Where the Priesthood is not, the people are expected to live according to the best knowledge they have; but even then they cannot with impunity commit many heinous faults. The Lord more readily overlooks them in consequence of their unenlightened condition, and there is a kingdom prepared for them. 10:286.

When a man merely from a spirit of conviction goes forth to build up the kingdom of God—to reform the nations of the earth, he can go so far as morality operates upon and enlightens him; but he is without authority from heaven. We are under no obligation to obey any man or being in matters pertaining to salvation, unless his words have the authority and sanction of the holy Priesthood. 8:122.

I never passed John Wesley's church in London without stopping to look at it. Was he a good man? Yes; I suppose him to have been, by all accounts, as good as ever walked on this earth, according to his knowledge. Has he obtained a rest? Yes, and greater than ever entered his mind to expect; and so have thousands of others of the various religious denominations. Why could he not build up the Kingdom of God on the earth? He had not the Priesthood; that was all the difficulty he labored under. Had the Priesthood been conferred upon him, he would have built up the Kingdom of God in his day as it is now being built up. He would have introduced the ordinances, powers, grades, and quorums of the Priesthood; but, not holding the Priesthood, he could not do it. Did the Spirit of God rest upon him? Yes, and does, more or less, at times, upon all people. 7:5.

Many persons think, if they see a Prophet they see one possessing all the keys of the Kingdom of God on the earth. This is not so; many persons have prophesied without having any Priesthood on them at all. It is no particular revelation or gift for a person to prophesy. You take a good statesman, for instance, he will tell you what will become of a nation by their actions. He foresees this and that, and knows the result of any line of policy that may be pursued. To be a prophet is simply to be a foreteller of future events; but an Apostle of the Lord Jesus Christ has the keys of the holy Priesthood and the power thereof is sealed upon his head, and by this he is authorized to proclaim the truth to the people, and if they receive it, well; if not, the sin be upon their own heads. 13:144.

Seek diligently to know the will of God. How can you know it? In matters pertaining to yourselves as individuals, you can obtain it directly from the Lord; but in matters pertaining to public affairs, his will is ascertained through the proper channel, and may be known by the general counsel that is given you from the proper source. 1:78.

I have already said that Christ set in his Church Apostles and Prophets; he also set in his Church evangelists, pastors and teachers; also the gifts of the Spirit, such as diverse tongues, healing the sick, discernment of spirits, and various other gifts. Now, I would ask the whole world, who has received revelation that the Lord has discontinued these offices and gifts in his Church? I have not. I have had revelation that they should be in the Church, and that there is no Church without them. I have had many revelations proving to me that the Old and New Testaments are true. Their doctrines are comprised in the Gospel that we preach, which is the power of God unto salvation to all who believe. 13:144.

I plead with the Elders of Israel day by day, when I have an opportunity, to live their religion—to live so that the Holy Ghost will be their constant companion; and then they will be qualified to be judges in Israel, to preside as Bishops, presiding Elders, and High Councilors, and as men of God, to take their families and friends by the hand and lead them in the path of truth and virtue, and eventually into the Kingdom of God. 6:331.

The First Presidency—In the setting forth of items of doctrine which pertain to the progress and further building up of the Kingdom of God upon the earth, and the revealing of his mind and will, he has but one mouth through which to make known his will to his people. When the Lord wishes to give a revelation to his people, when he wishes to reveal new items of doctrine to them, or administer chastisement, he will do it through the man whom he has appointed to that office and calling. The rest of the offices and callings of the Church are helps and governments for the edifying of the body of Christ and the perfection of the Saints, etc., every president, bishop, elder, priest, teacher, deacon and member standing in his order and officiating in his standing and degree of Priesthood as ministers of the words of life as shepherds to watch over departments and sections of the flock of God in all the world, and as helps to strengthen the hands of the Presidency of the whole Church. 11:135.

The Lord Almighty leads this Church, and he will never suffer you to be led astray if you are found doing your duty. You may go home and sleep as sweetly as a babe in its mother's arms, as to any danger of your leaders leading you astray, for if they should try to do so the Lord would quickly sweep them from the earth. Your leaders are trying to live their religion as far as they are capable of doing so. 9:289.

The First Presidency have of right a great influence over this people; and if we should get out of the way and lead this people to destruction, what a pity it would be! How can you know whether we lead you correctly or not? Can you know by any other power than that of the Holy Ghost? I have uniformly exhorted the people to obtain this living witness, each for themselves; then no man on earth can lead them astray. 6:100.

Be careful, all the world, and touch not the anointed of the Lord. Afflict not the people who have the oracles of salvation for all the human family. 8:195.

To possess and retain the spirit of the Gospel, gather Israel, redeem Zion, and save the world must be attended to first and foremost, and should be the prevailing desire in the hearts of the First Presidency, of the Elders of Israel, and of every officer in the Church and Kingdom of God. 7:174.

Perhaps it may make some of you stumble, were I to ask you a question—Does a man's being a Prophet in this Church prove that he shall be the President of it? I answer, No! A man may be a Prophet, Seer, and Revelator, and it may have nothing to do with his being the President of the Church. Suffice it to say, that Joseph was the President of the Church, as long as he lived. He always filled that responsible station by the voice of the people. Can you find any revelation appointing him the President of the Church? The keys of the Priesthood were committed to Joseph, to build up the Kingdom of God on the earth, and were not to be taken from him in time or in eternity, but when he was called to preside over the Church, it was by the voice of the people; though he held the keys of the Priesthood, independent of their voice. 1:133.

I would beseech and pray the people to live so that if I do not magnify my office and calling, you will burn me by your faith and good works, and I shall be removed. 7:281.

The spirit of Joseph which fell upon me is ready to fall upon somebody else when I am removed. 5:57.

The first name I shall present to you is that of Brigham Young, President of the Church of Jesus Christ of Latter-day Saints. If any person can say that he should not be sustained in this office, say so. If there is no objection, as it is usual in the marriage ceremony of the Church of England, "Let them for ever afterwards hold their peace," and not go snivelling around saying that you would like to have a better man, and one who is more capable of leading the Church. 7:228.

Suppose that Sidney Rigdon and Frederick G. Williams had been taken away or had apostatized, as one of them did soon after the revelation I have referred to was given, and there had been only Joseph Smith left of the First Presidency, would he alone have had authority to set in order the Kingdom of God on the earth? Yes. Again: Suppose that eleven of the Twelve had been taken away by the power of the Adversary, that one Apostle has the same power that Joseph had, and could preach, baptize, and set in order the whole Kingdom of God upon the earth, as much so as the Twelve, were they all together. Again: If in the providence of God he should permit the enemy to destroy these two first Quorums, and then destroy the Quorum of the Seventy, all but one man, what is his power? It would be to go and preach, baptize, confirm, lay on hands, ordain, set in order, build up, and establish the whole Kingdom of God as it is now. Suppose the enemy had power to destroy all but one of the High Priests from the face of the earth, what would that one possess in the power of his Priesthood? He would have power and authority to go and preach, baptize, confirm, ordain, and set in order the Kingdom of God in all its perfection of the earth. Could he do this without revelation? No. Could the Seventies? No. Could the Twelve? No. And we ask, could Joseph Smith or the First Presidency do this without revelation? No. Not one of them could do such a work without revelation direct from God. I can go still further. Whoever is ordained to the office of an Elder to a certain degree possesses the keys of the Melchizedek Priesthood; and suppose only one Elder should be left on the earth, could he go and set in order the Kingdom of God? Yes, by revelation. 9:88.

Although Brothers Willard Richards, Heber C. Kimball, and myself are out of the Quorum of the Twelve, our Apostleship has not been taken from us. I preached considerable upon this subject in Nauvoo, to give the people the understanding of the different callings of men. 6:320.

Many may think that a man in my standing ought to be perfect; no such thing. If you would only think of it for a moment you would not have me perfect, for if I were perfect the Lord would take me to Paradise quicker than you would be willing to have me go there. I want to stay with you; and I expect to be just nearly perfect enough to lead you on. 10:212.

I had the promise, years ago, that I never should apostatize and bring an evil upon this people. God revealed that through Joseph, long before he died; and if I am not doing right, you may calculate that the Lord is going to take me home. He will not send me to hell, but he will take me home to himself. "I will take you up here, Brigham, and give you a few lessons." 9:142.

(After putting the motion for himself to be sustained as "Prophet, Seer, and Revelator," the President remarked):

I will say that I never dictated the latter part of that sentence. I make this remark, because those words in that connection always made me feel as though I am called more than I am deserving of. I am Brigham Young, an Apostle of Joseph Smith, and also of Jesus Christ. If I have been profitable to this people, I am glad of it. The brethren call me so; and if it be so, I am glad. 5:296.

The Apostle and Melchizedek Priesthood—The calling of an Apostle is to build up the Kingdom of God in all the world; it is the Apostle that holds the keys of this power, and nobody else. If an Apostle magnifies his calling, he is the word of the Lord to his people all the time. 6:282.

It is the duty and privilege of the Twelve Apostles to have the Holy Ghost for their constant companion, and live always in the Spirit of Revelation, to know their duty and understand their calling; this is also the duty and privilege of the First Presidency of the Church. 11:135.

I can tell you the spirit of the Twelve, which will be a consolation to you, and also to the Twelve. If I could see every one of the Elders with their wives and children as obedient to every requirement made of them—the children to the parents, the wives to the husbands, and the husbands to the Priesthood—as the Twelve are—my soul would be happy. I will say further: those of the Twelve that travel the most and serve God, are the most obedient. 10:310.

In the last week's *News* I published a portion of a revelation, showing the authority of the First Presidency of the Church, composed at first of Joseph Smith, Sidney Rigdon, and Frederick G. Williams. When this revelation was given, the two last-named brethren were Joseph Smith's counselors, and this First Presidency possessed the power and authority of building up the Kingdom of God upon all the earth, and of setting the Church in order in its perfection. You read in the revelation alluded to that when the Twelve were called and ordained, they possessed the same power and authority as the three First Presidents; and in reading further you find that there must needs be appendages and helps growing out of this Priesthood. The Seventies possess the same power and authority; they hold the keys of establishing, building up, regulating, ordaining and setting in order the Kingdom of God in all its perfections upon the earth. We have a Quorum of High Priests, and there are a great many of them. They are a local body—they tarry at home; but the Seventies travel and preach; so also do the High Priests, when they are called upon. They possess precisely the same Priesthood that the Seventies and the Twelve and the First Presidency possess; but are they ordained to officiate in all the authority, power, and keys of this Priesthood? No, they are not. Still they are High Priests of God; and if they magnify their Priesthood, they will receive at some time all the authority and power that it is possible for men to receive. 9:87.

The Bishopric by right belongs to the literal descendants of Aaron, but we shall have to ordain from the other tribes, men who hold the High Priesthood, to act in the Lesser, until we find a literal descendant of Aaron, who is prepared to receive it.

The Lesser Priesthood, then, you perceive, comes within the purview of the Apostleship, because a man that holds it has a right to act or officiate as a High Priest, as one of the High Council, as a Patriarch, as a Bishop, Elder, Priest, Teacher, and Deacon, and in every other office and calling that is in the Church, from first to last, when duty demands it. 1:136.

Now will it cause some of you to marvel that I was not ordained a High Priest before I was ordained an Apostle? Brother Kimball and myself were never ordained High Priests. How wonderful! I was going to say how little some of the brethren understood the Priesthood, after the Twelve were called. In our early career in this Church, on one occasion, in one of our Councils, we were telling about some of the Twelve wanting to ordain us High Priests, and what I said to Brother Patten when he wanted to ordain me in York State: said I, Brother Patten, wait until I can lift my hand to heaven and say, I have magnified the office of an Elder. After our conversation was over in the Council, some of the brethren began to query, and said we ought to be ordained High Priests; at the same time I did not consider that an Apostle needed to be ordained a High Priest, an Elder, or a Teacher. I did not express my views on the subject, at that time, but thought I would hear what brother Joseph would say about it. It was William E. McLellin who told Joseph that I and Heber were not ordained High Priests, and wanted to know if it should not be done. Said Joseph, "Will you insult the Priesthood? Is that all the knowledge you have of the office of an Apostle? Do you not know that the man who receives the Apostleship, receives all the keys that ever were, or that can be, conferred upon mortal man? What are you talking about? I am astonished!" Nothing more was said about it.

I have tried to show you, brethren, as briefly as possible, the order of the Priesthood. When a man is ordained to be an Apostle, his Priesthood is without beginning of days, or end of life, like the Priesthood of Melchizedek; for it was his Priesthood that was spoken of in this language and not the man. 1:136.

Twenty-seven years ago, on the 5th of this month, in the year 1834, a company started for Kirtland to redeem the land of Zion. Brother Heber C. Kimball and my brother Joseph were in that camp. There had not then been ordained any Twelve Apostles, nor any Seventies, although there was a revelation pertaining to the Apostles and Seventies. There were High Priests, but no High Priests' Quorum. I am relating this as a little matter of history that will no doubt be interesting to those who were not there.

After we returned from Missouri, my brother Joseph Young and myself had been singing after preaching in a meeting; and when the meeting was dismissed, Brother Joseph Smith said, "Come, go down to my house with me." We went and sung to him a long time, and talked with him. He then opened the subject of the Twelve and Seventies for the first time I ever thought of it. He said, "Brethren, I am going to call out Twelve Apostles. I think we will get together. by-and-by, and select Twelve Apostles, and select a Quorum of Seventies from those who have been up to Zion, out of the camp boys." In 1835 the last of January or in February, or about that time, we held our meetings from day to day, and Brother Joseph called out Twelve Apostles at that time. He had a revelation when we were singing to him. Those who were acquainted with him knew when the Spirit of Revelation was on him, for his countenance wore an expression peculiar to himself while under that influence. He preached by the Spirit of Revelation, and taught in his council by it, and those who were acquainted with him could discover it at once, for at such times there was a peculiar clearness and transparency in his face. He followed up that revelation until he organized the Church, and so along until the baptism for the dead was revealed. 9:89.

How came these Apostles, these Seventies, these High Priests, and all this organization we now enjoy? It came by revelation. Father Cahoon, who lately died in your neighborhood, was one of the first ordained to the office of High Priests in this Kingdom. In the year 1831 the Prophet Joseph went to Ohio. He left the State of New York on the last of April, if my memory serves me, and arrived in Kirtland sometime in May. They held a General Conference, which was the first General Conference ever called or held in Ohio. Joseph then received a revelation, and ordained High Priests. You read in the book of Doctrine and Covenants how he received the Priesthood in the first place. It is there stated how Joseph received the Aaronic Priesthood. John the Baptist came to Joseph Smith and Oliver Cowdery. When a person passes behind the veil, he can only officiate in the spirit-world; but when he is resurrected he officiates as a resurrected being, and not as a mortal being. You read in the revelation that Joseph was ordained, as it is written. When he received the Melchizedek Priesthood, he had another revelation. Peter, James, and John came to him. You can read the revelation at your leisure. When he received this revelation in Kirtland, the Lord revealed to him that he should begin and ordain High Priests; and he then ordained quite a number, all whose names I do not now recollect; but Lyman Wight was one; Fathers Cahoon and Morley, John Murdock, Sidney Rigdon, and others were also then ordained. These were the first that were ordained to this office in the Church. I relate this to show you how Joseph proceeded step by step in organizing the Church. At that time there were no Seventies nor Twelve Apostles. 9:88-89.

Joseph Smith never would permit the Seventies to get together and believe themselves a separate body from the rest of the Church. I never cared much about this, for I was not a particle afraid that they would get any power that truly does not belong to them; for, if they did, I was always satisfied that it would be blown to the four winds. I want to inform the Seventies living in Bishop Miller's Ward (and what I now say applies to all the other Wards and Bishops) if he calls on them to act as Teachers, it is their imperative duty to act as Teachers, seeking to benefit and bless the people by enlarging their understanding, that they may prove themselves before God and one another. There is a world of intelligence to impart, and the Priesthood (in its various callings, appointments, helps, and governments) is the means, through its ministers, of imparting it to the people. It is not a duty of a Seventy or High Priest, who is appointed a Teacher or a Bishop, to neglect the duties of those callings to attend a Seventies' or High Priests' meeting. Attend to the wishes of your Bishop, and never ask who has the most power. The man who has the most power with God will wield it, and earth and hell cannot hinder it. Every man who has true influence has obtained it before God through faithfulness, and in all such cases there is not the least danger but what he will have it before the Saints. It is the man who converses with the heavens, who delights in doing so, and knows for himself that this is the Kingdom of God, who has true influence. 9:92.

There is no retrograde movement in ordaining a High Priest to the office of a Bishop, for, properly speaking, he is set apart to act in that office. 10:96.

We shall dissolve the present High Council of this Stake. Many of them are far advanced in years, and some of them live at considerable distances from this city. They have labored according to the best of their ability. 7:337.

The Bishop and the Aaronic Priesthood—The office of a Bishop belongs to the lesser Priesthood. He is the highest officer in the Aaronic Priesthood, and has the privilege of using the Urim and Thummim—has the administration of angels, if he has faith, and lives so that he can receive and enjoy the blessings Aaron enjoyed. At the same time, could Aaron rise up and say, "I have as much power and authority as you, Moses?" No; for Moses held the keys and authority above all the rest upon the earth. He holds the keys of the Priesthood of Melchizedek, which is the Priesthood of the Son of God, which holds the keys of all these Priesthoods, dispensing the blessings and privileges of both Priesthoods to the people, as he did in the days of the Children of Israel when he led them out of Egypt. 9:87.

I will say a few words with regard to a Bishop. Except we find a literal descendant of Aaron, a man has to be ordained to the High Priesthood to administer as did Aaron and his sons. Can the Bishop baptize the people, according to his Bishopric? He can. When the people he has baptized assemble for confirmation, can he confirm them? He cannot, under the power of his Bishopric, but as he has been ordained to the office of a High Priest, after the order of Melchizedek, to prepare him to act in the office of a Bishop, in the Priesthood of Aaron, when he has baptized the people under the authority of his Bishopric, he has a right as a High Priest to confirm them into the Church by the laying on of hands. 9:280.

A Bishop in his calling and duty is with the Church all the time; he is not called to travel abroad to preach, but is at home; he is not abroad in the world, but is with the Saints. 2:89.

In the capacity of a Bishop, has any person a right to direct the spiritual affairs of the Kingdom of God? No. In that capacity his right is restricted to affairs in a temporal and moral point of view. He has a right to deal with the transgressor. I do not care what office a transgressor bears in the Church and Kingdom of God, if he should be one of the Twelve Apostles, and come into a Bishop's neighborhood, and purloin his neighbor's books, defile his neighbor's bed, or commit any breach of the moral law, the Bishop has a right to take that man before himself and his council, and there hold him to answer for the crime he has been guilty of, and deal with him for his fellowship in the Church. 9:91.

Who, then, has the greatest power? Those who best do the will of God. When a Bishop calls upon a man to officiate as an assistant to him, he does not call upon him as a Seventy or as a High Priest, but as one of his own family—as a member of his Ward. 9:93.

Instead of my believing for a moment that Paul wished to signify to Timothy that he must select a man to fill the office of a Bishop that would have but one wife, I believe directly the reverse; but his advice to Timothy amounts simply to this—it would not be wise for you to ordain a man to the office of a Bishop unless he has a wife; you must not ordain a single or unmarried man to that calling. 2:88.

The Bishops should be a perfect example to their Wards in all things. 16:44.

Let each Bishop attend faithfully to his Ward, and see that every man and woman is well and faithfully and profitably employed; that the sick and aged are properly cared for that none suffer. Let each

Bishop be a tender and indulgent father to his Ward, administering a word of comfort and encouragement here, a word of advice and counsel there, and a word of chastisement in another place, where needed, without partiality, wisely judging between man and man, caring for and seeking earnestly the welfare of all, watching over the flock of God with the eye of a true shepherd, that wolves and dogs may not enter among the flock to rend them. 11:252.

The Bishops should, through their teachers, see that every family in their Wards, who is able, should donate what they would naturally consume on the fast day to the poor. 12:116.

If a Bishop will act to the extent of his calling and office, and magnify it, there will not be an individual in his Ward that is not employed to the best advantage. He would see that all lived as they should, walking humbly with their God. There would not be a person in his Ward that he does not know, and he would be acquainted with their circumstances, conduct, and feeling. 8:146.

The Bishops should set those whom they have confidence in, those whom they know to be honest, to be watchmen on the tower, and let them find out who are suffering. 3:245.

There are many of the Bishops here today, and my advice to them is for them to be honest with me, to be honest with their God, to keep their covenants sacred, and to make a clean breast of all their business transactions that their consciences may be void of offense towards God and man. 8:316.

When your Bishop calls upon you, or advises you to do anything that will be for your good, do not call that oppression. All the instruction he gives will be calculated to do you good, to raise you in that scale of intelligence that will make of you wise men and wise women. When we are recommended to do that which will lead to good, that cannot very well be construed into oppression. 10:313.

If the people of a Ward are living in the faithful performance of their several duties, their faith and their prayers will be concentrated before the Lord, in the name of Jesus, for and in behalf of their Bishop, that he may know his business and be made fully capable to fulfil the duties of his calling to the honor of God and the salvation of the people. 11:135.

You have often heard me and my brethren say that if the people in the capacity of a Ward, for instance, would let their faith be perfectly united, and their whole desires rise to the Father, through the name of Jesus Christ, and hold their Bishop in his calling between God and them, it would hardly be possible for that Bishop to do wrong, for he would be filled with wisdom. 6:98-99.

Do our Bishops labor for pay? No, if they are not capable of getting a living and sustaining themselves and families, and of filling the office of Bishop without pay, they are hardly worthy of the Bishopric. If a High Priest is called to be a president or to travel and preach the Gospel to the nations of the earth, he must do it without pay; and we think that any man who is not able to keep himself and family and travel and preach one-half or two-thirds of his time without being paid, is not so good a financier as he ought to be. 14:108.

I say to the Bishop who has just addressed us, won't you do as I have formerly directed you, and appoint good, wise, judicious men to go through your Ward, to find out what is in that Ward, and the situation of every family, whether they have money, flour, or costly clothing or whether they are destitute and suffering? This is your business and calling. Do not let there be one place, in the habitations of the Saints in your Wards, about which you are uninformed. Brother Woolley has reported the circumstances of a Bishop finding a woman who had been living upon the charity of her neighbors, and who, at the same time, had valuable property, and money hid up. I can refer you to scores of like circumstances, and what is more, to some of the Elders, those who are supposed to be among the best of our Elders. 3:244.

Bishops' Counselors should be examples to the Church; they should be like fathers to the Church. If they are really the Counselors of the Bishop, they should practice everything that is good that he practices; and if the Bishop himself should neglect any duty, they should perform their duty as counselors, and should teach, guide, direct, and counsel the Bishop to improve in his life. 13:275.

The Wards will be organized hereafter; Bishops will be placed over them, with their two Counselors, all of whom will be ordained High Priests, if not already so ordained, and then be set apart to act in their several offices. They then will form a court; and all the other quorums of Priesthood will be set in order. 19:43.

Church Organization and Government—The living oracles of the Lord, * * * are always in the midst of his people. 10:302.

Teach the people true knowledge, and they will govern themselves. 10:190.

The government of this Church is based upon true principles, and the reason people fall out by the way is because of their ignorance —because they do not thoroughly canvass their acts, and wisely ponder the probable results. 7:65.

We shall never have the keys of authority committed to us to be rulers until we will rule just as God would rule if he were here himself. 14:97.

But the Kingdom of heaven, when organized upon the earth,

will have every officer, law and ordinance necessary for the managing of those who are unruly, or who transgress its laws, and to govern those who desire to do right, but cannot quite walk to the line; and all these powers and authorities are in existence in the midst of this people. 15:161.

I am for the Kingdom of God. I like a good government, and then I like to have it wisely and justly administered. The government of heaven, if wickedly administered, would become one of the worst governments upon the face of the earth. No matter how good a government is, unless it is administered by righteous men, an evil government will be made of it. 10:177.

"But we thought that the government you are talking about was a theocratic government." It is; and it is the only true form of government on the earth—the only one that possesses all the true principles of republicanism. It puts every man and woman right, puts everything in its place, and gives to each one his due according to his work; for so will they be judged in that day. 7:8.

People have reason to fear the bogus or spurious theocracy. There are but few upon the earth who do not in their hearts acknowledge a Supreme Being, and also believe that Being to be holy; and if they could be dictated by that Being, and be sure that they were dictated by the influence from him, there are but few who would object to that influence, and that government. 7:147.

I wish you to build up every man who is in the faith of the Gospel—who is in the faith of God, angels, and good men; and if you strive to pull down good men who are around you, you are sure to fall yourselves. 8:71.

There is only one way to obtain power and influence in the Kingdom of God, and only one way to obtain foreknowledge, and that is to live so that that influence will come from our Creator, enlightening the mind and revealing things that are past, present and future pertaining to the earth and its inhabitants, and to the dealings of God with the children of men; in short, there is no source of true information outside of the Spirit of Revelation; it maketh manifest all things, and revealeth the dispositions of communities and of individuals. By possessing this Spirit, mankind can obtain power that is durable, beneficial, and that will result in a higher state of knowledge, of honor and of glory. This can be obtained only by strictly marking the path of truth, and walking faithfully therein. 10:104.

It is the right and privilege of every Elder in Israel to enjoy the Holy Ghost, and the light of it, to know everything which concerns himself and his individual duties, but it is not his right and privilege to dictate his superior in office, nor to give him counsel, unless he is called upon to do so, then he may make suggestions. 11:135.

Now ask yourselves, and let me ask you, who has been to you, individually, and told you to vote just as you have voted here today? Has any man visited your habitations to tell you that when you come to this house you must all vote precisely alike? I will pause right here and will request that, if any person present has been so instructed, he or she will let us know it. I do not see any person rise, and I need not look for any one to do so, from the simple fact that not a word on this subject has been said to the Latter-day Saints. Our doctrine is true and we like it; our faith is one and we are one in it, our object is one and we unitedly pursue the straight and narrow path that leads to it. 14:91.

If the time was that the Elders of Israel could not be chastened and corrected for their wrongs, and be set right, you may know that they have proved recreant to the faith. And if those who are appointed to lead this people dare not rise up and tell them of their iniquity and chastise them therefor, and teach them the way of life and salvation, you may know that your leaders have fallen from their station. 5:124.

We will first present the Authorities of the Church; and I sincerely request the members to act freely and independently in voting —also in speaking if it be necessary. There has been no instance in this Church of a person's being in the least curtailed in the privilege of speaking his honest sentiments. It cannot be shown in the history of this people that a man has ever been injured, either in person, property, or character, for openly expressing, in the proper time and place, his objections to any man holding authority in this Church, or for assigning his reasons for such objections. Persons have frequently ruined their own characters by making false accusations. 7:227-228.

Our ecclesiastical government is the government of heaven.

No person possesses intelligence, in any degree, that he has not received from the God of heaven, or, in other words, from the Fountain of all intelligence, whether he acknowledges his God in it or not. No man, independent of the Great Ruler of the universe, is capable of devising that which we see and are well acquainted with. All mechanism, good government, wholesome principle, and true philosophy of whatever name or nature, flows from God to finite man. What for? To determine what he will do with it. It is for his improvement and advancement in the arts of civilized life, mortality, and true religion. This has been taught you from the beginning as the unmistakable features of our holy religion. 7:141.

Let the Presidents and Apostles and Elders do the work the Lord has set them to do, and obey the counsel which is given them, and the Kingdom will continue to roll, to increase in strength, in importance, in magnitude and in power, in wisdom, intelligence and glory; and no one need be concerned, for it is the Kingdom which the Lord our God has established, and has sustained by his matchless wisdom and power from the beginning to this day. 11:253.

It is a common adage, "Old men for counsel, and young men for war." Until men born in the Priesthood grow old therein in faithfulness, I would say, with comparatively few exceptions, "Young men for counsel, and young men for war." For knowledge and understanding, I would rather, as a general thing, select young men from eighteen years of age—the sons of men who have been in this Church from the beginning, than to select their fathers. Their minds have been but little, if any, trammeled with erroneous traditions and teachings. Let the yoke of the Gospel be put upon those young men Brother Joseph referred to in his remarks, who have been sowing their wild oats for years, and they are generally better and more correct in the offices of the Priesthood than many of the gray-haired fathers. They understand more about God, about Jesus Christ, and the government of God on the earth, than do many of the fathers and grandfathers. 7:335.

It is true that under some circumstances we may have to look at the others. For instance, here is the High Council, they are called to act upon cases that come before them. Of course their duty, then, is to examine into the conduct of their brethren and sisters; and this is required of them. And if they do it without prejudice, without selfishness, by the power of the Holy Ghost, divested of every improper feeling, judging righteous judgment between man and man, the performance of this duty will purify them just as much as any other labor. 11:292.

It may be considered that we are a mixed congregation, consisting of Bishops, Seventies, High Priests, Elders, the Twelve, and the First Presidency; but I consider we are, strictly speaking, a meeting of the Elders of Israel; for if we were to be instructed in the duties of any one of these Quorums, that instruction would be equally good for all. 6:314.

High Councilors, do you have any trials before you? "Yes." Have the brethren complained of each other? "Yes." Are their feelings alienated one from the other? Is there a party spirit manifested in the Council? "Sometimes." Do the brethren go off satisfied with the decisions of the Council? Bishops, do you have any trials? Are the feelings of the brethren in your Wards alienated?

"Yes." What should they do in such cases? They should follow the rules laid down, and be reconciled to their brethren forthwith. I think that it can be shown that the great majority of difficulties between brethren arises from misunderstandings rather than from malice and a wicked heart, and instead of talking the matter over with each other in a saint-like spirit, they will contend with each other until a real fault is created, and they have brought a sin upon themselves. When we have done good ninety-nine times and then do an evil, how common it is, my brethren and sisters, to look at that one evil all the day long and never think of the good. Before we judge each other we should look at the design of the heart, and if it is evil, then chasten that individual, and take a course to bring him back again to righteousness. 12:173.

When you are rebuked by each other—when brethren meet you and say, "This is wrong in you," you should receive it kindly, and express your thanks for the reproof, and acknowledge the wrong frankly, and admit that you may frequently do wrong when you do not know it, and say, "I wish you to enlighten my mind, to take me by the hand, and let me go along hand-in-hand and strengthen and sustain each other." What, in your weaknesses? Yes. Do you expect to see a perfect man? Not while you stay here. 8:367.

You may, figuratively speaking, pound one Elder over the head with a club, and he does not know but what you have handed him a straw dipped in molasses to suck. There are others, if you speak a word to them, or take a straw and chasten them, whose hearts are broken; they are as tender in their feelings as an infant, and will melt like wax before the flame. You must not chasten them severely; you must chasten according to the spirit that is in the person. Some you may talk to all day long, and they do not know what you are talking about. There is a great variety. Treat people as they are. 8:367.

Just a few words to the Presidency of this Stake of Zion. It is now their duty to see that the officers within their jurisdiction perform their several duties, it is sufficient for them, too, if they will attend to it. The High Council, I hope, will not have much business to do. I am told that there have only been three cases during the last twenty-three years, that have gone for trial before the High Council from Farmington. That is doing very well. To the now acting Bishops, who will be ordained Bishops in the county, I will say that you will now be required to look after your several Wards more assiduously than heretofore; see that Teachers are diligent in the performance of their duties, and that all difficulties that may arise among the brethren of the Ward be settled, if possible, by the Teachers; and also see that all who claim membership in this Church observe the moral law of our religion. We shall not expect to hear of people breaking the Sabbath, and a hundred other things all of which are inconsistent with our holy callings, and opposed to the accomplishment of the work that the Father has given us to do. You are called upon now to make yourselves familiar with the revelations and commandments that have been given us of the Lord for our perfection, for our sanctification preparatory to our exaltation, and so live that our acts and conversations may conform to the same. You are called upon now to improve your ways, to seek with all earnestness for an increase of faith that you may live according to the higher laws, which is your privilege to do, and which is so necessary for our peace and comfort and for the good order of society and for the salvation of the Latter-day Saints. 19:43.

Chapter XIII

THE FIRST PRINCIPLES OF THE GOSPEL

Importance of the Principles of the Gospel—By faithfully attending to the first principles of the Gospel laid down in the New Testament, you are introduced into the knowledge of the works of God in the dispensation of the fulness of time. 1:244.

To understand the first principles of the Gospel—to rightly understand them, a man must have the wisdom that comes from above; he must be enlightened by the Holy Ghost; his mind must be in open vision; he must enjoy the blessings of salvation himself, in order to impart them to others. 6:283.

Need of Ordinances—There is no ordinance that God has delivered by his own voice, through his Son Jesus Christ, or by the mouths of any of his Prophets, Apostles or Evangelists, that is useless. Every ordinance, every commandment and requirement is necessary for the salvation of the human family. 13:215.

With regard to the ordinances of God, we may remark that we yield obedience to them because he requires it; and every iota of his requirements has a rational philosophy with it. We do not get up things on a hypothesis. That philosophy reaches to all eternity, and is the philosophy that the Latter-day Saints believe in. Every particle of truth that every person has received is a gift of God. We receive these truths, and go on from glory to glory, from eternal lives to eternal lives, gaining a knowledge of all things, and becoming Gods, even Sons of God. These are the celestial ones. These are they whom the Lord has chosen through their obedience. They have not spurned the truth, when they have heard it. These are they that have not spurned the Gospel, but have acknowledged the angels in their true character. These are they that work for the salvation of the human family. 19:50.

Because we believe in the ordinance of baptism, the ordinance of the sacrament is not to be done away. To learn that, if you believe in the laying on of hands for the reception of the Holy Ghost, you are not to deny the laying on of hands for the healing of the sick. It is not for people to take only part of the religion of Christ, and say, "It is all we require;" but take the whole truth wherever you find it. It is good; claim it, take it to yourself, and cleave to it, for it will do you good. Cease to separate truth from truth. 8:260.

However much we may profess attachment to God and his cause

we are not entitled to the blessings and privileges of his Kingdom until we become citizens therein. How can we do this? By repenting of our sins, and obeying the requirements of the Gospel of the Son of God which has been delivered to us. Hundreds and thousands of people have believed on the Lord Jesus Christ and repented of their sins, and have had the Holy Spirit to witness unto them that God is love, that they loved him and that he loved them, and yet they are not in his Kingdom. They have not complied with the necessary requirements, they have not entered in at the door. 13:57.

Faith—The Gospel that we preach is the power of God unto salvation; and the first principle of that Gospel is, as I have already said, faith in God, and faith in Jesus Christ his Son, our Savior. We must believe that he is the character he is represented to be in the Holy Scriptures. Believe that he told the truth when he said to his disciples, "Go ye forth and preach the Gospel to every creature; he that believeth and is baptized shall be saved, but he that believeth not shall be damned." We must believe that this same Jesus was crucified for the sins of the world, that is for the original sin, not the actual individual transgressions of the people; not but that the blood of Christ will cleanse from all sin, all who are disposed to act their part by repentance, and faith in his name. But the original sin was atoned for by the death of Christ, although its effect we still see in the diseases, distempers and every species of wickedness with which the human family is afflicted. 13:143.

Faith is an eternal principle; belief is an admission of the fact. Faith, to us, is the gift of God; belief is inherent in the children of men, and is the foundation for the reception of faith. Belief and unbelief are independent in men, the same as other attributes. Men can acknowledge or reject, turn to the right or to the left, rise up or remain seated, you can say that the Lord and his Gospel are not worthy of notice, or you can bow to them. 8:16.

Belief is inherent in the creature—implanted within him for his use and benefit—to believe or disbelieve. Your own experience may satisfy you that faith is not brought into requisition by the presentation of either facts or falsehoods to the external senses, or to the inward perceptions of the mind. If we speak of faith in the abstract, it is the power of God by which the worlds are and were made, and is a gift of God to those who believe and obey his commandments. On the other hand, no living, intelligent being, whether serving God or not, acts without belief. He might as well undertake to live without breathing as to live without the principle of belief. But he must believe the truth, obey the truth, and practice the truth, to obtain the power of God called faith. 8:259-260.

When men are in the habit of philosophising upon every point, only relying upon what we call human reason, they are constantly liable to error. But place a man in a situation where he is obliged or compelled, in order to sustain himself, to have faith in the name of Jesus Christ, and it brings him to a point where he will know for himself; and happy are those who pass through trials, if they maintain their integrity and their faith to their calling. 7:158.

When you believe the principles of the Gospel and attain unto faith, which is a gift of God, he adds more faith, adding faith to faith. He bestows faith upon his creatures as a gift; but his creatures inherently possess the privilege of believing the Gospel to be true or false. 8:17.

If the people will only be full of good works, I will insure that they will have faith in time of need. 3:154.

There is no saving faith merely upon the principles of believing or acknowledging a fact. Take a course to let the Spirit of God leave your hearts, and every soul of you would apostatize. 7:55.

It is the easiest thing in the world to believe the truth. It is a great deal easier to believe truth than error. It is easier to defend the truth than to defend error. 19:42.

We are under obligation to trust in our God; and this is the ground-work of all we can do ourselves. 4:356.

The first principle of the Gospel is faith in God—faith in a Supreme Being. This is a point that meets the infidel, and is one upon which I have reflected and talked a great deal, and I have come to this conclusion—that good, solid, sound sense teaches me never to judge a matter until I understand it, and infidels should never pass their opinion with regard to the character of a Supreme Being until they know whether there is one or not. If this principle were an article in the creed of the infidel world, I think they would not be quite so skeptical as they are; I think we should not meet with any person who would deny the existence of a Deity. The infidel looks abroad and sees the works of nature, in all their diversity—the mountain piercing the clouds with its snowy peaks, the mighty river, fertilizing, in its course to the seea, the valleys and plains in every direction, the sun in his glory at mid-day, the moon in her silvery splendor, and the myriad organizations from man to the minutest form of insect life, all giving the most irrefutable evidence of a Designer and Creator of infinite wisdom, skill and power, and yet he says there is no Deity, no Supreme Ruler, but all is the result of blind chance. How preposterous! Now, here is a book called the Bible. It is enclosed in what we call the cover, consisting of boards, paper and leather. Within the covers, we see a vast amount of writing—syllables, words and sentences;

now if we say there never was a person to compose, write, print or bind this book, but that it is here wholly as the result of chance, we shall only give expression to the faith, if faith it can be called, of those who are termed infidels; in fact this is infidelity. I do not want to say much about it, it is too vain! 13:142.

When you read the revelations, or when you hear the will of the Lord concerning you, for your own sakes never receive that with a doubtful heart. 3:336.

To explain how much confidence we should have in God, were I using a term to suit myself, I should say *implicit* confidence. I have faith in my God, and that faith corresponds with the works I produce. I have no confidence in faith without works. 4:24.

My faith is, when we have done all we can, then the Lord is under obligation, and will not disappoint the faithful; he will perform the rest. 4:91.

A great many good people, who possess much of the Spirit of the Lord, are naturally given to doubting, having so little self-reliance that they sometimes doubt whether they are Saints in truth or not. These often doubt when they should not. So long as they are walking humbly before God, keeping his commandments, and observing his ordinances, feeling willing to give all for Christ, and do everything that will promote his Kingdom, they need never doubt, for the Spirit will testify to them whether they are of God or not. There are some who are always fearful, trembling, doubting, wavering, and at the same time doing everything they can for the promotion of righteousness. Yet, they are in doubt whether they are doing the best possible good, and they fear and fail here and there, and will doubt their own experience and the witness of the Spirit to them. 12:169.

When a person is placed in circumstances that he cannot possibly obtain one particle of anything to sustain life, it would then be his privilege to exercise faith in God to feed him, who might cause a raven to pick up a piece of dried meat from some quarter where there was plenty, and drop it over the famishing man. When I cannot feed myself through the means God has placed in my power, it is then time enough for him to exercise his providence in an unusual manner to administer to my wants. But while we can help ourselves, it is our duty to do so. If a Saint of God be locked up in prison, by his enemies, to starve to death, it is then time enough for God to interpose, and feed him. 1:108.

Are you full of faith? You can tell whether I am or not by looking at me. You can tell whether the brethren who have been speaking to you are full of faith in the Gospel by the look of their countenances. You can see this if there is not a word spoken; we can tell by our feelings when we look at a congregation whether they have faith or not. I see there is a great amount of faith in the midst of the Latter-day Saints, and I wish there was a little more patience and obedience. 15:37.

If the Latter-day Saints will walk up to their privileges, and exercise faith in the name of Jesus Christ, and live in the enjoyment of the fulness of the Holy Ghost constantly day by day, there is nothing on the face of the earth that they could ask for, that would not be given to them. The Lord is waiting to be very gracious unto this people, and to pour out upon them riches, honor, glory and power, even that they may possess all things according to the promises he has made through his Apostles and Prophets. 11:114.

When faith springs up in the heart, good works will follow, and good works will increase that pure faith within them. 3:155.

The expression, "true believer," needs qualifying, for many believe who do not obey—I will qualify it by saying, a believer in Jesus Christ, who manifests his faith to God, angels, and his brethren, by his obedience. Not but that there are believers who do not obey, but the only true believers are they who prove their belief by their obedience to the requirements of the Gospel. 1:234.

Our Heavenly Father does not always reveal to his children the secret workings of his providences, nor does he show them the end from the beginning; for they have to learn to trust in him who has promised to fight our battles, and crown us with victory, if we are faithful as was faithful Abraham. 11:13.

Repentance—Sin consists in doing wrong when we know and can do better, and it will be punished with a just retribution, in the due time of the Lord. 2:133.

Though we may do the best we know how at this time, can there be no improvement made in our lives? There can. If we do wrong ignorantly, when we learn it is wrong, then it is our duty to refrain from that wrong immediately and for ever, and the sin of ignorance is winked at, and passes into oblivion. 2:130.

When men truly and heartily repent, and make manifest to the heavens that their repentance is genuine by obedience to the requirements made known to them through the laws of the Gospel, then are they entitled to the administration of salvation, and no power can withhold the good spirit from them. 10:18.

Now, my brethren, you who have sinned, repent of your sins. I can say to you in regard to Jesus and the atonement (it is so written, and I firmly believe it), that Christ has died for all. He had paid the full debt, whether you receive the gift or not. But if we continue to sin, to lie, steal, bear false witness, we must repent of and forsake that sin to have the full efficacy of the blood of Christ. Without this it will be of no effect; repentance must come, in order that the atonement may prove a benefit to us. Let all who are doing wrong cease doing wrong; live no longer in transgression, no matter of what kind; but live every day of your lives according to the revelations given, and so that your examples may be worthy of imitation. Let us remember that we never get beyond the purview of our religion—never, never! 11:375.

Some of our old traditions teach us that a man guilty of atrocious and murderous acts may savingly repent when on the scaffold; and upon his execution will hear the expression, "Bless God! he has gone to heaven, to be crowned in glory, through the all-redeeming merits of Christ the Lord." This is all nonsense. Such a character never will see heaven. Some will pray, "O that I had passed through the veil on the night of my conversion!" This proves the false ideas and vain notions entertained by the Christian world. 8:61.

When I first came into the Church it was a subject of considerable thought to me why people whom I knew to be as good and moral as they could be, should have to repent. But I could see afterwards that if they had nothing else to repent of they could and ought to repent of their false religions, of their narrow, contracted creeds in which they were bound, of the ordinances of men, and get something better. These narrow, contracted religions have spread infidelity in the world. They should repent of these and take hold of the things of God and receive the truths of heaven. "Well," say the ministers, "we have lived according to the light we have received." We say, are you willing to receive more? If so, here is more for you. So far as your faith in Christ goes, and your mortality, we say, Amen. But here is something more. 16:43.

The Savior has warned us to be careful how we judge, forgiving each other seven times seventy in a day, if we repent, and confess our sins one to another. Can we be more merciful and forgiving than our Father in Heaven? We cannot. Therefore let people do the best they can, and they will pave the way for the rising generation to walk up into the light, wisdom, and knowledge of the angels, and of the redeemed from this earth, to say nothing of other earths, and they will be prepared to enjoy in the resurrection all the blessings which are for the faithful, and enjoy them in the flesh. 2:132.

We should never cease reforming and seeking to the Lord our God. 4:269.

All I have ever asked for or contended for is a reformation in the life of this people; that the thief should stop his stealing, the swearer his swearing, the liar his lying, the deceiver his deceiving, and the man who loves the world more than his God and his religion wean his affections from those objects and place them where they of right belong. I do not wish anybody to cherish a wild enthusiasm, so common in the world, which is produced by the excitement of animal passions, and makes people weep and cry out in an insane manner. I wish the people to make themselves acquainted with facts pertaining to God, to heaven, to mankind upon the earth, their errand here, for what they are created, the nature of their organization, who has power over them, who controls them, how much they can control themselves, etc., etc.; and then let us see whether we can be men and conduct ourselves like Saints, or live and act like the wicked. 9:103.

Keep your follies that do not concern others to yourselves, and keep your private wickedness as still as possible; hide it from the eyes of the public gaze as far as you can. I wish to say this upon this particular point in regard to people's confessing. We wish to see people honestly confess as they should and what they should. 8:362.

If I have injured any person, I ought to confess to that person and make right what I did wrong. 8:361.

But if you have stolen your neighbor's cattle, own it, and restore the property, with fourfold if it is requested. If you have taken your neighbor's spade, own it, and return it, with fourfold if he requires it. I believe in coming out and being plain and honest with that which should be made public, and in keeping to yourselves that which should be kept. If you have your weaknesses, keep them hid from your brethren as much as you can. You never hear me ask the people to tell their follies. But when we ask the brethren, as we frequently do, to speak in sacrament meetings, we wish them, if they have injured their neighbors, to confess their wrongs; but do not tell about your nonsensical conduct that nobody knows of but yourselves. Tell to the public that which belongs to the public. If you have sinned against the people, confess to them. If you have sinned against a family or a neighborhood, go to them and confess. If you have sinned against your Ward, confess to your Ward. If you have sinned against one individual, take that person by yourselves and make your confession to him. And if you have sinned against your God, or against yourselves, confess to God, and keep the matter to yourselves, for I do not want to know anything about it. 8:362.

Baptism—We, the Latter-day Saints, believe in being baptized by immersion for the remission of sins, according to the testimony of the disciples of Jesus and the revelations of the Lord given in these last days. Infants are pure, they have neither sorrow of heart, nor sins to repent of and forsake, and consequently are incapable of being baptized for the remission of sin. If we have sinned, we must know good from evil; an infant does not know this, it cannot know it; it has not grown into the idea of contemplation of good and evil; it has not the capacity to listen to the parent or teacher or to the priest when they tell what is right or wrong or what is injurious; and until these things are understood a person cannot be held accountable and consequently cannot be baptized for the remission of sin. 13:237.

The Lord has instituted laws and ordinances, and all have their peculiar design and meaning. And though we may not know the origin of the necessity of being baptized for the remission of sins, it answers that portion of the law we are now under to teach the people in their ignorance that water is designed for purification, and to instruct them to be baptized therein for the remission of their sins. If the people could fully understand this matter, they would perceive that it is perfectly reasonable and has been the law to all worlds. 7:162-163.

What is required of us as soon as we come to the years of accountability? It is required of us, for it is an institution of heaven, the origin of which you and I cannot tell, for the simple reason that it has no beginning, it is from eternity to eternity—it is required of us to go down into the waters of baptism. Here is a fountain or element, typical of the purity of the eternities. Go down into the waters, and there be baptized for the remission of sins, and then have hands laid upon us to confirm us members of the Church of Jesus Christ of Latter-day Saints. Then receive the Spirit of Truth, or the Holy Ghost. Then live according to every word that proceeds out of the mouth of God, through those men whom he has appointed here upon the earth, until we are perfect. 19:48.

If you have been righteous from your birth up, and have never committed known sins and transgressions, be baptized to fulfil all righteousness, as Jesus was. If you can say you have no sins to repent of, forsake your false theories, and love and serve God with an undivided heart. 14:281.

Has water, in itself, any virtue to wash away sin? Certainly not; but the Lord says, "If the sinner will repent of his sins, and go down into the waters of baptism, and there be buried in the likeness of being put into the earth and buried, and again be delivered from the water, in the likeness of being born—if in the sincerity of his heart he will do this, his sins shall be washed away." Will the water of itself wash them away? No; but keeping the commandments of God will cleanse away the stain of sin. 2:4.

In the beginning God cursed the earth; but did he curse all things pertaining to it? No, he did not curse the water, but he blessed it.

Pure water is cleansing—it serves to purify; and you are aware that the ancient Saints were very tenacious with regard to their purification by water. From the beginning the Lord instituted water for that purpose among others. I do not mean from the beginning of this earth alone; and although we have no immediate concern in inquiring into the organization of other earths that do not come within reach of our investigation, yet I will say that water has been the means of purification in every world that has been organized out of the immensity of matter. 7:162.

All Latter-day Saints enter the new and everlasting covenant when they enter this Church. They covenant to cease sustaining, upholding and cherishing the kingdom of the Devil and the kingdoms of this world. They enter the new and everlasting covenant to sustain the Kingdom of God and no other kingdom. They take a vow of the most solemn kind, before the heavens and earth, and that, too, upon the validity of their own salvation, that they will sustain truth and righteousness instead of wickedness and falsehood, and build up the Kingdom of God, instead of the kingdoms of this world. 12:230.

You have not the power to baptize yourselves, neither have you power to resurrect yourselves; and you could not legally baptize a second person for the remission of sins until some person first baptized you and ordained you to this authority. 6:275.

Gift of the Holy Ghost—In the New Testament and Book of Mormon, we learn that when the Gospel is preached the people are taught to believe on the Lord Jesus Christ, to repent of their sins, be baptized for the remission of sin, and receive the Holy Ghost by the laying on of hands; the Holy Ghost is then the special gift of the Father and is his minister. He also gives intelligence by angels, as well as by the inspiration of the Holy Spirit, and by opening the minds of the Saints to behold in vision things as they are in eternity. When true doctrines are advanced, though they may be new to the hearers, yet the principles contained therein are perfectly natural and easy to be understood, so much so that the hearers often imagine that they had always known them. This arises from the influence of the Spirit of Truth upon the spirit of intelligence that is within each person. The influence that comes from heaven is all the time teaching the children of men. 9:254.

We believe we are entitled to the gift of the Holy Ghost in extent according to the discretion and wisdom of God and our faithfulness; which gift brings all things to our remembrance, past, present, and to come, that are necessary for us to know, and as far as our minds are prepared to receive the knowledge of God revealed by that all-wise Agent. The Holy Ghost is God's minister, and is delegated to visit the sons and daughters of men. All intelligent beings pertaining to this earth are instructed from the same source. 9:254.

The Holy Ghost reveals unto you things past, present, and to come; it makes your minds quick and vivid to understand the handiwork of the Lord. Your joy is made full in beholding the footsteps of our Father going forth among the inhabitants of the earth; this is invisible to the world, but it is made visible to the Saints, and they behold the Lord in his providences, bringing forth the work of the last days. 4:22.

My knowledge is, if you will follow the teachings of Jesus Christ and his Apostles, as recorded in the New Testament, every man and woman will be put in possession of the Holy Ghost; every person will become a Prophet, Seer, and Revelator, and an expounder of truth. They will know things that are, that will be, and that have been. They will understand things in heaven, things on the earth, and things under the earth, things of time, and things of eternity, according to their several callings and capacities. 1:243.

There is a variety of blessings; a different blessing being probably given to one, two, three or four of this congregation. Thus, one will have faith to lay on hands upon the sick and rebuke disease, and drive it from the person afflicted. Many may receive this blessing of faith, the gift of healing. Some may receive faith to the discerning of spirits; they can discern the spirit of a person, wether it is good or evil. They have such power that when a person enters this congregation they can tell the spirit of such person; then they have received the gift of discerning of spirits. Some may receive the gift of tongues, that they will get up and speak in tongues, and speak in many other languages beside their mother tongue, the language that they were brought up in, that they were first taught, and be able to proclaim the Gospel of life and salvation that all men could understand it. These are the blessings; but others might receive the gift of prophecy, get up and prophesy what is to befall this nation, what will befall this or that individual, and what will befall the different nations of the earth, etc. 16:164.

The gifts of the Gospel are given to strengthen the faith of the believer. 10:324.

Suppose you obey the ordinances of the Gospel, and do not speak in tongues today, never mind that. Suppose you do not have the spirit of prophecy, no matter. Suppose you do not receive any particular gift attended by the rushing of a mighty wind, as on the day of Pentecost, there is no particular necessity that you should. On the day of Pentecost there was special need for it, it was a peculiarly trying time. Some special and powerful manifestation of the power of the Almighty was necessary to open the eyes of the people and let them know that Jesus has paid the debt, and that they had actually crucified him who, by his death, had become the Savior of the world. It required this at that time to convince the people. 14:14.

The gift of seeing with the natural eyes is just as much a gift as the gift of tongues. The Lord gave that gift and we can do as we please with regard to seeing; we can use the sight of the eye to the glory of God, or to our own destruction. 3:364.

The gift of communicating one with another is the gift of God, just as much so as the gift of prophecy, of discerning spirits, of tongues, of healing, or any other gift, though sight, taste, and speech, are so generally bestowed that they are not considered in the same miraculous light as are those gifts mentioned in the Gospel.

We can use these gifts and every other gift God has given us, to the praise and glory of God, to serve him, or we can use them to dishonor him and his cause; we can use the gift of speech to blaspheme his name. 3:364.

Healing the Sick—We lay hands on the sick and wish them to be healed, and pray the Lord to heal them, but we cannot always say that he will. 4:284.

I am here to testify to hundreds of instances, of men, women, and children being healed by the power of God, through the laying on of hands, and many I have seen raised from the gates of death, and brought back from the verge of eternity; and some whose spirits had actually left their bodies, returned again. I testify that I have seen the sick healed by the laying on of hands, according to the promise of the Savior. 1:240.

When I lay hands on the sick, I expect the healing power and influence of God to pass through me to the patient, and the disease to give way. I do not say that I heal everybody I lay hands on; but many have been healed under my administration. Jesus said, on one occasion, "Who has touched me?" A woman had crept up behind him in the crowd, and touched the hem of his garment, and he knew it, because virtue had gone from him. Do you see the reason and propriety of laying hands on each other? When we are prepared, when we are holy vessels before the Lord, a stream of power from the Almighty can pass through the tabernacle of the administrator to the system of the patient, and the sick are made whole; the headache, fever or other disease has to give way. My brethren and sisters, there is virtue in us if we will do right; if we live our religion we are the temples of God wherein he will dwell; if we defile ourselves, these temples God will destroy. 14:72.

Instead of calling for a doctor you should administer to them by the laying on of hands and anointing with oil, and give them mild food, and herbs, and medicines that you understand; and if you want the mind and will of God at such a time, get it, it is just as much your privilege as of any other member of the Church and Kingdom of God. It is your privilege and duty to live so that you know when the word of the Lord is spoken to you and when the mind of the Lord is revealed to you. I say it is your duty to live so as to know and understand all these things. 18:71.

Many people are unwilling to do one thing for themselves in case of sickness, but ask God to do it all. 4:25.

I am sent for continually, though I only go occasionally, because it is a privilege of every father, who is an Elder in Israel, to have faith to heal his family, just as much so as it is my privilege to have faith to heal my family; and if he does not do it he is not living up to his privilege. It is just as reasonable for him to ask me to cut his wood and maintain his family, for if he had faith himself he would save me the trouble of leaving other duties to attend to his request. 3:46.

You may go to some people here, and ask what ails them, and they answer, "I don't know but we feel a dreadful distress in the stomach and in the back; we feel all out of order, and we wish you to lay hands on us." Have you used any remedies?" No. "We wish the Elders to lay hands upon us, and we have faith that we shall be healed." That is very inconsistent according to my faith. If we are sick, and ask the Lord to heal us, and to do all for us that is necessary to be done, according to my understanding of the Gospel of salvation, I might as well ask the Lord to cause my wheat and corn to grow without my plowing the ground and casting in the seed. It appears consistent to me to apply every remedy that comes within the range of my knowledge, and to ask my Father in Heaven, in the name of Jesus Christ, to sanctify that application to the healing of my body; to another this may appear inconsistent.

But supposing we were traveling in the mountains, and all we had or could get, in the shape of nourishment, was a little venison, and one or two were taken sick, without anything in the world in the shape of healing medicine within our reach, what should we do? According to my faith, ask the Lord Almighty to send an angel to heal the sick. This is our privilege, when so situated that we cannot get anything to help ourselves. Then the Lord and his servants can do all. But it is my duty to do, when I have it in my power. 4:24.

Chapter XIV

THE SABBATH; MEETINGS; THE SACRAMENT

How to Spend the Sabbath Day—Spend the Sabbath day prudently, in the love and fear of God. 19:65.

Persons professing to be Saints should assemble themselves together on the Lord's day, except those who may be necessarily detained at home to keep the house, take care of the children, or to perform some work of necessity and mercy; the rest should assemble in the place appointed for worship and the offering up of our sacraments. 10:284.

You take this book (the book of Doctrine and Covenants) and you will read here that the Saints are to meet together on the Sabbath day. It is what we call the first day of the week. No matter whether it is the Jewish Sabbath or not. I do not think there is anybody who can bring facts to prove which is the seventh day, or when Adam was put in the garden, or the day about which the Lord spoke to Moses. This matter is not very well known, so we call the day on which we rest and worship God the first day of the week. This people called Latter-day Saints, are required by the revelations that the Lord has given to assemble themselves together on this day. In this commandment we are required to come together and repent of our sins and confess our sins and partake of the bread and of the wine, or water, in commemoration of the death and sufferings of our Lord and Savior. 16:168.

Instead of suffering our labors to occupy the Sabbath—instead of planning our business to infringe upon the first day of the week, we should do as little as possible; if it is necessary to cook food, do so; but even if that could be dispensed with, it would be better. As to keeping the Sabbath according to the Mosaic law, indeed, I do not; for it would be almost beyond my power. Still, under the new covenant, we should remember to preserve holy one day in the week as a day of rest—as a memorial of the rest of the Lord and the rest of the Saints; also for our temporal advantage, for it is instituted for the express purpose of benefiting man. It is written in this book (the Bible), that the Sabbath was made for man. It is a blessing to him. As little labor as possible should be done upon that day; it should be set apart as a day of rest, to assemble together in the place appointed, according to the revelation, confessing our sins, bringing our tithes and offerings, and presenting ourselves before the Lord, there to commemorate the death and sufferings of our Lord Jesus Christ. 6:277-278.

Now, remember, my brethren, those who go skating, buggy riding or on excursions on the Sabbath day—and there is a great deal of this practiced—are weak in the faith. Gradually, little by little, little by little, the spirit of their religion leaks out of their hearts and their affections, and by and by they begin to see faults in their brethren, faults in the doctrines of the Church, faults in the organization, and at last they leave the Kingdom of God and go to destruction. I really wish you would remember this, and tell it to your neighbors. 15:83.

The Lord has directed his people to rest one-seventh part of the time, and we take the first day of the week, and call it our Sabbath. This is according to the order of the Christians. We should observe this for our own temporal good and spiritual welfare. When we see a farmer in such a hurry, that he has to attend to his harvest, and to haying, fence-making, or to gathering his cattle on the Sabbath day, as far as I am concerned, I count him weak in the faith. He has lost the spirit of his religion, more or less. Six days are enough for us to work, and if we wish to play, play within the six days; if we wish to go on excursions, take one of those six days, but on the seventh day, come to the place of worship, attend to the Sacrament, confess your faults one to another and to our God, and pay attention to the ordinances of the house of God. 15:81.

I said yesterday to a Bishop who was mending a breach in the canal, and expressed a wish to continue his labor on the following Sabbath, as his wheat was burning up, let it burn, when the time comes that is set apart for worship, go up and worship the Lord. 3:331.

The Lord has planted within us a divinity; and that divine immortal spirit requires to be fed. Will earthly food answer for that purpose? No; it will only keep this body alive as long as the spirit stays with it, which gives us an opportunity of doing good. That divinity within us needs food from the Fountain from which it emanated. It is not of the earth, earthy, but is from heaven. Principles of eternal life, of God and godliness, will alone feed the immortal capacity of man and give true satisfaction. 7:138.

We are under the necessity of assembling here from Sabbath to Sabbath, and in Ward meetings, and besides, have to call our solemn assemblies, to teach, talk, pray, sing, and exhort. What for? To keep us in remembrance of our God and our holy religion. Is this custom necessary? Yes; because we are so liable to forget—so prone to wander, that we need to have the Gospel sounded in our ears as much as once, twice, or thrice a week, or, behold, we will turn again to our idols. 6:195.

If you can make as good a beginning as did an old lady, you will do well. She went to a schoolhouse, and, on her return, called at a neighbor's who inquired where she had been. She replied, "I have been to meeting." "Has there been a meeting?" "Oh, yes, and a glorious one, too." "Dear me, we did not hear of it. Were there many there?" "No, there were not many." "Who was there?" "Why, the Lord was there, and I was there, and had a blessed good meeting." If you cannot get any person to meet with you, be sure and have the Lord meet with you, and you will soon gain confidence in yourselves and have influence with your brethren. 8:65.

Worship on Every Day—Monday, Tuesday, Wednesday, Thursday, Friday, and Saturday must be spent to the glory of God, as much as Sunday, or we shall come short of the object of our pursuit. 13:261.

The Lord knows the wants of his mortal children, and has appointed unto them one-seventh part of the time for rest, though we cannot say, in every sense of the word, that this is a day of rest to the Latter-day Saints or to the professing Christians, some of whom are in the habit of rising at sunrise to hold prayer-meetings; they then eat breakfast and hurry away to the morning service until noon; in the afternoon they again have meetings, and class meetings, prayer meetings, confessing meetings, etc., and so continue until nine in the evening. To such persons I cannot consider it really a day of rest. 10:187.

Coming to this Tabernacle to worship and do the will of God for one day in the week, and following our own inclination and doing our own will at all other times, is a folly; it is useless, and a perfect burlesque on the service of God. We should do the will of God, and spend all our time for the accomplishment of his purposes, whether we are in this Tabernacle or elsewhere. 12:34.

If I had my own mind, I would devote the time for meetings like this within the measure of the six days, and on the seventh rest from all my labors, for the express purpose of renewing the mental and physical power of man. They require it, as the Lord well knew; hence he established a day of rest. The natural tendency of the physical powers of man is to decay; and to preserve them as long as possible, they need this retirement from labor—this rest—this ease. 8:58.

Preaching and Listening in Meetings—While we have the privilege of speaking to each other, let us speak words of comfort and consolation. When you are influenced by the Spirit of holiness and purity, let your light shine; but if you are tried and tempted and buffeted by Satan, keep your thoughts to yourselves—keep your mouths closed; for speaking produces fruit, either of a good or evil character. 7:268.

As we have met in the capacity of a General Conference, we shall expect to hear instructions from the Elders pertaining to the building up of the Kingdom of God on earth. This is our calling, this is the labor devolving upon us, and it should occupy our attention day by day from morning until evening and from week to week; in fact, we have no other calling or business. 13:260.

Today we are able to meet together to speak to each other, to strengthen and do each other good; and by forsaking our fields for a season, to gather together to worship our God, I can assure you that our crops will be better than they would be if we were to spend all our time in our fields. We may water and plant and toil, but we should never forget that it is God who gives the increase; and by meeting together, our health and spirits will be better, we will look better, and the things of this world will increase around us more, and we will know better how to enjoy them. 11:116.

I will take the liberty of suggesting to my brethren who address the congregation that our sermons should be short, and if they are not filled with life and spirit let them be shorter, for we have not time at this Conference to let all the Elders who speak preach a long sermon, but we have time to say a few words in bearing testimony, to give a few words of counsel to encourage the Saints, to strengthen the weak, to endeavor to confirm those who are wavering, and so forward the Kingdom of God. 12:27.

Brethren and sisters, I will make one request of you. When you speak, speak so that we can hear and understand you, whether it be much or little, good or bad. If you have nothing to say, take my counsel, and keep your seat. If you have anything to say, say it; and when you get through, stop. Let your feelings be governed and controlled by the principles of eternal life, as should the children of God, delighting in truth and righteousness. 7:270.

Many have a foreboding in their hearts; a fearfulness, a tremor comes over them, when they arise to address a congregation. They think that it will not do to tell the people just what they understand, but talk about it and talk about it. In this way they darken counsel. Do not darken counsel by your words. 4:368.

When people assemble to worship they should leave their worldly cares where they belong, then their minds are in a proper condition to worship the Lord, to call upon him in the name of Jesus, and to get his Holy Spirit, that they may hear and understand things as they are in eternity, and know how to comprehend the providences of our God. This is the time for their minds to be open, to behold the invisible things of God, that he reveals by his Spirit. 3:53.

Every person should be silent when we meet here to worship God. Remember and try to keep perfectly quiet, and do not whisper, talk, nor scrape your feet; and do not let your children cry if you can help it. 14:44.

My greatest desire to my Father and God is that I may so speak that my remarks will be acceptable to him and beneficial to those who hear me. 7:131.

I am responsible for the doctrine I teach; but I am not responsible for the obedience of the people to that doctrine. 13:1.

The same weakness is in me, that is common to the most of my brethren who address you from this stand, that is, a degree of timidity, which arises from a sense of the importance of the work in which we are engaged; but my resolution overbalances this. 1:334.

I am extremely anxious so to convey my ideas to the people that they will understand them as I do. Our language is deficient, and I do not possess in this particular the natural endowment that some men enjoy. I am a man of few words, and unlearned in the learning of this generation. 9:287.

I have never yet seen the time that I had wisdom, strength, and ability enough to preach a Gospel discourse—to commence it, and finish it, setting before the people the plan of salvation sufficiently full, that thereby they might be saved. But it is only given in portions —a little here, and a little there, by feeble man. 6:283.

When I have endeavored to address a congregation, I have almost always felt a repugnance in my heart to the practice of premeditation, or of pre-constructing a discourse to deliver to the people, but let me ask God my Heavenly Father, in the name of Jesus Christ, to give me his Spirit, and put into my heart the things he wishes me to speak whether they be for better or worse. These have been my private feelings, as a general thing. 1:264.

I need the attention of the congregation and the faith of those who have faith; I need the wisdom of God and his Spirit to be in my heart to enable me to speak to the edification of the people. Although I have been a public speaker for thirty-seven years, it is seldom that I rise before a congregation without feeling a child-like timidity; if I live to the age of Methuselah I do not know that I shall outgrow it. There are reasons for this which I understand. When I look upon the faces of intelligent beings I look upon the image of the God I serve. There are none but what have a certain portion of divinity within them; and though we are clothed with bodies which are in the image of our God, yet this mortality shrinks before that portion of divinity which we inherit from our Father. This is the cause of my timidity, and of all others who feel this embarrassment when they address their fellow beings. 13:139.

In addressing a congregation, though the speaker be unable to say more than half a dozen sentences, and those awkwardly constructed, if his heart is pure before God, those few broken sentences are of more value than the greatest eloquence without the Spirit of the Lord and of more real worth in the sight of God, angels, and all good men. In praying, though a person's words be few and awkwardly expressed, if the heart is pure before God, that prayer will avail more than the eloquence of a Cicero. What does the Lord, the Father of us all, care about our mode of expression? The simple, honest heart is of more avail with the Lord than all the pomp, pride, splendor, and eloquence produced by men. When he looks upon a heart full of sincerity, integrity, and child-like simplicity, he sees a principle that will endure forever—"That is the spirit of my own kingdom—the spirit I have given to my children." 8:283-284.

I believe, according to my feelings, that if I had all the mastery of language that has ever been obtained by the learned, my spirit would delight more in childlike conversation, and that too, in a simple language, than in the most learned literary style that is used. A plain, clear method of expressing ideas is the most pleasing to me. 4:341.

I believe it is our duty to imitate everything that is good, lovely, dignified and praiseworthy. We ought to imitate the best speakers, and study to convey our ideas to each other in the best and choicest language, especially when we are dispensing the great truths of the Gospel of peace to the people. I generally use the best language I can command. 11:255.

Testimony Meetings—You know that the first Thursday in each month we hold as a fast day. How many here know the origin of this day? Before tithing was paid, the poor were supported by donations. They came to Joseph and wanted help, in Kirtland, and he said there should be a fast day, which was decided upon. It was to be held once a month, as it is now,* and all that would have been eaten that day, of flour, or meat, or butter, or fruit, or anything else, was to be carried to the fast meeting and put into the hands of a person selected for the purpose of taking care of it and distributing it among the poor. 12:115.

Do not hesitate to tell your feelings. 4:368.

In our fast-day meetings, the Saints meet to express their feelings and to strengthen each other in their faith in the holy Gospel. 7:267.

*At present the first Sunday of the month is designated fast day.

We wish the Latter-day Saints to meet at their respective houses, erected for that purpose, on the day appointed for a fast, and take with them of their substance to feed the poor and the hungry among us, and, if it is necessary, to clothe the naked. We expect to see the sisters there; for they are generally first and foremost in deeds of charity and kindness. Let the hearts of the poor be made glad, and let their prayers and thanksgiving ascend unto God, and receive an answer of rich blessings upon our heads. 12:126.

Do you not receive as much of the spirit of intelligence, of the spirit of knowledge, and the consoling influences of the Holy Ghost, to have people rise and testify of the things of God which they do know, of those things which they have experienced themselves? Does not that vividly bring to your minds the goodness of the Lord in revealing to you the truths of the Gospel? Does not that strengthen your faith, give you an increase of confidence and witness to you that you are a child of God? Most assuredly it does. Therefore, when any testify of the things of God, it strengthens their brethren, precisely as it did in days of old when they observed the counsel to, "Speak often one to another," "strengthen the brethren," and so on. 4:367.

If any of you feel that there is no life in your meetings, as I occasionally hear some of the brethren say, then it becomes your duty to go and instill life into that meeting, and do your part to produce an increase of the Spirit and power of God in the meetings in your locality. 10:309.

I always feel to urge our youth to attend meetings when strangers preach, that they may be able to understand that which is not of God, and learn the difference between the doctrine taught by us and others. 13:323.

Now, then, if our brethren of the Presbyterians, Methodists or any others visit here and want to preach to you, certainly let them preach, and have your children hear them. They will tell you to keep the Sabbath and to love your father and mother; they will tell you to be true, honest, industrious, to be faithful to your studies, to read the Bible and all good books, to study the sciences, etc., which is all good, and as far as such teaching goes just as good as it can be. I say, parents, do not be afraid of having your children learn everything that is worth learning. And if any of our Christian brethren want to go into our Sabbath schools to teach our children, let them do so. They will not teach them anything immoral in the presence of those who are in charge of the schools. 14:196.

Whether we are poor or rich, if we neglect our prayers and our sacrament meetings, we neglect the Spirit of the Lord, and a spirit of darkness comes over us. 10:300.

When a man opens or closes a meeting with prayer, every man, woman, and child in the congregation who professes to be a Saint should have no desire or words in their hearts and mouths but what are being offered by the man who is mouth for all the congregation. 6:42.

The Sacrament of the Lord's Supper—The revelations of God to Joseph Smith instruct the Latter-day Saints to live their religion day by day, and to meet on the first day of the week to break bread, confess their faults one to another and pray with and for each other. I would like this tradition fastened not only upon the people generally, but particularly upon the Bishops and other leaders of this Church. 9:369.

I say to the brethren and sisters, in the name of the Lord, it is our duty and it is required of us, by our Father in Heaven, by the spirit of our religion, by our covenants with God and each other, that we observe the ordinances of the house of God, and especially on the Sabbath day, to attend to the Sacrament of the Lord's Supper. Then attend the Ward meetings and the Quorum meetings. 15:82.

In the ordinance we here attend to in the afternoon, we show to the Father that we remember Jesus Christ, our Elder Brother; we testify to him that we are willing to take upon us his name. When we are doing this, I want the minds here as well as the bodies. I want the whole man here when you come to meeting. 8:137.

This is a very solemn ordinance. The Christian world accepts it, in preference to any other, as one of the ordinances of the house of God. With some, this ordinance is the first and the last; and with others this ordinance is not thought to be of sufficient importance to be attended to. I wish to say to the Latter-day Saints, and also to those who do not believe in the fulness of the Gospel, that this ordinance, which we are now attending to this afternoon, is, in reality, no more sacred than any other ordinance of the house of God in the eyes of him who has instituted the same. The validity of one divine law is the same as the validity of another with our Father and God. 11:39-40.

I would exhort my brethren and sisters to receive this ordinance every Sabbath, when they meet together, as is our practice; not following the customs of others, for with some denominations this is administered once a month, with others once in three months, with others never, they not believing in outward ordinances. We are in the habit of partaking of the contents of the cup each Sabbath when we meet together, and I do pray you, my brethren and sisters, to contemplate this ordinance thoroughly, and seek unto the Lord with all your hearts that you may obtain the promised blessings by obedience to it. Teach its observance to your children; impress upon them its necessity. Its observance is as necessary to our salvation as any other of the ordinances and commandments that have been instituted in order that the people may be sanctified, that Jesus may bless them and give unto them his spirit and guide and direct them that they may secure unto themselves life eternal. Impress the sacredness of this important ordinance upon the minds of your children. 19:91.

We do this in remembrance of the death of our Savior; it is required of his disciples until he comes again, no matter how long that may be. No matter how many generations come and go, believers in him are required to eat bread and drink wine in remembrance of his death and sufferings until he comes again. Why are they required to do this? To witness unto the Father, to Jesus and to the angels that they are believers in and desire to follow him in the regeneration, keep his commandments, build up his Kingdom, revere his name and serve with an undivided heart, that they may be worthy to eat and drink with him in his Fathers' Kingdom. This is why the Latter-day Saints partake of the ordinance of the Lord's Supper.

I know that in the Christian world sermon after sermon is preached on this subject; yet people there differ in their belief concerning these emblems. The Mother Church of the Christian world believes that the bread becomes the actual flesh of Jesus, and that the wine becomes his blood; this is preposterous to me. It is bread, and it is wine; but both are blessed to the souls of those who partake thereof. But to be followers of the Lord Jesus more is required than merely to partake of the bread and wine—the emblems of his death and suffering—it is necessary that strict obedience be rendered to his requirements. 13:139-140.

In what consists the benefit we derive from this ordinance? It is in obeying the commands of the Lord. When we obey the commandments of our Heavenly Father, if we have a correct understanding of the ordinances of the house of God, we receive all the promises attached to the obedience rendered to his commandments. 2:3.

It is one of the greatest blessings we could enjoy, to come before the Lord, and before the angels, and before each other, to witness that we remember that the Lord Jesus Christ has died for us. This proves to the Father that we remember our covenants, that we love his Gospel, that we love to keep his commandments, and to honor the name of the Lord Jesus upon the earth. 6:277.

In the days of ancient Israel, while in the land of Palestine, they were not blessed so profusely as we are with the crystal streams from the mountains. They were in the habit of drinking a great deal of wine, and among the few who have continued to inhabit that land, this habit, I believe, has been kept up to the present time. It is a wine country. But the Lord has said to us it mattered not what we partake of when we administer the cup to the people, inasmuch as we do it with an eye single to the glory of God; it is then acceptable to him. Consequently we use water as though it were wine; for we are commanded to drink not of wine for this sacred purpose except it be made by our own hands. 19:92.

In some of our Wards and settlements the administering of the Sacrament has been introduced in the Sunday schools. It is very pleasing and gratifying to the spirit that I possess, for the parents to see that their children attend Sunday school and receive the proper instruction with regard to their faith. After the Sunday school is over, let the parents take the pains to bring their children to meetings. 19:92.

I will now express a wish in relation to all who may rise here to ask a blessing on the bread and water of the Sacrament, or to preach to such large congregations as assemble here. When the Elders rise here to speak, I want them to raise their voices so that the people can hear them, that the audience may be able to say "Amen" to all the good; and if there is evil, refuse it. When any one rises to preach, pray, sing, exhort, or bless the Sacramental emblems, let him do so with voice sufficient for all to hear. 8:183.

Chapter XV

TITHING; THE UNITED ORDER

The Law of Tithing—One thing is required at the hands of this people, and to understand which there is no necessity for receiving a commandment every year, viz.: to pay their tithing. I do not suppose for a moment, that there is a person in this Church, who is unacquainted with the duty of paying tithing, neither is it necessary to have revelation every year upon the subject. There is the Law—pay one-tenth. 1:278.

I like the term, because it is scriptural, and I would rather use it than any other. The Lord instituted tithing; it was practiced in the days of Abraham, and Enoch and Adam and his children did not forget their tithes and offerings. You can read for yourselves with regard to what the Lord requires. I want to say this much to those who profess to be Latter-day Saints—if we neglect our tithes and offerings we will receive the chastening hand of the Lord. We may just as well count on this first as last. If we neglect to pay our tithes and offerings we will neglect other things and this will grow upon us until the spirit of the Gospel is entirely gone from us, and we are in the dark, and know not whither we are going. 15:163.

If the Lord requires one-tenth of my ability to be devoted to building temples, meetinghouses, schoolhouses, to schooling our children, gathering the poor from the nations of the earth, bringing home the aged, lame, halt and blind, and building houses for them to live in, that they may be comfortable when they reach Zion, and to sustaining the Priesthood, it is not my prerogative to question the authority of the Almighty in this, nor of his servants who have charge of it. If I am required to pay my tithing it is my duty to pay it. In the days of Joseph, when my circumstances were very, very straitened, I never had $500, $100, one dollar, fifty cents or twenty-five cents, but what, if it were wanted, it went as free as a cup of water from a well—Joseph was welcome to it. Was I tried in this? Yes, for many and many has been the time in my poverty, when if I had a dollar or fifty cents in my possession I have thought, "I can buy a pint or a half pint of molasses for my children to sop their bread in," but it was called for, and it went as free as the water of the river here would be to a thirsty person. And as for my time, from the day that I entered this Church until now, I have paid no attention to any business except that of building up this Kingdom. The question may be asked, "Do you not attend to your private affairs and business?" Yes, when I can, but I do not know that I have ever spent one minute in attending to business belonging to Brigham Young, when the business of the Church and Kingdom of God on the earth required his attention. Yet I would not say that this is any excuse for not strictly paying my tithing. I have paid a great deal of tithing, more perhaps than any other man, or any other ten men who were ever in the Church, and yet my tithing is not paid. But I pay tithing, and when the grain upon my farm is ripened, or the cattle upon it are matured, I say to my men, "Be sure and pay the tithing on whatever we have raised." But in some instances I have found that it was neglected. 16:111.

It is very true that the poor pay their tithing better than the rich do. If the rich would pay their tithing we should have plenty. The poor are faithful and prompt in paying their tithing, but the rich can hardly afford to pay theirs—they have too much. If he has only ten dollars he can pay one; if he has only one dollar he can pay ten cents; it does not hurt him at all. If he has a hundred dollars he can possibly pay ten. If he has a thousand dollars he looks over it a little and says, "I guess I will pay it; it ought to be paid anyhow"; and he manages to pay his ten dollars or his hundred dollars. But suppose a man is wealthy enough to pay ten thousand, he looks that over a good many times and says, "I guess I will wait until I get a little more, and then I will pay a good deal." And they wait and wait, like an old gentleman in the East; he waited and waited and waited to pay his tithing until he went out of the world, and this is the way with a great many. They wait and continue waiting, until, finally, the character comes along who is called Death, and he slips up to them and takes away their breath, then they are gone and cannot pay their tithing, they are too late, and so it goes. 15:163-164.

The Saints abroad are required to pay their tithing. 8:182.

When men are Saints, they will bring their thousands and lay them at the feet of the Bishops, Apostles, and Prophets, saying, "Here is my money; it is now where it should be." 6:175.

When a man wishes to give anything, let him give he best he has got. The Lord has given to me all I possess; I have nothing in reality, not a single dime of it is mine. You may ask, "Do you feel as you say?" Yes, I actually do. The coat I have on my back is not mine, and never was; the Lord put it in my possession honorably, and I wear it; but if he wishes for it, and all there is under it, he is welcome to the whole. I do not own a house, or a single farm of land, a horse, mule, carriage, or wagon, or wife, nor child, but what the Lord gave me, and if he wants them, he can take them at his pleasure, whether he speaks for them, or takes them without speaking. 2:307.

When my Bishop came to value my property, he wanted to know what he should take my tithing in. I told him to take anything I had, for I did not set my heart upon any one thing; my horses, cows, hogs, or any other thing he might take; my heart is set upon the work of my God, upon the public good of his great Kingdom. 1:376.

If we live our religion we will be willing to pay tithing. 10:283.

Here is a character—a man—that God has created, organized, fashioned and made,—every part and particle of my system from the top of my head to the soles of my feet, has been produced by my Father in Heaven; and he requires one-tenth part of my brain, heart, nerve, muscle, sinew, flesh, bone, and of my whole system, for the building of temples, for the ministry, for sustaining missionaries and missionaries' families, for feeding the poor, the aged, the halt and blind, and for gathering them home from the nations and taking care of them after they are gathered. He has said, "My son, devote one-tenth of yourself to the good and wholesome work of taking care of your fellow-beings, preaching the Gospel, bringing people into the Kingdom; lay your plans to take care of those who cannot take care of themselves; direct the labors of those who are able to labor; and one-tenth part is all-sufficient if it is devoted properly, carefully and judiciously for the advancement of my Kingdom on the earth." 16:69.

The Lord Has Given All—It is not for me to rise up and say that I can give to the Lord, for in reality I have nothing to give. I seem to have something. Why? Because the Lord has seen fit to bring me forth, and has blessed my efforts in gathering things which are desirable, and which are termed property. 2:300.

We are not our own, we are bought with a price, we are the Lord's; our time, our talents, our gold and silver, our wheat and fine flour, our wine and our oil, our cattle, and all there is on this earth that we have in our possession is the Lord's, and he requires one-tenth of this for the building up of his Kingdom. Whether we have much or little, one-tenth should be paid in for tithing. 14:88.

What object have I in saying to the Latter-day Saints, do this, that or the other? It is for my own benefit, it is for your benefit; it is for my own wealth and happiness, and for your wealth and happiness that we pay tithing and render obedience to any requirement of Heaven. We can not add anything to the Lord by doing these things. Tell about making sacrifices for the Kingdom of heaven. There is no man who ever made a sacrifice on this earth for the Kingdom of heaven, that I know anything about except the Savior. He drank the bitter cup to the dregs, and tasted for every man and for every woman, and redeemed the earth and all things upon it. But he was God in the flesh, or he could not have endured it. "But we suffer, we sacrifice, we give something, we have preached so long." What for? "Why, for the Lord." I would not give the ashes of a rye straw for the man who feels that he is making sacrifice for God. We are doing this for our own happiness, welfare and exaltation, and for nobody else's. This is the fact, and what we do, we do for the salvation of the inhabitants of the earth, not for the salvation of the heavens, the angels, or the Gods. 16:114.

I do not expect to see the day when I am perfectly independent, until I am crowned in the celestial kingdom of my Father, and made as independent as my Father in Heaven. I have not yet received my inheritance as my own, and I expect to be dependent until I do, for all that I have is lent to me. 3:245.

We own nothing but the talents God has given to us to improve upon, to show him what we will do with them. 8:293.

People Not Compelled to Pay Tithing—The people are not compelled to pay their tithing, they do as they please about it, it is urged upon them only as a matter of duty between them and their God. 12:36.

We do not ask anybody to pay tithing, unless they are disposed to do so; but if you pretend to pay tithing, pay it like honest men. 8:202.

Some complain and say that they are taxed by tithing. We ask no tithing of any man. In this we are as independent as the Lord is. I say, do not pay another dollar in tithing unless you want to. 8:345.

Pay your tithing, just because you like to, not unless you want to. They say we cut people off the Church for not paying tithing; we never have yet, but they ought to be. God does not fellowship them. The law of tithing is an eternal law. The Lord Almighty never had his Kingdom on the earth without the law of tithing being in the midst of his people, and he never will. It is an eternal law that God has instituted for the benefit of the human family, for their salvation and exaltation. This law is in the Priesthood, but we do not want any to observe it unless they are willing to do so. 14:89.

Use of Tithing—It may be supposed by some that the tithing is used to sustain and feed the First Presidency and the Twelve; this is a false impression. I can say, without boasting, that there is not another man in this Kingdom has done more in dollars and cents to build it up than I have, and yet I have not done a farthing's worth of myself, for the means I have handled God has given me; it is not mine, and if it ever is mine it will be when I have overcome and gained my exaltation and received it from him who rightfully owns all things. 10:270.

The little moiety that is now paid on tithing is used to bring the poor here, to find them houses to live in, bread to eat, and wood to burn. Now, suppose we had a little more of this surplus on hand, could we not help the brethren on their way to preach the Gospel to the nations? Yes, we could. Some of them will leave families that will, probably, be destitute, and if we had means on hand we could donate to help them, and to prevent them from running continually to the Bishops. 12:36.

The Lord requires one-tenth of that which he has given me; it is for me to pay the one-tenth of the increase of my flocks and of all that I have, and all the people should do the same. The question may arise, "What is to be done with the tithing?" It is for the building of temples to God; for the enlarging of the borders of Zion; sending Elders on missions to preach the Gospel and taking care of their families. By and by we shall have some temples to go into, and we will receive our blessings, the blessings of heaven, by obedience to the doctrine of tithing. We shall have temples built throughout these mountains, in the valleys of this Territory and the valleys of the next Territory, and finally, all through these mountain valleys. We expect to build temples in a great many valleys. We go to the Endowment House, and before going, we get a recommendation from our Bishop that we have paid our tithing. 16:168.

In regard to this whining of the world about Brigham's handling the tithing, I can say that he has put in ten dollars where he has taken one out of the treasury, and he has paid more tithing than any other man in the Church. Everybody should pay their tenth. A poor woman ought to pay her tenth chicken, if she has to draw out ten times its value for her support. It is all the Lord's and we are only his stewards. 16:45.

It is my business to control the disbursements of the tithing paid by the Saints, and not the business of every Elder in the Kingdom who thinks the tithing belongs to him. 8:170.

The United Order—The Lord has declared it to be his will that his people enter into covenant, even as Enoch and his people did, which of necessity must be before we shall have the privilege of building the Center Stake of Zion, for the power and glory of God will be there, and none but the pure in heart will be able to live and enjoy it. 18:263.

When the Lord gave the revelation instructing us in our duty as to consecrating what we have, if the people then could have understood things precisely as they are, and had obeyed that revelation, it would have been neither more nor less than yielding up that which is not their own, to him to whom it belongs. And so it is now. 2:303.

When they bow down to worship the Lord, they acknowledge

that the earth is his, and the cattle upon a thousand hills; and tell the Lord there is no sacrifice they are not willing to make for the sake of the religion of Jesus Christ. The people were crying this continually among the churches when the Book of Mormon came forth, and the Lord spoke through Joseph, revealing the law of consecration, to see whether they were willing to do as they said in their prayers. 2:305.

There is another revelation still prior to this time, stating that it is the duty of all people who go to Zion to consecrate all their property to the Church of Jesus Christ of Latter-day Saints. This revelation was referred to at the April Conference in 1854. It was one of the first commandments or revelations given to this people after they had the privilege of organizing themselves as a Church, as a body, as the Kingdom of God on the earth. I observed then, and I now think, that it will be one of the last revelations which the people will receive into their hearts and understand, of their own free will and choice, and esteem it as a pleasure, a privilege, and a blessing unto them to observe and keep most holy. 2:299.

I have said, and say today, that according to the age of the people we have improved as fast as the church of Enoch. I trust we improve faster, for we have not as much time as they had. In some of the first revelations which were given to this Church, the Order of Enoch was given for a pattern to this people; and Enoch patterned after the heavens. In the commencement of the Church, the Latter-day Saints could not receive it, and they were driven from city to city, as the Lord said they should be, through the mouth of his servant Joseph, until they should be willing to receive this Order. 12:210.

Will the time ever come that we can commence and organize this people as a family? It will. Do we know how? Yes; what was lacking in these revelations from Joseph to enable us to do so was revealed to me. Do you think we will ever be one? When we get home to our Father and God, will we not wish to be in the family? Will it not be our highest ambition and desire to be reckoned as the sons of the living God, as the daughters of the Almighty, with a right to the household, and the faith that belongs to the household, heirs of the Father, his goods, his wealth, his power, his excellency, his knowledge and wisdom? 11:326.

I will say, first, that the Lord Almighty has not the least objection in the world to our entering into the Order of Enoch. I will stand between the people and all harm in this. He has not the least objection to any man, every man, all mankind on the face of the earth turning from evil and loving and serving him with all their hearts. With regard to all those orders that the Lord has revealed, it depends upon the will and doings of the people, and we are at liberty, from this Conference, to go and build up a settlement, or we can join ourselves together in this city, do it legally—according to the laws of the land—and enter into covenant with each other by a firm agreement that we will live as a family, that we will put our property into the hands of a committee of trustees, who shall dictate the affairs of this society. 16:8.

And when this people become one, it will be one in the Lord. They will not look alike. We will not all have grey, blue, or black eyes. Our features will differ one from another, and in our acts, dispositions, and efforts to accumulate, distribute, and dispose of our time, talents, wealth and whatever the Lord gives to us, in our journey through life, we will differ just as much as in our features. The point that the Lord wishes to bring us to is to obey his counsel and observe his word. Then every one will be dictated so that we can act as a family. 12:57.

But to the text. We want to see a community organized in which every person will be industrious, faithful and prudent. What will you do with the children? We will bring them up until they are of legal age, then say, "Go where you please. We have given you a splendid education, the advantage of all the learning of the day, and if you do not wish to stay with the Saints, go where you please." What will you do with those who apostatize after having entered into covenant and agreement with others, that their property shall be one, and be in he hands of trustees, and shall never be taken out? If any of these parties apostatize, and say we wish to withdraw from this community, what will you do with them? We will say to them, "Go, and welcome," and if we are disposed to give them anything, it is all right. 15:226.

I know how to start such a society, right in this city, and how to make its members rich. I would go now, and buy out the poorest Ward in this city, and then commence with men and women who have not a dollar in the world. Bring them here from England, or any part of the earth, set them down in this Ward and put them to work, and in five years we would begin to enter other Wards, and we would buy this house and that house, and the next house, and we would add Ward to Ward until we owned the whole city, every dollar's worth of property there is in it. We could do this, and let the rich go to California to get gold, and we would buy their property. Would you like to know how to do this? I can tell you in a very few words—never want a thing you cannot get, live within your means, manufacture that which you wear, and raise that which you eat. Raise every calf and lamb; raise the chickens, and have your eggs, make your butter and cheese, and always have a little to spare. The first year we raise a crop, and we have more than we want. We buy nothing, we sell a little. The next year we raise more; we buy nothing and we sell more. In this way we could pile up the gold and silver and in twenty years a hundred families working like this could buy out their neighbors. I see men who earn four, five, ten or fifteen dollars a day and spend every dime of it. Such men spend their means foolishly, they waste it instead of taking care of it. They do not know what to do with it, and they seem to fear that it will burn their pockets, and they get rid of it. If you get a dollar, sovereign, half-eagle or eagle, and are afraid it will burn your pockets, put it into a safe. It will not burn anything there, and you will not be forced to spend, spend, spend as you do now. 16:11.

I have looked upon the community of Latter-day Saints in vision and beheld them organized as one great family of heaven, each person performing his several duties in his line of industry, working for the good of the whole more than for individual aggrandizement; and in this I have beheld the most beautiful order that the mind of man can contemplate, and the grandest results for the upbuilding of the Kingdom of God and the spread of righteousness upon the earth. Will this people ever come to this order of things? Are they now prepared to live according to that patriarchal order that will be organized among the true and faithful before God receives his own? We all concede the point that when this mortality falls off, and with it its cares, anxieties, love of self, love of wealth, and love of power, and all the conflicting interests which pertain to this flesh, that then, when our spirits have returned to God who gave them, we will be subject to every requirement that he may make of us, that we shall then live together as one great family; our interest will be a general, a common interest. Why can we not so live in this world? 12:153.

Chapter XVI

THE WORD OF WISDOM

Moderation—By temperance and moderation lay the foundation for the development of the mind. 19:68.

Indulgence of appetite is not worthy the notice of men and women, though the body must be sustained, for that is a duty God has placed upon us. 8:141.

Satisfying the appetite brings to an end the pleasure of eating; and where food is partaken of chiefly to gratify the pleasurable sensation derived from eating, disease is engendered, and true misery springs out of this unwise gratification. Some healthy, strong-constitutioned persons can eat large quantities of food with apparent impunity; but, in so doing, the tax they place upon their systems will ultimately bring disease and death. 8:139.

As I said to the brethren the other day in the Thirteenth Ward schoolhouse, with regard to worldly pleasure, comfort, and enjoyment: you may take as much as you please of the Spirit of the Lord, and it will not make your stomach or head ache. You may drink nine cups of strong spiritual drink, and it will not hurt you; but if you drink nine cups of strong tea, see what it will do for you. Let a person that is very thirsty and warm satiate his appetite with cold water, and when he gets through he will perhaps have laid the foundation for death, and may go to an untimely grave, which is frequently done. Excessive eating, drinking, or exercise all tend to the grave. 11:329.

The blessings of food, sleep, and social enjoyment are ordained of God for his glory and our benefit, and it is for us to learn to use them and not abuse them, that his Kingdom may advance on the earth, and we advance in it. 6:149.

The Word of Wisdom—This Word of Wisdom prohibits the use of hot drinks and tobacco. I have heard it argued that tea and coffee are not mentioned therein; that is very true; but what were the people in the habit of taking as hot drinks when the revelation was given? Tea and coffee. We were not in the habit of drinking water very hot, but tea and coffee—the beverages in common use. And the Lord said hot drinks are not good for the body nor the belly, liquor is not good for the body nor the belly, but for the washing of the body, etc. Tobacco is not good, save for sick cattle, and for bruises and sores, its cleansing properties being then very useful. 13:277.

I know that some say the revelations upon these points are not given by way of commandment. Very well, but we are commanded to observe every word that proceeds from the mouth of God. 13:3.

Now I want you should recollect—Bishops, Elders of Israel, High Priests, Seventies, the Twelve Apostles, the First Presidency, and all the House of Israel, hearken ye, O my people! keep the word of the Lord, observe the Word of Wisdom, sustain one another, sustain the household of faith, and let our enemies alone. 12:29.

Now, Elders of Israel, if you have the right to chew tobacco, you have a privilege I have not; if you have a right to drink whiskey, you have a right that I have not; if you have a right to transgress the Word of Wisdom, you have a right that I have not. 12:30.

I said to the Saints at our last annual Conference, the Spirit whispers to me to call upon the Latter-day Saints to observe the Word of Wisdom, to let tea, coffee, and tobacco alone, and to abstain from drinking spirituous drinks. This is what the Spirit signifies through me. If the Spirit of God whispers this to his people through their leader, and they will not listen nor obey, what will be the consequences of their disobedience? Darkness and blindness of mind with regard to the things of God will be their lot; they will cease to have the spirit of prayer, and the spirit of the world will increase in them in proportion to their disobedience until they apostatize entirely from God and his ways. 12:118.

In the name of the Lord Jesus Christ, I command the Elders of Israel—those who have been in the habit of getting drunk—to cease drinking strong drink from this time henceforth. But some may think they need it as soon as they go out of this house. Let me be your physician in this matter. So long as you are able to walk and attend to your business, it is folly to say that you need ardent spirits to keep you alive. The constitution that a person has should be nourished and cherished; and whenever we take anything into the system to force and stimulate it beyond its natural capacity, it shortens life. I am physician enough to know that. When you are tired and think you need a little spirituous liquor, take some bread and butter or bread and milk, and lie down and rest. Do not labor so hard as to deem it requisite to get half drunk in order to keep up your spirits. If you will follow this counsel, you will be full of life and health, and you will increase your intelligence, your joy, and comfort. 7:337.

I now again request the authorities of this Church in their various localities to sever from this society those who will not cease getting drunk. 7:338.

It is my positive counsel and command that drinking liquor be stopped. If I had the influence the world gives me credit for, I would not have a single drunkard, thief, or liar in this society. I do not profess to have that influence, but I can raise my voice against those evils. 1:337.

This Word of Wisdom which has been supposed to have become stale, and not in force, is like all the counsels of God, in force as much today as it ever was. There is life, everlasting life in it—the life which now is and the life which is to come. 12:209.

It is a piece of good counsel which the Lord desires his people to observe, that they may live on the earth until the measure of their creation is full. This is the object the Lord had in view in giving that Word of Wisdom. To those who observe it he will give great wisdom and understanding, increasing their health, giving strength and endurance to the faculties of their bodies and minds until they shall be full of years upon the earth. This will be their blessing if they will observe his word with a good and willing heart and in faithfulness before the Lord. 12:156.

Mankind would not become attached to these unnecessary articles were it not for the poison they contain. The poisonous or narcotic properties in spirits, tobacco and tea are the cause of their being so much liked by those who use them. 13:276.

I say to all the Elders of Israel, if it makes you sick and so sleepy that you cannot keep out of bed unless you have tobacco, go to bed and there lie. How long? Until you can get up and go to your business like rational men, like men who have heads on their shoulders and who are not controlled by their foolish appetites. I have said to my family, and I now say to all the sisters in the Church, if you cannot get up and do your washing without a cup of tea in the morning, go to bed, and there lie. How long? Until the influence of tea is out of the system. Will it take a month? No matter if it does; if it takes three months, six months, or a year, it is better to lie there in bed until the influence of tea, coffee and liquor is out of the system, so that you may go about your business like rational persons, than to give way to these foolish habits. They are destructive to the human system; they filch money from our pockets, and they deprive the poor of the necessaries of life. 13:278.

The sisters may inquire, "What can we do?" Rule your own passions, and exercise faith until you can govern and control your appetites, instead of drinking tea, coffee, and hot drinks. That is one of the smallest duties I can think of. Permit your bodies to have natural forms; also take pains to have the bodies of your daughters grow naturally, and teach them what they are made for, and that they, through faith, must overcome every besetting sin and every unholy passion and appetite. 8:283.

And now that we have commenced to observe the Word of

Wisdom, never treat resolution with a cup of tea or coffee, for as sure as you treat resolution once, it will plead hard for a treat again. Keep the Word of Wisdom—help the poor, feed the hungry, and clothe the naked. Never let it be said of the Territory of Utah that a poor person had to go to the second house for a morsel to eat. 12:54-55.

Many of our sisters thing they cannot live without tea. I will tell you what we can do—I have frequently said it to my brethren and sisters—if they cannot live without tea, coffee, brandy, whisky, wine, beer, tobacco, etc., they can die without them. This is beyond controversy. If we had the determination that we should have, we would live without them or die without them. Let the mother impregnate her system with these narcotic influences when she is bringing forth a family on the earth, and what does she do? She lays the foundation of weakness, palpitation of the heart, nervous affections, and many other ills and diseases in the system of her offspring that will afflict them from the cradle to the grave. Is this righteous or unrighteous, good or evil? Let my sisters ask and answer the question for themselves, and the conclusion which each and every one of them may come to is this, "If I do an injury to my child, I sin." 13:276.

Last week I received a note in which was enclosed three dollars from a sister; I cannot tell her name, for she did not give it. She said she had not drunk any tea since Conference, and she had saved about three dollars, which she enclosed for me to do good with. I felt "God bless her," and she will be blessed as sure as she lives. 12:52.

If you observe faithfully the Word of Wisdom, you will have your dollar, your five dollars, your hundred dollars, yea, you will have your hundreds of dollars to spend for that which will be useful and profitable to you. Why should we continue to practice in our lives those pernicious habits that have already sapped the foundation of the human constitution, and shortened the life of man to that degree that a generation passes away in the brief period of from twenty-seven to twenty-nine years? The strength, power, beauty and glory that once adorned that form and constitution of man have vanished away before the blighting influences of inordinate appetite and love of this world. The health and power and beauty that once adorned the noble form of man must again be restored to our race; and God designs that we shall engage in this great work of restoration. Then let us not trifle with our mission, by indulging in the use of injurious substances. These lay the foundation of disease and death in the systems of men, and the same are committed to their children, and another generation of feeble human beings is introduced into the world. Such children have insufficient bone, sinew, muscle, and constitution, and are of little use to themselves, or to their fellow creatures; they are not prepared for life. 12:118.

A man who indulges in any habit that is pernicious to the general good in its example and influence, is not only an enemy to himself but to the community so far as the influence of that habit goes. A man who would not sacrifice a pernicious habit for the good it would do the community is, to say the least of it, lukewarm in his desires and wishes for public and general improvement.

So we see that almost the very first teachings the first Elders of this Church received were as to what to eat, what to drink, and how to order their natural lives that they might be united temporarily as well as spiritually. This is the great purpose which God has in view in sending to the world, by his servants, the Gospel of life and salvation. 12:158.

There is more strength and nutriment in a bowl of water gruel than there is in tea; and there is no unhealthy influence in the water gruel, but there is in tea and coffee. 11:350.

Live Long—Take care of yourselves, and live as long as you can, and do all the good you can. 4:302.

The first principle that pertains to the intelligence God has bestowed upon us is to know how to preserve the present organization with which we are endowed. It is man's first duty to his existence, a knowledge of which would cause him to use all prudent efforts for the preservation of his life on the earth until his work here is completed. 8:281.

Prepare to die, is not the exhortation in this Church and Kingdom; but prepare to live is the word with us, and improve all we can in the life hereafter, wherein we may enjoy a more exalted condition of intelligence, wisdom, light, knowledge, power, glory, and exaltation. Then let us seek to extend the present life to the uttermost, by observing every law of health, and by properly balancing labor, study, rest, and recreation, and thus prepare for a better life. Let us teach these principles to our children, that, in the morning of their days, they may be taught to lay the foundation of health and strength and constitution and power of life in their bodies. 11:132.

This is the duty of the human family, instead of wasting their lives and the lives of their fellow-beings, and the precious time God has given us to improve our minds and bodies by observing the laws of life, so that the longevity of the human family may begin to return. By and by, according to the Scriptures, the days of a man shall be like the days of a tree. But in those days people will not eat and drink as they do now; if they do their days will not be like a tree, unless it be a very short-lived tree. This is our business. 14:89.

We are trying to become natural in our habits, and are striving to fulfil the end and design of our creation. 13:233.

The fathers and mothers have laid the foundation for many of these diseases, from generation to generation, until the people are reduced to their present condition. True, some live to from fifty to ninety years of age, but it is an unusual circumstance to see a man an hundred years old, or a woman ninety. The people have laid the foundation of short life through their diet, their rest, their labor, and their doing this, that, and the other in a wrong manner, with improper motives, and at improper times. 2:269.

You, mothers and daughters in Israel, who are taking this course, how do you expect to live to accomplish the work the Lord has assigned you? You get up in the morning and have your cup of tea, your fried ham, your cold beef and mince pies, and everything you can possibly cram into the stomach, until you surfeit the system and lay the foundation for disease and earthly death. Says the mother—"Do eat, my little daughter, you are sick; take a piece of pie, toast, or meat, or drink a little tea or coffee; you must take something or other." Mothers in Israel, such a course engenders disease, and you are laying a foundation that will cut off one-half or two-thirds of the lives of your children. 12:37.

Eating for Health—Instead of doing two days' work in one day, wisdom would dictate to our sisters, and to every other person, that if they desire long life and good health, they must, after sufficient exertion, allow the body to rest before it is entirely exhausted. When exhausted, some argue that they need stimulants in the shape of tea, coffee, spirituous liquors, tobacco, or some of those narcotic substances which are often taken to goad on the lagging powers to greater exertions. But instead of these kinds of stimulants they should recruit by rest. Work less, wear less, eat less, and we shall be a great deal wiser, healthier, and wealthier people than by taking the course we now do. It is difficult to find anything more healthy to drink than good cold water, such as flows down to us from springs and snows of our mountains. This is the beverage we should drink. It should be our drink at all times. If we constantly drink even malt liquor made from our barley and wheat, our health would be injured more or less thereby. It may be remarked that some men who use spirituous liquors and tobacco are healthy, but I argue that they would be much more healthy if they did not use it, and then they are entitled to the blessings promised to those who observe the advice given in the "Word of Wisdom." Some few persons who have been addicted to the use of hot drinks, etc., have reached the age of eighty, eighty-three, and eighty-four years, but had they not been addicted to such habits of living they might have reached the age of an hundred or an hundred and five years. 12:122.

I do not mean to go without food and go to fasting. This is the other extreme. A sufficient amount of food that will agree with the stomach is healthy, and should be partaken of. Aged or middle-aged, youth or children, never should go without food until their stomachs are faint, demanding something to sustain their systems, and continue to undergo this; for this lays the foundation of weakness, and this weakness will tempt disease. But keep the stomach in perfectly healthy condition. Now I do not mean fasting, but eating moderately; and if my sisters will go home and commence to adopt this rule, you will find that you begin to get better, your children and neighbors will get better. We do not expect all to be free from sickness. I have had a great deal of sickness in my life. I do not expect to be free from ills, the weakness, debility and disease that prey upon the human family, but we can amend our ways, and amend our life by being prudent; and I wish the sisters to understand this, and to adopt these instructions. 19:68.

The citizens of this city are tolerably comfortable; a great many of them have an abundance of fruit, and they enjoy it. It is very healthy for them and their children to eat in the season thereof. 11:141.

As we got richer and built warm houses, and have lived more richly, indulging in sweet cake, plum pudding, roast beef and so on, we have had more or less disease among us. 13:142.

Go into their houses and you will find beef, pork, apple pie, custard pie, pumpkin pie, mince pie, and every luxury, and they live so as to shorten their days and the days of their children. You may think that these things are not of much importance; no more they are, unless they are observed, but let the people observe them and they lay the foundation for longevity, and they will begin to live out their days, not only a hundred years, but, by and by, hundreds of years on the earth. Do you think they will stuff themselves then with tea and coffee, and perhaps with a little brandy sling before breakfast and a little before going to bed, and then beef, pork, mutton, sweet meats, and pastry, morning, noon and night? No; you will find they will live as our first parents did, on fruits and on a little simple food, and they will never overload the stomach. 12:37.

Suppose I happen to say, "Come, wife, let us have a good dinner today;" what does she get? Pork and beef boiled, stewed, roasted, and fried potatoes, onions, cabbage and turnips, custard, eggs, pies of all kinds, cheese and sweet meats. 2:269.

A thorough reformation is needed in regard to our eating and drinking, and on this point I will freely express myself, and shall be glad if the people will hear, believe and obey. If the people were willing to receive the true knowledge from heaven in regard to their diet they would cease eating swine's flesh. I know this as well as Moses knew it, and without putting it in a code of commandments. The beef fed upon our mountain grasses is as healthy food as we need at present. Beef, so fattened, is as good as wild meat, and is quite different in its nature from stall-fed meat. But we can eat fish; and I ask the people of this community, Who hinders you from raising fowls for their eggs? Who hinders you from cultivating fruit of every variety that will flourish in the different parts of this Territory? There has not been a day through the whole winter that I have not had fresh peaches, and plenty of apples and strawberries. Who hinders any person in this community from having these different kinds of food in their families? Fish is as healthy a food as we can eat, if we except vegetables and fruit, and with them will become a very wholesome diet. 12:192.

When we go on a trip to the settlements and stop at the brethren's houses, it is, "Brother Brigham, let us manifest our feelings towards you and your company." I tell them to do so, but give me a piece of Johnny-cake; I would rather have it than their pies and tarts and sweet meats. Let me have something that will sustain nature and leave my stomach and whole system clear to receive the Spirit of the Lord and be free from headache and pains of every kind.

The Americans, as a nation, are killing themselves with their vices and high living. As much as a man ought to eat in half an hour they swallow in three minutes, gulping down their food like the canine quadruped under the table, which, when a chunk of meat is thrown down to it, swallows it before you can say "twice." If you want a reform, carry out the advice I have just given you. Dispense with your multitudinous dishes, and, depend upon it, you will do much towards preserving your families from sickness, disease and death.

If this method were adopted in this community, I will venture to say that it would add ten years to the lives of our children. That is worth a great deal. 13:153-154.

If the days of man are to begin to return, we must cease all extravagant living. When men live to the age of a tree, their food will be fruit. Mothers, to produce offspring full of life and days, must cease drinking liquor, tea, and coffee, that their systems may be free from bad effects. If every woman in this Church will now cease drinking tea, coffee, liquor, and all other powerful stimulants, and live upon vegetables, etc., not many generations will pass away before the days of man will again return. But it will take generations to eradicate entirely the influences of deleterious substances. 8:63.

Living out-of-Doors—People need not be afraid of living out-of-doors, nor sleeping out-of-doors. This country is much healthier than the lowlands in the States, or than many places in the Old World. 4:92.

Good pure air is the greatest sustainer of animal life. Other elements of life we can dispense with for a time, but this seems to be essential every moment; hence the necessity of well-ventilated dwelling-houses, especially the rooms occupied for sleeping. You can live without water and food longer than you can without air, and water is of more importance than meat and bread. 8:168.

The out-door air is what the people need for health, it is good for them to camp out. Close houses are injurious to the health; if our houses were every one of them levelled to the ground, and we were obliged to live in our wagons and tents, the people would be healthier, from year to year, than they are now. Good houses are comfortable and very convenient, and please our feelings, and are tolerably healthful when properly ventilated. 2:284.

What gives the people colds and makes them sick? You hear many say, "I had not had a cold this fall until I came into our new house." Brethren and sisters that have come into the city from living in the canyons, and those who have arrived from the States this season, have not been troubled with colds until they came into warm houses; that gives them colds, by depriving their lungs of the benefit they are organized to receive from the atmosphere. 4:91.

We should have plenty of pure, fresh air. If children are kept in close bedrooms, they become puny and weakly. Let them sleep where they can have abundance of pure air, in well-ventilated rooms, or out-of-doors, in the summer time, in a safe place; it will be most beneficial for their health. 12:218.

Exercise and Mental Vigor—Do you know that it is your privilege so to live that your minds may all the time be perfectly within your control? Study to preserve your bodies in life and health, and you will be able to control your minds. 8:135.

My mind becomes tired, and perhaps some of yours do. If so, go and exercise your bodies. 6:148.

In the eastern country there was a man who used to go crazy, at times, and then come to his senses again. One of his neighbors asked him what made him go crazy; he replied, "I get to thinking, and thinking, until finally I think so far that I am not always able to think back again." Can you think too much for the spirit which is put in the tabernacle? You can, and this is a subject which I wish the brethren instructed upon, and the people to understand. The spirit is the intelligent part of man, and is intimately connected with the tabernacle. Let this intelligent part labor to excess, and it will eventually overcome the tabernacle, the equilibrium will be destroyed, and the whole organization deranged. Many people have deranged themselves by thinking too much.

The thinking part is the immortal or invisible portion, and it is that which performs the mental labor; then the tabernacle, which is formed and organized for that express purpose, brings about or effects the result of that mental labor. Let the body work with the mind, and let them both labor fairly together, and, with but few exceptions, you will have a strong-minded, athletic individual, powerful both physically and mentally.

When you find the thinking faculty perfectly active, in a healthy person, it should put the physical organization into active operation, and the result of the reflection is carried out, and the object is accomplished. In such a person you will see mental and physical health and strength combined, in their perfection. 3:247.

As for health, it is far healthier to walk than to ride, and better every way for the people. 4:103.

Many persons are so constituted, that if you put them in a parlor, keep a good fire for them, furnish them tea, cake, sweet meats, etc., and nurse them tenderly, soaking their feet, and putting them to bed, they will die in a short time; but throw them into snow banks, and they will live a great many years. Brother Heywood would have been in his grave long ago, if he had not led an out-door life, and such is the case with others; but he is again here, and we have the privilege of seeing him. 4:295.

Physiological Differences—The study and practice of anatomy and surgery are very good; they are mechanical, and are frequently needed. Do you not think it is necessary to give medicine sometimes? Yes, I can see the faces of this congregation, but I do not see two alike; and if I could look into your nervous systems and behold the operations of disease, from the crowns of your heads to the soles of your feet, I should behold the same difference that I see in your physiognomy—there would be no two precisely alike. Doctors make experiments, and if they find a medicine that will have the desired effect on one person, they set it down that it is good for everybody, but it is not so, for upon the second person that medicine is administered to, seemingly with the same disease, it might produce death. If you do not know this, you have not had the experience that I have. I say that unless a man or woman who administers medicine to assist the human system to overcome disease, understands, and has that intuitive knowledge, by the Spirit, that such an article is good for that individual at that very time, they had better let him alone. Let the sick do without eating, take a little of something to cleanse the stomach, bowels and blood, and wait patiently, and let nature have time to gain the advantage over the disease. 15:225.

Feeding Children—Now, mothers, if you want to do good, do not let your sons and daughters drink either tea of coffee, while under your protection. 11:352.

Some mothers, when bearing children, long for tea and coffee, or for brandy and other strong drinks, and if they give way to that influence the next time they will want more, and the next still more, and thus lay the foundation for drunkenness in their offspring. An appetite is engendered, bred, and born in the child, and it is a miracle if it does not grow up a confirmed drunkard. 2:270.

Infants, children, youth, young men, and young women, thousands and tens of thousands of them, go to an untimely grave through the diseases engendered in their systems by their progenitors. 13:276.

Sisters, will you take notice, and instruct those who are not here today, to adopt this rule—stop your children from eating meat, and especially fat meat; let them have composition* to drink, instead of unhealthy water; let them eat a little more porridge; let them eat sparingly and not oppress the stomach so as to create a fever. No matter whether it is a child or a middle-aged person, whenever the stomach is over-loaded and charged with more than is required it creates a fever; this fever creates sickness, until death relieves the sufferer. 19:68.

Many husbands are made sick and many children are sent to an untimely grave through eating badly prepared food, the result of ignorance or carelessness. 10:28.

Children should have milk, bread, water, and potatoes; and everything that would lay the foundation for disease should be strenuously kept from their stomachs, that no appetites may be formed for pernicious substances, which, when formed, cannot be overcome easily, if at all. 2:21.

I will tell you how you can enjoy health. You let your children have a little milk in the morning. Give them a little bread with it—not soft bread, teach your children to eat crust—hard-baked bread, that the Americans would call stale, but the English would not. Teach them to eat this, and to eat sparingly. Instead of drinking unhealthy water, boil such water, and let it stand until it is cool. If the children are in the least troubled with summer complaint, and are weak in their bowels, make a weak composition tea, sweeten it

***Define Composition.**

with loaf sugar and put a little nice cream in it; and let the children make a practice of drinking composition instead of cold water. Mothers, keep the children from eating meat; and let them eat vegetables that are fully matured, not unripe, and bread that is well-baked, not soft. Do not put your loaf into the oven with a fire hot enough to burn it before it is baked through, but with a slow heat, and let it remain until it is perfectly baked; and I would prefer, for my own eating, each and every loaf to be not thicker than my two hands—you tell how thick they are—and I would want the crust as thick as my hand. 19:67.

Be careful of your bodies; be prudent in laying out your energies, for when you are old you will need the strength and power you are now wasting. Preserve your lives. Until you know and practice this, you are not thoroughly good soldiers nor wise stewards. 8:136-137.

CHAPTER XVII

THE FAMILY

Virtue—Purity preserves, sustains and increases. 16:108.

The principle of pure affection is the gift of God, and it is for us to learn to control it and exercise proper dominion over it. 6:149.

Learn the will of God, keep his commandments and do his will, and you will be a virtuous person. 3:204.

Any man who humbles a daughter of Eve to rob her of her virtue, and cast her off dishonored and defiled, is her destroyer, and is responsible to God for the deed. If the refined Christian society of the nineteenth century will tolerate such a crime, God will not; but he will call the perpetrator to an account. He will be damned; in hell he will lift up his eyes, being in torment, until he has paid the uttermost farthing, and made a full atonement for his sins. 11:268.

The defiler of the innocent is the one who should be branded with infamy and cast out from respectable society, and shunned as a pest, or, as a contagious disease, is shunned. The doors of respectable families should be closed against him, and he should be frowned upon by all high-minded and virtuous persons. Wealth, influence and position should not screen him from their righteous indignation. His sin is one of the blackest in the calendar of crime, and he should be cast down from the high pinnacle of responsibility and consideration, to find his place among the worst of felons. 11:267.

I would rather follow her to the grave, and send her home pure, than suffer my daughter to be prostituted. I will not suffer any female member of my family to be polluted through the corruptions of wicked men. 2:322.

Ever since I knew that my mother was a woman I loved the sex, and delighted in their chastity. The man who abuses, or tries to bring dishonor upon the female sex is a fool, and does not know that his mother and his sisters were women. 12:194.

Marriage—Let every man in the land over eighteen years of age take a wife, and then go to work with your hands and cultivate the earth, or labor at some mechanical business, or some honest trade to provide an honest living for yourselves and those who depend upon you for their subsistence; observing temperance, and loving truth and virtue; then would the woman be cared for, be nourished, honored and blest, becoming honorable mothers of a race of men and women farther advanced in physical and mental perfection than their fathers. This would create a revolution in our country, and would produce results that would be of incalculable good. 12:194-195.

Young men, fit you up a little log cabin, if it is not more than ten feet square, and then get you a bird to put in your little cage. You can then work all day with satisfaction to yourself considering that you have a home to go to, and a loving heart to welcome you. You will then have something to encourage you to labor and gather around you the comforts of life, and a place to gather them to. Strive to make your little home attractive. Use lime freely, and let your houses nestle beneath the cool shades of trees, and be made fragrant with perfume of flowers. 12:204.

The Lord says—Let my servants and handmaidens be sealed, and let their children be sealed. 12:164.

We understand that we are to be made kings and priests unto God; now if I be made the king and lawgiver to my family, and if I have many sons, I shall become the father of many fathers, for they will have sons, and their sons will have sons, and so on, from generation to generation, and, in this way, I may become the father of many fathers, or the king of many kings. This will constitute every man a prince, king, lord, or whatever the Father sees fit to confer upon us.

In this way we can become king of kings, and lord of lords, or father of fathers, or prince of princes, and this is the only course, for another man is not going to raise up a kingdom for you. 3:265-266.

But the whole subject of the marriage relation is not in my reach, nor in any other man's reach on this earth. It is without beginning of days or end of years; it is a hard matter to reach. We can tell some things with regard to it; it lays the foundation for worlds, for angels, and for the Gods; for intelligent beings to be crowned with glory, immortality, and eternal lives. In fact, it is the thread which runs from the beginning to the end of the holy Gospel of Salvation—of the Gospel of the Son of God; it is from eternity to eternity. 2:90.

When a man and woman have received their endowments and sealings,* and then had children born to them afterwards, those children are legal heirs to the Kingdom and to all its blessings and promises, and they are the only ones that are on this earth. There is not a young man in our community who would not be willing to travel from here to England to be married right, if he understood things as they are; there is not a young woman in our community, who loves the Gospel and wishes its blessings, that would be married in any other way; they would live unmarried until they could be married as they should be, if they lived until they were as old as Sarah before she had Isaac born to her. Many of our brethren have married off their children without taking this into consideration, and

*In the Temple—For Eternity.

thinking it a matter of little importance. I wish we all understood this in the light in which heaven understands it. 11:118.

Our children who are born in the Priesthood are legal heirs, and entitled to the revelations of the Lord, and as the Lord lives, his angels have charge over them, though they may be left to themselves occasionally. 12:174.

There is no ecclesiastical law that you know anything about, to free a wife from a man to whom she has been sealed, if he honors his Priesthood. 8:345.

I will give each of the young men in Israel, who have arrived at an age to marry, a mission to go straightway and get married to a good sister, fence a city lot, lay out a garden and orchard and make a home. This is the mission that I give to all young men in Israel. And I say to you, sisters, if you do not know how to milk a cow, you can soon learn. If you do not know how to feed the cows, you can learn. If you do not know how to feed the chickens, get them and learn how, and if your husband takes you to live in ever so small and humble a cottage, make it neat and nice and clean, and set out flowers around the doors, and let the husband plant fruit trees and shade trees, and let wives help their husbands that they may be encouraged to take hold of more important business that will create an income sufficient to sustain their wives, and by economy and care become wealthy in a short time, and have your carriage to ride in. What a satisfaction it will be to you to know that what you possess is the result of your industry and economy. 12:200-201.

Do Not Marry Unbelievers—Be careful, O ye mothers in Israel, and do not teach your daughters in future, as many of them have been taught, to marry out of Israel. Woe to you who do it; you will lose your crowns as sure as God lives. 12:97.

What was the cause of the first, or one of the first, curses that came upon Israel? I will tell you. One of the first transgressions of the family called Israel, was their going to other families or other nations to select partners. This was one of the great mistakes made by the children of Abraham, Isaac and Jacob, for they would go and marry with other families, although the Lord had forbidden them to do so, and had given them a very strict and stringent law on the subject. He commanded them not to marry among the Gentiles, but they did and would do it. Inasmuch as they would not do what he required of them, then he gave them what I call a portion of the law of carnal commandments. This law told them what they might and whom they might not marry. It was referred to by the Savior and his Apostles and it was a grievous yoke to place on the necks of any people; but as the children of this family would run after Babylon, and after the pride and the vanity and evils of the world, and seek to introduce them into Israel, the Lord saw fit to place this burden upon them. 16:111.

How is it with you, sisters? Do you distinguish between a man of God and a man of the world? It is one of the strangest things that happens in my existence, to think that any man or woman can love a being that will not receive the truth of heaven. The love this Gospel produces is far above the love of women; it is the love of God—the love of eternity—of eternal lives. 8:199-200.

Birth Control—There are multitudes of pure and holy spirits waiting to take tabernacles, now what is our duty?—To prepare tabernacles for them; to take a course that will not tend to drive those spirits into the families of the wicked, where they will be trained in wickedness, debauchery, and every species of crime. It is the duty of every righteous man and woman to prepare tabernacles for all the spirits they can. 4:56.

This is the reason why the doctrine of plurality of wives was revealed, that the noble spirits which are waiting for tabernacles might be brought forth. 4:56.

To check the increase of our race has its advocates among the influential and powerful circles of society in our nation and in other nations. The same practice existed forty-five years ago, and various devices were used by married persons to prevent the expenses and responsibilities of a family of children, which they must have incurred had they suffered nature's laws to rule pre-eminent. That which was practiced then in fear and against reproving conscience, is now boldly trumpeted abroad as one of the best means of ameliorating the miseries and sorrows of humanity. Infanticide is very prevalent in our nation. It is a crime that comes within the purview of the law, and is therefore not so boldly practiced as is the other equally great crime, which, no doubt, to a great extent, prevents the necessity of infanticide. The unnatural style of living, the extensive use of narcotics, the attempts to destroy and dry up the fountains of life, are fast destroying the American element of the nation; it is passing away before the increase of the more healthy, robust, honest, and less sinful class of the people which are pouring into the country daily from the Old World. The wife of the servant man is the mother of eight or ten healthy children, while the wife of his master is the mother of one or two poor, sickly children, devoid of vitality and constitution, and, if daughters, unfit, in their turn, to be mothers, and the health and vitality which nature has denied them through irregularities of their parents are not repaired in the least by their education. 12:120-121.

The Husband—Let the father be the head of the family, the

master of his own houshold; and let him treat them as an angel would treat them; and let the wives and the children say amen to what he says, and be subject to his dictates, instead of their dictating the man, instead of their trying to govern him. 4:55.

Now let me say to the First Presidency, to the Apostles, to all the Bishops in Israel, and to every quorum, and especially to those who are presiding officers, Set that example before your wives and your children, before your neighbors and this people, that you can say: "Follow me, as I follow Christ." When we do this, all is right, and our consciences are clear. 15:229.

I exhort you, masters, fathers, and husbands, to be affectionate and kind to those you preside over. And let them be obedient, let the wife be subject to her husband, and the children to their parents. Mothers, let your minds be sanctified before the Lord, for this is the commencement, the true foundation of a proper education in your children, the beginning point to form a disposition in your offspring, that will bring honor, glory, comfort, and satisfaction to you all your lifetime. 1:69.

Let the husband and father learn to bend his will to the will of his God, and then instruct his wives and children in this lesson of self-government by his example as well as by precept, and his neighbors also, showing them how to be brave and steadfast, in subduing the rebellious and sinful disposition. Such a course as this will eventually subdue that unhallowed influence which works upon the human heart. 9:256.

It is for the husband to learn how to gather around his family the comforts of life, how to control his passions and temper, and how to command the respect, not only of his family but of all his brethren, sisters, and friends. It is the calling of the wife and mother to know what to do with everything that is brought into the house, laboring to make her home desirable to her husband and children, making herself an Eve in the midst of a little paradise of her own creating, securing her husband's love and confidence, and tying her offspring to herself, with a love that is stronger than death, for an everlasting inheritance. 10:28.

Let the husband make an improvement upon his kitchen and pantry and upon his bedrooms for the benefit of his family, and improve his gardens, walks, etc., beautifying your habitations and their surroundings, making pavements and planting shade trees. 10:177.

I have been into houses which have not had the least convenience for the women, not so much as a bench to set their water pails on, and they have to set them on the floor, and yet their husbands will sit there year after year, and never make so much improvement as a bench to set the pail on. Yet they have the ability, but they will not exercise it. 18:75.

The father should be full of kindness, and endeavor to happify and cheer the mother, that her heart may be comforted and her affections unimpaired in her earthly protector, that her love for God and righteousness may vibrate throughout her whole being, that she may bear and bring forth offspring impressed and endowed with all the qualities necessary to a being designed to reign king of kings and lord of lords. 8:62.

The Wife—You cannot read in the Bible that women take the lead—that the responsibility is upon the women, for it is not so. 9:143.

One thing is very true and we believe it, and that is that a woman is the glory of the man; but she was not made to be worshiped by him. As the Scriptures say, Man is not without the woman, neither is woman without the man in the Lord. Yet woman was not made to be worshiped anymore than was man. Woman has her influence, and she should use that in training her children in the way they should go; if she fails to do this she assumes fearful responsibilities. 14:106.

I have a word to say to my sisters. When I reflect upon the duties and responsibilities devolving upon our mothers and sisters, and the influence they wield, I look upon them as the mainspring and soul of our being here. It is true that man is first. Father Adam was placed here as king of the earth, to bring it into subjection. But when Mother Eve came she had a splendid influence over him. A great many have thought it was not very good; I think it was excellent.

Now, I say the women have great influence. Look at the nations of the earth. Any nation you like, no matter which, and you enlist the sympathies of the female portion of it and what is there you cannot perform? If the government wants soldiers, they are on hand; if means, it is forthcoming. If you want influence and power, and have the ladies on your side, they will give it you. 14:102.

Now, a few words directly to my sisters here in the Kingdom of God. We want your influence and power in helping to build up that Kingdom and what I wish to say to you is simply this, if you will govern and control yourselves in all things in accordance with good, sound, common sense and the principles of truth and righteousness, there is not the least fear but what father, uncle, grandfather, brothers, and sons will follow in the wake. 14:102.

You ought to love a woman only so far as she adorns the doctrine you profess. 3:360.

The mothers are the moving instruments in the hands of Providence to guide the destinies of nations. Let the mothers of any nation teach their children not to make war, the children would grow up and never enter into it. Let the mothers teach their children, "War, war upon your enemies, yes, war to the hilt!" and they will be filled with this spirit. Consequently, you see at once what I wish to impress upon your minds is, that the mothers are the machinery that gives zest to the whole man, and guide the destinies and lives of men upon the earth. 19:72.

It is the right of the mother who labors in the kitchen, with her little prattling children around, to enjoy the Spirit of Christ, and to know her duty with regard to those children; but it is not her duty and privilege to dictate to her husband in his duties and business. If that mother or wife enjoys the gift and power of the Holy Ghost, she will never intrude upon the rights of her husband. It is the right and privilege of the husband to know his duty with regard to his wives and children, his flocks and his herds, his fields and his possessions; though I have seen women who, I thought, actually knew more about the business of life than their husbands themselves did, and were really more capable of directing a farm, the building of a house, and the management of flocks and herds, etc., than the men were; but if men were to live up to their privileges this would not be the case; for it is their right to claim the light of truth and that intelligence and knowledge necessary to enable them to carry on every branch of their business successfully. 11:135.

Study order and cleanliness in your various occupations. Adorn your city and neighborhood. Make your homes lovely, and adorn your hearts with the grace of God. 8:297.

You may say that it is hard work to please a man; yes, and woman too. But when a man does his duty in providing for a family, there can reasonably be but little complaint on the part of any sensible woman. 4:314.

Many of the sisters grieve because they are not blessed with offspring. You will see the time when you will have millions of children around you. If you are faithful to your covenants, you will be mothers of nations. 8:208.

It is your right, wives, to ask your husbands to set out beautiful shade and fruit trees, and to get you some vines and flowers with which to adorn the outside of your dwellings; and if your husbands have not time, get them yourselves and plant them out. Some perhaps, will say, "Oh, I have nothing but a log house, and it is not worth that." Yes; it is worth it. Whitewash and plaster it up, and get vines to run over the door, so that everybody who passes will say, "What a lovely little cottage!" This is your privilege and I wish you to exercise yourselves in your own rights. 14:105.

It is not my general practice to counsel the sisters to disobey their husbands, but my counsel is—obey your husbands; and I am sanguine and most emphatic on that subject. But I never counselled a woman to follow her husband to the Devil. If a man is determined to expose the lives of his friends, let that man go to the Devil and to destruction alone. 1:77.

A few words to the sisters, you mothers who are trifling with the ordinances of the house of God, and the blessings that are proffered to you, I will say that the time will come, if you persist in doing so, when you will mourn, and will be willing to give worlds, if you possessed them, for the privilege of living your lives over again. Some of you are treating with contempt the oracles of the Kingdom of God upon the earth, and in the commission of this sin you trifle with your own salvation, as well as the salvation of your children. Repent, and turn unto God, and teach your children the importance of doing the same, and of the sacredness of the ordinances and the laws of God. 18:263.

The duty of the mother is to watch over her children and give them their early education, for impressions received in infancy are lasting. You know, yourselves, by experience, that the impressions you have received in the dawn of your mortal existence, bear, to this day, with the greatest weight upon your mind. The child reposes implicit confidence in the mother, you behold in him a natural attachment, no matter what her appearance may be, that makes him think his mother is the best and handsomest mother in the world. I speak for myself. Children have all confidence in their mothers; and if mothers would take proper pains, they can instill into the hearts of their children what they please. You will, no doubt, recollect reading, in the Book of Mormon, of two thousand young men, who were brought up to believe that, if they put their whole trust in God, and served him, no power would overcome them. You also recollect reading of them going out to fight, and so bold were they, and so mighty their faith, that it was impossible for their enemies to slay them. This power and faith they obetained through the teachings of their mothers.

These duties and responsibilities devolve upon mothers far more than upon fathers, for you know the latter are often in the field or canyon, and are frequently away from home, sometimes for several days together, attending to labors which compel them to be absent from home. But the mother is at home with the children continually; and if they are taught lessons of usefulness it depends upon her. 14:105.

Mothers, remember that when your husbands are engaged in the service of the Church, and are all the time occupied in the duties of the Priesthood, so that they have not time to instruct their children, the duty devolves upon you. Then bring your children up in the ways of truth, and be to them both a father and mother, until they are old enough to perform duties by the side, and under the immediate eye, of their father. I like to see mothers bring their children to meeting, as soon as they can be brought without injuring them, and when they can tell what they want, and call for water when they are faint. As soon as they are old enough to receive instruction, bring them here to be taught. 2:21.

Were I a woman possessed of great powers of mind, filled with wisdom, and, upon the whole, a magnanimous woman, and had been privileged with my choice, and had married a man, and found myself deceived, he not answering my expectations, and I being sorry that I had made such a choice, let me show my wisdom by not complaining about it. A woman's wisdom and judgment has failed her once in the choice of a husband, and it may again, if she is not very careful. By seeking to cast off her husband—by withdrawing her confidence and good will from him, she casts a dark shade upon his path, when, by pursuing a proper course of love, obedience, and encouragement, he might attain to that perfection she had anticipated in him. 7:280.

Is it not a blessing to you, mothers, to raise up Prophets and Apostles—men filled with the glory of God, to go forth and extend the work of our God? 8:92.

I can say to the sisters, if you have superior talents, arise and let your light shine. Prove to your neighbors and the community that you are capable of teaching those sisters whom you deem to be ignorant or neglectful. 7:162.

Children—I wish to say to the children, obey your parents, be good, never suffer yourselves to do that which will mortify you through life, and that will cause you to look back with regret. While you are pure and spotless preserve yourselves in the integrity of your souls. Although you are young you know good from evil, and live so that you can look back on your lives and thank the Lord that he has preserved you, or has enabled you to preserve yourselves, so that you have no misconduct to regret or mourn over. Take this course and you will secure to yourselves an honorable name on earth among the good and the pure; you will maintain your integrity before heaven, and prove yourselves worthy of a high state of glory when you get through with this world. 14:200.

You may say to yourselves, "If I can do as well as my parents, I think I shall do well, and be as good as I want to be, and I should not strive to excel them." But if you do your duty you will far excel them in everything that is good—in holiness, in physical and intellectual strength, for this is your privilege, *and it becomes your duty*. 2:18.

Our young folks who have arrived at years of maturity should think and act for themselves. They are citizens of the earth; they have a share here, and have a part to bear—a character to form and frame and present to the world, or they will sink into oblivion and forgetfulness. 13:263.

The spirits which are reserved have to be born into the world, and the Lord will prepare some way for them to have tabernacles. 3:264.

I can pick out scores of men in this congregation who have driven their children from them by using the wooden rod. Where there is severity there is no affection or filial feeling in the hearts of either party; the children would rather be away from the father than be with him. 9:196.

Those whom I once knew as little boys are growing out of my recollection; these young men know nothing but "Mormonism." They are in some instances called wild and ungovernable; but these wild boys, properly guided and directed, will make the greatest men who have ever lived upon this earth; and I want them to throw aside their diffidence and come up and shake hands with me, and say, "How do you do, Brother Brigham?" for I feel warmly towards them. 11:118.

Family Life—If every person who professes to be a Latter-day Saint, was actually a Saint, our home would be a paradise, there would be nothing heard, nothing felt, nothing realized, but praise to the name of our God, doing our duty, and keeping his commandments. 3:254.

To gain the spiritual ascendancy over ourselves, and the influences with which we are surrounded, through a rigid course of self-discipline, is our first consideration, it is our first labor, before we can pave the way for our children to grow up without sin unto salvation. 2:131.

In my experience I have learned that the greatest difficulty that exists in the little bickerings and strifes of man with man, woman with woman, children with children, parents with children, brothers with sisters, and sisters with brothers, arises from the want of rightly understanding each other. 4:368.

In our daily pursuits in life, of whatever nature and kind, Latter-day Saints, and especially those who hold important positions in the Kingdom of God, should maintain a uniform and even temper, both when at home and when abroad. They should not suffer reverses and unpleasant circumstances to sour their natures and render them fretful and unsocial at home, speaking words full of bitterness and biting acrimony to their wives and children, creating gloom and sorrow in their habitations, making themselves feared rather than loved by their families. Anger should never be permitted to rise in our bosoms, and words suggested by angry feelings should never be permitted to pass our lips. "A soft answer turneth away wrath, but grievous words stir up anger." "Wrath is cruel, and anger is outrageous"; but "the discretion of a man deferreth his anger; and it is his glory to pass over a transgression." 11:136.

Fathers, mothers, brothers and sisters are no more to me than are any other persons, unless they embrace this work. Here are my fathers, my mothers, my sisters, and my brethren in the Kingdom, and I have none outside of it, neither in any part of the earth, nor in all the eternity of the Gods. In this Kingdom are my acquaintances, relatives, and friends,—my soul, my affections, my all. 8:199.

If a child or relative of mine forsakes the Gospel, the holy Priesthood, his God, and the Kingdom of God, farewell to that child or relative, whether near or distant. I own none as relatives, only those who love and serve our Lord and Savior, Jesus Christ. All that belong to my Father's house I own. I love them, I delight in their society, no matter whether they are poor or rich, learned or unlearned, if they observe the laws of the Kingdom of God and live according to it. 9:155.

If children have sinned against their parents, or husbands against their wives, or wives against their husbands, let them confess their faults one to another and forgive each other, and there let the confession stop; and then let them ask pardon from their God. Confess your sins to whoever you have sinned against, and let it stop there. If you have committed a sin against the community, confess to them. If you have sinned in your family, confess there. Confess your sins, iniquities, and follies, where that confession belongs, and learn to classify your actions. 4:78.

Let us live so that the spirit of our religion will live within us, then we have peace, joy, happiness and contentment, which makes such pleasant fathers, pleasant mothers, pleasant children, pleasant households, neighbors, communities and cities. That is worth living for, and I do think that the Latter-day Saints ought to strive for this. 15:135.

I will illustrate the method of establishing confidence in each other by taking, for example, the child of four or five years of age. The mother allows that child to own a small chest in which to keep his little trinkets, such as little bosom pins, ribbons, doll clothes, etc. This is considered by all the family the child's chest. Now let none go into that chest and take anything from it, without the consent of the child. This is a very small matter, some may think; but begin at as small a point as this to create confidence, and let it grow up from little to much. Wives, let your husbands' stores alone, if they have not committed them to your charge. Husbands, commit that to your wives that belongs to them, and never search their boxes without their consent. I can boast of this. I have lived in the marriage relation nearly thirty years, and I never was the man to open my wife's chest, without her consent, except once, and that was to get out a likeness that I wanted on the instant, and she was not at home to get it for me. That was the first time I ever opened a trunk in my life, that belonged to my wife, or to my child. The child's little chest, with its contents, is as sacred to him, as mine is to me. If this principle were strictly carried out by every man, woman, and child among the Saints, it would make them a blessed people indeed. 1:315.

I wish the daughters of Israel to far exceed their mothers in wisdom. And I wish these young men and boys to far exceed their fathers. I wish my sons to far exceed me in goodness and virtue. 2:17.

I say to our young men, be faithful, for you do not know what is before you, and abstain from bad company and bad habits. Let me say to the boys sixteen years old and even younger, make up your minds to mark out the path of rectitude for yourselves, and when evil is presented, let it pass by unnoticed by you, and preserve yourselves in truth, in righteousness, virtue and holiness before the Lord. You were born in the Kingdom of God; it is to be built up; the earth has to be renovated, and the people sanctified, after they are gathered from the nations, and it requires considerable skill and ability to do this; let our young men prepare themselves to aid and do their part in this great work. I want you to remember this teaching with regard to our youth. 11:118.

Importance of Early Training—We see the infant in its mother's arms. What is this infant here for? What is the design in the creation of this little infant child? It lies here in its mother's arms; it would not resist, in the least, if it were dropped into a caldron of boiling oil; if it were thrown into fire it would not know it until it felt the flames; it might be laid down here, and the wolf might come and lick its face, and it would not know but that its mother was soothing it. You see this foundation, the starting point, the germ of intelligence embodied in this infant, calculated to grow and expand into manhood, then to the capacity of an angel, and so onward to eternal exaltation. But here is the foundation. Sent to school, the child learns to read, and continues to improve as long as it lives. Is this the end of the knowledge of man? No. It is only the beginning. It is the first stage of all the intelligence that the philosopher in his reflections, taking the starry world before him, and looking into the immensity of the creations of God, can imagine. Here is the first place where we learn, this is the foot of the hill. 19:46.

When children are old enough to labor in the field, then the father will take them in charge. If children are not taught by their mothers, in the days of their youth, to revere and follow the counsels of their fathers, it will be hard indeed for the father ever to control them. 1:68.

Parents, have you ever noticed that your children have exercised faith for you when you have been sick? The little daughter, seeing you sick, will lift her heart with a pure, angelic-like prayer to heaven; and disease is rebuked when that kind of faith is exercised. God bless the children! I pray that they may live and be reared up in righteousness, that God may have a people that will spread and establish one universal reign of peace, and possess the powers of the world to come. 8:117.

Influence of the Mother—Let mothers commence to teach their children while in their laps, there do you teach them to love the Lord, and keep his commandments. Teach them to keep your commandments, and you will teach them to keep the commandments of your husbands. It is not the prerogative of a child to dictate to his mother, or his father; and it is not the prerogative of the father to rise up and dictate to his God whom he serves. 1:68.

If you mothers, will live your religion, then in the love and fear of God teach your children constantly and thoroughly in the way of life and salvation, training them up in the way they should go, when they are old they will not depart from it. I promise you this, it is as true as the shining sun, it is an eternal truth. In this duty we fail; we do not bring up our children in the way they should go, or there would be no turning away, wandering here and there from the society of the Saints. We let our children do too much as they have a mind to; if they want this or that their wishes must be granted. 19:92.

If a mother wishes to control her child, in the first place let her learn to control herself, then she may be successful in bringing the child into perfect subjection to her will. 14:277.

The first thing that is taught by the mother to the child should be true; we should never allow ourselves to teach our children one thing and practice another. 13:244.

I have often thought and said, "How necessary it is for mothers, who are the first teachers of their children and who make the first impressions on their young minds, to be strict." How careful they should be never to impress a false idea on the mind of a child! They should never teach them anything unless they know it is correct in every respect. They should never say a word, especially in the hearing of a child, that is improper. How natural it is for women to talk baby talk to their children; and it seems just as natural for the men to do so. It is just as natural for me as to draw my breath to talk nonsense to a child on my lap, and yet I have been trying to break myself of it ever since I began to have a family. 14:105.

Teach Children the Gospel—If we do not take the pains to train our children, to teach and instruct them concerning these revealed truths, the condemnation will be upon us, as parents, or at least in a measure. 19:92.

Teach your children from their youth, never to set their hearts immoderately upon an object of this world. 3:357.

Bring up your children in the love and fear of the Lord; study their dispositions and their temperaments, and deal with them accordingly, never allowing yourself to correct them in the heat of passion; teach them to love you rather than to fear you, and let it be your constant care that the children that God has so kindly given you are taught in their early youth the importance of the oracles of God, and the beauty of the principles of our holy religion, that when they grow to the years of man and womanhood they may always cherish a tender regard for them and never forsake the truth. I do not wish you to lay the stress and importance upon outward ceremonies that many do. Parents, teach your children by precept and example, the importance of addressing the Throne of grace; teach them how to live, how to draw from the elements the necessaries of life, and teach them the laws of life that they may know how to preserve themselves in health and be able to minister to others. And when instructing them in the principles of the Gospel, teach them that they are true, truth sent down from heaven for our salvation, and that the Gospel incorporates every truth whether in heaven, in earth, or in hell; and teach them, too, that we hold the keys of eternal life, and that they must obey and observe the ordinances and laws pertaining to this holy Priesthood, which God has revealed and restored for the exaltation of the children of men. 19:221.

If the law of Christ becomes the tradition of this people, the children will be brought up according to the law of the celestial kingdom, else they are not brought up in the way they should go. 3:327.

Latter-day Saints, have your children come to meeting. Sisters, let your little girls go to Sunday school or come to meeting! Brethren, let your children go to Sunday school, or to meeting, and advise your neighbors to do the same. 14:118.

In the morning, it is true, there are many in the Sunday School, and that we recommend; but in the afterpart of the day, where are these schoolchildren? Are they playing in the streets, or are they visiting? In going to Sunday school they have done their duty so far; but they ought to be here. In their youth they ought to learn the principles and doctrines of their faith, the arguments for truth, and the advantages of truth. 15:83.

Teach your children honesty and uprightness, and teach them also never to injure others. As I say to my sisters sometimes, "Look here, my dear sister, if your child quarrels with your neighbor's child, do not chasten your neighbor's child. Go and make peace, be a peace-maker. Teach your child never to do a wrong; and if your neighbor's child has injured you or yours, or taken anything from you, never mind. You stop until you find out. Perhaps the child has meant no wrong. You should learn the facts in the case, and go with a meek, humble, quiet spirit, and peace will result." 13:252.

Parents Should Teach by Example: If parents will continually set before their children examples worthy of their imitation and the approval of our Father in Heaven, they will turn the current, and the tide of feelings of their children, and they, eventually, will desire righteousness more than evil. 14:195.

Let the father and mother, who are members of this Church and Kingdom, take a righteous course, and strive with all their might never to do a wrong, but to do good all their lives; if they have one child or one hundred children, if they conduct themselves towards them as they should, binding them to the Lord by their faith and prayers, I care not where those children go, they are bound up to their parents by an everlasting tie, and no power of earth or hell can separate them from their parents in eternity; they will return again to the fountain from whence they sprang. 11:215

We should never permit ourselves to do anything that we are not willing to see our children do. We should set them an example that we wish them to imitate. Do we realize this? How often we see parents demand obedience, good behavior, kind words, pleasant looks, a sweet voice and a bright eye from a child or children when they themselves are full of bitterness and scolding! How inconsistent and unreasonable this is! 14:192.

Parents should never drive their children, but lead them along, giving them knowledge as their minds are prepared to receive it. Chastening may be necessary betimes, but parents should govern their children by faith rather than by the rod, leading them kindly by good example into all truth and holiness. 12:174.

Our children will have the love of the truth, if we but live our religion. Parents should take that course that their children can say, "I never knew my father to deceive or take advantage of a neighbor; I never knew my father to take to himself that which did not belong to him, never, never! No, but he said, 'Son, or daughter, be honest, true, virtuous, kind, industrious, prudent and full of good works.'" Such teachings from parents to their children will abide with them forever, unless they sin against the Holy Ghost, and some few, perhaps, will do this. 14:195.

Guides for Child Training—We can guide, direct, and prune a tender sprout, and it inclines to our direction, if it is wisely and skilfully applied. So, if we surround a child with healthy and salutary influences, give him suitable instruction and store his mind with truthful traditions, may be that will direct his feet in the way of life. 9:248.

A child loves the smiles of its mother, but hates her frowns. I tell the mothers not to allow the children to indulge in evils, but at the same time to treat them with mildness. If a child is required to step in a certain direction, and it does not seem willing to do so, gently put it in the desired way, and say, There, my little dear, you must step when I speak to you. Children need directing and teaching what is right in a kind, affectionate manner. 8:74.

You cannot break down the indomitable will of the human family. I have known children to be so abused and whipped as to render them almost or entirely worthless, and still the indomitable will remained. 6:332.

Now understand it—when parents whip their children for reading novels, and never let them go to the theater, or to any place of recreation and amusement, but bind them to the moral law, until duty becomes loathsome to them; when they are freed by age from the rigorous training of their parents, they are more fit for companions to devils, than to be the children of such religious parents. 2:94.

It never hurts my feelings to see young exuberant life and animation manifest themselves. Do not be discouraged about the follies of the young. 7:336.

You see, hear and witness a good deal of contention among children—some of you do, if not all—and I will give you a few words with regard to your future lives, that you may have children that are not contentious, not quarrelsome. Always be good-natured yourselves, is the first step. Never allow yourselves to become out of temper and get fretful. Why, mother says, "this is a very mischievous little boy or little girl." What do you see? That amount of vitality in those little children that they cannot be still. If they cannot be anything else they will tip over the chairs, cut up and pull away at anything to raise a row. They are so full of life that they cannot contain themselves; and they are something like ourselves—boys. They have so much vitality in them that their bones fairly ache with strength. They have such an amount of vitality—life, strength and activity, that they must dispose of them; and the young ones will contend with each other. Do not be out of temper yourselves. Always sympathize with them and soothe them. Be mild and pleasant. 19:69.

I believe in indulging children, in a reasonable way. If the little girls want dolls, shall they have them? Yes. But must they be taken to the dressmaker's to be dressed? No. Let the girls learn to cut and sew the clothing for their dolls, and in a few years they will know how to make a dress for themselves and others. Let the little boys have tools, and let them make their sleds, little wagons, etc., and when they grow up, they are acquainted with the use of tools and can build a carriage, a house, or anything else. 9:173.

Be careful of the clothing you have. Do not let your children's clothing lie underfoot when you undress them at night, but teach your boys and girls, when they come into the house, to find a place for their hats, cloaks, and bonnets, that, when they want them, they can put their hands upon them in a moment. When they take off their boots and shoes, let them be deposited where they can be found in the dark, that, if the children are obliged to get up at night, perhaps in case of fire, they can find their clothing, and not be under the necessity of being turned out naked. If a person can put his hand on his clothing, he can dress in the dark. 9:172-173.

What did you promise your little girl if she would do so and so? Did you promise her a present for well-doing? "Yes." Have you recollected it? "No, it has gone from my mind," says the mother. If she does ill have you promised her a chastisement? "Yes." Did you keep your word? You have not, and the child forms the conclusion in its own mind directly that the mother tells that which is not true—she says she will do this or that, and she does not do it. It is an easy lesson for mothers to learn to pass their time with their children and never give them a false impression. Think before you speak; promise your children nothing. If you wish to make them presents, do so; if you promise a chastisement, keep your word, but be cautious! 13:244.

Mothers, will you be missionaries? We will appoint you a mission to teach your children their duty, and instead of ruffles and fine dresses to adorn the body, teach them that which will adorn their minds. Let what you have to clothe them with be neat and clean and nice. Teach them cleanness and purity of body and the principles of salvation, and they will delight to come to these meetings. 14:220.

I delight to see the mother teach her daughters to be housekeepers, to be particular, clean, and neat; to sew, spin, and weave; to make butter and cheese; and I have no objection to their learning to cultivate flowers, herbs, and useful shrubs in the gardens. It is good for their health to rise early in the morning and work in the soil an hour or two before breakfast, this practice is especially beneficial to those who have weak lungs. And while you delight in raising flowers, etc., do not neglect to learn how to take care of the cream, and how to make of it good wholesome butter, and of the milk good healthy nutritious cheese; neither forget your sewing, spinning, and weaving; and I would not have them neglect to learn music and would encourage them to read history and the Scriptures, to take up a newspaper, geography, and other publications, and make themselves acquainted with the manners and customs of distant kingdoms and nations, with their laws, religion, geographical location on the face of the world, their climate, natural productions, the extent of their commerce, and the nature of their political organization; in fine, let our boys and girls be thoroughly instructed in every useful branch of physical and mental education. Let this education begin early. Teach little children the principles of order; the little girl to put the broom in its right place, to arrange the stove furniture in the neatest possible way, and everything in its own place. Teach them to lay away their clothing neatly, and where it can be found; and when they tear their frocks and aprons teach them how to mend the rent so neatly that the place cannot be seen at a short distance; and instead of asking your husbands to buy them ribbons and frills, teach them to make them of the material we can produce. Teach the little boys to lay away the garden hoe, the spade, etc., where they will not be destroyed by rust; and let them have access to tools that they may learn their use, and develop their mechanical skill while young; and see that they gather up the tools when they have done with them, and deposit them in the proper place. Let both males and females encourage within them mechanical ingenuity, and seek constantly to understand the world they are in, and what use to make of their existence. 9:188-189.

I would like to see the time when our sisters will take more pains to beautify their children. When your children arise in the morning, instead of sending them out of doors to wash in cold, hard water, with a little soft soap, and wiping them as though you would tear the skin off them, creating roughness and darkness of skin, take a piece of soft flannel, and wipe the faces of your children smooth and nice, dry them with a soft cloth; and instead of giving them pork for their breakfast, give them good wholesome bread and sweet milk, baked potatoes and also buttermilk if they like it, and a little fruit, and I would have no objections to their eating a little rice. Rice is an excellent food for children, and I wish some of the brethren would cultivate it in these valleys. Upland rice will flourish in this country. Train up your children to be beautiful and fair, instead of neglecting them until they are sunburned and become like the natives of our mountains. 12:201.

Need of Parent Training—You should go to work to study and see what you can do for the recovery of your children. If a child is taken sick with fever, give it something to stay that fever or relieve the stomach and bowels, so that mortification may not set in. Treat the child with prudence and care, with faith and patience, and be careful in not overcharging it with medicine. If you take too much medicine into the system, it is worse than too much food. But you will always find that an ounce of preventive is worth a pound of cure. Study and learn something for yourselves. It is the privilege of a mother to have faith and to administer to her child; this she can do herself, as well as sending for the Elders to have the benefit of their faith. 13:155.

CHAPTER XVIII

SOME WOMANLY DUTIES

The Housewife—I am addressing myself to the ladies of the Kingdom of God, to those who know how to keep their houses, furniture and beds pure and clean, who can cook food for their husbands, and children in a way that it will be clean, tasteful and wholesome. The woman that can do this I call a lady. In this view I differ from the world generally; for the lady of the world is not supposed to know anything about what is going on in the kitchen; her highest ambition is to be sure and be in the fashion, at no matter what cost to her husband or father; she considers that she may as well be out of the world as out of the fashion. 11:138.

A good housewife, whether she possesses much or little, will have a place for everything she has in the house, and make her house orderly and comfortable, and everything when wanted can be found in its place. 9:157.

If I had nothing but a piece of an old newspaper folded for a holder I would have it where I could put my hand on it in a moment, in the dark if I wanted it. And so with the dishcloth, the broom, the chairs, tables, sofas, and everything about the house, so that if you had to get up in the night you could lay your hand on whatever you wanted instantly. Have a place for everything and everything in its place. 14:89.

When I go into a house, I can soon know whether the woman is an economical housekeeper or not; and if I stay a few days, I can tell whether a husband can get rich or not. If she is determined on her own course, and will waste and spoil the food entrusted to her, that man will always be poor. 4:313.

It is an old saying that a woman can throw out of the window with a spoon as fast as a man can throw into the door with a shovel; but a good housekeeper will be saving and economical and teach her children to be good housekeepers, and how to take care of everything that is put in their charge. 12:195.

Ladies, if you are the means of plunging this whole people into debt so as to distress them, will there be anything required of you? I think there will, for you will be judged according to your works. Are not the men as extravagant as the women? Yes, certainly they are, and just as foolish. I could point out instances by the score and by the hundred of men who are just as unwise, shortsighted, and foolish as the women can be; but a condemnation of the male portion of the community will not justify the female portion of it. 14:105.

Now, sisters, if you will consider these things you will readily see that time is all the capital stock there is on the earth; and you should consider your time golden, it is actually wealth, and, if properly used, it brings that which will add to your comfort, convenience, and satisfaction. Let us consider this, and no longer sit with hands folded, wasting time, for it is the duty of every man and of every woman to do all that is possible to promote the Kingdom of God on the earth. 18:77.

If there are women who want to do good, let them do their own work, and save their sixpences and dollars for the building of temples, tabernacles, meetinghouses, schoolhouses, educating the youth, preaching the Gospel, and gathering the poor. 11:351.

What I say of housewives will fully apply to farmers and mechanics. I labored many years as a mechanic, and in the darkest night I could put my hand upon any tool I used. You may call this boasting, but it is not. It is merely mentioning the order in which I kept my shop. 8:296.

Count the steps that a woman takes when she is doing her work, let them be measured, and it will be found that in many instances she had taken steps enough to have traveled from fifteen to twenty miles a day; I will warrant this to be the case. 4:101.

Woman's Fashions—Beauty must be sought in the expression of the countenance, combined with neatness and cleanliness and graceful manners. 18:75.

Anything is ridiculous, more or less, that is not comely. 14:17.

Let the beauty of your adorning be the work of your hands. 19:75.

I love to see the human form and the human face adorned, but let the adorning be the workmanship of our hands, from the elements with which we are constantly surrounded. I love beauty whether adorned or unadorned. I love chaste and refined manners, especially when they are founded upon virtue. 10:6.

In the works of God, you see an eternal variety, consequently we do not ask the people to become Quakers, and all the men wear wide-brimmed hats, and the ladies wear drab or cream-colored silk bonnets projecting in the front, perhaps six or seven inches, rounded on the corners, with a cape behind. 14:17.

The daughters of Israel should understand what fashions they should have, without borrowing from the impure and unrighteous. 12:220.

Create your own fashions, and make your clothing to please yourselves, independent of outside influences; and make your hats and bonnet to shade you. I wish you, sisters, to listen to these counsels, and place yourselves in a condition to administer to the poor. Get your husbands to provide you with a little of this and a little of that of which you can make something by adding your own labor. I do not mean that you shall apply to them for five dollars and ten dollars to spend for that which is of no profit, but manufacture something that will be useful as well as beautiful and comely. 12:202.

Not flaunting, flirting and gossiping, as a great many are, and thinking continually of their dresses, and of this and that and the other that will minister to and gratify their vanity. Such women seldom think of their prayers. 15:162.

I am ashamed to see the tight clothes—to see the shape of the ladies. 19:75.

Ask your mothers, then, to make your clothes suitable and becoming; and keep your hair smooth and nice. The hair is given to the female for adornment; and therefore let the ladies, young and old, adorn their heads with their hair. Mothers should study and children should study to preserve the skin of the children from being ruined by dirt, and the heat of a scorching sun, and to keep themselves clean and pure. 19:65.

If I were a lady and had a piece of cloth to make me a dress, I would cut it so as to cover my person handsomely and neatly; and whether it was cut according to the fashion or not, custom would soon make it beautiful. 15:38.

It adds no beauty to a lady, in my opinion, to adorn her with fine feathers. When I look at a woman, I look at her face, which is composed of her forehead, cheeks, nose, mouth and chin, and I like to see it clean, her hair combed neat and nice, and her eyes bright and sparkling; and if they are so, what do I care what she has on her head, or how or of what material her dress is made? Not the least in the world. 18:74.

The Lord instructs us in a revelation, to let our clothing be plain: "Let all thy garments be plain, and their beauty the beauty of the work of thine own hands." He never said to us, "Do not make a silk or satin ribbon, or fine broadcloth," but he has said to us, "Make the articles of clothing that you wear;" if we do not, we shall find by and by that we shall not be able to get them. 10:311.

Let the sisters take care of themselves, and make themselves beautiful, and if any of you are so superstitious and ignorant as to say that this is pride, I can say that you are not informed as to the pride which is sinful before the Lord, you are also ignorant as to the excellency of the heavens, and of the beauty which dwells in the society of the Gods. Were you to see an angel, you would see a beautiful and lovely creature. Make yourselves like angels in goodness and beauty.

Let the mothers in Israel make their sons and daughters healthy and beautiful, by cleanliness and a proper diet. Whether you have much or little clothing for your children, it can be kept clean and healthy, and be made to fit their persons neatly. Make your children lovely and fair that you may delight in them. Cease to send out your children to herd sheep with their skins exposed to the hot sun, until their hands and faces appear as though they lived in an ash heap. I call upon my sisters to lead out in these things. 12:201.

It is a disgrace to a community to drag their cloth in the dirt. How many women are there here today who walked to this Tabernacle without throwing dirt every step they took, not only on themselves but upon those who walked near them? I shun them; when I see them coming. I try to make my way in some other direction in order to avoid their dust. I can get enough of it without receiving it from them. If there is a nuisance in the path, they are sure to wipe up a portion of it with their dress, and then trail it on to their carpet or into the bedrooms and distribute it through the house.

On the other hand I will say, ladies, if we ask you to make your dresses a little shorter, do not be extravagant and cut them so short that we can see the tops of your stockings. Bring them down to the tops of your shoes, and have them so that you can walk and clear the dust, and do not expose your persons. Have your dresses neat and comely, and conduct yourselves, in the strictest sense of the word, in chastity. 12:299.

If my mother and her grandmother got one silk dress, and they lived to a hundred years old, it was all that they wanted. I think my grandmother's silk dress came down to her children. She put her silk dress on when I went to see her. It was, I think, her wedding dress, and she had been married some seventy years. 19:74.

That which is convenient should be beautiful. 15:38.

As for fashion, it does not trouble me, my fashion is convenience and comfort. 14:21.

Some Duties of the Relief Societies—These societies are for the improvement of our manners, our dress, our habits, and our methods of living. 19:68.

The sisters in our Female Relief Societies have done great good. Can you tell the amount of good that the mothers and daughters in Israel are capable of doing? No, it is impossible. And the good they will do will follow them to all eternity. 13:34.

As I have often told my sisters in the Female Relief Societies, we have sisters here who, if they had the privilege of studying, would make just as good mathematicians or accountants as any man; and we think they ought to have the privilege to study these branches of knowledge that they may develop the powers with which they are endowed. We believe that women are useful, not only to sweep houses, wash dishes, make beds, and raise babies, but that they should stand behind the counter, study law or physic, or become good bookkeepers and be able to do the business in any counting house, and all this to enlarge their sphere of usefulness for the benefit of society at large. In following these things they but answer the design of their creation. 13:61.

Now, ladies, go to and organize yourselves into industrial societies, and get your husbands to produce you some straw, and commence bonnet and hat making. If every Ward would commence and continue this and other industrial pursuits, it would not be long before the females of the Wards of our Territory would have stores in their Wards, and means sufficient to send and get the articles which they need, that cannot yet be manufactured here and which they may want to distribute. 12:195.

When the sisters, for instance, meet together at a quilting or for a visit, if every one speaks, believes and loves the truth, and there is nothing in them that is deceptive, how easy it is to converse and pass the time! We all delight in the truth; and if a wrong, or that which is false, is manifested it must be corrected or banished, and truth be adopted in the place thereof. It is the easiest life to lead on the face of the earth. How do I know it? By experience; I never tried the opposite much. 14:76.

I will here say to the Latter-day Saints, if you will feed the poor with a willing heart and ready hand, neither you nor your children will ever be found begging bread. In these things the people are right; they are right in establishing Female Relief Societies, that the hearts of the widow and orphan may be made glad by the blessings which are so abundantly and so freely poured out upon them. 12:171.

Sisters, do you see any children around your neighborhood poorly clad and without shoes? If you do, I say to you, Female Relief Societies, pick up these children and relieve their necessities, and send them to school. And if you see any young, middle-aged or old ladies in need find them something to do that will enable them to sustain themselves; but don't relieve the idle, for relieving those who are able but unwilling to work is ruinous to any community. The time we spend here is our life, our substance, our capital, our fortune, and that time should be used profitably. Take these old ladies, there are a great many of them around rather poor, and give them something to do; that is their delight. You will hardly find an old lady in the community who has not been brought up to work; and they would rather knit stockings or do some other useful labor than eat the bread of charity. Relieve the wants of every individual in need in your neighborhoods. This is in the capacity and in the power of the Female Relief Societies when it is not in the power of the Bishops. 14:107.

I wish to call the attention of our sisters to our Relief Societies. We are happy to say that many of them have done a great deal. We wish them to continue and progress. In our Relief Societies we wish to introduce many improvements. We wish our sisters of experience to teach the young girls not to be so anxious for the gratification of their imaginary wants, but to confine themselves more to their real necessities. Fancy has no bounds, and I often think it is without form and comeliness. We are too apt to give way to the imagination of our hearts, but if we will be guided by wisdom, our judgment will be corrected, and we will find that we can improve very much. We can improve the language we use. 12:298.

The ladies can learn to keep books as well as the men; we have some few, already, who are just as good accountants as any of our brethren. Why not teach more of them to keep books and sell goods, and let them do this business, and let the men go to raising sheep, wheat, or cattle, or go and do something or other to beautify the earth and help to make it like the Garden of Eden, instead of spending their time in a lazy, loafing manner? 12:374-375.

I have a short sermon for my sisters. I wish you, under the direction of your Bishops and wise men, to establish your Relief Societies, and organize yourselves under the direction of the brethren, and establish yourselves for doing business, gathering up your little amounts of means that would otherwise go to waste, and put them to usury, and make more of them, and thus keep gathering in. Let this be commenced forthwith. 12:201.

Chapter XIX

OBEDIENCE

Counsel—How my heart longs to see the brethren and sisters in a condition that when the words of truth and virtue—righteous words of counsel—are poured upon them, they will meet like drops of water meeting each other. How I long to see the brethren, when they hear the words of truth poured upon them, ready to receive those words because they are perfectly congenial to their feelings, and every soul exclaim, "Those words savor of the Spirit that is in me; they are my delight, my meat, and my drink; they are the streams of eternal life. How congenial they are, instead of their being contrary to my feelings." 9:3.

If we hearken to counsel, we shall be the best people in the world; we shall be as a bright light set upon a hill, that cannot be hid, or like a candle upon a candlestick. 12:173.

If I or any other man give counsel that meets with opposition, that intrudes upon the affections, meditations, and feelings of the people, and is harsh to their ears, bitter to their souls, it is either not the words of truth, or they have not the fountain of life within them, one of the two. If the Lord speaks from the heavens, reveals his will, and it comes in contact with our feelings and notions of things, or with our judgments, we are destitute of that fountain of truth which we should possess. If our hearts are filled with the Spirit of truth, with the Spirit of the Lord, no matter what the true words from heaven are, when God speaks, all his subjects should shout, "Hallelujah! praise God! We are ready to receive those words, for they are true." 9:3-4.

Every man in the Kingdom of God would give the same counsel upon each subject, if he would wait until he had the mind of Christ upon it. Then all would have one word and mind, and all men would see eye to eye. 5:100.

If you would always pause and say, I have no counsel for you, I have no answer for you on this subject, because I have no manifestation of the Spirit, and be willing to let everybody in the world know that you are ignorant when you are, you would become wise a great deal quicker than to give counsel on your own judgment, without the Spirit of revelation. 5:100.

The Latter-day Saints who hearken to the words of the Lord, given to them touching their political, social, and financial concerns, I say, and say it boldly, that they will have wisdom which is altogether superior to the wisdom of the children of darkness, or the children of this world. I know this by the revelations of the Lord Jesus Christ, and by the results of my own actions. They who have hearkened to the counsels given to them in temporal matters, have invariably bettered their condition temporally and spiritually. 12:118.

Obedience—When the Lord commands the people, let them obey. 2:123.

Every son and daughter of God is expected to obey with a willing heart every word which the Lord has spoken, and which he will in the future speak to us. It is expected that we hearken to the revelations of his will, and adhere to them, cleave to them with all our might; for this is salvation, and any thing short of this clips the salvation and the glory of the Saints. 2:2.

Obedience is one of the plainest, most every-day and home principles that you ever thought or know anything about. In the first place, learn that you have a father, and then learn strict obedience to that parent. Is not that a plain, domestic, home principle? 6:173.

I cannot save you. I can tell you how to save yourselves, but you must do the will of God. 10:317.

How shall we know what to do? By being obedient to every requirement of the Gospel. 8:148.

A mere theory amounts to but little, while practice and obedience have to do with stern realities. 9:330.

Every good and wholesome law we should obey strictly, and do it with a good and honest heart. 11:134.

Blessed are they who obey when the Lord gives a direct commandment, but more blessed are they who obey without a direct commandment. 12:128.

Do you think that people will obey the truth because it is true, unless they love it? No, they will not. Truth is obeyed when it is loved. Strict obedience to the truth will alone enable people to dwell in the presence of the Almighty. 7:55.

The Lord has sent forth his laws, commandments, and ordinances to the children of men, and requires them to be strictly obeyed, and we do not wish to transgress those laws, but to keep them. We do not wish to change his ordinances, but to observe them; we do not wish to break the everlasting covenant, but to keep that with our fathers, with Jesus, with our Father in Heaven, with holy angels, and to live according to them. 16:31.

If a man is called to go and labor for the poor, if his Bishop calls upon him to go into the canyon after a load of wood for the poor, and he goes there, with his heart uplifted to God, and with his eye single to the building up of the Kingdom, and gets the load of wood and lays it at the door of the Bishop for the poor, for the widow or for those who cannot help themselves, he is just as much in the line of his duty in so doing as though he were on his knees praying. 11:293.

This people have got to become of one heart and one mind. They have to know the will of God and do it, for to know the will of God is one thing, and to bring our wills, our dispositions, into subjection to that which we do understand to be the will of God is another. 3:54-55.

We believe in obeying the laws of the land, we should also obey the laws of God. 16:45.

Some of you may ask, "Is there a single ordinance to be dispensed with? Is there one of the commandments that God has enjoined upon the people, that he will excuse them from obeying? Not one, no matter how trifling or small in our own estimation. No matter if we esteem them non-essential, or least or last of all the commandments of the house of God, we are under obligation to observe them. 8:339.

With regard to the obedience of heavenly beings, to which reference has been made to-day; they live pure and holy, and they have attained unto this power through suffering. Many of them have drunk of the bitter cup even to the dregs. They have learned that righteousness will prevail, that truth is the foundation of their very existence. 11:15.

The most effectual way to establish the religion of Heaven is to live it, rather than to die for it: I think I am safe in saying that there are many of the Latter-day Saints who are more willing to die for their religion than to live it faithfully. There is no other proof can be adduced to God, angels, and men, that a people faithfully live their religion, than that they repent truly of their sins, obey the law of baptism for the remission of sins, and then continue to do the works of righteousness day by day. 9:333.

There are a great many texts which might be used, very comprehensive and full of meaning, but I know of none, either in the Old or New Testament, more so than that saying, said to have been made by the Savior, and I have no doubt it was, "If ye love me, keep my commandments."

"How long? For a day? Keep the commandments of the Lord for a week? Observe and do his will for a month or a year? There is no promise to any individual, that I have any knowledge of, that he shall receive the reward of the just, unless he is faithful to the end. If we fully understand and faithfully carry out in our lives the sayings of Jesus, "If ye love me, keep my commandments," we shall be prepared to go back and dwell in the presence of the Father and the Son.

What are his commandments? Did he ever teach the people anything that is wrong? If we read the requirements made by Jesus, by the Father, or by any messenger sent from the heavens to the children of men, we shall find nothing that will injure any human being or that will destroy the soul of one of the sons or daughters of Adam and Eve. Many think that the sayings and doings of some of the prophets and servants of God, in ancient and modern times, said and done in obedience to the commands of the Lord Almighty, tend to evil; but it is not so. All God's requirements tend to do good to his children. Any notion to the contrary is the result of ignorance. The human family are enveloped in ignorance, so far as the origin and object of their existence here is concerned. Their ignorance, superstition, darkness and blindness are very apparent to all who are in the least enlightened by the Spirit of truth. They seek to hide themselves in ignorance and blindness rather than learn who they are and the object of their being here. What do the human family know of God or Jesus, or of the words which I have quoted, "If ye love me, keep my commandments?" "Search the Scriptures, for in them ye think ye have eternal life," says Jesus, "and they are they which testify of me." They testify of the Savior, of his doctrines and requirements, and of the ordinances of his house; the plan of salvation is there portrayed, and any person who follows its dictation may redeem himself from the thraldom of sin, and know, by the Spirit, that Jesus is the Christ. All who will take this course will know by revelation that God is our Father; they will understand the relationship they hold to him and to their fellow-beings. The world may in vain ask the question, "Who are we?" But the Gospel tells us that we are the sons and daughters of that God whom we serve. Some say, "We are the children of Adam and Eve." So we are, and they are the children of our Heavenly Father. We are all the children of Adam and Eve, and they are the offspring of him who dwells in the heavens, the highest Intelligence that dwells anywhere that we have any knowledge of. Here we find ourselves, and when infants, the most helpless, and needing the most care and attention of any creatures that come into being on the face of the earth. Here we find in ourselves the germ and the foundation, the embryo of exaltation, glory, immortality and eternal lives. As we grow up we receive strength, knowledge and wisdom, some more and some less; but only by keeping the commands of the Lord Jesus can we have the privilege of knowing the things pertaining to eternity and our relationship to the heavens. 13:310.

The most excellent human or divine laws are of no use to earthly or heavenly beings, unless they are faithfully observed. Law is for the protection of the law-abider; and the penalty of the law is for the law-breaker. 9:332.

People will never be taken and sacrificed for their ignorance, when they have had no opportunity to know and understand the truth. Such a proceeding would be contrary to the economy of heaven. But after we receive and understand things as they are, if we then disobey, we may look for the chastening hand of the Almighty. 3:246.

Walk up, O ye Latter-day Saints, and wake up! Come to the Lord, forsake your covetousness, your back-slidings, forsake the spirit of the world, and return to the Lord with full purpose of heart until you get the Spirit of Christ within you, that you, like others, can cry, "Abba Father, the Lord, he is God, and I am his servant." 15:6.

We have nothing to sacrifice. All we have to do is to love and serve our God, and do everything we can to bring knowledge to ourselves and to the people. 6:196.

When the Gospel is preached to the honest in heart they receive it by faith, but when they obey it labor is required. To practice the Gospel requires time, faith, the heart's affections and a great deal of labor. Here many stop. They hear and believe, but before they go on to practice they begin to think that they were mistaken, and unbelief enters into their hearts. 16:40.

When we get to understand all knowledge, all wisdom, that it is necessary for us to understand in the flesh, we will be like clay in the hands of the potter, willing to be moulded and fashioned according to the will of him who has called us to this great and glorious work, of purifying ourselves and our fellow-beings, and of preparing the nations of the earth for the glory that awaits them through obedience. 19:93.

I believe that it is a hell intolerable for a people, a family or a single person, to strive to grasp truth with one hand, and error with the other, to profess to walk in obedience to the commandments of God, and, at the same time, mingle heart and hand with the wicked. 3:254.

Effect of Obedience—Great peace have they who love the law of the Lord and abide in his commandments. 8:121.

If you wish to receive and enjoy the favor of our Heavenly Father, do his will. 8:33.

When will this people become Saints indeed? Not until they observe every counsel that is given to them of this kind, doing with their might the things that are required of them. 11:139.

All who receive eternal life and salvation will receive it on no other condition than believing in the Son of God and obeying the principles that he has laid down. Can we devise any other means and plan of salvation? We cannot. 13:213.

The Saints who live their religion will be exalted, for they never will deny any revelation which the Lord has given or may give, though, when there is a doctrine coming to them which they cannot comprehend fully, they may be found saying, "The Lord sendeth this unto me, and I pray that he will save and preserve me from denying anything which proceedeth from him, and give me patience to wait until I can understand it for myself."

Such persons will never deny, but will allow those subjects which they do not understand, to remain until the visions of their minds become open. This is the course which I have invariably pursued, and if anything came that I could not understand, I would pray until I could comprehend it.

Do not reject anything because it is new or strange, and do not sneer nor jeer at what comes from the Lord, for if we do, we endanger our salvation. It is given to us, as agents, to choose or refuse, as brother S. W. Richards has set before you, but we are agents within limits; if it were not so there would be no law. 3:266.

By obeying the ordinances of God, mankind glorify God, but if they do not obey him, they do not detract one particle from his glory and power. The commandments of God are given to us expressly for our benefit, and if we live in obedience to them we shall live so as to understand the mind and will of God for ourselves, and concerning ourselves as individuals. 12:126.

How shall we know that we obey him? There is but one method by which we can know it, and that is by the inspiration of the Spirit of the Lord witnessing unto our spirit that we are his, that we love him, and that he loves us. It is by the spirit of revelation we know this. We have no witness to ourselves internally, without the spirit of revelation. We have no witness outwardly, only by obedience to the ordinances. 12:99.

Law is made for the lawless. Let the Saints live their religion, and there is not a law that can justly infringe upon them. 8:140.

There is no law against doing good. There is no law against love. There is no law against serving God. There is no law against charity and benevolence. There is no law against the principles of eternal life. Live them, and no righteous law of man can reach you. 8:140.

When the law of God is written on the hearts of a people, every person will know his place. 8:296.

When men and women talk about giving everything for the salvation which they anticipate and live for, behold, they have nothing to give; nor have they anything to do, only to do their duty. And what is that? To improve upon that which is committed to their possession—to prove themselves worthy to their Father and God, that ere long they may be worthy to receive crowns of glory, immortality and eternal life. Then we shall be beyond the power of Satan. 6:196.

So long as the Latter-day Saints will live their religion, they shall never be confounded, worlds without end. Never be afraid; your hearts are brave, your arms are strong, and God is our defense. 10:40.

Those who live their religion will enjoy the Spirit, and that enjoyment will increase; and if we will be faithful, the Lord will make our feet as firm in these valleys as are the everlasting riches in these mountains, and no power can remove us. He will give us a sure place in these mountains until we go forth and redeem Zion. Do right, be faithful, and make no calculations about removing before the time comes. 8:285.

Obedience and Free Agency—Here is a brother who says, "Why, yes, you may have some of my property or even take it all; but I want to be a man for myself; I do not want to be dictated; I want to preserve my own freedom; I do not want to be a slave." What an idea! It is from the enemy, and because a person has not the Spirit of the Lord to see how things are. There is not a man of us but what is willing to acknowledge at once that God demands strict obedience to his requirements. But in rendering that strict obedience, are we made slaves? No, it is the only way on the face of the earth for you and me to become free, and we shall become slaves of our own passions, and of the wicked one, and servants to the Devil, if we take any other course, and we shall be eventually cast into hell with the devils. Now to say that I do not enjoy the volition of my own will just as much when I pray as I would to swear, is a false principle, it is false ground to take. You take the man who swears, and he has no more freedom, and acts no more on his own will than the man who prays; the man who yields strict obedience to the requirements of Heaven, acts upon the volition of his own will and exercises his freedom just as much as when he was a slave to passion; and I think it is much better and more honorable for us, whether children or adults, youthful, middle-aged or old, it is better to live by and better to die by, to have our hearts pure, and to yield strict obedience to the principles of life which the Lord has revealed, than to be a slave to sin and wickedness. All that the Lord requires of us is strict obedience to the laws of life. All the sacrifice that the Lord asks of his people is strict obedience to our own covenants that we have made with our God, and that is to serve him with an undivided heart. 18:246.

One of the simplest things in the world is to control a people.

Is there any particular art in making this people obedient? There is just one. If you, Elders of Israel, can get the art of preaching the Holy Ghost into the hearts of the people, you will have an obedient people. This is the only art required. Teach the people truth, teach them correct principles; show them what is for their greatest good and don't you think they will follow in that path? They will, just as far as it is consistent with their weaknesses and the power of darkness that is over the inhabitants of the earth—with us as with others. 12:257.

A person before he can understand the law and government of God must see and understand the propriety of it and see its beauties. So it is with the whole system of salvation. Not that I would say we are machines, for we have our agency; but God has placed us here, and he exacts strict obedience to his laws before we can derive the benefit and blessings their observance will yield. You may take a beautiful machine of any kind you please, and when the machinist has finished his work and set it in perfect order, how could it be expected to operate satisfactorily if a hook here or a journal yonder were to say, I am not going to stay here, or, I am going to jump out of place and am going somewhere else; and then another piece of the machinery would jump out of its place into another part of the machine. What would be the state of such a machine? Confusion and disorganization would soon result and the machinist might very properly say, what a pity that I bestowed so much labor on such unruly members of my machine. 13:241.

The world will not receive the Gospel, unless they can have it on their own terms, and will persecute the few that do receive it. 9:331.

We as a people, will be chastened until we can wholly submit ourselves to the Lord and be Saints indeed. 5:354.

Effects of Disobedience—When light comes, if the people reject that light, it will condemn them, and will add to their sorrow and affliction. 6:288.

If we live our religion we shall prosper, and if we live in the neglect of our duty, and continue to do so, there will be tribulation and anguish here, and the chastening hand of the Almighty will be on this people. 3:340.

I feel in my heart to bless you; it is full of blessings and not cursing. It is something that does not occupy my feelings to curse any individual, but I will modify this by saying those who ought not to be cursed. Who ought to be? Those who know their Master's will, and do it not; they are worthy of many stripes; it is not those who do not know, and do not do, but those who know it, and do not do it—they are the ones to be chastised. 1:248.

As soon as you are overcome by the spirit of the world, you forget every good deed and kindness that has been extended to you, and you only remember the transpiring and infliction of what you deemed to be evil that would have resulted in good, had you done right. 3:358.

It is the misapplied intelligence God has given us that makes all the mischief on the earth. That intelligence he designed to carry out the purposes of his will, and endowed it with capabilities to grow, spread abroad, accumulate, and endeavor to enjoy greater happiness, glory, and honor, and continue to expand wider and wider, until eternity is comprehended by it; if not applied to this purpose, but to the grovelling things of earth, it will be taken away, and given to one who has made better use of this gift of God. 2:124-125.

If we will only practice what we profess, I tell you we are at the defiance of hell. 2:186.

For a man to undertake to live a Saint and walk in darkness is one of the hardest tasks that he can undertake. You cannot imagine a position that will sink a person more deeply in perplexity and trouble than to try to be a Saint without living as a Saint should—without enjoying the spirit of his religion. It is our privilege to live so as to enjoy the spirit of our religion. That is designed to restore us to the presence of the Gods. Gods exist, and we had better strive to be prepared to be one with them. 7:238.

Anything that is impure must, sooner or later, perish; no matter whether it is in the faith and practice of an individual, town, nation, or government. That kingdom, principality, power or person that is not controlled by principles that are pure and holy must eventually pass away and perish. 14:75.

I know it is hard to receive chastisement, for no chastisement is joyous, but grievous at the time it is given; but if a person will receive chastisement and pray for the Holy Spirit to rest upon him, that he may have the Spirit of truth in his heart, and cleave to that which is pleasing to the Lord, the Lord will give him grace to bear the chastisement, and he will submit to and receive it, knowing that it is for his good. 3:47.

Men must quit swearing and taking the name of God in vain; they must refrain from lying, stealing, cheating, and doing that which they know they ought not to do, or they must be severed from this Church and Kingdom. 4:307.

The Latter-day Saints, in all their travels, have not been as rebellious as the Children of Israel were. 11:279.

Chapter XX

GRATITUDE, HUMILITY, DEVOTION, LIBERALITY, HONESTY

Gratitude—I do not know of any, excepting the unpardonable sin, that is greater than the sin of ingratitude. 14:277.

We rejoice because the Lord is ours, because we are sown in weakness for the express purpose of attaining to greater power and perfection. In everything the Saints may rejoice—in persecution, because it is necessary to purge them, and prepare the wicked for their doom; in sickness and in pain, though they are hard to bear, because we are thereby made acquainted with pain, with sorrow, and with every affliction that mortals can endure, for by contact all things are demonstrated to our senses. We have reason to rejoice exceedingly that faith is in the world, that the Lord reigns, and does his pleasure among the inhabitants of the earth. Do you ask if I rejoice because the Devil has the advantage over the inhabitants of the earth, and has afflicted mankind? I most assuredly answer in the affirmative; I rejoice in this as much as in anything else. I rejoice because I am afflicted. I rejoice because I am poor. I rejoice because I am cast down. Why? Because I shall be lifted up again. I rejoice that I am poor because I shall be made rich; that I am afflicted, because I shall be comforted, and prepared to enjoy the felicity of perfect happiness, for it is impossible to properly appreciate happiness except by enduring the opposite. 1:359.

Humility—I delight extremely in plain simplicity. 4:341.

The humble will live, their spirits will be buoyant, and they will live to a great age. 8:181.

We have to humble ourselves and become like little children in our feelings—to become humble and childlike in spirit, in order to receive the first illuminations of the spirit of the Gospel, then we have the privilege of growing, of increasing in knowledge, in wisdom, and in understanding. 3:192.

The hearts of the meek and humble are full of joy and comfort continually. 4:22.

When a person sees things as they are, flattery and reproach are all the same to him, he sees no difference. If he finds that he is pleasing God and his brethren, he is exceedingly rejoiced, and feels an increase of humility and resignation. When a man is proud and arrogant, flattery fills him with vanity and injures him; but it is not so when he is increasing in the faith of God. 12:50.

I exhort the brethren not to boast over our enemies' downfall. Boast not, brethren. God has come out of his hiding-place, and has commenced to vex the nations that have rejected us, and he will vex them with a sore vexation. 8:324.

Devotion to the Gospel—To the Latter-day Saints I say, live your religion, sanctify the Lord God in your hearts, live every word that proceeds from the mouth of God, and we shall be prospered. 13:318.

A man, or a woman, desiring to know the will of God, and having an opportunity to know it, will apply their hearts to this wisdom until it becomes easy and familiar to them, and they will love to do good instead of evil. 3:363.

To enjoy the protection of the Almighty, we have got to live our religion—to live so that we have the mind of Christ within us. 4:358.

All I ask of you is to apply your hearts to the Gospel of Jesus Christ and be Saints. I will not ask anything else on this earth of you, only to live so as to know the mind and will of God when you receive it, and then abide in it. If you will do that, you will be prepared to do a great many things, and you will find that there is much good to be done. 3:375.

When you know how to be a Saint today, you are in a fair way to know how to be a Saint tomorrow. And if you can continue to be a Saint today, you can through the week, and through the year, and you can fill up your whole life in performing the duty and labor of a Saint. 2:53.

If I am organized and capacitated to receive this glory and this exaltation, I must be the friend of him who has brought me forth and instituted this exaltation for me; I must not be his enemy at any time. 4:198.

I have sought to teach you how to get rich, but I never taught you to neglect your duty; I never instructed you nor taught you to forsake the Lord; and today I would rather not own one farthing, and take my valise in my hand, as I did at the rise of the Church, and travel among the nations of the earth, and beg my bread from door to door, than to neglect my duty and lose the Spirit of Almighty God. If I have wealth and cannot use it to the glory of God and the building up of his Kingdom, I ask the Lord to take it from me. 13:280.

There is not a wicked man on the face of the earth but what reveres a pure servant of God. They may not acknowledge it with their organs of speech, but in their hearts, sentiments and feelings they revere such a character. When they see a pure and holy man or woman, say they, "I wish I was as good as you are." Then let us take a pride in acknowledging our religion and living it, by being virtuous, true and good in everything, and then take pride in educating your minds until you can conquer and control yourselves in everything. Educate your children in all the knowledge the world can give them. God has given it to the world, it is all his. Every true principle, every true science, every art, and all the knowledge that men possess, or that they ever did or ever will possess, is from God. We should take pains and pride to instill this knowledge into the minds of our neighbors, and our brethren, and rear our children so that the learning and education of the world may be theirs, and that virtue, truth and holiness may crown their lives that they may be saved in the Kingdom of God. 12:326.

I say to this community, Be humble, be faithful to your God, true to his Church, benevolent to the strangers that may pass through our Territory, and kind to all people, serving the Lord with all your might, trusting in him; but never fear the frowns of an enemy, nor be moved by the flatteries of friends or of enemies from the path of right. Serve your God; believe in him, and never be ashamed of him, and sustain your character before him.

I say to the aged, to the middle-aged, and to the young—All be true to your God, true to your brethren, and kind to all, serving God with all your heart. And may he bless you for Jesus' sake. Amen. 1:146.

While speaking the other day to the people, I observed that "the race was not to the swift, nor the battle to the strong," neither riches to men of wisdom. I happened to cast my eyes upon Ira Ames, who was sitting in the congregation. I knew he had been in the Church a considerable length of time, I have been personally acquainted with him for twenty years. My eye also caught many more of the first Saints at the same time. These men know that "Mormonism" is true, they have moved steadily forward, and have not sought to become noted characters as many have; but, unseen as it were, they have maintained their footing steadily in the right path. I could place my hand upon many in this congregation, who will win the race, though they are not very swift, to outward appearance, and they make no great pretensions; they are found continually attending to their own business. They do not appear to be great warriors, or as if they were likely to win the battle. But what is their true character? They have faith today, they are filled with faith, their words are few, but they are full of integrity. You will find them tomorrow as they were yesterday, or are today. Visit them when you will, or under what circumstances, and you find them unalterably the same; and finally when you have spent your life with them, you will find that their lives throughout have been well spent, full of faith, hope, charity, and good works, as far as they have had the ability. These are the ones who will win the race, conquer in the battle, and obtain the peace and righteousness of eternity. 1:89.

You may examine from the beginning to this day, and continue to watch in the future, and where you find a man who wishes to steady the ark of God, without being called to do so, you will find a dark spot in him. The man full of light and intelligence discerns that God steadies his own ark, dictates his own affairs, guides his people, controls his kingdom, governs nations, and holds the hearts of all living in his hands, and turns them hither and thither at his pleasure, not infringing upon their agency. There is not the least danger of disagreeing with persons enjoying the Holy Spirit. 8:66.

To be great is to be good before the Heavens and before all good men. 10:111.

Give Freely—Let us not love the things of this world above the things of God, but strip for the race and harness for the battle of the Gospel plan of salvation. 10:328.

How contracted in mind and short-sighted we must be to permit the perishable things of this world to swerve us in the least degree from our fidelity to the truth. It shows that we lack knowledge which we should possess. 11:283.

Suppose that you are required to do ten pieces of work, but of the ten only one is necessary for the promotion of the Kingdom of God; which had you better do—perform the ten pieces of labor, to be sure of doing the right piece, or neglect the whole ten because you do not know which the right one is? Had you not better do the whole ten pieces, that you may be sure of performing that which the Lord really requires at your hands? 8:12-13.

I wish you to understand, however, that a man giving his means to build up the Kingdom of God is no proof to me that he is true in heart. I have long since learned, that a person may give a gift with an impure design. 10:268.

Man may think, and some of them do, that we have a right to work for ourselves; but I say we have no time to do that in the narrow, selfish sense generally entertained when speaking about working for self. We have no time allotted to us here on the earth to work for ourselves in that sense; and yet when laboring in the most disinterested and fervent manner for the cause and Kingdom of God, it is all for ourselves. Though our time be entirely occupied in laboring for the advancement of the Kingdom of God on the earth we are in reality laboring most effectually for self, for all our interest and welfare, both in time and eternity, are circumscribed and bound up in that Kingdom. 14:101.

Be Honest—Woe to those who profess to be Saints and are not honest. Only be honest with yourselves, and you will be honest to the brethren. 2:53.

Men must be honest, they must live faithfully before their God, and honor their calling and being on the earth. You ask if that is possible? Yes; the doctrine which we have embraced takes away the stony hearts. 3:118-119.

We need to learn, practice, study, know and understand how angels live with each other. When this community comes to the point to be perfectly honest and upright, you will never find a poor person; none will lack, all will have sufficient. Every man, woman, and child will have all they need just as soon as they all become honest. When the majority of the community are dishonest, it maketh the honest portion poor, for the dishonest serve and enrich themselves at their expense. 6:76.

It is much better to be honest; to live here uprightly, and forsake and shun evil, than it is to be dishonest. It is the easiest path in the world to be honest,—to be upright before God; and when people learn this, they will practice it. 5:295.

Honest hearts produce honest actions—holy desires produce corresponding outward works.

Fulfil your contracts and sacredly keep your word. 10:97.

I have no fellowship for a man that will make a promise and not fulfil it. 13:301.

Simple truth, simplicity, honesty, uprightness, justice, mercy, love, kindness, do good to all and evil to none, how easy it is to live by such principles! A thousand times easier than to practice deception! 14:76.

Honesty in Labor—I have tried to suppress dishonesty in individuals, and have tried thereby to make them honest. If I hire a carpenter and pay him three dollars a day, and he is three days in making a six-panel door that a good workman can make in one, or even a door and a half, I do not want to pay him three dollars a day for the labor. 6:73.

We want the Saints to increase in goodness, until our mechanics, for instance, are so honest and reliable that this Railroad Company will say, "Give us a 'Mormon' Elder for an engineer, then none need have the least fear to ride, for if he knows there is danger he will take every measure necessary to preserve the lives of those entrusted to his care." I want to see our Elders so full of integrity that they will be preferred by this Company for their engine builders, watchmen, engineers, clerks, and business managers. If we live our religion and are worthy the name of Latter-day Saints, we are just the men that all such business can be entrusted to with perfect safety; if it can not it will prove that we do not live our religion. 12:300.

If you see honest persons, you see those who are ready to take hold and labor with their might, even though they have but one potato in a day; they will suffer rather than impoverish the Church. 3:340.

One liar is like a bad king. A corrupt and wicked king can corrupt a whole nation. One liar can deceive thousands. 16:30.

A very simple person can tell the truth, but it takes a very smart person to tell a lie and make it appear like the truth. 11:304.

Consistency and Sincerity—O, consistency, thou art one of the fairest jewels in the life of a Saint. 11:136.

If we teach righteousness, let us also practice righteousness in every sense of the word; if we teach morality, let us be moral; let us see to it that we preserve ourselves within the bounds of all the good which we teach to others. I am sure this course will be good to live by and good to die by, and when we get through the journey of life, here, what consolation it will be to us to know that we have done as we have wished others to do by us in all respects. 11:130.

There is not one man in this city, nor in the Territory, who hates the truth and the Latter-day Saints, whose influence I dread, no, not even the hundredth part, as I do a smooth, slick hypocrite who professes to be a Latter-day Saint. The former cannot sow the seeds of infidelity and unbelief in the hearts of the people; but the latter can. 18:359.

A person who is a thief, a liar, and a murderer in his heart, but professes to be a Saint, is more odious in the sight of God, angels and good men, than a person who comes out and openly declares that he is our enemy. I know how to take such a man, but a devil with a Saint's cloak on is one of the meanest characters you can imagine. I say, blessings on the head of a wicked Gentile who is my avowed enemy, far sooner than upon an enemy cloaked with a Saint's profession. 3:120.

But I hope and trust in the Lord my God that I shall never be left to praise this people, to speak well of them, for the purpose of cheering and comforting them by the art of flattery; to lead them on by smooth speeches day after day, week after week, month after month, and year after year, and let them roll sin as a sweet morsel under their tongues, and be guilty of transgressing the law of God. I hope I shall never be left to flatter this people, or any people, on the earth, in their iniquity, but far rather chasten them for their wickedness and praise them for their goodness. 4:22.

The religion that we have embraced must last a man from Monday morning until Monday morning, and from Saturday night until Saturday night, and from one new year until another; it must be in all our thoughts and words, in all our ways and dealings. We come here to tell the people how to be saved; we know how, consequently we can tell others. Suppose our calling tomorrow is to conduct a railroad, to go into some philosophical business, or no matter what, our minds, our faith or religion, our God and his Spirit are with us; and if we should happen to be found in a room dedicated for purposes of amusement and an accident should occur, and an Elder engaged in the dance is called upon to go and lay hands on the sick, if he is not prepared to exercise his calling and his faith in God as much there as at any other time and in any other place, he never should be found there, for none have a legal right to the amusements which the Lord has ordained for his children except those who acknowledge his hand in all things and keep his commandments. 14:117.

Chapter XXI

HAPPINESS AND SOCIAL ENJOYMENTS

Saints Should be Happy—Then learn to be happy when you have the privilege. 5:294.

The whole world are after happiness. It is not found in gold and silver, but it is in peace and love. 12:314.

What will give a man joy? That which will give him peace. 7:3.

If the heart is cheerful, all is light and glorious within; there is no sorrow. 6:41.

When man is industrious and righteous, then is he happy. 9:244.

The person who enjoys the experience of the knowledge of the Kingdom of God on the earth, and at the same time has the love of God within him, is the happiest of any individuals on the earth. 18:236.

What principal object have human beings in view? Happiness. Give me glory, give me power, give me wealth, give me a good name, give me influence with my fellow-men, give me all these, and it does not follow that I am thereby made happy; that depends altogether upon what principle those acquisitions were gained. 7:3.

The only heaven for you is that which you make yourselves. My heaven is here (laying his hand upon his heart). I carry it with me. When do I expect it in its perfection? When I come up in the resurrection; then I shall have it, and not till then. 4:57.

You never saw a true Saint in the world that had sorrow, neither can you find one. If persons are destitute of the fountain of living water, or the principles of eternal life, then they are sorrowful. If the words of life dwell within us, and we have the hope of eternal life and glory, and let that spark within us kindle to a flame, to the consuming of the least and last remains of selfishness, we never can walk in darkness and are strangers to doubt and fear. 6:41.

If this is the work of God, let us understand its beauty and glory. I do not say that all are like myself; but from the day I commenced preaching the Gospel to this present moment, I never had a feeling in my heart to occupy much time in preaching hell to the people, or in telling them much about being damned. There are the kingdoms and worlds which God has prepared, and which are waiting for the just. There are more beauty, glory, excellency, knowledge, power, and heavenly things than I have time to talk about, without spending my time in talking about the hells prepared for the damned. I have not time to talk much about them. 8:42.

It does make the Devil mad. That is true, it makes him mad that he cannot afflict this people so as to make them have a sad countenance. 4:299.

To make ourselves happy is incorporated in the great design of man's existence. I have learned not to fret myself about that which I cannot help. If I can do good, I will do it; and if I cannot reach a thing, I will content myself to be without it. This makes me happy all the day long. 2:95.

Where is happiness, real happiness? Nowhere but in God. By possessing the spirit of our holy religion, we are happy in the morning, we are happy at noon, we are happy in the evening; for the spirit of love and union is with us, and we rejoice in the spirit because, it is of God, and we rejoice in God, for he is the giver of every good thing. Every Latter-day Saint, who has experienced the love of God in his heart, after having received the remission of his sins, through baptism, and the laying on of hands, realizes that he is filled with joy, and happiness, and consolation. He may be in pain, in error, in poverty, or in prison, if necessity demands, still, he is joyful. This is our experience, and each and every Latter-day Saint can bear witness to it. 18:213.

Truly happy is that man or woman, or that people, who enjoys the privileges of the Gospel of the Son of God, and who know how to appreciate his blessings. 1:309.

Men and women, for slight causes, make shipwreck of faith, lose the spirit of the Gospel, losing the object for which they left their homes and their friends. We are all searching for happiness; we hope for it, we think we live for it, it is our aim in this life. But do we live so as to enjoy the happiness we so much desire? There is only one way for Latter-day Saints to be happy, which is simply to live their religion, or in other words believe the Gospel of Jesus Christ in every part, obeying the gospel of liberty with full purpose of heart, which sets us free indeed. If we will, as a community, obey the law of God, and comply with the ordinances of salvation, then we may expect to find the happiness we so much desire, but if we do not pursue this course we cannot enjoy the unalloyed happiness which is to be found in the Gospel. To profess to be a Saint, and not enjoy the spirit of it, tries every fibre of the heart, and is one of the most painful experiences that man can suffer. 12:168.

Social Amusements—There is no true enjoyment in life—nothing that can be a blessing to an individual or to a community, but what is ordained of God to bless his people. 6:143.

We want to see every countenance full of cheerfulness, and every eye bright with the hope of future happiness. 12:314.

We are made to enjoy all that God enjoys, to inherit all he inherits, to possess all the power that he possesses, all the excellency with which he is endowed—all things are to be brought into subjection to him by his faithful children, that they may enjoy all things with him; these considerations bring peace to the heart that is opened to understanding. 10:171.

A gathering and social spirit seems to be the order of heaven—of the spirit that is in the Gospel we have embraced. Though it may be esteemed as a fault—as an unwarrantable act to separate ourselves from those who do not believe as we believe, yet such is the nature of a portion of our religion pertaining to the performance of outward duties. If the Latter-day Saints can associate together, free from the contaminating influences that are in the world, it is a blessing and a great privilege. What would induce a child to grow up in the wickedness of the wicked world, if it never saw or heard any of it? 7:267.

Is there anything immoral in recreation? If I see my sons and daughters enjoying themselves, chatting, visiting, riding, going to a party or a dance, is there anything immoral in that? I watch very closely, and if I hear a word, see a look, or a sneer at divine things or anything derogatory to a good moral character, I feel it in a moment, and I say, "If you follow that it will not lead to good, it is evil; it will not lead to the fountain of life and intelligence; follow, only, the path that leads to life everlasting."

It is the privilege of the Saints to enjoy every good thing, for the earth and its fulness belong to the Lord, and he has promised all to his faithful Saints; but it must be enjoyed without spirit of covetousness and selfishness—without the spirit of lust, and in the spirit of the Gospel; then the sun will shine sweetly upon us; each day will be filled with delight, and all things will be filled with beauty, giving joy, pleasure, and rest to the Saints. 8:82.

We are to learn how to enjoy the things of life—how to pass our mortal existence here. There is no enjoyment, no comfort, no pleasure, nothing that the human heart can imagine, with all the spirit of revelation we can get, that tends to beautify, happify, make comfortable and peaceful, and exalt the feelings of mortals, but what the Lord has in store for his people. He never objected to their taking comfort. He never revealed any doctrine, that I have any knowledge of, but, what in its nature is calculated to fill with peace and glory, and lift every sentiment and impulse of the heart above every low, sad, deathly, false and grovelling feeling. The Lord wishes us to live that we may enjoy the fulness of the glory that pertains to the upper world, and bid farewell to all that gloomy, dark, deathly feeling that is spread over the inhabitants of the earth. 8:128-129.

Our organism makes us capable of exquisite enjoyment. Do I not love my wife, my son, my daughter, my brother, my sister, my father, and my mother? And do I not love to associate with my friends? I do, and love to reflect and talk on eternal principles. 7:138.

We say to the Bishops and to everybody, exercise yourselves, provide innocent amusement for the youth, attract the minds of the children, and get the upper hand of them and be on the lead. I see mothers right among us whose course is very imprudent with their children. You ought always to take the lead of your children in their minds and affections. Instead of being behind with the whip, always be in advance, then you can say, "Come along," and you will have no use for the rod. They will delight to follow you, and will like your words and ways, because you are always comforting them and giving them pleasure and enjoyment. If they get a little naughty, stop them when they have gone far enough. We say to the brethren, humor your wives and children as far as you can, but when they transgress, and transcend certain bounds we want them to stop. If you are in the lead they will stop, they cannot run over you; but if you are behind they will run away from you. Husbands, always be in advance of your wives, and then if they undertake to do something that is very displeasing to you they will run right against you, and then stop and sit down because they can't go any further. Do you know how to do this? "No," says one, "I don't know that I do." Well, then, learn by searching after truth, according to the revelations given in this book. Search after truth in all good books, and learn the wisdom of the world and the wisdom of God, and put them together and you will be able to benefit yourselves. 12:313.

Our work, our every-day labor, our whole lives are within the scope of our religion. This is what we believe and what we try to practice. Yet the Lord permits a great many things that he never commands. I have frequently heard my old brethren in the Christian world make remarks about the impropriety of indulging in pastimes and amusements. The Lord never commanded me to dance, yet I have danced: you all know it, for my life is before the world. Yet while the Lord has never commanded me to do it, he has permitted it. I do not know that he ever commanded the boys to go and play at ball, yet he permits it. I am not aware that he ever commanded us to build a theater, but he has permitted it, and I can give the reason why. Recreation and diversion are as necessary to our well-being as the more serious pursuits of life. There is not a man in the world but what, if kept at any one branch of business or study, will become like a machine. Our pursuits should be so diversified as to develop every trait of character and diversity of talent. If you would develop every power and faculty possessed by your children, they must have the privilege of engaging in and enjoying a diversity of amusements and studies; to attain great excellence, however, they cannot all be kept to any one individual branch of study. I recollect once while in England, in the district of country called the "Potteries," seeing a man pass along the street, his head, perhaps, within sixteen or eighteen inches of the ground. I inquired what occupation he had followed for a living, and learned that he had never done anything in his life but turned a teacup, and he was then seventy-four years of age. How do we know but what, if he had had the privilege, he would have made a statesman or a fine physician, an excellent mechanic, or a good judge? We cannot tell. This shows the necessity of the mind being kept active and having the opportunity of indulging in every exercise it can enjoy in order to attain to a full development of its powers. 13:61.

Little boys play with their wagons, tops, marbles, etc.; little girls with their dolls, cradles, and skipping ropes. They are in the height of their enjoyment, while there sits the mother whose mind comprehends all the children can enjoy, and then she can see enjoyment far beyond what they are then capable of enjoying. Perhaps her vision is open to see forward into the eternity before her, and that she will be able to preserve her identity in her future existence. Do you not see how easy it is for her to circumscribe all those little children can enjoy? Her feeling is, "I am delighted: it is a great satisfaction to see my children enjoy themselves." But how would she like to engage in their plays? "It is my joy to see them enjoy themselves." Do you like to get together in your parties? How are you looked upon by beings in the eternal worlds? Precisely as a mother looks upon her children when they are enjoying themselves and passing their time so kindly with each other. Says the mother, "I do delight in seeing my children enjoy themselves." I also delight in enjoying myself with the brethren and sisters, and giving to my natural organization the food that the natural body requires. The body requires food, and the immortal spirit requires food; the whole organization requires something to feast upon, and we get up amusements to satisfy it. 8:358-359.

I repeat that it is not your lawful privilege to yield to anything in the shape of amusement, until you have performed every duty, and obtained the power of God to enable you to withstand and resist all foul spirits that might attack you, and lead you astray; until you have command over them, and by your faith, obtained, through prayer and supplication, the blessings of the Holy Spirit, and it rests upon, and abides continually with you. 1:113.

In all your social communications, or whatever your associations are, let all the dark, discontented, murmuring, unhappy, miserable feelings—all the evil fruit of the mind, fall from the tree in silence and unnoticed; and so let it perish, without taking it up to present to your neighbors. But when you have joy and happiness, light and intelligence, truth and virtue, offer that fruit abundantly to your neighbors, and it will do them good, and so strengthen the hands of your fellow-beings, even though you may be looked upon as an outcast, vile people, not worthy of the society of what are commonly deemed the intelligent portion of the world. 7:269.

I have frequently told the people at our places of recreation, if they cannot go there with the Spirit of the Lord, they had better stay at home. 11:283.

On every such occasion, it is right, reasonable, and necessary, that every heart be directed to the Lord. When we have had sufficient recreation for our good, let that suffice. It is all right; then let our minds labor instead of our bodies; and in all our exercises of body and mind, it is good to remember the Lord. 1:30.

I am most perfectly satisfied to associate with those whose hearts are filled with peace, with praise and adoration to our God, and whose lives are full of good works. Their voices to me are like sweet music. I have not the least desire to mingle with or look upon the faces of those who hate God and his cause. 8:57.

We are now enjoying our pastimes. We often meet together and worship the Lord by singing, praying, and preaching, fasting, and communing with each other in the Sacrament of the Lord's Supper. Now we are met in the capacity of a social community—for what? That our minds may rest, and our bodies receive that recreation which is proper and necessary to keep up an equilibrium, to promote healthy action to the whole system.

Let our minds sing for joy, and let life diffuse itself into every avenue of the body; for the object of our meeting is for its exercise, for its good.

This party was gotten up by the members of the Legislature, to rest their minds, to convene in a social capacity, and enjoy the society of each other, with their families, and to give renewed activity and energy, which will invigorate and strengthen them in the discharge of the arduous duties devolving upon them. 1:29.

Our present situation, and the enjoyments of this evening, will become subjects of pleasant and agreeable reflection, when we shall be separated from this community, and go to the right and to the left; then these moments of festive joy will be remembered with pleasing emotions, and cherished in fond memory in afteryears. 1:30.

Is there any harm in Sunday school parties? No! It is one of the most harmless kinds of enjoyment when conducted aright. If they wish to dance, let them dance; let them talk and play; but not do any wrong. They must not get angry with each other; and if any do wrong instruct them to do right. If our children are thus taught, they will be patterns of piety and their conduct will be worthy of imitation. 12:239.

One of the most useful amusements we could have would be for the Seventies and High Priests to meet here, instead of in their small halls, and lecture. Which is the most delightful, to satisfy the wants of the natural body, or those of the intelligent part within us? Which is the most precious? Both. 8:358.

My first remarks will be concerning such exercises as we have seen here this morning. The Latter-day Saints have many pastimes, and they enjoy themselves in social society with one another. Yet I think, in my reflections, that we should have an increase—and we are having partially an increase of recreation for our youth. We have very few holidays. When the 4th of July comes, we have our amusements and exercises. When the 24th of July comes, we hail it as the anniversary of a day of deliverance. On reflection, I have come to the conclusion that it would be better if we would pay more attention to these public exercises, and direct the minds of our children by observing them, taking a course to have them avoid getting into the habit of drinking and every kind of rowdyism, and other things that are unbecoming; and in all of our amusements have objects of improvement that are worthy of pursuit. We should have more of the children attend Sunday school, and the teachers should continually place objects before them that will lead them to study to improve in their manners, in their words, in their looks and in their behavior; and that will guide their minds aright. You will find we can place before them objects that will do them much good in their thoughts and reflections, that will improve their young and tender minds, and have an influence upon their future lives for good; and we can thus bring them up in the nurture and admonition of the Lord by taking a course to lead their minds. 12:238-239.

I am satisfied that those persons who stamp, clap hands, whistle, and make other noisy and boisterous demonstrations in the theaters, so untimed and uncalled for, have but little sense, and know not the difference between a happy smile of satisfaction to cheer the countenance of a friend, or a contemptuous sneer that brings the curses of man upon man. 9:290.

Never give way to vain laughter. I have seldom laughed aloud for twenty or thirty years without regretting it, and I always blush for those who laugh aloud without meaning. 9:290.

Dancing—Those that have kept the covenants and served their God, if they wish to exercise themselves in any way to rest their minds and tire their bodies, go and enjoy yourselves in the dance, and let God be in all your thoughts in this as in all other things, and he will bless you. 6:149.

There are many of our aged brethren and sisters, who, through the traditions of their fathers and the requirements of a false religion, were never inside a ball-room or a theater until they became Latter-day Saints, and now they seem more anxious for this kind of amusement than are our children. This arises from the fact they have been starved for many years for that amusement which is designed to buoy up their spirits and make their bodies vigorous and strong, and tens of thousands have sunk into untimely graves for want of such exercises to the body and the mind. They require mutual nourishment to make them sound and healthy. Every faculty and power of both body and mind is a gift from God. Never say that means used to create and continue healthy action of body and mind are from hell. 9:244.

I want it distinctly understood, that fiddling and dancing are no part of our worship. The question may be asked, What are they for, then? I answer, that my body may keep pace with my mind. My mind labors like a man logging, all the time; and this is the reason why I am fond of these pastimes—they give me a privilege to throw everything off, and shake myself, that my body may exercise, and my mind rest. What for? To get strength, and be renewed and quickened, and enlivened, and animated, so that my mind may not wear out. Experience tells us that the most of the inhabitants of the earth wear out their bodies without wearing their minds at all, through the suffering they endure from hard labor, with distress, poverty, and want. While on the other hand, a great portion of mankind wear out their bodies without laboring, only in anxiety. But when men are brought to labor entirely in the field of intelligence, there are few minds to be found possessing strength enough to bear all things; the mind becomes overcharged, and when this is the case, it begins to wear upon the body, which will sink for want of the proper exercises. This is the reason why I believe in and practice what I do. 1:30.

There is no music in hell, for all good music belongs to heaven. Sweet harmonious sounds give exquisite joy to human beings capable of appreciating music. I delight in hearing harmonious tones made by the human voice, by musical instruments, and by both combined. Every sweet musical sound that can be made belongs to the Saints and is for the Saints. Every flower, shrub and tree to beautify, and to gratify the taste and smell, and every sensation that gives to man joy and felicity are for the Saints who receive them from the Most High. 9:244.

If you happen to be in a party where I am and wearing dresses made with your own hands, I shall take pleasure in dancing with you in preference to the lady dressed in silks and satins. 9:100.

I am opposed to making a cotillion hall a place of worship. 9:194.

I am opposed to having cotillions or theatrical performances in this Tabernacle. I am opposed to making this a fun hall, I do not mean for wickedness, I mean for the recuperation of our spirits and bodies. I am not willing that they should convert the house that has been set apart for religious meetings into a dancing hall. 9:195.

Those who cannot serve God with a pure heart in the dance should not dance. 6:148.

If you want to dance, run a foot race, pitch quoits, or play at ball, do it, and exercise your bodies, and let your minds rest. 6:149.

If you wish to dance, dance; and you are just as much prepared for a prayer meeting after dancing as ever you were, if you are Saints. If you desire to ask God for anything, you are as well prepared to do so in the dance as in any other place, if you are Saints. Are your eyes open to know that everything in the earth, in hell, or in heaven, is ordained for the use of intelligent beings? 6:148.

The Theater—Is there evil in the theater; in the ball room; in the place of worship; in the dwelling; in the world? Yes, when men are inclined to do evil in any of these places. There is evil in persons meeting simply for a chitchat, if they will allow themselves to commit evil while thus engaged. 9:243.

I built that theater to attract the young of our community and to provide amusement for the boys and girls, rather than have them running all over creation for recreation. Long before that was built I said to the Bishops, "Get up your parties and pleasure grounds to amuse the people." 12:312-313.

Upon the stage of a theater can be represented in character, evil and its consequences, good and its happy results and rewards; the weakness and the follies of man, the magnanimity of virtue and the greatness of truth. The stage can be made to aid the pulpit in impressing upon the minds of a community an enlightened sense of a virtuous life, also a proper horror of the enormity of sin and a just dread of its consequences. The path of sin with its thorns and pitfalls, its gins and snares can be revealed, and how to shun it. 9:243.

Tragedy is favored by the outside world; I am not in favor of it. I do not wish murder and all its horrors and the villainy leading to it portrayed before our women and children; I do not want the child to carry home with it the fear of the fagot, the sword, the pistol, or the dagger, and suffer in the night from frightful dreams. I want such plays performed as will make the spectators feel well; and I wish those who perform to select a class of plays that will improve the public mind, and exalt the literary taste of the community. 9:245.

Excursions—If the people should conclude to take short excursions with their families, except the smallest children, it would be much to their comfort and would cheer them up. 2:283.

I would be very pleased to learn that your Bishop, Brother Miller, was preparing a place for parties; with a little pond to float boats on, and other means of enjoyment, where the people could assemble to have their exercises. Get the young minds to follow after you in these things, and they will follow after you in every precept that is good. And I would like to hear of other Bishops taking steps to prepare suitable places for the same purpose. 12:239.

Chapter XXII

EDUCATION

Knowledge and Intelligence—Education is a good thing, and blessed is the man who has it, and can use it for the dissemination of the Gospel without being puffed up with pride. 11:214.

When we speak upon education, it is not to be understood that it alone consists in a man's learning the letters of the alphabet, in being trained in every branch of scholastic lore, in becoming a proficient in the knowledge of the sciences, and a classical scholar, but also in learning to classify himself and others. 1:66.

Find a true philosopher and you find one who has the true principles of Christianity. He delights in them; and sees and understands the hand of Providence guiding and directing in all the affairs of this life. 14:82.

A firm, unchangeable course of righteousness through life is what secures to a person true intelligence. 8:32.

Intelligent beings are organized to become Gods, even the Sons of God, to dwell in the presence of the Gods, and become associated with the highest intelligences that dwell in eternity. We are now in the school, and must practice upon what we receive. 8:160.

When we have faith to understand that he must dictate, and that we must be perfectly submissive to him, then we shall begin to rapidly collect the intelligence that is bestowed upon the nations, for all this intelligence belongs to Zion. All the knowledge, wisdom, power, and glory that have been bestowed upon the nations of the earth, from the days of Adam till now, must be gathered home to Zion. 8:278.

This people have embraced the philosophy of eternal lives, and in view of this we should cease to be children and become philosophers, understanding our own existence, its purpose and intimate design, then our days will not become a blank through ignorance, but every day will bring with it its useful and profitable employment. God has placed us here, given us the ability we possess, and supplied the means upon which we can operate to produce social, national, and eternal happiness. 9:100.

When a man is capable of correcting you, and of giving you light, and true doctrine, do not get up an altercation, but submit to be taught like little children, and strive with all your might to understand. 1:47.

Learning a, b, c, d, does not hinder me learning e, f, g. 16:27.

A Religion of Improvement—Ours is a religion of improvement; it is not contracted and confined; but is calculated to expand the minds of the children of men and lead them up into the state of intelligence that will be an honor to our being. 10:290.

Every art and science known and studied by the children of men is comprised within the Gospel. Where did the knowledge come from which has enabled man to accomplish such great achievements in science and mechanism within the last few years? We know that knowledge is from God, but why do they not acknowledge him? Because they are blind to their own interests, they do not see and understand things as they are. Who taught men to chain the lightning? Did man unaided of himself discover that? No, he received the knowledge from the Supreme Being. From him, too, has every art and science proceeded, although the credit is given to this individual, and that individual. But where did they get the knowledge from, have they it in and of themselves? No, they must acknowledge that, if they cannot make one spear of grass grow, nor one hair white or black without artificial aid, they are dependent upon the Supreme Being just the same as the poor and the ignorant. Where have we received the knowledge to construct the labor-saving machinery for which the present age is remarkable? From Heaven. Where have we received our knowledge of astronomy, or the power to make glasses to penetrate the immensity of space? We received it from the same Being that Moses, and those who were before him, received their knowledge from; the same Being who told Noah that the world should be drowned and its people destroyed. From him has every astronomer, artist and mechanician that ever lived on the earth obtained his knowledge. By him, too, has the power to receive from one another been bestowed, and to search into the deep things pertaining to this earth and every principle connected with it. 12:257.

It is highly gratifying to the Lord, to angels, and to all good men, to see intelligent beings organized to receive a great amount of intelligence—seeking to possess eternal life. 8:136.

The Lord has chosen the poor of this world,—rich in faith—and the time will come when he will give the earth to his poor for an everlasting inheritance. I speak this for the comfort of my brethren and sisters who have been poor. They have come here, and what do we see? The youth, the middle-aged and the old improving in letters, in mechanism and in the arts and sciences. We bring them here to improve them, and if the Lord will bless us sufficiently, and the people will bless themselves, we will have a nation that understands all things pertaining to the earth that it is possible for man to grasp. Will this people be praiseworthy? Yes, and honored and honorable. Will they be looked to as examples? Yes; and it is the duty of the Latter-day Saints to live their religion so that all the world can say there is a pattern for us, not only in our business and worship, but in our knowledge of things that are, things that have been and of things that are yet to come, until the knowledge of Zion shall reach the uttermost parts of the earth, and the kings and great men shall say, "Let us go to Zion and learn wisdom." 12:257.

The greatest difficulty we have to meet is what may be termed ignorance, or want of understanding in the people. 7:63.

Not only does the religion of Jesus Christ make the people acquainted with the things of God, and develop within them moral excellence and purity, but it holds out every encouragement and inducement possible, for them to increase in knowledge and intelligence, in every branch of mechanism, or in the arts and sciences, for all wisdom, and all the arts and sciences in the world are from God, and are designed for the good of his people. 13:147.

Knowledge to be Sought—The religion embraced by the Latter-day Saints, if only slightly understood, prompts them to search diligently after knowledge. There is no other people in existence more eager to see, hear, learn, and understand truth. 8:6.

Let there be a mutual desire in every man to disseminate knowledge, that all may know. I have always followed out the rule of dispensing what I know to others, and been blessed in so doing. 9:370.

Put forth your ability to learn as fast as you can, and gather all the strength of mind and principle of faith you possibly can, and then distribute your knowledge to the people. 8:146.

We, who believe in and have obeyed this Gospel, look forward with the anticipation of obtaining a great amount of knowledge and wisdom. When we embraced the Gospel, the spirit opened up to our minds the fact that the wisdom, the knowledge and the power of God would increase in the midst of the Saints. This is our experience, knowing for myself, what the Spirit of the Lord brings to the understanding, testify what it reveals to others. 18:236.

Let us train our minds until we delight in that which is good, lovely and holy, seeking continually after that intelligence which will enable us effectually to build up Zion, which consists in building houses, tabernacles, temples, streets, and every convenience and necessity to embellish and beautify, seeking to do the will of the Lord all the days of our lives, improving our minds in all scientific and mechanical knowledge, seeking diligently to understand the great design and plan of all created things, that we may know what to do with our lives and how to improve upon the facilities placed within our reach. 10:177.

If we wish to be taught, to receive, and understand, we must train ourselves. 6:99.

We are in a great school, and we should be diligent to learn, and continue to store up the knowledge of heaven and of earth, and read good books, although I cannot say that I would recommend the reading of all books, for it is not all books which are good. Read good books, and extract from them wisdom and understanding as much as you possibly can, aided by the Spirit of God. 12:124.

Every man and woman that has talent and hides it will be called a slothful servant. Improve day by day upon the capital you have. In proportion as we are capacitated to receive, so it is our duty to do. 7:7.

It is our duty and calling, as ministers of the same salvation and Gospel, to gather every item of truth and reject every error. Whether a truth be found with professed infidels, or with the Universalists, or the Church of Rome, or the Methodists, the Church of England, the Presbyterians, the Baptists, the Quakers, the Shakers, or any other of the various and numerous different sects and parties, all of whom have more or less truth, it is the business of the Elders of this Church (Jesus, their Elder Brother, being at their head) to gather up all the truths in the world pertaining to life and salvation, to the Gospel we preach, to mechanism of every kind, to the sciences, and to philosophy, wherever it may be found in every nation, kindred, tongue, and people and bring it to Zion. 7:283.

Continuous Education—This is our labor, our business, and our calling—to grow in grace and in knowledge from day to day and from year to year. 6:268.

I shall not cease learning while I live, nor when I arrive in the spirit-world; but shall there learn with greater facility; and when I again receive my body, I shall learn a thousand times more in a thousand times less time; and then I do not mean to cease learning, but shall continue my researches. 8:10.

We shall never see the time when we shall not need to be taught, nor when there will not be an object to be gained. I never expect to see the time that there will not be a superior power and a superior knowledge, and, consequently, incitements to further progress and further improvements. 10:221.

If I do not learn what is in the world, from first to last, somebody will be wiser than I am. I intend to know the whole of it, both good and bad. Shall I practice evil? No; neither have I told you to practice it, but to learn by the light of truth every principle there is in existence in the world. 2:94.

We need constant instruction, and our great heavenly Teacher requires of us to be diligent pupils in his school, that we may in time reach his glorified presence. If we will not lay to heart the rules of education which our Teacher gives us to study, and continue to advance from one branch of learning to another, we never can be scholars of the first class and become endowed with the science, power, excellency, brightness and glory of the heavenly hosts; and unless we are educated as they are, we cannot associate with them. 10:266.

And inasmuch as the Lord Almighty has designed us to know all that is in the earth, both the good and the evil, and to learn not only what is in heaven, but what is in hell, you need not expect ever to get through learning. Though I mean to learn all that is in heaven, earth, and hell. Do I need to commit iniquity to do it? No. If I were to go into the bowels of hell to find out what is there, that does not make it necessary that I should commit one evil, or blaspheme in any way the name of my Maker 2:94.

The extent of knowledge incorporated within the salvation extended to the children of men, will vastly exceed the researches of the human family, and when they have passed the veil, they will then understand that they have but just commenced to learn. Brother Morley says he never expects to be too old to learn; I believe that doctrine.

Could we live to the age of Methuselah, and eat the fruits which the earth would produce in her strength, as did Adam and Eve before the transgression, and spend our lives in searching after the principles of eternal life, we would find, when one eternity had passed to us, that we had been but children thus far, babies just commencing to learn the things which pertain to the eternities of the Gods.

We might ask, when shall we cease to learn? I will give you my opinion about it: never, never. 3:202.

If we continue to learn all that we can, pertaining to the salvation which is purchased and presented to us through the Son of God, is there a time when a person will cease to learn? Yes, when he has sinned against God the Father, Jesus Christ the Son, and the Holy Ghost—God's minister; when he has denied the Lord, defied him and committed the sin that in the Bible is termed the unpardonable sin—the sin against the Holy Ghost. That is the time when a person will cease to learn, and from that time forth, will descend in ignorance, forgetting that which they formerly knew. They will cease to increase, but must decrease. These are the only characters who will ever cease to learn, both in time and eternity. 3:203.

I ask, have the great and learned men completed their education? No, they are ever learning, and never able to come to the knowledge of the truth. 1:70.

I will not say, as do many, that the more I learn the more I am satisfied that I know nothing; for the more I learn the more I discern an eternity of knowledge to improve upon.

One scholar in a school may far outstrip the rest; but give them sufficient time, and they can learn what the quick, bright scholar has learned so easily and quickly. If we are capacitated to learn one thing today, we can learn another tomorrow. It is the height of folly to say that a man can only learn so much and no more. The further literary men advance in their studies, the more they discern there is to learn, and the more anxious they are to learn.

We may live here year after year, and store up knowledge all the time, and yet not have an opportunity of exhibiting it to others; it is on hand; whenever the time comes it should be used. 6:274.

Experience has taught us that it requires time to acquire certain branches of mechanism, also all principles and ideas that we wish to become masters of. The closer people apply their minds to any correct purpose the faster they can grow and increase in the knowledge of the truth. When they learn to master their feelings, they can soon learn to master their reflections and thoughts in the degree requisite for attaining the objects they are seeking. But while they yield to a feeling or spirit that distracts their minds from a subject they wish to study and learn, so long they will never gain the mastery of their minds. 6:94.

No matter what your circumstances are, whether you are in prosperity or in adversity, you can learn from every person, transaction, and circumstance around you. 4:287.

Effects of Education—The results of the education and traditions of the inhabitants of the earth, are interwoven with their feelings, and are like a cloak that envelopes them, in the capacity of societies, neighborhoods, people, and pursue that course collectively or individually, that seemeth good to themselves. 3:88.

Every principle of true philosophy convinces a person who understands the spirit of the Gospel and has received the good word of life, that the darkness is in proportion to the light that has been forsaken. Rear a child in a cell which only admits a small glimmer of light, and the child will pass its time with some degree of satisfaction, when a person accustomed to the bright of day could not at first see anything. And the greater the light bestowed upon an individual or upon a people, the greater the darkness when that light is forsaken. 8:121.

Will education feed and clothe you, keep you warm on a cold day, or enable you to build a house? Not at all. Should we cry down education on this account? No. What is it for? The improvement of the mind; to instruct us in all arts and sciences, in the history of the world, in the laws of nations; to enable us to understand the laws and principles of life, and how to be useful while we live. 14:83.

What is the religion of the day? What are all the civil laws and governments of the day? They are merely traditions, without a single exception. Do the people realize this—that it is the force of their education that makes right and wrong with them? It is not the line which he Lord has drawn out; it is not the law which the Lord has given them; it is not the righteousness which is according to the character of him who has created all things, and by his own law governs and controls all things; but by the prejudice of education—the prepossessed feeling that is begotten in the hearts of the children of men, by surrounding objects. 9:86.

If I should hear a man advocate the erroneous principles he has imbibed through education, and oppose those principles, some might imagine that I was opposed to that man, when, in fact, I am only opposed to every evil and erroneous principle he advances. 6:331.

There is not a law of God, nor a law of any nation that exercises so strong an influence upon us as do our traditions at times, to bind us to certain customs, habits and ceremonies. 8:58.

Educate our Children—Believe on the Lord Jesus Christ, obey his doctrine, cease your warring and contention, beat your swords into plowshares and your spears into pruning hooks; make railroads, build colleges, teach the children, give them the learning of the world and the things of God; elevate their minds, that they may not only understand the earth we walk upon, but the air we breathe, the water we drink, and all the elements pertaining to the earth; and then search other worlds, and become acquainted with the planetary system, the dwellings of the angels and the heavenly beings, that they may ultimately be prepared for a higher state of being, and finally be associated with them. I wish we would do it; I pray the Lord to do it, but he will not, unless we help him. 14:210.

The education of our children is worthy of our attention, and the instruction of the Elders from this stand. It is a subject that should be thoroughly impressed upon the minds of parents and the rising generation; and those who wish to preach from this text may do so. 13:262.

It is a duty we owe our children to educate and train them in every principle of honor and good manners, in a knowledge of God and his ways, and in popular school education. I am happy to hear the little children sing, and hope they are also learning to read and write, and are progressing in every useful branch of learning. 11:111.

See that your children are properly educated in the rudiments of their mother tongue, and then let them proceed to higher branches of learning; let them become more informed in every department of true and useful learning than their fathers are. When they have become well acquainted with their language, let them study other languages, and make themselves fully acquainted with the manners, customs, laws, governments and literature of other nations, peoples, and tongues. Let them also learn the truth pertaining to the arts and sciences, and how to apply the same to their temporal wants. Let them study things that are upon the earth, that are in the earth, and that are in the heavens. 8:9.

I wish this people to pay particular attention to the education of their children. If we can do no more, we should give them the facilities of a common education, that when our sons are sent into the world as ministers of salvation and as representatives of the Kingdom of God in the mountains, they can mingle with the best society and intelligibly and sensibly present the principles of truth to mankind, for all truth is the offspring of heaven, and is incorporated in the religion which we have embraced.

Every accomplishment, every polished grace, every useful attainment in mathematics, music, and in all science and art belongs to the Saints, and they should avail themselves as expeditiously as possible of the wealth of knowledge the sciences offer to every diligent and persevering scholar. 10:224.

The education of youth is an important text for the brethren to preach from. A very high value should be placed upon it by the Saints. We have the privilege of enjoying the spirit of revelation and the knowledge which comes from above, and in addition to this, every branch of education known in the world should be taught among and acquired by us. 13:263.

My policy is to keep everybody busy in building up this Kingdom; in building houses; in breaking up land; in setting out fruit and ornamental trees; in laying out fine gardens, pleasant walks, and beautiful groves; and in building academies and other places of learning.

There are hundreds of young men here who can go to school, which is far better than to waste their time. Study languages, get knowledge and understanding; and while doing this, get wisdom from God, and forget it not, and learn how to apply it, that you may be good with it all the days of your lives. 2:145.

Establish Schools—Is it not a blessing to have schools in our community, where our teachers can teach our children correct principles, and impart to them education that will be useful? 8:92.

Let a few schools be started by those who are capable of teaching the sciences. The science of architecture, for instance, is worthy the attention of every student. It yields a great amount of real pleasure to be able to understand the grand architectural designs of those magnificent structures that are scattered over Europe and other countries. 9:173.

Go to work and start some schools, go to school and study; have the girls go, and teach them chemistry, so that they can take any of these rocks and analyze them. The sciences can be learned without much difficulty. I want to have schools to entertain the minds of the people and draw them out to learn the arts and sciences. Send the old children to school, and the young ones also; there is nothing I would like better than to learn chemistry, botany, geology, and mineralogy, so that I could tell what I walk on, the properties of the air I breathe, what I drink, etc. 16:170.

Let our teachers ask the Father, in the name of Jesus, to bestow upon them and upon their scholars the Spirit of wisdom and intelligence from heaven; ask for skill and control and ability to teach on the part of the teacher, and willingness to be controlled and adaptability to be taught on the part of the scholars. Let parents aid the teacher in his labors, by seeing that their children attend school punctually, with a proper supply of books, slates, pencils, etc., and permit not a good diligent, faithful schoolteacher to suffer for the common necessaries of life, while he is laboring to educate and bless their children. 9:369.

I will now urge it upon the people—the young men and middle-aged—to get up schools and study. If they are disposed to study physics or surgery, all right; they will know then what to do if a person is sickly, or has his elbow, wrist, or shoulder put out of joint, or his arm or any bone broken. It is just as important to learn such things as it is to learn to plant potatoes. Pay more attention to arithmetic and other things that are useful, instead of acquiring a little French and German and other fanciful studies that are not of so much practical importance. I do not know how long it will be before we call upon the brethren and sisters to enter upon business in an entirely different way from what they have done. I have been an advocate for our printing to be done by females, and as for men being in stores, you might as well set them to knitting stockings as to sell tape. Such business ought to be done by the sisters. It would enable them to sustain themselves, and would be far better than for them to spend their time in the parlor or in walking the streets. Hardy men have no business behind the counter; they who are not able to hoe potatoes, go to the canyon, cut down the trees, saw the lumber, etc., can attend to that business. Study arithmetic and bookkeeping. Introduce stenography into every school; it is an excellent thing to learn. By its means we can commit our thoughts and reflections to paper with ease and rapidity, and thus preserve that which will be of benefit to ourselves and others, and which would otherwise be forever lost. Introduce every kind of useful studies into our schools. Get up classes for the study of law. The laws of this Territory, of the United States, of the different States, of England, and foreign lands. Do this instead of riding over the prairies hunting and wasting your time, which is property that belongs to the Lord our God, and if we do not make good use of it we shall be held accountable. 12:31-32.

Let good schools be established throughout all the settlements of the Saints in Utah. Let good teachers, who are Latter-day Saints in principle and at heart, be employed to educate our children. A good schoolteacher is one of the most essential members in society; he relieves parents, in part, of a great responsibility and labor; we should, therefore, make the business of schoolteaching a permanent institution, and the remuneration should be in amount and in kind equal to the receipts of our best mechanics; it should also be promptly and willingly paid, and school commissioners and trustees should see to it that teachers are properly qualified and do earn their pay. Could I have my wish, I would introduce into our system of education every real improvement. 10:225.

Understand men and women as they are, and not understand them as you are. 8:37.

What to Study—It is our privilege and our duty to search all things upon the face of the earth, and learn what there is for man to enjoy, what God has ordained for the benefit and happiness of mankind, and then make use of it without sinning against him. 9:243.

Learn everything that the children of men know, and be prepared for the most refined society upon the face of the earth, then improve upon this until we are prepared and permitted to enter the society of the blessed—the holy angels that dwell in the presence of God, for our God, because of his purity, is a consuming fire. 16:77.

We should be a people of profound learning pertaining to the things of the world. We should be familiar with the various languages, for we wish to send missionaries to the different nations and to the islands of the sea. We wish missionaries who may go to France to be able to speak the French language fluently, and those who may go to Germany, Italy, Spain, and so on to all nations, to be familiar with the languages of those nations.

We also wish them to understand the geography, habits, customs, and laws of nations and kingdoms, whether they be barbarians or civilized. This is recommended in the revelations given to us. In them we are taught to study the best books, that we may become as well acquainted with the geography of the world as we are with our gardens, and as familiar with the people—so far at least as they are portrayed in print—as we are with our families and neighbors. 8:40.

How gladly would we understand every principle pertaining to science and art, and become thoroughly acquainted with every intricate operation of nature, and with all the chemical changes that are constantly going on around us! How delightful this would be, and what a boundless field of truth and power is open for us to explore! We are only just approaching the shores of the vast ocean of information that pertains to this physical world, to say nothing of that which pertains to the heavens, to angels and celestial beings, to the place of their habitation, to the manner of their life, and their progress to still higher degrees of perfection. 9:167.

Our education should be such as to improve our minds and fit us for increased usefulness; to make us of greater service to the human family; to enable us to stop our rude methods of living, speaking, and thinking. 14:83.

Learn to be good for something. 11:298.

If we could only learn enough to be self-preserving and self-sustaining, we should then have learned what the Gods have learned before us, and what we must eventually learn before we can be exalted. 9:169.

Learn all you can. Learn how to raise calves, chickens, lambs, and all kinds of useful fowls and animals; learn how to till the ground to the best advantage for raising all useful products of the soil; and learn how to manufacture molasses and sugar from the sugar cane. Raise flax, husbands, and let your wives learn to manufacture fine linen. 9:173.

Let the boys from ten to twenty years of age get up schools to learn sword exercise, musket and rifle exercise, and, in short, every act of war. Shall we need this knowledge? No matter; it is good to be acquainted with this kind of exercise. 9:173.

If I could get my own feelings answered I would have law in our schoolbooks, and have our youth study law at school. Then lead their minds to study the decisions and counsels of the just and the wise, and not forever be studying how to get the advantage of their neighbor. This is wisdom. 16:9.

I have a few things to lay before the Conference, one of which is—and I think my brethren will agree with me that this is wise and practicable—for from one to five thousand of our young and middle-aged men to turn their attention to the study of law. I would not speak lightly in the least of law, we are sustained by it; but what is called the practice of law is not always the administration of justice, and would not be so considered in many courts. 16:9.

Every Elder should have at least one trade, and if possible more than one. 10:77.

I am happy to see our children engaged in the study and practice of music. Let them be educated in every useful branch of learning, for we, as a people, have in the future to excel the nations of the earth in religion, science and philosophy. Great advancement has been made in knowledge by the learned of this world, still there is yet much to learn. The hidden powers of nature which give life, growth, and existence to all things have not yet been approached by the wisdom of this world. There exists around us, in the works of God, an everlasting variety—no two leaves, no two blades of grass are alike. Natural philosophy, so far as known, marks these phenomena of nature, and reveals her wonders, but is incapable of revealing the modus operandi of the production.

Let the children in our schools be taught everything that is necessary with regard to doctrine and principle, and then how to live; and let mothers teach their daughters regarding themselves, and how they should live in their sphere of existence, that they may be good wives and good mothers. Let the sisters study economy in the labor and management of their homes. I am satisfied that more than one-half of the labor that is done in our houses can be saved by a judicious exercise of thought and good judgment. Then be wise in these things, and we shall not need tea and coffee, or any other stimulant stronger than our natural food. 12:122-123.

Study to apply your labor to advantage, and you will accomplish much more, without wearing yourselves out so fast. If you have to roll a log, cut down a tree, etc., study how to take advantage of the work. Contrive to accomplish your work with the least expenditure of strength. 8:297.

I would advise you to read books that are worth reading; read reliable history, and search wisdom out of the best books you can procure. 9:173.

"Shall I sit down and read the Bible, the Book of Mormon, and the Book of Covenants all the time?" says one. Yes, if you please, and when you have done, you may be nothing but a sectarian after all. It is your duty to study to know everything upon the face of the earth in addition to reading those books. We should not only study good, and its effects upon our race, but also evil, and its consequences. 2:93-94.

All men should study to learn the nature of mankind, and to discern that divinity inherent in them. A spirit and power of research is planted within, yet they remain undeveloped. 7:1.

Novel reading—is it profitable? I would rather that persons read novels than read nothing. 9:173.

I hope to see the time when we shall have a reformation in the orthography of the English language, among this people, for it is greatly needed. Such a reformation would be a great benefit, and would make the acquirement of an education much easier than at present. 12:174.

I long for the time that a point of the finger, or motion of the hand, will express every idea without utterance. When a man is full of the light of eternity, then the eye is not the only medium through which he sees, his ear is not the only medium by which he hears, nor the brain the only means by which he understands. When the whole body is full of the Holy Ghost, he can see behind him with as much ease, without turning his head, as he can see before him. If you have not that experience, you ought to have. It is not the optic nerve alone that gives the knowledge of surrounding objects to the mind, but it is that which God has placed in man—a system of intelligence that attracts knowledge, as light cleaves to light, intelligence to intelligence, and truth to truth. It is that which lays in man a proper foundation for all education. I shall yet see the time that I can converse with this people, and not speak to them, but the expression of my countenance will tell the congregation what I wish to convey, without opening my mouth.

Religious Education—We have established a school in Salt Lake City for the instruction of the Elders of Israel in the doctrines which are contained in the Bible, Book of Mormon, and book of Doctrine and Covenants, etc., and that is also the place where questions may be asked, and instructions given touching all doctrines and principles that may be entertained by them. That is also the place where correction may be given and explanations be made upon all matters which pertain to the temporal and spiritual lives of the Saints. It is about two months since that school was established. 12:159.

We are starting the School of the Prophets. We have been in this school all the time. The revelations of the Lord Jesus Christ to the human family are all the learning we can ever possess. Much of this knowledge is obtained from books which have been written by men who have contemplated deeply on various subjects, and the revelations of Jesus have opened their minds, whether they knew it or acknowledged it or not. We will start this School of the Prophets to increase in knowledge. 12:116.

There are a great many branches of education: some go to college to learn languages, some to study law, some to study physics, and some to study astronomy, and various other branches of science. We want every branch of science taught in this place that is taught in the world. But our favorite study is that branch which particularly belongs to the Elders of Israel — namely, theology. Every Elder should become a profound theologian—should understand this branch better than all the world. 6:317.

The Christian world is actually coming to the point that they will dismiss the Bible from their schools; and by and by they will dismiss it from their pulpits and get one to suit themselves; they will hew out for themselves cisterns that will hold no water. 13:213.

Science and Religion—I am not astonished that infidelity prevails to a great extent among the inhabitants of the earth, for the religious teachers of the people advance many ideas and notions for truth which are in opposition to and contradict facts demonstrated by science, and which are generally understood. You take, for instance, our geologists, and they tell us that this earth has been in existence for thousands and millions of years. They think, and they have good reason for their faith, that their researches and investigations enable them to demonstrate that this earth has been in existence as long as they assert it has; and they say, "If the Lord, as religionists declare, made the earth out of nothing in six days, six thousand years ago, our studies are all vain; but by what we can learn from nature and the immutable laws of the Creator as revealed therein, we know that your theories are incorrect and consequently we must reject your religions as false and vain; we must be what you call infidels, with the demonstrated truths of science in our possession; or, rejecting those truths, become enthusiasts in, what you call, Christianity.

In these respects we differ from the Christian world, for our religion will not clash with or contradict the facts of science in any particular. You may take geology, for instance, and it is true science; not that I would say for a moment that all the conclusions and deductions of its professors are true, but its leading principles are; they are facts—they are eternal; and to assert that the Lord made this earth out of nothing is preposterous and impossible. God never made something out of nothing; it is not in the economy or law by which the worlds were, are, or will exist. There is an eternity before us, and it is full of matter; and if we but understand enough of the Lord and his ways we would say that he took of this matter and organized this earth from it. How long it has been organized it is not for me to say, and I do not care anything about it. As for the Bible account of the creation we may say that the Lord gave it to Moses. If we understood the process of creation there would be no mystery about it, it would be all reasonable and plain, for there is no mystery except to the ignorant. This we know by what we have learned naturally since we have had a being on the earth. We can now take a hymn book and read its contents; but if we had never learned letters and knew nothing about type or paper or their uses, and should take up a book and look at it, it would be a great mystery; and still more so would it be to see a person read line after line, and give expression therefrom to the sentiments of himself or others. But this is no mystery to us now, because we have learned our letters, and then learned to place those letters into syllables, the syllables into words, and the words into sentences.

Fifty or a hundred years ago, if any one had told the people of the East Indies that water could be congealed, and form ice so thick and hard that you could walk on and drive teams over it, they would probably have said, "We do not believe a word of it." Why? Because they did not know anything about it. A proper reply for all mankind to make under similar circumstances would be, "We do not know anything about what you say, and do not know whether we should have faith in it or not. Perhaps we should, but we have no evidence at present on which to found such a belief." You go down south here among some of our native Indian tribes, where some of the very best of blankets are made, and you will find them twisting their yarn with their fingers and little sticks, and their loom attached to the limbs of trees for weaving purposes. Show them a loom such as white people use, and it would be a perfect mystery to them. Sixty or seventy years ago a loom worked by water power would have been a mystery to an American, but there is no mystery in that today, because the process is understood. So it is with the East Indians and ice, for the chemist now, by a chemical process, will congeal the water and make ice of it before their eyes, and it is in this way, by testimony, evidence, and demonstration that ignorance and prejudice are removed, faith implanted and knowledge acquired. It is so with regard to all the facts in existence that we do not understand. 14:115-117.

There is no ingenious mind that has ever invented anything beneficial to the human family but what he obtained it from the one Source, whether he knows or believes it or not. There is only one Source whence men obtain wisdom, and that is God, the Fountain of all wisdom; and though men may claim to make their discoveries by their own wisdom, by meditation and reflection, they are indebted to our Father in Heaven for all. 13:148.

It has been observed here this morning that we are called fanatics. Bless me! That is nothing. Who has not been called a fanatic who has discovered anything new in philosophy or science? We have all read of Galileo, the astronomer, who, contrary to the system of astronomy that had been received for ages before his day, taught that the sun, and not the earth, was the center of our planetary system? For this the learned astronomer was called "fanatic," and subjected to persecution and imprisonment of the most rigorous character. So it has been with others who have discovered and explained new truths in science and philosophy which have been in opposition to long-established theories; and the opposition they have encountered has endured until the truth of their discoveries has been demonstrated by time. The term "fanatic" is not applied to professors of religion only. How was it with Dr. Morse, when shut up in the attic of an old building in Baltimore for more than a year, with a little wire stretched around the room, experimenting upon it with his battery, he told a friend that by means of that he could sit there and talk to Congress in Washington? Was he not considered a fanatic, and wild, and crazy? Certainly he was; and so it was with Robert Fulton, when he was conducting his experiments with steam and endeavoring to apply it so as to propel a vessel through the water. And all great discoveries in art, science, or mechanism have been denounced as fanatics and crazy; and it has been declared by their contemporaries that they did not know what they were saying, and they were thought to be almost as wild and incoherent as the generality of the people now think George Francis Train to be. 13:270.

How difficult it is to teach the natural man, who comprehends nothing more than that which he sees with the natural eye! How hard it is for him to believe! How difficult would be the task to make the philosopher, who, for many years, has argued himself into the belief that his spirit is no more after his body sleeps in the grave, believe that his intelligence came from eternity, and is as eternal, in its nature, as the elements, or as the Gods. Such doctrine by him would be considered vanity and foolishness, it would be entirely beyond his comprehension. It is difficult, indeed, to remove an opinion or belief into which he has argued himself from the mind of the natural man. Talk to him about angels, heavens, God, immortality, and eternal lives, and it is like sounding brass, or a tinkling cymbal to his ears; it has no music to him; there is nothing in it that charms his senses, soothes his feelings, attracts his attention, or engages his affections, in the least; to him it is all vanity. 1:2.

True principles will abide, while all false principles will fall with those who choose and cleave to them. 7:65.

We should seek substantial information, and trust little to that kind of so-called learning that is based upon theory. We should pluck fruit from the tree of knowledge, and taste, then shall our eyes be open to see, our ears to hear and our hearts to understand. I would recommend the same course to those who have not embraced and tasted the sweets of "Mormonism." We should get wisdom by reading and by study. We should introduce the best books into our schools for the education and improvement of our children. Let our schoolteachers seek constantly to fasten upon the young mind useful information, and banish from their schools, every study that only tends to perplex the student and waste his valuable time. 9:369.

The Body and the Mind—Some think too much, and should labor more, others labor too much and should think more, and thus maintain an equilibrium between the mental and physical members of the individual; then you will enjoy health and vigor, will be active, and ready to discern truly, and judge quickly. Men who do much thinking, philosophers for instance, should apply their bodies to more manual labor in order to make their bodies more healthy and their minds more vigorous and active. 3:248.

Studies in Sunday Schools—We wish in our Sunday and day schools, that they who are inclined to any particular branch of study may have the privilege to study it. 13:61.

Wisdom—The person that applies his heart to wisdom, and seeks diligently for understanding, will grow to be mighty in Israel. 3:363.

Let wisdom be sown in your hearts, and let it bring forth a bountiful harvest. It is more profitable to you than all the gold and silver and other riches of earth. Let wisdom spring up in your hearts, and cultivate it. 8:140.

After all our endeavors to obtain wisdom from the best books, etc., there still remains an open fountain for all: "If any man lack wisdom let him ask of God." Let every Latter-day Saint constantly practice himself in the performance of every good word and work, to acknowledge God to be God, to be strict in keeping his laws, and learning to love mercy, eschew evil and delight in constantly doing that which is pleasing to God. This is the only sure way to obtain influence with God and all good men. 9:370.

As we prepare materials to build a house or temple, so man can prepare himself for the reception of eternal wisdom. We go where the materials for a house are, and prepare them to answer our purpose;

so we may go to where eternal wisdom dwells and there diligently seek to possess it, for its price is above rubies. 9:250.

Who is it that understands wisdom before God? In some respects we have to define it for ourselves—each for himself—according to our own views, judgment and faith, and the observance of the Word of Wisdom or the interpretation of God's requirements on this subject, must be left partially, with the people. 14:20.

It is our privilege to be as wise in our generation as the children of this world; and not only so, but it is our duty to be as wise in our generation as the children of this world. We have the true light and knowledge and we ought to know as much as the philosophical world, or as any other people on the earth. We ought at least to know as much about politics as do the political world, or as do any other people. I expect that we do; and if we only apply our minds in the proper time and channel, we know as much about the Christian world as do any other people, and we ought to know as much about the whole world as do any other people. In fact, we ought to know more upon all those matters than any other people; for we are privileged with far superior advantage, through faith and obedience to the Gospel. 4:356.

We pray for wisdom, but God will as soon put bread and meat in our cupboards without any endeavor of ours, as he will give us wisdom without our trying to get it. If a man wants a farm, let him make it; if he wishes an orchard he plants it; if he wants a house for his family to live in, he must gather the materials and build it. He will give us wisdom in these things, but he will not come down to do the manual labor. 9:250.

This people are increasing in the wisdom which cometh from God, and their power to organize the crude elements around them into the necessaries of life is in ratio to their increase of intelligence and application of labor. In this way we ought to understand these great principles. We need not seek for a revelation to know how to make cloth, when the mode is plainly marked before our eyes. Sheep produce a textile material, and how to make it into cloth has been known time out of mind; we can raise sheep in abundance. I do not look for power from the heavens that will produce for us wool, cloth, iron, food, or anything we need, without being made with hands. We should understand what is required of us to sustain ourselves. 9:255.

It is the privilege of man to search out the wisdom of God pertaining to the earth and the heavens. 9:242.

Real wisdom is a real pleasure; real wisdom, prudence, and understanding, is a real comfort. 19:96.

I want our children to go and hear all there is to hear, for the whole sum of it will be wound up as I once heard one of the finest speakers America has ever produced say, when speaking on the soul of man. After laboring long on the subject, he straightened himself up—he was a fine-looking man—and, said he, "My brethren and sisters, I must come to the conclusion that the soul of man is an immaterial substance." Said I, "Bah!" 14:198.

Chapter XXIII

SELF-CONTROL

The Will of Man—You call it will. It is the divinity God has placed in his intelligent creatures. 8:209.

Have we a will? Yes, it is an endowment, a trait of the character of the Gods, with which all intelligence is endowed, in heaven and on earth,—the power to accept or reject. 9:106.

God has placed within us a will, and we should be satisfied to have it controlled by the will of the Almighty. Let the human will be indomitable for right. It has been the custom of parents to break the will until it is weakened, and the noble, God-like powers of the child are reduced to a comparative state of imbecility and cowardice. Let that heaven-born property of human agents be properly tempered and wisely directed, instead of pursuing the opposite course, and it will conquer in the cause of right. Break not the spirit of any person, but guide it to feel that it is its greatest delight and highest ambition to be controlled by the revelations of Jesus Christ, then the will of man becomes God-like in overcoming the evil that is sown in the flesh, until God shall reign within us to will and do of his good pleasure. 9:150.

Take people in every capacity of life, and their wills are first and foremost. You can gain and lead the affections of the people, but you cannot scare them, nor whip them, nor burn them to do right against their wills. The human family will die to gratify their wills. Then learn to rightly direct those wills, and you can direct the influence and power of the people. 8:363.

There is no man or woman on the earth in the habit of stealing, but what can cease the practice right square if they are disposed. And so with the liar, he can stop lying, and lie no more, and tell the truth. It only wants the will to do it, and that will brought into exercise to enable the liar to be truthful, the thief to be honest, and the swearer to stop his evil speaking. 18:77.

We want the spirit, knowledge, power and principle within us to govern and control our tempers; there is no danger of having too much if we will only control them by the Spirit of the Almighty. Every intelligent being on the earth is tempered for glory, beauty, excellency and knowledge here, and for immortality and eternal lives in the worlds to come. But every being who attains to this must be sanctified before God and be completely under the control of his Spirit. If I am thus controlled by the Spirit of the Most High,

I am a king. I am supreme so far as the control of self is concerned; and it also enables me to control my wives and children. And when they thus see that I am under the government and control of the good Spirit, they will be perfectly submissive to my dictates. 13:272.

Now I charge you again, and I charge myself not to get angry. Never let anger arise in your hearts. No, Brigham, never let anger arise in your heart, never, never! Although you may be called upon to chastise and to speak to the people sharply, do not let anger arise in you, no, never! 14:146.

Self-Control Necessary—We are trying to govern ourselves, and if we continue trying and faint not, we shall assuredly conquer. 11:256.

Let the people study to bring their thinking or reflecting faculties into subjection. 6:94.

Learn to control yourselves; learn to be in the hands of God as clay in the hands of the potter; and if he will turn our enemies away, praised be his name. But if it should become a duty to take the sword, let us do it manfully and in the strength of Israel's God. 5:229.

I answer, it is the absolute and imperative duty of the Elders of Israel to try and control themselves and their families and their brethren, until they can hold control over all things in righteousness. 10:333.

I have frequently said that the greatest endowment God ever gave to man is good, sound, solid sense to know how to govern ourselves. 9:250.

No man can ever become a ruler in the Kingdom of God, until he can perfectly rule himself; then is he capable of raising a family of children who will rise up and call him blessed. 9:334.

No man ever did, or ever will rule judiciously on this earth, with honor to himself and glory to his God, unless he first learn to rule and control himself. A man must first learn to rule himself rightly before his knowledge can be fully brought to bear for the correct government of a family, a neighborhood, or nation, over which it is his lot to preside. 3:256.

In this probation, we have evil to contend with, and we must overcome it in ourselves, or we never shall overcome it anywhere else. 6:99.

You have been taught the standard of right. Now subdue your rebellious passions, dismiss everything that you know or consider to be wrong, and embrace that which is better. 6:74.

Let each person be determined, in the name of the Lord Jesus Christ, to overcome every besetment—to be the master of himself, that the Spirit God has put in your tabernacles shall rule; then you can converse, live, labor, go here or there, do this or that, and converse and deal with your brethren as you ought. 8:139.

You cannot inherit eternal life, unless your appetites are brought in subjection to the spirit that lives within you, that spirit which our Father in Heaven gave. I mean the Father of your spirits, of those spirits which he has put into these tabernacles. The tabernacles must be brought in subjection to the spirit perfectly, or your bodies cannot be raised to inherit eternal life; if they do come forth, they must dwell in a lower kingdom. Seek diligently, until you bring all into subjection to the law of Christ. 4:200.

We often hear people excuse themselves for their uncouth manners and offensive language, by remarking "I am no hypocrite," thus taking to themselves credit for that which is really no credit to them. When evil arises within me, let me throw a cloak over it, subdue it, instead of acting it out upon the false presumption that I am honest and no hypocrite. Let not thy tongue give utterance to the evil that is in thine heart, but command thy tongue to be silent until good shall prevail over the evil, until thy wrath has passed away and the good Spirit shall move thy tongue to blessings and words of kindness. So far I believe in being a hypocrite. This is practical with me. When my feelings are aroused to anger by the ill-doings of others, I hold them as I would hold a wild horse, and I gain the victory. Some think and say that it makes them feel better when they are mad, as they call it, to give vent to their madness in abusive and unbecoming language. This, however, is a mistake. Instead of its making you feel better, it is making bad worse. When you think and say it makes you better you give credit to a falsehood. When the wrath and bitterness of the human heart are moulded into words and hurled with violence at one another, without any check or hindrance, the fire has no sooner expended itself than it is again rekindled through some trifling course, until the course of nature is set on fire; "and it is set on fire of hell." 11:255.

Be patient; do not murmur at the dealings of Providence. The Lord rules in the heavens and works his pleasure upon the earth. Can you comprehend the meaning of the Prophet Amos in the question: "Shall there be evil in the city, and the Lord hath not done it?" His providences are constantly ruling and overruling, to a greater or less degree, in the affairs of the children of men. 7:237.

The sooner an individual resists temptation to do, say, or think wrong, while he has light to correct his judgment, the quicker he will gain strength and power to overcome every temptation of evil. 6:94.

I am trying to civilize myself. Are you trying to do the same?

If we have succeeded in this, then we have control over our words and over our actions, and also so far as our influence goes, over our associates. If we are civilized ourselves, we shall be partially prepared to receive the things that our Father and God has in store for all such as prepare themselves to become recipients of his choice gifts—for enlightenment, for intelligence, for glory, for power, and for every qualification he wishes to bestow upon his children here upon the earth, to prepare them to dwell in mansions of eternal light. 8:7.

Until we can subdue our own passions, and bring every human feeling and aspiration into subjection to the will of God, we are not really capable of guiding and dictating others to the full possession of victory in the Kingdom of God. To conquer and subdue, and school ourselves until we bring everything into subjection to the law of Christ, is our work. 11:13.

The thousands and tens of thousands of incidents that make up the sum of human lives, whether for good or evil, depend on a momentary watchfulness and care. 8:52.

A righteous person will never be discouraged, but will constantly contend against his evil passions, and against evil in his family and neighborhood; and the Lord will utterly cleanse his thrashing floor as with the besom of destruction. 8:151.

Many men will say they have a violent temper, and try to excuse themselves for actions of which they are ashamed. I will say, there is not a man in this house who has a more indomitable and unyielding temper than myself. But there is not a man in the world who cannot overcome his passion, if he will struggle earnestly to do so. If you find passion coming on you, go off to some place where you cannot be heard; let none of your family see you or hear you, while it is upon you, but struggle till it leaves you; and pray for strength to overcome. As I have said many times to the Elders, pray in your families; and if, when the time for prayer comes, you have not the spirit of prayer upon you, and your knees are unwilling to bow, say to them, "Knees, get down there"; make them bend, and remain there until you obtain the Spirit of the Lord. If the spirit yields to the body, it becomes corrupt; but if the body yields to the spirit it becomes pure and holy. 11:290.

Thirty years' experience has taught me that every moment of my life must be holiness to the Lord, resulting from equity, justice, mercy, and uprightness in all my actions, which is the only course by which I can preserve the Spirit of the Almighty to myself. 9:220.

Check Your Words—If you first gain power to check your words, you will then begin to have power to check your judgment, and at length actually gain power to check your thoughts and reflections. 6:98.

You should succeed in bringing your tongues into subjection, so as never to let them speak evil, so that they will perfectly obey your judgment and the discretion God has given you, and are perfectly obedient to the will of the holy Gospel. 3:195.

There is an old maxim, and in many cases an excellent one. It is, "Think twice before you speak, and three times before you act." If we train ourselves to think what we are about to do, before we do it, and have understanding to know, and power to perform the good, we can thereby avoid the evil that is present with us. 1:92.

It is also a precious gift, that some people seem to be possessed of, to have knowledge enough not to talk until they can say something to advantage and benefit to themselves, or others, or both. 9:86.

If any are in the habit of taking the name of God in vain, cease doing so today, tomorrow and throughout the coming week, and so continue, and you will soon gain strength to overcome the habit entirely; you will gain power over your words. Some are in the habit of talking about their neighbors, of vending stories they know nothing about, only that Aunt Sally said that Cousin Fanny told Aunt Betsy that old Aunt Ruth said something or other, or somebody had had a dream; and by the time the story or dream reaches you, it has assumed the semblance of a fact, and you are very foolishly spending your time in talking about things that amount to nothing, or that you have no concern with. A report is started that such a one has done wrong, and, by the time it has gone its round, has become anointed with the salve of the backbiter and tale-bearer — become endowed with their spirit. One and another falls in with it and says, "That is true—your cause is just, you are exactly right, and the other is surely wrong," when they know nothing about the matter, thereby engendering entirely groundless ill feelings against each other. Before we condemn, we should wait until the heavens clearly indicate a fault in a father, brother, sister, wife, husband, or neighbor. And if heaven declares a fault, wait until the Holy Ghost manifests to you that such is a fault. Let the Father reveal to you that the person you are thinking or talking about is actually wrong. Traduce no person. When you know what right is, and are capable of correcting a person that is wrong, then it is time enough for you to judge. 6:97-98.

Cease Your Anger—No man or people possessing wisdom will give vent to wrath, for that is calculated to weaken, to destroy, to blot out of existence. 7:10.

Cease your anger, and sullenness of temper, and serve the Lord with cheerfulness, and singleness of heart. You need not expect salvation, except you can administer the same salvation to others, both in precept and example. If you expect compassion from me, administer the same to me. If you wish kind words and kind treatment from me, give me the same blessing you desire yourself; and that is the way you will be saved. 1:245.

Do not get so angry that you cannot pray; do not allow yourselves to become so angry that you cannot feed an enemy—even your worst enemy, if an opportunity should present itself. There is a wicked anger, and there is a righteous anger. The Lord does not suffer wicked anger to be in his heart; but there is anger in his bosom, and he will hold a controversy with the nations, and will sift them, and no power can stay his hand. 5:228.

If you give way to your angry feelings, it sets on fire the whole course of nature, and is set on fire of hell; and you are then apt to set those on fire who are contending with you. When you feel as though you would burst, tell the old boiler to burst, and just laugh at the temptation to speak evil. If you will continue to do that, you will soon be such masters of yourselves as to be able, if not to tame, to control your tongues—able to speak when you ought, and to be silent when you ought. 6:75.

Learn to Know Ourselves—The greatest lesson you can learn is to know yourselves. When we know ourselves, we know our neighbors. When we know precisely how to deal with ourselves, we know how to deal with our neighbors. You have come here to learn this. You cannot learn it immediately, neither can all the philosophy of the age teach it to you; you have to come here to get a practical experience and to know yourselves. You will then begin to learn more perfectly the things of God. No being can thoroughly know himself, without understanding more or less of the things of God; neither can any being learn and understand the things of God, without knowing himself: he must know himself, or he never can know God. 8:334.

But people cannot judge themselves as they can others, nor look upon their own conduct as they do upon the conduct of others. We must learn to look at ourselves, to judge ourselves, and know how to deal with ourselves and that will enable us to bring ourselves into perfect subjection to the law of Christ. 6:73.

There is a trait in the character of man which is frequently made manifest in the Saints. It is simply this—to see faults in others when we do not examine our own. When you see people, professing to be Latter-day Saints, examining the faults of others, you may know that they are not walking in the path of obedience as strictly as they should. 11:292.

Let Us Mind Our Own Business—I will repeat part of the "Mormon Creed," viz: "Let every man mind his own business." If this is observed, every man will have business sufficient on hand, so as not to afford time to trouble himself with the business of other people. 2:92-93.

If we will faithfully mind our own concerns, live our religion, do good to all men, preach the Gospel to the nations of the earth, gather up the honest in heart, build up and establish Zion in the earth, and send the Gospel to the House of Israel, and live and serve God in all things, all will be well with us, we have no cause for fear in the least. 19:5.

The question may be asked: "Are we never to know the doings of others? Are we never to look to see how others are walking and progressing in this Gospel? Must we forever and forever confine our minds to thinking of ourselves, and our eyes to looking at ourselves?" I can merely say that if persons only understand the path of duty and walk therein, attaining strictly to whatever is required of them, they will have plenty to do to examine themselves and to purify their own hearts; and if they look at their neighbors and examine their conduct, they will look for good and not for evil. 11:292.

My position in the presence of God, before the angels and upon the face of the earth, is that it is easier and more delightful to serve God than to serve ourselves and the Devil. 13:1.

Chapter XXIV

OUR FELLOW MEN

Love Each Other—Go on until we are perfect, loving our neighbor more than we love ourselves. 19:49.

Put away all unkind feelings, and let all your meditations be correct. 8:72.

It is folly in the extreme for persons to say that they love God; when they do not love their brethren; and it is of no use for them to say that they have confidence in God, when they have none in righteous men. 4:297.

We are not here isolated and alone, differently formed and composed of different material from the rest of the human race. We belong to and are part of this family, consequently we are under obligations one to another, and the Latter-day Saints in these mountains are under obligations to their brethren and sisters scattered in the nations who, through indigent circumstances, are unable to gather to themselves in the comforts of life. 13:301.

Be just as independent as a God to do good. Love mercy, eschew evil, be a savior to yourselves and to your families, and to your fellow beings just as much as you possibly can, and go on with your independence and do not yield yourselves servants to obey an evil principle or an evil being. 15:7.

It should be satisfactory evidence that you are in the path of life, if you love God and your brethren with all your hearts. You may see, or think you see, a thousand faults in your brethren; yet they are organized as you are; they are flesh of your flesh, bone of your bone; they are of your Father who is in heaven; we are all His children, and should be satisfied with each other as far as possible. The main difficulty in the hearts of those who are dissatisfied is, they are not satisfied with themselves. 8:287.

We should commence our labors of love and kindness with the family to which we belong; and then extend them to others. 11:288.

A man or woman who has embraced, and who enjoys, the principles of this Church, ought to live like an angel. They ought never to be angry with each other, but live in the light of the truth continually, and every man be kind to his neighbor. 1:245.

The Latter-day Saints have got to learn that the interest of their brethren is their own interest, or they never can be saved in the celestial kingdom of God. 3:331.

Let us have compassion upon each other, and let the strong

tenderly nurse the weak into strength, and let those who can see guide the blind until they can see the way for themselves. 10:213.

When you see a neighbor begin to slip, pray for him that he may have the Spirit of the Gospel as he once had. And if you feel this Spirit within yourselves, pray for an increase of that light you received when you first received the Gospel, and you will save yourself and house. 8:164.

Envy not those who do better than you do; do not pursue them with malice, but try to shape and frame your life by theirs. 11:256.

Reason as to why it is that you can remember an injury better than a kindness; why you can retain hatred longer than love. Is it through your fallen nature? Is it because you were begotten and born in sin? Or is it not rather because the power of the tempter has control over you, and because the world is full of evil principles, and you have adhered to them? Yes, this is the cause, and you must acknowledge it. The whole world is contaminated with the spirit to remember evil and forget the good. 3:356.

I have examined myself very closely; I have been trying to know myself, to govern myself, and purify my own heart. The worst evil I can imagine or wish to come upon the enemies of truth is, that they be obliged to live by holy principles, and to deal by their fellow-creatures as they would wish to be dealt by. 8:13-14.

Be kind to all as our Father in Heaven is kind. He sends his rain upon the just and the unjust; and gives the sun to shine upon the evil and the good. So let our goodness extend to all the works of his hands, where we can; but do not yield to the spirit and influence of evil. Do not encourage wickedness in our midst. 12:220.

Do I say, Love your enemies? Yes, upon certain principles. But you are not required to love their wickedness; you are only required to love them so far as concerns a desire and effort to turn them from their evil ways, that they may be saved through obedience to the Gospel. 8:71.

If there is nothing in the heart which governs us, and controls to an evil effect, the tongue of itself will never produce evil. 3:196.

Let Us Be Merciful—The genius of our religion is to have mercy upon all, do good to all, as far as they will let us do good to them. 11:282.

God bless the humble and the righteous, and may He have compassion upon us because of the weakness that is in our nature. And considering the great weakness and ignorance of mortals, let us have mercy upon each other. 9:158.

Let us be just, merciful, faithful and true, and let us live our religion, and we shall be taught all things pertaining to the building up of Zion. 10:177.

The merciful man shall find mercy. When a man designedly does wrong, he ought to be chastised for that wrong, receiving according to his works. If a man does wrong through ignorance, and manifests sincere sorrow for the wrong, he is the one whom we should forgive seventy times in a day, if necessary, and not the one who has designedly done wrong and repents not. 7:244.

Men should act upon the principle of righteousness, because it is right, and is a principle which they love to cherish and see practiced by all men. They should love mercy, because of its benevolence, charity, love, clemency, and all of its lovely attributes, and be inspired thereby to deal justly, fairly, honorably, meting out to others their just deservings. 1:119.

When we hold unrighteous, ungodly persons in fellowship, it injures the whole body of Christ; but we do it because we have compassion for them. 10:284.

Be steadfast, always abiding in the truth. Never encourage malice or hatred in your hearts; that does not belong to a Saint. I can say in truth, that with all the abuse I have ever met, driven from my home, robbed of my substance, I do not know that a spirit of malice has ever rested in my heart. I have asked the Lord to mete out justice to those who have oppressed us, and the Lord will take His own time and way for doing this. It is in His hands, and not mine, and I am glad of it, for I could not deal with the wicked as they should be dealt with. 10:297.

Show Charity—Only a few men on the earth understand the charity that fills the bosom of our Savior. We should have charity; we should do all we can to reclaim the lost sons and daughters of Adam and Eve, and bring them back to be saved in the presence of our Father and God. If we do this, our charity will extend to the utmost extent that it is designed for the charity of God to extend in the midst of this people. 8:175.

Let all Latter-day Saints learn that the weaknesses of their brethren are not sins. When men or women undesignedly commit a wrong, do not attribute that to them as a sin. Let us learn to be compassionate one with another; let mercy and kindness soften every angry and fretful temper, that we may become long-suffering and beneficial in all our communications one with another. 9:334.

Let us be patient with one another. I do not altogether look at things as you do. My judgment is not in all things like yours, nor yours like mine. When you judge a man or woman, judge the intentions of the heart. It is not by words, particularly, nor by actions, that men will be judged in the great day of the Lord; but, in connection with words and actions, the sentiments and intentions of the heart will be taken, and by these will men be judged. 8:10.

Ye mighty men of God, make sure the path for your own feet to walk to eternal life, and take as many with you as you can. Take them as they are, understand them as they are, and deal with them as they are; look at them as God looks at them, and then you can judge them as he would judge them. 8:10.

Respect one another; do not speak lightly of each other. Some, if they get a little pique against an individual, are disposed to cast him down to hell, as not worthy of a place upon earth. O fools! not to understand that those you condemn are the workmanship of God, as well as yourselves! God overlooks their weaknesses; and so far as they do good, they are as acceptable as we are. Thank God that you know better, and be full of mercy and kindness. 8:149.

Suppose that in this community there are ten beggars who beg from door to door for something to eat, and that nine of them are impostors who beg to escape work, and with an evil heart practice imposition upon the generous and sympathetic, and that only one of the ten who visit your doors is worthy of your bounty; which is best, to give food to the ten, to make sure of helping the truly needy one, or to repulse the ten because you do not know which is the worthy one? You will all say, administer charitable gifts to the ten, rather than turn away the only truly worthy and truly needy person among them. If you do this, it will make no difference in your blessings, whether you administer to worthy or unworthy persons, inasmuch as you give alms with a single eye to assist the truly needy. 8:12.

My experience has taught me, and it has become a principle with me, that it is never any benefit to give, out and out, to man or woman, money, food, clothing, or anything else, if they are able-bodied, and can work and earn what they need, when there is anything on the earth for them to do. This is my principle, and I try to act upon it. To pursue a contrary course would ruin any community in the world and make them idlers. People trained in this way have no interest in working; "but," say they, "we can beg, or we can get this, that, or the other." No, my plan and counsel would be, let every person, able to work, work and earn what he needs; and if the poor come around me—able-bodied men and women—take them and put them into the house. "Do you need them?" No; but I will teach this girl to do housework, and teach that woman to sew and do other kinds of work, that they may be profitable when they get married or go for themselves. "Will you give them anything to wear?" O, yes, make them comfortable, give them plenty to eat and teach them to labor and earn what they need; for the bone and sinew of men and women are the capital of the world. 11:297.

To give to the idler is as wicked as anything else. Never give anything to the idler. 16:19.

Set the poor to work—setting out orchards, splitting rails, digging ditches, making fences, or anything useful, and so enable them to buy meal and flour and the necessaries of life. 12:60-61.

Have the poor got greedy eyes? Are they covetous and penurious? I shall go a little too far if I am not careful. I must guard myself, because the Lord has chosen the poor of this world. But what kind of poor? Now the poor may be divided into three classes. In the first place there is the Lord's poor, of which you may pick up one here and another there, one in a city, two in a family. Is there any other kind? Yes, you come across a certain class that may be called the Devil's poor. Is there any other class? Yes, there is another class, who, long before I ever mentioned them, were denominated poor devils. Hence we have the Lord's poor, the Devil's poor, and poor devils. 12:57.

Establish Confidence—Preserve your honor, and your integrity, and ever cherish the confidence that men repose in you. 11:256.

Want of confidence is the parent of moral imbecility and intellectual weakness. 10:20.

But if we lack confidence in each other, and be jealous of each other, our peace will be destroyed. If we cultivate the principles of unshaken confidence in each other, our joy will be full. 1:33.

If we could obtain that faith and confidence in each other, and in our God, that when we ask a favor, we could do so with a full assurance and knowledge that we should receive, do you not perceive that it would lead us directly to do as we would be done by, in every transaction and circumstance of life? It would prompt us to do, not only as much as requested, but more. If your brother should request you to go with him a mile, you should go two; if he should sue you for your coat, you would give him your cloak also. This principle prompts us to do all we can to promote the interest of each other, the cause of God on the earth, and whatever the Lord desires us to do; makes us ready and willing to perform it at once. 1:115.

If you wish to establish a confidence such as the Gods enjoy, let us cease from every evil act, and from the contemplation of every evil design; never infringe upon another's rights, but let each one sustain his brother in the enjoyment of his privileges and rights, holding them as sacred as our own salvation. If confidence has been lost, this is the surest and only successful way to restore it. Hear it, ye preachers, ye Apostles, and Prophets; ye Elders, High Priests, and Seventies; ye

Priests, Teachers, Deacons, and Bishops; every man and woman in the Church of God throughout the world; commence to preach this discourse at home, beginning with your own heart; then teach your wives and your children; then let it spread its warning and cheering influence, like the genial sunbeam, from family to family, until the whole Church of Jesus Christ of Latter-day Saints is united as the heart of one man. 1:315.

Let us from this time forth live so as to create confidence in all men with whom we deal and come in contact; and treasure up each particle of confidence we obtain as one of the most precious possessions mortals can possibly possess. When by my good actions I have created confidence in my neighbor towards me, I pray that I may never do anything that will destroy it. 11:256.

The work in which you and I have enlisted is to restore confidence in the minds of the people; and when I hear of circumstances transpiring in which brethren forfeit their word I regard it as a blot upon the character of this people. We should keep our word with each other. And if we have difficulty or misunderstanding with each other, talk it over, canvass the subject thoroughly, seriously and discreetly, and we shall find that all difficulties will be remedied in this way easier than any other; and we shall also find that nearly every difficulty that arises in the midst of the inhabitants of the earth, is through misunderstanding; and if a wrong in intent and design really exists, if the matter is canvassed over, the wrongdoer is generally willing to come to terms. 14:278.

Avoid Contention—I consider it as a disgrace to the community, and in the eyes of the Lord, and of angels, and in the eyes of all the Prophets and Revelators that have ever lived upon the earth, when a community will descend to a low, degraded state of contention with each other. 1:32.

I wish men would look upon that eternity which is before them. In the great morning of the resurrection, with what grief would they look upon their little trifling affairs of this probation; they would say, "O! do not mention it, for it is a source of mortification to me to think that I ever should be guilty of doing wrong, or of neglecting to do good to my fellow men, even if they have abused me." 1:32.

When a difference of judgment exists between two parties, let them come together and lay their difficulties at each other's feet, laying themselves down in the cradle of humility, and say, "Brother (or sister), I want to do right; yea, I will even wrong myself, to make you right." Do you not think that a man or woman, acting in that manner towards his or her neighbor, would be justified by the law of righteousness? Their judgments come together, and they are agreed:

there would, consequently, be no need of calling in a third person to settle the difference. After taking this course, if you cannot come together, then call in a third person and settle it. 6:319.

Contentions frequently arise to so alienating a degree that brethren have no faith in each other's honesty and integrity, when, perhaps, both parties have stumbled over a little, selfish, ignorant, personal misunderstanding, are carrying it to the extent of wishing to cut each other off from the Church. Very frequently such cases are presented before me. Unravel the difficulty, and it is found to have started in a trifling misunderstanding in relation to some small matter; all the trouble has arisen from a most frivolous cause. Avoid nursing misunderstandings into difficulties. Some talk with a heavy, deep stress upon their words, without intending anything harsh or unkind. 8:72.

If your neighbors talk about you, and you think that they do wrong in speaking evil of you, do not let them know that you ever heard a word, and conduct yourselves as if they always did right, and it will mortify them, and they will say, "We'll not try this game any longer." 19:70.

Let us make ourselves capable of doing at least a little good, and this will occupy our minds upon something that is indeed profitable to others, and will somewhat divert our attention from worshipping ourselves and blaming everybody that does not do the same. 10:205.

Now, if you do not want to quarrel, take measures to prevent it. 12:315.

Do Not Deal Out Judgment—Cease looking at others. Cease to judge each other. 6:74.

Kindness, love, and affection are the best rod to use upon the refractory. 9:195.

Away with all little meannesses, and deal out kindness to all. Chasten, where chastening will answer best; but try persuasion before you try the rod. 8:63.

Do not throw away a man or a woman, old or young. If they commit an evil today, and another tomorrow, but wish to be Saints and to be forgiven, do you forgive them, not only seven times, but seventy times seven in a day, if their hearts are fully set to do right. Let us make it a point to pass over their weaknesses and say, "God bless you in trying to be better in time to come," and act as wise stewards in the Kingdom of God. 8:368.

You are not as you should be, unless you can correct every person you know to be wrong, without having personal ill-feelings against them. 8:191.

Judge not, that ye be not judged. Let no man judge his fellow being, unless he knows he has the mind of Christ within him. We ought to reflect seriously upon this point; how often it is said—"Such a person has done wrong, and he cannot be a Saint, or he would not do so." How do you know? We hear some swear and lie; they trample upon the rights of their neighbor, break the Sabbath by staying away from meeting, riding about the city, hunting horses and cattle, or working in the canyons. Do not judge such persons, for you do not know the design of the Lord concerning them; therefore, do not say they are not Saints. What shall we do with them? Bear with them. The brethren and sisters from the old countries frequently place great confidence in the American Elders who have been their pastors, but some trifling thing occurs that does not appear right to them, and they say in a moment, "That Elder is not a Latter-day Saint." Judge no man. A person who would say another is not a Latter-day Saint, for some trifling affair in human life proves that he does not possess the Spirit of God. Think of this, brethren and sisters; write it down, that you may refresh your memories with it; carry it with you and look at it often. If I judge my brethren and sisters, unless I judge them by the revelations of Jesus Christ, I have not the Spirit of Christ; if I had, I should judge no man. 1:339.

I am very thankful that it is not our province, in our present condition, to judge the world; if it were, we would ruin everything. We have not sufficient wisdom, our minds are not filled with the knowledge and power of God; the spirit needs to contend with the flesh a little more until it shall be successful in subduing its passions, until the whole soul is brought into perfect harmony with the mind and will of God. And we must also acquire the discretion that God exercises in being able to look into futurity, and to ascertain and know the results of our acts away in the future, even in eternity, before we will be capable of judging. 19:7.

If you are ever called upon to chasten a person, never chasten beyond the balm you have within you to bind up. 9:124-125.

When a man has power over his neighbor, over his fellow-being, and puts him in torment, which is like the flames of everlasting fire, so that he never dares to speak his mind, or walk across the street, or attend to any branch of business without a continual fear of his oppressor, and of the rod hanging over him for punishment, it is worse than to kill and eat him. That is as the torment of hell. 2:140.

Respect for Neighbors—Treat the passing strangers with kindness and respect; treat all kindly and respectfully who respect you and your rights as American citizens. 10:249.

Here is truth—here are life and salvation. Will you have them? If you say, "Nay," all right; for you have the privilege of making your own choice. It has never altered my feelings towards individuals, as men or as women, whether they believe as I do or not. Can you live as neighbors with me? I can with you; and it is no particular concern of mine whether you believe with me or not. 7:165.

In our intercourse with outsiders—do not call them Gentiles—let our example be such as is worthy of imitation; then every one among them who is honest will say, "I guess you are right, I think I will come and stay with you." 12:273.

Lady and Gentleman Defined—Now, my brethren and sisters, from the high and from the lower circles of life, find if you can on the face of the earth a gentleman or lady, in the strict sense of the word, and you will find a man or woman that would border very closely on an angel. Every word that they speak will be seasoned with grace; every act of their lives would be as nigh as mortals can come to angels; nothing pertaining to them low, degrading or disgraceful. You find a gentleman and you will find a man who possesses a heart full of charity, faith and love, full of good works, whose hand is always open to do good to every creature. You find a lady, and she is one who is ready to impart wisdom, knowledge, truth, and every virtuous and holy principle to her sisters and her fellow beings. These are the true lady and gentleman; but they are of a higher order than those we now call ladies and gentlemen. 12:259.

The Negro—The seed of Ham, which is the seed of Cain descending through Ham, will, according to the curse put upon him, serve his brethren, and be a "servant of servants" to his fellow-creatures, until God removes the curse; and no power can hinder it. 2:184.

The Generous Nature—It floods my heart with sorrow to see so many Elders of Israel who wish everybody to come to their standard and be measured by their measure. Every man must be just so long, to fit their iron bedstead, or be cut off to the right length; if too short, he must be stretched, to fill the requirement.

The faithful will exercise faith, and pray always for all who are within the reach of mercy. The good desire good to all. 11:273.

If they see an erring brother or sister, whose course does not comport with their particular ideas of things, they conclude at once that he or she cannot be a Saint, and withdraw their fellowship, concluding that, if they are in the path of truth, others must have precisely their weight and dimensions.

The ignorance I see, in this particular, among this great people is lamentable. Let us not narrow ourselves up; for the world, with all its variety of useful information and its rich hoard of hidden treasure, is before us; and eternity, with all its sparkling intelligence, lofty aspirations, and unspeakable glories, is before us, and ready to aid us in the scale of advancement and every useful improvement. 8:9.

Serve the Lord, and try not to find fault with each other. Live so that you will not have any fault to find with yourselves, and never mind the faults of your brethren, for each person has enough of his own to attend to. 8:291.

To be gentle and kind, modest and truthful, to be full of faith and integrity, doing no wrong is of God; goodness sheds a halo of loveliness around every person who possesses it, making their countenances beam with light, and their society desirable because of its excellency. They are loved of God, of holy angels, and of all the good on earth, while they are hated, envied, admired and feared by the wicked. 11:240.

We ought to be ourselves and not anybody else. We do not wish to be anybody else, neither do we wish to be anybody but Saints. 3:363.

Every moment of human life should be devoted to doing good somewhere and in some way. 9:296.

If every person in the community would correct his own errors each day he lives, the errors of the whole would continually be effectually corrected. It is an individual business, over which each man must preside, until every fault in our whole lives is corrected and we are sanctified before the Lord. 6:316.

It is good to hold on to an old friend; and, no matter how many new friends I have, I always hold fast to the old ones, and never let them go, unless their wicked conduct breaks the thread of fellowship between us. 10:42.

What comes of litigation? Poverty and degradation to any community that will encourage it. Will it build cities, open farms, build railroads, erect telegraph lines and improve a country? It will not; but it will bring any community to ruin. 11:259.

He will bless any man, any family, or any people who is liberal. As it is written in the good book, "The liberal man deviseth liberal things," and if he deviseth liberal things by his liberality he shall stand. The Lord will bless that people that is full of charity, kindness and good works. 13:279.

I also say, Cease speaking evil one of another, and cease being dishonest. Masters, deal honestly and justly with those whom you hire, and who are called servants. Servants, deal honestly and uprightly with those who employ you, who are called masters, that confidence and the spirit of brotherhood may be kindled, where now, in too many instances, the desire to take advantage exists. 18:233.

Chapter XXV

UNITY AND CO-OPERATION

Be of One Mind and One Heart—I pray, my brethren, the Bishops, the Elders, the Seventies, the Apostles, yea, every man and woman and child who has named the name of Christ, to be of one heart and of one mind, for if we do not become of one heart and mind we shall surely perish by the way. 12:156.

If we were one, we should then prove to heaven, to God our Father, to Jesus Christ our Elder Brother, to the angels, to the good upon the earth, and to all mankind that we are the disciples of the Lord Jesus Christ. If we are not one, we are not in the true sense of the word the disciples of the Lord Jesus. 11:273.

When truth comes, receive it as from the Lord, and let everything be simplified to us as unto children, for the Lord has ordained that we may grow in grace, and in the knowledge of the truth, and be able to receive more knowledge, wisdom, and understanding, and it is not possible for us to receive it any other way, only as we apply our hearts strictly to overcome every evil and cleave to that which is pleasing to the Lord—to that which tends to life and salvation. This is the only channel in which we can become of one heart, and of one mind. 3:355.

Jesus offered up one of the most essential prayers that could possibly be offered up by a human or heavenly being—no matter who, pertaining to the salvation of the people, and embodying a principle without which none can be saved, when he prayed the Father to make His disciples one, as He and His Father were one. He knew that if they did not become one, they could not be saved in the celestial Kingdom of God. If persons do not see as he did while in the flesh, hear as he heard, understand as he understood, and become precisely as he was, according to their several capacities and calling, they can never dwell with Him and His Father. 6:96.

The Church of Jesus Christ could not exist, and be divided up into parties. Where such disunion exists in any government, it ultimately becomes the means of the utter overthrow of that government or people, unless a timely remedy is applied. Party spirit once made its appearance in heaven, but was promptly checked. 9:332.

That perfect union, which must ultimately be enjoyed by the Latter-day Saints, can only be brought about by every man and woman living so as to keep their minds pure and unspotted like a piece of clean, white paper, being constantly free from the love of the world, that the spirit of revelation may easily indite upon the heart whatever is the mind and will of the Lord. We cannot be truly the members of Christ's mystical body without living in this way, that the Spirit may indite as easily upon the heart the things of God, as these brethren, our reporters, can write with ink on paper. 11:19.

Perfect Oneness Will Save a People—We must become of one heart and mind, in order to fully enjoy the blessings we anticipate. 6:41.

If we are united, we are independent of the powers of hell and of the world. 5:257.

Unity of purpose and action, in carrying out the will of our Father, has been my theme all the day long. 18:356.

A perfect oneness will save a people, because intelligent beings cannot become perfectly one, only by acting upon principles that pertain to eternal life. Wicked men may be partially united in evil; but, in the very nature of things, such a union is of short duration. The very principle upon which they are partially united will itself breed contention and disunion to destroy the temporary compact. Only the line of truth and righteousness can secure to any kingdom or people, either of earthly or heavenly existence, an eternal continuation of perfect union; for only truth and those who are sanctified by it can dwell in celestial glory. 7:277.

The Savior sought continually to impress upon the minds of His disciples that a perfect oneness reigned among all celestial beings—that the Father and the Son and their Minister, the Holy Ghost, were one in their administration in heaven and among the people pertaining to this earth. Between them and all the heavenly hosts there can be no disunion, no discord, no waverings on a suggestion, on a thought or reflection, on a feeling or manifestation; for such a principle would differ widely from the character of him who dictates them, who makes his throne the habitation of justice, mercy, equity, and truth. If the heavenly hosts were not one, they would be entirely unfit to dwell in the eternal burnings with the Father and Ruler of the universe. 7:276.

All who keep the faith are of one heart and one mind, and this testimony is so confirmed to all that we cannot be mistaken. 18:231.

How is it that the Latter-day Saints feel and understand alike, are of one heart and one mind, no matter where they may be when they receive the Gospel, whether in the north, or the south, the east or the west, even to the uttermost parts of the earth? They receive that which was promised by the Savior when He was about to leave the earth, namely, the Comforter, that holy function from on high which recognizes one God, one faith, one baptism, whose mind is the will of God the Father, in whom there dwelleth unity of faith and action, and in whom there cannot be division or confusion; when they received this further light, it matters not whether they have seen each other or not, they have at once become brothers and sisters, having been adopted into the family of Christ through the bonds of the everlasting covenant, and all can then exclaim, in the beautiful language of Ruth, "Thy people shall be my people, and thy God my God!" And the fact that we receive this Comforter, the Holy Ghost, is proof that the spirit in warring with the flesh has overcome, and by continuing in this state of victory over our sinful bodies we become the sons and daughters of God. Christ having made us free, and whoever the Son makes free is free indeed. Having fought the good fight we then shall be prepared to lay our bodies down to rest to await the morning of the resurrection when they will come forth and be reunited with the spirits, the faithful, as it is said, receiving crowns, glory, immortality and eternal lives, even a fulness with the Father, when Jesus shall present His work to the Father, saying, "Father, here is the work thou gavest me to do." Then will they become Gods, even the sons of God; then will they become eternal fathers, eternal mothers, eternal sons and eternal daughters; being eternal in their organization they go from glory to glory, from power to power; they will never cease to increase and to multiply, worlds without end. When they receive their crowns, their dominions, they then will be prepared to frame earths like unto ours and to people them in the same manner as we have been brought forth by our parents, by our Father and God. 18:259.

To be a Saint is to be as Jesus was; to be assimilated to the spirit and character which He exhibited while here on earth. 12:310.

Unity in God's Work, the Strength of Zion—Who can resist the power possessed by the Latter-day Saints in their union? And the stronger our union, the more mighty are the bands of our strength. 9:241.

I wish the people to understand that they have no interest apart from the Lord our God. The moment you have a divided interest, that moment you sever yourselves from eternal principles. 4:31.

The faith of the Gospel of Jesus Christ is calculated to unite the people in one, and to bring them back to the unity and faith of those who obeyed the Gospel anciently, and finally to bring them back to glory. 5:228.

We have not in our society an aristocratic circle. Whether a brother wears a coon skin cap or a fine beaver hat is all the same to us. If a person is a faithful servant of God we do not object to his coming to meeting, though he has only a piece of buffalo skin to wear on his head. We partake of the Sacrament with him, hail him in the street as a brother and a friend, converse with him, meet him in social parties and greet him as an equal. 9:188.

We have been gathered from many nations, and speak many languages; we have been ruled by different nationalities, and educated in different religions, yet we dwell together in Utah under one government, believe in the same God and worship Him in the same way, and we are all one in Christ Jesus. The world wonder at this, and fear the union that prevails among this, as they are called, singular people. Why is this? It is because the Spirit of the Lord Almighty is in the people, and they follow its dictates, and they hearken to the truth, and live by it; this unites them in one, and causeth them to dwell together in peace. 11:124.

I will give you a text: Except I am one with my good brethren, do not say that I am a Latter-day Saint. We must be one. Our faith must be concentrated in one great work—the building up of the Kingdom of God on the earth, and our works must aim at the accomplishment of that great purpose. 7:280.

We have come here to build up Zion. How shall we do it? I have told you a great many times. There is one thing I will say in regard to it. We have got to be united in our efforts. We should go to work with a united faith like the heart of one man; and whatever we do should be performed in the name of the Lord, and we will then be blessed and prospered in all we do. We have a work on hand whose magnitude can hardly be told. 13:155.

Now, besides being our duty to pray, it is our duty to live in peace with one another. It is also our duty to love the Gospel and the spirit of the Gospel, so that we can become one in the Lord, not out of Him, that our faith, our affections for truth, the kingdom of heaven, our acts, all our labor will be concentrated in the salvation of the children of men, and the establishment of the Kingdom of God on the earth. This is co-operation on a very large scale. This is the work of redemption that is entered into by the Latter-day Saints. Unitedly we perform these duties, we stand, we endure, we increase and multiply, we strengthen and spread abroad, and shall continue so to do until the kingdoms of this world are the kingdoms of our God and His Christ. 15:63.

To Saint and sinner, believer and unbeliever, I wish here to offer one word of advice and counsel, by revealing the mystery that abides with this people called Latter-day Saints; it is the Spirit of the living God that leads them; it is the Spirit of the Almighty that binds them together, it is the influence of the Holy Ghost that makes them love each other like little children; it is the Spirit of Jesus Christ that makes them willing to lay down their lives for the cause of Truth; and it was that same Spirit that caused Joseph, our martyred Prophet, to lay down his life for the testimony of what the Lord revealed to him. This mystery, the great mystery of "Mormonism," is, that the Spirit of the Lord binds the hearts of the people together. Let the world look at it. 1:145.

If we will live so that Christ can make us one through our obedience, where are wars and contentions? All will cease. Where is the spirit of bickering? There will be no more of it. 14:209.

The religion of heaven unites the hearts of the people and makes them one. You may gather a people together, and no matter how widely they differ in politics, the Gospel of Jesus Christ will make them one, even if among them were found members of all the political parties in the country. If members of all these various organizations were to obey the Gospel and gather together, the religion of heaven would clear their hearts of all political rubbish and make them one in voting for principles and measures, instead of men, and I think that any religion that will not do this is very feeble in its effects. 14:159.

Advantage of Temporal Unity—Would you like to live at ease and get rich? Would you like to keep your homes in this city? I know you would. You can do so by being one in all things. 11:278.

I want you to be united. If we should build up and organize a community, we would have to do it on the principle of oneness, it is one of the simplest things I know of. A city of one hundred thousand or a million of people could be united into a perfect family, and they would work together as beautifully as the different parts of the carding machine work together. Why, we could organize millions into a family under the Order of Enoch. 16:170.

I can see no good accruing to this community in maintaining a divided interest; our interest must be one throughout, in order to produce the good we desire.

If we will work unitedly, we can work ourselves into wealth, health, prosperity and power, and this is required of us. It is the duty of a Saint of God to gain all the influence he can on this earth, and to use every particle of that influence to do good. If this is not his duty, I do not understand what the duty of man is. 12:376.

If we would work together in our farming, in our mechanism, be obedient and work as a family for the good of all, it would be almost impossible for anybody to guess the success we would have. But we have got to do it in the Lord. We must not do it with a covetous heart. Always be ready and willing that the Lord should have it all, and do what he pleases with it. I have asked a favor of the Lord in this thing, and that is not to place me in such circumstances that what He has given me shall go into the hands of our enemies. God forbid that! But let it go for the preaching of the Gospel, to sustain and to gather the poor, to build factories, make farms, and set the poor to work, as I have hundreds and thousands that had not anything to do. I have fed and clothed them and taken care of them until they have become comparatively independent. I have made no man poor, but thousands and thousands rich, that is, the Lord has, through your humble servant. 15:166.

Suppose there was a union of effort in every political and financial matter undertaken for the benefit of the whole people, who cannot see the good that would result? We have tried this to some extent in relation to our markets here; but suppose we were fully agreed on the point, we could demand a fair price for our products, and we need not be imposed upon by traders and traffickers. If we were agreed we could supply ourselves from distant markets, say with our clothing, at a far less cost than now. 12:35.

Now the object is to improve the minds of the inhabitants of the earth, until we learn what we are here for, and become one before the Lord, that we may rejoice together and be equal. Not to make all poor, no. The whole world is before us. The earth is here, and the fulness thereof is here. It was made for man; and one man was not made to trample his fellow man under his feet, and enjoy all his heart desires, while the thousands suffer. We will take a moral view, a political view, and we see the inequality that exists in the human family. We take the inhabitants of the civilized world, and how many laboring men are there in proportion to the inhabitants? About one to every five that are producers, and the supposition is that ten hours' work by the one to three persons in the twenty-four hours will support the five. It is an unequal condition to mankind. We see servants that labor early and late, and that have not the opportunity of measuring their hours ten in twenty-four. They cannot go to school, nor hardly get clothing to go to meeting in on the Sabbath. I have seen many cases of this kind in Europe, when the young lady would have to take her clothing on a Saturday night and wash it, in order that she might go to meeting on the Sunday with a clean dress on. Who is she laboring for? For those who, many of them, are living in luxury. And, to serve the classes that are living on them, the poor, laboring men and women are toiling, working their lives out to earn that which will keep a little life within them. Is this equality? No. What is going to be done? The Latter-day Saints will never accomplish their mission until this inequality shall cease on the earth. 19:46.

Unity Does Not Mean Individual Uniformity—How could you ever get a people equal with regard to their possessions? They never can be, no more than they can be in the appearances of their faces. 4:29.

We never shall become one to that extent that we shall look alike or possess precisely the same mental power and ability; this is not the design of heaven. But we expect to become one in all our operations to bring for the fulness of the Kingdom of God on the earth, that Jesus may come and reign King of nations as He does King of Saints. Shall we call this a union for political purposes? I say it is good policy for people to be of one heart and mind in all their operations. 12:35.

The Co-operative Movement—This co-operative movement is only a stepping stone to what is called the Order of Enoch, but which is in reality the Order of Heaven. It was revealed to Enoch when he built up his city and gathered the people together and sanctified them, so that they became so holy and pure that they could not live among the rest of the people and the Lord took them away. 13:2.

Now, I tell you the facts about this movement. We started the co-operative system here when we thought we would wait no longer; we opened the Wholesale Co-operative Store, and since that, retail stores have been established, although some of the latter were opened before the wholesale store was opened. I know this, that as soon as this movement was commenced the price of goods came down from twenty to thirty percent. I recollect very well, after our vote last October Conference, that it was soon buzzed around, "Why, you can get a calico down street at eighteen and seventeen cents a yard"; and it came down to sixteen. But when it came down to sixteen cents, who had a chance to buy any? Why, nobody unless it was just a few yards that were sold to them as a favor. But when it came to the Wholesale Co-operative Store the price was put at sixteen cents, and retail stores are selling it today at seventeen and a half or eighteen cents a yard. 12:373.

What I have in mind with regard to this co-operative business is this: There are very few people who cannot get twenty-five dollars to put into one of these co-operative stores. There are hundreds and thousands of women who, by prudence and industry, can obtain this sum. And we say to you, put your capital into one of these stores. What for? To bring you interest for your money. Put your time and talents to usury. We have the parable before us. If we have one, two, three or five talents, of what advantage will they be if we wrap them in a napkin and lay them away? None at all. Put them out to usury. These co-operative stores are instituted to give the poor a little advantage as well as the rich. 12:375.

Brethren, if you will start here and operate together in farming, in making cheese, in herding sheep and cattle and every other kind of work, and get a factory here and co-operative store—I have been told there is no co-operative store here—get a good co-operative store, and operate together in sheep-raising, store-keeping, manufacturing and everything else, no matter what it is, by-and-by, when we can plant ourselves upon a foundation that we cannot be broken up, we shall then proceed to arrange a family organization for which we are not yet quite prepared. You now, right here in this place, commence to carry on your business in a co-operative capacity. In every instance I could show every one of you what a great advantage would be gained in working together; I cannot reason it out here just how much advantage there is in co-operation in your lumbering and in your herding. You have men here, I suppose, who have had an arm shot off; they cannot go into the canyons and get out wood. Another, perhaps, has had a leg cut off; he cannot run here and there like some of you; but he can do something; he will make a first-rate shopman, and at keeping books, perhaps, he will be one of the best. He cannot take the scythe and mow; he cannot attend to a threshing machine; he cannot go into the woods lumbering; he could not herd well,—but he could go into the factory, and he can do many things. Well, we can do this and keep up co-operation. I can take fifty men who have not a cent, and if they would do as I would wish them to do, they would soon be worth their thousands, every one of them. 16:169.

I am prepared to prove to any sensible congregation, any good philosopher or thinking person or people, who have steady brain and nerve to look at things as they are, that can tell white from black and daylight from midnight darkness, that the closer the connection in a business point of view that a community hold themselves together, the greater will be their joy and wealth. I am prepared to prove, from all the facts that have existed or that now exist in all branches of human affairs, that union is strength, and that division is weakness and confusion. 13:267.

If the people called Latter-day Saints do not become one in temporal things, as they are in spiritual things, they will not redeem and build up the Zion of God upon the earth. This co-operative movement is a stepping stone. We say to the people, take advantage of it, it is your privilege. Instead of giving it into the hands of a few individuals to make their hundreds and thousands, let the people generally, enjoy the benefit arising from the sale of merchandise.

I have already told you that this will stop the operation of many little traders, but it will make them producers as well as consumers. You will find that if the people unitedly hearken to the counsel that is given them, it will not be long before the hats, caps, bonnets, boots and shoes, pants, coats, vests and underclothing of this entire community will all be made in our midst. 13:3.

Chapter XXVI

THRIFT AND INDUSTRY

Faith and Works—They who secure eternal life are doers of the word as well as hearers. 14:37.

The grand difficulty with the people is they do not do quite as well as they know how; it is that which hinders us from accomplishing the work given us to do. 19:220.

Unless you improve upon it, every correct principle advanced through the authority of the holy Priesthood becomes to you a dead letter. But if you have the life within you, you will grow, whether you stay at home or come to meeting; and every true principle, power, and manifestation that God gives you, you will improve upon and treasure up in your hearts. 8:120.

Know whether you ought to do a thing or not, and if you ought not, let it alone. That is the way to live. 14:161.

Time Should Be Spent Wisely—What have we? Our time. Spend it as you will. Time is given to you; and when this is spent to the best possible advantage for promoting truth upon the earth, it is placed to our account, and blessed are you; but when we spend our time in idleness and folly it will be placed against us. 19:75.

We have to give an account of the days we spend in folly. 19:75.

Idleness and wastefulness are not according to the rules of heaven. Preserve all you can, that you may have abundance to bless your friends and your enemies. 14:44.

Do those things that are necessary to be done and let those alone that are not necessary, and we shall accomplish more than we do now. 3:160.

Of the time that is allotted to man here on the earth there is none to lose or to run to waste. After suitable rest and relaxation there is not a day, hour or minute that we should spend in idleness, but every minute of every day of our lives we should strive to improve our minds and to increase the faith of the holy Gospel, in charity, patience, and good works, that we may grow in the knowledge of the truth as it is spoken and prophesied of and written about. 13:310.

I told them that we brought nothing but knowledge to direct them in their labors and to teach them how to employ their time. This is the greatest wealth we possess—to know how to direct our labors rightly, spending every hour advantageously for the benefit of our wives and children and neighbors. 12:172.

Labor Indispensable—Is not the upbuilding of the Kingdom of

God on earth a temporal labor all the time? It will be built up by physical force and means, by manual labor more than by any particular mental effort of the mind. 3:122.

Everything connected with building up Zion requires actual, severe labor. It is nonsense to talk about building up any kingdom except by labor; it requires the labor of every part of our organization, whether it be mental, physical, or spiritual, and that is the only way to build up the Kingdom of God. 3:122.

If we are to build up the Kingdom of God, or establish Zion upon the earth, we have to labor with our hands, plan with our minds, and devise ways and means to accomplish that object. 3:51.

You count me out fifty, a hundred, five hundred, or a thousand of the poorest men and women you can find in this community; with the means that I have in my possession, I will take these ten, fifty, hundred, five hundred, or a thousand people, and put them to labor; but only long enough to benefit their health and to make their food and sleep sweet unto them, and in ten years I will make that community wealthy. In ten years I will put six, a hundred, or a thousand individuals, whom we have to support now by donations, in a position not only to support themselves, but they shall be wealthy, shall ride in their carriages, have fine houses to live in, orchards to go to, flocks and herds and everything to make them comfortable. 14:88.

As was observed this morning, in a wholesome, lovely, excellent discourse, we will have to go to work and get the gold out of the mountains to lay down, if we ever walk in streets paved with gold. The angels that now walk in their golden streets, and they have the tree of life within their paradise, had to obtain that gold and put it there. When we have streets paved with gold, we will have placed it there ourselves. When we enjoy a Zion in its beauty and glory, it will be when we have built it. If we enjoy the Zion that we now anticipate, it will be after we redeem and prepare it. If we live in the city of the New Jerusalem, it will be because we lay the foundation and build it. If we do not as individuals complete that work, we shall lay the foundation for our children and our children's children, as Adam has. If we are to be saved in an ark, as Noah and his family were, it will be because we build it. If the Gospel is preached to the nations, it is because the Elders of Israel in their poverty, without purse or scrip, preach the Gospel to the uttermost parts of the earth. 8:354-355.

My faith does not lead me to think the Lord will provide us with roast pigs, bread already buttered, etc.; he will give us the ability to raise the grain, to obtain the fruits of the earth, to make habitations, to procure a few boards to make a box, and when harvest comes, giving us the grain, it is for us to preserve it—to save the wheat until we have one, two, five, or seven years' provisions on hand, until there is enough of the staff of life saved by the people to bread themselves and those who will come here seeking for safety. 10:293.

Let Nothing Go To Waste—Take things calm and easy, pick up everything, let nothing go to waste. 14:88.

Never let anything go to waste. Be prudent, save everything, and what you get more than you can take care of yourselves, ask your neighbors to help you consume. 1:250.

Never consider that you have bread enough around you to suffer your children to waste a crust or a crumb of it. If a man is worth millions of bushels of wheat and corn, he is not wealthy enough to suffer his servant girl to sweep a single kernel of it into the fire; let it be eaten by something and pass again into the earth, and thus fulfil the purpose for which it grew. Remember it, do not waste anything, but take care of everything. 1:253.

There is not a family in this city, where there are two, three, four, or five persons, but what can save enough from their table, from the waste made by the children, and what must be swept in the fire and out of the door, to make pork sufficient to last them through the year, or at least all they should eat. 4:314.

Go to the poorest family in this community, and I will venture to say that they waste rags enough every year to buy the schoolbooks that are needed for their children, and do even more. 16:16.

If you wish to get rich, save what you get. A fool can earn money; but it takes a wise man to save and dispose of it to his own advantage. 11:301.

It is to our advantage to take good care of the blessings God bestows upon us; if we pursue the opposite course, we cut off the power and glory God designs we should inherit. It is through our own carefulness, frugality, and judgment which God has given us, that we are enabled to preserve our grain, our flocks and herds, wives and children, houses and lands, and increase them around us, continually gaining power and influence for ourselves as individuals and for the Kingdom of God as a whole. 9:171.

You may see some little girls around the streets here with their mothers' skirts on, or their sun bonnets, and with their aprons full of dirt. Your husbands buy you calico, but you do not know what to do with it. It is to be carefully worn until the last thread is worn out, and then put into the rag bag to make paper with. 4:319.

It is good policy and economy to sustain each other. 12:63.

Use just enough of your earnings to make your bodies and your families happy and comfortable, and save the residue. 9:295.

We Must be a Self-Sustaining People—We want you henceforth to be a self-sustaining people. Hear it, O Israel! hear it, neighbors, friends and enemies, this is what the Lord requires of this people. 12:285.

Ye Latter-day Saints, learn to sustain yourselves, produce everything you need to eat, drink or wear; and if you cannot obtain all you wish for today, learn to do without that which you cannot purchase and pay for; and bring your minds into subjection that you must and will live within your means. 12:231.

Who are deserving of praise? The persons who take care of themselves or the ones who always trust in the great mercies of the Lord to take care of them? It is just as consistent to expect that the Lord will supply us with fruit when we do not plant the trees; or that when we do not plow and sow and are saved the labor of harvesting, we should cry to the Lord to save us from want, as to ask him to save us from the consequences of our own folly, disobedience and waste. 12:243-244.

Implied faith and confidence in God is for you and me to do everything we can to sustain and preserve ourselves; and the community that works together, heart and hand, to accomplish this, their efforts will be like the efforts of one man. 4:25.

Brethren, learn. You have learned a good deal, it is true; but learn more; learn to sustain yourselves; lay up grain and flour, and save it against a day of scarcity. Sisters, do not ask your husbands to sell the last bushel of grain you have to buy something for you out of the stores, but aid your husbands in storing it up against a day of want, and always have a year's, or two, provision on hand. 12:204.

Instead of searching after what the Lord is going to do for us, let us inquire what we can do for ourselves. 9:172.

The first revelation given to Adam was of a temporal nature. Most of the revelations he received pertained to his life here. That was also the case in the revelations of Noah. We have but very few of the instructions the Lord gave to Enoch, concerning his city; but, doubtless, most of the revelations he received pertained to a temporal nature and condition. And certainly the revelation Noah received, so far as in our possession, almost exclusively pertained to this life. The same principle was carried out in the days of Moses, and in the days of his fathers, Abraham, Isaac, and Jacob. We may say that eight or nine-tenths of the doctrines and principles set forth in the revelations given to those men were of a temporal nature.

As soon as Moses was called upon to go and deliver Israel, the revelations the Lord gave to him were of a temporal nature, pertaining to the temporal life of the children of Israel—instructing Moses how to deliver them from bondage and lead them from the servile state in which they then were. He taught them in the same manner while they were traveling through the wilderness; and so it continued down to the days of the judges, and then to Saul, whom the Lord permitted them to make a king, and then through the teachings of the Prophets. 6:170.

Whatever the Latter-day Saints have gained has been obtained by sheer wrestling and unconquerable resolution. 13:93.

As an instance, we have men who quarry rock out of the mountains; and we would say to those men, can you go and quarry rock without the suitable instruments? Says one, "I must have so many picks and wedges, and I must have so many drills of different sizes, and so many sledges and hammers." Another man says, "I am going to make the tools; I have the ability, and I will make the instruments from ore in the mountains." You remember what Nephi did. When he came to the sea, and prepared to build his barge, the Lord showed him the ore, and Nephi made the tools with which he formed his barge. He did not have to go back to Jerusalem to get tools. I would like to see a little more of that skill displayed here than I do at the present time. I am using this comparison to show that we, in our poverty, have this work to do. 8:354.

The Elements of Wealth are Around Us—I say to my brethren and sisters, come let us learn how to gather around us from the elements an abundance of every comfort of life, and convert them to our wants and happiness. Let us not remain ignorant, with the ignorant, but let us show the ignorant how to be wise. 10:6.

The Lord has done his share of the work; he has surrounded us with elements containing wheat, meat, flax, wool, silk, fruit, and everything with which to build up, beautify and glorify the Zion of the last days, and it is our business to mould these elements to our wants and necessities, according to the knowledge we now have and the wisdom we can obtain from the heavens through our faithfulness. In this way will the Lord bring again Zion upon the earth, and in no other. 9:283.

While we have a rich soil in this valley, and seed to put in the ground, we need not ask God to feed us, nor follow us round with a loaf of bread begging of us to eat it. He will not do it, neither would I, were I the Lord. We can feed ourselves here; and if we are ever placed in circumstances where we cannot, it will then be time enough for the Lord to work a miracle to sustain us. 1:108.

It is our duty to be active and diligent in doing everything we can to sustain ourselves, to build up His Kingdom, to defend ourselves against our enemies, to lay our plans wisely, and to prosecute every method that can be devised to establish the Kingdom of God on the earth, and to sanctify and prepare ourselves to dwell in His presence. Yet, after all this, if the Lord should not help—if he should not lend his aid to our endeavors, all our labors will prove in vain. 2:279-280.

This world is before us. The gold, silver and precious stones are in the mountains, in the rivers, in the plains, in the sands and in the waters, they all belong to this world, and you and I belong to this world. Is there enough to make each of us a finger ring? Certainly there is. Is there enough to make us a breast pin? Certainly there is. Is there enough to make jewelry for the ladies to set their diamonds and precious stones in? Certainly there is. Is there enough to make the silver plate, the spoons, platters, plates and knives and forks? There is. There is plenty of it in the earth for all these purposes. Then what on earth are you and I quarreling about it for? Go to work systematically and take it from the mountains, and put it to use that we want it, without contending against each other, and filching the pockets of each other. The world if full of it. If it goes from my pocket it is still in the world, it still belongs to this little ball, this little speck in God's creation, so small that from the sun I expect you would have to have a telescope that would magnify it many times to see it; and from any of the fixed stars I do not expect that it has ever been seen, only by the celestials—mortals could not see this earth at that distance. And here people are contending, quarrelling, seeking how to get the advantage of each other, and how to get all the wealth there is in the world; wanting to rule nations, wanting to be president, king or ruler. What would they do if they were? Most of them would make everybody around them miserable, that is what they would do. There are very few men on the earth who try to make people happy. Occasionally there have been emperors and monarchs who have made their people happy but they have been very rare. But suppose we go to work to gather up all that there is in the bosom and upon the surface of our mother earth and bring it into use, is there any lack? There is not, there is enough for all. Then do look at these things as they are, Latter-day Saints, and you who are not Latter-day Saints, look at things as they are. And I do hope and pray for your sakes, outsiders, and for the sakes of those who profess to be Latter-day Saints, that we shall have good peace for a time here, so that we can build our furnaces, open our mines, make our railroads, till the soil, follow our mercantile business uninterrupted; that we may attend to the business of beautifying the earth. 15:19.

Agriculture—The increase of our children, and their growing up to maturity, increases our responsibilities. More land must be brought into cultivation to supply their wants. This will press the necessity of digging canals to guide the waters of our large streams over the immense tracts of bench and bottom lands which now lie waste. We want our children to remain near us, where there is an abundance of land and water, and not go hundreds of miles away to seek homes. In these great public improvements the people should enter with heart and soul, and freely invest in them their surplus property and means, and thus prepare to locate the vast multitudes of our children which are growing up, and strengthen our hands, and solidify still more—make still more compact our present organized spiritual and national institutions. 11:116.

You have a living off an acre and a quarter of land. Such a little farm well tilled and well managed, and the products of it economically applied, will do wonders towards keeping and educating a small family. Let the little children do their part, when they are not engaged in their studies, in knitting their stockings and mittens, braiding straw for their hats, or spinning yarn for their frocks and underclothing. If this people would strictly observe these simple principles of economy, they would soon become so rich that they would not have room sufficient to hold their abundance; their storehouses would run over with fulness. 11:142.

Now, cultivate your farms and gardens well, and drive your stock to where they can live through the winter, if you have not feed for them. Do not keep so many cattle, or, in other words, more than you can well provide for and make profitable to yourselves and to the Kingdom of God. We have hundreds and thousands of fat cattle upon the ranges, and yet we have no beef to eat, or very little. Kill your cattle when they are fat, and salt down the meat, that you may have meat to eat in the winter and some to dispose of to your neighbors for their labor to extend your improvements. Lay up your meat, and not let it die on your hands. Such a course is not right. Cattle are made for our use, let us take care of them. 11:142.

I intend to plant and sow, not only in the month of May, but in the month of June, and in the month of July, and I will continue my labors to raise what is necessary to sustain life as long as the season lasts. 2:280.

Let groves of olive trees be planted, and vineyards of the most approved varieties of grapes, and let sweet potatoes be raised in abundance, and all trees and roots that bear fruit in the ground and above the ground that can be used as food for man and beast. that plenty may flow in the land like a river, and contentment be enthroned in every household, while industry, frugality, and peace prevail everywhere. 10:227.

Instead of people being poor, we already have too much, unless we take better care of it. I heard a man who is living in this city—one who has always been well off—state that he used to keep twelve cows when he first came here, and was often nearly destitute of milk and butter. After a few years, the number of his cows was reduced to six, and he said that the six did him more good than the twelve had done. In two years more, they were reduced to two, and the two cows have done him much more good than the twelve or the six did, for they could be and were more properly attended to. 4:317.

Everything which we use to feed the life of man or beast, not a grain of it should be permitted to go to waste, but should be made to pass through the stomach of some animal; everything, also, which will fertilize our gardens and our fields should be sedulously saved and wisely husbanded, that nothing may be lost which contains the elements of food and raiment for man and sustenance for beast. 11:130.

Save your hay; save your chaff; save your straw; save your wheat; save your oats; save your barley, and everything that can be saved and preserved against a day of want. 12:241.

Wives, go into the garden and raise the salad and numerous other articles within your judgment and strength. Who hindered you from making a little vinegar last year? People are frequently running round and asking, "Where can I buy some vinegar?" When I was keeping a house, if my neighbors had a million hogsheads of vinegar, I had no need to buy a spoonful of it, for I would make a plenty for my own use, and would have eggs, butter, and pork, of my own production, and manage to secure beef, and salt it away nicely, and we had all the essentials for comfortable diet. 4:318.

What hinders you from raising something to feed a cow? Nothing. Who hinders you from planting your garden with corn, and having the suckers and the fodder? Who hinders you from raising carrots, parsnips, etc., to feed a cow with through the winter? This you can do on a little more than a quarter of an acre, but will you do it? 4:317.

The riches of a kingdom or nation do not consist so much in the fulness of its treasury as in the fertility of its soil and the industry of its people. 10:266.

Our wants are many, but our real necessities are very few. Let us govern our wants by our necessities, and we shall find that we are not compelled to spend our money for naught. Let us save our money to enter and pay for our land, to buy flocks of sheep and improve them, and to buy machinery and start more woolen factories. 12:289.

We are not anxious to obtain gold; if we can obtain it by raising potatoes and wheat, all right. "Can't you make yourselves rich by speculating?" We do not wish to. "Can't you make yourselves rich by going to the gold mines?" We are right in the midst of them. "Why don't you dig the gold from the earth?" Because it demoralizes any community or nation on the earth to give them gold and silver to their hearts' content; it will ruin any nation. But give them iron and coal, good hard work, plenty to eat, good schools and good doctrine, and it will make them a healthy, wealthy and happy people. 13:176.

Purchase cows, for if we have not already supplied you with cows, we are able and willing to do so. Most, if not all, have already been furnished with cows. What did you do with the calves? "We sold them for a trifle." Why did you not raise them? Do you not know that they would very soon be valuable? No, but you waste your calves, neglect buying pigs, and live without milk, and many of the easily procured comforts of life. 4:315.

The time will come that gold will hold no comparison in value to a bushel of wheat. 1:250.

When a farmer has done with his ploughs, he should put them under shelter until they are again wanted. When harness is taken off, it should be so hung up that you can go at any time of night and find it, or a saddle, bridle, saddle-blanket, or any other trapping, and be ready at once. 8:296.

Manufacturing—I pray the Lord to hedge up the way and shut down the gate so that we may be compelled to depend upon our own manufacturing for the comforts of life. 7:67.

Also raise flax, and prepare it for the women to manufacture into summer clothing. 4:316.

Save your wool, and send it to the factory. If we want a little cotton cloth, we can raise it in the southern country; and we could raise some here as well as in some other places. We can raise about two gatherings. 19:73.

I want them to save their wool and to keep it in this Territory. If we have not factories sufficient to work up all the wool that grows in this Territory, and in these mountains, we will send and get more machinery, and build more factories, and work up the wool for the people. 15:159.

Go and build a tannery, that the hides that come off our beef cattle, may be made into leather. 19:73.

We want glass. Some man will come along, by-and-by, and take the quartz rock, rig up a little furnace and make glass. 9:31.

By-and-by some man will come along, not worth fifty dollars, and take the feldspar, which enters so largely into our granite rock, and make the best of chinaware. 9:31.

Dye-stuffs have opened another drain through which considerable of our money has passed off. Wherever Indian corn will flourish madder can be produced in great quantities, yet we have been paying out our money to strangers for this article. Indigo can be successfully and profitably raised in this region. 10:226.

Importing sugar has been a great drain upon our floating currency. I am satisfied that it is altogether unnecessary to purchase sugar in a foreign market. The sorghum is a profitable crop, in Great Salt Lake and the adjoining counties, for the manufacture of molasses; in this section it can be profitably raised for the manufacture of sugar. I have tasted samples of sugar produced from the sorghum raised in the south of Utah, and a better quality of raw sugar I never saw. Let some enterprising persons prosecute this branch of home-production, and thus effectually stop another outlet for our money. Sugar ranks high among the staples of life, and should be produced in great abundance. 10:226.

Go to and raise silk. You can do it, and those who cannot set themselves to work we will set them to work gathering straw, and making straw hats and straw bonnets; we will set others to gathering willow, and others to making baskets; we will set others to gathering flags and rushes, and to making mats, and bottoming chairs and making carpets. 12:202.

As I told the people, when we first came into this valley in 1847, there is plenty of silk in the elements here, as much so as in any other part of the earth. 9:32.

The capitalists may say, "What are we to do with our means?" Go and build factories and have one, two, or three thousand spindles going. Send for fifty, a hundred, or a thousand sheep and raise wool. Some of you go to raising flax and build a factory to manufacture it, and do not take every advantage and pocket every dollar that is to be made. You are rich and I want to turn the stream so as to do good to the whole community. 13:36.

Commerce—It may be said that we shall always be poor without commerce; we shall always be poor with it, unless we command it; and unless we can do this, we are better without. 11:134.

But, again, with regard to this railroad; when it is through, even in ordinary times it opens to us the market, and we are at the door of New York, right at the threshold of the emporium of the United

States. We can send our butter, eggs, cheese, and fruits and receive in return oysters, clams, codfish, mackerel, oranges, and lemons. Let me say more to you—do up your peaches in the best style, for they will want them. 12:54.

Whatsoever administers to the sustenance, comfort and health of mankind forms the basis of the commerce of the world. Gold and silver in coin are only valuable as mediums to facilitate exchange. They can be made useful to us and add to our comfort when made into cups, plates, etc., in our household economy. 10:227.

Recollect that in trading there is great advantage in turning over your capital often. 13:35.

Are our merchants honest? I could not be honest and do as they do; they make five hundred percent on some of their goods, and that, too, from an innocent, confiding, poor, industrious people. 11:114.

Capital and Labor—All the capital there is upon the earth is the bone and sinew of workingmen and women. Were it not for that, the gold and the silver and precious stones would remain in the mountains, upon the plains and in the valleys, and never would be gathered or brought into use. The timber would continue to grow, but none of it would be brought into service, and the earth would remain as it is; but it is the activity and labor of the inhabitants of the earth that bring forth the wealth. Labor builds our meetinghouses, temples, courthouses, fine halls for music and fine schoolhouses; it is labor that teaches our children, and makes them acquainted with the various branches of education, that makes them proficient in their own language and in other languages, and in every branch of knowledge understood by the children of men; and all this enhances the wealth and glory and the comfort of any people on the earth. 16:66.

We say to the Latter-day Saints, work for these capitalists, and work honestly and faithfully, and they will pay you faithfully. I am acquainted with a good many of them, and as far as I know them, I do not know but every one is an honorable man. They are capitalists, they want to make money, and they want to make it honestly and according to the principles of honest dealing. If they have means and are determined to risk it in opening mines you work for them by the day. Haul their ores, build their furnaces and take your pay for it, and enter your lands, build homes, improve your farms, buy your stock, and make yourselves better off. 14:85.

There are many in the city of New York who never went to school a day in their lives; they are wallowing in the gutter, ragged, dirty, and filthy. They learn sharpness, it is true; but where do they sleep? By the wayside, or crawl into some old building—girls and boys, and live there by the thousand. They have not a shelter to place their heads under, but when night comes their only refuge is old buildings, hovels, and corners of streets forsaken by the police, and there they must spend the night. Why not take such characters and bring them out to this country, or to California, Oregon, or to the plains of Illinois, Wisconsin, etc., and make a town, settle up the country, and make these poor, miserable creatures better off? You would prove yourselves worthy of existence on the earth if you would. 14:84.

To pay people the wages they want here would prevent us from raising silk profitably. We look forward to the period when the price of labor here will be brought to a reasonable and judicious standard. 12:202.

Time and the ability to labor are the capital stock of the whole world of mankind, and we are all indebted to God for the ability to use time to advantage, and he will require of us a strict account of the disposition we make of this ability; and he will not only require an account of our acts, but our words and thoughts will also be brought into judgment. 18:73.

A young woman, compelled to labor for her daily bread, applies for work to some lady in comfortable circumstances. The lady perhaps says, "What wages do you want?" "I do not know. What will you give me?" The reply is, probably, "Well, I will give you fifty cents a week and your board, but I shall want you to do my washing, ironing, milking, scrubbing, and cooking," the whole of it, most likely, keeping the poor girl at work from five o'clock in the morning until ten at night. Yet her poverty leaves her no choice, and she is compelled to become a slave in order to procure, day by day, her breakfast, dinner, and supper. It is probable that if her father be alive he is too poor to help her; and if she has a mother she may be a widow and unable to rescue her from a life of toil and slavery. A lady, whom I knew in my youth, the wife of a minister, where I used to attend meeting, said once to some of her sisters in the church, "Do you suppose that we shall be under the necessity of eating with our hired help when we get into heaven? We do not do it here, and I have an idea that there will be two tables in heaven." Yet she was a lady of refinement and education, still the traditions that had been woven into her very being proved the folly she possessed to ask such a question. 14:99.

Let mechanics and every man who has capital create business and give employment and means into the hands of laborers; build good and commodious houses, magnificent temples, spacious tabernacles, lofty halls, and every other kind of structure that will give character and grandeur to our cities and create respect for our people. Let us make mechanics of our boys, and educate them in every useful branch of science and in the history and laws of kingdoms and nations, that they may be fitted to fill any station in life, from a ploughman to a philosopher. 10:270.

The non-producer must live on the products of those who labor. There is no other way. If we all labor a few hours a day, we could then spend the remainder of our time in rest and the improvement of our minds. This would give an opportunity to the children to be educated in the learning of the day, and to possess all the wisdom of man. 19:47.

Do not oppress the poor, but trust in God, and you will go neither hungry, naked, nor thirsty. If you oppress the poor, the day will come when you will be naked, thirsty, and hungry, and will not be able to get anything to supply your wants. 8:73.

Build Good Houses and Beautiful Cities—Let the people build good houses, plant good vineyards and orchards, make good roads, build beautiful cities in which may be found magnificent edifices for the convenience of the public, handsome streets skirted with shade trees, fountains of water, crystal streams, and every tree, shrub and flower that will flourish in this climate, to make our mountain home a paradise and our hearts wells of gratitude to the God of Joseph, enjoying it all with thankful hearts, saying constantly, "not mine but thy will be done, O Father." 10:3.

Beautify your gardens, your houses, your farms; beautify the city. This will make us happy, and produce plenty. The earth is a good earth, the elements are good if we will use them for our own benefit, in truth and righteousness. Then let us be content, and go to with our mights to make ourselves healthy, wealthy, and beautiful, and preserve ourselves in the best possible manner, and live just as long as we can, and do all the good we can. 15:20.

Every improvement that we make not only adds to our comfort but to our wealth. 16:64.

Make good houses; learn how to build; become good mechanics and business men, that you may know how to build a house, a barn, or a storehouse, how to make a farm, and how to raise stock, and take every care of it by providing proper shelter and every suitable convenience for keeping it through the winter; and prove yourselves worthy of the greater riches that will be committed to you than this valley and what it can produce. 8:289.

Accumulate Property—Efforts to accumulate property in the correct channel are far from being an injury to any community, on the contrary, they are highly beneficial, provided individuals, with all that they have, always hold themselves in readiness to advance the interests of the Kingdom of God on the earth. Let every man and woman be industrious, prudent, and economical in their acts and feelings, and while gathering to themselves, let each one strive to identify his or her interests with the interests of this community, with those of their neighbor and neighborhood, let them seek their happiness and welfare in that of all, and we will be blessed and prospered. 3:330.

To do right can be reduced to perfect simplicity in a few words, viz., from this time henceforth, let no person work, or transact any kind of business whatever, that he cannot do in the name of the Lord. 1:337.

This life is worth as much as any life that any being can possess in time or in eternity. There is no life more precious to us in the eye of eternal wisdom and justice than the life which we now possess. Our first duty is to take care of this life. 11:113.

To be prudent and saving, and to use the elements in our possession for our benefit and the benefit of our fellow beings is wise and righteous; but to be slothful, wasteful, lazy and indolent, to spend our time and means for naught, is unrighteous. 16:16.

We all believe that the Lord will fight our battles; but how? Will he do it while we are unconcerned and make no effort whatever for our own safety when an enemy is upon us? If we make no efforts to guard our towns, our houses, our cities, our wives and children, will the Lord guard them for us? He will not; but if we pursue the opposite course and strive to help him to accomplish his designs, then will he fight our battles. We are baptized for the remission of sins; but it would be quite as reasonable to expect remission of sins without baptism, as to expect the Lord to fight our battles without our taking every precaution to be prepared to defend ourselves. The Lord requires us to be quite as willing to fight our own battles as to have him fight them for us. If we are not ready for an enemy when he comes upon us, we have not lived up to the requirements of him who guides the ship of Zion, or who dictates the affairs of his Kingdom. 11:131.

Debt—Pay your debts, we will help you to do so, but do not run into debt any more. 14:105.

Be prompt in everything, and especially to pay your debts. 14:279.

A man who will run into debt, when he has no prospect of paying it back again, does not understand the principles that should prevail in a well-regulated community, or he is wilfully dishonest. 11:258.

A man who will not pay his honest debts is no Latter-day Saint, if he has the means to pay them. 11:258.

It is bad enough, quite bad enough, to borrow from an enemy and not to repay him; to do this is beneath the character of any human being; but all who will borrow from a friend, and especially from the poor, are undeserving the fellowship of the Saints if they do not repay. 14:276.

Chapter XXVII

WEALTH

Wealth Belongs to the Lord—Earthly riches are concealed in the elements God has given to man, and the essence of wealth is power to organize from these elements every comfort and convenience of life for our sustenance here, and for eternal existence hereafter. The possession of all the gold and silver in the world would not satisfy the cravings of the immortal soul of man. The gift of the Holy Spirit of the Lord alone can produce a good, wholesome, contented mind. Instead of looking for gold and silver, look to the heavens and try to learn wisdom until you can organize the native elements for your benefit; then, and not until then, will you begin to possess the true riches. 10:35.

There is any amount of property, and gold and silver in the earth and on the earth, and the Lord gives to this one and that one—the wicked as well as the righteous—to see what they will do with it, but it all belongs to him. He has handed over a goodly portion to this people, and, through our faith, patience and industry, we have made us good, comfortable homes here, and there are many who are tolerably well off, and if they were in many parts of the world they would be called wealthy. But it is not ours, and all we have to do is to try and find out what the Lord wants us to do with what we have in our possession, and then go and do it. If we step beyond this, or to the right or to the left, we step into an illegitimate train of business. Our legitimate business is to do what the Lord wants us to do with that which he bestows upon us, and dispose of it just as he dictates, whether it is to give all, one-tenth, or the surplus. 16:10.

No person on the earth can truly call anything his own, and never will until he has passed the ordeals we are all now passing, and has received his body again in a glorious resurrection, to be crowned by him who will be ordained and set apart to set a crown upon our heads. Then will be given to us that which we now only seem to own, and we will be forever one with the Father and the Son, and not until then. 9:106.

The elements are to be brought into shape and operation for the benefit, happiness, beauty, excellency, glory, and exaltation of the children of men that dwell upon the earth. 9:242.

Uncertainty of Temporal Possessions—Do you not know that the possession of your property is like a shadow, or the dew of the morning before the noonday sun, that you cannot have any assurance of its control for a single moment! It is the unseen hand of Providence that controls it. 1:114.

We cannot trust to the certainty of mortal possessions; they are transitory, and a dependence upon them will plunge into hopeless disappointment all those who trust in them. 2:122.

We should find that the things of this world called riches, are in reality not riches. We should find they are like mirages to the ignorant, mere phenomena to the inhabitants of the earth; to-day they are, to-morrow they are not; they were, but now they are gone, it is not known where. The earthly king upon his throne, who reigns triumphantly over his subjects, is blasted, with all his kingdom, and brought to naught at one breath of him who possesses true riches. Let him who possesses the true riches say to the elements around that kingdom, "produce no wheat, nor oil, nor wine, but let there be a famine upon that people," in such a circumstance where is the wealth of that king, his power, his grandeur, and his crown? There is no bread, no oil, there are no flocks, no herds, for they have perished upon the plains, his wheat is blasted, and all his crops are mildewed. What good does his wealth do him? His subjects are lying all around him lifeless for want of bread; he may cry to them, but in vain; his wealth, power, and influence have vanished, they are swept away like the flimsy fabric of a cobweb. 1:266.

The Sin of Covetousness—How the Devil will play with a man who so worships gain! 10:174.

I am more afraid of covetousness in our Elders than I am of the hordes of hell. 5:353.

Those who are covetous and greedy, anxious to grasp the whole world, are all the time uneasy, and are constantly laying their plans and contriving how to obtain this, that, and the other. 3:119.

Men are greedy for the vain things of this world. In their hearts they are covetous. It is true that the things of this world are designed to make us comfortable, and they make some people as happy as they can be here; but riches can never make the Latter-day Saints happy. Riches of themselves cannot produce permanent happiness; only the Spirit that comes from above can do that. 7:135.

When I cast my eyes upon the inhabitants of the earth and see the weakness, and I may say, the height of folly in the hearts of the kings, rulers, and the great, and those who should be wise and good and noble; when I see them grovelling in the dust; longing, craving, desiring, contending for the things of this life, I think, O foolish men, to set your hearts on the things of this life! To-day they are seeking after the honors and glories of the world, and by the time the sun is hidden by the western mountains the breath is gone out of their nostrils, they sink to their mother earth. Where are their riches then? Gone forever. As Job says, "Naked I came into the world." Destitute and forlorn, they have to travel the path that is untried and unknown to them, and wend their way into the spirit world. They know not where they are going nor for what. The designs of the Creator are hidden from their eyes; darkness, ignorance, mourning and groaning take hold of them and they pass into eternity. And this is the end of them concerning this life as far as they know. A man or a woman who places the wealth of this world and the things of time in the scales against the things of God and the wisdom of eternity, has no eyes to see, no ears to hear, no heart to understand. What are riches for? For blessings, to do good. Then let us dispense that which the Lord gives us to the best possible use for the building up of his Kingdom, for the promotion of the truth on the earth, that we may see and enjoy the blessings of the Zion of God here upon this earth. I look around among the world of mankind and see them grabbing, scrambling, contending, and every one seeking to aggrandize himself, and to accomplish his own individual purposes, passing the community by, walking upon the heads of his neighbors —all are seeking, planning, contriving in their wakeful hours, and when asleep dreaming, "How can I get the advantage of my neighbor? How can I spoil him, that I may ascend the ladder of fame?" This is entirely a mistaken idea. You see that nobleman seeking the benefit of all around him, trying to bring, we will say, his servants, if you please, his tenants, to his knowledge, to like blessings, that he enjoys, to dispense his wisdom and talent among them and to make them equal with himself. As they ascend and increase, so does he, and he is in the advance. All eyes are upon that king or that nobleman, and the feelings of those around him are, "God bless him! How I love him! How I delight in him! He seeks to bless and to fill me with joy, to crown my labors with success, to give me comfort, that I may enjoy the world as well as himself." But the man who seeks honor and glory at the expense of his fellow-men is not worthy of the society of the intelligent. 15:18.

I hope to see the day when there will be no such thing as one man taking usury from another. 13:92.

True Riches—There is no such thing as a man being truly rich until he has power over death, hell, the grave, and him that hath the power of death, which is the Devil. For what are the riches, the wealth possessed by the inhabitants of the earth? Why, they are a phantom, a mere shadow, a bubble on the wave, that bursts with the least breath of air. Suppose I possessed millions on millions of wealth of every description I could think of or ask for, and I took a sudden pain in my head, which threw me entirely out of my mind, and baffled the skill of the most eminent physicians, what good would that money do me, in the absence of the power to say to the pain, "Depart"? But suppose I possessed power to say to the pain, "Go thou to the land from whence thou comest"; and say, "Come, health, and give strength to my body"; and when I want death, to say, "Come you, for I have claim upon you, a right, a warranty deed, for this body must be dissolved"; says death, "I want it, to prey upon"; but again I can say to death, "Depart from me, thou canst not touch me"; would I not be rich indeed? How is it now? Let the slightest accident come upon one of the human family, and they are no more. Do we then possess true riches in this state? We do not. 1:271.

To possess this world's goods is not in reality wealth, it is not riches, it is nothing more nor less than that which is common to all men, to the just and the unjust, to the Saint and to the sinner. The sun rises upon the evil and the good; the Lord sends his rain upon the just and upon the unjust; this is manifest before our eyes, and in our daily experience. Old King Solomon, the wise man, says, the race is not to the swift, nor the battle to the strong, neither riches to men of wisdom. The truth of this saying comes within our daily observation. Those whom we consider swift are not always the ones that gain the mastery in the race, but those who are considered not so fleet, or not fleet at all, often gain the prize. It is, I may say, the unseen hand of Providence, that overruling power that controls the destinies of men and nations, that so ordains these things. The weak, trembling, and feeble, are the ones frequently who gain the battle; and the ignorant, foolish, and unwise will blunder into wealth. This is all before us, it is the common lot of man; in short, I may say, it is the philosophical providence of a philosophical world. 1:267.

Gold is Not Wealth—What use is gold when you get enough to eat, drink, and wear without it? 1:250.

There is no happiness in gold, not in the least. It is very convenient as an article of exchange, in purchasing what we need; and instead of finding comfort and happiness in gold, you exchange it to obtain happiness, or that which may conduce to it. There is no real wealth in gold. People talk about being wealthy—about being rich; but place the richest banking company in the world upon a barren rock, with their gold piled around them, with no possible chance of exchanging it, and destitute of the creature comforts, and they would be poor indeed. Where then is their joy, their comfort, their great wealth? They have none. 8:168.

True wealth consists in the skill to produce conveniences and comforts from the elements. All the power and dignity that wealth can bestow is a mere shadow, the substance is found in the bone and sinew of the toiling millions. Well-directed labor is the true power that supplies our wants. It gives regal grandeur to potentates, education and supplies to religious and political ministers, and supplies the wants of the thousands of millions of earth's sons and daughters. There are conditions and panics in society that all the power of earthly wealth cannot avert. 10:189.

It has been supposed that wealth gives power. In a depraved state of society, in a certain sense it does, if opening a wild field for unrighteous monopolies, by which the poor are robbed and oppressed and the wealthy are more enriched, is power. In a depraved state of society money can buy positions and titles, can cover up a multitude of incapabilities, can open wide the gates of fashionable society to the lowest and most depraved of human beings; it divides society into castes without any reference to goodness, virtue or truth. It is made to pander to the most brutal passions of the human soul; it is made to subvert every wholesome law of God and man, and to trample down every sacred bond that should tie society together in a national, municipal, domestic and every other relationship. Wealth thus used is used out of its legitimate channel. 10:3.

How to Become Wealthy—When men act upon the principles which will secure to them eternal salvation, they are sure of obtaining all their hearts' desire, sooner or later; if it does not come today, it may come tomorrow; if it does not come in this time, it will in the next. 2:122.

I am not for hoarding up gold and other property to lie useless, I wish to put everything to a good use. I never keep a dollar lying idle by me, for I wish all the means to be put into active operation. 3:160.

I can witness one fact, and so can others, that by paying attention to the building up of the Kingdom of God alone we have got rich in the things of this world; and if any man can tell me how we can get rich in any other way, he can do more than I can. We leave our business and our families and go out to preach the peaceable things of the Kingdom, and pay attention to that, never thinking of our business or our families, except when we ask the Lord to bless our families in common with all the families of the Saints everywhere. 11:116.

Do you want wealth? If you do, do not be in a hurry. Do you want the riches pertaining to this world? Yes, we acknowledge we do. Then, be calm, contented, composed; keep your pulses correct, do not let them get up to a hundred and twenty, but keep them as high as you can, ranging from seventy to seventy-six; and when there is an appointment for a meeting be sure to attend that meeting. If there is to be a two-days' meeting, come to it; spend the time here and learn what is going on. Watch closely, hear every word that is spoken, let every heart be lifted to God for wisdom, and know and understand every word of prophecy, every revelation that may be given, every counsel that may be presented to the people, that you may be able to weigh, measure, comprehend and decide between that which is of God and that which is not of God. Refuse the evil, learn wisdom, and grow in grace and in the knowledge of the truth. 15:35.

The course pursued by men of business in the world has a tendency to make a few rich, and to sink the masses of the people in poverty and degradation. 11:348.

This is the counsel I have for the Latter-day Saints today. Stop, do not be in a hurry. I do not know that I could find a man in our community but what wishes wealth, would like to have everything in his possession that would conduce to his comfort and convenience. Do you know how to get it? "Well," replies one, "if I do not, I wish I did; but I do not seem to be exactly fortunate—fortune is somewhat against me." I will tell you the reason of this—you are in too much of a hurry; you do not go to meeting enough, you do not pray enough, you do not read the Scriptures enough, you do not meditate enough, you are all the time on the wing, and in such a hurry that you do not know what to do first. This is not the way to get rich. I merely use the term "rich" to lead the mind along, until we obtain eternal riches in the celestial kingdom of God. Here we wish for riches in a comparative sense, we wish for the comforts of life. If we desire them let us take a course to get them. Let me reduce this to a simple saying—one of the most simple and homely that can be used—"Keep your dish right side up," so that when the shower of porridge does come, you can catch your dish full. 15:36.

These are a few words of consolation to the brethren who wish to keep their riches, and with them I promise you leanness of soul, darkness of mind, narrow and contracted hearts, and the bowels of your compassion will be shut up, and by and by you will be overcome with the spirit of apostasy and forsake your God and your brethren. 12:127.

My policy is to get rich; I am a miser in eternal things. Do I want to become rich in the things of this earth? Yes, if the Lord wishes me to have such riches, and I can use them to good advantage. My policy is to keep every man, woman, and child busily employed, that they may have no idle time for hatching mischief in the night, and for making plans to accomplish their own ruin. 2:144.

I told you the other day what makes me rich, it is the labor of those whom I feed and clothe; still I do not feel that I have a dollar in the world that is my own, it is the Lord's and he has made me a steward over it; and if I can know where the Lord is pleased to have it appropriated, there it shall go. 3:118.

One-third or one-fourth of the time that is spent to procure a living would be sufficient, if your labor were rightly directed. People think they are going to get rich by hard work—by working sixteen hours out of the twenty-four; but it is not so. A great many of our brethren can hardly spend time to go to meeting. Six days is more time than we need to labor. 8:355.

The great majority of men and women do not know how to take care of themselves. Let me refer the whole of you to a circumstance in Winter Quarters. We left Nauvoo in February, 1846, made our own roads through Iowa, except some 40 or 50 miles, built bridges, cut down timber, turned out 500 men to go to Mexico, came this side of the Missouri river, and there wintered. How did you live there? Do you know how you got anything to eat? Brethren came to me, saying, "We must go to Missouri. Can we not take our families and go to Missouri, and get work?" Do you know, to this day, how you lived? I will tell you, and then you will remember it. I had not five dollars in money to start with; but I went to work and built a mill, which I knew we should want only for a few months, that cost 3,600 dollars. I gave notice that I would employ every man and pay him for his labor. If I had a sixpence, I turned it into 25 cents; and a half-bushel of potatoes I turned into a half-a-bushel of wheat. How did I do that? By faith. I went to Brother Neff, who had just come in the place, and asked him for and received 2,600 dollars, though he did not know where the money was going. He kept the mill another year, and it died on his hands. I say, God bless him forever! for it was the money he brought from Pennsylvania that preserved thousands of men, women, and children from starving. I handled and dictated it, and everything went off smoothly and prosperously. 6:173.

Shall I give you my ideas in brief with regard to business and business transactions? Here for instance, a merchant comes to our neighborhood with a stock of goods; he sells them at from two to ten hundred per cent above what they cost. As a matter of course he soon becomes wealthy, and after a time he will be called a millionaire, when perhaps he was not worth a dollar when he commenced to trade. You will hear many say of such person, what a nice man he is, and what a great financier he is! My feeling of such a man is, he is a great cheat, a deceiver, a liar! He imposes on the people, he takes that which does not belong to him, and is a living monument of falsehood. Such a man is not a financier! The financier is he that brings the lumber from the canyons and shapes it for the use of his fellow man, employing mechanics and laborers to produce from the elements and the crude material everything necessary for the sustenance and comfort of man; one who builds tanneries to work up the hides instead of letting them rot and waste or be sent out of the country to be made into leather and then brought back in the shape of boots and shoes; and that can take the wool, the furs and straw and convert the same into cloth, into hats and bonnets, and that will plant out mulberry trees and raise the silk, and thus give employment to men, women and children, as you have commenced to do here, bringing the elements into successful use for the benefit of man, and reclaiming a barren wilderness, converting it into a fruitful field, making it to blossom as the rose; such a man I would call a financier, a benefactor of his fellow man. But the great majority of men who have amassed great wealth have done it at the expense of their fellows. 19:97.

Wealth Must Be Used—Few men know what to do with riches when they possess them. 1:250.

You know very well that it is against my doctrine and feelings for men to scrape together the wealth of the world and let it waste and do no good. 9:186.

Then do not hoard up your gold; if you do, it will canker, but put out every dollar to usury. Instead of your souls being bound up in your cattle and other property, put it all where it should be placed for the benefit of the Kingdom of God on earth and for his glory. 9:191.

A man has no right with property, which, according to the laws of the land, legally belongs to him, if he does not want to use it; he ought to possess no more than he can put to usury, and cause to do good to himself and his fellow man. When will a man accumulate money enough to justify him in salting it down, or, in other words, laying it away in the chest, to lock it up, there to lie, doing no manner of good either to himself or his neighbor? It is impossible for a man ever to do it. No man should keep money or property by him that he cannot put to usury for the advancement of that property in value or amount, and for the good of the community in which he lives; if he does, it becomes a dead weight upon him. Every man who has got cattle, money, or wealth of any description, bone and sinew, should put it out to usury. If a man has the arm, body, head, the component parts of a system to constitute him a laboring man, and has nothing in the world to depend upon but his hands, let him put them to usury. Never hide up anything in a napkin, but put it forth to bring an increase. If you have got property of any kind, that you do not know what to do with, lay it out in making a farm, or building a sawmill or a woolen factory, and go to with your mights to put all your property to usury.

If you have more oxen and other cattle than you need, put them in the hands of other men, and receive their labor in return, and put that labor where it will increase your property value. 1:252.

If a man comes in the midst of this people with money, let him use it in beautifying his inheritance in Zion, and in increasing his capital by thus putting out his money to usury. Let him go and make a great farm, and stock it well, and fortify all around with a good and efficient fence. What for? Why, for the purpose of spending his money. Then let him cut it up into fields, and adorn it with trees, and build a fine house upon it. What for? Why, for the purpose of spending his money. What will he do when his money is gone? The money thus spent, with a wise and prudent hand, is in a situation to accumulate and increase a hundred-fold. When he has done making his farm, and his means still increase by his diligent use of it, he can then commence and build a woolen factory for instance; he can send and buy the sheep and have them brought here, and have them herded here, and shear them here, and take care of them, then set the boys and girls to cleaning, carding, spinning, and weaving the wool into cloth, and thus employ hundreds and thousands of the brethren and sisters who have come from the manufacturing districts of the old country, and have not been accustomed to dig in the earth for their livelihood, who have not learned anything else but to work in the factory. This would feed them and clothe them, and put within their reach the comforts of life; it would also create at home a steady market for the produce of the agriculturist, and the labor of the mechanic. 1:253.

Wealth Brings Happiness Only When Used for the Gospel— All the real business we have on hand is to promote our religion. 4:355.

If you come naked and barefooted (I would not care if you had naught but a deer skin around you when you arrive here), and bring your God and your religion, you are a thousand times better than if you come with wagonloads of silver and gold and left your God behind. 4:204.

If, by industrious habits and honorable dealings, you obtain thousands or millions, little or much, it is your duty to use all that is put in your possession, as judiciously as you have knowledge, to build up the Kingdom of God on the earth. 4:29.

If we are destroyed through the possession of wealth, it will be because we destroy ourselves. If we possessed hundreds of millions of coin and devoted that means to building up the Kingdom of God and doing good to his creatures, with an eye single to his glory, we would be as much blessed and as much entitled to salvation as the poor beggar that begs from door to door; the faithful rich man is as much entitled to the revelations of Jesus Christ as is the faithful poor man. 10:300.

We must watch and pray, and look well to our walk and conversation, and live near to our God, that the love of this world may not choke the precious seed of truth, and feel ready, if necessary, to offer up all things, even life itself, for the Kingdom of Heaven's sake. 11:111.

Look out, ye men of Israel, and be careful that you love not the world or the things of the world in their present state, and in your loftiness and pride, forget the Lord your God. We ought to care no more for the silver and the gold, and the property that is so much sought for by the wicked world, than for the soil or the gravel upon which we tread. 11:18.

I do not care what becomes of the things of this world, of the gold, of the silver, of the houses and of the lands, so we have power to gather the House of Israel, redeem Zion, and establish the Kingdom of God on the earth. I would not give a cent for all the rest. True, these things which the Lord bestows upon us are for our comfort, for our happiness and convenience, but everything must be devoted to the upbuilding of the Kingdom of God on the earth. 3:361.

It is thought by many that the possession of gold and silver will produce for them happiness, and, hence, thousands hunt the mountains for the precious metals; in this they are mistaken. The possession of wealth alone does not produce happiness, although it will produce comfort, when it can be exchanged for the essentials and luxuries of life. When wealth is obtained by purloining, or in any other unfair and dishonorable way, fear of detection and punishment robs the possessor of all human happiness. When wealth is honorably obtained by man, still the possession of it is embittered by the thought that death will soon strip them of it and others will possess it. What hopes have they in the future, after they get through with this sorrowful world? They know nothing about the future; they see nothing but death and hell. Solid comfort and unalloyed joy are unknown to them. 11:15.

Men and women who are trying to make themselves happy in

the possession of wealth or power will miss it, for nothing short of the Gospel of the Son of God can make the inhabitants of the earth happy, and prepare them to enjoy heaven here and hereafter. 11:329.

It matters little, though we have many times left our houses and other possessions, having been driven from them by our enemies; for the earth is the Lord's and the fulness thereof; the gold and silver they are taking from the earth are all in his hands to dispose of at his pleasure. He sets up kingdoms and casts them down at his pleasure. The fulness of the earth is in his hands, but it cannot be enjoyed, in the full sense of the term, without enjoying it in connection with his Kingdom. 8:161-162.

Though I possessed millions of money and property, that does not excuse me from performing the labor that it is my calling to perform, so far as I have strength and ability, any more than the poorest man in the community is excused. The more we are blessed with means, the more we are blessed with responsibility; the more we are blessed with wisdom and ability, the more we are placed under the necessity of using that wisdom and ability in the spread of righteousness, the subjugation of sin and misery, and the amelioration of the condition of mankind. The man that has only one talent and the man that has five talents have responsibility accordingly. If we have a world of means, we have a world of responsibility. If we have an eternity of knowledge, we shall have an eternity of business to transact and to occupy every particle of the knowledge bestowed upon us. 9:172.

Some Dangers of Wealth—The question will not arise with the Lord, nor with the messengers of the Almighty, how much wealth a man has got, but how has he come by this wealth and what will he do with it? 11:294.

If the Lord ever revealed anything to me, he has shown me that the Elders of Israel must let speculation alone and attend to the duties of their calling, otherwise they will have little or no power in their missions or upon their return. 8:179.

The Latter-day Saints who turn their attention to money-making soon become cold in their feelings toward the ordinances of the house of God. They neglect their prayers, become unwilling to pay any donations; the law of tithing gets too great a task for them; and they finally forsake their God, and the providences of heaven seem to be shut from them—all in consequence of this lust after the things of this world, which will certainly perish in handling, and in their use they will fade away and go from us. 18:213.

If I had only seen in my young days an interest manifested by those who had wealth, power and influence to reach down a hand to take the suffering, ignorant, poor and elevate them to the standard they occupied, and to place them in possession of every comfort, it would have been a matter of great joy to me. But it was not so then, neither is it now. Men generally use their wealth for selfish purposes, and do not seek to devote it to God and to the glory of his name. 13:147.

Do not be anxious to have this people become rich, and possess the affection of the world. I have been fearful lest we come to fellowship the world. 10:298.

Some say, "If we had a gold mine, we would do well." If I knew where there was a gold mine, I would not tell you. I do not want you to find one, and I do not mean that you shall; or, if you do, it shall be over my faith. We have gold enough in the world, and it is the Lord's, and we do not deserve more than we get. Let us make good use of that, and send out the Elders. 8:204.

I would as soon see a man worshiping a little god made of brass or of wood as to see him worship his property. 6:196.

Never pray for riches; do not entertain such a foolish thought. In my deep poverty, when I knew not where I could procure the next morsel of food for myself and family, I have prayed God to open the way that I might get something to keep myself and family from dying. Those who do more than this are off, more or less, from the track that leads to life eternal. 7:138.

We are the greatest speculators in the world. We have the greatest speculation on hand that can be found in all the earth. I never denied being a speculator. I never denied being a miser, or of feeling eager for riches; but some men will chase a picayune five thousand miles when I would not turn round for it, and yet we are preachers of the same Gospel, and brethren in the same Kingdom of God. You may consider this is a little strong; but the speculation I am after, is to exchange this world, which, in its present state, passes away, for a world that is eternal and unchangeable, for a glorified world filled with eternal riches, for the world that is made an inheritance for the Gods of eternity. 1:326.

The Poor—The poor are the people of God, and they shall inherit the earth. 8:186.

The Gospel of life and salvation does not reduce those who obey it to beggary; but it takes the poor and the ignorant, makes them wise and happy, and surrounds them with the comforts of life and everything desirable, and teaches them to serve God with all their hearts. 14:121.

If a man comes to me and says he is out of food, what of that? He is out of food; that is all. If a man comes along and says, "My family is destitute of food and clothing," what of that? Simply that they are destitute of food and clothing, and still they may be gentlemen and ladies, for all that, and be honoring their tabernacles and being on the earth.

The customs of the world have made it degrading to ask for food, but it is not, when a person cannot honestly procure it in any other way. The man who is hungry and destitute has as good a right to my food as any other person, and I should feel as happy in associating with him, if he had a good heart, as with those who have an abundance, or with the princes of the earth. They all are esteemed by me, not according to the wealth and position they hold, but according to the character they have. 3:245

The Lord's poor do not forget their covenants, while the Devil's poor pay no regard to their promises. 3:2.

What causes poverty among this people? It is the want of discretion, calculation, sound judgment. I am paying men more or less by the day, and where do you see those who get the least wages? Seated back in the barber's chair three or four times a week. Next at a store to get a box of blacking to put upon fifteen dollar boots, if they can get them. They must have four or five dollar handkerchiefs, as fine things for their wives and children, and as much in quantity as any other man has. At the end of the year there are two or three hundred dollars on the debit side of their accounts. 9:297.

Let the poor, those who have to depend upon their brethren for bread, after they have done all they can to obtain it themselves, be thankful, and take no more than they require to use in a frugal manner. 3:375.

The poor are filled with idolatry as well as the rich, and covet the means of those who have helped them; the rich also have the same spirit of idolatry, and stick to what they have. Let the poor be honest, let the rich be liberal, and lay their plans to assist the poor, to build up the Kingdom of God, and at the same time enrich themselves, for that is the way to build up God's Kingdom. 3:6.

Poor men, or poor women, who have nothing, and covet that which is not their own, are just as wicked in their hearts, as the miserly man who hoards up his gold and silver, and will not put it out to use. I wish the poor to understand, and act as they would wish others to act towards them in like circumstances. 2:52.

If the poor had all the surplus property of the rich many of them would waste it on the lusts of the flesh, and destroy themselves in using it. For this reason the Lord does not require the rich to give all their substance to the poor. It is true that when the young man came to Jesus to know what he must do to be saved, he told him, finally, "sell all that thou hast and distribute unto the poor, and thou shalt have treasure in heaven, and come, follow me"; and a great many think that he told the young man to give away all that he had, but Jesus did not require any such thing, neither did he say so, but simply, "distribute to the poor." If the poor knew what to do with what they have many, yea very many, in this land would have all that is necessary to make them comfortable. 13:302.

If they had the privilege of dictating the affairs of this people, or of any other, they would divide the substance of the rich among the poor, and make all what they call equal. But the question would arise with me at once, how long would they remain equal? Make the rich and the poor of this community, or of any other, equal by the distribution of their earthly substance, and how long would it be before a certain portion of them would be calling upon the other portion, for something with which to sustain themselves? The cry would soon be—"I have no bread, no house, no team, no farm; I have nothing." And in a very few years, at the most, large properties would thus pass from the hands of such individuals, and would be distributed among those who know how to accumulate wealth and to preserve it when accumulated. 12:56.

It is a disgrace to every man and woman that has sense enough to live, not to take care of their own relatives, their own poor, and plan for them to do something they are able to do. 8:145.

Chapter XXVIII

MISSIONARY WORK

The Gospel to be Preached to all Men—The Gospel must be preached to the world, that the wicked may be left without excuse. 4:58.

It is necessary that all have the privilege of receiving or rejecting eternal truth, and that they may be prepared to be saved, or be prepared to be damned. 7:139.

Our Father in Heaven, Jesus, our Elder Brother and the Savior of the world, and the whole heavens, are calling upon this people to prepare to save the nations of the earth, also the millions who have slept without the Gospel. 18:77.

The Lord has called me to this work, and I feel as though I will do it. We will send the Gospel to the nations; and when one nation turns us away we will go to another and gather up the honest in heart, and the rest we care not for until we come on Mount Zion as saviors, to attend to the ordinances of the house of God for them. 8:230-231.

The Lord has restored the Priesthood in our day for the salvation of Israel. Does he design to save anybody else? Yes; he will save the House of Esau, and I hope to live until I see Mount Zion established, and saviors come up to save those poor, miserable beings who are continually persecuting us—all who have not sinned against the Holy Ghost. Our labor is to save ourselves, to save the House of Israel, to save the House of Esau, and all the Gentile nations—every one that can be saved. 7:281.

This Kingdom or work is proffered to the whole of the human family, even to all who will accept it, upon the terms of strict obedience to all its ordinances and requirements, and to its organization of Prophets and Apostles, gifts and blessings and graces. 11:249.

There are, doubtless, millions of just as honest people among the several religious denominations as are amongst the professedly Latter-day Saints. But they have not the Gospel, they are in darkness with regard to the plan of salvation, and their teachers are blind guides, totally unable to give the people the living word, the way of life. If they live up to the best light and knowledge they have and can get, they are safe, and in a saved condition. What is the sin of the ministry and people of the present Christian denominations? It is that light has come to them and they reject it. The condemnation of the Jewish nation was that light had come into the world, but they chose darkness rather than light, because their deeds were evil; so says the Savior. The same Gospel that Jesus taught to those who rejected him is entrusted to us to preach to the whole world with the same consequences which must reach them at some time, in some condition. 17:262.

I shall be very happy when I can know that the people of the East Indian Archipelago, and the people on every island and continent, both the high and the low, the ignorant and intelligent, have received the words of eternal life, and have had bestowed upon them the power of the eternal Priesthood of the Son of God, by which they may become truly civilized. 8:7.

The day will come when the Gospel will be presented to the kings and queens and great ones of the earth; but it will be presented with a different influence from that with which it has been presented to the poor, but it will be the same Gospel. We shall not present any other Gospel; it is the same from everlasting to everlasting. 13:150.

The Elders have also preached through the different nations of Europe as far as they were allowed to do so. In some countries the law would not permit them; but the Lord will yet revolutionize those nations until the door will be opened and the Gospel will be preached to all. 12:256.

Had I the choice whether to go to the States and gather Saints, or to go where the Gospel was preached by the ancient Apostles of the Lord Jesus Christ, among the children of the people who have formerly had the Gospel preached to them, I would engage to go to the States and gather one hundred Saints to one that could be gathered from among the children of those who heard Peter, Paul, and others of the ancient Apostles preach the Gospel. 4:306.

Though the people in the States are daily becoming more hardened against the truth, yet if I were in New York this day, and it was my business to be there, I would not be there long before I would have many Elders preaching through different parts of that city; I would have them preaching in the English, Danish, French, German, and other languages. And soon would have Elders dispersed all over the State, and would raise up new friends enough to sustain me, that is, if the Lord would help me, and if he did not, I would leave. 4:37.

Help to Save Every Person—What is Babylon? It is the confused world: come out of her, then, and cease to partake of her sins, for if you do not you will be partakers of her plagues. 12:282.

If to all eternity you could praise God, through being the means of saving one soul, I may say the least or most inferior intelligence upon the earth, pertaining to the human family—if you could be the means of saving one such person, how great would be your joy in the heavens! Then let us save many, and our joy will be great in proportion to the number of souls we save. Let us destroy none. 9:124.

A true servant of God takes more pleasure in saving the meanest capacity organized in human form upon the face of the earth than a wicked person can in leading hosts astray. Let a Prophet of God, an Apostle, or any servant of the Lord Jesus have the privilege of bringing the very smallest degree of organized intelligence up higher and higher until it is capable of receiving the intelligence of angels, and it will give more consolation and happiness than to lead all the posterity of Adam into a wrong path. 8:59.

We had better gather nine that are unworthy than to neglect the tenth if he is worthy. 15:18.

We gather the poorest of the people, the unlearned, and a few of the learned; but generally, we gather those who are poor, who wish to be redeemed; who feel the oppression the high and the proud have made them endure; they have felt a wish to be delivered, and consequently their ears were open to receive the truth. Take those who are in the enjoyment of all the luxuries of this life, and their ears are stopped up; they cannot hear. 12:256.

And when you are called to preach the Gospel on foreign missions, take a course to save every person. There is no man or woman within the pale of saving grace but that is worth saving. There is no intelligent being, except those who have sinned against the Holy Ghost, but that is worth, I may say, all the life of an Elder to save in the Kingdom of God. 9:124.

This people are mostly gathered from what are termed the laboring and middle classes. We have not gathered into this Church men that are by the world esteemed profound in their principles, ideas, and judgment. We have none in this Church that are called by them expert statesmen. How frequently it is cast at the Elders, when they are abroad preaching, that Joseph Smith, the founder of their Church and religion, was only a poor illiterate boy. That used to be advanced as one of the strongest arguments that could be produced against the doctrine of salvation, by the wise and learned of this world, though it is no argument at all. The Lord should have revealed himself to some of the learned priests or talented men of the age, say they, who could have done some good and borne off the Gospel by their influence and learning, and not to a poor, ignorant, unlettered youth. Not many wise, not many mighty, not many noble, speaking after the manner of men, are called; but God hath chosen the foolish things of the world to confound the wise, the weak things of the world to confound the things that are mighty; and base things of the world

—things which are despised by the world, hath God in his wisdom chosen; yea, and things which are not, to bring to naught things that are, that no flesh should glory in his presence. 6:70.

It is the House of Israel we are after, and we care not whether they come from the east, the west, the north, or the south; from China, Russia, England, California, North or South America, or some other locality; and it is the very lad on whom Father Jacob laid his hands, that will save the House of Israel. The Book of Mormon came to Ephraim, for Joseph Smith was a pure Ephraimite. 2:268.

If this net does not gather the good and the bad we should have no idea that it is the net that Jesus spoke about when he said that it should gather of all kinds. 14:78.

I may say that this Gospel is to spread to the nations of the earth, Israel is to be gathered, Zion redeemed, and the land of Joseph, which is the land of Zion, is to be in the possession of the Saints, if the Lord Almighty lets me live; and if I go behind the veil somebody else must see to it. My brethren must bear it off shoulder to shoulder. 3:361.

Words of Departing Missionaries—We wish the brethren to understand the facts just as they are; that is, there is neither man or woman in this Church who is not on a mission. That mission will last as long as they live, and it is to do good, to promote righteousness, to teach the principles of truth, and to prevail upon themselves and everybody around them to live those principles that they may obtain eternal life. 12:19.

When I came into this Church, I started right out as a missionary, and took a text, and began to travel on a circuit. Truth is my text, the Gospel of salvation my subject, and the world my circuit. 9:137.

We do not wish a man to enter on a mission, unless his soul is in it. 2:267.

The brethren who have been called upon foreign missions we expect to respond to the call cheerfully. 4:264.

Go forth and preach the Gospel, gain an experience, learn wisdom, and walk humbly before your God, that you may receive the Holy Ghost to guide and direct you, and teach you all things past, present, and to come. 8:176.

Go trusting in God, and continue to trust in him, and he will open your way and multiply blessings upon you, and your souls will be satisfied with his goodness. I cannot promise you any good in taking an unrighteous course; your lives must be examples of good works. 8:73.

I think that the brethren were required to go and preach "without purse and scrip," and that is what I am now trying to get them to do—to go "without purse and scrip," and not beg the poor Saints to death. Let us support the Elders, instead of making the poor do it. We are able to send these men out to preach the Gospel, and they may go "without purse or scrip." 8:169.

I wish the Elders to go forth as I have taught them. If you have a clean shirt and one to be washed, then be satisfied. If you are clothed so as to be comfortable, be satisfied, and do not let your minds reach out after anything, only to preach the Gospel and gather the souls of men. That is all the business you have upon your hands—it is your whole mission; and trust in God to get home—trust in the Lord to go from place to place, and the way will be opened for you. 8:185.

Those who now go forth upon missions will feel more of the power of God than they ever had, and will speak as men having authority, asking no odds of the wicked. 8:172.

I would like to impress upon the minds of the brethren, that he who goes forth in the name of the Lord, trusting in him with all his heart, will never want for wisdom to answer any question that is asked him, or to give any counsel that may be required to lead the people in the way of life and salvation, and he will never be confounded worlds without end. Go in the name of the Lord, trust in the name of the Lord, lean upon the Lord, and call upon the Lord fervently and without ceasing, and pay no attention to the world. You will see plenty of the world—it will be before you all the time—but if you live so as to possess the Holy Ghost you will be able to understand more in relation to it in one day than you could in a dozen days without it, and you will at once see the difference between the wisdom of men and the wisdom of God, and you can weigh things in the balance and estimate them at their true worth. 12:34.

If the Elders cannot go with clean hands and pure hearts, they had better stay here. Do not go thinking, when you arrive at the Missouri River, at the Mississippi, at the Ohio, or at the Atlantic, that then you will purify yourselves; but start from here with clean hands and pure hearts, and be pure from the crown of the head to the soles of your feet; then live so every hour. Go in that manner, and in that manner labor, and return again as clean as a piece of pure white paper. This is the way to go; and if you do not do that, your hearts will ache.

Will you be liable to fall into temptation and be overtaken by sin? Yes, unless you live so as to have the revelation of Jesus Christ continually, not only to live in it today or while you are preaching, in a prayer meeting, or in a conference; and when you are out of these meetings, when you are guarded more particularly by the Spirit, say that you can get along without the Holy Ghost. You must have it all the time—on Sunday, Monday, Tuesday, and every day through the week, and from year to year, from the time you leave home until you return; so that when you come back, you may not be afraid if the Lord Almighty should come into the midst of the Saints and reveal all the acts and doings and designs of your hearts in your mission; but be found clean like a piece of white paper. That is the way for the Elders to live in their ministry at home and abroad. 6:273-274.

I want to say for the consolation of the Elders of Israel and those who go forth to preside, you need have no trouble with regard to the building up of this Kingdom, only do your duty in the sphere to which you are assigned. 14:79.

Elders who go forth to proclaim the Gospel, unless they do something to clip their faith, or cause them to apostatize from their religion, so that they are left in the dark, are generally on the increase in improvement, grow in grace and in knowledge. They are advancing in the principles of truth, while the world are receding from the truth they once had; consequently, it appears to the Elders, and to those who go from the Saints into the world, that it is growing wicked faster than it really is, and the Elders do not always realize that their advancement in truth produces much of the appearance of the great distance between them and the world. 3:221-222.

If those who are going to preach do not go with that faith that pertains to eternal life, and that spirit that is like a well of water, springing up into everlasting life, their labors will be vain. They may be the best theoretical theologians in the world—may be able to preach a Bible and a half in a sermon, to read history without a book, and understand all the dealings with men from the days of Adam till now; and, without the Spirit of the living God to guide them, they will not be able to accomplish anything to their credit towards building up his Kingdom. They must realize that success in preaching the Gospel springs not from the wisdom of this world. They must so live as to enjoy the power of God. 8:70-71.

Don't carry your wives or your children in your hearts or in your affections with you one rod. Dedicate them to the Lord God of Israel, and leave them at home; and when you are in England, or among other nations, no matter where, when you pray for your families, pray for them as being in the Great Salt Lake Valley, and do not bring them close to you, as though they were in your carpet-bag. Pray for them where they are. You must feel—if they live, all right; if they die, all right; if I die, all right; if I live, all right; for we are the Lord's, and we shall soon meet again. 6:276.

I wish to say to you that are left here, whose husbands and fathers are going away for a season—don't cling to them one particle, but let them go as cheerfully as you would give a weary traveler a cup of cold water. If you live, it is all right; and if you fall asleep before they return, it is all right. Don't send your hearts after them one step, nor suffer your spirits to cling to them one moment. Then you, wives, in very deed will be blessed and be helpmeets to your husbands. 6:276.

Many have such feelings, that they are greater who are in the world preaching the Gospel than those who remain here. It is a grand mistake. 6:274.

Look over the history of the Church of the living God on the earth from the days of Adam until now, and I will ensure that you cannot find the equal to the excessive labor of the Elders of Israel in our day in spreading the Truth through the world to save mankind. I have no idea that it was done in the days of Enoch; for the human family had then spread over the earth but little, and the Elders did not have to travel scores of thousands of miles without purse or scrip among the wicked. So also in the days of Noah; they had but a short distance to travel. In the days of the Israelites, of the Prophets, of Jesus Christ, and the Apostles, what was their labor in the extent of its field, compared with that of this people? Very small. You may trace the course of their travel, and you will find that it was far less than that of the Elders of Israel in our day. 5:351.

If you go on a mission to preach the Gospel with lightness and frivolity in your hearts, looking for this and that, and to learn what is in the world, and not having your minds rivited—yes, I may say riveted—on the cross of Christ, you will go and return in vain. Go forth weeping, bearing precious seed, full of the power of God, and full of faith to heal the sick even by the touch of your hand, rebuking and casting out foul spirits, and causing the poor among men to rejoice, and you will return bringing your sheaves with you. Let your minds be centered on your missions and labor earnestly to bring souls to Christ. 12:33-34.

Advice to Missionaries in the Field—The travels and labors of the Elders about to go on missions will throw them into positions which will cause them to seek unto the Lord. They need to live their religion, to go forth with pure hearts and clean hands, and then preach the Gospel by the power of God sent down from heaven. They should touch not and taste not of sin, and when they return they should come pure and clean, ready to meet the Saints with open countenances. 8:178.

When you reach your respective fields of labor in the States, in England, or elsewhere, do not begin to pull down your predecessors.

So far as their conduct will permit, speak of them as your brethren, and as men who have done the best they knew how. Testify that you know them to be good men, when you know that they have been doing according to their best judgment and understanding; and do not say hard words about your predecessors in the vineyard. Not one who does this will gain anything by it. Do not discourage, deride, or bring anything against any of your predecessors to lessen the character of any one who has done the best he knew how. 8:181.

Gather the Saints, but do not flatter; invite, but do not urge, and by no means compel any one. 8:72.

If you have a happy influence with your brethren and sisters, preserve it, for it is more choice than fine gold. How many times have I told the Elders, "When you go on missions, be careful to preserve your God-like dignity and integrity." 8:346.

The Elders who are going abroad should deal out kindness to those they are sent to watch over, and your smiles will be far better than your cursings could be. 8:74.

You know that I have said that, if it were now my calling to go and preach the Gospel, I could make as many converts as I ever did; for I would go in such a manner that the bitterly prejudiced would have to labor hard to find out that I was a "Mormon" until I had induced them to love the truth. Then they would say, "If that is 'Mormonism' I want it." 5:5.

I wish the Elders of Israel to understand mankind as they are—to go to the people and take them as they are. 9:121.

I wish you all to understand that no Elders go to any place among the world but what the wicked find fault with the people of God. 4:78.

Let me now say to my brethren, the Elders of Israel, it is always proper to ask kindly and affectionately the people to perform what you wish performed, instead of ordering them to do it. This principle is always good for parents and teachers to observe. 10:228.

Elders of Israel, learn to be spiritual physicians. Carry the medicine with you to deal out to every patient as he needs it. If a patient has chills and fever in his spirit, you must carry the medicine to cure it. 9:125.

Never suffer yourselves to mingle in any of those recreations that tend to sin and iniquity, while you are away from the body of the Church, where you cannot so fully control yourselves. 1:48.

I recollect, in England, sending an Elder to Bristol, to open a door there, and see if anybody would believe. He had a little more than thirty miles to walk; he starts off one morning, and arrives at Bristol; he preached the Gospel to them, and sealed them all up to damnation, and was back next morning. He was just as good a man, too, as we had. It was want of knowledge caused him to do so. I go and preach to the people, and tell them at the end of every sermon, He that believeth and is baptized, shall be saved; and he that believeth not, shall be damned. I continue preaching there day after day, week after week, and month after month, and yet nobody believes my testimony, that I know of, and I don't see any signs of it. "What shall I do in this case, if I am sent to preach there?" you may inquire. You must continue to preach there, until those who sent you shall tell you to leave that field of labor; and if the people don't manifest by their works, that they believe, as long as they come to hear me, I will continue to plead with them until they bend their disposition to the Gospel? Why? Because I must be patient with them, as the Lord is patient with me; as the Lord is merciful to me, I will be merciful to others; as he continues to be merciful to me, consequently I must continue in long-suffering to be merciful to others—patiently awaiting, with all diligence, until the people will believe, and until they are prepared to become heirs to a celestial kingdom, or angels to the Devil. 3:91.

In the first place, I want to say to the Elders who go forth to preach the Gospel—no matter who may apply to you for baptism, even if you have good reason to believe they are unworthy, if they require it, forbid them not, but perform that duty and administer the ordidance for them; it clears the skirts of your garments, and the responsibility is upon them. 14:78.

The meek and lowly Jesus sent his disciples without purse or scrip; and when the honest in heart see our Elders go in the same manner that Jesus' disciples did, with the doctrine that he delivered to his disciples, and preach without purse or scrip, our Elders will find plenty of honest-hearted persons who will receive their testimony. But when the Elders go into the great cities, hire large halls and hire carriages to ride to their pulpit in, the people say it is a speculation, and such Elders do not have much of the Spirit of the Lord to preach to the people. 13:90.

When you reach your fields of labor, do the best you can; and when the enemy comes along and tells you that you are somebody, say, "Mr. Devil, it is none of your business. What I have spoken is what the Lord gave to me. I have presented it to the people, and that is all I have to do with it." If you cannot preach as nicely and smoothly as you wish, and a feeling rises that you cannot preach at all—that you had better return home, tell Satan to get behind you—that he has no power to dictate whether you preach a word or not, for you are in the Lord's service. So live that the Spirit of the Lord can instruct your minds at all times, and you can then defy the Devil and all his emissaries. If you have nothing from the Lord to present to the people, be as willing to be silent as you would to preach what might be termed a splendid discourse. 8:55.

I do not think there was worse said about the Savior and his disciples in ancient days than has been said about the people of Utah in modern times. Take no notice of this, but attend to the business about which you have been sent. Tell this generation the truth, and pass along. Do not contend or argue much but pass along peaceably and preach the first principles of the Gospel. 8:56.

If you should have visits here from those professing to be Christians, and they intimate a desire to preach to you, by all means invite them to do so. Accord to every reputable person who may visit you, and who may wish to occupy the stands of your meeting houses to preach to you, the privilege of doing so, no matter whether he be a Catholic, Presbyterian, Congregationalist, Baptist, Free-will Baptist, Methodist, or whatever he may be; and if he wishes to speak to your children let him do so. Of course you have the power to correct whatever false teachings or impressions, if any, your children may hear or receive. 14:195.

When men enjoy the spirit of their missions and realize their calling and standing before the Lord and the people, it constitutes the happiest portions of their lives. 8:53.

Some inquire, "Why cannot we serve God in other countries as well as here?" You can just as well in England, in France, in Germany, in Italy, on the islands of the sea, in the United States, in California, or anywhere else, as you can here. 2:253.

The Returned Missionary—Come home with your heads up. Keep yourselves clean, from the crowns of your heads to the soles of your feet; be pure in heart,—otherwise you will return bowed down in spirit and with a fallen countenance, and will feel as though you never could rise again. 8:55.

I wish to make this request: that the Elders who return from missions consider themselves just as much on a mission here as in England or in any other part of the world. 14:220.

We frequently call the brethren to go on missions to preach the Gospel, and they will go and labor as faithfully as men can do, fervent in spirit, in prayer, in laying on hands, in preaching to and teaching the people how to be saved. In a few years they come home, and throwing off their coats and hats, they will say, "Religion, stand aside, I am going to work now to get something for myself and my family." This is folly in the extreme. When a man returns from a mission where he has been preaching the Gospel he ought to be just as ready to come to this pulpit to preach as if he were in England, France, Germany, or on the islands of the sea. And when he has been at home a week, a month, a year, or ten years, the spirit of preaching and the spirit of the Gospel ought to be within him like a river flowing forth to the people in good words, teachings, precepts, and examples. If this is not the case he does not fill his mission. 14:100.

Do not come from your missions leaving behind you people whom you have oppressed, from whom you have begged their money. I would work my way there and back again, or beg from strangers, before I would take one dime from the Saints, unless they of their own free will and accord wished to make me presents, and were able to do so without distressing themselves. True, I have seen the time, and so have many of my brethren, when my heart has ached to see men and women go without food day after day for the sake of feeding me, when I could feed myself; but any other course would not satisfy them. Under such circumstances you must humor the people and yield to their feelings. 8:55.

Those faithful Elders who have testified of this work to thousands of people on the continents and islands of the seas will see the fruits of their labors, whether they have said five words or thousands. They may not see these fruits immediately, and perhaps, in many cases, not until the Millennium; but the savor of their testimony will pass down from father to son. 8:142.

The Gospel is Preached With Authority—When a man who is called and ordained of God goes forth he preaches the ordinances, faith in Christ and obedience to him as our Savior. He declares that the first step to be taken, after believing in the Father and the Son, is to go down into the waters of baptism and there be immersed in the water, and come up out of the water as Jesus did. Some may inquire why the Latter-day Saints are so strenuous on this point? We do it for the remission of sins; Jesus did this to fulfil all righteousness. 14:96.

Perhaps some may say that I have too much faith in the prophecies of God, in the latter-day work, and in the administration of individuals that now live and have lived on the earth in our day. Be it so, no matter to me. I am here to testify in the name of the God of Israel that for many years past there have been men traveling through the length and breadth of the earth who possess the same power and authority as that with which Jesus endowed his Apostles when he told them to go into all the world and "preach the Gospel to every creature, and he that believeth and is baptized shall be saved, but he that believeth not shall be damned, and these signs shall follow them that believe. In my name they shall cast out devils, heal the sick, speak with new tongues," etc. 14:131.

The Spirit, Not Logic or Debate, Makes Converts—Let one go forth who is careful to prove logically all he says by numerous quotations from the revelations, and let another travel with him who can say, by the power of the Holy Ghost, Thus saith the Lord, and tell what the people should believe—what they should do—how they should live, and teach them to yield to the principles of salvation—though he may not be capable of producing a single logical argument, though he may tremble under a sense of his weakness, cleaving to the Lord for strength, as such men generally do, you will invariably find that the man who testifies by the power of the Holy Ghost will convince and gather many more of the honest and upright than will the merely logical reasoner. 8:53.

However good and useful a classical education may be in the possession of a good and wise man, yet it is not essentially necessary for him to have it, to tell the simple truth which is given to mankind by the revelations of God, because it can be told by the simple and the unlearned. 11:215.

Debate and argument have not that saving effect that has testifying to the truth as the Lord reveals it to the Elder by the Spirit. I think you will agree with me in this; at least, such is my experience. I do not wish to be understood as throwing a straw in the way of the Elders storing their minds with all the arguments they can gather to urge in defense of their religion, nor do I wish to hinder them in the least from learning all they can with regard to religions and governments. The more knowledge the Elders have the better. 8:53.

I had only traveled a short time to testify to the people, before I learned this one fact, that you might prove doctrine from the Bible till doomsday, and it would merely convince a people, but would not convert them. You might read the Bible from Genesis to Revelation, and prove every iota that you advance, and that alone would have no converting influence upon the people. Nothing short of a testimony by the power of the Holy Ghost would bring light and knowledge to them—bring them in their hearts to repentance. Nothing short of that would ever do. You have frequently heard me say that I would rather hear an Elder, either here or in the world, speak only five words accompanied by the power of God, and they would do more good than to hear long sermons without the Spirit. That is true, and we know it. 5:327.

When a false theory has to be maintained, it requires to be set forth with much care; it requires study, and learning, and cunning sophistry to gild over a falsehood and give it the semblance of truth, and make it plausible and congenial to the feelings of the people; but the most simple and unlearned person can tell you the truth. A child can tell you the truth, in child-like language, while falsehood requires the lawyer and the priest to tell it to make it at all plausible; it requires a scholastic education to make falsehood pass for truth. 11:214.

The servants of God have truth, and nothing but truth, to present to the world, that the world may be sanctified by the truth. The truth needeth no polish to make it lovely and desirable to those who love it. 11:234.

They must eventually either acknowledge that he is the Son of God and that his Gospel is the only Gospel, or they must take infidelity. Sooner or later the sects, one after another, will deny the Savior and every one of the ordinances of his Gospel, until they are all enveloped in infidelity, or they must accept the whole. Strange as it may appear, they are now following shadows, phantoms of the brain, and mischievous manifestations. 14:74.

What should the wicked hear? They should hear a man testify that Joseph Smith was and is a Prophet of God, that he was a good man, and that he did plant and establish the Kingdom of God on the earth, and we know it. "How shall I know?" says one. By obeying the commandments given to you. The Lord has said, go into the waters of baptism and be baptized for the remission of your sins, and you shall receive a witness that I am telling you the truth. How? By baptism and the laying on of hands alone? No. By seeing the sick healed? No, but by the Spirit that shall come unto you through obedience, which will make you feel like little children, and cause you to delight in doing good, to love your Father in Heaven and the society of the righteous. Have you malice and wrath then? No, it is taken from you, and you feel like the child in its mother's lap. You will feel kind to your children, to your brothers and sisters, to your parents and neighbors, and to all around you; you will feel a glow, as of fire, burning within you; and if you open your mouths to talk you will declare ideas which you did not formerly think of; they will flow into your mind, even such as you have not thought of for years. The Scriptures will be opened to you, and you will see how clear and reasonable everything is which this or that Elder teaches you. Your hearts will be comforted, you can lie down and sleep in peace, and wake up with feelings as pleasant as the breezes of summer. This is a witness to you. 3:211.

The Latter-day Saints realize that there is no period of man's existence not incorporated with the plan of salvation, and directly pointing to a future existence. Consequently, when we stand here to speak to the people, let every man speak what is in his heart. If one of our Elders is capable of giving us a lecture upon any of the sciences, let it be delivered in the spirit of meekness—in the spirit of the holy Gospel. If, on the Sabbath day, when we are assembled here to worship the Lord, one of the Elders should be prompted to give us a lecture on any branch of education with which he is acquainted, is it outside the pale of our religion? I think not. If any of the Elders are disposed to give a lecture to parents and children on letters, on the rudiments of the English language, it is in my religion, it is a part of my faith. Or if an Elder shall give us a lecture upon astronomy, chemistry, or geology, our religion embraces it all. It matters not what the subject be, if it tends to improve the mind, exalt the feelings, and enlarge the capacity. The truth that is in all the arts and sciences forms a part of our religion. Faith is no more a part of it than any other true principle of philosophy. Were I to give you a lecture today upon farming, would I be speaking upon a matter that transcends the bounds of our religion? Agriculture is a part of it as well as any other truth. Were I to lecture on business principles of any kind, our religion embraces it; and what it does not circumscribe, it would be well for us to dispense with at once and forever. 1:334.

Humility and Devotion, the Essentials—The Kingdom of our God, that is set upon the earth, does not require men of many words and flaming oratorical talents, to establish truth and righteousness. It is not the many words that accomplish the designs of our Father in Heaven, with him it is the acts of the people more than their words; this I was convinced of before I embraced the Gospel. Had it not been that I clearly saw and understood that the Lord Almighty would take up the weak things of this world to confound the mighty, the wise, and the talented, there was nothing that could have induced me, or persuaded me, to have ever become a public speaker. 4:20.

On the other hand, I do not wish any of the brethren to be discouraged, for if you feel that you cannot say a single word, no matter, if you will only be faithful to your God and to your religion, and be humble, and cleave unto righteousness, and forsake iniquity and sin, the Lord will guide you and give you words in due season. 2:268.

I have known some of the Elders when they thought they would be called out to preach, keep away from meetings lest they should be called upon, for they feel their littleness, their nothingness, their inability to rise up and preach to the people. They do not feel that they are anybody, and why should they expose their weaknesses? I have noticed one thing in regard to this—quite a number of these men become giants in the cause of truth, as there are of any other class; for when they get away they begin to lean on the Lord, and to seek unto him, and feeling their weaknesses, they ask him to give them wisdom to speak to the people as occasion may require. Others can rise up here and preach a flaming discourse, insomuch that you would think they were going to tear down the nations; but when they go out into the world they often accomplish but little. 2:267.

Preach Only That Which is Known—With regard to doctrinal points, that which we do not understand should not be talked about in this stand; and the Elders of Israel should never contend about any point of doctrine that does not pertain to the present day's salvation. 7:47.

I will give a caution to my brethren, the Elders—never undertake to teach a thing that you do not understand. Such things will come into your minds; but without launching out on such subjects, questions may be asked and answered, and we gain knowledge from each other. There is plenty within the scope of our own brains that, by the assistance of the Spirit of the Lord, will enable us to tell many things—more than the world, or even more than the Saints can receive. 13:263.

If you do not understand a doctrine or a portion of Scripture, when information is asked of you, say that the Lord has not revealed that to you, or that he has not opened your understanding to grasp it, and that you do not feel safe in giving an interpretation until he does. 8:56.

Hints for Preachers—Short sermons fitly spoken, are better than long ones ill spoken. 3:249.

The spirit of truth will do more to bring persons to light and knowledge, than flowery words. 4:21.

I wish to see the Elders get up here and manifest their spirits, and speak as they feel when they are alone in their meditations. 3:237.

I car little for a man's language, if his spirit proves to me that he has the love of God within him. 9:290.

The preacher needs the power of the Holy Ghost to deal out to each heart a word in due season, and the hearers need the Holy Ghost to bring forth the fruits of the preached word of God to his glory. 8:167.

No man ever preached a Gospel sermon, except by the gift and power of the Holy Ghost sent down from heaven. Without this power, there is no light in the preaching. 8:138.

Elders in this Church—men who have been members for years,—often speak of principles in the abstract, when they would be better understood if they spoke of them in connection with other kindred principles. 8:259.

Perfection in conveying ideas is not yet given to the children of men. Our language is altogether inadequate for always conveying our ideas with unmistakable precision, and the same ideas are generally advanced in different words by different persons. 8:259.

When a person opens his mouth, no matter what he talks about, to a person of quick discernment he will disclose more or less of his true sentiments. You cannot hide the heart, when the mouth is open. If you want to keep your heart secret, keep your mouth shut. 6:74.

There are two thousand persons in this assembly, and if only half a dozen of them have done wrong, I could not chastise them without appearing to chastise the whole congregation, which in reality is not so. By chastising the guilty, however, it is impossible to spot the conscience of good men and women, whose hearts are clean and pure as a piece of white paper. 1:92.

We can form some kind of an idea how a man feels by looking at him, but if you wish a man to portray himself faithfully you must get him to talk, and I will insure that the organs of speech will show out the true state of the mind, sooner or later, and reveal the fruit of his heart. No man can hide it if he is allowed to talk; he will be sure to manifest his true feelings. 3:237.

If you wish to impress on the minds of individuals or an audience anything that you desire them to remember, you will have to use language accordingly. 14:193.

When we hear a man that can speak of heavenly things, and present them to the people in a way that they can be understood, you may know that to that man the avenue is open, and he, by some power, has communication with heavenly beings; and when the highest intelligence is exhibited, he, perhaps, has communication with the highest intelligence that exists. 8:206.

I do not like to hear men make excuses, although it is natural, and I put up with it. I wish they could see and understand that they have had advantages above many of their brethren—that they have been greatly blessed, and should never complain, but should stand up here and exercise themselves according to the best of their ability, and do all the good possible for them to do. 5:97.

The truth is easily understood, and as easily told. The agriculturist and the mechanic can tell the truth, and become efficient ministers of it, by living faithfully in accordance with what they know of the Gospel; for in this way they obtain the Holy Ghost, which giveth utterance. 11:214.

When people are hungry they need substantial food; when they are thirsty they need substantial drink. Moses' smiting the rock would not have benefited the people in the least, if water had not gushed out. It is the duty of the true minister of Christ to instruct the people of God how to get their food today, and to teach them by precept and example how to become an independent nation. 11:133.

It is my business to teach mankind how to live, how to honor their present existence, how to treat their bodies so as to live to a good old age on the earth, and have power to do good and not evil all their days, and be ready to enter into the rest prepared for the Saints. 10:27.

It yields solid satisfaction to hear men testify of the truth of the Gospel. It is always peculiarly interesting to me to hear the Saints tell their experience. It is to me one of the best sermons to hear men and women relate to each other how the Lord has wrought upon their understanding and brought them into the path of truth, life, and salvation. I would rather hear men tell their own experiences, and testify that Joseph was a Prophet of the Lord, and that the Book of Mormon, the Bible, and other revelations of God, are true; that they know it by the gift and power of God; that they have conversed with angels, have had the power of the Holy Ghost upon them, giving them visions and revelations, than hear any kind of preaching that ever saluted my ears. 1:89.

A man who wishes to receive light and knowledge, to increase in the faith of the Holy Gospel, and to grow in the knowledge of the truth as it is in Jesus Christ, will find that when he imparts knowledge to others he will also grow and increase. Be not miserly in your feelings, but get knowledge and understanding by freely imparting it to others; and be not like a man who selfishly hoards his gold; for that man will not thus increase upon the amount, but will become contracted in his views and feelings. So the man who will not impart freely of the knowledge he has received, will become so contracted in his mind that he cannot receive truth when it is presented to him. Wherever you see an opportunity to do good, do it, for that is the way to increase and grow in the knowledge of the truth. 2:267.

If a congregation wish to be instructed so as to understand alike and alike receive an increase of wisdom and knowledge, their minds must be intent on the subject before them. They must not suffer their thoughts to be roaming over the earth; they must not permit their minds to be scanning and traversing their every-day duties and avocations. 6:93-94.

Elders of Israel and Bishops, be fathers, and take a course by which you will win the affections of the people. How? With your silken lips? No, no; but with the fear of the Almighty. Do you know that men and women of God love truth? They do not love sophistry, it is an abomination to them. 4:283.

A few words now, with regard to preaching. The greatest and loudest sermon that can be preached, or that ever was preached on the face of the earth, is practice. No other is equal to it. 12:271-272.

If you will reflect upon what class of speakers have most edified you, no matter whether they are taught or untaught in the learning of the schools, you will readily discover that it has been those whose minds were stored with good ideas, and who spoke so that you could readily and easily understand them, whether their language was couched in the most approved style or not. When you hear individuals speak whose minds are stored with rich ideas, do they not benefit you the most? I care but little about your language, hand out the ideas, and let us know what you have stored in your minds. 3:243-244.

I have the same diffidence in my feelings that most public speakers have, and am apt to think that others can speak better and more edifying than I can. There are but few public speakers but what feel more or less timidity. That is probably not so much a man-fearing spirit as it is a natural delicacy or timidity. All of you have doubtless to some extent realized the same feeling, either in large or small assemblies, and also in social conversation. People generally are more or less disturbed and thrown off their balance by the sound of their own voices, especially when speaking to an audience, even after being much used to addressing assemblies. Some of our most eloquent and interesting speakers would rather do almost anything than speak to the congregations that assemble here. That diffidence or timidity we must dispense with. When it becomes our duty to talk, we ought to be willing to talk. If we never exhibit the knowledge within us, the people will not know really whether we have any. 6:93.

If an Elder in preaching the Gospel, does not feel that he has the power to preach life and salvation, and legally to administer the ordinances, and that, too, by the power of God, he will not fill his mission to his own credit, nor to the good of the people, and the advancement and honor of the Kingdom of God. From all I can read, from all I can gather, from the revelations from God to man, and from the revelations of the Spirit to me, no man can successfully preach the Gospel and be owned, blessed, and acknowledged by the heavens, unless he preaches by the power of God through direct revelation. Not but that, in a great many instances, a man may not be manifestly under the immediate and powerful influences and direction of revelation to dictate him all the time in his meditations and reasonings, and yet can advance many good ideas that he has gathered by means of his natural reasoning. But to magnify and make honorable the calling of an Elder in this Church, I cannot conceive, in my understanding, any other true principle by which it can be done, only when perfectly controlled by the Spirit of the Lord. 8:52-53.

When a "Mormon" Elder offers evidence of this great work to unbelievers, they tell him that he is a party concerned, and his evidence cannot be taken with regard to Joseph Smith's mission. I ask the Christian world, Where are your witnesses that Jesus is the Christ? Who are those who testified of his mission, and how many are there? Eight persons testified of him, and their testimony is recorded, and they were his disciples and parties concerned; yet at this day all the Christian world is ready to receive their testimony. I testify that this work of God in which we are engaged has been commenced to gather the House of Israel and establish Zion in the last days, and has more outward and weighty evidence to prove that it is of God than there was in the days of Jesus to prove that he was the Christ. When the Book of Mormon came forth it was testified to by twelve witnesses, and who can dispute their testimony? No living person on the earth can do it, and besides the testimony of these twelve witnesses, hundreds and thousands have received a witness to themselves from the heavens, and who can dispute their testimony? No living person on the earth can do it. This infidel world inquires, "Where do you get your testimony?" We answer, we get it from the heavens. Were we to ask them where they get the knowledge they possess, they reply, "We do not know; it came to us; we know not its source." We have testimony that the Bible is true, that the prophecies contained in it are true, that Jesus is the Son of God, and came to redeem the world. Have the so-called Christian world this kind of testimony? They have not. All the testimony they can boast of is the testimony of eight men who lived nearly two thousand years ago. The infidel world cannot receive their testimony, because they were parties concerned. 12:208.

Brother Whiting says that he is a man of but few words. I am satisfied that there is greater wisdom with many who say but little, than there is with those who talk so much; as for the multitude of words, they are but of little consequence, the ideas are by far the greatest importance. 4:20.

Chapter XXIX

VISIONS, MYSTERIES AND MIRACLES

Visions of a Personal Nature—I ask, Is there a reason for men and women being exposed more constantly and more powerfully, to the power of the enemy, by having visions than by not having them? There is and it is simply this—God never bestows upon his people, or upon an individual, superior blessings without a severe trial to prove them, to prove that individual, or that people, to see whether they will keep their covenants with him, and keep in remembrance what he has shown them. Then the greater the vision, the greater the display of the power of the enemy.

So when individuals are blessed with visions, revelations, and great manifestations, look out, then the Devil is nigh you, and you will be tempted in proportion to the visions, revelation, or manifestation you have received. 3:205-206.

If the Lord Almighty should reveal to a High Priest, or to any other than the head, things that are true, or that have been and will be, and show him the destiny of this people twenty-five years from now, or a new doctrine that will in five, ten, or twenty years hence become the doctrine of this Church and Kingdom, but which has not yet been revealed to this people, and reveal it to him by the same Spirit, the same messenger, the same voice, the same power that gave revelations to Joseph when he was living, it would be a blessing to that High Priest, or individual; but he must rarely divulge it to a second person on the face of the earth, until God reveals it through the proper source to become the property of the people at large. Therefore when you hear Elders say that God does not reveal through the President of the Church that which they know, and tell wonderful things, you may generally set it down as a God's truth that the revelation they have had is from the Devil, and not from God. If they had received from the proper source, the same power that revealed to them would have shown them that they must keep the things revealed in their own bosoms, and they seldom would have a desire to disclose them to the second person. 3:318.

Leave Mysteries Alone—Now, brethren, preach the things that we verily believe, and when we come to points of doctrine that we do not know, even if we have good reason to believe them, if our philosophy teaches us they are true, pass them by and teach only to the people that which we do know. 13:265.

What is a mystery? We do not know, it is beyond our comprehension. When we talk about mystery, we talk about eternal obscurity; for that which is known, ceases to be a mystery; and all that is known, we may know as we progress in the scale of our intelligence. That which is eternally beyond the comprehension of all our intelligence is mystery. 1:274.

These are the mysteries of the Kingdom of God upon the earth, to know how to purify and sanctify our affections, the earth upon which we stand, the air we breathe, the water we drink, the houses in which we dwell and the cities we build, that when strangers come into our country they may feel a hallowed influence and acknowledge a power to which they are strangers. 10:176.

Jesus said to his disciples, to them it was given to know the mysteries of the Kingdom of Heaven, but to them that were without, it was not given. If we were to examine the subject closely, we should learn that a very scanty portion of the things of the Kingdom were ever revealed, even to the disciples. If we were prepared to gaze upon the mysteries of the Kingdom, as they are with God, we should then know that only a very small portion of them has been handed out here and there. God, by his Spirit, has revealed many things to his people, but, in almost all cases, he has straightway shut up the vision of the mind. He will let his servants gaze upon eternal things for a moment, but straightway the vision is closed, and they are left as they were, that they may learn to act by faith, or as the Apostle has it, not walking by sight, but by faith. 1:264.

You may now be inclined to say, "We wish to hear the mysteries of the kingdoms of the Gods who have existed from eternity, and of all the kingdoms in which they will dwell; we desire to have these things portrayed to our understandings."

Allow me to inform you that you are in the midst of it all now, that you are in just as good a kingdom as you will ever attain to, from now to all eternity, unless you make it yourselves by the grace of God, by the will of God, which is a code of laws perfectly calculated to govern and control eternal matter. 3:336.

If they will only live up to it, there has already been enough taught the brethren who have lived here for years to prepare them to enter into the strait gate and into New Jerusalem, and be prepared to enjoy the society of the holy angels. 8:177.

Providences of God, All Miracles—The providences of God are all a miracle to the human family until they understand them. There are no miracles, only to those who are ignorant. A miracle is supposed to be a result without a cause, but there is no such thing. There is a cause for every result we see; and if we see a result without understanding the cause we call it a miracle. 14:79.

The Gospel plan is so devised, that a miracle to make people believe would only be a condemnation to them. When you hear people tell what they have seen—that they have seen great and powerful miracles wrought, and they could not help believing, remember that "devils believe and tremble," because they cannot help it. When the voice of the Good Shepherd is heard, the honest in heart believe and receive it. It is good to taste with the inward taste, to see with the inward eyes, and to enjoy with the sensations of the ever-living spirit. No person, unless he is an adulterer, a fornicator, covetous, or an idolater, will ever require a miracle, in other words, no good honest person ever will. 8:42.

You have gathered the idea from me that it is not the miracles that are performed before a person's eyes that convince him that one is of God, or of the Devil; yet, if the Lord designs that a person should heal the sick, the individual can do so; but is that to convince the wicked that the operator is sent of God? No, it is a blessing on the Saints, and the wicked have nothing to do with it, they have no business to hear of it; that is for the Saints, it is especially for their benefit, and theirs alone. 3:211.

This, in my own mind, is argued out perfectly, upon natural principles. It is natural for me to believe that, if I plough the ground and sow wheat, in the proper season I shall reap a crop of wheat; this is the natural result. It was precisely so with the miracles that Jesus wrought upon the earth. At the wedding in Cana of Galilee, when they had drunk all the wine, they went to the Savior and asked him what they should do. He ordered them to fill up their pots with water, and after having done so they drew forth of that water and found that it was wine. I believe that was real wine; I do not believe that it was done on the principle that such things are done in these days by wicked men, who, by means of what they term psychology, electro-biology, mesmerism, etc., influence men and make them believe that water is wine, and other things of a similar character. The Savior converted the water into wine. He knew how to call the necessary elements together in order to fill the water with the properties of wine. The elements are all around us; we eat, drink and breathe them, and Jesus, understanding the process of calling them together, performed no miracle except to those who were ignorant of that process. It was the same with the woman who was healed by touching the hem of his garment; she was healed by faith, but it was no miracle to Jesus. He understood the process, and although he was pressed by the crowd, behind and before, and on each side, so that he could scarcely make his way through it, the moment she touched him he felt virtue leave him and enquired who touched him. This was no miracle to him. He had the issues of life and death in his power; he had power to lay down his life and power to take it up again. This is what he says, and we must believe this if we believe the history of the Savior and the sayings of the Apostles recorded in the New Testament. Jesus had this power in and of himself; the Father bequeathed it to him; it was his legacy, and he had the power to lay down his life and take it again. He had the streams and issues of life within him and when he said "*Live*" to individuals, they lived. The diseases that are and ever have been prevalent among the human family are from beneath, and are entailed upon them through the fall—through the disobedience of our first parents; but Jesus, having the issues of life at his command, could counteract those diseases at his pleasure. The case of the Centurion's servant is a striking instance of this. The Centurion sent and besought Jesus to heal his servant. "Say in a word," said he, "and my servant shall be healed." Jesus, seeing the man's earnestness and solicitude, said, "I have not found so great faith, no, not in Israel." And it is said that they who were sent, returned to the Centurion's house and found the servant healed. Jesus counteracted the disease preying upon the system of this man but to himself, knowing the principle by which the disease was rebuked, it was no miracle. 13:140-141.

As quick as I admit that the history Moses gives of himself is true, I cannot have any question in the world but what in ancient days they understood in a measure how to command the elements. The magicians of Egypt were instructed in things pertaining to true riches, and had obtained keys and powers enough to produce a bogus in opposition to the true coin, as it were, and thus they deceived the king and the people. They could cause frogs to come upon the land, as well as Moses could. They could turn the waters of Egypt into blood, and in many more things compete with Moses. There was one thing, however, they could not do, though they produced a very good bogus, but it was not quite the true coin. When they threw their staffs on the floor before the king, these could not swallow the staff of Moses, but the staff of Moses swallowed the staffs of the magicians. I have no doubt that men can perform many such wonders by the principles of natural philosophy. 1:270.

Miracles for Believers—Miracles, or these extraordinary manifestations of the power of God, are not for the unbeliever; they are to console the Saints, and to strengthen and confirm the faith of those who love, fear, and serve God, and not for outsiders. 12:97.

"Why do not the people speak with tongues?" We do, and we speak with tongues that you can understand, and Paul says he would rather speak five or ten words in a language that can be understood, than many in a language that cannot be. This is what may be conveyed. 15:133.

Faith Not Dependent on Miracles—I do not want to see a miracle to confirm the truth of any doctrine or saying that is revealed to me. If I can see that it is calculated to purify the hearts of the people and to sanctify their affections, and to reconcile them to God and to his law and government, it satisfies me; and so far as this goes, I might say that I am like the Christian world, in the belief that miracles are no longer needed. But I believe that miracles are as absolutely necessary now as they ever were. 13:140.

Take the case of the Children of Israel and the miracles that were wrought in their deliverance from the land of Egypt. The question arises, was it through their faith, or because of the promises which God had made to their fathers? * * * It was not because of the righteousness of the Children of Israel, but because of the promises of the Lord to Abraham, Isaac, and Jacob, for he must fulfil the promises made to his servants. He wanted at one time to destroy the whole people, and told Moses to let him alone that he might destroy them because of their wickedness and rebellion, and he would make of him (Moses) a great nation; but Moses pleaded in their behalf, and called upon the Lord to remember his promises, and they were preserved. 12:242-243.

Do you suppose that Jesus Christ healed every person that was sick, or that all the devils were cast out in the country where he sojourned? I do not. Working miracles, healing the sick, raising the dead, and the like, were almost as rare in his day as in this our day. Once in a while the people would have faith in his power, and what is called a miracle would be performed, but the sick, the blind, the deaf and dumb, the crazy, and those possessed with different kind of devils were around him, and only now and then could his faith have power to take effect, on account of the want of faith in the individuals. 3:45-46.

If we have faith to feel that the issues of life and death are in our power, we can say to disease, "Be ye rebuked in the name of Jesus, and let life and health come into the system of this individual, from God, to counteract this disease"; and our faith will bring this by the laying on of hands by administering the ordinance of the holy Gospel. 13:141.

Men who have professedly seen the most, known and understood the most, in this Church, and who have testified in the presence of large congregations, in the name of Israel's God, that they have seen Jesus, etc., have been the very men who have left this Kingdom, before others who had to live by faith. 3:205.

You will recollect that I have often told you that miracles would not save a person, and I say that they never should. If I were to see a man come in here this day, and say, "I am the great one whom the Lord has sent," and cause fire to come down in our sight, through the ceiling that is over our heads, I would not believe any more for that. It is no matter what he does, I cannot believe any more on that account. What will make me believe? What made the twelve Apostles of Jesus Christ witnesses? What constituted them Apostles —special witnesses to the world? Was it seeing miracles? No. What was it? The visions of their minds were opened, and it was necessary that a few should receive light, knowledge, and intelligence, that all the powers of earth and hell could not gainsay or compete with. That witness was within them, and yet, after all that was done for them, after all that Jesus showed them, and after all the power of the spirit of revelation which they possessed, you find that one of them apostatized, turned away and sold his Lord and Master for thirty pieces of silver, in consequence of his not being firm to his covenant in the hour of darkness and temptation. Another of them was ready to say, "I do not know anything about the Lord Jesus Christ," and denied him.

Some are apt now to say, "I don't know anything about this Mormonism, I don't know about the Priesthood." Did you not once know? "I thought I did, but now I find myself deceived." What is the reason? Because they give way to temptation; they may have had great light, knowledge, and understanding, the visions of their minds may have been opened and eternity exhibited to their view, but when this is closed up, in proportion to the light given to them, so is the darkness that comes upon them to try them. 3:206-207.

A sister who received the gift of tongues is not thereby empowered to dictate her president, or the Church. All gifts and endowments given of the Lord to members of his Church are not given to control the Church; but they are under the control and guidance of the Priesthood, and are judged by it. Some have erred upon this point, and have been led captive by the Devil. 11:136.

If you say that you want mysteries, commandments, and revelations, I reply that scarcely a Sabbath passes over your heads, those of you who come here, without your having the revelations of Jesus Christ poured upon you like water on the ground. 3:336-337.

Some are very anxious that I should have visions. I have all that the Lord gives to me; and all that he keeps back he may; for that is no concern of mine. We are on the old ship Zion; and if God is not at the helm, the old ship will wreck and go to the Devil. As for my taking charge of the Kingdom of God on the earth, exclusively and independently of direction from heaven, I shall not do any such thing. If the Lord does not direct the old ship and act as captain and pilot, it will go to destruction.

He is at the helm, and will stay there. If you and I will bring our feelings to the point I have just spoken of, he will continue to guide the welfare of Zion and all its rights. 5:352.

Chapter XXX

TRIALS AND PERSECUTION

Trials are Necessary—We are now in a day of trial to prove ourselves worthy or unworthy of the life which is to come. 12:167.

If we have correct doctrines, and will fashion our lives to them, we may sanctify ourselves without being chastened. 12:310.

The people of the Most High God must be tried. It is written that they will be tried in all things, even as Abraham was tried. If we are called to go upon mount Moriah to sacrifice a few of our Isaacs, it is no matter; we may just as well do that as anything else. I think there is a prospect for the Saints to have all the trials they wish for, or can desire. 4:369.

All intelligent beings who are crowned with crowns of glory, immortality, and eternal lives must pass through every ordeal appointed for intelligent beings to pass through, to gain their glory and exaltation. Every calamity that can come upon mortal beings will be suffered to come upon the few, to prepare them to enjoy the presence of the Lord. If we obtain the glory that Abraham obtained, we must do so by the same means that he did. If we are ever prepared to enjoy the society of Enoch, Noah, Melchizedek, Abraham, Isaac, and Jacob, or of their faithful children, and of the faithful Prophets and Apostles, we must pass through the same experience, and gain the knowledge, intelligence, and endowments that will prepare us to enter into the celestial kingdom of our Father and God. How many of the Latter-day Saints will endure all these things, and be prepared to enjoy the presence of the Father and the Son? You can answer that question at your leisure. Every trial and experience you have passed through is necessary for your salvation. 8:150.

Should our lives be extended to a thousand years, still we may live and learn. Every vicissitude we pass through is necessary for experience and example, and for preparation to enjoy that reward which is for the faithful. 9:292.

If Adam had not sinned, and if his posterity had continued upon the earth, they could not have known sin, or the bitter from the sweet, neither would they have known righteousness, for the plain and simple reason that every effect can only be fully manifested by its opposite. If the Saints could realize things as they are when they are called to pass through trials, and to suffer what they call sacrifices, they would acknowledge them to be the greatest blessings that could be bestowed upon them. But put them in possession of true principles and true enjoyments, without the opposite, and they could not know enjoyment, they could not realize happiness. They could not tell light from darkness, because they have no knowledge of darkness and consequently are destitute of a realizing sense of light. If they should not taste the bitter, how could they realize the sweet? They could not. 2:301-302.

You will learn this in the Bible, the Book of Mormon, and in the revelations given through Joseph. We must know and understand the opposition that is in all things, in order to discern, choose, and receive that which we do not know will exalt us to the presence of God. You cannot know the one without knowing the other. This is a true principle. 4:373.

Now if you possess the light of the Holy Spirit, you can see clearly that trials in the flesh are actually necessary. 2:8.

Purpose of Persecution—Let any people enjoy peace and quiet, unmolested, undisturbed,—never be persecuted for their religion, and they are very likely to neglect their duty, to become cold and indifferent, and lose their faith. 7:42.

He led this people in different parts of the United States, and the finger of scorn has been pointed at them. Officers of the Government of the United States have lifted their heels against them, and this people have been driven from town to town, from county to county, and from state to state. The Lord has his design in this. You may ask what his design is. You all know that the Saints must be made pure, to enter into the celestial kingdom. It is recorded that Jesus was made perfect through suffering. If he was made perfect through suffering, why should we imagine for one moment that we can be prepared to enter into the kingdom of rest with him and the Father, without passing through similar ordeals? 8:66.

We are infinitely more blessed by the persecutions and injustice we have suffered, than we could have been if we had remained in our habitations from which we have been driven—than if we had been suffered to occupy our farms, gardens, stores, mills, machinery and everything we had in our former possessions. 10:38.

Persecution May Be Expected—I wish to inform you, brethren and sisters, who have just arrived in these valleys, that all your trials hitherto are but trifling in comparison to the trials you will now be called to meet and pass through. 8:163.

War has been declared against the Saints over twenty-seven years, and our enemies have only fallen back so as to gain strength and pretexts for making another attack. Will that spirit increase? If it does, and we love our religion, let me tell you that we will increase faster than our enemies will. 5:340.

Only be faithful, brethren and sisters, and I promise that you shall have all such privileges as shall be for your good. You need not be discouraged, or mourn, because you were not in Jackson County persecutions, or were not driven from Ohio, Missouri, and Illinois, and stripped, robbed and plundered of all your property. Do not mourn and feel bad, because you were not in Nauvoo; have no fears, for if the word of the Lord is true, you shall yet be tried in all things; so rejoice, and pray without ceasing, and in everything give thanks, even if it is in the spoiling of your goods, for it is the hand of God that leads us, and will continue so to do. Let every man and woman sanctify themselves before the Lord, and every providence of the Almighty shall be sanctified for good to them. 1:279.

The ancient Saints were, and the Saints of latter days have been, driven from pillar to post, their name a hiss and a by-word, and their character traduced to the lowest degree. I will appeal to men in this congregation, who have lived for years in the society of the world, who are judges, magistrates, sheriffs, merchants, mechanics, and farmers, if anything was ever alleged against their character until they joined the Latter-day Saints. But where are your characters now in the world? Your former friends now have found out that you always were miserable creatures, they now declare they never had any confidence in you, for you always were enthusiastic beings, and knew not what you were doing. They always believed you would prove yourselves dishonest, etc. This has been the character given to the Saints by the world in all ages. 1:236.

Meet Trials Cheerfully—We are the happiest people when we have what are called trials; for then the Spirit of God is more abundantly bestowed upon the faithful. If the Lord requires it, I would as soon consume all I have and go into the mountains with my family as to do a good many other things. 5:332.

I say to the Latter-day Saints, all we have to do is to learn of God. Let the liars lie on, and let the swearers swear on, and they will go to perdition. All we have to do is to go onward and upward, and keep the commandments of our Father and God; and he will confound our enemies. 19:50.

There is not a hardship, there is not a disappointment, there is not a trial, there is not a hard time, that comes upon this people in this place, but that I am more thankful for than I am for full granaries. 4:51.

We have passed through a great many scenes, we may say, of tribulation, though I would have all my brethren understand that I do not take this to myself, for all that I have passed through has been joy and joyful to me; but we have seemingly sacrificed a great deal, and passed through many scenes of trial and temptations, no doubt of this. We have had to suffer temptations, more or less, and we have taken the spoiling of our goods joyfully. I have, myself, five times before I came to this valley, left everything that the Lord had blessed me with pertaining to this world's goods, which, for the country where I lived, was not a very little. 18:237.

As to trials, why bless your hearts, the man or woman who enjoys the spirit of our religion has no trials; but the man or woman who tries to live according to the Gospel of the Son of God, and at the same time clings to the spirit of the world, has trials and sorrows acute and keen, and that, too, continually.

Cast off the yoke of the enemy, and put on the yoke of Christ, and you will say that his yoke is easy and his burden is light. This I know by experience. 16:123.

I have heard a great many tell about what they have suffered for Christ's sake. I am happy to say I never had occasion to. I have enjoyed a great deal, but so far as suffering goes I have compared it a great many times, in my feelings and before congregations, to a man wearing an old, worn-out, tattered and dirty coat, and somebody comes along and gives him one that is new, whole and beautiful. This is the comparison I draw when I think of what I have suffered for the Gospel's sake—I have thrown away an old coat and have put on a new one. No man or woman ever heard me tell about suffering. "Did you not leave a handsome property in Ohio, Missouri, and Illinois?" Yes. "And have you not suffered through that?" No, I have been growing better and better all the time, and so have this people. And you may take the history of the world from the days of Adam down, and I am at the defiance of any historian to prove that the Saints have ever suffered as much as the sinners. This is my belief about the religion of Jesus Christ. Some may say, "Did not the children of Israel suffer?" Yes. "Why?" Because of their iniquity. They transgressed the laws God had given them; they changed the ordinances and broke the everlasting covenant, and for their sin and disobedience they were led into captivity. If they had been obedient, I reckon they would have been led direct to the Holy Land, and stayed there. Some may say, "Now, Mr. Speaker, you have been driven from your home, was it for righteousness?" No, I expect not. I expect it was to chasten me and make me better. 13:147.

Cause of Persecution—Hatred and persecution have been the lot of every man that ever lived upon the earth holding the oracles of the Kingdom of Heaven to deliver to the children of men. Wicked men, Satan, and all the powers of hell and hate are at war with every holy principle that God wishes to place in the possession of his children. That is the true reason of the hatred and persecution meted out to us. 8:13.

Do you know that that very principle caused the death of all the Prophets, from the days of Adam until now? Let a Prophet arise upon the earth, and never reveal the evils of men, and do you suppose that the wicked would desire to kill him? No, for he would cease to be a Prophet of the Lord, and they would invite him to their feasts, and hail him as a friend and brother. Why? Because it would be impossible for him to be anything but one of them. It is impossible for a Prophet of Christ to live in an adulterous generation without speaking of the wickedness of the people, without revealing their faults and their failings, and there is nothing short of death that will stay him from it, for a Prophet of God will do as he pleases. 3:48.

The false religion that is in the world, is what raises this "hue and cry," misguides the people, and opposes itself against the Kingdom of God on the earth. Now if we would only fall in with the wicked all would be right, and then no person would wish to persecute us. 2:181.

Why should we have enemies? "Why is it," say our objectors, "that you cannot mingle and mix in society like other religious denominations?" It has been seen that the people would not permit us to dwell in their midst in peace. We have been universally driven by illegal force, by mobs, murderers, and assassins, as unworthy of having a place amongst the abodes of civilized man, until, as a last resort, we found peace in these distant valleys. It is because our religion is the only true one. It is because we have the only true authority, upon the face of the whole earth, to administer in the ordinances of the Gospel. It is because the keys of this dispensation were committed by messengers sent from the Celestial world unto Joseph Smith, and are now held on the earth by this people. It is because Christ and Lucifer are enemies, and cannot be made friends; and Lucifer, knowing that we have this Priesthood, this power, this authority, seeks our overthrow. 2:177.

All hell is moved against this people, because we are of one heart and of one mind. 5:228.

It is light, intelligence, the power of God that make the wicked tremble and wish "Mormonism" out of the way. If it were a false doctrine or a false theory, the Devil would not endeavor to disturb it, wicked men would not fear it, Heaven would not smile upon it, nor give a revelation to any man or woman to believe it, and we should have poor success; and Heaven forbid that we should have success or gain influence upon any other principle than the revelation of Jesus Christ. 7:160.

We were not persecuted because we believed in having many wives, for that principle was not known to our persecutors until we came to these mountains, although the revelation was received by Joseph Smith and written a year before his death. 14:119.

We are Christians professedly, according to our religion. People have gathered to themselves certain ideas, and laid them down as systems, calling them religion, all professing to believe and obey the Scriptures. Their religions are peculiar to themselves—our religion is peculiar to God, to angels, and to the righteous of time and eternity. Why are we persecuted because of our religion? Why was Joseph Smith persecuted? Why was he hunted from neighborhood to neighborhood, from city to city, from state to state, and at last suffered death? Because he received revelations from the Father, from the Son, and was ministered to by holy angels, and published to the world the direct will of the Lord concerning his children on the earth. Again, why was he persecuted? Because he revealed to all mankind a religion so plain and so easily understood, consistent with the Bible, and so true. It is now as it was in the days of the Savior; let people believe and practice these simple, God-like truths, and it will be as it was in the old world, they will say, if this man be let alone he will come and take away our peace and nation. 18:231.

Disobedience Causes Persecution—When we look at the Latter-day Saints, we ask, is there any necessity of their being persecuted? Yes, if they are disobedient. Is there any necessity of chastening a son or a daughter? Yes, if they are disobedient. But suppose they are perfectly obedient to every requirement of their parents, is there any necessity of chastening them then? If there is, I do not understand the principle of it. I have not yet been able to see the necessity of chastening an obedient child, neither have I been able to see the necessity of chastisement from the Lord upon a people who are perfectly obedient. Have this people been chastened? Yes, they have. 12:308.

We have been persecuted, driven, smitten, cast out, robbed and hated; and I may say it was for our coldness and neglect of duty; and if we did not exactly deserve it, there have been times when we did deserve it. If we did not deserve it at the time, it was good for and gave us an experience, though I must say that one of the hardest lessons for me to learn on earth is to love a man who hates me and would put me to death if he had the power. I do not think I have got this lesson by heart, and I do not know how long I shall have to live to learn it. I am trying. 14:97.

Those who turn away from the holy commandments will meet trials that are trials indeed. They will feel the wrath of the Almighty upon them. Those who are still and are good children will receive the rich blessings of their Father and God. Be still, and let your faith rest on the Lord Almighty. 7:136.

Result of Persecution—Every time you kick "Mormonism" you kick it upstairs; you never kick it downstairs. The Lord Almighty so orders it. 7:145.

Can you destroy a true religion by persecuting it? No. 7:145.

Joseph could not have been perfected, though he had lived a thousand years, if he had received no persecution. If he had lived a thousand years, and led this people, and preached the Gospel without persecution, he would not have been perfected as well as he was at the age of thirty-nine years. You may calculate, when this people are called to go through scenes of affliction and suffering, are driven from their homes, and cast down, and scattered, and smitten, and peeled, the Almighty is rolling on his work with greater rapidity. 2:7.

Well, do you think that persecution has done us good? Yes. I sit and laugh, and rejoice exceedingly when I see persecution. I care no more about it than I do about the whistling of the north wind, the croaking of the crane that flies over my head, or the crackling of the thorns under the pot. The Lord has all things in his hand; therefore let it come, for it will give me experience. 2:8.

Every time they persecute and try to overcome this people, they elevate us, weaken their own hands, and strengthen the hands and arms of this people. And every time they undertake to lessen our number, they increase it. And when they try to destroy the faith and virtue of this people, the Lord strengthens the feeble knees, and confirms the wavering in faith and power in God, in light, and intelligence. Righteousness and power with God increase in this people in proportion as the Devil struggles to destroy it. 8:225-226.

If we did not have to bear the iron hand of persecution, the principles we believe in, which attract the attention of the good and the evil upon the earth and which occupy so many tongues and circumscribe their philosophy, would be embraced by thousands who are now indifferent to them. The evildoer would crowd upon our borders; and we have plenty of them now without receiving any more. They would crowd into this Church. 18:359.

I say the same now. Let us alone, and we will send Elders to the uttermost parts of the earth, and gather out Israel, wherever they are; and if you persecute us, we will do it the quicker, because we are naturally dull when let alone, and are disposed to take a little sleep, a little slumber, and a little rest. If you let us alone, we will do it a little more leisurely; but if you persecute us, we will sit up nights to preach the Gospel. 2:320.

Moses was not to blame because Pharaoh's heart became more and more hard. He was not to blame because an overwhelming destruction came upon that devoted army. Neither is God, Jesus Christ, Joseph Smith, myself, or the Apostles and Prophets of this last dispensation to blame for the unbelief of this nation, and for the dark and lowering tempest that now threatens to overthrow them with a terrible destruction. Still, as Pharaoh's heart became harder and harder, so will it be with the persecutors of God's people and purposes in the latter times, until they are utterly destroyed. 10:4.

Cannot Overtake Falsehood—We have been asked a good many times, "Why do you not publish the truth in regard to these lies which are circulated about you?" We might do this if we owned all the papers published in Christendom. Who will publish a letter from me or my brethren? Who will publish the truth from us? If it gets into one paper, it is slipped under the counter or somewhere else; but it never gets into a second. They will send forth lies concerning us very readily. The old adage is that a lie will creep through the keyhole and go a thousand miles while truth is getting out of doors; and our experience has proved this. We have not the influence and power necessary to refute the falsehoods circulated about us. We depend on God, who sits in the heavens. Our trust is in him who created the heavens, who formed the earth, and who has brought forth his children on the earth, and who has given the intelligence which they possess. 13:177.

If I had in my possession one hundred million dollars in cash, I could buy the favor of the publishers of newspapers and control their presses; with that amount I could make this people popular, though I expect that popularity would send us to hell. 3:160.

Danger of Persecuting the Saints—When men lift their hands against the Latter-day Saints, they lift them against the Almighty. 11:119.

He who lifts his heel against the Lord and against his anointed will find himself a poor, pusillanimous, weak instrument in the hands of the Devil to accomplish his designs. 8:33.

When men operate against this people, they may spend all they possess and all their ability, and it will pass away like an empty sound, and they will be forgotten. Such persons have always come to naught, and all who fight against the people of the Most High will continue to come to naught. 3:259.

Tell the world—sound it in the ears of kings and rulers, that they are persecuting a people to whose God they will have to pay every debt they contract; they will be brought into judgment for every act against this Kingdom. This is the Kingdom of God; these are the people of God, as are all who receive the truth and follow its principles. As to parentage, we are no more the children of God than are the rest of the inhabitants of the earth. Originally, as to our parents, as to our organization and that which pertains to our life, we are all the children of one Father, whether we be Jew or Gentile, bond or free, black or white, noble or ignoble. The difference we see arises in consequence of the different use made of the agency given to man. 8:194-195.

The sufferings that have come upon the Latter-day Saints, through persecution, will not compare in severity with the sufferings which have come upon the wicked in our own day. 11:274.

Persecution Comes From Efforts of Few—Now to tell the truth, there are but few, in comparison with the numbers that now live, who are rabid against and seek to destroy the Kingdom of God. A great portion of the human family are honorable men and women, and they would just as soon that "Mormonism" should live as any other ism. The few who seek to destroy the Kingdom of God are priests, politicians, and office seekers, and they would care nothing about it, only they are afraid we will take away their place and station. 11:323.

Chapter XXXI

POLITICAL GOVERNMENT

Theocratic Government—I believe in a true republican theocracy, and also in a true democratic theocracy, as the term democratic is now used; for they are to me, in their present use, convertible terms. 6:346.

What do I understand by a theocratic government? One in which all laws are enacted and executed in righteousness, and whose officers possess that power which proceedeth from the Almighty. That is the kind of government I allude to when I speak of a theocratic government, or the Kingdom of God upon the earth. It is, in short, the eternal powers of the Gods. 6:346-347.

If the Kingdom of God, or a theocratic government, was established on the earth, many practices now prevalent would be abolished.

One community would not be permitted to array itself in opposition to another to coerce them to their standard; one denomination would not be suffered to persecute another because they differed in religious belief and mode of worship. Every one would be fully protected in the enjoyment of all religious and social rights, and no state, no government, no community, no person would have the privilege of infringing on the rights of another; one Christian community would not rise up and persecute another. 6:343.

But few, if any, understand what a theocratic government is. In every sense of the word, it is a republican government, and differs but little in form from our National, State, and Territorial Governments; but its subjects will recognize the will and dictation of the Almighty. The Kingdom of God circumscribes and comprehends the municipal laws for the people in their outward government, to which pertain the Gospel covenants, by which the people can be saved; and those covenants pertain to fellowship and faithfulness.

The Gospel covenants are for those who believe and obey; municipal laws are for both Saint and sinner.

The Constitution and laws of the United States resemble a theocracy more closely than any government now on the earth, or that ever has been so far as we know, except the government of the Children of Israel to the time when they elected a king.

All governments are more or less under the control of the Almighty, and, in their forms, have sprung from the laws that he has from time to time given to man. Those laws, in passing from generation to generation, have been more or less adulterated, and the result has been the various forms of government now in force among the nations; for, as the Prophet says of Israel, "They have transgressed the laws, changed the ordinances, and broken the everlasting covenant."

Whoever lives to see the Kingdom of God fully established upon the earth will see a government that will protect every person in his rights. If that government was now reigning upon this land of Joseph, you would see the Roman Catholic, the Greek Catholic, the Episcopalian, the Presbyterian, the Methodist, the Baptist, the Quaker, the Shaker, the Hindo, the Mahometan, and every class of worshipers most strictly protected in all their municipal rights and in the privileges of worshiping who, what, and when they pleased, not infringing upon the rights of others. Does any candid person in his sound judgment desire any greater liberty? 6:342-343.

In the sincere observances of the principles of true religion and virtue, we recognize the base, the only sure foundation of enlightened society and well-established government. 2:178.

I have had some people ask me how I manage and control the people. I do it by telling them the truth and letting them do just as they have a mind to. 14:162.

Republican Government—There is no other platform that any government can stand upon and endure, but the platform of truth and virtue. 10:108.

How can a republican government stand? There is only one way for it to stand. It can endure; but how? It can endure, as the government of heaven endures, upon the eternal rock of truth and virtue; and that is the only basis upon which any government can endure. 9:4.

What is a true republican government is easily answered. It is a government or institution that is perfect—perfect in its laws and ordinances, having for its object the perfection of mankind in righteousness. This is true democracy. 7:10.

Individual self-government lies at the root of all true and effective government, whether in heaven or on earth. Those who govern should be wiser and better than the governed, that the less may be blessed of the greater. Were this so, then the people would willingly repose their dearest interests to the trusts of their rulers or leaders, and with a feeling of pleasure bow to and carry out to the letter their insrtuctions and conclusions on all matters that pertained to the general good. This will apply to great kingdoms and mighty nations, to small companies of immigrants crossing the plains, or to the home circle. A republican government in the hands of a wicked people must terminate in woe to that people, but in the hands of the righteous it is everlasting, while its power reaches to heaven. 10:19.

Suppose this people inhabiting these mountains are broken off entirely from the nations of the world, rendering no allegiance to any earthly power combined or isolated; free to make laws, to obey them, or to break them; free to act, to choose, and to refuse, and, in every sense of the word, to do as they please, without any fixed order of government whatever, and they make a constitution a system of government for mutual protection and advancement in the principles of right, to be framed according to the best wisdom that can be found in this community;—I say, let them govern themselves by a republican system of government, selecting a man from their midst to preside over them. 7:11.

A true system of civilization will not encourage the existence of every abomination and crime in a community but will lead them to observe the laws Heaven has laid down for the regulation of the life of man. There is no other civilization. A truly civilized person is one who is a real gentleman or lady; in language and manners he is truly refined, and gives way to no practice that is unhallowed or uncomely. This is what we are after, and trying to attain to. 12:287.

I believe in a true republican government; but where is the man capable of exhibiting in their true character the principles of such a government? 7:10.

The man who fights with coolness and calculation in moral and domestic reform will win every time. 10:205.

God and Governments—Every government not ordained of God as we have just been hearing, will, in its time, crumble to the dust and be lost in the fog of forgetfulness. 14:93.

If your eyes were opened, you would see his hand in the midst of the nations of the earth in the setting up of governments and in the downfall of kingdoms—in the revolutions, wars, famine, distress, and wretchedness among the inhabitants of the earth. In these manifestations you would discern the footsteps of the Almighty just as plainly as you may see the footsteps of your children upon the soft earth. 7:144.

Why are they thus led to sow the seeds of their own destruction? Because the kingdoms of this world are not designed to stand. When men are placed at the head of governments who are actually controlled by the power of God—by the Holy Ghost—they can lay plans, they can frame constitutions, they can form governments and laws that have not the seeds of death within them, and no other men can do it. 4:267.

In the laws of every government now on this earth, there are certain principles in their constitutions that will ere long sap the foundations of their existence; and so it will be, so long as men continue to persist in ruling and making laws, in regulating and controlling by human wisdom alone, and in issuing their mandates and sending their officers to administer laws, made by the wisdom of man. 4:267.

If a nation transgresses wholesome laws and oppresses any of its citizens or another nation, until the cup of iniquity is full, through acts that are perfectly under its own control, God will hurl those who are in authority from their power, and they will be forgotten; and he will take another people, though poor and despised, a hiss and a by-word among the popular nations, and instill into them power and wisdom; and they will increase and prosper, until they in turn become a great nation on the earth. 6:146.

Great and mighty empires are raised to the summit of human greatness by him, to bring to pass his inscrutable purposes, and at his pleasure they are swept from existence and lost in the oblivion of antiquity. All these mighty changes are pointing to and preparing the way for the introduction of his Kingdom in the latter times, that will stand forever and grow in greatness and power until a holy, lasting, religious and political peace shall make the hearts of the poor among men exult with joy in the Holy One of Israel, and that his Kingdom is everywhere triumphant. 9:368.

Fitness of Rulers—No being is fit to rule, govern, and dictate, until he has been controlled, governed, and dictated,—has yielded obedience to law, and proved himself worthy, by magnifying the law that was over him, to be master of that law. 8:324.

What is the reign of a king who cannot control his passions? Will not his subjects sorrow? Yes, they will feel the weight of his wrath, and their backs will ache, and their heads will ache, and they will receive the lash from a heavy hand. 8:324.

Labor and Politics—Put a community in possession of knowledge by means of which they can obtain what they need by the labor of their bodies and their brains, then, instead of being paupers they will be free, independent and happy, and these distinctions of classes will cease, and there will be but one class, one grade, one great family. 16:20.

Do you wish to possess enlarged influence in a political point of view? Gather around you the poor and honest of mankind and bestow your charity on them, not by giving them in the way that charity is almost universally understood, but supply them labor that will pay an interest on the outlay of means and, at the same time, afford food, raiment and shelter to the laborer; in this way the man of means becomes a benefactor to his race. 10:193.

If you wish to gain power in the minds of any people, give them the same opportunity that you possess to become independent and self-sustaining, and endow them with all the wisdom and knowledge that they are capable of receiving, and let them increase with you and unitedly grow and become strong. 10:190.

Saints and Politics—I stand for Constitutional law, and if any transgress, let them be tried by it, and, if guilty, suffer its penalty. 10:109.

I say God speed everybody that is for freedom and equal rights! I am with you. Whom do we want to fill our public offices? We want the best men that we can find for governor, president and statesmen, and for every other office of trust and responsibility; and when we have obtained them, we will pray for them and give them our faith and influence to do the will of God and to preserve themselves and the people in truth and righteousness. 13:274.

If we live our religion, honor our God and his Priesthood, then we shall honor every wholesome government and law there is upon the earth and become aliens to all unrighteous, unjust and unlawful administrators, wherever they may be found. In the various nations, kingdoms and governments of the world are to be found laws, ordinances and statutes as good as can be made for mortal man. 10:41.

Are we a political people? Yes, very political indeed. But what party do you belong to or would you vote for? I will tell you whom we will vote for: we will vote for the man who will sustain the principles of civil and religious liberty, the man who knows the most and who has the best heart and brain for a statesman; and we do not care a farthing whether he is a whig, a democrat, a barnburner, a republican, a new light or anything else. These are our politics. 13:149.

If nobody will speak for us, let us speak for ourselves; if no person else will do anything for us, let us do something for ourselves. This is right; it is politically right, religiously right, nationally right, socially and morally right, and it is right in every sense of the word for us to sustain ourselves. 11:140.

Let those called Latter-day Saints so learn wisdom as to carry out the true principles of government, that they may be able to govern and control all things wisely. 7:64.

The Constitution of the United States, an Inspired Document—We mean to sustain the Constitution of the United States and all righteous laws. 9:157.

We will cling to the Constitution of our country, and to the government that reveres that sacred charter of freemen's rights; and, if necessary, pour out our best blood for the defense of every good and righteous principle. 10:41.

It was observed this morning that the Government of the United States was the best or most wholesome one on the earth, and the best adapted to our condition. That is very true. 2:310.

To accuse us of being unfriendly to the Government, is to accuse us of hostility to our religion, for no item of inspiration is held more sacred with us than the Constitution under which she acts. As a religious society, we, in common with all other denominations, claim its protection. 2:175.

The signers of the Declaration of Independence and the framers of the Constitution were inspired from on high to do that work. But was that which was given to them perfect, not admitting of any addition whatever? No; for if men know anything, they must know that the Almighty has never yet found a man in mortality that was capable, at the first intimation, at the first impulse, to receive anything in a state of entire perfection. They laid the foundation, and it was for aftergenerations to rear the superstructure upon it. It is a progressive—a gradual work. 7:14.

The general Constitution of our country is good, and a wholesome government could be framed upon it, for it was dictated by the invisible operations of the Almighty; he moved upon Columbus to launch forth upon the trackless deep to discover the American Continent; he moved upon the signers of the Declaration of Independence; and he moved upon Washington to fight and conquer in the same way as he moved upon ancient and modern Prophets, each being inspired to accomplish the particular work he was called to perform in the times, seasons, and dispensations of the Almighty. God's purposes, in raising up these men and inspiring them with daring sufficient to surmount every opposing power, was to prepare the way for the formation of a true republican government. They laid its foundation; but when others came to build upon it, they reared a superstructure far short of their privileges, if they had walked uprightly as they should have done. 7:13.

We believe that the Lord has been preparing that when he should bring forth his work, that, when the set time should fully come, there might be a place upon his footstool where sufficient liberty of conscience should exist, that his Saints might dwell in peace under the broad panoply of constitutional law and equal rights. In this view we consider that the men in the Revolution were inspired by the Almighty, to throw off the shackles of the mother government, with her established religion. For this cause were Adams, Jefferson, Franklin, Washington, and a host of others inspired to deeds of resistance to the acts of the King of Great Britain, who might also have been led to those aggressive acts, for aught we know, to bring to pass the purposes of God, in thus establishing a new government upon a principle of greater freedom, a basis of self-government allowing the free exercise of religious worship.

It was the voice of the Lord inspiring all those worthy men who bore influence in those trying times, not only to go forth in battle but to exercise wisdom in council, fortitude, courage, and endurance in the tented field, as well as subsequently to form and adopt those wise and efficient measures which secured to themselves and succeeding generations, the blessings of a free and independent government.

This government, so formed, has been blessed by the Almighty until she spreads her sails in every sea, and her power is felt in every land. 2:170.

This, then, is our position towards the Government of the United States and towards the world, to put down iniquity, and exalt virtue; to declare the word of God which he revealed unto us, and build up his Kingdom upon the earth. And, know all men, Governments, Nations, Kindreds, Tongues, and People, that this is our calling, intention, and design. We aim to live our religion, and have communion with our God. We aim to clear our skirts of the blood of this generation, by our faithfulness in preaching the truth of heaven in all plainness and simplicity; and I have often said, and repeat it now, that all other considerations of whatever name or nature, sink into insignificance in comparison with this. To serve God and keep his commandments, are first and foremost with me. If this is higher law, so be it. As it is with me, so should it be with every department of the Government; for this doctrine is based upon the principles of virtue and integrity; with it, the Government, her Constitution, and free institutions are safe; without it no power can avert their speedy destruction. It is the life-giving power to the Government; it is the vital element on which she exists and prospers; in absence she sinks to rise no more. 2:176.

The Saints Will Yet Save the Constitution — When the day comes in which the Kingdom of God will bear rule, the flag of the United States will proudly flutter unsullied on the flagstaff of liberty and equal rights, without a spot to sully its fair surface; the glorious flag our fathers have bequeathed to us will then be unfurled to the breeze by those who have power to hoist it aloft and defend its sanctity. 2:317.

How long will it be before the words of the prophet Joseph will be fulfilled? He said if the Constitution of the United States were saved at all it must be done by this people. It will not be many years before these words come to pass. 12:204.

When the Constitution of the United States hangs, as it were, upon a single thread, they will have to call for the "Mormon" Elders to save it from utter destruction; and they will step forth and do it. 2:182.

The present Constitution, with a few alterations of a trifling nature, is just as good as we want; and if it is sustained on this land of Joseph, it will be done by us and our posterity. 8:324.

I expect to see the day when the Elders of Israel will protect and sustain civil and religious liberty and every constitutional right bequeathed to us by our fathers, and spread these rights abroad in connection with the Gospel for the salvation of all nations. I shall see this whether I live or die. 11:262.

Religious Liberty Should be Observed—The Government of the United States, and the President of the United States ought to treat the religion of the Latter-day Saints as they do Methodism, Presbyterianism, Quakerism, Shakerism, and many other isms, and say, "Here, I wish you to hold your tongue about the 'Mormons,' for they have just as good a right to their religion as you have to yours." And when the people petition for this or that (as the right of petition should never be denied), it is the duty of those who are addressed to hearken to the petitions of the people. 2:186.

Are not our religious sentiments as sacred to us as to any other portion of the community? And should it not be the duty, as well as the pride, of every American citizen to extend that provision of the Constitution to us which he claims for himself? And is not that sacred instrument invaded and broken as much in debarring and excluding this people from its privilege, rights, and blessings, as it would be if your rights and privileges were thus invaded? No, gentlemen, we have broken no laws, our glorious Constitution guarantees unto us all that we claim. Under its broad folds, in its obvious meaning and intents, we are safe, and can always rejoice in peace. All that we have ever claimed, or wish to, on the part of the Government, is the just administration of the powers and privileges of the National Compact. 2:172.

I pause now to ask, Had not Joseph Smith a right to promulgate and establish a different, a new religion and form of worship in this Government? Every one must admit he had. This right was always held sacred, for upon it was based the religious liberty of every citizen of the Republic. It was a privilege held sacred in the bosom of every class of people; no judge dared invade its holy precincts. No legislator nor governor ventured to obstruct the free exercise thereof. Whenever the iron hand of oppression and persecution has fallen upon this people, our opposers have broken their own laws, set at defiance and trampled under foot every principle of equal rights, justice, and liberty found written in that rich legacy of our fathers. *The Constitution of the United States.* 2:171.

Whether our religion is believed by any other people or not, it is by us, and no power or authority in the Government can lawfully or righteously molest us in the peaceable and quiet enjoyment thereof. It cannot be done without law, and surely the Government has no right to make any law concerning it, or to prevent the free exercise thereof. 2:177.

The Government of the United States has never engaged in a crusade against us as a people, although she has remained silent, or refused us, when appealed to for redress of grievances. She has permitted us to be driven from our own lands, for which she had taken our money, and that too with her letters patent in our hands, guaranteeing to us peaceable possession. She has calmly looked on and permitted one of the fundamental and dearest provisions of the Constitution to be broken; she has permitted us to be driven and trampled under foot with impunity. Under these circumstances, what course is left for us to pursue? I answer that, instead of seeking to destroy the very best Government in the world, as seems to be the fears of some, we, like all other good citizens, should seek to place those men in power, who will feel the obligations and responsibilities they are under to a mighty people; who would feel and realize the important trusts reposed in them by the voice of the people who call them to administer law under the solemn sanction of an oath of fidelity to that heaven-inspired instrument, to the inviolate preservation of which we look for the perpetuity of our free institutions. 2:175.

Opposed to Corrupt Administrators of Law—I do not lift my voice against the great and glorious Government guaranteed to every citizen by our Constitution, but against those corrupt administrators who trample the Constitution and just laws under their feet. 5:232.

It is a pretty bold stand for this people to take, to say that they will not be controlled by the corrupt administrators of our general Government. We will be controlled by them, if they will be controlled by the Constitution and laws; but they will not. Many of them do not care any more about the Constitution and the laws that they make than they do about the laws of another nation. That class trample the rights of the people under their feet, while there are many who would like to honor them. All we have ever asked for is our Constitutional rights. We wish the laws of our Government honored, and we have ever honored them; but they are trampled under foot by administrators. 5:231.

I repeat that the Constitution, laws, and institutions of our

Government are as good as can be, with the intelligence now possessed by the people. But they, as also the laws of other nations, are too often administered in unrighteousness; and we do not and cannot love and respect the acts of the administrators of our laws, unless they act justly in their offices. 6:344.

The President of the United States—As I have already stated, the President of the United States should be a perfect pattern for all the people to walk after; so also should the Vice-President, the members of the Cabinet, and of Congress, the Governors of States and Territories, and in fine, all the officers in the Government, be patterns for the people to imitate. 2:183.

And the people should concentrate their feelings, their influence, and their faith to select the best man they can find to be their President, if he has nothing more to eat than potatoes and salt—a man who will not aspire to become greater than the people who appoint him, but be contented to live as they live, be clothed as they are clothed, and in every good thing be one with them. 7:12-13.

When the best man is elected President, let him select the best men he can find for his counselors or cabinet; and let all the officers within the province of the Chief Magistrate to appoint, be selected upon the same principle to officiate wisely in different parts of the nation. 6:345.

The Government of the United States is republican in form, and should be in its administration, and requires a man for President who is capable of communicating to the understanding of the people, according to their capacity, information upon all points pertaining to the just administration of the Government. He should understand what administrative policy would be most beneficial to the nation. He should also have the knowledge and disposition to wisely exercise the appointing power, so far as it is constitutionally within his control, and select only good and capable men for the office. He should not only carry out the legal and just wishes of his constituents, but should be able to enlighten their understanding and correct their judgment. And all good officers in a truly republican administration will constantly labor for the security of the rights of all, irrespective of sect or party. 7:63.

In the free and independent Government of the United States, who in the eyes of the Almighty ought to have the privilege of sitting in the Presidential chair, to be countenanced, adored, loved, and reverenced in his capacity, and be justified therein by the heavenly hosts? It is that man who is sanctified before God, and who loves the Lord Jesus with all his heart, or in other words, who is endowed with wisdom from on high, and has revelations, visions, and dreams, giving him understanding to provide for the welfare of every portion of the nation, and a willingness to preserve to every one their fair and just religious rights, as well as political, for the good and benefit of all. In the eyes of eternal justice, only such a man has a right to that office. They are afraid to put a man there who is a professor of religion, lest he favor his own party. A man is a fool that would do that, when he has laws to preserve and keep inviolate towards all religious denominations. 2:188-189.

In our Government a President is elected for four years, and by custom re-elected but once, thus limiting the time of any one person to but eight years at most. Would it not be better to extend that period during life or good behavior; and when the people have elected the best man to that office, continue him in it as long as he will serve them?

Would it not be better for the States to elect their Governors upon the same principle; and if they officiate unjustly, hurl them from office? If a good man is thus elected and continues to do his duty, he will keep in advance of the people; and if he does not, he does not magnify his office. Such is the Kingdom of God, in comparison. 6:345.

Is a man fit to be President of the United States, who will bow and succumb to the whims of the people? No. A President should learn the true situation of his constituents, and deal out even-handed justice to all, utterly regardless of the clamor of party. 5:126.

We want men to rule the nation who care more for and love better the nation's welfare than gold and silver, fame, or popularity. 7:12.

Who is the most suitable judge between man and man? The man who is the most capable of judging between right and wrong; let him sit upon the judgment seat, and do not ask him whether he is a Democrat, a Whig, a Tory, or a Republican. Is he a just man, and will he render an impartial judgment? If so, I care not to what political party he belongs; I am content that he should adjudicate between me and my neighbor. 10:193.

Political Parties—It has been told me from my youth up that opposition is the life of business, especially in the political arena. It is opposition that has ruined our nation, and has been, is and will be the ruin of all nations. 10:190.

When the people's affections are interwoven with a republican government administered in all its purity, if the administrators act not in virtue and truth it is but natural that the people become disaffected with mal-administration, and divide and sub-divide into parties, until the body politic is shivered to pieces. 10:108.

Parties in our Government have no better idea than to think the Republic stands all the firmer upon opposition; but I say that it is not so. A republican government consists in letting the people rule by their united voice, without a dissension,—in learning what is for the best, and unitedly doing it. That is true republicanism. 5:228.

States' Rights—Suppose there is a division between the North and South, and the fifteen slave States try to form a permanent government, can they do it? I tell you they cannot. How long will it be before some other States, perhaps New York, forms a separate government? And if a State has a right to secede, so has a Territory, and so has a county from a State or Territory, and a town from a county, and a family from a neighborhood, and you will have perfect anarchy. 8:322.

If we are what we profess to be—a republican Government, there is no State in the Union but what should be amenable to the general Government holding to the old English rights in Rhode Island. Then Congress, with the President at their head, could meet and veto every act made by any department of the Government, if it was necessary. So let Congress come together when any of the States transcend the bounds of right and hold them amenable for their actions. The general Government should never give any portion of the nation license to say they are free and independent. This should only apply to the nation as a whole. 7:13.

So it is with States and Territories. Let them be unduly fostered and sustained by the general Government, and it will lead them into idleness, inactivity, and corruption; they will not be as spirited and active as when they are made to rely upon their own resources. 2:321.

Forebodings of the Civil War—The nation that gave me and many of you birth is very nigh to the hours of sorrow. Their cup is very nigh filled to the brim. They reject the servants of God; they reject the Gospel of salvation; they turn away from the principles of truth and righteousness; and they are sinking in their own sins and corruptions. I would that they would have mercy on themselves. I will pray the Lord to have mercy on them, but I pray them to have mercy on themselves to return to the Lord, forsake their wickedness and learn righteousness, and then God would have mercy on them, and bestow his blessings upon them, if they would receive them. 4:371.

What will be their condition when the Spirit of the Lord is withdrawn? They will whet the knife to cut each other's throats, and as Brother Hooper remarked, try to make Mason and Dixon's the dividing line; but that will not remain, for they will cross it to destroy each other, and the sword and fire will be prevalent in the land. 8:147-148.

Yes, his mercy yearns over the Nation that has striven for a score of years to rid the earth of the Priesthood of the Son of God and to destroy the last Saint. He has mercy upon them, he bears with them, he pleads with them by his Spirit, and occasionally sends his angels to administer to them. Marvel not, then, that I pray for every soul that can be saved. 8:124.

War—If I had my wish, I should entirely stop the shedding of human blood. 10:108.

There is a spirit which prompts the nations to prepare for war, desolation, and bloodshed—to waste each other away. 8:174.

From the authority of all history, the deadly weapons now stored up and being manufactured will be used until the people are wasted away, and there is no help for it. The spirit of revolution goes on through the nations: it never goes back. 8:157.

Do not be discouraged when you hear of wars, and rumors of wars, and tumults, and contentions, and fighting, and bloodshed; for behold they are at the thresholds of our doors. 4:369.

Does one nation rise up to war with another without having motives, and those which they will substantiate as being good and sufficient? Will one people rise up to war with another people, except the motive that moves them is of a nature to justify them in their own minds and judgment for doing so? No. There is not a people upon the face of this earth that would do so; they all calculate to do that which seemeth good to them. 3:88.

The difficulty with the whole world in their divisions and subdivisions, is that they have no more confidence in each other than they have in their God, and that is none at all, no, not one particle. This confuses nations, and breaks them up; it weakens them, and they tumble to pieces. It disturbs cities and counties, and really the seeds of destruction are within those kingdoms where the people have not confidence in each other. 4:296.

Wars, commotions, tumults, strife, nation contending against nation, and people against people, have all been governed and controlled by him whose right it is to control such matters.

Among wicked nations, or among Saints, among the ancient Israelites, Philistines, and Romans, the hand of the Lord was felt; in short, all the powers that have been upon the earth, have been dictated, governed, controlled, and the final issue of their existence has been brought to pass, according to the wisdom of the Almighty. Then my testimony is, it is all right. 1:163.

Of one thing I am sure; God never institutes war; God is not the author of confusion or of war; they are the results of the acts of the children of men. Confusion and war necessarily come as the results of the foolish acts and policy of men; but they do not come because God desires they should come. If the people, generally, would turn to the Lord, there would never be any war. Let men turn from their iniquities and sins, and, instead of being covetous and wicked, turn to God and seek to promote peace and happiness throughout the land, and wars would cease. We expect to see the day when swords shall be turned into ploughshares, spears into pruning hooks, and when men shall learn war no more. This is what we want. We are for peace, plenty and happiness to all the human family. 13:149.

Our traditions have been such that we are not apt to look upon war between two nations as murder; but suppose that one family should rise up against another and begin to slay them, would they not be taken up and tried for murder? Then why not nations that rise up and slay each other in a scientific way be equally guilty of murder? "But observe the martial array, how splendid! See the furious war horses, with their glittering trappings. Then the honor and glory and pride of the reigning king must be sustained, and the strength and power and wealth of the nation must be displayed in some way; and what better way than to make war upon neighboring nations, under some slight pretext?" Does it justify the slaying of men, women, and children that otherwise would have remained at home in peace, because a great army is doing the work? No: the guilty will be damned for it. 7:137.

The very Indians who massacre men, women, and children on the plains, have their religious ceremonies and pray to their God for success in killing men, women, and children. The French and Austrians meet and slay one another by hundreds and thousands; and thousands of women and children who were not engaged in battle are also sacrificed by the folly of those Christian wars. The instigators of those wars are just as guilty of murder, before God, as the Indians are for killing the men, women, and children who are passing through their country. What is the difference in the eyes of our Father and God? It is just as much murder to kill, unjustly, a million at a blow as it is to kill one, though Dr. Young has stated that "One murder makes a villain; millions make a hero." Were I to make war upon an innocent people, because I had the power, to possess myself of their territory, their silver, gold, and other property, and be the cause of slaying, say fifty thousand strong, hale, hearty men, and devolving consequent suffering upon one hundred thousand women and children, who would suffer through privation and want, I am very much more guilty of murder than is the man who kills only one person to obtain his pocket-book. 7:137.

Woman Suffrage—Now, sisters, I want you to vote also, because women are the characters that rule the ballot box. 1:218.

Chapter XXXII

DEATH AND RESURRECTION

The Body Must Return to Mother Earth—Every person possessing the principle of eternal life should look upon his body as of the earth earthy. Our bodies must return to their mother earth. True, to most people it is a wretched thought that our spirits must, for a longer or shorter period, be separated from our bodies, and thousands and millions have been subject to this affliction throughout their lives. If they understood the design of this probation and the true principles of eternal life, it is but a small matter for the body to suffer and die. 7:240.

The Lord has pleased to organize tabernacles here, and put spirits into them, and they then become intelligent beings. By and by, sooner or later, the body, this that is tangible to you, that you can feel, see, handle, etc., returns to its mother dust. Is the spirit dead? No. You believe the spirit still exists, when this body has crumbled into the earth again, and the spirit that God puts into the tabernacle goes into the world of spirits. What is their situation? Is there any opportunity for them whatever? Yes, there is. 2:138.

"Well," says Mr. B.: If you have not this great power, and can heal the sick by the laying on of hands, come with me and heal the sick in our neighborhood; or how is it that any of you 'Mormons' die at all?" Take your time, Mr. B. The Bible teaches me I am dust, and to dust I must return. It is not for me to thwart the plans of Jehovah, or do away with any item of doctrine the Lord has taught me. From dust I am, and to dust I must return. So it is with the rest of us, we shall all die and be buried in the silent grave. 1:240.

We shall suffer no more in putting off this flesh and leaving the spirit houseless than the child, in its capacity, does in its first efforts to breathe the breath of this mortal life. 8:28.

Our bodies are composed of visible, tangible matter, as you all understand; you also know that they are born into this world. They then begin to partake of the elements adapted to their organization and growth, increase to manhood, become old, decay, and pass again into the dust. Now in the first place, though I have explained this many times, what we call death is the operation of life, inherent in the matter of which the body is composed, and which causes the decomposition after the spirit has left the body. Were that not the fact, the body, from which has fled the spirit, would remain to all eternity, just as it was when the spirit left it, and would not decay.

What is commonly called death does not destroy the body, it

only causes a separation of spirit and body, but the principle of life, inherent in the native elements, of which the body is composed, still continues with the particles of that body and causes it to decay, to dissolve itself into the elements of which it was composed, and all of which continues to have life. When the spirit given to man leaves the body, the tabernacle begins to decompose. Is that death? No, death only separates the spirit and body, and a principle of life still operates in the untenanted tabernacle, but in a different way, and producing different effects from those observed while it was tenanted by the spirit. There is not a particle of element which is not filled with life, and all space is filled with element; there is no such thing as empty space, though some philosophers contend that there is.

Life in various proportions, combinations, conditions, etc., fills all matter. Is there life in a tree when it ceases to put forth leaves? You see it standing upright, and when it ceases to bear leaves and fruit you say it is dead, but that is a mistake. It still has life, but that life operates upon the tree in another way, and continues to operate until it resolves it to the native elements. It is life in another condition that begins to operate upon man, upon animal, upon vegetation, and upon minerals when we see the change termed dissolution. There is life in the material of the fleshly tabernacle, independent of the spirit given of God to undergo this probation. There is life in all matter, throughout the vast extent of all the eternities; it is in the rock, the sand, the dust, in water, air, the gases, and in short, in every description and organization of matter, whether it be solid, liquid, or gaseous, particle operating with particle.

I have heard some philosophers argue that because no body could move without displacing other matter, therefore there must be empty space. That reasoning is nonsense to me, because eternity is, was, and will continue to be full of matter and life. We put a ship in motion on the water, and have we created an empty space? No, we have only changed the position of matter. Men and animals move upon the earth, birds and fishes cleave the elements they are organized to operate in, but do they leave a track of empty space? No, for all eternity is full of matter and life. True, element is capable of contraction and expansion, but that does not by any means imply empty space. You see life in human beings and in the growing vegetation, and when that spirit of life departs, another condition of life at once begins to operate upon the organization which remains. By way of illustration I will quote one passage from the Book of Job, who in his afflictions was visited by several friends, and after he had concluded that they were all miserable comforters, he exclaimed, "Though worms destroy this body, yet in my flesh shall I see God."

To make this passage clearer to your comprehension, I will paraphrase it, Though my spirit leave my body, and though worms destroy its present organization, yet in the morning of the resurrection I shall behold the face of my Savior, in this same tabernacle; that is my understanding of the idea so briefly expressed by Job. 3:276-277.

Man Should Live Out His Days—It is not the design of the Father that the earthly career of any should terminate until they have lived out their days; and the reason that so few do live out their days is because of the force of sin in the world and the power of death over the human family. To these causes, and not to the design of the Creator, may be attributed the fact that disease stalks abroad, laying low the aged, middle-aged, youth, and infants, and the human family generally by millions. 14:230.

So live that when you wake in the spirit-world you can truthfully say, "I could not better my mortal life, were I to live it over again." I exhort you, for the sake of the House of Israel, for the sake of Zion which we are to build up, to so live, from this time, henceforth, and forever, that your characters may with pleasure be scrutinized by holy beings. Live godly lives, which you cannot do without living moral lives. 8:164.

We Should Not Mourn for the Righteous Dead—Those who have honored their calling and Priesthood to the end die in the Lord, and their works do follow them. 13:75.

It is a great cause of joy and rejoicing and comfort to his friends to know that a person has passed away in peace from this life, and has secured to himself a glorious resurrection. The earth and the fulness of the earth and all that pertains to this earth in an earthly capacity is no comparison with the glory, joy and peace and happiness of the soul that departs in peace. 12:186.

Mourning for the righteous dead springs from the ignorance and weakness that are planted within the mortal tabernacle, the organization of this house for the spirit to dwell in. No matter what pain we suffer, no matter what we pass through, we cling to our mother earth, and dislike to have any of her children leave us. We love to keep together the social family relation that we bear one to another, and do not like to part with each other; but could we have knowledge and see into eternity, if we were perfectly free from the weakness, blindness, and lethargy with which we are clothed in the flesh, we should have no disposition to weep or mourn. 4:131.

Nothing remains here for us but to pay our last respects to that which came from mother earth. It was formed and fashioned and the spirit was put into it, and it has grown and become what it is, and the spirit having departed, the body lies ready to return to the bosom of its mother, there to rest until the morning of the resurrection. But the life and intelligence which once dwelt in that body still live, and Sister Aurelia moves, talks, walks, enjoys and beholds that which we cannot enjoy and behold while we are in these tabernacles of clay. She is in glory; she has passed the ordeals and has reached a position in which the power of Satan has no influence upon her. The advantage of this Priesthood is that when persons yield obedience to it, they secure to themselves the sanction of him who is its author, and who has bestowed it upon the children of men. His power is around them and defends them; and when they pass into the spirit world they are out of the reach of the power of Satan. Where the pure in heart are the wicked cannot come. This is the state of the spirit world. 14:229.

When death is past, the power of Satan has no more influence over a faithful individual; that spirit is free, and can command the power of Satan. The penalty demanded by the fall has been fully paid; all is accomplished pertaining to it, when the tabernacle of a faithful person is returned to the earth. All that was lost is passed away, and that person will again receive his body. When he is in the spirit world, he is free from those contaminating and condemning influences of Satan that we are now subject to. Here our bodies are subject to being killed by our enemies—our names to being cast out as evil. We are persecuted, hated, not beloved: though I presume that we are as much beloved here as the spirits of the Saints are in the spirit world by those spirits who hate righteousness. It is the same warfare, but we will have power over them. Those who have passed through the veil have power over the evil spirits to command, and they must obey. 7:240-241.

Shall we rejoice that we have the opportunity of paying the last respects due to this lifeless clay, which a few days ago was alive and active, full of spirit, attending the High Council, giving decisions full of knowledge? Yes, we will rejoice. It is a matter of rejoicing more than the day of his birth. It is true it is grievous to part with our friends. We are creatures of passion, of sympathy, of love, and it is painful for us to part with our friends. We would keep them in the mortal house, though they should suffer pain. Are we not selfish in this? Should we not rather rejoice at the departure of those whose lives have been devoted to doing good, to a good old age? Brother Spencer has lived beyond what is counted to be the common age of man some four or five years; his judgment was as active as it was twenty-five years ago. He has been faithful in this holy war. He instructed all with whom he met in the way of life. He never gave counsel but what marked the way to life everlasting. 13:75.

Our Identity Will Be Preserved—And the thought of being annihilated—of being blotted out of existence—is most horrid, even to that class called infidels. 5:53.

This intelligence must endure. We must preserve our identity before the Lord, who has sent his Son and angels, and is sending the Holy Ghost, and his ministers, and revelations, to comfort, cheer, guide, and direct the affairs of his Kingdom on the earth. 8:155.

I am after life; I want to preserve my identity, so that you can see Brigham in the eternal worlds just as you see him now. I want to see that eternal principle of life dwelling within us which will exalt us eternally in the presence of our Father and God. 7:57.

The Gospel of life and salvation reveals to each individual who receives it that this world is only a place of temporary duration, existence, trials, etc. Its present fashion and uses are but for a few days, while we were created to exist eternally. The wicked can see no further than this world is concerned. We understand that when we are unclothed in this present state, then we are prepared to be clothed upon with immortality—that when we put off these bodies we put on immortality. These bodies will return to dust, but our hope and faith are that we will receive these bodies again from the elements —that we will receive the very organization that we have here, and that, if we are faithful to the principles of freedom, we shall then be prepared to endure eternally. 5:53.

Our Bodies Will be Resurrected—After the spirit leaves the body, it remains without a tabernacle in the spirit world until the Lord, by his law that he has ordained, brings to pass the resurrection of the dead. When the angel who holds the keys of the resurrection shall sound his trumpet, then the peculiar fundamental particles that organized our bodies here, if we do honor to them, though they be deposited in the depths of the sea, and though one particle is in the north, another in the south, another in the east, and another in the west, will be brought together again in the twinkling of an eye, and our spirits will take possession of them. We shall then be prepared to dwell with the Father and the Son, and we never can be prepared to dwell with them until then. Spirits, when they leave their bodies, do not dwell with the Father and the Son, but live in the Spirit world, where there are places prepared for them. Those who do honor to their tabernacles, and love and believe in the Lord Jesus Christ, must put off this mortality, or they cannot put on immortality. This body must be changed, else it cannot be prepared to dwell in the glory of the Father. 8:28.

The only true riches in existence are for you and me to secure for ourselves a holy resurrection. 1:272.

After the body and spirit are separated by death, what, pertaining to this earth, shall we receive first? The body; that is the first object of a divine affection beyond the grave. We first come in possession of the body. The spirit has overcome the body, and the body is made subject in every respect to that divine principle God has planted in the person. The spirit within is pure and holy, and goes back pure and holy to God, dwells in the spirit world pure and holy, and, by and by, will have the privilege of coming and taking the body again. Some person holding the keys of the resurrection, having previously passed through that ordeal, will be delegated to resurrect our bodies, and our spirits will be there and prepared to enter into their bodies. Then, when we are prepared to receive our bodies, they are the first earthly objects that bear divinity personified in the capacity of the man. Only the body dies; the spirit is looking forth. 9:139.

But this our place of abode is only temporary; we are on a journey; we have only to winter and summer, as it were. Brother Grant has got through here, and has gone to his spiritual place of abode for a season. Not that he has reached his journey's end, nor will he, until he has again received this body that now lies before me. Every material part and portion pertaining to his body, to the temporal organization that constitutes the man, will clothe his spirit again, before he is prepared to receive the place and habitation that is prepared for him; yet he has gone to his spiritual home for a season. 4:129.

Yes, we will lay down these bodies in the grave. What for? That the dust, our mother earth, that composes the house of the spirit, may be purified by passing through this ordeal, and be prepared to be called up and united with the intelligent heavenly body that God has prepared. This is nothing but a change. It is not the dissolution of the creature; it is merely putting off the flesh that pertains to this world.

The particles of this earth that now compose this body will be rearranged, and the spirit will be clothed with an immortal tabernacle. Let the spirit reign predominant over the flesh, and bring into subjection the whole man, every feeling and every desire of his heart, and let him be devoted wholly, body and spirit, to the end for which he has been created. When the flesh is brought into subjection, it is made worthy through that means. 8:43.

We are here in circumstances to bury our dead according to the order of the Priesthood. But some of our brethren die upon the ocean; they cannot be buried in a burying ground, but they are sewed up in canvas and cast into the sea, and perhaps in two minutes after they are in the bowels of the shark, yet those persons will come forth in the resurrection, and receive all the glory of which they are worthy, and be clothed upon with all the beauty of resurrected Saints, as much so as if they had been laid away in a gold or silver coffin, and in a place expressly for burying the dead. 9:193.

The resurrection from the dead may also, with propriety, be called a birth. 8:260.

The blood he spilled upon Mount Calvary he did not receive again into his veins. That was poured out, and when he was resurrected, another element took the place of the blood. It will be so with every person who receives a resurrection; the blood will not be resurrected with the body, being designed only to sustain the life of the present organization. When that is dissolved, and we again obtain our bodies by the power of the resurrection, that which we now call the life of the body, and which is formed from the food we eat and the water we drink will be supplanted by another element; for flesh and blood cannot inherit the Kingdom of God. 7:163.

Jesus, the Firstfruits of the Resurrection—Jesus is the first begotten from the dead, as you will understand. Neither Enoch, Elijah, Moses, nor any other man that ever lived on earth, no matter how strictly he lived, ever obtained a resurrection until after Jesus Christ's body was called from the tomb by the angel. He was the first begotten from the dead. He is the Master of the resurrection—the first flesh that lived here after receiving the glory of the resurrection. 8:260.

You read about a first resurrection. If there is a first, there is a second. And if a second, may there not be a third, and a fourth, and so on? Yes; and happy are they who have a part in the first resurrection. Yes, more blessed are they than any others. But blessed also are they that will have part in the second resurrection, for they will be brought forth to enjoy a kingdom that is more glorious than the sectarian world ever dreamed of. 7:287.

The Resurrected Body—We bear the image of our earthly parents in their fallen state, but by obedience to the Gospel of salvation, and the renovating influences of the Holy Ghost, and the holy resurrection, we shall put on the image of the heavenly, in beauty, glory, power and goodness. Jesus Christ was so like the Father that on one occasion in answer to a request, "Show us the Father," he said, "He that hath seen me hath seen the Father." 11:123.

In the resurrection everything that is necessary will be brought from the elements to clothe and to beautify the resurrected Saints, who will receive their reward. I do not trouble myself about my dead. If they are stripped of their clothing, I do not want to know it. 9:192.

When the body comes forth again, it will be divine, God-like according to the capacity and ordinations of the Lord. Some are fore-ordained to one station, and some to another. We want a house, and when we get it and our spirits enter into it, then we can begin to look forth—for what? For our friends. We want them resurrected. Here is this friend and that friend, until by and by all are on the earth that has abided the law by which it was made. Then that which you and I respect, are fond of, and love with an earthly love, will become divine, and we can then love it with that affection which it is not now worthy of. 9:140.

Our bodies are now mortal. In the resurrection there will be a reunion of the spirits and bodies, and they will walk, talk, eat, drink, and enjoy. Those who have passed these ordeals are society for angels—for the Gods, and are the ones who will come into the Temple of the Lord that is to be built in the latter days, when saviors shall come up upon Mount Zion, and will say, "Here, my children, I want this and this done. Here are the names of such and such ones, of our fathers, and mothers—our ancestors; we will bring them up. Go forth, you who have not passed the ordeals of death and the resurrection—you who live in the flesh, and attend to the ordinances for those who have died without the law." Those who are resurrected will thus dictate in the temple. When the Saints pass through death, they cannot officiate in this sinful world, but they will dictate those who are here. "Go, now, and be baptized for the honorable—for those who would have received the law of God and the true religion, if they had lived; be baptized for the heathen—for all who were honest; officiate for them, and save them, and bring them up. Be baptized for them, anointed for them, washed and sealed for them, and fulfil all the ordinances which cannot be dispensed with." They will all be performed for the living and the dead upon Mount Zion. 8:225.

Resurrection Necessary to Full Salvation—No man can enter the celestial kingdom and be crowned with a celestial glory, until he gets his resurrected body; but Joseph and the faithful who have died have gained a victory over the power of the Devil, which you and I have not yet gained. So long as we live in these tabernacles, so long we will be subject to the temptations and power of the Devil; but when we lay them down, if we have been faithful, we have gained the victory so far; but even then we are not so far advanced at once as to be beyond the neighborhood of evil spirits. 3:371.

Chapter XXXIII

THE SPIRIT WORLD

All Go to the Spirit World — When we get through this state of being, to the next room, I may call it, we are not going to stop there. We shall still go on, doing all the good we can, administering and officiating for all whom we are permitted to administer and officiate for, and then go on to the next, and to the next, until the Lord shall crown all who have been faithful on this earth, and the work pertaining to the earth is finished, and the Savior, whom we have been helping, has completed his task, and the earth, with all things pertaining to it, is presented to the Father. Then these faithful ones will receive their blessings and crowns, and their inheritances will be set off to them and be given to them, and they will then go on, worlds upon worlds, increasing for ever and ever. 16:70.

No spirit of Saint or sinner, of the Prophet or him that kills the Prophet, is prepared for their final state; all pass through the veil from this state and go into the world of spirits; and there they dwell waiting for their final destiny. 6:294.

Where Is the Spirit World?—Is the spirit world here? It is not beyond the sun, but is on this earth that was organized for the people that have lived and that do and will live upon it. No other people can have it, and we can have no other kingdom until we are prepared to inhabit this eternally. 3:372.

When you lay down this tabernacle, where are you going? Into the spiritual world. Are you going into Abraham's bosom? No, not anywhere nigh there but into the spirit world. Where is the spirit world? It is right here. Do the good and evil spirits go together? Yes, they do. Do they both inhabit one kingdom? Yes, they do. Do they go to the sun? No. Do they go beyond the boundaries of the organized earth? No, they do not. They are brought forth upon this earth, for the express purpose of inhabiting it to all eternity. Where else are you going? Nowhere else, only as you may be permitted. 3:369.

You are in the presence of God, and when your eyes are opened you will understand it. Brother Grant's spirit is in the presence of God; and he is with Joseph, when he is not required to be somewhere else. He is at work for the benefit of Zion, for that is all the business that Joseph and the Elders of this Church have on hand. 4:133.

It reads that the spirit goes to God who gave it. Let me render this scripture a little plainer; when the spirits leave their bodies they are in the presence of our Father and God, they are prepared then to see, hear and understand spiritual things. But where is the spirit world? It is incorporated within this celestial system. Can you see it with your natural eyes? No. Can you see spirits in this room? No. Suppose the Lord should touch your eyes that you might see, could you then see the spirits? Yes, as plainly as you now see bodies, as did the servant of Elisha. If the Lord would permit it, and it was his will that it should be done, you could see the spirits that have departed from this world, as plainly as you now see bodies with your natural eyes. 3:368.

The Prophet lays down his body, he lays down his life, and his spirit goes to the world of spirits; the persecutor of the Prophet dies, and he goes to Hades; they both go to one place, and they are not to be separated yet. Now understand, that this is part of the great sermon the Lord is preaching in his providence, the righteous and the wicked are together in Hades.

If we go back to our mother country, the States, we find there the righteous, and we there find the wicked; if we go to California, we there find the righteous and the wicked; all dwelling together; and when we go beyond this veil, and leave our bodies which were taken from mother earth, and which must return, our spirits will pass beyond the veil; we go where both Saints and sinners go; they all go to one place. 3:94.

If the wicked wish to escape from his presence, they must go where he is not, where he does not live, where his influence does not preside. To find such a place is impossible, except they go beyond the bounds of time and space. 2:94.

Labors in the Spirit World—They must go into prison, both Saints and sinners. The good and bad, the righteous and the unrighteous must go to the house of prison, or Paradise, and Jesus went and opened the doors of salvation to them. And unless they lost the keys of salvation on account of transgression, as has been the case on this earth, spirits clothed with the Priesthood have ministered to them from that day to this. And if they lost the keys by transgression, some one who had been in the flesh, Joseph, for instance, had to take those keys to them. And he is calling one after another to his aid, as the Lord sees he wants help. 4:285.

Compare those inhabitants on the earth who have heard the Gospel in our day, with the millions who have never heard it, or had the keys of salvation presented to them, and you will conclude at once as I do, that there is an almighty work to perform in the spirit world. Joseph has not yet got through there. When he finishes his mission in the spirit world, he will be resurrected, but he has not yet done there. Reflect upon the millions and millions and millions of people that have lived and died without hearing the Gospel on the earth, without the keys of the Kingdom. They were not prepared for celestial glory, and there was no power that could prepare them without the keys of this Priesthood. 4:285.

Jesus was the first man that ever went to preach to the spirits in prison, holding the keys of the Gospel of salvation to them. Those keys were delivered to him in the day and hour that he went into the spirit world, and with them he opened the door of salvation to the spirits in prison. 3:370.

Father Smith and Carlos and Brother Partridge, yes, and every other good Saint, are just as busy in the spirit world as you and I are here. They can see us, but we cannot see them unless our eyes were opened. What are they doing there? They are preaching, preaching all the time, and preparing the way for us to hasten our work in building temples here and elsewhere, and to go back to Jackson County and build the great temple of the Lord. They are hurrying to get ready by the time we are ready, and we are all hurrying to get ready by the time our Elder Brother is ready. 3:369-370.

When men overcome as our faithful brethren have, and go where they see Joseph, who will dictate them and be their head and Prophet all the time, they have power over all disembodied evil spirits, for they have overcome them. Those evil spirits are under the command and control of every man that has had the Priesthood on him, and has honored it in the flesh, just as much as my hand is under my control. 4:132.

Every faithful man's labor will continue as long as the labor of Jesus, until all things are redeemed that can be redeemed, and presented to the Father. There is a great work before us. 13:77.

The spirits that dwell in these tabernacles on this earth, when they leave them go directly into this world of spirits. What? A congregated mass of inhabitants there in spirit, mingling with each other, as they do here? Yes, brethren, they are there together, and if they associate together, and collect together, in clans and in societies as they do here, it is their privilege. No doubt they yet, more or less, see, hear, converse and have to do with each other, both good and bad. If the Elders of Israel in these latter times go and preach to the spirits in prison, they associate with them, precisely as our Elders associate with the wicked in the flesh, when they go to preach to them. 2:137.

If a person is baptized for the remission of sins, and dies a short time thereafter, he is not prepared at once to enjoy a fulness of the glory promised to the faithful in the Gospel; for he must be schooled, while in the spirit, in the other departments of the house of God, passing on from truth to truth, from intelligence to intelligence, until he is prepared to again receive his body and to enter into the presence of the Father and the Son. We cannot enter into celestial glory in our present state of ignorance and mental darkness. 7:332.

Suppose, then, that a man is evil in his heart—wholly given up to wickedness, and in that condition dies, his spirit will enter into the spirit world intent upon evil. On the other hand, if we are striving with all the powers and faculties God has given us to improve upon our talents, to prepare ourselves to dwell in eternal life, and the grave receives our bodies while we are thus engaged, with what disposition will our spirits enter their next state? They will be still striving to do the things of God, only in a much greater degree—learning, increasing, growing in grace and in the knowledge of the truth. 7:333.

If we are faithful to our religion, when we go into the spirit world, the fallen spirits—Lucifer and the third part of the heavenly hosts that came with him, and the spirits of wicked men who have dwelt upon this earth, the whole of them combined will have no influence over our spirits. Is not that an advantage? Yes. All the rest of the children of men are more or less subject to them, and they are subject to them as they were while here in the flesh. 7:240.

Spirits are just as familiar with spirits as bodies are with bodies, though spirits are composed of matter so refined as not to be tangible to this coarser organization. They walk, converse, and have their meetings; and the spirits of good men like Joseph and the Elders, who have left this Church on earth for a season to operate in another sphere, are rallying all their powers and going from place to place preaching the Gospel, and Joseph is directing them, saying, go ahead, my brethren, and if they hedge up your way, walk up and command them to disperse. You have the Priesthood and can disperse them, but if any of them wish to hear the Gospel, preach to them.

Can they baptize them? No. What can they do? They can preach the Gospel, and when we have the privilege of building up Zion, the time will come for saviors to come up on Mount Zion. Some of those who are not in mortality will come along and say, "Here are a thousand names I wish you to attend to in this temple, and when you have got through with them I will give you another thousand;" and the Elders of Israel and their wives will go forth to officiate for their forefathers, the men for the men, and the women for the women. 3:371-372.

Life in the Spirit World—We have more friends behind the veil than on this side, and they will hail us more joyfully than you were ever welcomed by your parents and friends in this world; and you will rejoice more when you meet them than you ever rejoiced to see a friend in this life; and then we shall go on from step to step, from rejoicing to rejoicing, and from one intelligence and power to another, our happiness becoming more and more exquisite and sensible as we proceed in the words and powers of life. 6:349.

When the breath leaves the body, your life has not become extinct; your life is still in existence. And when you are in the spirit world, everything there will appear as natural as things now do. Spirits will be familiar with spirits in the spirit world—will converse, behold, and exercise every variety of communication with one another as familiarly and naturally as while here in tabernacles. There, as here, all things will be natural, and you will understand them as you now understand natural things. You will there see that those spirits we are speaking of are active; they sleep not. And you will learn that they are striving with all their might—laboring and toiling diligently as any individual would to accomplish an act in this world—to destroy the children of men. 7:239.

I can say with regard to parting with our friends, and going ourselves, that I have been near enough to understand eternity so that I have had to exercise a great deal more faith to desire to live than I ever exercised in my whole life to live. The brightness and glory of the next apartment is inexpressible. It is not encumbered so that when we advance in years we have to be stubbing along and be careful lest we fall down. We see our youth, even, frequently stubbing their toes and falling down. But yonder, how different! They move with ease and like lightning. If we want to visit Jerusalem, or this, that, or the other place—and I presume we will be permitted if we desire—there we are, looking at its streets. If we want to behold Jerusalem as it was in the days of the Savior; or if we want to see the Garden of Eden as it was when created, there we are, and we see it as it existed spiritually, for it was created first spiritually and then temporally, and spiritually it still remains. And when there we may behold the earth as at the dawn of creation, or we may visit any city we please that exists upon its surface. If we wish to understand how they are living here on these western islands, or in China, we are there; in fact, we are like the light of the morning, or, I will not say the electric fluid, but its operations on the wires. God has revealed some little things, with regard to his movements and power, and the operation and motion of the lightning furnish a fine illustration of the ability of the Almighty.

When we pass into the spirit world we shall possess a measure of his power. Here, we are continually troubled with ills and ailments of various kinds. In the spirit world we are free from all this and enjoy life, glory, and intelligence; and we have the Father to speak to us, Jesus to speak to us, and angels to speak to us, and we shall enjoy the society of the just and the pure who are in the spirit world until the resurrection. 14:231.

Chapter XXXIV

ETERNAL JUDGMENT

Judgment According to Works—This is a subject I have reflected upon a great deal, and I have come to the conclusion that we shall be judged according to the deeds done in the body and according to the thoughts and intents of the heart. 14:99.

There are none ticketed for the pit, unless they fill up that ticket themselves through their own misconduct. 4:268.

I do know that the trying day will soon come to you and to me; and ere long we will have to lay down these tabernacles and go into the spirit world. And I do know that as we lie down, so judgment will find us, and that is scriptural; "as the tree falls so it shall lie," or, in other words, as death leaves us so judgment will find us. 4:52.

The sectarian doctrine of final rewards and punishments is as strange to me as their bodiless, partless, and passionless God. Every man will receive according to the deeds done in the body, whether they be good or bad. All men, excepting those who sin against the Holy Ghost, who shed innocent blood or who consent thereto, will be saved in some kingdom; for in my Father's house, says Jesus, are many mansions. 11:125.

How many kingdoms there are has not been told to us; they are innumerable. The disciples of Jesus were to dwell with him. Where will the rest go? Into kingdoms prepared for them, where they will live and endure. Jesus will bring forth, by his own redemption, every son and daughter of Adam, except the sons of perdition, who will be cast into hell. Others will suffer the wrath of God —will suffer all the Lord can demand at their hands, or justice can require of them; and when they have suffered the wrath of God till the utmost farthing is paid, they will be brought out of prison. Is this dangerous doctrine to preach? Some consider it dangerous; but it is true that every person who does not sin away the day of grace, and become an angel to the Devil, will be brought forth to inherit a kingdom of glory. 8:154.

How many glories and kingdoms will there be in eternity? You will see the same variety in eternity as you see in the world. 6:293.

We read in the Bible that there is one glory of the sun, another glory of the moon, and another glory of the stars. In the book of Doctrine and Covenants, these glories are called telestial, terrestrial, and celestial, which is the highest. These are worlds, different departments, or mansions, in our Father's house. Now those men, or those women, who know no more about the power of God, and the influences of the Holy Spirit, than to be led entirely by another person, suspending their own understanding, and pinning their faith upon another's sleeve, will never be capable of entering into the celestial glory, to be crowned as they anticipate; they will never be capable of becoming Gods. They cannot rule themselves, to say nothing of ruling others, but they must be dictated to in every trifle, like a child. They cannot control themselves in the least, but James, Peter, or somebody else must control them. They never can become Gods, nor be crowned as rulers with glory, immortality, and eternal lives. They never can hold sceptres of glory, majesty, and power in the celestial kingdom. Who will? Those who are valiant and inspired with the true independence of heaven, who will go forth boldly in the service of their God, leaving others to do as they please, determined to do right, though all mankind besides should take the opposite course. 1:312.

More will prove faithful than will apostatize. A certain class of this people will go into the celestial kingdom, while others cannot enter there, because they cannot abide a celestial law; but they will attain to as good a kingdom as they desire and live for. 8:39.

The punishment of God is God-like. It endures forever, because there never will be a time when people ought not to be damned, and there must always be a hell to send them to. How long the damned remain in hell, I know not, nor what degree of suffering they endure. If we could by any means compute how much wickedness they are guilty of, it might be possible to ascertain the amount of suffering they will receive. They will receive according as their deeds have been while in the body. God's punishment is eternal, but that does not prove that a wicked person will remain eternally in a state of punishment. 9:147.

You hear some of them preach and teach that which I never taught; you hear them preach people into hell. Such doctrine never entered my heart; but you hear others preach, that people will go there to dwell throughout the endless ages of eternity. Such persons know no more about eternity, and are no more capable of instructing others upon that subject, than a little child. 1:352.

But when the light of the knowledge of God comes to a man, and he rejects it, that is his condemnation. 2:140.

All who believe, have honest hearts, and bring forth fruits of righteousness, are the elect of God and heirs to all things. All who refuse to obey the holy commandments of the Lord and the ordinances of his house will be judged out of their own mouths, will condemn themselves as they do now, will be accounted unworthy and will have no part or lot with the righteous. 8:83.

"Well," says one, "if I am pretty sure to get a state of glory better than this, I guess I will not take the trouble to inherit anything more." Well, run the risk of it, every man on the earth has the privilege. The Gospel is preached, sin revives, some die and some contend against it—some receive it and some do not; but this is the sin of the people—truth is told them and they reject it. This is the sin of the world. "Light has come into the world, but men love darkness rather than light, because their deeds are evil." So said Jesus in his day. We say, here is the Gospel of life and salvation, and everyone that will receive it, glory, honor, immortality and eternal life are theirs; if they reject it, they take their chance. 15:128.

Honesty in Action Will Temper Judgment—A man or woman must know the ways of God before they can become ungodly. Persons may be sinners, may be unrighteous, may be wicked, who have never heard the plan of salvation, who are even unacquainted with the history of the Son of Man, or who have heard of the name of the Savior, and perhaps, the history of his life while on the earth, but have been taught unbelief through their tradition and education; but to be ungodly, in the strict sense of the word, they must measurably understand godliness. 4:58.

Don't cast them down to hell for their honest belief. 2:140.

If you do evil ignorantly and in good faith, I promise you it shall result in good. 7:139.

It has appeared to me, from my childhood to this day, as a piece of complete nonsense, to talk about the inhabitants of the earth being thus irretrievably lost—to talk of my father and mother, and yours, or our ancestors, who have lived faithfully according to the best light they had; but because they had not the everlasting covenant and the holy Priesthood in their midst, that they should go to hell and roast there to all eternity. It is nonsense to me; it always was, and is yet. 6:291.

So far as mortality is concerned, millions of the inhabitants of the earth live according to the best light they have—according to the best knowledge they possess. I have told you frequently that they will receive according to their works; and all, who live according to the best principles in their possession, or that they can understand, will receive peace, glory, comfort, joy and a crown that will be far beyond what they are anticipating. They will not be lost. 6:332.

I say to every priest on the face of the earth, I do not care whether they be Christian, Pagan or Mohammedan, you should live according to the best light you have; and if you do you will receive all the glory you ever anticipated. We should not be prejudiced against you in the least; even if you are against us and declare falsehoods about us we should not retaliate. But how prone we are to rebuke if we are rebuked, or if we receive a sharp word to return one. The Latter-day Saints have to overcome this; and the world may cry out and say all manner of evil against us, but, my brethren and sisters, let us so live that it will be said falsely. 14:151.

The very heathen we were talking about; if they have a law, no matter who made it, and do the best they know how, they will have a glory which is beyond your imagination, by any description I might give; you cannot conceive of the least portion of the glory of God prepared for his beings, the workmanship of his hands. 3:93.

None will become angels to the Devil except those who have sinned against the Holy Ghost. 11:271.

Hell Defined—Any person knowing and understanding the Scriptures as they are, and understanding the mind and will of God, can understand at once that when he is shut out from the presence of the Lord, when he does not hear his voice, sees not his face, receives not the ministering of his angels or ministering spirits, and has no messenger from the heavens to visit him, he must surely be in hell. 2:137.

Were the wicked, in their sins, under the necessity of walking into the presence of the Father and Son, hand-in-hand with those who believe that all will be saved—that Jesus will leave none, their condition would be more excruciating and unendurable than to dwell in the lake that burns with fire and brimstone. The fatalist's doctrine consigns to hell the infant not a span long, while the adulterer, whoremonger, thief, liar, false swearer, murderer, and every other abominable character, if they but repent on the gallows or their deathbeds, are by the same doctrine, forced into the presence of the Father and the Son, which, could they enter there would be a hell to them. 8:153-154.

There is not a man or woman, who violates the covenants made with their God, that will not be required to pay the debt. The blood of Christ will never wipe that out, your own blood must atone for it; and the judgments of the Almighty will come, sooner or later, and every man and woman will have to atone for breaking their covenants. To what degree? Will they have to go to hell? They are in hell enough now. I do not wish them in a greater hell, when their consciences condemn them all the time. Let compassion reign in our bosoms. Try to comprehend how weak we are, how we are organized, how the spirit and the flesh are continually at war. 3:247.

Will I prophesy evil? No. Let us prophesy good. But the justice and mercy of God must have their demands. 8:195.

The Second Death—What is that we call death, compared to the agonies of the second death? If people could see it, as Joseph and Sidney saw it, they would pray that the vision be closed up; for they could not endure the sight. Neither could they endure the sight of the Father and the Son in their glory, for it would consume them. 18:217.

It is a curious idea, but one in favor of which there is much testimony, that when people take the downward road, one that is calculated to destroy them, they will actually in every sense of the word be destroyed. Will they be what is termed annihilated? No, there is no such thing as annihilation, for you cannot destroy the elements of which things are made. 2:302.

None will be lost or turned away except those who sin against the Holy Ghost. 16:32.

Measure of Human Judgment—Every man and woman has got to have clean hands and a pure heart, to execute judgment, else they had better let the matter alone. 3:247.

I have a certain knowledge within me that the Elders of Israel will never be permitted to lay judgment to the line and righteousness to the plummet, with regard to the wicked and ungodly, until they understand righteous principles, and live to them. 7:46.

You may judge of the truth you hear today and of that which you will hear in times to come; for we shall be judges of ourselves as well as of our enemies, and we shall also judge angels. 5:258.

When the judgment is given to the Saints, it will be because of their righteousness, because they will judge even as the angels and as the Gods, and not as the wicked do. 19:7.

Chapter XXXV

SALVATION

Universal Salvation—Salvation is the full existence of man, of the angels, and the Gods, it is eternal life—the life which was, which is, and which is to come. And we, as human beings, are heirs to all this life, if we apply ourselves strictly to obey the requirements of the law of God, and continue in faithfulness. 12:111.

The economy of heaven is to gather in all, and save everybody who can be saved. 11:262.

People should understand that there is no man born upon the face of the earth but what can be saved in the Kingdom of God, if he is disposed to be. 8:160.

I have heard a great many sermons, prayers and exhortations for people to go and get religion and have their names written in the "Lamb's Book of Life." I want to inform the whole world, all the sons and daughters of Adam, that their names are written there, and there they will remain to all eternity unless they by their evil acts blot them out. 13:149.

There never was any person over-saved; all who have been saved, and that ever will be in the future, are only just saved, and then it is not without a struggle to overcome, that calls into exercise every energy of the soul. 2:132.

All that have lived or will live on this earth will have the privilege of receiving the Gospel. They will have Apostles, Prophets, and ministers there, as we have here, to guide them in the ways of truth and righteousness, and lead them back to God. All will have a chance for salvation and eternal life. 6:149.

If our faith is one, and we are united to gain one grand object, and I, as an individual, can possibly get into the celestial kingdom, you and every other person, by the same rule, can also enter there. 2:132.

How many shall be preserved? All who do not deny and defy the power and character of the Son of God—all who do not sin against the Holy Ghost. 6:292.

The heathen nations that now exist and that have existed on the earth will all be blessed, will see the time when they will have the privilege of receiving the blessings of the covenant established on the earth by the Son of God, and through it will be brought into glory and rest. 8:83.

The names of every son and daughter of Adam are already written in the Lamb's Book of Life. Is there ever a time when they will be taken out of it? Yes, when they become sons of perdition, and not till then. Every person has the privilege of retaining it there for ever and ever. If they neglect that privilege, then their names will be erased, and not till then. All the names of the human family are written there, and the Lord will hold them there until they come to the knowledge of the truth, that they can rebel against him, and can sin against the Holy Ghost; then they will be thrust down to hell, and their names be blotted out from the Lamb's Book of Life. 6:297.

Now, the inquiry on our minds is, are all the world going to share in these blessings? Yes, all the world. Are there none going to be lost? Are there none going to suffer the wrath of the Almighty? I can say, in the first place, as I have said all my life, where I have been preaching, I never had the spirit to preach hell and damnation to the people. I have tried a great many times—I tried last Sabbath, and I have tried today to come to that point—the sufferings of the wicked. They will suffer, it seems; but I cannot get my heart upon anything else, only salvation for the people. All nations are going to share in these blessings; all are incorporated in the redemption of the Savior. He has tasted death for every man; they are all in his power, and he saves them all, as he says, except the sons of perdition; and the Father has put all the creations upon this earth in his power. The earth itself, and mankind upon it, the brute beasts, the fish of the sea, and the fowls of heaven, the insects, and every creeping thing, with all things pertaining to this earthly ball,—all are in the hands of the Savior, and he has redeemed them all. 6:296-297.

Where God and Christ dwell, that is a kingdom of itself—the celestial kingdom. 7:288.

How many Gods there are, and how many places there are in their kingdoms, is not for me to say; but I can say this, which is a source of much comfort, consolation, and gratification to me: Behold the goodness, the long-suffering, the kindness, and the strong parental feeling of our Father and God in preparing the way and providing the means to save the children of men—not alone the Latter-day Saints—not alone those who have the privilege of the first principles of the celestial law, but to save all. It is a universal salvation—a universal redemption. 8:35.

It will be a pleasure to know that we have saved all the Father gave into our power. Jesus said that he lost none except the sons of perdition. He will lose none of his brethren, except sons of perdition. Let us save all the Father puts in our power. 9:124.

All heaven is anxious that the people should be saved. The

heavens weep over the people, because of their hard-heartedness, unbelief, and slowness to believe and act. 4:196.

Our religion is adapted to the capacity of the whole human family. It does not send a portion of the people to howl in torment for ever and ever, but it reaches after the last son and daughter of Adam and Eve, and will pluck them from the prison, unlock the doors, and burst the bonds and bring forth every soul who will receive salvation. 12:309.

The salvation that Jesus has purchased will reach the whole human family and save, in a kingdom or in some place where they will enjoy to the extent of their capacity, those who reject not the Gospel and despise not the Savior. 14:133.

There is a chance for those who have lived and for those who now live. The Gospel has come. Truth and light and righteousness are sent forth into the world, and those who receive them will be saved in the celestial kingdom of God. And many of those who, through ignorance, through tradition, superstition, and the erroneous precepts of the fathers, do not receive them, will yet inherit a good and glorious kingdom, and will enjoy more and receive more than ever entered into the heart of man to conceive, unless he has had a revelation. 8:36.

The Way to Salvation—You will be no more perfect in your sphere, when you are exalted to thrones, principalities, and powers, than you are required to be and are capable of being in your sphere today. 6:99.

No man will be saved and come into the presence of the Father, only through the Gospel of Jesus Christ—the same for one as the other. The Lord has his cause, his ways, his work; he will finish it up. Jesus is laboring with his might to sanctify and redeem the earth and to bring back his brethren and sisters into the presence of the Father. We are laboring with him for the purification of the whole human family, that we and they may be prepared to dwell with God in his Kingdom. 13:150.

No matter what the outward appearance is—if I can know of a truth that the hearts of the people are fully set to do the will of their Father in Heaven, though they may falter and do a great many things through the weakness of human nature, yet they will be saved. 5:256.

And if we accept salvation on the terms it is offered to us, we have got to be honest in every thought, in our reflections, in our meditations, in our private circles, in our deals, in our declarations, and in every act of our lives, fearless and regardless of every principle of error, of every principle of falsehood that may be presented. 5:124.

To look for salvation fifty years hence and do nothing for salvation at the present time is preposterous. God has placed the means of salvation within our reach, and the volition of the creature is at his own disposal. When his sons and daughters avail themselves of the means he has supplied for their salvation, doing good for themselves, it is gratifying to him. 10:221.

Salvation an Individual Work—Though our interest is one as a people, yet remember, salvation is an individual work; it is every person for himself. I mean more by this than I have time to tell you in full, but I will give you a hint. There are those in the Church who calculate to be saved by the righteousness of others. They will miss their mark. They are those who will arrive just as the gate is shut, so in that case you may be shut out; then you will call upon some one, who, by their own faithfulness, through the mercy of Jesus Christ, have entered in through the celestial gate, to come and open it for you; but to do this is not their province. Such will be the fate of those persons who vainly hope to be saved upon the righteousness and through the influence of Brother Somebody. I forewarn you therefore to cultivate righteousness and faithfulness in yourselves, which is the only passport into celestial happiness. 2:132.

If Brother Brigham shall take a wrong track, and be shut out of the Kingdom of heaven, no person will be to blame but Brother Brigham. I am the only being in heaven, earth, or hell, that can be blamed.

This will equally apply to every Latter-day Saint. Salvation is an individual operation. I am the only person that can possibly save myself. When salvation is sent to me, I can reject or receive it. In receiving it, I yield implicit obedience and submission to its great Author throughout my life, and to those whom he shall appoint to instruct me; in rejecting it, I follow the dictates of my own will in preference to the will of my Creator. There are those among this people who are influenced, controlled, and biased in their thoughts, actions, and feelings by some other individual or family, on whom they place their dependence for spiritual and temporal instruction, and for salvation in the end. These persons do not depend upon themselves for salvation, but upon another of their poor, weak, fellow mortals. 1:312.

Many Degrees of Salvation—When God revealed to Joseph Smith and Sidney Rigdon that there was a place prepared for all, according to the light they had received and their rejection of evil and practice of good, it was a great trial to many, and some apostatized because God was not going to send to everlasting punishment heathens and infants, but had a place of salvation, in due time, for all, and would bless the honest and virtuous and truthful, whether they ever belonged to any church or not. It was a new doctrine to this generation, and many stumbled at it. 16:42.

These words set forth the fact to which Jesus referred when he said, "In my Father's house are many mansions." How many I am not prepared to say; but here are three distinctly spoken of: the celestial, the highest; the terrestrial, the next below it, and the telestial, the third. If we were to take the pains to read what the Lord has said to his people in the latter days we should find that he has made provision for all the inhabitants of the earth; every creature who desires, and who strives in the least, to overcome evil and subdue iniquity within himself or herself, and to live worthy of a glory, will possess one. We who have received the fulness of the Gospel of the Son of God, or the Kingdom of heaven that has come to earth, are in possession of those laws, ordinances, commandments and revelations that will prepare us, by strict obedience, to inherit the celestial kingdom, to go into the presence of the Father and the Son. 14:148.

There are millions and millions of kingdoms that the people have no conception of. The Christians of the day have no knowledge of God, of godliness, of eternity, of the worlds that are, and that have been, and that are coming forth. There are myriads of people pertaining to this earth who will come up and receive a glory according to their capacity. 6:347.

Is it not a glorious thought that there are kingdoms, mansions of glory and comfortable habitations prepared for all the sons and daughters of Adam, except the sons of perdition? All will not have part in the first resurrection, and perhaps many will not appear in the second; but all will be resurrected, and, except the sons of perdition, enter kingdoms, the least of which I presume is more glorious than ever John Wesley saw in vision. 8:196-197.

Exaltation Proportioned to Capacity—The man or woman who lives worthily is now in a state of salvation. 1:6.

Is every man and woman capable of receiving the highest glory of God? No. 9:104.

Are all spirits endowed alike? No, not by any means. Will all be equal in the celestial kingdom? No. Some spirits are more noble than others; some are capable of receiving more than others. There is the same variety in the spirit world that you behold here, yet they are of the same parentage, of one Father, one God. 4:268.

Some are not capable of the same exaltation as are others, arising from the difference in the conduct and capacities of people. There is also a difference in the spirit world. It is the design, the wish, the will, and mind of the Lord that the inhabitants of the earth should be exalted to thrones, kingdoms, principalities, and powers, according to their capacities. In their exaltation, one may be capable of presiding over ten cities, while another may not be capable of presiding over more than five, another over only two, and another over but one. They must all first be subjected to sin and to the calamities of mortal flesh, in order to prove themselves worthy; then the Gospel is ready to take hold of them and bring them up, unite them, enlighten their understandings, and make them one in the Lord Jesus, that their faith, prayers, hopes, affections, and all their desires may ever be concentrated in one. 6:97.

The Celestial Kingdom—The celestial is the highest of all. The telestial and terrestrial are also spoken of; and how many more kingdoms of glory there are, is not for me to say. I do not know that they are not innumerable. This is a source of great joy to me. 8:35.

The Kingdom that this people are in pertains to the celestial kingdom; it is a Kingdom in which we can prepare to go into the presence of the Father and the Son. 8:197.

The men and women, who desire to obtain seats in the celestial kingdom, will find that they must battle every day. 11:14.

As for a person being saved in the celestial kingdom of God without being prepared to dwell in a pure and holy place, it is all nonsense and ridiculous; and if there be any who think they can gain the presence of the Father and the Son by fighting for, instead of living, their religion, they will be mistaken, consequently the quicker we make up our minds to live our religion the better it will be for us. 14:157.

Who can define the divinity of man? Only those who understand the true principles of eternity—the principles that pertain to life and salvation. Man, by being exalted, does not lose the power and ability naturally given to him; but, on the contrary, by taking the road that leads to life, he gains more power, more influence and ability during every step he progresses therein. 7:274.

Our spirits, thousands of years ago, were first begotten; and at the consummation of all things, when the Savior has finished his work and presented it to the Father, he will be crowned. None of you will receive your crowns of glory, immortality, and eternal lives before he receives his. He will be crowned first, and then we shall be crowned, every one in his order; for the work is finished, and the spirit is complete in its organization with the tabernacle. The world is the first to be redeemed, and the people last to be crowned upon it. 6:282.

Chapter XXXVI

TEMPLES AND SALVATION FOR THE DEAD

Saints Always Commanded to Build Temples—We are going to build temples. This law is given to the children of men. 14:95.

Concerning revelations pertaining to building temples, I will give you the words of our beloved Prophet while he was yet living upon the earth. Many of us that are here today, were with him from the commencement of the Church. He was frequently speaking upon the building of temples in Kirtland, Missouri, and Illinois. When the people refused in Kirtland to build a temple, unless by a special revelation, it grieved his heart that they should be so penurious in their feelings as to require the Lord to command them to build a house to his name. It was not only grievous to him, but to the Holy Spirit also. He frequently said that if it were not for the covetousness of the people, the Lord would not give revelations concerning the building of temples, for we already knew all about them; the revelations giving us the order of the Priesthood made known to us what is wanted in that respect at our hands. 1:277.

We that are here are enjoying a privilege that we have no knowledge of any other people enjoying since the days of Adam, that is, to have a temple completed, wherein all the ordinances of the house of God can be bestowed upon his people. Brethren and sisters, do you understand this? It seems that a great many of the people know nothing about it. It is true that Solomon built a temple for the purpose of giving endowments, but from what we can learn of the history of that time they gave very few if any endowments, and one of the high priests was murdered by wicked and corrupt men, who had already begun to apostatize, because he would not reveal those things appertaining to the Priesthood that were forbidden him to reveal until he came to the proper place. I will not say but what Enoch had temples and officiated therein, but we have no account of it. We know that he raised up a people so pure and holy that they were not permitted to remain with the wicked inhabitants of the earth, but were taken to another place. 18:303.

The earth, the Lord says, abides its creation; it has been baptized with water, and will, in the future, be baptized with fire and the Holy Ghost, to be prepared to go back into the celestial presence of God, with all things that dwell upon it which have, like the earth, abided the law of their creation. Taking this view of the matter, it may be asked why we build temples. We build temples because there is not a house on the face of the whole earth that has been reared to God's name which will in anywise compare with his character, and that he can consistently call his house. There are places on the earth where the Lord can come and dwell, if he pleases. They may be found on the tops of high mountains, or in some cavern or places where sinful man has never marked the soil with his polluted feet.

He requires his servants to build him a house that he can come to and where he can make known his will. 10:252.

We enjoy the privilege of entering into a temple, built to the name of God, and receiving the ordinances of his house, with all the keys and blessings preparatory to entering into the "lives"; we also enjoy the privilege of administering for our fathers and mothers, our grandfathers and grandmothers, for those who have slept without the Gospel. 19:22.

In the spirit world those who have got the victory go on to prepare the way for those who live in the flesh, fulfilling the work of saviors on Mount Zion.

To accomplish this work there will have to be not only one temple but thousands of them, and thousands and tens of thousands of men and women will go into those temples and officiate for people who have lived as far back as the Lord shall reveal. If we are faithful enough to go back and build that great temple which Joseph has written about, and should the Lord acknowledge the labor of his servants, then watch, for you will see somebody whom you have seen before, and many of you will see him whom you have not seen before, but you will know him as soon as you see him. 3:372.

Temples Indispensable for Higher Ordinances—In consequence of our having been driven from our homes, and because of our destitute circumstances, the Lord has permitted us to do what we have done, namely, to use this Endowment House for temple purposes. But since, through the mercies and blessings of God, we are able to build temples, it is the will and commandment of God that we do so. 18:263.

Do we need a temple? We do, to prepare us to enter in through the gate into the city where the Saints are at rest. Ordinances necessary to this have not yet been performed and cannot be in the absence of a suitable place. We wish a temple, not for the public congregation, but for the Priesthood, wherein to arrange and organize fully the Priesthood in its order and degrees, to administer the ordinance of the Priesthood to the Saints for their exaltation. 9:240.

We cannot now administer the further ordinances of God, in the fullest sense of the word, legally unto the people, neither shall we be able to do so until we have a temple built for that purpose. Some may consider that I am notifying our common foe in saying this, but it is true, notwithstanding, and our common foe knows it. We must be situated in local circumstances wherein we can efficiently administer in those ordinances of the house of God that cannot be administered to a people while they are scattered abroad among the nations of the wicked. 12:162.

There are some of the sealing ordinances that cannot be administered in the house that we are now using; we can only administer in it some of the first ordinances of the Priesthood pertaining to the endowment. There are more advanced ordinances that cannot be administered there; we would, therefore, like a temple, but I am willing to wait a few years for it. I want to see the temple built in a manner that it will endure through the Millennium. This is not the only temple we shall build; there will be hundreds of them built and dedicated to the Lord. This temple will be known as the first temple built in the mountains by the Latter-day Saints. And when the Millennium is over, and all the sons and daughters of Adam and Eve, down to the last of their posterity, who come within the reach of the clemency of the Gospel, have been redeemed in hundreds of temples through the administration of their children as proxies for them, I want that temple still to stand as a proud monument of the faith, perseverance and industry of the Saints of God in the mountains, in the nineteenth century. 10:254.

We have often told you that we want to build a temple, but not for convening promiscuous congregations. I inform you, long before you see the walls reared and the building completed, that it will be for the purpose of the Priesthood, and not for meetings of the people; we shall not hold public meetings in it. I should like to see the temple built, in which you will see the Priesthood in its order and true organization, each Quorum in its place. 8:202-203.

Endowments Given in Temples—The commandments contained in the New Testament with regard to the ordinances of the house of God are obligatory upon us. 13:314.

Every individual who is prepared for the celestial kingdom must go through the same things. 3:195.

It is absolutely necessary that the Saints should receive the further ordinances of the house of God before this short existence shall come to a close, that they may be prepared and fully able to pass all the sentinels leading into the celestial kingdom and into the presence of God. 12:163-164.

Then go on and build the temples of the Lord, that you may receive the endowments in store for you, and possess the keys of the eternal Priesthood, that you may receive every word, sign, and token, and be made acquainted with the laws of angels, and of the kingdom of our Father and our God, and know how to pass from one degree to another, and enter fully into the joy of your Lord. 2:315.

Some of us are not dependent on the temple for our endowment blessings, for we have received them under the hands of Joseph the Prophet, and know where to go to bestow the same on others. You may ask me whether the leaders of this Church have received all their endowment blessings. I think that we have got all that you can get in your probation, if you live to be the age of Methuselah; and we can give what we possess to others who are worthy. 10:254.

A great many of you have had your endowments, and you know what a vote with uplifted hands means.

It is a sign which you make in token of your covenant with God and with one another, and it is for you to perform your vows. When you raise your hands to heaven and let them fall and then pass on with your covenants unfulfilled, you will be cursed.

I feel sometimes like lecturing men and women severely who enter into covenants without realizing the nature of the covenants they make, and who use little or no effort to fulfil them.

Some Elders go to the nations and preach the Gospel of life and salvation, and return without thoroughly understanding the nature of the covenant. It is written in the Bible that every man should perform his own vows, even if to his own hurt; in this way you will show to all creation and to God that you are full of integrity. 3:332.

Most of you, my brethren, are Elders, Seventies, or High Priests; perhaps there is not a Priest or Teacher present. The reason of this is that when we give the brethren their endowments, we are obliged to confer upon them the Melchizedek Priesthood; but I expect to see the day, when we shall be so situated that we can say to a company of brethren, You can go and receive the ordinances pertaining to the Aaronic order of Priesthood, and then you can go into the world and preach the Gospel, or do something that will prove whether you will honor that Priesthood before you receive more. Now we pass them through the ordinances of both Priesthoods in one day, but this is not as it should be and would, if we had a temple wherein to administer these ordinances. But this is all right at present; we should not be satisfied in any other way, and consequently we do according to the circumstances we are placed in. 10:309.

The ordinances of the house of God are for the salvation of the human family. We are the only ones on the earth at the present time, that we have any knowledge of, who hold the keys of salvation committed to the children of men from the heavens by the Lord Almighty; and inasmuch as there are those who hold these keys, it is important that they should be acted upon for the salvation of the human family. The building of temples, places in which the ordinances of salvation are administered, is necessary to carry out the plan of redemption, and it is a glorious subject upon which to address the Saints. 13:262.

Giving endowments to a great many proves their overthrow, through revealing things to them which they cannot keep. They are not worthy to receive them. 4:372.

Were it not for what is revealed concerning the sealing ordinances, children born out of the covenant could not be sealed to their parents. 18:249.

The ordinances of the house of God are expressly for the Church of the Firstborn. 8:154.

I would rather see this people cleansed, and give the righteous their endowments after they have waited awhile. Let the poor, and those who are humble before the Lord, have the first chance. 2:144.

Vicarious Work for the Dead in Temples—We are preaching to them the Gospel of Salvation—to the dead—through those who have lived in this dispensation. 3:90.

There is an opportunity for men who are in the spirit to receive the Gospel. Jesus, while his body lay in the grave two nights and one day, went to the world of spirits to show the brethren how they should build up the kingdom, and bring spirits to the knowledge of the truth in the spirit world; he went to set them the pattern there, as he had done on this earth. Hence you perceive that there, spirits have the privilege of embracing the truth.

You may ask if they are baptized there? No. Can they have hands laid upon them for the gift of the Holy Ghost? No. None of the outward ordinances that pertain to the flesh are administered there, but the light, glory, and power of the Holy Ghost are enjoyed just as freely as upon this earth; and there are laws which govern and control the spirit world, and to which they are subject. 2:138.

Now a few words to the brethren and sisters upon the doctrine and ordinances of the house of God. All who have lived on the earth according to the best light they had, and would have received the fulness of the Gospel had it been preached to them, are worthy of a glorious resurrection, and will attain to this by being administered for, in the flesh, by those who have the authority. All others will have a resurrection, and receive a glory, except those who have sinned against the Holy Ghost. It is supposed by this people that we have all the ordinances in our possession for life and salvation, and exaltation, and that we are administering in these ordinances. This is not the case. We are in possession of all the ordinances that can be administered in the flesh; but there are other ordinances and administrations that must be administered beyond this world. I know you would ask what they are. I will mention one. We have not, neither can we receive here, the ordinance and the keys of the resurrection. They will be given to those who have passed off this stage of action and have received their bodies again, as many have already done and many more will. They will be ordained, by those who hold the keys of the resurrection, to go forth and resurrect the Saints, just as we receive the ordinance of baptism, then the keys of authority to baptize others for the remission of their sins. This is one of the ordinances we cannot receive here, and there are many more. We hold the authority to dispose of, alter and change the elements; but we have not received authority to organize native element, to even make a spear of grass grow.

We have no such ordinance here. We organize according to men in the flesh. By combining the elements and planting the seed, we cause vegetables, trees, grain, etc., to come forth. We are organizing a Kingdom here according to the pattern that the Lord has given for people in the flesh, but not for those who have received the resurrection, although it is a similitude. Another item: We have not the power in the flesh to create and bring forth or produce a spirit; but we have the power to produce a temporal body; the germ of this, God has placed within us. And when our spirits receive our bodies, and through our faithfulness we are worthy to be crowned, we will then receive authority to produce both spirit and body. But these keys we cannot receive in the flesh. Herein, brethren, you can perceive that we have not finished, and cannot finish our work, while we live here, no more than Jesus did while he was in the flesh.

We cannot receive, while in the flesh, the keys to form and fashion kingdoms and to organize matter, for they are beyond our capacity and calling, beyond this world. In the resurrection, men who have been faithful and diligent in all things in the flesh, have kept their first and second estate, and are worthy to be crowned Gods, even the Sons of God, will be ordained to organize matter. How much matter do you suppose there is between here and some of the fixed stars which we can see? Enough to frame many, very many millions of such earths as this, yet it is now so diffused, clear and pure, that we look through it and behold the stars. Yet the matter is there. Can you form any conception of this? Can you form any idea of the minuteness of matter? 15:136.

Do you recollect that in about the year 1840-41, Joseph had a revelation concerning the dead? He had been asked the question a good many times: "What is the condition of the dead, those that lived and died without the Gospel? It was a matter of inquiry with him. He considered this question for himself, and for the brethren and the Church, "What is the condition of the dead? What will be their fate? Is there no way today by which they can receive their blessings as there was in the days of the Apostles, and when the Gospel was preached upon the earth in ancient days?" When Joseph received the revelation that we have in our possession concerning the dead, the subject was opened to him, not in full, but in part, and he kept on receiving. When he had first received the knowledge by the spirit of revelation how the dead could be officiated for, there are brethren and sisters, here, I can see quite a number here who were in Nauvoo, and you recollect that when this doctrine was first revealed, and in hurrying in the administration of baptism for the dead, that sisters were baptized for their male friends, were baptized for their fathers, their grandfathers, their mothers and their grandmothers, etc. I just mention this so that you will come to understanding, that as we knew nothing about this matter at first, the old Saints recollect, there was little by little given and the subject was made plain, but little was given at once. Consequently, in the first place people were baptized for their friends and no record was kept. Joseph afterwards kept a record. Then women were baptized for men and men for women, etc. It would be very strange, you know, to the eyes of the wise and those that understood the things pertaining to eternity, if we were called upon to commence a work that we could not finish. This, therefore, was regulated and all set in order; for it was revealed that if a woman was baptized for a man, she could not be ordained for him, neither could she be made an Apostle or a Patriarch for the man, consequently the sisters are to be baptized for their own sex only.

This doctrine of baptism for the dead is a great doctrine, one of the most glorious doctrines that was revealed to the human family; and there are light, power, glory, honor and immortality in it. 16:165.

There are many of the ordinances of the house of God that must be performed in a temple that is erected expressly for the purpose. There are other ordinances that we can administer without a temple. You know that there are some which you have received—baptism, the laying on of hands for the gift of the Holy Ghost, such as the speaking in and interpretation of tongues, prophesying, healing, discerning of spirits, etc., and many blessings bestowed upon the people, we have the privilege of receiving without a temple. There are other blessings, that will not be received, and ordinances that will not be performed according to the law that the Lord has revealed, without their being done in a temple prepared for that purpose. We can, at the present time, go into the Endowment House and be baptized for the dead, receive our washings and anointing, etc., for there we have a font that has been erected, dedicated expressly for baptizing people for the remission of sins, for their health and for their dead friends; in this the Saints have the privilege of being baptized for their friends. We also have the privilege of sealing women to men, without a temple. This we can do in the Endowment House; but when we come to other sealing ordinances, ordinances pertaining to the holy Priesthood, to connect the chain of the Priesthood from Father Adam until now, by sealing children to their parents, being sealed for our forefathers, etc., they cannot be done without a temple. When the ordinances are carried out in the temples that will be erected, men will be sealed to their fathers, and those who have slept, clear up to Father Adam. This will have to be done, because of the chain of the Priesthood being broken upon the earth. The Priesthood has left the people, but in the first place the people left the Priesthood. They transgressed the laws, changed the ordinance, and broke the everlasting covenant, and the Priesthood left them; but not until they had left the Priesthood. This Priesthood has been restored again, and by its authority we shall be connected with our fathers, by the ordinance of sealing, until we shall form a perfect chain from Father Adam down to the closing up scene. This ordinance will not be performed anywhere but in a temple; neither will children be sealed to their living parents in any other place than a temple. For instance, a man and his wife come into the Church, and they have a family of children. These children have been begotten out of the covenant, because the marriage of their parents is not recognized by the Lord as performed by his authority; they have, therefore, to be sealed to their parents, or else they cannot claim them in eternity; they will be distributed according to the wisdom of the Lord, who does all things right. When we had a temple prepared in Nauvoo, many of the brethren had their children, who were out of the covenant, sealed to them, and endowments were given. Then parents, after receiving their endowments and being sealed for time and eternity, and they have other children; they are begotten and born under the covenant, and they are the rightful heirs to the kingdom, they possess the keys of the kingdom. Children born unto parents, before the latter enter into the fulness of the covenants, have to be sealed to them in a temple to become legal heirs of the Priesthood. It is true they can receive the ordinances, they can receive their endowments, and be blessed in common with their parents; but still the parents cannot claim them legally and lawfully in eternity unless they are sealed to them. Yet the chain would not be complete without this sealing ordinance being performed.

Now, to illustrate this, I will refer to my own father's family. My father died before the endowments were given. None of his children have been sealed to him. If you recollect, you that were in Nauvoo, we were very much hurried in the little time we spent there after the temple was built. The mob was there ready to destroy us; they were ready to burn our houses, they had been doing it for a long time; but we finished the temple according to the commandment that was given to Joseph, and then took our departure. Our time, therefore, was short, and we had no time to attend to this. My father's children, consequently, have not been sealed to him. Perhaps all of his sons may go into eternity, into the spirit world, before this can be attended to; but this will make no difference; the heirs of the family will attend to this if it is not for a hundred years.

It will have to be done sometime. If, however, we get a temple prepared before the sons of my father shall all have gone into the spirit world, if there are any of them remaining, they will attend to this, and as heirs be permitted to receive the ordinances for our father and mother. This is only one case, and, to illustrate this subject perfectly, I might have to refer to hundreds of examples for each case. 16:186.

We trust in God. I reckon he will fight our battles and we will be baptized for and in behalf of the human family during a thousand years; and we will have hundreds of temples and thousands of men and women officiating therein for those who have fallen asleep, without having had the privilege of hearing and obeying the Gospel, that they may be brought forth and have a glorious resurrection, and enjoy the kingdom which God has prepared for them. The Devil will fight hard to hinder us, and we shall not take an inch of ground except by obedience to the power of, and faith in, the Gospel of the Son of God. The whole world is opposed to this doctrine. But is there any harm in it? If they could only see it as it is in the Lord, they would rejoice in it, and instead of fighting it, they would praise God for having revealed so glorious a doctrine. Suppose that the notion entertained by some is true, that after the death of our bodies our spirits sleep an eternal sleep, and I am baptized for my father, grandfather, and so on, above, beneath, or around about the earth! All will admit that no harm would be done in practicing these ordinances. Then let us alone if our practices will do no harm, why oppose us in their observance? The result might possibly affect beneficially our progenitors, and then you who oppose would be found fighting against God. Better let the Gospel have its course. 13:330.

Let me say to you, if it is true that no man can enter the kingdom of God unless he is born of the water and of the Spirit, God must provide a plan by which those who have died ignorant of the Gospel may have the privilege of doing so, or he would appear to be a partial being. Has he provided that way? He has. The Christian world have taught, preached, contemplated, meditated, sung about and prayed for the Millennium. What are you going to do during that period, Christians? Do you know what the Millennium is for, and what work will have to be done during that period? Suppose the Christian world were now one in heart, faith, sentiment and works, so that the Lord could commence the Millennium in power and glory, do you know what would be done? Would you sit and sing yourselves away to everlasting bliss? No, I reckon not. I think there is a work to be done then which the whole world seems determined we shall not do. What is it? To build temples. We never yet commenced to lay the foundation of a temple but what all hell was in arms against us. That is the difficulty now. We have commenced the foundation of this temple. What are we going to do in these temples? Anything to be done there? Yes, and we will not wait for the Millennium and the fulness of the glory of God on the earth; we will commence as soon as we have a temple, and work for the salvation of our forefathers; we will get their genealogies as far as we can. By and by, we shall get them perfect. In these temples we will officiate in the ordinances of the Gospel of Jesus Christ for our friends, for no man can enter the Kingdom of God without being born of the water and of the Spirit. We will officiate for those who are in the spirit world, where Jesus went to preach to the spirits, as Peter has written in the third chapter, verses 18, 19, 20, of his first epistle.

We will also have hands laid on us for the reception of the Holy Ghost; and then we will receive the washing and anointings for and in their behalf, preparatory to their becoming heirs of God and joint-heirs with Christ. Are you going to do this, Latter-day Saints? Yes. What will the Christian world do with their dead? Let them sleep an eternal sleep, for there are no provisions made for them in the Gospel they believe in and have taught to them. 13:329.

We will bring up all the inhabitants of the earth, except those who have sinned against the Holy Ghost, and save them in some kingdom where they will receive more glory and honor than ever the Methodist contemplated. This should be a comfort and a consolation to all the inhabitants of the earth. They will not save themselves, millions have not had a chance, and millions now living, through the strength of their traditions, will not do it; their consciences and feelings are bound up in their systems and creeds, whereas if they felt as independent as they should feel, they would break loose and receive the truths; but they will live and die in bondage, and we calculate to officiate for them. Many a man I know of, who has fallen asleep, we have been baptized for, since the Church was organized—good, honest, honorable men, charitable to all, living good, virtuous lives. We will not let them go down to hell; God will not. The plan of salvation is ample to bring them all up and place them where they may enjoy all they could anticipate. 14:97.

Can we do anything for them? Yes. What are we trying to build a temple for? And we shall not only build a temple here, if we are successful, and are blessed and preserved, but we shall probably commence two or three more, and so on as fast as the work requires, for the express purpose of redeeming our dead. When I get a revelation that some of my progenitors lived and died without the blessings of the Gospel, or even hearing it preached, but were as honest as I am, as upright as I am, or as any man or woman could be upon the earth; as righteous, so far as they knew how, as any Apostle or Prophet that ever lived, I will go and be baptized, confirmed, washed, and anointed, and go through all the ordinances and endowments for them, that their way may be opened to the celestial kingdom.

As I have frequently told you, that is the work of the Millennium. It is the work that has to be performed by the seed of Abraham, the chosen seed, the royal seed, the blessed of the Lord, those the Lord made covenants with. They will step forth, and save every son and daughter of Adam who will receive salvation here on the earth; and all the spirits in the spirit world will be preached to, conversed with, and the principles of salvation carried to them, that they may have the privilege of receiving the Gospel; and they will have plenty of children here on the earth to officiate for them in those ordinances of the Gospel that pertain to the flesh. 2:138.

What do you suppose the fathers would say if they could speak from the dead? Would they not say, "We have lain here thousands of years, here in this prison house, waiting for this dispensation to come? Here we are, bound and fettered, in the association of those who are filthy?" What would they whisper in our ears? Why, if they had the power the very thunders of heaven would be in our ears, if we could but realize the importance of the work we are engaged in. All the angels in heaven are looking at this little handful of people, and stimulating them to the salvation of the human family. So also are the devils in hell looking at this people, too, and trying to overthrow us, and the people are still shaking hands with the servants of the devil, instead of sanctifying themselves and calling upon the Lord and doing the work which he has commanded us and put into our hands to do. When I think upon this subject, I want the tongues of seven thunders to wake up the people. 18:304.

We are trying to save the living and the dead. The living can have their choice, the dead have not. Millions of them died without the Gospel, without the Priesthood, and without the opportunities that we enjoy. We shall go forth in the name of Israel's God and attend to the ordinances for them. And through the Millennium, the thousand years that the people will love and serve God, we will build temples and officiate therein for those who have slept for hundreds and thousands of years—those who would have received the truth if they had had the opportunity; and we will bring them up, and form the chain entire, back to Adam. 14:97.

If we preserve ourselves in the truth and live so that we shall be worthy of the celestial kingdom, by and by we can officiate for those who have died without the Gospel—the honest, honorable, truthful, virtuous and pure. By and by it will be said unto us, Go ye forth and be baptized for them and receive the ordinances for them, and the hearts of the children will be turned to the fathers who have slept in their graves, and they will secure to them eternal life. This must be, lest the Lord come and smite the earth with a curse. The children will go forth and revive this law for those who have slept for thousands of years who died without the Gospel. Jesus will prepare a way to bring them up into his presence. But were it not for the few who will be prepared here on the earth to officiate when the Lord shall come to reign King of nations, what would be the condition of the world? They would sleep and sleep on; but the way is prepared for their redemption. 14:151.

Hundreds of millions of human beings have been born, lived out their short earthly span, and passed away, ignorant alike of themselves and of the plan of salvation provided for them. It gives great consolation, however, to know that this glorious plan devised by Heaven follows them into the next existence, offering for their acceptance eternal life and exaltation to thrones, dominions, principalities, and powers in the presence of their Father and God, through Jesus Christ, his Son. 9:148.

If we obey this law, preserve it inviolate, live according to it, we shall be prepared to enjoy the blessings of a celestial kingdom. Will any others? Yes, thousands and millions of the inhabitants of the earth who would have received and obeyed the law that we preach, if they had had the privilege. When the Lord shall bring again Zion, and the watchmen shall see eye to eye, and Zion shall be established, saviors will come upon Mount Zion and save all the sons and daughters of Adam that are capable of being saved, by administering for them. 8:35.

Our enemies will yet be glad to come to us for safety and salvation; and we will do as Brother Kimball has said—we will save the old veteran fathers; and the time will come when we will be baptized for them, while those who trample upon the rights of their fellow men will be weltering in hell. Yes, we will bring up those old revolutionary sires and save them; for God loves men who are true to each other and are true to him. 5:212.

Who Should Represent the Dead—A man is ordained and receives his washings, anointings, and endowments for the male portion of his and his wife's progenitors, and his wife for the female portion. 3:372.

For instance, a man and his wife come into the Church; he says, "My father and mother were good people; I would like to officiate for them." "Well, have you any other friends in the Church?" "Nobody but myself and my wife." Well, now, the wife is not a blood relation, consequently she is not in reality the proper person, but she can be appointed the heir if there are no other relatives—if there are no sisters, this wife of his can officiate for the mother; but if the man has a sister in the Church, it is the privilege and place of the sister of this man, the daughter of those parents that are dead, to go and officiate—be baptized, to go and be sealed with her brother for her father and mother. If this man and woman have a daughter old enough to officiate for her grandmother, she is a blood relation, and is the heir, and can act; but if there is no daughter, the man's wife can be appointed as the heir. 16:188.

Some brethren here are anxious to know whether they can receive endowments for their sons or for their daughters. No, they cannot until we have a temple; but they can officiate in the ordinances so far as baptism and sealing are concerned. A man can be baptized for a son who died before hearing the Gospel. A woman can be baptized for her daughter, who died without the Gospel. Suppose that the father of a dead son wishes to have a wife sealed to his son; if the young woman desired as a wife is dead and have a mother or other female relative in the Church, such mother is the heir, and she can act in the sealing ordinances in the stead of her daughter. But if the young woman desired as a wife have no relative in the Church, to act in her behalf, then the mother of the young man can be baptized for her, and act as proxy for her in the sealing ordinances. We can attend to these ordinances now before the temple is built here; but no one can receive endowments for another, until a temple is prepared in which to administer them. We administer just so far as the law permits us to do. In reality we should have performed all these ordinances long ago, if we had been obedient; we should have had temples in which we could attend to all these ordinances. Now, the brethren have the privilege of being baptized for their dead friends—when I say the brethren, I mean the brethren and sisters—and these friends can be sealed. 16:187.

We will operate here, in all the ordinances of the house of God which pertains to this side of the veil, and those who pass beyond and secure to themselves a resurrection pertaining to the lives will go on and receive more and more, more and more, and will receive one after another until they are crowned Gods, even the sons of God. This idea is very consoling. We are now baptizing for the dead, and we are sealing for the dead, and if we had a temple prepared we should be giving endowments for the dead—for our fathers, mothers, grandfathers, grandmothers, uncles, aunts, relatives, friends and old associates, the history of whom we are now getting from our friends in the East. The Lord is stirring up the hearts of many there, and there is a perfect mania with some to trace their genealogies and to get up printed records of their ancestors. They do not know what they are doing it for, but the Lord is prompting them; and it will continue and run on from father to father, father to father, until they get the genealogy of their forefathers as far as they possibly can. 15:138.

We want to sacrifice enough to do the will of God in preparing to bring up those who have not had the privilege of hearing the Gospel while in the flesh, for the simple reason that, in the spirit world, they cannot officiate in the ordinances of the house of God. They have passed the ordeals, and are beyond the possibility of personally officiating for the remission of their sins and for their exaltation, consequently they are under the necessity of trusting in their friends, their children and their children's children to officiate for them, that they may be brought up into the celestial kingdom of God. 18:238.

"Saviors on Mount Zion"—We have a work to do just as important in its sphere as the Savior's work was in its sphere. Our fathers cannot be made perfect without us; we cannot be made perfect without them. They have done their work and now sleep. We are now called upon to do ours; which is to be the greatest work man ever performed on the earth. Millions of our fellow creatures who have lived upon the earth and died without a knowledge of the Gospel must be officiated for in order that they may inherit eternal life (that is, all that would have received the Gospel). And we are called upon to enter into this work. 18:213.

We are called, as it has been told you, to redeem the nations of the earth. The fathers cannot be made perfect without us; we cannot be made perfect without the fathers. There must be this chain in the holy Priesthood; it must be welded together from the latest generation that lives on the earth back to Father Adam, to bring back all that can be saved and placed where they can receive salvation and a glory in some kingdom. This Priesthood has to do it; this Priesthood is for this purpose. 13:280.

Can the fathers be saved without us? No. Can we be saved without them? No, and if we do not wake up and cease to long after the things of this earth, we will find that we as individuals will go down to hell, although the Lord will preserve a people unto himself. Now, we are ready to give endowments, do you have any feelings for those who have died without having the Gospel? 18:304.

The ordinance of sealing must be performed here man to man, and woman to man, and children to parents, etc., until the chain of generation is made perfect in the sealing ordinances back to Father Adam; hence, we have been commanded to gather ourselves together, to come out of Babylon, and sanctify ourselves, and build up the Zion of our God, by building cities and temples, redeeming countries from the solitude of nature, until the earth is sanctified and prepared for the residence of God and angels. 12:165.

The doctrines of the Savior reveal and place the believers in possession of principles whereby saviors will come upon Mount Zion to save the House of Esau, which is the Gentile nations, from sin and death,—all except those who have sinned against the Holy Ghost. Men and women will enter into the temples of God, and be, in comparison, pillars there, and officiate year after year for those who have slept thousands of years. 6:344.

When his Kingdom is established upon the earth, and Zion built up, the Lord will send his servants as saviors upon Mount Zion. The servants of God who have lived on the earth in ages past will reveal where different persons have lived who have died without the Gospel, give their names, and say, "Now go forth, ye servants of God, and exercise your rights and privileges; go and perform the ordinances of the house of God for those who have passed their probation without the Gospel, and for all who will receive any kind of salvation; bring them up to inherit the celestial, terrestrial, and telestial kingdoms," and probably many other kingdoms not mentioned in the Scriptures; for every person will receive according to his capacity and according to the deeds done in the body, whether good or bad, much or little. 6:347.

Who will possess the earth and all its fulness? Will it not

be those whom the Lord has reserved to this honor? And they will come upon Mount Zion as saviors to labor through the Millennium to save others. 8:191.

Suppose we are ready to go into the temples of God to officiate for our fathers and our grandfathers—for our ancestors back for hundreds of years, who are all looking to see what their children are doing upon the earth. The Lord says, I have sent the keys of Elijah the Prophet—I have imparted that doctrine to turn the hearts of the fathers to the children, and the hearts of the children to the fathers. Now, all you children, are you looking to the salvation of your fathers? Are you seeking diligently to redeem those that have died without the Gospel, inasmuch as they sought the Lord Almighty to obtain promises for you? For our fathers did obtain promises that their seed should not be forgotten. O ye children of the fathers, look at these things. You are to enter into the temples of the Lord and officiate for your forefathers.

Suppose we are ready to enter into the temple to be baptized and attend to the ordinances for one hundred of our best forefathers, and Thomas should say to John, "John, take this affair and see to it; I want to go to this ferry to make a little money;" or, "Joseph, you know the names of our ancestors better than I do; won't you go and see to their salvation? I have not time myself; I want to build a bridge." "James, are you ready to perform your duties for the dead?" "No; I want to go and keep a grocery." And you know the language that is common to such places; the name of the Lord is blasphemed, and his servants are cursed with bitter oaths.

What do you think of it, gentlemen, Elders in Israel? What would money have to do with you, if you were now upon the threshold of eternity, and eternity open to you? Would you have the apostasy, as you have now? A little money is more to such persons than the salvation of all the sons and daughters of Adam. I wish I had a voice like ten thousand earthquakes, that all the world might hear and know the loving kindness of the Lord. 6:296.

What is going to be done with them? By and by Zion will be built up; temples are going to be reared, and the holy Priesthood is going to take effect and rule, and every law of Christ will be obeyed, and he will govern and reign King of nations as he now does King of Saints. Pretty soon you will see temples reared up, and the sons of Jacob will enter into the temples of the Lord. What will they do there? They will do a great many things. When you see Zion redeemed and built up—when you see the people performing the ordinances of salvation for themselves and for others, (and they will hereafter,) you will see simply this (but I have not time this morning to tell you, only a little part of it): About the time that the temples of the Lord will be built and Zion is established—pretty nigh this time, you will see (those who are faithful enough,) the first you know, there will be strangers in your midst, walking with you, talking with you; they will enter into your houses and eat and drink with you, go to meeting with you, and begin to open your minds, as the Savior did the two disciples who walked out in the country in the days of old.

About the time the temples are ready, the strangers will be along and will converse with you, and will inquire of you, probably, if you understand the resurrection of the dead. You might say you have heard and read a great deal about it, but you do not properly understand it; and they will then open your minds and tell you the principles of the resurrection of the dead and how to save your friends; they will point out Scriptures in the Old and New Testament, in the Book of Mormon, and other revelations of God, saying, "Don't you recollect reading so and so, that saviors should come up on Mount Zion?" etc., and they will expound the Scriptures to you. You have got your temples ready; now go forth and be baptized for those good people. There are your father and your mother—your ancestors for many generations back—the people that have lived upon the face of the earth since the Priesthood was taken away, thousands and millions of them, who have lived according to the best light and knowledge in their possession. They will expound the Scriptures to you, and open your minds, and teach you of the resurrection of the just and the unjust of the doctrine of salvation, they will use the keys of the holy Priesthood, and unlock the door of knowledge, to let you look into the palace of truth. You will exclaim, That is all plain: why did I not understand it before? and you will begin to feel your heart burn within you, as they walk and talk with you.

You will enter into the temple of the Lord and begin to offer up ordinances before the Lord for your dead. Says this or that man, I want to save such a person—I want to save my father; and he straightway goes forth in the ordinance of baptism, and is confirmed, and washed, and anointed, and ordained to the blessings of the holy Priesthood for his ancestors? Before his work is finished, a great many of the Elders of Israel in Mount Zion will become pillars in the temple of God, to go no more out. They will eat and drink and sleep there; and they will often have occasion to say, "Somebody came to the temple last night; we did not know who he was, but he was no doubt a brother, and told us a great many things we did not before understand. He gave us the names of a great many of our forefathers that are not on record, and he gave me my true lineage and the names of my forefathers for hundreds of years back. He said to me, you and I are connected in one family; there are the names of your ancestors; take them and write them down, and be baptized and confirmed, and save such and such ones, and receive of the blessings of the eternal Priesthood for such and such an individual, as you do for yourselves." This is what we are going to do for the inhabitants of the earth. When I look at it, I do not want to rest a great deal, but be industrious all the day long; for when we come to think upon it, we have no time to lose, for it is a pretty laborious work. 6:294-295.

Then in the spirit world they will say, "Do you not see somebody at work for you? The Lord remembers you and has revealed to his servants on the earth what to do for you." 3:372.

When the Lord shall usher in the morning of rest, we may enter into our labors to officiate for our dead friends back to Adam. 6:149.

Powers of Evil Opposed to Temple Building—Some say, "I do not like to do it, for we never began to build a temple without the bells of hell beginning to ring." I want to hear them ring again. All the tribes of hell will be on the move, if we uncover the walls of this temple. But what do you think it will amount to? You have all the time seen what it has amounted to. 8:355-356.

I can say, for my comfort and consolation, and for yours, too, that we did build two temples, and commenced another. We completed a temple in Kirtland and in Nauvoo; and did not the bells of hell toll all the time we were building them? They did, every week and every day. 8:356.

The Salt Lake Temple—This I do know—there should be a temple built here. I do know it is the duty of this people to commence to build a temple. Now, some will want to know what kind of a building it will be. Wait patiently, brethren, until it is done, and put forth your hands willingly to finish it. I know what it will be. I scarcely ever say much about revelations, or visions, but suffice it to say, five years ago last July I was here, and saw in the spirit the temple not ten feet from where we have laid the chief cornerstone. I have not inquired what kind of a temple we should build. Why? Because it was represented before me. I have never looked upon that ground, but the vision of it was there. I see it as plainly as if it was in reality before me. Wait until it is done. I will say, however, that it will have six towers, to begin with, instead of one. Now do not any of you apostatize because it will have six towers, and Joseph only built one. It is easier for us to build sixteen, than it was for him to build one. The time will come when there will be one in the centre of temples, we shall build, and, on the top, groves and fish ponds. But we shall not see them here, at present. 1:132.

I have determined, by the help of the Lord and this people, to build him a house. You may ask, "Will he dwell in it?" He may do just as he pleases; it is not my prerogative to dictate to the Lord. But we will build him a house, that, if he pleases to pay us a visit, he may have a place to dwell in, or if he should send any of his servants, we may have suitable accommodations for them. I have built myself a house, and the most of you have done the same, and now, shall we not build the Lord a house? 1:376.

"Does the Lord require the building of a temple at our hands?" I can say that he requires it just as much as ever he required one to be built elsewhere. If you should ask, "Brother Brigham, have you any knowledge concerning this; have you ever had a revelation from heaven upon it?" I can answer truly, it is before me all the time, not only today, but it was almost five years ago, when we were on this ground looking for locations, sending out scouting parties through the country, to the right and to the left, to the north and the south, to the east and the west; before we had any returns from any of them, I knew, just as well as I now know, that this was the ground on which to erect a temple—it was before me. 1:277.

We shall attempt to build a temple to the name of our God. This has been attempted several times, but we have never yet had the privilege of completing and enjoying one. Perhaps we may in this place, but if, in the providence of God, we should not, it is all the same. It is for us to do those things which the Lord requires at our hands, and leave the result with him. It is for us to labor with a cheerful good will; and if we build a temple that is worth a million of money, and it requires all our time and means, we should leave it with cheerful hearts, if the Lord in his providence tells us so to do. If the Lord permits our enemies to drive us from it, why, we should abandon it with as much cheerfulness of heart as we ever enjoy a blessing. It is no matter to us what the Lord does, or how he disposes of the labor of his servant. But when he commands, it is for his people to obey. We should be as cheerful in building this temple, if we knew beforehand that we should never enter into it when it was finished, as we would though we knew we were to live here a thousand years to enjoy it. 1:277.

I want this temple that we are now building to the name of our God to stand for all time to come as a monument of the industry, faithfulness, faith, and integrity of the Latter-day Saints who were driven into the mountains. I want to see the temple finished as soon as it is reasonable and practicable. Whether we go in there to work or not makes no difference; I am perfectly willing to finish it to the last leaf of gold that shall be laid upon it, and to the last lock that should be put on the doors, and then lock every door, and there let it stand until the earth can rest before the Saints commence their labors there. They receive more in the house of the Lord now than is their due. Our brethren and sisters, baptized three, four, or six months ago, go and get their endowments, the sealing blessings for all eternity, the highest that can be conferred upon them, yet how lightly they are treated! Many do not consider, they do not realize these things. They have not the spirit of revelation, they do not live for it, hence they do not see these things in their proper light, and we are not in such a hurry as many think we ought to be. 11:372.

The temple will be for the endowments—for the organization and instruction of the Priesthood. If you want to build a temple on these conditions, you can have the privilege. But I never again want to see one built to go into the hands of the wicked. I have asked my Father to give me power to build a temple on this block, but not until I can forever maintain my rights in it. I would rather see it burnt than to see it go into the hands of devils. I was thankful to see the temple in Nauvoo on fire. Previous to crossing the Mississippi river, we had met in that temple and handed it over to the Lord God of Israel; and when I saw the flames, I said, "Good, Father, if you want it to be burned up." I hoped to see it burned before I left, but I did not. I was glad when I heard of its being destroyed by fire, and of the walls having fallen in, and said, "Hell, you cannot now occupy it." When the temple is built here, I want to maintain it for the use of the Priesthood; if this cannot be, I would rather not see it built, but go into the mountains and administer there in the ordinances of the holy Priesthood, which is our right and privilege. I would rather do this than to build a temple for the wicked to trample under their feet. 8:203.

Address at the Laying of the Cornerstone of the Salt Lake Temple—This morning we have assembled on one of the most solemn, interesting, joyful, and glorious occasions that ever have transpired, or will transpire among the children of men, while the earth continues in its present organization, and is occupied for its present purposes. And I congratulate my brethren and sisters that it is our unspeakable privilege to stand here this day, and minister before the Lord on an occasion which has caused the tongues and pens of Prophets to speak and write for many scores of centuries which are past.

When the Lord Jesus Christ tabernacled in the flesh—when he had left the most exalted regions of his Father's glory, to suffer and shed his blood for sinning, fallen creatures, like ourselves, and the people crowded around him, a certain man said unto him, "Master, I will follow thee whithersoever thou goest." Jesus said unto him,

"Foxes have holes, and the birds of the air have nests; but the Son of Man hath nowhere to lay his head." And we find no record that this man followed him any farther.

Why had not the Son of Man where to lay his head? Because his Father had no house upon the earth—none dedicated to him, and preserved for his exclusive use, and the benefit of his obedient children.

The Ark containing the covenant—or the Ark of the Covenant in the days of Moses, containing the sacred records, was moved from place to place in a cart. And so sacred was that Ark, if a man stretched forth his hand to steady it, when the cart jostled, he was smitten and died. And would to God that all who attempt to do the same in this day, figuratively speaking, might share the same fate. And they will share it sooner or later, if they do not keep their hands, and tongues, too, in their proper places, and stop dictating the order of the Gods of the Eternal Worlds.

When the Ark of the Covenant rested, or when the Children of Israel had an opportunity to rest (for they were mobbed and harassed somewhat like the Latter-day Saints), the Lord, through Moses, commanded a tabernacle to be built, wherein should rest and be stationed, the Ark of the Covenant. And particular instructions were given by revelation to Moses, how every part of said tabernacle should be constructed, even to the curtains—the number thereof, and of what they should be made; and the covering, and the wood for the boards, and for the bars, and the court, and the pins, and the vessels, and the furniture, and everything pertaining to the tabernacle. Why did Moses need such a particular revelation to build a tabernacle? Because he had never seen one, and did not know how to build it without revelation, without a pattern.

Thus the Ark of the Covenant continued until the days of David, King of Israel, standing or occupying a tabernacle, or tent. But to David, God gave commandment that he should make preparation for a house, wherein he, himself, might dwell, or which he might visit, and in which he might commune with his servants when he pleased.

From the day the Children of Israel were led out of Egypt to the days of Solomon, Jehovah had no resting place upon the earth (and for how long a period before that day, the history is unpublished), but walked in a tent or tabernacle, before the Ark, as it seemed him good, having no place to lay his head.

David was not permitted to build the house which the Lord told him should be built, because he was a "man of blood," that is, he was beset by enemies on every hand, and had to spend his days in war and bloodshed to save Israel (much as the Latter-day Saints have done, only he had the privilege of defending himself and the people from mobocrats and murderers, while we have hitherto been denied that privilege), and, consequently, he had no time to build a house unto the Lord, but, commanded his son Solomon, who succeeded him on the throne, to erect the temple at Jerusalem, which God had required at his hands.

The pattern of this temple, the length and breadth, and height of the inner and outer courts, with all the fixtures thereunto appertaining, were given to Solomon by revelation, through the proper source. And why was this revelation-pattern necessary? Because Solomon had never built a temple, and did not know what was necessary in the arrangement of the different apartments, any better than Moses did what was needed in the tabernacle.

This temple, called Solomon's temple, because Solomon was the master workman, was completed some time previous to the appearance of the Son of Man on the earth, in the form of the babe of Bethlehem, and had been dedicated as the house of the Lord, and accepted as a finished work by the Father, who commanded it to be built, that his Son might have a resting place on the earth, when he should enter on his mission.

Why, then, did Jesus exclaim to the man who volunteered to follow him wheresoever he went, that "the Son of Man hath not where to lay his head?" Jesus knew the pretended saint and follower to be a hypocrite, and that if he told him plainly that he would not fare as well as the birds and foxes, he would leave him at once, and that would save him much trouble.

But how could Jesus' saying, that he had "not where to lay his head," be true? Because the house which the Father had commanded to be built for his reception, although completed, had become polluted, and hence the saying, "My house is the house of prayer; but ye have made it a den of thieves," and he made a scourge of cords, and drove the money-changers, and dove-sellers, and faro-gamblers, all out of his house, and overthrew their tables; but that did not purify the house, so that he could not sleep in it, for an holy thing dwelleth not in an unholy temple.

If Jesus could not lay his head in an unholy polluted temple, how can the Latter-day Saints expect that the Holy Spirit will take and abide its residence with them, in their tabernacles and temples of clay, unless they keep themselves pure, spotless, and undefiled?

It is no wonder that the Son of Man, soon after his resurrection from the tomb, ascended to his Father, for he had no place on earth to lay his head; his house still remaining in the possession of his enemies, so that no one had the privilege of purifying it, if they had the disposition, and otherwise the power, to do it; and the occupants thereof were professors in name, but hypocrites and apostates, from whom no good thing can be expected.

Soon after the ascension of Jesus, through mobocracy, martyrdom, and apostasy, the Church of Christ became extinct from the earth, the Man Child,—the Holy Priesthood, was received up into heaven from whence it came, and we hear no more of it on the earth, until the angels restored it to Joseph Smith, by whose ministry the Church of Jesus Christ was restored, reorganized on earth, twenty-three years ago this day, with the title of Latter-day Saints to distinguish them from the Former-day Saints.

Soon after, the Church, through our beloved Prophet Joseph, was commanded to build a temple to the Most High, in Kirtland, Ohio. Joseph not only received revelation and commandment to build a temple, but he received a pattern also, as did Moses for the tabernacle, and Solomon for his temple; for without a pattern, he could not know what was wanted, having never seen one, and not having experienced its use.

Without revelation, Joseph could not know what was wanted, any more than any other man, and, without commandment, the Church were too few in number, too weak in faith, and too poor in purse, to attempt such a mighty enterprise. But by means of all these stimulants, a mere handful of men, living on air, and a little hominy and milk, and often salt or no salt, when milk could not be had; the great Prophet Joseph, in the stone quarry, quarrying rock with his own hands; and the few then in the Church, following his example of obedience and diligence wherever most needed; with laborers on the walls, holding the sword in one hand to protect themselves from the mob, while they placed the stone and moved the trowel with the other, the Kirtland temple—the second house of the Lord, that we have any published record of on the earth, was so far completed as to be dedicated. And those first Elders who helped to build it, received a portion of their first endowments, or we might say more clearly, some of the first, or introductory, or initiatory ordinances, preparatory to an endowment.

The preparatory ordinances there administered, though accompanied by the ministrations of angels, and the presence of the Lord Jesus, were but a faint similitude of the ordinances of the house of the Lord in their fulness; yet many, through the instigation of the Devil, thought they had received all, and knew as much as God; they have apostatized, and gone to hell. But be assured, brethren, there are but few, very few of the Elders of Israel, now on earth, who know the meaning of the word endowment. To know, they must experience; and to experience, a temple must be built.

Let me give you a definition in brief. Your endowment is, to receive all those ordinances in the house of the Lord, which are necessary for you, after you have departed this life, to enable you to walk back to the presence of the Father, passing the angels who stand as sentinels, being enabled to give them the key words, the signs and tokens, pertaining to the holy Priesthood, and gain your eternal exaltation in spite of earth and hell.

Who has received and understands such an endowment, in this assembly? You need not answer. Your voices would be few and far between, yet the keys to these endowments are among you, and thousands have received them, so that the Devil, with all his aids, need not suppose he can again destroy the holy Priesthood from the earth, by killing a few, for he cannot do it. God has set his hand, for the last time, to redeem his people, the honest in heart, and Lucifer cannot hinder him.

Before these endowments could be given at Kirtland, the Saints had to flee before mobocracy. And, by toil and daily labor, they found places in Missouri, where they laid the cornerstones of temples, in Zion and her stakes, and then had to retreat to Illinois, to save the lives of those who could get away alive from Missouri, where fell the Apostle David W. Patten, with many like associates, and where were imprisoned in loathsome dungeons, Joseph and Hyrum, and many others. But before all this had transpired, the temple at Kirtland had fallen into the hands of wicked men, and by them been polluted, like the temple at Jerusalem, and consequently it was disowned by the Father and the Son.

At Nauvoo, Joseph dedicated another temple, the third on record. He knew what was wanted, for he had previously given most of the prominent individuals then before him their endowment. He needed no revelation then, of a thing he had long experienced, any more than those now do, who have experienced the same things. It is only where experience fails, that revelation is needed.

Before the Nauvoo temple was completed, Joseph was murdered —murdered at sunlight, under the protection of the most noble Government that then existed, and that now exists, on our earth. Has his blood been atoned for? No! And why? A martyr's blood to true religion was never atoned for on our earth. No man, or nation of men, without the Priesthood, has power to make atonement for such sins. The souls of all such, since the days of Jesus, are "under the altar," and are crying to God, day and night, for vengeance. And shall they cry in vain? God forbid! He has promised he will hear them in his own due time, and recompense a righteous reward.

But what of the temple in Nauvoo? By the aid of sword in one hand, and trowel and hammer in the other, with firearms at hand, and a strong band of police, and the blessings of heaven, the Saints, through hunger, and thirst, and weariness, and watchings, and prayings, so far completed the temple despite the devices of the mob, that many received a small portion of their endowment, but we know of no one who received it in its fulness. And then, to save the lives of all the Saints from cruel murder, we removed westward, and being led by the all-searching eye of the great Jehovah, we arrived at this place.

Of the journey hither, we need say nothing, only, God led us. Of the sufferings of those who were compelled to, and did, leave Nauvoo in the winter of 1846, we need say nothing. Those who experienced it know it, and those who did not, to tell them of it would be like exhibiting a beautiful painting to a blind man.

We will not stop to tell you of the sufferings of widows and orphans on Omaha lands, while their husbands and fathers were traversing the burning plains of the south, to fight the battles of a country which had banished them from civilization, for they secured the land on which we dwell, from our Nation's foe, exposed the gold of California, and turned the world upside down. All these things are before you, you know them, and we need not repeat them.

While these things were transpiring with the Saints in the wilderness, the temple at Nauvoo passed into the hands of the enemy, who polluted it to that extent the Lord not only ceased to occupy it, but he loathed to have it called by his name, and permitted the wrath of its possessors to purify it by fire, as a token of what will speedily fall upon them and their habitations unless they repent.

But what are we here for, this day? To celebrate the birthday of our religion! To lay the foundation of a temple to the Most High God, so that when his Son, our Elder Brother, shall again appear, he may have a place where he can lay his head, and not only spend a night or a day, but find a place of peace, that he may stay till he can say, "I am satisfied."

Brethren, shall the Son of Man be satisfied with our proceedings this day? Shall we have a house on the earth which he can call his own? Shall we have a place where he can lay his head, and rest over night, and tarry as long as he pleases, and be satisfied and pleased with his accommodations?

These are questions for you to answer. If you say yes, you have got to do the work, or it will not be done. We do not want any whiners about this temple. If you cannot commence cheerfully, and go through the labor of the whole building cheerfully, start for California, and the quicker the better. Make you a golden calf, and worship it. If your care for the ordinances of salvation, for yourselves, your living, and dead, is not first and foremost in your hearts, in your actions, and in everything you possess, go! Pay your debts, if you have any, and go in peace, and prove to God and all his Saints that you are what you profess to be, by your acts.

But if you are what you profess to be, do your duty—stay with the Saints, pay your tithing, and be prompt in paying, as you are in feeding your family; and the temple, of which we have now laid the southeast cornerstone, will arise in beauty and grandeur, in a manner and time which you have not hitherto known or contemplated.

The Saints of these valleys have grown in riches, and abundance of the comforts of life, in a manner hitherto unparalleled on the page of history, and if they will do by their Heavenly Father as he has done by them, soon will this temple be inclosed. But if you go in for a speculation with passers-by, as many have hitherto done, you will not live to see the topstone of this temple laid; and your labors and toils for yourselves and friends, dead and alive, will be worse than though you had no existence.

We dedicate this, the southeast cornerstone of this temple, to the Most High God. May it remain in peace till it has done its work, and until he who has inspired our hearts to fulfil the prophecies of his holy Prophets, that the house of the Lord should be reared in the "Tops of the Mountains" shall be satisfied, and say, "It is enough." And may every tongue, pen, and weapon, that may rise against this or any other cornerstone of this building, feel the wrath and scourging of an incensed God! May sinners in Zion be afraid, and fearfulness surprise the hypocrite, from this hour. And may all who do not feel to say Amen, go speedily to that long night of rest from which no sleeper will awake, till roused by the trump of the second resurrection. 2:29-33.

St. George Temple—Now we have a temple which will all be finished in a few days, and of which there is enough completed to commence work therein, which has not been done since the days of Adam, that we have any knowledge of. 18:304.

We have dedicated this spot of ground upon which we expect to erect a temple in which to administer the ordinances of the House of God. Into this house, when it is completed, we expect to enter to enjoy the blessings of the Priesthood, and receive our washings, our anointings, our endowments, and our sealings; and the brethren will be sealed to connect the links and make perfect the chain from ourselves to Father Adam. This is the object of the temple which we are about to commence building at this place. 19:33.

Never have I seen to so great an extent that willingness to labor for the cause of righteousness, which was witnessed in the temple at St. George last winter. The Spirit of God pervaded the hearts of the brethren and sisters, and how willing they were to labor! This work will continue, and the brethren and sisters will go into the temples of the Lord, to officiate for those who have died without the Gospel from the days of Father Adam to the winding up scene, until every one is officiated for; who can or will receive the Gospel so that all may have the opportunity and privileges of life and salvation.

Don't you think we have a work to perform? Yes, and it will take a thousand years to accomplish it. In the temple last winter the brethren and sisters enjoyed themselves the best that they ever did in their lives. So they said. And our children, just old enough to work, how happy they were! They would exclaim, "I never knew anything about 'Mormonism' before!" If you were in the temple of God working for the living and the dead, your eyes and hearts would not be after the fashions of the world, nor the wealth of the world. Yet the whole of this world's wealth belongs to the Lord, and he can give to whomsoever he pleases. 19:45.

I am aware that you wish to hear something of our labors in the south. I will say that we have had a blessed time, such a time as no other people on the earth have enjoyed for many centuries, that we have any knowledge of. We have been permitted to enjoy privileges for the possession of which we have been striving and laboring for many years. For almost half a century we have been exerting ourselves that we might have the privilege of entering into a temple of God, there to officiate and receive the ordinances of his holy house, both for ourselves and for our friends that have slept without the Gospel. This privilege and blessing we have not enjoyed until within a very few months past. The feeling experienced by those who have participated in the blessings administered in the temple is something which cannot be described to your understanding. Those only who have shared with us in the temple ordinances know for themselves the satisfaction there is in realizing that we are indeed co-workers with our Lord and Savior; that we bear a humble part in the great work of salvation; that we have the privilege of receiving and obeying the truth, and of securing to ourselves that happiness which the Gospel alone affords; and not only of performing these ordinances for ourselves, but of doing the necessary work for our parents and forefathers who have slept without the Gospel, that they may partake also of the waters of life, and be judged according to men in the flesh. This is a privilege, a blessing, which no one can sense unless he is in possession of it. We are happy to know by our faith and feelings through the spirit of revelation within us that our labors have been accepted of the Lord. We have enjoyed ourselves exceedingly in the society of each other; the aged, the middle-aged and the youth have rejoiced and been made glad in this glorious work. 19:1.

"We are now prepared to attend to baptizing and giving endowments, and shall appoint Tuesdays and Wednesdays for baptisms, and Thursdays and Fridays for endowments and sealings, as a standing appointment for the present." 18:305.

I am so thankful we have completed our temple, it is the greatest blessing that could be bestowed upon us. I know of nothing that could equal it. But we are not satisfied with this one, we must hurry the building of another one, and thus another one and so on, and perform the great work therein that is required at our hands. 19:222.

We enjoy privileges that are enjoyable by no one else on the face of the earth. Suppose we were awake to this thing, namely, the salvation of the human family, this house would be crowded, as we hope it will be, from Monday morning until Saturday night. This house (St. George) was built here in this place purposely, where it is warm and pleasant in the winter time, and comfortable to work, also for the Lamanites, and also those coming from the south, and other places to receive their endowments, and other blessings. 18:304.

Chapter XXXVII

MAN'S SEARCH FOR TRUTH AND SALVATION

Man Desires Salvation—Honest hearts, the world over, desire to know the right way. They have sought for it, and still seek it. There have been people upon the earth all the time who sought diligently with all their hearts to know the ways of the Lord. Those individuals have produced good, inasmuch as they had the ability. And to believe that there has been no virtue, no truth, no good upon the earth for centuries, until the Lord revealed the Priesthood through Joseph the Prophet, I shall say is wrong. There has been more or less virtue and righteousness upon the earth at all times from the days of Adam until now. That we all believe. 6:170.

Until they sin away the day of grace, there is something in all persons that would delight to rise up and reject the evil and embrace the truth. There is not a person on the earth so vile but, when he looks into his own heart, honors the man of God and the woman of God—the virtuous and holy—and despises his comrades in iniquity who are like himself. There is not a man upon the earth, this side of saving grace, unless he has sinned so far that the Spirit of the Lord has ceased to strive with him and enlighten his mind, but delights in the good, in the truth, and in the virtuous. 8:326.

Reflect for a moment upon the sensitive faculty implanted within us. We know when we touch anything with our hands. When we discern an object with our eyes, we know that we see. How do we know? By a principle common to all intelligent beings — by the sensations God has placed within us. Were it not for this, the eye could not see, nor sensation be communicated by touch. Were it not for the intelligent principle God has placed within us, we could neither feel, see, hear, taste, nor smell.

It is recorded that some have eyes to see, and see not; ears to hear, and hear not; hearts have they, but they understand not. You who are spiritually-minded, who have the visions of your minds opened—have studied yourselves, your organizations, the power by which you have been organized, and the influences that act upon you, can understand that the power that has given you physical sensation is the power of the same God that gives you understanding of the truth. The latter power is inward. My inward eyes see, my inward hands handle, my inward taste tastes of the word of God. The Apostle used this language. He spoke of tasting the good word of God and the powers of the world to come. Do you taste? Yes, by the sensations God has planted within you. Thousands and thousands know, by their inward and invisible sensation, things that have been, things that are, and things that are in the future, as well as they know the color of a piece of cloth by means of their outward or physical vision. When this inner light is taken from them, they become darker than they were before, they cannot understand, and turn away from the things of God. 8:41.

Descend from the busy, wealth-seeking middle classes, to the humbler grade of society, and follow them in their various occupations and pursuits, and each one of them is seeking earnestly that which he imagines to be salvation. The poor, ragged, trembling mendicant, who is forced by hunger and cold to drag his feeble body from under some temporary shelter, to seek a bit of bread, or a coin from his more fortunate fellow-mortal, if he can only obtain a few crusts of bread to satisfy the hunger-worm that gnaws his vitals, and a few coppers to pay his lodgings, he has attained to the summit of his expectations, to what he sought for—salvation, and he is comparatively happy, but his happiness vanishes with the shades of night, and his misery comes with the morning light. From the matchmaker up to the tradesman, all have an end in view, which they suppose will bring to them salvation. King, courtier, commanders, officers, and common soldiers, the commodore, and sailor before the mast, the fair-skinned Christian, and the dark-skinned savage, all, in their respective grades and spheres of action, have a certain point in view, which, if they can obtain, they suppose will put them in possession of salvation. 1:1.

Humanity Loves Truth and Righteousness—What would satisfy the children of men, if they had it in their possession? Only truth and the true principles and conduct flowing from its observance. True, certain classes of the inhabitants of the earth are pretty well satisfied with themselves, through their researches in the philosophies of the day; and yet they are not fully satisfied. What will satisfy us? If we understood all principles and powers that are, that have been, and that are to come, and had wisdom sufficient to control powers and elements with which we are associated, perhaps we would then be satisfied. If this will not satisfy the human mind, there is nothing that will. 7:2.

The spirit which inhabits these tabernacles naturally loves truth, it naturally loves light and intelligence, it naturally loves virtue, God and godliness; but being so closely united with the flesh their sympathies are blended, and their union being necessary to the possession of a fulness of joy to both, the spirit is indeed subject to be influenced by the sin that is in the mortal body, and to be overcome by it and by the power of the Devil, unless it is constantly enlightened by that spirit which enlighteneth every man that cometh into the world, and by the power of the Holy Ghost which is imparted through the Gospel. In this, and this alone, consists the warfare between Christ and the Devil. 11:237.

The greater portion of the inhabitants of the earth are inclined to do right. That is true. There is a monitor in every person that would reign there triumphantly, if permitted so to do, and lead to truth and virtue. 8:320.

As to the mortals of the world, I have said it a great many times and still say that there are just as good men and women on the earth in other societies and communities as we have here, as far as they understand; and we are after such ones. 12:326.

There are as honest men in other churches as there are in ours. 8:357.

Human Family Alike in Sentiments—In reality, the inhabitants of the earth do not vary so much in their sentiments as they do in the explaining of them to each other. This I have good reason to believe; when feelings and ideas are explained, people vary more in language than in sentiment, yet they differ widely in their sentiments, feelings, customs, habits, and manner of life. 1:74.

When we see and comprehend things in the spirit, we ofttimes realize an utter inability to simplify and tell them in our language, to others; though we may receive principles, and convey the same to others, to some extent. It would be a great consolation to me, inasmuch as faith comes by hearing the word of God, if I had language to express my feelings. No man can tell all that he can see in the spirit, when the vision of the spirit is upon him. He can see and understand in the spirit only. He cannot tell it, yet many things may be given, in part, to others. 1:115.

A Variety of Human Gifts—I am sensible that people are not gifted and capacitated alike. There is not that depth of understanding and intensity of thought in some that there is in others, neither is there the same scope of perception. Some are quick to apprehend, while others are slow. 6:93.

We all enjoy the power of sight, but how differently we look at and comprehend things! And we are very much like the people who have lived before us. We are a strange and curious composition—no two alike. Of all the faces before me this afternoon there are no two alike. We might possibly find those whose judgment would be pretty much alike on various subjects, still there are no two whose judgments are precisely the same. Human life is a great stage, and it contains a very great variety of scenes and scenery, of thought and of action. 16:23.

There is quite a diversity in men as to their capacity for learning, and also in regard to retaining what they learn. Some comprehend their lessons quickly, while others are not so gifted. I have also noticed that some children commit their lessons quickly and well; but ask them the meaning and intent of what they have committed, and they cannot answer you; while others pay more attention to the intent and meaning of what they learn. Such is the case with all persons, no matter what their age; and some are capacitated to receive more and faster than others. 8:158.

Let the people bring out their talents, and have the variety within them brought forth and made manifest so that we can behold it, like the variety in the works of nature. See the variety God has created—no two trees alike, no two leaves, no two spears of grass alike. The same variety that we see in all the works of God, that we see in the features, visages and forms, exists in the spirits of men. Now let us develop the variety within us, and show to the world that we have talent and taste, and prove to the heavens that our minds are set on beauty and true excellence, so that we can become worthy to enjoy the society of angels, and raise ourselves above the level of the wicked world and begin to increase in faith, and the power that God has given us, and to show to the world an example worthy of imitation. 11:305.

Man's Powers are Limited—The inhabitants of the earth have the pleasure of performing the labors they list to do, but they have never enjoyed the privilege of controlling the results of their labors, and never will until they are crowned with glory, immortality and eternal lives. We have the privilege of going to the gold mines, or staying at home; of serving God, or not serving him; but the result of our acts is not in our hands, it is in the hands of our Father and God. So it is with individuals, with neighborhoods, with communities, and with the nations of the earth. 10:331.

If the Latter-day Saints and all the world understood the philosophy of their own being, they would bow in humble reverence to him who is the Author of our being and the Author of all wisdom and all knowledge known among the children of men. It is very little comparatively that we do know, and but very little we can really comprehend. It is believed that our scientists and philosophers are very far advanced, and that wonderful progress has been made in the nineteenth century; but notwithstanding all the knowledge and power of philosophy which so distinguish our age, who among our most learned can create as simple a thing as a spear of grass, or the leaf of a tree? No one; this can only be done through the natural process; no one can organize the simplest particle of element independent of the laws of nature. When the philosopher of the age reaches that perfection that one can waft himself to the moon or to the North star, or to any other of the fixed stars, and be there in an instant, in the same manner that Jesus did when he ascended to the Father in heaven and returned to the earth again, then we may begin to think we know a little. When we shall possess the power and knowledge to cause heavenly planets to take their position, giving them their laws and boundaries which they must obey, and which they cannot pass, then we may begin to feel that we possess a little wisdom and power. 18:259.

If I look through my telescope, and my friends inquire how far I can see, I tell them I can see anything in sight, no matter how far from me the object may be; but I cannot see anything out of sight, or that which is beyond the power of the instrument. So it is in the intellectual faculties of mankind; it is easy for them to see that which is before their eyes, but when the object is out of sight, it is a difficult matter for them to see it; and they are at a loss how to form an estimate of it, or what position to put themselves in, so as to see the object they desire to see. 1:351.

There is but a hair's breadth between the vulgar and sublime. There is but a hair's breadth between the depths of infidelity and the heights of the faith of the Gods. Man is here like a feather trembling between the two, liable continually to be operated upon by the power of the enemy; and it is through that power that the children of men are made to doubt the evidences of their own senses, when, at the same time, if they would reflect for a moment and listen to the intelligence which God has placed within them, they would know, when they saw what is termed a miracle, the power by which it is wrought; they would know when they have seen with their eyes and felt with their hands, or when they have had a heavenly vision. 7:163-164.

Man Must Have Confidence in Himself—We must be ourselves. 3:365.

There are a great many men who know but little about what they can do, and there are a great many women that never consider what they can perform; people do not fully reflect upon their own acts, upon their own ability, and therefore do not understand what they are capable of doing. 4:101.

It is not for any man to think he is a cipher—that what he can do will not tell in this matter, and say, "They will get along well enough without me." 1:53.

When a person is thinking all the time he is little better than a machine, he perverts the purpose of his organization, and injures both mind and body. Why? Because the mental labor does not find vent through the organism of the tabernacle, and has not that scope—that field of labor which it desires, and which it was wisely designed that it should have. Think according to your labor, labor according to your thinking. 3:248.

Man Always Dependent—Shall we ever see the time we shall be perfectly independent of every other being in all the eternities? No; we shall never see that time. Many have fallen on as simple ground as this, and were I to use a Western term, I would say, "They are troubled with a big head." Such persons think they have power to do this, that, and the other, but they are left to themselves, and the Lord loves to show them they have no power. 1:338.

We Must Fight Our Battles—But some may say, "I have faith the Lord will turn them away." What ground have we to hope this? Have I any good reason to say to my Father in Heaven, "Fight my battles," when he has given me the sword to wield, the arm and the brain that I can fight for myself? Can I ask him to fight my battles and sit quietly down waiting for him to do so? I cannot. I can pray the people to hearken to wisdom, to listen to counsel; but to ask God to do for me that which I can do for myself is preposterous to my mind. 12:240-241.

How to Know Oneself—No man can know himself unless he knows God, and he cannot know God unless he knows himself. 16:75.

Our Good Character Must Be Cherished—When a man by his course in life has acquired a character that is spotless, it is a priceless jewel, and nothing should induce him to barter it away. If the wicked try to bring a blemish or cast a stain upon it their efforts will not be successful. They may throw their mud, but it will not stain the garments of the pure and holy. 13:218.

"Are our characters our own?" We may say, "Yes, we form these characters." Suppose that we are fortunate enough to form a good, honest character in the minds and in the faith of those who are acquainted with us, do not those characters belong to our neighbors, although we may be the framers of them? And I would like to ask, have we the right to destroy them? It is a serious question with me. If we have confidence in each other, and our conduct has been such that we have created confidence in the feelings of our neighbors toward us, have we a right to destroy that confidence? Is it not sacrilege? I will simply reply by giving my views with regard to myself. According to the knowledge which I possess it is a great deal easier for an individual to preserve a good character than to frame and make one if it is lost. It is much easier to keep a fort when it is well armed and defended than to give it into the hands of the enemy and then regain it. Consequently, we had better keep our characters, if they are good, than to suffer the enemy to rob us of them. 14:277.

The Need of Leaders—The whole world are sadly in want of what they call a master-spirit. 6:44.

When I say rule, I do not mean with an iron hand, but merely to take the lead—to lead them in the path I wish them to walk in. They may be determined not to answer my will, but they are doing it all the time without knowing it. 9:195.

It is not every man that is capable of filling every station, though there is no man but what is capable of filling his proper station, and that, too, with dignity and honor to himself. When you find a person that is capable of receiving light and wisdom, one that can descend to the capacity of the weakest of the weak, and can comprehend the highest and most noble intelligence that can be obtained by man, can receive it with all ease, and comprehend it, circumscribe it, understand it from first to last, that is the man that can ripen for eternity in a few years; that is the individual who is capable of occupying stations that many cannot occupy. 4:130.

Let the people see to it that they get righteous men to be their leaders, who will labor with their hands and administer to their own necessities, sit in judgment, legislate, and govern in righteousness; and officers that are filled with peace; and see to it that every man that goes forth among the people as a traveling officer is full of the fear of the Lord, and would rather do right at a sacrifice than do wrong for a reward. 7:12.

Duty and Responsibility of Man—"To mind your own business" incorporates the whole duty of man. 10:295.

What is the duty of a Latter-day Saint? To do all the good he can upon the earth, living in the discharge of every duty obligatory upon him. 10:295.

His labor is to build up, not to destroy; to gather together, not to scatter abroad; to take the ignorant and lead them to wisdom; to pick up the poor and bring them to comfortable circumstances. This is our labor—what we have to do. 10:316.

It is the business of a Latter-day Saint, in passing through the street, if he sees a fence pole down, to put it up; if he sees an animal in the mud to stop and help get it out. 10:296.

The greater our privileges and the greater the blessings bestowed upon us, the more faithfulness and diligence are required in our callings to save the children of men. 7:274.

There are men upon whom God has bestowed gifts and graces, and women who are endowed with strong mental ability, and yet they cannot receive the truth; and then the truth condemns them; it leaves them in darkness. When they cannot receive every truth, let it be ever so important or unimportant to them, their neglect to grasp in their faith and truth God reveals for their benefit weakens them, comparatively, from the crowns of their heads to the soles of their feet, and the enemy may have the advantage over them in an hour when they think not. 8:59.

Strive to be righteous, not for any speculation, but because righteousness is lovely, pure, holy, beautiful, and exalting; it is designed to make the soul happy and full of joy, to the extent of the whole capacity of man, filling him with light, glory, and intelligence. 8:172.

If we do the best we know how, and yet commit many acts that are wrong and contrary to the counsel given to us, there is hope in our case. 2:132.

Chapter XXXVIII

THE TESTIMONY OF THE TRUTH

All Latter-day Saints May Know the Gospel Is True—It is a special privilege and blessing of the holy Gospel to every true believer, to know the truth for himself. 1:234.

It is both the duty and privilege of the Latter-day Saints to know that their religion is true. 8:148.

We are the witnesses of this great work which the Lord has commenced in the latter days. 11:213.

Let every one get a knowledge for himself that this work is true. We do not want you to say that it is true until you know that it is; and if you know it, that knowledge is as good to you as though the Lord came down and told you. 8:142.

There is not a man or a woman on this earth who receives the spirit of the Gospel but what can testify to its truth. 11:213.

We must have the testimony of the Lord Jesus to enable us to discern between truth and error, light and darkness, him who is of God, and him who is not of God, and to know how to place everything where it belongs. That is the only way to be a scientific Christian; there is no other method or process which will actually school a person so that he can become a Saint of God, and prepare him for a celestial glory; he must have within him the testimony of the spirit of the Gospel. 3:155.

If you are satisfied, in your sensitive powers and faculties, that God has revealed the holy Priesthood, established his Kingdom upon the earth, restored the fulness of the Gospel, and set his hand to gather the House of Israel, this will answer your purpose just as well as though you went into heaven to see for yourselves. 8:261.

If I attain to the knowledge of all true principles that have ever existed, and do not govern myself by them, they will damn me deeper in hell than if I had never known anything about them. 1:244.

How a Witness of the Truth Is Won—I do not want men to come to me or my brethren for testimony as to the truth of this work; but let them take the Scriptures of divine truth, and there the path is pointed out to them as plainly as ever a guideboard indicated the right path to the weary traveler. There they are directed to go, not to Brothers Brigham, Heber, or Daniel, to any Apostle or Elder in Israel, but to the Father in the name of Jesus, and ask for the information they need. Can they who take this course in honesty and sincerity receive information? Will the Lord turn away from the honest heart seeking for truth? No, he will not; he will prove to them, by the revelations of his Spirit, the facts in the case. And when the mind is open to the revelations of the Lord it comprehends them quicker and keener than anything that is seen by the natural eye. It is not what we see with our eyes—they may be deceived—but what is revealed by the Lord from heaven that is sure and steadfast, and abides forever. We do not want the people to rely on human testimony, although that cannot be confuted and destroyed; still, there is a more sure word of prophecy that all may gain if they will seek it earnestly before the Lord. 12:96.

You and I must have the testimony of Jesus within us, or it is of but little use for us to pretend to be servants of God. We must have that living witness within us. 4:368.

I will now make a few remarks upon testimony. I have heard a great many Elders in this Church, and people who were professing Christians before this work was revealed, testifying of the things of God. Men rise up here and say they do know that this is the work of God, that Joseph was a Prophet, that the Book of Mormon is true, that the revelations through Joseph Smith are true, and this is the last dispensation and the fulness of times, wherein God has set his hand to gather Israel for the last time, and redeem and build up Zion on this land. How do they know this? Persons know and will continue to know and understand many things by the manifestations of the Spirit, that through the organization of the tabernacle it is impossible otherwise to convey. Much of the most important information is alone derived through the power and testimony of the Holy Ghost in the speaker, revealing itself to the understanding and spirit of the hearer. This is the only way you can convey a knowledge of the invisible things of God. 8:41.

A man or woman desirous of knowing the truth, upon hearing the Gospel of the Son of God proclaimed in truth and simplicity, should ask the Father, in the name of Jesus, if this is true. If they do not take this course, they try and argue themselves into the belief that they are as honest as any man or woman can be on the face of the earth; but they are not, they are careless as to their own best interests. 12:95.

On the other hand, nothing short of the power of the Almighty, nothing short of the Holy Spirit of Jesus Christ, can prove to you that this is the work of God. Men uninspired of God cannot by their worldly wisdom disprove it, or prevail against it; neither can they by wisdom alone prove it to be true, either to themselves or to others. Their not being able to prevail against it does not prove it to be the Kingdom of God, for there are many theories and systems on the earth, incontrovertible by the wisdom of the world, which are nevertheless false. Nothing less than the power of the Almighty, enlightening the understanding of men, can demonstrate this glorious truth to the human mind. 1:310.

How are we to know the voice of the Good Shepherd from the voice of a stranger? Can any person answer this question? I can. It is very easy. To every philosopher upon the earth, I say, your eye can be deceived, so can mine; your ear can be deceived, so can mine; the touch of your hand can be deceived, so can mine; but the Spirit of God filling the creature with revelation and the light of eternity, cannot be mistaken—the revelation which comes from God is never mistaken. When an individual, filled with the Spirit of God, declares the truth of heaven, the sheep hear that, the Spirit of the Lord pierces their inmost souls and sinks deep into their hearts; by the testimony of the Holy Ghost light springs up within them, and they see and understand for themselves. This is the way the Gospel should be preached by every Elder in Israel, and by this power every hearer should hear; and if we would know the voice of the Good Shepherd, we must live so that the Spirit of the Lord can find its way to our hearts. 16:74.

Peter was blessed, because he had eyes to see; and when he saw with his spiritual eyes, he acknowledged it. He was not so proud and high-minded as to turn round and deny. If the conviction of their own minds had free course, and were not trammeled through their erroneous traditions, millions and millions would hail this day with thanksgiving. 7:8.

If there is a person in the midst of the Latter-day Saints—one who has named the name of Christ as a Latter-day Saint, that can ask for any more literal testimony than we have, I do not know what he would ask. He might wish to see some person that had power to bring fire down from heaven. Should such a person appear, the exercise of that power would by no means prove that he was a messenger of salvation. Or suppose that I should see a man capable of raising the dead every hour in a day, could I merely for that believe he was sent of God? No. Some may think it strange, but should I see a man come along here and cast his cane on the floor, and it became a serpent and ran out of the door, would I any more believe that man to be sent of God? No, I would not. Were I to see a person fill the air with living creatures, turn the dust into life; or the river Jordan into blood, do you suppose I would any more for that consider that man sent of God? Not in the least. There is but one witness—one testimony, pertaining to the evidence of the Gospel of the Son of God, and that is the Spirit that be diffused among his disciples. Do his will, and we shall know whether he speaks by the authority of the Father or of himself. Do as he commands us to do, and we shall know of the doctrine, whether it is of God or not. It is only by the revelations of the Spirit that we can know the things of God. 9:2.

Many men and women who have obeyed the Gospel, and have not received from the Lord these striking testimonies, will say, "Well, I really do not know that I can tell whether the Gospel is true or not." To all such I say, Then you are no philosopher at all, for upon the rational principles of common philosophy you can tell whether it is true or not. Does it contain the seeds of life? Does it promote the plants and yield the fruits of life, or does it produce the plants and yield the fruits of death? Not that I wish to make a mere historical convert, or a people who believe historically, mathematically, or philosophically; but I know and understand that the Lord never leaves his children without a witness. 14:112.

The older portion of this community embraced the truth through the conviction of it, and prayed unto the Lord for the light of it, and they received the testimony of the Spirit of God; but our children do not know the greatness of their blessings and privileges. They are entitled to the spirit of the Gospel from their mothers' wombs; they have it with them all the time; they are born in it. 11:215.

A great many come to me and say, "I wish to do exactly as the Lord shall direct through you, Brother Brigham." If I had the word of the Lord, I would not dare give it to them, unless I knew it was an absolute duty. They never would obey it, because they are taught the word of the Lord here all the time, but do they hearken to it? Those who have wisdom within themselves, who have in possession the spirit of the Gospel, know what they hear from this stand. They know truth from error; they are satisfied, and never ask the Lord to give them more revelation, but to give them grace to observe and keep what they have received. 3:338.

Truth commends itself to every honest person, it matters not how simply it is told, and when it is received it seems as though we had been acquainted with it all our lives. It is the testimony of the majority of the Latter-day Saints that when they first heard the Gospel preached, as contained in the Bible and Doctrine and Covenants, although entirely new to them, it seemed as though they already understood it, and that they must have been "Mormons" from the beginning. 19:42.

I frequently think that the only way for a man to prove any fact in the world is by experience. We go, for instance, into an orchard and some says there is a sweet apple tree, and he may say the same of other trees, but without tasting, how shall I know they are sweet? Unless I taste of them I cannot know it. I may take the testimony of others who have tasted them, as to whether they are sweet, sour or bitter, but without tasting it cannot prove to my senses that they are so. Now, as I understand it, it is the same with all facts that have come to the knowledge of all beings in heaven, or on earth—all facts are proved and made manifest by their opposite. 13:59.

My testimony is based upon experience, upon my own experience, in connection with that obtained by observing others. To me it has become positively true—no doubt remains upon my mind, whatever, as to the power of the revealed will of heaven to man upon the minds of the people, when the principles of salvation are set before them by the authorized ministers of heaven. The heavenly truth commends itself to every person's judgment and to their faith; and more especially to the sense of those who wish to be honest with themselves, with their God, and with their neighbor. Yet I must admit that all men are not operated upon alike; the evidence of truth comes more forcibly to the understandings of some than others. This is owing to numerous influences. The Gospel may be preached to an individual, and the truth commend itself to the conscience of that person, creating but a little faith in its truth, to which there may be an addition made. If persons can receive a little, it proves they may receive more. If they can receive the first and second principles with an upright feeling, they may receive still more, and the words of the prophet be fulfilled. 2:1-2.

My testimony is positive. I know that there are such cities as London, Paris, and New York—from my own experience or from that of others; I know that the sun shines, I know that I exist and have a being, and I testify that there is a God, and that Jesus Christ lives, and that he is the Savior of the world. Have you been to heaven and learned to the contrary? I know that Joseph Smith was a Prophet of God, and that he had many revelations. Who can disprove this testimony? Any one may dispute it, but there is no one in the world who can disprove it. I have had many revelations; I have seen and heard for myself, and know these things are true, and nobody on earth can disprove them. The eye, the ear, the hand, all the senses may be deceived, but the Spirit of God cannot be deceived; and when inspired with that Spirit, the whole man is filled with knowledge, he can see with a spiritual eye, and he knows that which is beyond the power of man to controvert. What I know concerning God, concerning the earth, concerning government, I have received from the heavens, not alone through my natural ability, and I give God the glory and the praise. Men talk about what has been accomplished under my direction, and attribute it to my wisdom and ability; but it is all by the power of God, and by intelligence received from him. I say to the whole world, receive the truth, no matter who presents it to you. 16:46.

Why Some Men Reject the Gospel—I have often heard men say they were convinced that "Mormonism" was true, and that they would cleave to it; but as for their hearts being converted, it is altogether another thing. 6:321.

Wherever the Gospel of Jesus Christ has been preached, either in these or former days, it has met with a class of men to whom the truth looked lovely and God-like, and the spirit within would prompt them to embrace it; but they find themselves so advantageously connected in the world, and have so many interests at stake if they should embrace it, they conclude that it will not do, and here comes the warfare again. Some few will overcome the reasonings of the flesh, and follow the dictates of the spirit; while the great majority of this class of persons are won over by sordid considerations and cleave to their idols. 11:237.

They would come now by thousands and thousands, if the Latter-day Saints were only popular. "What, these honorable men?" Yes, they would say, "I want to be baptized. I admire your industry, and your skill in governing. You have a system of governing that is not to be found anywhere else. You know how to govern cities, territories, or the world, and I would like to join you." But take care if you join this people without the love of God in your soul it will do you no good. If they were to do this, they would bring in their sophistry, and introduce that which would poison the innocent and honest and lead them astray. I look at this, and I am satisfied that it will not do for the Lord to make this people popular. Why? Because all hell would want to be in the Church. The people must be kept where the finger of scorn can be pointed at them. Although it is admitted that we are honest, industrious, truthful, virtuous, self-denying, and, as a community, possess every moral excellence, yet we must be looked upon as ignorant and unworthy, and as the offscouring of society, and be hated by the world. What is the reason of this? Christ and Baal can not become friends. When I see this people grow and spread and prosper, I feel that there is more danger than when they are in poverty. Being driven from city to city or into the mountains is nothing compared to the danger of our becoming rich and being hailed by outsiders as a first-class community. I am afraid of only one thing. What is that? That we will not live our religion, and that we will partially slide a little from the path of rectitude, and go part of the way to meet our friends. 12:272.

Testimony Not Built Upon a Man—Some men declare that they wish to have such confidence in their leaders as not to enquire whether this or that is right, but to perform what they are bid to do. No man will have that degree of confidence, unless it is founded in truth. 4:296.

Joseph Smith a Witness of the Truth—The Devil and his emissaries thought if they could only destroy Joseph Smith, that the system he had laid the foundation to build upon would crumble and fall to rise no more; but it is evident to all, that since the death of Joseph, the system has flourished with greater vigor than before, for where there is a testament in full force, there must also of necessity be the death of the testator, for a testament is of force after men are dead. 10:304.

Whosoever confesseth that Joseph Smith was sent of God to reveal the holy Gospel to the children of men, and lay the foundation for gathering Israel, and building up the Kingdom of God on the earth, that spirit is of God, and every spirit that does not confess that God has sent Joseph Smith, and revealed the everlasting Gospel to and through him, is of Antichrist, no matter whether it is found in a pulpit or on a throne. 8:176.

This whole people were cast out for believing that God spake to Joseph Smith and chose him to be his messenger—his Apostle—to this generation. I testify to you that we were not cast out for teaching and practicing the Patriarchal doctrine, as our enemies now declare, for at that time it had not been published to the world, but it was for believing, preaching, and practicing the doctrines of the New Testament; for believing in the events to take place in the latter days, as foretold by the ancient Prophets; and, for believing the declarations of Joseph Smith, that Jesus was indeed the Christ and the Savior of all men, but especially of them that believe, and that he had set his hand the second time to gather his people, to establish his Kingdom, to build up Zion, redeem Jerusalem, empty the earth of wickedness and bring in everlasting righteousness. 9:366.

A Duty to Listen to the Truth—Do not say, "You are Mormons, and we do not want to hear anything about you." Wait until you have searched and researched and have obtained wisdom to understand what we preach, or to prove it to be untrue. If you cannot prove it untrue and are not disposed to receive it, let it alone. If it is the work of God, it will stand. What do you say, outsiders? What do you say, Christian world and heathen world? If we have the truth to present to you, which will do you good here and hereafter, which will save you today and tomorrow and every day, until it saves you in the Kingdom of God and brings you to a perfect state of felicity and happiness in the presence of the Father, will you have it? 12:313-314.

In the Christian world, thousands and millions of them are as close to the truth as any man that ever lived upon the face of the earth, so far as moral, Christian deportment is concerned. I can find a great many of this community who live as moral lives as men and women can. Is there anything else necessary and important? Yes —so to live as to have the light of the Spirit of truth abiding within you day by day, that when you hear the truth, you know it as well as you know the faces of your father's family, and also understand every manifestation produced by erroneous principles. 6:331.

Chapter XXXIX

THE CHURCH AND KINGDOM OF GOD ON EARTH

Israel—Who was Israel? They are those who are of the seed of Abraham, who received the promise through their forefathers; and all the rest of the children of men, who receive the truth, are also Israel. My heart is always drawn out for them, whenever I go to the throne of grace. 1:107.

Israel is dispersed among all the nations of the earth; the blood of Ephraim is mixed with the blood of all the earth. Abraham's seed is mingled with the rebellious seed through the whole world of mankind. 16:75.

The Elders who have arisen in this Church and Kingdom are actually of Israel. 2:268.

Those islanders and the natives of this country are of the House of Israel—of the seed of Abraham, and to them pertain the promise; and every soul of them, sooner or later, will be saved in the Kingdom of God, or be destroyed root and branch. 6:199.

Again, if a pure Gentile firmly believes the Gospel of Jesus Christ, and yields obedience to it, in such a case I will give you the words of the Prophet Joseph: "The effect of the Holy Ghost upon a Gentile is to purge out the old blood, and make him actually of the seed of Abraham." 2:269.

We are to build up and establish Zion, gather the House of Israel, and redeem the nations of the earth. This people have this work to do, whether we live to see it or not. This is all in our hands. 8:68.

It is obligatory upon us to see that the House of Israel have the Gospel preached to them; to do all that is in our power to gather them to the land of their fathers, and to gather up the fulness of the Gentiles before the Gospel can go with success to the Jews. 12:113.

We are now gathering the children of Abraham who have come through the loins of Joseph and his sons, more especially through Ephraim, whose children are mixed among all the nations of the earth. The sons of Ephraim are wild and uncultivated, unruly, ungovernable. The spirit in them is turbulent and resolute; they are the Anglo-Saxon race, and they are upon the face of the whole earth, bearing the spirit of rule and dictation, to go forth from conquering to conquer. They search wide creation and scan every nook and corner of this earth to find out what is upon and within it. I see a congregation of them before me today. No hardship will discourage these men; they will penetrate the deepest wilds and overcome almost insurmountable difficulties to develop the treasures of the earth, to further their indomitable spirit for adventure. 10:188.

The Church and the Kingdom—Out of this Church will grow the Kingdom which Daniel saw. This is the very people that Daniel saw would continue to grow and spread and prosper; and if we are not faithful, others will take our places, for this is the Church and people that will possess the Kingdom for ever and ever. 8:143.

We shall preach on, we shall struggle on until the kingdoms of this world shall become the Kingdom of our God and his Christ. 11:240.

This is the Kingdom of God on the earth. The people that sit before me, in connection with the many thousands that are upon the earth, are the people of God. If we have become so taught that the Lord sees that we shall be capable of managing, governing, and controlling the Kingdom of God upon the earth in a more perfect manner than it has been heretofore, you may rest assured that this people are bound to victory. Just as fast as we are capable of rightly dispensing the principles of power, of light, of knowledge, of intelligence, of wealth, of heaven, and of earth, just so fast will they be bestowed upon this people. 5:327.

If this Gospel goes to the uttermost parts of the earth and fulfils its destiny as predicted by the Prophets, by Jesus and by the Apostles, it will eventually swallow up all the good there is on the earth; it will take every honest, truthful and virtuous man and woman and every good person and gather them into the fold of this Kingdom, and this society will enlarge, spread abroad and multiply, and will increase in knowledge until the members composing it know enough to lengthen out their days and man's longevity returns, and they begin to live as men did anciently. 11:303.

What will be the final result of the restoration of the Gospel, and the destiny of the Latter-day Saints? If they are faithful to the Priesthood which God has bestowed upon us, the Gospel will revolutionize the whole world of mankind; the earth will be sanctified, and God will glorify it, and the Saints will dwell upon it in the presence of the Father and the Son. 12:113.

An Object of the Church—We are exhorted to make our own heaven, our own paradise, our own Zion. 9:170.

We have an object in view, and that is to gain influence among all the inhabitants of the earth for the purpose of establishing the Kingdom of God in its righteousness, power and glory, and to exalt the name of the Deity, and cause that name by which we live to be revered everywhere that he may be honored, that his works may be honored, that we may be honored ourselves, and deport ourselves worthy of the character of his children. 11:274.

If the Latter-day Saints think, when the Kingdom of God is established on the earth, that all the inhabitants of the earth will join the Church called Latter-day Saints, they are mistaken. I presume there will be as many sects and parties then as now. Still, when the Kingdom of God triumphs, every knee shall bow and every tongue confess that Jesus is the Christ, to the glory of the Father. Even the Jews will do it then; but will the Jews and Gentiles be obliged to belong to the Church of Jesus Christ of Latter-day Saints? No; not by any means. Jesus said to his disciples, "In my Father's house are many mansions; were it not so I would have told you; I go to prepare a place for you, that where I am, there ye may be also," etc. There are mansions in sufficient numbers to suit the different classes of mankind, and a variety will always exist to all eternity, requiring a classification and an arrangement into societies and communities in the many mansions which are in the Lord's house, and this will be so for ever and ever. Then do not imagine that if the Kingdom of God is established over the whole earth, all the people will become Latter-day Saints. They will cease their persecutions against the Church of Jesus Christ, and they will be willing to acknowledge that the Lord is God, and that Jesus is the Savior of the world. 11:275.

The Kingdom of God to Develop Gradually—The Kingdom we are talking about, preaching about and trying to build up is the Kingdom of God on the earth, not in the starry heavens, nor in the sun. We are trying to establish the Kingdom of God on the earth to which really and properly everything that pertains to men—their feelings, their faith, their affections, their desires, and every act of their lives—belong, that they may be ruled by it spiritually and temporally. 10:328.

In that helpless infant upon its mother's breast we see a man, an Apostle, a Saint,—yea, generations of men with kingdoms, thrones, and dominions. Then the life of that little frail mortal is fraught with great and mighty results, and its value is inestimable.

If this be true of an infant, what may we expect to grow out of this infant Kingdom? We may look forward to all that belongs to greatness and goodness, to might and power, to dominion and glory. Then how jealously we ought to guard the rights of this infant power? How zealous and constant we should be in maintaining its interests and supporting its laws and sacred institutions! 9:170-171.

We are called to establish the Kingdom of God literally, just as much as we are spiritually. If we do not build it up in a temporal point of view, we will not accomplish what we are called to do; we will come short of our duty, and be removed out of the way, and others will be called to succeed us who will perform the labor we are called to do. 10:332.

I do not believe that the City of Enoch made greater advancement, in the same period of time, than this people have done in the twenty-six years of their career, which is saying a great deal for them. 3:374.

The Effect of the Kingdom of God—What is the Kingdom of God going to accomplish on the earth? It will revolutionize not only the United States, but the whole world, and will go forth from the morning to the evening, from the rising of the sun to the going down of the same, so shall be the ushering forth of the Gospel until the whole earth is deluged with it, and the righteous are gathered. 2:190.

No unrighteous person, no person who is filthy in his feelings will ever enter into the Kingdom of God. 3:275.

As this Kingdom of God grows, spreads, increases, and prospers in its course, it will cleanse, thoroughly purge, and purify the world from wickedness. He who supposes his house to be built upon a rock, and well calculated to withstand any test that may be applied to it, finds, when it is tried by the Gospel of the Kingdom, that its foundation proves to be sand, and the whole fabric appears nothing in which a man may securely trust for salvation. 1:190.

When the Kingdom of God is fully set up and established on the face of the earth, and takes the pre-eminence over all other nations and kingdoms, it will protect the people in the enjoyment of all their rights, no matter what they believe, what they profess, or what they worship. If they wish to worship a god of their own workmanship, instead of the true and living God, all right, if they will mind their own business and let other people alone. 2:310.

If we wish this Church and Kingdom of God upon earth, to be like a fine, healthy, growing tree, we should be careful not to let the dead branches remain too long. 3:274.

Government of the Kingdom of God—Every kingdom will be blotted out of existence, except the one whose ruling spirit is the Holy Ghost, and whose king is the Lord. 2:124.

It may be asked what I mean by the Kingdom of God. The Church of Jesus Christ has been established now for many years, and the Kingdom of God has got to be established, even that Kingdom which will circumscribe all the kingdoms of this world. It will yet give laws to every nation that exists upon the earth. This is the Kingdom that Daniel, the Prophet, saw should be set up in the last days. What Daniel saw should come to pass in the latter times is believed by nearly all the religious societies of Christendom. The only great difference between us and then is in the method of its establishment. 11:275.

When this Kingdom is organized in any age, the Spirit of it dwells in the hearts of the faithful, while its visible department exists among the people, with laws, ordinances, helps, governments, officers, administrators, and every other appendage necessary for its complete operation to the attainment of the end in view. 10:18.

The Lord designs to build up a Kingdom that will be both a spiritual and temporal Kingdom upon the earth. The earth and the kingdoms thereof will be given unto the Saints of the Most High God. Will they be rich then? Do you not think they will possess the gold mines and the treasures of the earth? Yes. But some cry out, "That is not yet." That is right. How long will it be until then? As soon as we are prepared to receive them. 10:332.

If we ever attain enough faith to obtain the Kingdom of God, as we anticipate, we shall obtain all the wealth there is for this Kingdom in time and eternity. We shall not rob other kingdoms, but we shall possess the eternity of matter that lies in the path of the onward progress of this Kingdom, and still eternity and its fulness will continue to stretch out before us. The great powers of eternal wisdom will be exercised to enhance the wealth, beauty, excellency and glory of this Kingdom, previous to its being introduced into the presence of the Father and the Son. This work we have to help perform. 10:301.

I have learned years ago that the Lord stands at the helm that guides Zion's ship. He is its Dictator; and unless we work exactly to the line that is marked out by him, our works will be in vain. This has been my experience from the beginning. In every branch and avenue of our lives we must learn to work to the line of truth. It is for us to know what ought to be done, and then do it. Though there should be no earthly prospect of accomplishing it, we can certainly try; and if we try with all our might, that act will prove at least a resolute and determined mind, adorned with patience and perseverance. And if, with all our resolute endeavors we are still unable to accomplish our purpose, the Lord will be very likely to stretch forth his hand and give the victory. 6:315.

If this people live to the principles they have embraced, they will be capable of counselling the nations; for we build upon a just foundation, and our principles are truth, righteousness, and holiness. Let us stand by those principles until they crush out folly from these valleys, and we become teachers of wisdom to the nations. 7:66.

It Will Continue—All is right. God can carry on his own work. This Kingdom will stand forever. 8:69.

The Lord will never suffer this people to dwindle down, and be hid up in a corner; it cannot be; neither does he want any person to help them but himself. 1:364.

God has commenced to set up his Kingdom on the earth, and all hell and its devils are moving against it. Hell is yawning and sending forth its devils and their imps. What for? To destroy the Kingdom of God from the earth. But they cannot do it. 5:75.

The soldiers of the Lord are in the mountains, in the canyons, upon the plains, on the hills, along the mighty streams, and by the rivulets. Thousands and thousands more are for us than those who are against us, and you need not have any fears. 5:57.

My heart is comforted. I behold the people of God, that they have been hunted, cast out, driven from the face of men. The powers of earth and hell have striven to destroy this Kingdom from the earth. The wicked have succeeded in doing so in former ages; but this Kingdom they cannot destroy, because it is the last dispensation—because it is the fulness of times. It is the dispensation of all dispensations, and will excel in magnificence and glory every dispensation that has ever been committed to the children of men upon the earth. The Lord will bring again Zion, redeem his Israel, plant his standard upon the earth, and establish the laws of his Kingdom, and those laws will prevail. 8:36.

If there are any hearts or spirits in this city, or elsewhere, that are fearfully wondering whether or not we are going to be destroyed, or whether this Church will endure and become the mighty power in the earth, according to the prediction of the servants of God, I will say to all such trembling souls, you need entertain no such fears. You need have only one fear, and that is with regard to yourselves, lest you should leave the light that the Lord has imparted to you and wander into darkness, returning to the beggarly elements of the world, lusting again after the things of the world in their sinful state. 19:3.

We cannot help being Saints; we cannot prevent the rolling forth of the work of God; in and of ourselves we have no power to control our own minds and passions; but the grace of God is sufficient to give us perfect victory. The power of the Lord our God helps us, and the Devil and his emissaries help us—the one on the one hand, the other on the other hand. We have power to receive the truth or reject it, and we have power to reject the evil or receive it. 8:226.

When the wicked have power to blow out the sun, that it shines no more; when they have power to bring to a conclusion the operations of the elements, suspend the whole system of nature, and make a footstool of the throne of the Almighty, they may then think to check "Mormonism" in its course, and thwart the unalterable purposes of heaven. Men may persecute the people who believe its doctrines, report and publish lies to bring tribulation upon their heads, earth and hell may unite in one grand league against it, and exert their malicious powers to the utmost, but it will stand as firm and immovable in the midst of it all as the pillars of eternity. Men may persecute the Prophet, and those who believe and uphold him, they may drive the Saints and kill them, but this does not affect the truths of "Mormonism" one iota, for they will stand when the elements melt with fervent heat, and the heavens are wrapt up like a scroll, and the solid earth is dissolved. "Mormonism" stands upon the eternal basis of omnipotence. Jehovah is the "Mormonism" of this people, their Priesthood and their power; and all who adhere to it will, in the appointed day, come up into the presence of the King Eternal, and receive a crown of life. 1:88.

The Business of Latter-day Saints—Our work is to bring forth Zion, and produce the Kingdom of God in its perfection and beauty upon the earth. 9:293.

We have no business here other than to build up and establish the Zion of God. It must be done according to the will and law of God, after that pattern and order by which Enoch built up and perfected the former-day Zion, which was taken away to heaven, hence the saying went abroad that Zion had fled. By and by it will come back again, and as Enoch prepared his people to be worthy of translation, so we, through our faithfulness, must prepare ourselves to meet Zion from above when it shall return to earth, and to abide the brightness and glory of its coming. 18:356.

I have Zion in my view constantly. We are not going to wait for angels, or for Enoch and his company to come and build up Zion, but we are going to build it. We will raise our wheat, build our houses, fence our farms, plant our vineyards and orchards, and produce everything that will make our bodies comfortable and happy, and in this manner we intend to build up Zion on the earth and purify it and cleanse it from all pollutions. Let there be an hallowed influence go from us over all things over which we have any power; over the soil we cultivate, over the houses we build, and over everything we possess; and if we cease to hold fellowship with that which is corrupt and establish the Zion of God in our hearts, in our own houses, in our cities, and throughout our country, we shall ultimately overcome the earth, for we are the lords of the earth; and, instead of thorns and thistles, every useful plant that is good for the food of man and to beautify and adorn will spring from its bosom. 9:284.

Individual Labor Required in the Kingdom of God—We have all kinds of fish in the Gospel net. 3:120.

The Lord will have a tried people. 16:28.

To be a Saint in the full sense of the word, is to be something very nearly perfect. If, however, we are striving to the utmost of the ability God has given us to prove that we are willing to serve him and perform our duties, we are justified. We have the Kingdom of God to build up, Zion to redeem; we have to sanctify ourselves so that we may be prepared to be caught up with the Church of the Firstborn, and if we improve every day and hour, then if we die we shall be found justified. But if we continue to live, we must become Saints in very deed, or come short of the fulness of the glory of God that is to be revealed. 16:41.

Many Latter-day Saints think when they have obeyed the Gospel, made a sacrifice in forsaking their homes, perhaps their parents, husbands, wives, children, farms, native lands, or other things held dear, that the work is done; but it is only just commenced. The work of purifying ourselves and preparing to build up the Zion of God on this continent has only just begun with us when we have got as far as that. 13:313.

A great many think that the Kingdom of God is going to bless them and exalt them, without any effort on their part. This is not so. Every man and woman is expected to aid the work with all the ability God has given them. Each person belonging to the human family has a portion of labor to perform in removing the curse from the earth and from every living thing upon it. When this work is performed, then will they possess all things. 10:301.

We have no correct individual interest separate from this Kingdom; if we have true interest at all, it is in the Kingdom of God. 3:154.

The Kingdom of God or Nothing—When the Kingdom of God is established, if each member of that Kingdom singly and individually will do his or her duty it will take care of itself, for it is a living, self-moving, self-sustaining, independent and heaven-ordained establishment. 11:249.

The Kingdom of God is all that is real worth. All else is not worth possessing, either here or hereafter. Without it, all else would be like a dry tree prepared for the burning—it is all consumed and the ashes are driven to the four winds. 8:185.

To me it is the Kingdom of God or nothing upon the earth. Without it I would not give a farthing for the wealth, glory, prestige and power of all the world combined; for like the dew upon the grass, it passeth away and is forgotten, and like the flower of the grass it withereth, and is not. Death levels the most powerful monarch with the poorest starving mendicant; and both must stand before the judgment seat of Christ to answer for the deeds done in the body. 11:126.

With us, it is the Kingdom of God, or nothing; and we will maintain it, or die in trying—though we shall not die in trying. It is comforting to many to be assured that we shall not die in trying; but we shall live in trying. We will maintain the Kingdom of God, living; and if we do not maintain it, we shall be found dying not only a temporal, but also an eternal death. Then take a course to live. 5:342.

If you give anything for the building up of the Kingdom of God, give the best you have. What is the best thing you have to devote to the Kingdom of God? It is the talents God has given you. How many? Every one of them. What beautiful talents! What a beautiful gift! It is more precious than fine gold that I can stand here and give you my ideas, and you can rise up and tell me what you think and feel, and thus exchange our ideas. It is one of the precious gifts bestowed upon human beings. Let us devote every qualification we are in possession of to the building up of God's Kingdom, and you will accomplish the whole of it. 8:346.

Chapter XL

SOME EFFECTS OF THE GOSPEL

The Nature of the Gospel—We have Zion in our view in her perfection. 4:270.

All knowledge and wisdom and every good that the heart of man can desire is within the circuit and circle of the faith we have embraced. 13:150.

The design of the Gospel is to reveal the secrets of the hearts of the children of men. 3:47-48.

Is there war in our religion? No; neither war nor bloodshed. Yet our enemies cry out "bloodshed," and "Oh, what dreadful men these Mormons are, and those Danites! how they slay and kill!" Such is all nonsense and folly in the extreme. The wicked slay the wicked, and they will lay it on the Saints. 12:30.

We offer life and salvation to the whole human family in the Gospel of the Son of God, and if they are not disposed to receive it they will suffer the consequence. It is for the Latter-day Saints to live their religion. 12:315.

Do you know that here is the standard, the nucleus, the fountain, the head for all the exercises of the Kingdom of God upon the face of the whole earth? Now, let the Saints in this congregation droop in their faith, and that spirit will spread before tomorrow morning throughout the vast domain of this creation. Every Elder that goes abroad is a witness of this fact. This spirit spreads through a telegraphic influence or force that is independent of wires. Let this people at the gathering-place wake out of their slumbers, gird on their armour, and go forth like men of war against wickedness, and every Branch throughout the Church feels the influence in a very short time—it is speedily imparted to all creation. The wires, as it were, are set, the lightnings flash over them, and all feel the influence, when we are doing our duty here. It all depends upon us here. 8:184.

The Gospel of life and salvation is the best institution that we, as mortal beings, can invest in. Go into the financial circles of the world, and you will find men gather and protect their plans for business, for railroads, for ship companies, for merchandizing, and various other pursuits. You will see those engaged in these companies associate together, confer with each other, lay their plans before each other, investigate them, scan every branch, and every part and particle of their business. We are engaged in a higher-toned branch of business than any merchants or railroad men, or any institution of an earthly nature, and it is pleasing to see the Latter-day Saints meet together to talk over this matter, and to learn the course they should pursue to gain the object of their pursuit. If an inquiry arises in any of your minds with regard to this, I will answer it by saying that we are in pursuit of all there is before us—life, light, wealth, intelligence, all that can be possessed on the earth by mortal man, and then in a higher state, where there will be more perfect development of the smattering knowledge than we received here, and all that can be enjoyed by intelligent beings in the celestial kingdoms of our God. 15:34.

The Latter-day Saints are a very peculiar people, and they are led in a peculiar way. We are brought into circumstances so as to be a stumbling block to the nations, through the failings and weaknesses of the Latter-day Saints. Jesus was a stumbling block to the nation of the Jews, and to the generation in which he lived, and to all that knew him, and how singular it is that Jesus Christ, at this late day, and at such a distance from the theater of his operations, should have attained such celebrity and fame; even his disciples are not only canonized, but almost deified, and looked upon as though they were Gods come down to dwell with men. Every circumstance connected with the Savior's life is looked upon as being divine. Christendom now acknowledge that Jesus was the Son of God; they look upon him as God manifested in the flesh according to the New Testament; yet the generation in which he lived did not see these tokens of divinity which this generation recognize. To them he was a "root out of dry ground"—"a stumbling block," "a rock of offense." So with the Latter-day Saints. They are a stumbling block to this generation. The world see all their weaknesses and faults, and see no divinity in the work in which they are engaged. Yet this is not to be wondered at, inasmuch as the world could not see it in Jesus when he dwelt in mortality. We are looked upon as a low, degraded, ignorant set of fanatics. This is the opinion of the great majority of the learned and refined world. Others say that our people are the dupes of a few. We do not claim to be very wise, but we do know that that portion of mankind called Christians in our day, who profess to be followers of the meek and lowly Jesus, are grossly ignorant of his character, and of the means and way of salvation which he offers to the world. The Latter-day Saints, as a people, may not be so far advanced in the knowledge of many of the sciences, as their neighbors; but they are learning how to take care of themselves, which is one of the greatest arts known to man. When the most learned and scientific among men scrutinize their own lives and experience, they are under the necessity of acknowledging that they are faulty, weak, ignorant; they are "strangers from the covenants of promise, having no hope, and without God in the world." 12:206-207.

There are professing Christians in our midst, who are so strict in their religious notions that they would rise in the morning at five o'clock and walk miles, if necessary, rather than miss their religious services; and they are those who are so zealous that they would measure the soil from here into old Jerusalem with their bodies if they could, to pay penance, as they call it. God does not require any such sacrifices as this; neither does he require any of these sacrifices which involve the shedding of blood or the loss of life. Such things do not belong to God's religion, they come through sin and transgression. Perhaps they who show such manifestations of their faith strengthen it and do themselves some good. All that is required of us is to sacrifice our feelings and to overcome the adversary by subduing the lust within us for anything but the Kingdom of God on the earth, the glory of God, and the salvation of our friends and families and of the human family from first to last; that our whole souls may be devoted to the building up of the Kingdom of God on the earth, and for the salvation of those who sleep, who died without the Gospel. 18:238.

Our religion is called "Mormonism" because the ancient records revealed to Joseph Smith were entitled, the Book of Mormon, according to the instructions given to him by the Lord; but I will call it the Plan of Salvation devised in the heavens for the redemption of mankind from sin, and their restoration to the presence of God.

It embraces every fact there is in the heavens and in the heaven of heavens—every fact there is upon the surface of the earth, in the bowels of the earth, and in the starry heavens; in fine, it embraces all truth there is in all the eternities of the Gods. 9:149.

Some of the Effects of the Gospel—The religion that we have embraced teaches us to prepare to live. 5:257.

But "Mormonism" has opened up light. Removing the curtain from the broad sunshine, it has lighted up the souls of hundreds of thousands, and they have been made to rejoice in the light of truth. 8:129.

With all the rest of the good that you can commit to memory, be sure to recollect that the Gospel of salvation is expressly designed to make Saints of sinners, to overcome evil with good, to make holy, good men of wicked, bad men, and to make better men of good. Wherein we are wicked, wherein we have evil passions, the Gospel will aid us in overcoming evil. It gives us the influence, the power, the knowledge, the wisdom, and the understanding to overcome our weaknesses and to purify ourselves before the Lord our God. 8:160.

When people receive the Gospel, their minds are opened; they see Zion in its glory; but they do not see the troubles on the plains, or the troubles with false brethren. 8:71.

What are the fruits of this Gospel when it is received into the heart of an individual? It will make a bad man good, and a good man better; it increases their light, knowledge, and intelligence, and enables them to grow in grace and in the knowledge of the truth, as the Savior did, until they understand men and things, the world and its doctrines, whether Christian, heathen or pagan, and will ultimately lead them to knowledge of things in heaven, on the earth or under the earth. 13:144.

Our religion teaches us truth, virtue, holiness, faith in God and in his Son Jesus Christ. It reveals mysteries, it brings to mind things past and present—unfolding clearly things to come. It is the foundation of mechanism; it is the spirit that gives intelligence to every living being upon the earth. All true philosophy originates from that Fountain from which we draw wisdom, knowledge, truth, and power. What does it teach us? To love God and our fellow creatures—to be compassionate, full of mercy, long-suffering, and patient to the forward and to those who are ignorant. There is a glory in our religion that no other religion that has ever been established upon the earth, in the absence of the true Priesthood, ever possessed. It is the fountain of all intelligence; it is to bring heaven to earth and exalt earth to heaven, to prepare all intelligence that God has placed in the hearts of the children of men—to mingle with the intelligence which dwells in eternity, and to elevate the mind above the trifling and frivolous objects of time, which tend downward to destruction. It frees the mind of man from darkness and ignorance, gives him that intelligence that flows from heaven, and qualifies him to comprehend all things. This is the character of the religion we believe in. 7:140-141.

Our belief will bring peace to all men and good will to all the inhabitants of the earth. It will induce all who sincerely follow its dictates to cultivate righteousness and peace; to live peaceably in their families; to praise the Lord morning and evening; to pray with their families, and will so fill them with the spirit of peace that they will never condemn or chasten any one unless it is well deserved. They will rise in the morning with their spirits as smooth and serene as the sun that is rising and giving life and heat to the world; just as calm and as smooth as the breeze on a summer evening. No anger, no wrath, no malice, contention or strife. If a wrong arises the party wronged will go to his neighbor and quietly investigate whether wrong was designed; and if the seeming transgressor is living according to the spirit of his religion, it will be found that he had designed no wrong, and that he will make ample amends, forgiveness will be accorded, and the trouble will end. This is the spirit and teaching of the Gospel.

How will perfection be obtained? By all persons in the Kingdom of God living so as to be revelators from the heavens for themselves and for all they preside over, that everything they have to perform in this life—every worldly care and duty, and all their walk and conversation before each other and before the Lord, may be marked out by the spirit of revelation. Is this the way to perfection? It is. This is the Gospel of our Lord Jesus Christ; this is the Gospel of life and salvation. 13:215.

We ought to understand that when our lives have been filled with all manner of wickedness, to turn and repent of our sins, to be baptized for the remission of them, and have our names written upon the Church records, does not prepare us for the presence of our Father and Elder Brother. What will? A continuation of faithfulness to the doctrines of Christ; nothing short of this will do it. 3:193-194.

It is very fortunate for those who receive this Gospel and the spirit of it in their hearts, for it awakes within them a desire to know and understand the things of God more than they ever did before in their lives, and they begin to inquire, read and search, and when they go to the Father in the name of Jesus he will not leave them without a witness. 14:135.

When people receive this Gospel, what do they sacrifice? Why, death for life. This is what they give: darkness for light, error for truth, doubt and unbelief for knowledge and the certainty of the things of God. 16:161.

The Saints in all ages have been protected, sustained and upheld by an Almighty Power in their sufferings, and the power of the religion of Jesus Christ has ever sustained them. The Jews anciently said, Let his blood be upon us and upon our children, and God took them at their word. 10:287.

You may as well undertake to terrify the Almighty on his throne, as to terrify a Latter-day Saint of the true stripe—one who has the true blood in him. 2:313.

The sound of the Gospel of life and salvation, to gather the House of Israel and redeem the children of men, is a terror to all nations. 8:13.

No blessing that is sealed upon us will do us any good, unless we live for it. 11:117.

Personal Joy in the Gospel—With me "Mormonism" is, "Out with the truth." 3:255.

The great object of my life is to establish the Kingdom of God upon the earth. 11:275.

It may be asked whether I have any idols? Yes, I have most darling idols—my God and my religion, and they are all the idols I wish to have. 9:106.

I feel happy. "Mormonism" has made me all I am, and the grace, the power, and the wisdom of God will make me all that I ever will be, either in time or eternity. 8:162.

You hear many talk about having made sacrifices; if I had that word in my vocabulary I would blot it out. I have never yet made what I call sacrifices; in my experience I know nothing about making them. 3:223.

Again, I say, if "Mormonism" is not all I anticipated it to be, it is nothing. If it is not in me, and I in it, if it is not all and in all to me, I am deceived in myself. It is everything in heaven and on earth to those who possess it truly. 2:128.

Our religion has been a continual feast to me. With me it is Glory! Hallelujah! Praise God! instead of sorrow and grief. Give me the knowledge, power, and blessings that I have the capacity of receiving, and I do not care how the Devil originated, nor anything about him; I want the wisdom, knowledge, and power of God. Give me the religion that lifts me higher in the scale of intelligence—that gives me the power to endure—that when I attain the state of peace and rest prepared for the righteous, I may enjoy to all eternity the society of the sanctified. 8:119.

The last time I spoke to you here I told you that I found my religion just as sweet to me in my private capacity, in my secret meditations upon my bed, and in my closet, in my office, or with my family, as it is when I am in this stand. I love it as well—esteem it as highly; it is as precious to my understanding, and it invigorates, buoys up, strengthens, and fills every power of my capacity with unspeakable joy, just as much at home as it does here. I hope this is the case with you all. If you live your religion, it is as dear to you when you are out of this Tabernacle as when you are here. 8:8.

I am happy; I am full of joy, comfort, and peace; all within me is light, for I desire nothing but to do the will of my Father in heaven. I delight not in unrighteousness, but in righteousness and truth. I seek to promote the good and happiness of myself and those with whom I am associated. 6:40.

My business is to save the people, not to oppress, plunder, and destroy them. It is also the duty of all the Elders to labor to save the people. 7:229.

I am so thankful that tongue cannot express what I feel, that I have the privilege of associating with the Saints, and of being a member in the Kingdom of God, and that I have friends in the Church of the Living God. 10:314.

I can say that I do not consider that I have ever suffered anything for this Kingdom—nothing in the least. I have never sacrificed anything, without it be the evil propensities that are sown in our nature, springing from the seed that was sown at the fall. 8:67.

The Lord has blessed me; he has always blessed me; from the time I commenced to build up Zion, I have been extremely blessed. I could relate circumstances of so extraordinary a character in regard to the providences of God to me, that my brethren and sisters would say in their hearts, "I can hardly give credence to this." But my heart has been set in me to do the will of God, to build up his Kingdom on the earth, to establish Zion and its laws, and to save the people; and I can say, truly and honestly, that the thought never came into my mind, in all my labors, what my reward will be, or whether my crown would be large or small, or any crown at all, a small possession, a large possession, or no possession. I have never had any thoughts or reflections upon this or cared the first thing about it. All that I have had in my mind has been that it was my duty to do the will of God, and to labor to establish his Kingdom on the earth. I do not love, serve or fear the Lord for the sake of getting rid of being damned, nor for the sake of getting some great gift or blessing in eternity, but purely because the principles which God has revealed for the salvation of the inhabitants of the earth are pure, holy and exalting in their nature. In them there is honor and eternal increase, they lead on from light to light, strength to strength, glory to glory, knowledge to knowledge, and power to power. 16:70.

"Mormonism" has done everything for me that ever has been done for me on the earth; it has made me happy; it has made me wealthy and comfortable; it has filled me with good feelings, with joy and rejoicing. Whereas, before I possessed the spirit of the Gospel I was troubled with that which I hear others complain of, that is, with, at times, feeling cast down, gloomy, and despondent; with everything wearing to me, at times, a dreary aspect.

But have the trees, the streams, the rocks, or any part of creation worn a gloomy aspect to me for one-half minute since I came in possession of the spirit of this Gospel? No, though before that time I might view the most beautiful gardens, buildings, cities, plantations, or anything else in nature, yet to me they all wore at times a shade of death.

They appeared at times as though a veil was brooding over them, which cast a dark shade upon all things, like the shade of the valley of death, and I felt lonesome and bad. But since I have embraced the Gospel not for one-half minute, to the best of my recollection, has anything worn to me a gloomy aspect; under all circumstances I have felt pleasant and cheerful.

When surrounded by mobs, with death and destruction threatening on every hand, I am not aware but that I felt just as joyful, just as well in my spirits, as I do now. Prospects might appear dull and very dark, but I have never seen a time in this Gospel but what I knew that the result would be beneficial to the cause of truth and the lovers of righteousness, and I have always felt to joyfully acknowledge the hand of the Lord in all things. 3:320.

I present myself before this congregation as a teacher of the way of life and salvation. 10:318.

Permit me to say, that I am proud of my religion. It is the only thing I pride myself in, on the earth. I may heap up gold and silver like the mountains; I may gather around me property, goods and chattels, but I could have no glory in that, compared with my religion; it is the foundation of light and intelligence; it swallows up the truth contained in all the philosophy of the world, both heathen and Christian; it circumscribes the wisdom of man; all the wisdom and power of the world; it reaches to that within the veil. Its bounds, its circumference, its end, its height, and depth, are beyond the comprehension of mortals, for it has none. 1:39.

I have an impulse within me to preach the Gospel of salvation. 4:43.

God, angels, and good men being my helpers, I will never cease to contend, inch by inch, until we gain the ground and possess the Kingdom. That is my feeling and faith, and we will accomplish it. I will prophesy, in the name of the Lord Jesus Christ, that we will possess the Kingdom of God upon the whole earth, and possess the earth. 8:166.

I know enough to let the Kingdom alone, and do my duty. It carries me, I do not carry the Kingdom. I sail in the old ship Zion, and it bears me safely above the raging elements; I have my sphere of action and duties to perform on board of that ship; to faithfully perform them should be my constant and unceasing endeavor. 11:252.

For nearly thirty years I have sought to know the truth, and to properly understand the principles of the holy Priesthood revealed from heaven through the Prophet Joseph; and I have ceased not, when I have had an opportunity, at the proper time and in the proper place, to present those principles to my fellow-men. 7:131.

I love to fight the devils, but I love to overcome them. 3:224.

We have forsaken the kingdom of darkness, have come out in open rebellion to the power of the Devil on this earth, and I for one will fight him, so help me God, as long as there is breath in my body, and do all in my power to overthrow his government and rule. And if he complains that I am infringing upon his ground, I shall very politely ask him to go to his own place, where he belongs. If any among this community want to sustain the government of the Devil in preference to the Kingdom of God, I wish them to go where they belong. I want to sustain the government of heaven, and shall stick fast to it, by the help of God. If we sustain it, it will build us up and crown us with victory and eternal life. 10:41.

But I am proud to say of my religion, I have studied it faithfully for twenty-two years, day and night, at home and abroad, upon the rivers, and upon the lakes, when traveling by sea and by land; have studied it in the pulpit; from morning till night; whatsoever might be my pursuit. I have studied it with as close an application as any college student ever did any subject he wished to commit to memory; and I can say I have only just got into the A B C of it; it leads the vision of my mind into eternity. 1:39.

Blessings Conditioned Upon Good Works—Every blessing the Lord proffers to his people is on conditions. These conditions are: "Obey my law, keep my commandments, walk in my ordinances, observe my statutes, love mercy, preserve the law that I have given to you inviolate, keep yourselves pure in the law, and then you are entitled to these blessings, and not until then." 16:162.

Good actions always result in blessings. The history of the people of God in all ages testifies that whenever they have listened to the counsel of heaven they have always been blessed. All this people are satisfied that they will be more blessed to hearken to good counsel than not to do so. 12:122.

Brethren and sisters, if we wish the blessings of heaven upon us, let us be faithful to our covenants and callings, faithful in paying tithing, in keeping the Word of Wisdom and in building temples. 16:69.

If the brethren will take hold and perform the labors devolving upon them, they shall be blessed in them. They will increase in health and in wealth. The Lord will bless the people in proportion as they bless themselves. 16:68.

I wish the people could realize that they walk, live, and abide in the presence of the Almighty. The faithful shall have eyes to see as they are seen, and you shall behold that you are in the midst of eternity and in the presence of holy beings, and be enabled ere long to enjoy their society and presence. You are greatly blessed. 8:200.

Do just as well as you know how in all things, never permitting yourself to commit an act unless the Spirit of God within you justifies you in doing it. And if you live every day of your lives according to the best light and understanding you possess, glorifying God, our Heavenly Father, just as far as your knowledge extends, I will promise you eternal life in the Kingdom of God. 19:220.

The man, or the woman, that mainly looks after the fruit, after the luxuries of life, good faith, fine apparel and at the same time professes to be a Latter-day Saint, if he does not get that spirit out of his heart, it will obtain a perfect victory over him; whereas he is required to obtain a victory over his lusts and over his unwise feelings. 4:52.

Increasing Blessings—Instead of the righteous being bound tighter and tighter, they will continue to have more and more liberty, as we are more and more faithful, and obtain more power with the heavens and more of the power of God upon us. Let us seek diligently unto the Lord until we obtain the faith of Jesus in its fulness, for those who possess this are free indeed. 10:288.

If the Lord had a people on the earth that he had perfect confidence in, there is not a blessing in the eternities of our God, that they could not bear in the flesh, that he would not pour out upon them. Tongue cannot tell the blessings the Lord has for a people who have proved themselves before him. 4:79.

The greatest blessing that can be bestowed on the children of men is power to civilize themselves after the order of the civilization of the heavens—to prepare themselves to dwell with heavenly beings who are capable of enduring the presence of the Gods. 8:7.

"Mormonism" keeps men and women young and handsome; and when they are full of the Spirit of God, there are none of them but what will have a glow upon their countenances; and that is what makes you and me young; for the Spirit of God is with us and within us. 5:210.

Personal Blessings Upon the People—Brethren and sisters, may God bless you! I bless you all the time, Hallelujah! Praise the name of Israel's God; for my soul exults in his name. 6:100.

I will say to you, my brethren and sisters, I bless you. I bless you according to the Priesthood that I hold and the keys thereof. I bless you in the name of Jesus Christ. 16:170.

God bless you! Peace be with you, and love be multiplied upon the people. I pray for the good all over the earth. My desire is to see the Kingdom of God prosper. 15:134.

May God bless you! Peace be upon you! Be fervent in spirit, humble, teachable, and prayerful, taking care of yourselves, endeavoring to save yourselves, and all you have any influence over, which is my continual prayer for you, in the name of Jesus Christ. Amen. 1:111.

Brethren and sisters, inasmuch as I have the right and privilege, through the Priesthood, I bless you in the name of the Lord, and say, be you blessed. These are my feelings to the Latter-day Saints, and would be to all the human family, if they would receive my blessings, in the name of Jesus Christ. Amen. 2:10.

May the Lord God Almighty bless the Saints, and every one who will permit his blessings to come upon them. I am under the same obligations to bless sinners as I am to bless Saints, if they will receive my blessings. I pray for the blessings of heaven upon the work of his hands, for we are all his children—the sons and daughters of our Parent who dwells in the heavens. 8:261.

God bless every good man. God bless the works of nature, God bless his own work, overthrow the wicked and ungodly and them that would destroy their fellow beings, that war and contentions may cease on the earth. O Lord, remove these from office and place good men at the head of the nations, that they may learn war no more, but go to, like rational and civilized beings, sustain peace on the earth and do good to each other. 12:289.

God bless you, and I pray that you may be blessed; but I pray you to bless yourselves. Brethren and sisters, let us bless ourselves, by doing the will of God, then we are right. 16:71.

I have experienced much in my life, and I will not ask you to do any better by one another, nor by me, that I do by you, and I will bless you all the time. I feel to bless you continually; my life is here, my interest, my glory, my pride, my comfort, my all are here, and all expect to have, to all eternity is wrapped up in the midst of this Church.

If I do not get it in this channel, I shall not have it at all. How do you suppose I feel? I feel as a father should feel towards his children. I have felt so for many years, even when I durst not say so; I have felt as a mother feels towards her tender offspring, and durst not express my feelings; but I have tried to carry out their expression in my life. May God bless you. Amen. 3:333.

I do not hate any man on earth or in hell. The worst wish I have for the wicked is that they may be obliged to live according to good and wholesome laws. 8:43.

There is not a man or woman on this earth that I hate; but I do most cordially hate their wicked acts. I am at war with false principles—with wickedness, sin, and abomination; and I expect to continue my warfare until I overcome. 7:6.

I feel happy; I feel at peace with all the inhabitants of the earth; I love my friends, and as for my enemies, I pray for them daily; and, if they do not believe I would do them good, let them call at my house, when they are hungry, and I will feed them; yea, I will do good to those who despitefully use and persecute me. I pray for them, and bless my friends all the time. 11:111.

If I had power, I certainly would bless the people with everything their hearts could wish if they would not sin. I would do, as I heard the mothers of some of my children say that went with me to St. George this winter, that I indulged them in everything they wanted. Why? Because they never manifested a desire for anything wrong. And if it were in my power I would bless all the inhabitants of the earth, with everything in which they could glorify God, and purify their own hearts. 18:362.

God bless you, my children, my little ones. I love you, I am a great lover of children and innocence and purity, and I am a hater of iniquity. I think very frequently, in looking upon the actions of men that I do not have compassion enough; but when I see the wolves among the lambs I am after them, to see that they do not destroy the lambs. I would have given worlds if I could have known the truth in my childhood, as I now hear it. I had a great desire to know it, and the priests were after me from the time I was eight years of age. I was infidel to their creeds, but not to the Bible, not to God, not to holiness, but to the creeds of the children of men I was infidel, and am to this day. I say, God bless you, my children. 19:65.

CHAPTER XLI

JOSEPH SMITH

A Prophet of God—I honor and revere the name of Joseph Smith. I delight to hear it; I love it. I love his doctrine. 13:216.

What I have received from the Lord, I have received by Joseph Smith; he was the instrument made use of. If I drop him, I must drop these principles; they have not been revealed, declared, or explained by any other man since the days of the Apostles. If I lay down the Book of Mormon, I shall have to deny that Joseph is a Prophet; and if I lay down the doctrine and cease to preach the gathering of Israel and the building up of Zion, I must lay down the Bible; and, consequently, I might as well go home as undertake to preach without these three items. 6:279-280.

I feel like shouting Hallelujah, all the time, when I think that I ever knew Joseph Smith, the Prophet whom the Lord raised up and ordained, and to whom he gave keys and power to build up the Kingdom of God on earth and sustain it. These keys are committed to this people, and we have power to continue the work that Joseph commenced, until everything is prepared for the coming of the Son of Man. This is the business of the Latter-day Saints, and it is all the business we have on hand. 3:51.

Not that Joseph was the Savior, but he was a Prophet. As he said once, when some one asked him, "Are you the Savior?" No, but L can tell you what I am—I am his brother." So we can say. 14:202.

Joseph Smith has laid the foundation of the Kingdom of God in the last days; others will rear the superstructure. 9:364.

I never saw any one, until I met Joseph Smith, who could tell me anything about the character, personality and dwelling-place of God, or anything satisfactory about angels, or the relationship of man to his Maker. Yet I was as diligent as any man need to be to try and find out these things. 16:46.

What is the nature and beauty of Joseph's mission? You know that I am one of his Apostles. When I first heard him preach, he brought heaven and earth together; and all the priests of the day could not tell me anything correct about heaven, hell, God, angels, or devils; they were as blind as Egyptian darkness. When I saw Joseph Smith, he took heaven, figuratively speaking, and brought it down to earth; and he took the earth, brought it up, and opened up, in plainness and simplicity, the things of God; and that is the beauty of his mission. I had a testimony, long before that, that he was a Prophet of the Lord, and that was consoling. Did not Joseph do the same to your understandings? Would he not take the Scriptures and make them so plain and simple that everybody could understand? Every person says, "Yes, it is admirable; it unites the heavens and the earth together," and as for time, it is nothing, only to teach us how to live in eternity. 5:332.

When you hear a man pour out eternal things, how well you feel, to what a nearness you seem to be brought with God. What a delight it was to hear Brother Joseph talk upon the great principles of eternity; he would bring them down to the capacity of a child, and he would unite heaven with earth, this is the beauty of our religion. 4:54.

There is not that being that ever had the privilege of hearing the way of life and salvation set before him as it is written in the New Testament, and in the Book of Mormon, and in the book of Doctrine and Covenants, by a Latter-day Saint, that can say that Jesus lives, that his Gospel is true, and at the same time say that Joseph Smith was not a Prophet of God. That is strong testimony, but it is true. No man can say that this book (laying his hand on the Bible) is true, is the word of the Lord, is the way, is the guide-board in the path, and a charter by which we may learn the will of God; and at the same time say, that the Book of Mormon is untrue; if he has had the privilege of reading it, or of hearing it read, and learning its doctrines. There is not that person on the face of the earth who has had the privilege of learning the Gospel of Jesus Christ from these two books, that can say that one is true, and the other is false. No Latter-day Saint, no man or woman, can say the Book of Mormon is true, and at the same time say that the Bible is untrue. If one be true, both are; and if one be false, both are false. If Jesus lives, and is the Savior of the world, Joseph Smith is a Prophet of God, and lives in the bosom of his father Abraham. Though they have killed his body, yet he lives and beholds the face of his Father in Heaven; and his garments are pure as the angels that surround the throne of God; and no man on the earth can say that Jesus lives, and deny, at the same time, my assertion about the Prophet Joseph. This is my testimony, and it is strong. 1:38.

Who can justly say aught against Joseph Smith? I was as well acquainted with him, as any man. I do not believe that his father and mother knew him any better than I did. I do not think that a man lives on the earth that knew him any better than I did; and I am bold to say that, Jesus Christ excepted, no better man ever lived or does live upon this earth. I am his witness. He was persecuted for the same reason that any other righteous person has been or is persecuted at the present day. 9:332.

I never have professed to be Brother Joseph, but Brother Brigham, trying to do good to this people. I am no better, nor any more important than another man who is trying to do good. If I am, I don't know it. If I improve upon what the Lord has given me, and continue to improve, I shall become like those who have gone before me; I shall be exalted in the celestial kingdom, and be filled to overflowing with all the power I can wield; and all the keys of knowledge I can manage will be committed unto me. What do we want more? I shall be just like every other man—have all that I can, in my capacity, comprehend and manage. 6:275-276.

Called and Directed by God—He called upon his servant Joseph Smith, Jr., when he was but a boy, to lay the foundation of his Kingdom for the last time. Why did he call upon Joseph Smith to do it? Because he was disposed to do it. Was Joseph Smith the only person on earth who could have done this work? No doubt there were many others who, under the direction of the Lord, could have done that work; but the Lord selected the one that pleased him, and that is sufficient. 11:253.

In all ages of the world that we have any knowledge of, when there was a people on the earth whom God acknowledged as his people, he has invariably dictated them in spiritual and in temporal things. This question was agitated year after year in the days of Joseph. The first two Bishops in the Church—Edward Partridge was the first—I was well acquainted with him, and Newel K. Whitney was the second—questioned the propriety of Joseph having anything to do with temporal things. Joseph would argue the case with them a little, and tell them how things were, and bring up scripture to show them that it could not be otherwise—that it was impossible for the Lord to dictate to people unless he dictated them in temporal affairs. The very first act after believing is a temporal act. After I hear the Gospel preached and believe it, I go down into the waters of baptism, which is a temporal act; it is an act that pertains to my will and my body; I will that my body shall go down into the water and be immersed for the remission of my sins; consequently, I have to go to the Elder who taught me the Gospel, the spiritual portion of the Kingdom, and apply to him to administer this temporal ordinance, and he has to do it; having taught the doctrine he officiate in the act and you will find through life, every circumstance, in every case, the man that dictates the spiritual Kingdom of God, must dictate the temporal affairs, it cannot be otherwise. I say this to you, because the idea in the minds of a few of the people is, "Brigham ought not to meddle with temporal affairs." They said so to Joseph, and they said so much about it, that I went into the temple at Kirtland, and challenged the men who were querying on this, to prove or bring up one instance where God did not manifest his will concerning temporal things whenever he made known his will to the children of men for establishing his Kingdom on the earth. They always came to the floor; they had to do it, there was nothing else for them; it prostrated every person. There was William E. McLellin, John F. Boynton, and Lyman Johnson who belonged to the Twelve, Frederick G. Williams, second counselor to Joseph, and two-thirds of the High Council, all talking about this, and I went into the temple and just challenged them to show wherein the Lord ever conferred upon any man in the world the power to dictate in spiritual affairs, that he did not in temporal affairs? They could not do it. I told them they could not draw the line between the spiritual and the temporal. All things were created first spiritual, and then temporal. Everything in the spirit world was presented as we see it now, and this temporal earth was presented there. We were in the spirit world, and we came here into this time, which is in eternity, nothing in the world only a change of time and seasons allotted to a change of being that makes it time to us. It is in eternity, and we are just as much in eternity now, as we shall be millions of years hence. But it is measured to finite beings, and it is changeable, and we call it temporal, while the fact is it is all spiritual in the first place, then temporal, then spiritual, and made immortal, consequently you cannot divide them. I say this for those to reflect upon who think that there is a difference between temporal and spiritual things. I do not say, for I do not know that there are any such here. 18:243.

Development of the Prophet—From the day that Joseph obtained the plates, and previous to that time, the Lord dictated him. He directed him day by day and hour by hour. 8:66.

Joseph continued to receive revelation upon revelation, ordinance upon ordinance, truth upon truth, until he obtained all that was necessary for the salvation of the human family. All the inhabitants of the earth are called of God; they are called to repent and be baptized for the remission of sins. 16:42.

We have passed from one thing to another, and I may say from one degree of knowledge to another. When Joseph first received the knowledge of the plates that were in the hill Cumorah, he did not then receive the keys of the Aaronic Priesthood, he merely received the knowledge that the plates were there, and that the Lord would bring them forth, and that they contained the history of the aborigines of this country. He received the knowledge that they were once in possession of the Gospel, and from that time he went on, step by step, until he obtained the plates, and the Urim and Thummim and had power to translate them. This did not make him an Apostle, it did not give to him the keys of the Kingdom, nor make him an Elder in Israel. He was a Prophet, and had the spirit of prophecy, and had received all this before the Lord ordained him. And when the Lord, by revelation, told him to go to Pennsylvania, he did so, and finished the translation of the Book of Mormon; and when the Lord, in another revelation, told him to come back, into New York State, and to go to old Father Whitmer's, who lived in a place opposite Waterloo, and there stop, he did so, and had meetings, and gathered up a few who believed in his testimony. He received the Aaronic Priesthood, and then he received the keys of the Melchizedek Priesthood, and organized the Church. He first received the power to baptize, and still did not know that he was to receive any more until the Lord told him there was more for him. Then he received the keys of the Melchizedek Priesthood, and had power to confirm after he had baptized, which he had not before. He would have stood precisely as John the Baptist stood, had not the Lord sent his other messengers, Peter, James and John, to ordain Joseph to the Melchizedek Priesthood. Then, after some of the brethren had been out preaching, he had a revelation that they should go up to the State of Ohio. I knew of them, though I was not acquainted with them before they went up there. They were seen by some of my family, my father saw and conversed with them. Then the way opened for a large gathering in the State of Ohio. Parley P. Pratt, Oliver Cowdery, Ziba Peterson, David Whitmer, John Whitmer, and a few others, went up there and preached the Gospel, and they came among the members of the society called Campbellites, formerly members of the Close Communion Baptists, their leader's name being Alexander Campbell. This man preached the doctrine that baptism was for the remission of sins, and that split the church; but when the brethren came to these societies and taught them, not only baptism for the remission of sins, but the laying on of hands for the reception of the Holy Ghost, they believed it, and were baptized for the remission of their sins, and received the laying on of hands for the Holy Ghost, and then received other ordinances.

At this time [1840] came a revelation that we could be baptized for our dead friends, but at first it was not revealed that a record should be kept of those who were baptized; but when he received an additional revelation to that effect, then a record was kept. Hundreds and thousands, I suppose, were baptized before any record was kept at all, and they were baptized over, and a record kept of the baptisms and the names of the administrator, those who acted for the dead, and of the dead, and of the witnesses. You can read in the book of Doctrine and Covenants, the letter that Joseph wrote, when he was away from home, in regard to having witnesses at these baptisms. I relate this to show you that the Lord did not reveal everything at once. But I need not dwell on this any longer. 18:239-240.

What Joseph Taught—All that Joseph Smith did was to preach the truth—the Gospel as the Lord revealed it to him—and tell the people how to be saved, and the honest-in-heart ran together and gathered around him and loved him as they did their own lives. He could do no more than to preach true principles, and that will gather the Saints in the last days, even the honest-in-heart. All who believe and obey the Gospel of Jesus Christ are his witnesses to the truth of these statements. 10:326.

The excellency of the glory of the character of Brother Joseph Smith was that he could reduce heavenly things to the understanding of the finite. When he preached to the people—revealed the things of God, the will of God, the plan of salvation, the purposes of Jehovah, the relation in which we stand to him and all the heavenly beings, he reduced his teachings to the capacity of every man, woman, and child, making them as plain as a well-defined pathway. This should have convinced every person that ever heard of him of his divine authority and power, for no other man was able to teach as he could, and no person can reveal the things of God, but by the revelations of Jesus Christ. 8:206.

No man was to be found who could teach repentance and baptism for the remission of sins, with authority to administer in the ordinances, until God commissioned Joseph Smith, and sent him forth with his commandment to the people. Previous to that time, I searched everything pertaining to the church; I searched high and low to find whether there was any such thing as pure religion upon the earth; I searched for a man that could tell me something of God, of heaven, of angels and of eternal life. I believed in God the Father, and in Jesus Christ, but I could not believe that the Church of Christ was upon the earth. The question was frequently asked, "Is the Methodist Church, the Quakers, or the Mother Church right?" No, I would reply, there is not a Bible church upon the earth. I might have continued to study the Bible and all the books that have been written, and without revelation from God I would have been like the sounding brass or tinkling cymbal, having no knowledge of God, of true religion, of the redemption of the living or of the dead; I would have lived and died in ignorance; and this was the condition of all the inhabitants of the earth. 10:311.

There was nothing of a temporal or spiritual nature suggested by Joseph Smith in his day, for the action of the Latter-day Saints that would not have been beneficial for them, if they had, with one heart and mind, performed all he desired them to do. 11:18.

Results of the Prophet's Labors—Joseph Smith, though he spent only fourteen years in presiding over this people, organizing the Church, proclaiming the Gospel and receiving revelations, yet had hundreds and thousands of men and women who were ready to go to the death with him. 14:149.

Now, as bad as myself and my brethren are, and as far as we are from the mark, and from the privileges we should enjoy, if Joseph Smith, Jr., the Prophet, could have seen the people in his day as willing to obey his voice, as they are today to obey the voice of their President, he would have been a happy man. He lived, labored, toiled, and worked; his courage was like the courage of an angel, and his will was like the will of the Almighty, and he labored till they killed him. 11:322.

Persecutions of the Prophet—Are there not scores of men and women here who are familiar with the death of our Prophet? Why did people hate him? Because of his influence. Did he gain or exercise an unrighteous influence? By no means. He possessed a righteous influence over the spirits, feelings, passions, and dispositions of all who delighted in truth and goodness, so far as he associated, and could guide them at his pleasure.

Am I hated for the same cause? I am. I am hated for teaching people the way of life and salvation—for teaching them principles that pertain to eternity, by which the Gods were and are, and by which they gain influence and power. Obtain that influence, and you will be hated, despised, and hunted like the roe upon the mountains. The way to obtain that influence is pointed out—by whom? By him through whom the worlds were created, and who has redeemed this earth and all things upon it. 7:3.

Our situation is peculiar at the present time. Has it not been peculiar ever since Joseph found the plates? The circumstances that surrounded him when he found the plates were singular and strange. He passed a short life of sorrow and trouble, surrounded by enemies who sought day and night to destroy him. If a thousand hounds were on this Temple Block, let loose on one rabbit, it would not be a bad illustration of the situation at times of the Prophet Joseph. He was hunted unremittingly. We have the privilege of believing the same Gospel that Joseph taught, and with him of being numbered with those whose names are cast out as evil. 10:315.

June 27, 1844, a little over fourteen years after the organization of this Church, Joseph Smith was slain. In his day there were but very few years of rest for the Saints. They occupied Nauvoo longer than any other one place; they lived there about seven years. We left Nauvoo in 1846, and from that time until now this Church has not been compelled to abandon their property and homes. We came here in the best and quickest way in our power, and have been building, fencing, planting, sowing, and making ourselves comfortable. It is now more than ten years since we first located here, unmolested and undisturbed. 7:42.

I lived close by where these plates were found. I knew that Joseph found them, from outward circumstances that transpired at the time. I shall not take time to relate but a little of the delicate, kind, benevolent, Christian-like, I will say anti-Godlike feelings of the priests and of the people who professed Christianity at the time that Joseph organized this Church. The very first thing that was circulated was this—"Did you know that Joe Smith and his followers got together last night, blew out the light, stripped themselves stark naked, and there they had the holy roll?" A great many of you do not understand this term. It came from the Shaking Quakers. I shall not attempt to relate here the conduct attributed to them, but from that sprung the peculiar phrase I have mentioned in your hearing this afternoon. In a very short time we were all thieves in the estimation of our so-called Christian neighbors. Said the priest to a beloved sister, "Sister, did you hear of such a man, he was a member of our church, a few days since, but he has joined old Joe Smith?" Says the sister, "No, can it be possible?" "Well, they say so," says the priest, and he himself had fabricated the entire story. This sister would tell it to another, and it would go all through the neighborhood that such a man, who only a few days before had been considered by them as good a brother as they had in their church, had become a chicken thief. But you cannot mention any crime that this people called Latter-day Saints have not been accused of committing by their so-called Christian neighbors; and these stories would generally commence by the priests whispering to some sister, "Did you hear of such and such a thing?" That was enough, all that was wanted, it became a solemn fact by the time it passed the third mouth. 16:67.

Had Joseph Smith been an impostor and of the world, the world would not have hated him, but would have loved its own. Had Joseph Smith made political capital of his religion and calling, and raised up a political party, he doubtless would have become celebrated and renowned in the world as a great man and as a great leader. 9:332.

Harassed by Lawsuits—He was poor, harassed, distressed, afflicted, and tormented with lawsuits, persecution upon persecution, and it cost thousands and hundreds of thousands of dollars to keep him alive, which a few had to sustain. Is this affliction upon them now? It is not. The scene is reversed. And as the people once thought, that many by one man could be made poor, they now believe, by one man many will be made rich. At the present day I do not know where the opportunity is to prove the people. 1:75.

Joseph Smith was arraigned before Judge Austin A. King, on a charge of treason. The Judge inquired of Mr. Smith, "Do you believe and teach the doctrine that in the course of time the Saints will possess the earth?" Joseph replied that he did. "Do you believe that the Lord will raise up a kingdom that will fill the whole earth and rule over all other kingdoms, as the Prophet Daniel has said?" "Yes, sir, I believe that Jesus Christ will reign King of nations as he does King of Saints." "Write that down, clerk; we want to fasten upon him the charge of treason, for if he believes this, he must believe that the State of Missouri will crumble and fall to rise no more." Lawyer Doniphan said to the Judge, "Judge, you had better make the Bible treason and have done with it." 9:331.

Joseph, our Prophet, was hunted and driven, arrested and persecuted, and although no law was ever made in these United States that would bear against him, for he never broke a law, yet to my certain knowledge he was defendant in forty-six lawsuits, and every time Mr. Priest was at the head of and led the band or mob who hunted and persecuted him. And when Joseph and Hyrum were slain in Carthage jail, the mob, painted like Indians, was led by a preacher. 14:199.

Joseph Smith, in forty-six prosecutions, was never proved guilty of one violation of the laws of his country. They accused him of treason, because he would not fellowship their wickedness. 10:111.

Of Good Character—We can find no person who presents a better character to the world, when the facts are known, than Joseph Smith, Jr., the Prophet, and his brother, Hyrum Smith, who was murdered with him. 14:203.

The history of Joseph and Mary is given to us by their best friends, and precisely as we will give the history of the Prophet Joseph. We know him to have been a good man, we know that he performed his mission, we know that he was an honorable man and dealt justly, we know his true character. 3:366.

But let his enemies give his character, and they will make him out one of the basest men that ever lived. Let the enemies of Joseph and Mary give their characters to us, and you would be strongly tempted to believe as the Jews believe. 3:366.

Why the Prophet Was Killed—If it be the will of the Lord for the people to live, they will live. If it had been the will of the Lord that Joseph and Hyrum should have lived, they would have lived. It was necessary for Joseph to seal his testimony with his blood. Had he been destined to live he would have lived. The Lord suffered his death to bring justice on the nation. The debt is contracted and they have it to pay. 13:95.

Many of the Prophets have sealed their testimony with their blood, that their testament might go forth with force and not return void. As in ancient days, so in modern days. When Joseph Smith sealed his testimony with his blood, his testament from that moment was in force to all the world; and woe to those who fight against it. 19:5.

Joseph Smith knew this, and when he went to Carthage he said, "I go to death; I go like a lamb to the slaughter; I go to my fate." 10:194.

If Brother Joseph Smith had taken a company and come to this country, as he intended to do, he could have been living here now, in spite of earth and hell. 5:342.

Forty-five years ago they were determined to kill the Prophet Joseph. I have lain upon the floor scores of nights ready to receive the mob who sought his life. This persecution commenced with a little neighborhood, then a town, then a county, then a state, and then the people of the United States; and by and by other nations will be just as bitter towards us and the doctrines we preach, as many of the people of our own nation now are. They will struggle and strive, and plan and devise, saying, "Let us take this course, and that course"; and they will struggle until they will come to a stop as though they were against a mountain of solid rock. They will do all they can to break us up, and even destroy us; this has been the case now for the last forty-five years. Joseph Smith had forty-six lawsuits, and I was with him through the most of them, and never was the first thing proved against him; he was never guilty of the first violation of the law or of good order. And when Governor Ford asked him to go to prison, as the mob were so enraged that he could not insure his life, that he might be safe until he returned from Nauvoo, he said: "I will pledge you the faith of the State of Illinois for your safety." But as soon as he was gone, the mob murdered both Joseph and his brother Hyrum, in the jail. That was to be so. I heard Joseph say many a time, "I shall not live until I am forty years of age." The spring before he was killed—his death occurred the 27th of June, 1844—he hurried off the first Elders of the Church. All right, I thought then, and I think so now. It is all in the hands of God. They killed Joseph, and what for? For the Gospel's sake. It was for no evil, for I was well acquainted with him. He testified to the truth, he sealed his testimony with his blood. Whether we believe in blood atonement or not, the Lord so ordered it, that Joseph, as well as others of the Prophets, sealed their testimony with their blood. 18:361.

Joseph's Work in the Spirit World—Jesus had a work to do on the earth. He performed his mission, and then was slain for his testimony. So it has been with every man who has been foreordained to perform certain important missions. Joseph truly said, "No power can take away my life, until my work is done." All the powers of earth and hell could not take his life, until he had completed the work the Father gave him to do; until that was done, he had to live. When he died he had a mission in the spirit world, as much so as Jesus had. 4:285.

Is Joseph glorified? No, he is preaching to the spirits in prison. He will get his resurrection the first of any one in this Kingdom, for he was the first that God made choice of to bring forth the work of the last days.

His office is not taken from him, he has only gone to labor in another department of the operations of the Almighty. He is still an Apostle, still a Prophet, and is doing the work of an Apostle and Prophet; he has gone one step beyond us and gained a victory that you and I have not gained, still he has not yet gone into the celestial kingdom, or, if he has, it has been by a direct command of the Almighty, and that, too, to return again so soon as the purpose has been accomplished. 3:371.

Nature of the Prophet and His Family—What of Joseph Smith's family? What of his boys? I have prayed from the beginning for Sister Emma and for the whole family. There is not a man in this Church that has entertained better feelings towards them. Joseph said to me, "God will take care of my children when I am taken." They are in the hands of God, and when they make their appearance before this people, full of his power, there are none but what will say, "Amen! we are ready to receive you." 8:69.

The Twelve, the Successors of the Prophet—At the death of Joseph, when the Twelve returned to Nauvoo, to use a comparison, the horses were all harnessed and the people were in the big carriage, and where were they going? They did not know. Who would gather up the lines and guide the team? No man would step forward, until I did. There was not one of the Twelve with me when I went to meet Sidney Rigdon on the meeting-ground. I went alone, and was ready alone to face and drive the dogs from the flock. 8:317.

Now, it is no more my duty to live so as to know the mind and will of the Lord than it is the duty of my brethren, the rest of the Twelve. I say the rest of the Twelve, because I am the President of the Quorum of the Twelve Apostles on the earth, and the only one that the Lord has acknowledged. It is true that Thomas B. Marsh was once President, but the Lord never acknowledged any man by revelation as President of that Quorum but myself. At the death of Joseph I stepped out from that position in the advance, according to the organization of the Church, for the sake of preserving the flock of God, but not according to my wishes, nor the desire of my heart, but it was my duty. When I heard of the Prophet's death I said, "What will become of the people? What will the Saints do now that the Prophet has gone?" It was my whole desire to preserve the sheep of the flock of God, and it is so today. Brother Kimball also stepped into the first Presidency, and we called others and ordained them to take our place for the time being, that the Church might be fully organized, and we expect to ordain more when we feel like it. 18:70.

Some Sayings of the Prophet—Joseph used to say, "When you get the Latter-day Saints to agree on any point, you may know it is the voice of God." 12:301.

Will the Constitution be destroyed? No, it will be held inviolate by this people; and, as Joseph Smith said, "The time will come when the destiny of the nation will hang upon a single thread. At this critical juncture, this people will step forth and save it from the threatened destruction." It will be so. 7:15.

Hundreds of people in this house are my witnesses, who heard Joseph say, when asked whether we should ever dare to leave Nauvoo, "The Saints will leave Nauvoo. I do not say they will be driven, as they were from Jackson County, Missouri, and from that State; but they will leave here and go to the mountains. And the next time the Saints remove, or are caused to remove, they will be turned out of the frying-pan, not into the fire, but into the middle of the floor." If this is not the middle of the floor, I do not know where you will find it. 8:356.

I recollect many times when Brother Joseph, reflecting upon how many would come into the Kingdom of God and go out again, would say, "Brethren, I have not apostatized yet, and don't feel like doing so." Many of you, no doubt, can call to mind his words. Joseph had to pray all the time, exercise faith, live his religion, and magnify his calling, to obtain the manifestations of the Lord, and to keep him steadfast in the faith. 2:257.

Who delivered Joseph Smith from the hands of his enemies to

the day of his death? It was God; though he was brought to the brink of death time and time again, and, to all human appearance, could not be delivered, and there was no probability of his being saved. When he was in jail in Missouri, and no person expected that he would ever escape from their hands, I had the faith of Abraham, and told the brethren, "As the Lord God liveth, he shall come out of their hands." Though he had prophesied that he would not live to be forty years of age, yet we all cherished hopes that that would be a false prophecy, and we should keep him forever with us; we thought our faith would outreach it, but we were mistaken—he at last fell a martyr to his religion. I said, "It is all right; now the testimony is in full force; he has sealed it with his blood, and that makes it valid." 1:364.

The question was asked a great many times of Joseph Smith, by gentlemen who came to see him and his people, "How is it that you can control your people so easily? It appears that they do nothing but what you say; how is it that you can govern them so easily?" Said he, "I do not govern them at all. The Lord has revealed certain principles from the heavens by which we are to live in these latter days. The time is drawing near when the Lord is going to gather out his people from the wicked, and he is going to cut short his work in righteousness, and the principles which he has revealed I have taught to the people and they are trying to live according to them, and they control themselves."

Gentlemen, this is the great secret now in controlling this people. It is thought that I control them, but it is not so. It is as much as I can do to control myself and to keep myself straight and teach the people the principles by which they should live. 13:176.

I recollect one remark that Brother Joseph used to make frequently, when talking to the Elders. No matter what he set them to do, whether he wanted them to go to a foreign land on a mission, or to go into business, he would say, "When you commence, go in at the little end of the horn; for if you do not, but enter at the big end, you will either have to turn round and come out at the end you went in at or go out at the small end, and be squeezed nigh unto death."

Let an Elder hire the best halls in large cities to begin with, and go to lecturing, and it will take him a long time to raise a Branch of this Church. But let him begin among the poor of the earth—those who live in the cellars, and garrets, and back streets; "for," says the Almighty, "I am going to take the weak things of the earth, and with them confound the wisdom of the wise." You will see that trait in every step of "Mormonism." God has chosen the obscure and weak, to bring them up and exalt them. Is not that the work of a God, the performance of this work without money and without price? The Gospel is sent to all the inhabitants of the earth—to the high and the low, the noble and the ignoble, the young and the old. "Here is the Gospel; you are welcome to it." "Don't you ask anything for it? Not a farthing. It has to go to the world, without money and price." Now, compare this with carrying the Gospel with your pockets full of money; and in the latter case, where is your glory and honor? 8:354.

I recollect, in Far West, Joseph, talking upon these matters, said, "The people cannot bear the revelations that the Lord has for them. There were a great many revelations if the people could bear them." I think it was the eighth day of July, 1831, Joseph had a revelation that the people should consecrate their surplus property for the building of a temple there in Far West, for the support of the Priesthood, for the paying of the debts of the Presidency, etc., which I could give an account of, for I was present when it came. Joseph was doing business in Kirtland, and it seemed as though all creation was upon him, to hamper him in every way, and they drove him from his business, and it left him so that some of his debts had to be settled afterwards; and I am thankful to say that they were settled up; still further, we have sent East to New York, to Ohio, and to every place where I had any idea that Joseph had ever done business, and inquired if there was a man left to whom Joseph Smith, Jr., the Prophet, owed a dollar, or a sixpence. If there was we would pay it. But I have not been able to find one. I have advertised this through every neighborhood and place where he formerly lived, consequently I have a right to conclude that all his debts were settled. 18:242.

Brother Kimball quoted a saying of Joseph the Prophet, that he would not worship a God who had not a Father; and I do not know that he would if he had not a mother; the one would be as absurd as the other. If he had a Father, he was made in his likeness. And if he is our Father we are made after his image and likeness. He once possessed a body, as we now do; and our bodies are as much to us, as his body to him. Every iota of this organization is necessary to secure for us an exaltation with the Gods. 9:286.

My name is had for good and evil upon the whole earth, as promised to me. Thirty years ago Brother Joseph, in a lecture to the Twelve said to me, "Your name shall be known for good and evil throughout the world," and it is so. The good love me, weak and humble as I am, and the wicked hate me; but there is no individual on the earth but what I would lead to salvation, if he would let me; I would take him by the hand, like a child, and lead him like a father in the way that would bring him to salvation. 10:297.

Chapter XLII

THE SETTLEMENT IN THE WEST

The Journey Across the Plains—A short recital of the reasons why these children before me were born here instead of being born in the States, I can give to you, and will endeavor to do so in a few words.

In 1830, forty-seven years ago last March, the Book of Mormon was printed and bound. Joseph Smith had received revelation, and plates on which were engraved characters from which the book was translated. Before the book was printed, before Joseph had the privilege of testifying to the truth of the latter-day work, persecution was raised against him. On the 6th day of April of the same year the Church of Jesus Christ was organized. Persecution increased and continued to increase. He left the State of New York and went to the State of Ohio. The Gospel was preached there and many received it. A settlement was formed, but Joseph had not the privilege of staying there long before they hunted him so determinedly that he was forced to leave Kirtland and the State of Ohio. He then went to Missouri. In the year 1838, in the month of March, in company with a number of brethren, myself included, Joseph arrived at Far West, Caldwell County, Missouri. We had not the privilege of staying there more than for a few months before the cry was raised against Joseph Smith, that he was guilty of high treason. This aroused the people and the government of the state; and in October, thirty-five hundred of the militia of the state of Missouri were marched against a few of us in Far West. They succeeded in taking Joseph and Hyrum and sixty-five others and putting them in prison. When Joseph had his trial, the great accusation against him was that he believed in the fulfilment of prophecy—the prophecies that had been made by Prophets of old and contained in Holy Writ. When Judge King asked Joseph if he believed the predictions of Daniel the Prophet, that in the latter-days the God of heaven would set up a kingdom which should succeed and finally rule and hold dominion over all other kingdoms, Joseph replied that he did believe this scripture as well as the rest. This was considered treason! Joseph's lawyer turned to Judge King and said, "Judge, I think you had better write it down that the Bible is treason," and this was all they found against him. But the mob continued until they drove the Latter-day Saints out of the state of Missouri. We were told if we remained there the people would be upon us. What we were guilty of we did not know, only that we believed in the Bible and the fulfilment of prophecy, or, in other words, in the literal reading of the word of God. They succeeded, after killing many of the Latter-day Saints—men, women, and children, cruelly massacring them—in driving us out of the state to the State of Illinois, where the people received us with open arms, especially the inhabitants of the city of Quincy; for which kindness the hearts of our people who passed through these scenes have ever been lifted to God, petitioning for blessings upon them. And they have been blessed. We lived in the State of Illinois a few years; and here, as elsewhere, persecution overtook us. It came from Missouri, centering itself upon Joseph, and fastened itself upon others. We lived in Illinois from 1839 to 1844, by which time they again succeeded in kindling the spirit of persecution against Joseph and the Latter-day Saints. Treason! Treason! Treason! they cried, calling us murderers, thieves, liars, adulterers, and the worst people on the earth. And this was done by the priests, those pious dispensers of the Christian religion whose charity was supposed to be extended to all men, Christian and heathen; they were joined by drunkards, gamblers, thieves, liars, in crying against the Latter-day Saints. They took Joseph and Hyrum, and as a guarantee for their safety, Governor Thomas Ford pledged the faith of the State of Illinois. They were imprisoned on the pretense of safekeeping, because the mob was so enraged and violent. The Governor left them in the hands of the mob, who entered the prison and shot them dead. John Taylor, who is present with us today, was in the prison, too, and was also shot, and was confined to his bed for several months afterwards. After the mob had committed these murders, they came upon us and burned our houses and grain. When the brethren would go out to put out the fire, the mob would lie concealed under fences, and in the darkness of the night, they would shoot them. At last they succeeded in driving us from the State of Illinois.

Three congressmen came in the fall of 1845, and had a conference with the Twelve and others; they were desirous that we should leave the United States. We told them we would do so, we had stayed long enough with them; we agreed to leave the State of Illinois in consequence of that religious prejudice against us that we could not stay in peace any longer. These men said the people were prejudiced against us. Stephen A. Douglas, one of the three, had been acquainted with us. He said, "I know you, I know Joseph Smith; he was a good man," and this people are a good people; but the prejudices of the priests and the ungodly are such that, said he, "Gentlemen, you cannot stay here and live in peace." We agreed to leave. We left Nauvoo in February, 1846. There remained behind a few of the very poor, the sick and the aged, who suffered again from the violence of the mob; they were whipped and beaten, and had their houses burned. We travelled west, stopping in places, building settlements, where we left the poor who could not travel any farther with the company. Exactly thirty years today myself, with others, came out of what we named Emigration Canyon; we crossed the Big and Little mountains, and came down the valley about three quarters of a mile south of this. We located, and we looked about, and finally we came and camped between the two forks of City Creek, one of which ran southwest and the other west. Here we planted our standard on this temple block and the one above it; here we pitched our camps and determined that here we would settle and stop. Still our brethren who tarried by the way were toiling through poverty and distress. At one time, I was told, they would have perished from starvation, had not the Lord sent quails among them. These birds flew against their wagons, and they either killed or stunned themselves, and the brethren and sisters gathered them up, which furnished them with food for days, until they made their way in the wilderness.

Children, we are the pioneers of this country, with one exception, west of the Mississippi river; we established the first printing press in every state from here to the Pacific Ocean, and we were the first to establish good schools; we were the first to plant out orchards and to improve the desert country, making it like the Garden of Eden. 19:60.

We wish strangers to understand that we did not come here out of choice, but because we were obliged to go somewhere, and this was the best place we could find. It was impossible for any person to live here unless he labored hard and battled and fought against the elements, but it was a first-rate place to raise Latter-day Saints, and we shall be blessed in living here, and shall yet make it like the Garden of Eden; and the Lord Almighty will hedge about his Saints and will defend and preserve them if they will do his will. The only fear I have is that we will not do right; if we do we will be like a city set on a hill, our light will not be hid. 14:121.

In the year 1845 I addressed letters to all the Governors of states and territories in the Union, asking them for an asylum, within their borders, for the Latter-day Saints. We were refused such privilege, either by silent contempt or a flat denial in every instance. They all agreed that we could not come within the limits of their territory or state. Three members of Congress came to negotiate with us to leave the confines of the United States, and of the public domain. It was understood that we were going to Vancouver Island; but we had our eyes on Mexico, and here we were located in the midst of what was then northern Mexico. 11:18.

When we were driven from Nauvoo, our Elders went to the east to lay our case before the judges, governors, and rulers of the different states to ask for an asylum; but none was offered us. We sent men through the eastern country to try and raise some means for the destitute women and children, whose husbands, fathers and brothers had gone into the Mexican war at the call of the general Government, leaving their wives and children and aged fathers and mothers upon the open prairies without home or shelter, and the brethren who went east hardly got enough to bear their expenses. The great men of the nation were asked if they would do anything for the Lord's people. No; not a thing would they do, but hoped they would perish in the wilderness. 11:17.

When I was written to in Nauvoo by the President of the United States, through another person, inquiring, "Where are you going, Mr. Young?" I replied that I did not know where we should land. We had men in England trying to negotiate for Vancouver's Island, and we sent a shipload of Saints round Cape Horn to California. Men in authority asked, "Where are you going to?" "We may go to California, or to Vancouver's Island." When the Pioneer company reached Green River, we met Samuel Brannan and a few others from California, and they wanted us to go there. I remarked, "Let us go to California, and we cannot stay there over five years; but let us stay in the mountains, and we can raise our own potatoes, and eat them; and I calculate to stay here." We are still on the backbone of the animal, where the bone and the sinew are, and we intend to stay here, and all hell cannot help themselves. 5:230-231.

Mark our settlements for six hundred miles in these mountains and then mark the path that we made coming here, building the bridges and making the roads across the prairies, mountains and canyons! We came here penniless in old wagons, our friends back telling us to "take all the provisions you can; for you can get no more! Take all the seed grain you can, for you can get none there!" We did this, and in addition to all this we have gathered all the poor we could, and the Lord has planted us in these valleys, promising that he would hide us up for a little season until his wrath and indignation passed over the nations. Will we trust in the Lord? Yes. 13:216.

The Saints were poor when they came into this valley, twenty-five years ago. They picked up a few buckskins, antelope skins, sheep skins, buffalo skins, and made leggings and moccasins of them, and wrapped the buffalo robes around them. Some had blankets and some had not; some had shirts, and I guess some had not. One man told me that he had not a shirt for himself or family. 15:158.

I will venture to say that not one of four out of my family had shoes to their feet when we came to this valley. 11:288.

We printed the first papers, except about two, set out the first orchards, raised the first wheat, kept almost the first schools, and made the first improvements in our pioneering, in a great measure, from the Mississippi river to the Pacific Ocean; and here we got at last, so as to be out of the way of everybody, if possible. We thought we would get as far as we could from the face of man; we wanted to get to a strange land, like Abraham, that we might be where we should not be continually wrong with somebody or other, and have them crying, "Oh, you Mormons!" and have the priests preaching, the press printing, the drunkard swearing, and all, high and low, rich and poor, wishing these poor "Mormons" were out of the way. We got out of the way as far as we could; and if we can get out of the way any farther and do any good, we are ready to get out of the way; but I think we are as far out of the way as we need to be; and we have got on the highway which has been cast up, and I think we had better stay here. 14:208.

Mormon Battalion—When we were right in the midst of Indians, who were said to be hostile, five hundred men were called to go to Mexico to fight the Mexicans, and, said Mr. Benton—"If you do not send them we will cover you up, and there will be no more of you." I do not want to think of these things, their authors belong to the class I referred to yesterday—the enemies of mankind, those who would destroy innocence, truth, righteousness and the Kingdom of God from the earth. We sent these five hundred men to fight the Mexicans, and those of us who remained behind labored and raised all that we needed to feed ourselves in the wilderness. We had to pay our own schoolteachers, raise our own bread and earn our own clothing, or go without, there was no other choice. We did it then, and we are able to do the same today. 16:19.

With regard to our going into the wilderness, and our there being called upon to turn out five hundred able-bodied men to go to Mexico, we had then seen every religious and political right trampled under foot by mobocrats; there were none left to defend our rights; we were driven from every right which freemen ought to possess. In forming that battalion of five hundred men, brother Kimball and myself rode day and night, until we had raised the full number of men the Government called for. Captain Allen said to me, using his own words, "I have fallen in love with your people. I love them as I never loved a people before." He was a friend to the uttermost. When he had marched that Mormon Battalion as far as Fort Leavenworth, he was thrown upon a sickbed where I then believed, and do now, he was nursed, taken care of, and doctored to the silent tomb, and the battalion went on with God for their friend.

That battalion took up their line of march from Fort Leavenworth by way of Santa Fe, and over the desert and dreary route, and planted themselves in the lower part of California, to the joy of all the officers and men that were loyal. At the time of their arrival, General Kearney was in a straitened position, and Colonel P. St. George Cooke promptly marched the battalion to his relief, and said to him, "We have the boys here now that can put all things right." The boys in that battalion performed their duty faithfully. I never think of that little company of men without the next thoughts being, "God bless them for ever and for ever." All this we did to prove to the Government that we were loyal. Previous to this, when we left Nauvoo, we knew that they were going to call upon us, and we were prepared for it in our faith and in our feelings. I knew then as well as I do now that the Government would call for a battalion of men out of that part of Israel, to test our loyalty to the Government. Thomas H. Benton, if I have been rightly informed, obtained the requisition to call for that battalion, and, in case of non-compliance with that requisition, to call on the militia of Missouri and Iowa, and other states, if necessary, and to call volunteers from Illinois, from which state we had been driven, to destroy the camp of Israel. This same Mr. Benton said to the President of the United States, in the presence of some other persons, "Sir, they are a pestilential race, and ought to become extinct." 10:106.

Have not this people invariably evinced their friendly feelings, disposition, and patriotism towards the Government by every act and proof which can be given by any people?

Permit me to draw your attention, for a moment, to a few facts in relation to raising the battalion for the Mexican war. When the storm cloud of persecution lowered down upon us on every side, when every avenue was closed against us, our leaders treacherously betrayed and slain by the authorities of the Government in which we lived, and no hope of relief could penetrate through the thick darkness and gloom which surrounded us on every side, no voice was raised in our behalf, and the general Government was silent to our appeals. When we had been insulted and abused all the day long, by those in authority requiring us to give up our arms, and by every other act of insult and abuse which the prolific imagination of our enemies could devise to test, as they said, our patriotism, which requisitions, be it known, were always complied with on our part; and when we were finally compelled to flee, for the preservation of our lives and the lives of our wives and children, to the wilderness; I ask, had we not reason to feel that our enemies were also in favor of our destruction? Had we not, I ask, some reason to consider them all, both in people and the Government, alike our enemies?

And when, in addition to all this, and while fleeing from our enemies, another test of fidelity and patriotism was contrived by them for our destruction, and acquiesced in by the Government (through the agency of a distinguished politician who evidently sought, and thought he had planned, our overthrow and total annihilation) consisting of a requisition from the war department, to furnish a battalion of five hundred men to fight under their officers, and for them, in the war then existing with Mexico, I ask again, could we refrain from considering both people and Government our most deadly foes? Look a moment at our situation, and the circumstances under which this requisition was made. We were migrating, we knew not whither, except that it was our intention to go beyond the reach of our enemies. We had no home, save our wagons and tents, and no store of provisions and clothing; but had to earn our daily bread by leaving our families in isolated locations for safety, and going among our enemies to labor. Were we not, even before this cruel requisition was made, unmercifully borne down by oppression and persecution past endurance by any other community? But under these trying circumstances we were required to turn out of our traveling camps five hundred of our most efficient men, leaving the old, the young, the women upon the hands of the residue, to take care of and support; and in case we refused to comply with so unreasonable a requirement, we were to be deemed enemies to the Government, and fit only for the slaughter.

Look also at the proportion of the number required of us, compared with that of any other portion of the Republic. A requisition of only thirty thousand from a population of more than twenty millions was all that was wanted, and more than was furnished, amounting to only one person and a half to a thousand inhabitants. If all other circumstances had been equal, if we could have left our families in the enjoyment of peace, quietness, and security in the houses from which we had been driven, our quota of an equitable requisition would not have exceeded four persons. Instead of this, five hundred must go, thirteen thousand percent above an equal ratio, even if all other things had been equal, but under the peculiar circumstances in which it was made comparison fails to demonstrate, and reason itself totters beneath its enormity. And for whom were we to fight? As I have already shown, for those that we had every reason to believe were our most deadly foes. Could the Government have expected our compliance therewith? Did they expect it? Did not our enemies believe that we would spurn, with becoming resentment and indignation, such an unhallowed proposition? And were they not prepared to make our rejection of it a pretext to inflame the Government still more against us, and thereby accomplish their hellish purposes upon an innocent people, in their utter extinction? And how was this proposition received, and how was it responded to by this people? I went myself, in company with a few of my brethren, between one and two hundred miles along the several routes of travel, stopping at every little camp, using our influence to obtain volunteers, and on the day appointed for the rendezvous the required complement was made up; and this was all accomplished in about twenty days from the time that the requisition was made known.

Our battalion went to the scene of action, not in easy berths on steamboats, nor with a few months' absence, but on foot over two thousand miles across trackless deserts and barren plains, experiencing every degree of privation, hardship, and suffering during some two years' absence before they could rejoin their families. Thus was our deliverance again effected by the interposition of that All-wise Being who can discern the end from the beginning, and overrule the wicked intentions of men to promote the advancement of his cause upon the earth. Thus were we saved from our enemies by complying with their, as hitherto, unjust and unparalleled exactions; again proving our loyalty to the Government.

Here permit me to pay a tribute of respect to the memory of Captain Allen, the bearer of this requisition from the Government. He was a gentleman full of humane feelings, and, had he been spared, would have smoothed the path, and made easy the performance of this duty, so far as laid in his power. His heart was wrung with sympathy when he saw our situation, and filled with wonder when he witnessed the enthusiastic patriotism and ardor which so promptly complied with his requirement; again proving, as we had hundreds of times before proved, by our acts, that we were belied by our enemies, and that we were as ready, and even more so than any other inhabitants of the Republic, to shoulder the musket, and go forth to fight the battles of our common country, or stand in her defense. History furnishes no parallel, either of the severity or injustice of the demand, or in the alacrity, faithfulness, and patriotism with which it was answered and complied. Thus can we cite instance after instance of persons holding legal authority, being moved upon, through the misrepresentation and influence of our enemies to insult us as a people, by requiring a test of our patriotism. How long must this state of things continue? So long as the people chose to remain in wilful ignorance with regard to us; so long as they choose to misinterpret our views, misrepresent our feelings, and misunderstand our policy. 2:173.

We made and broke the road from Nauvoo to this place. Some of the time we followed Indian trails, some of the time we ran by the compass; when we left the Missouri river we followed the Platte. And we killed rattlesnakes by the cord in some places; and made roads and built bridges till our backs ached. Where we could not build bridges across rivers, we ferried our people across, until we arrived here, where we found a few naked Indians, a few wolves and rabbits, and any amount of crickets; but as for a green tree or a fruit tree, or any green field, we found nothing of the kind, with the exception of a few cottonwoods and willows on the edge of City Creek. For some 1200 or 1300 miles we carried every particle of provision we had when we arrived here. When we left our homes we picked up what the mob did not steal of our horses, oxen and calves, and some women drove their own teams here. Instead of 365 pounds of breadstuff when they started from the Missouri river, there was not half of them had half of it. We had to bring our seed grain, our farming utensils, bureaus, secretaries, sideboards, sofas, pianos, large looking glasses, fine chairs, carpets, nice shovels and tongs and other fine furniture, with all the parlor, cook stoves, etc., and we had to bring these things piled together with some women and children, helter-skelter, topsy-turvy, with broken-down horses, ring-boned, spavined, pole evil, fistula and hipped; oxen with three legs, and cows with one teat. This was our only means of transportation, and if we had not brought our goods in this manner we would not have had them, for there was nothing here. You may say this is a burlesque. Well, I mean it as such, for we, comparatively speaking, really came here naked and barefoot. 12:286-287.

Settlement in the Great Salt Lake Valley—In the days of Joseph we have sat many hours at a time conversing about this very country. Joseph has often said, "If I were only in the Rocky Mountains with a hundred faithful men, I would then be happy, and ask no odds of mobocrats." 11:16.

I do not wish men to understand I had anything to do with our being moved here, that was the providence of the Almighty; it was the power of God that wrought out salvation for this people, I never could have devised such a plan. 4:41.

I did not devise the great scheme of the Lord's opening the way to send this people to these mountains. Joseph contemplated the move for years before it took place, but he could not get here, for there was a watch placed upon him continually to see that he had no communication with the Indians. This was in consequence of that which is written in the Book of Mormon; one of the first evils alleged against him was that he was going to connive with the Indians; but did he ever do anything of the kind? No, he always strove to promote the best interest of all, both red and white. Was it by any act of ours that this people were driven into their midst? We are now their neighbors, we are on their land, for it belongs to them as much as any soil ever belonged to any man on earth; we are drinking their water, using their fuel and timber, and raising our food from their ground. 4:41.

We have faith, we live by faith; we came to these mountains by faith. We came here, I often say, though to the ears of some the expression may sound rather rude, naked and barefoot, and comparatively this is true. 13:172.

We had to have faith to come here. When we met Mr. Bridger on the Big Sandy River, said he, "Mr. Young, I would give a thousand dollars if I knew an ear of corn could be ripened in the Great Basin." Said I, "Wait eighteen months and I will show you many of them." Did I say this from knowledge? No, it was my faith; but we had not the least encouragement—from natural reasoning and all that we could learn of this country—of its sterility, its cold and frost, to believe that we could ever raise anything. But we travelled on, breaking the road through the mountains and building bridges until we arrived here, and then we did everything we could to sustain ourselves. We had faith that we could raise grain; was there any harm in this? Not at all. If we had not had faith, what would have become of us? We would have gone down in unbelief, have closed up every resource for our sustenance and should never have raised anything. 13:173.

I cannot help being here. We might have gone to Vancouver's Island; and if we had, we should probably have been driven away or used up before this time. But here we are in the valleys of the mountains, where the Lord directed me to lead the people. The brethren who are in foreign countries desire to gather to the gathering-place of the Saints, and they have for the present to come to Great Salt Lake City. They cannot help that. Why did we not go to San Francisco? Because the Lord told me not: "For there are lions in the way, and they will devour the lambs, if you take them there." What now can we do? Why, instead of being merchants, instead of going to St. Louis to buy goods, we can go down to our Dixie land, the southern part of our Territory, and raise cotton and manufacture goods for ourselves. 9:105.

A great many wanted to go to the Gila River; that was proposed when we first came to this valley. It was said to be a lovely country, and that men could live there almost without labor. What if we had gone there? You see what has followed us here; but what would have been the result, if we had gone there? Long before this time we would have been outnumbered by our enemies; there would have been more against us than for us in our community. Suppose we had gone to Texas, where Lyman Wight went? He tried to make all the Saints believe that Joseph wanted to take the whole Church there. Long before this, we would have been killed, or compelled to leave the country. We could not have lived there. 4:344.

We came to these mountains because we had no other place to go to. We had to leave our homes and possessions on the fertile lands of Illinois to make our dwelling places in these desert wilds, on barren, sterile plains amid lofty, rugged mountains. None dare come here to live until we came here, and we now find it to be one of the best countries in the world for us. 10:223.

Five years ago we were menaced on every side by the cruel persecutions of our inveterate enemies; hundreds of families, who had been forced from their homes, and compelled to leave behind them their all, were wandering as exiles in a state of abject destitution; but, by the favor of heaven, we have been enabled to surmount all these difficulties, and can assemble here today in the chamber of these mountains, where there are none to make us afraid, far from our persecutors, far from the turmoil and confusion of the old world. 1:376.

Seven years ago tomorrow, about eleven o'clock, I crossed the Mississippi River, with my brethren, for this place, not knowing, at that time, whither we were going, but firmly believing that the Lord had in reserve for us a good place in the mountains, and that he would lead us directly to it. It is but seven years since we left Nauvoo, and we are now ready to build another temple. I look back upon our labors with pleasure. Here are hundreds and thousands of people that have not had the privileges that some of us have had. Do you ask, what privileges? Why, of running the gauntlet, of passing through the narrows. They have not had the privilege of being robbed and plundered of their property, of being in the midst of mobs and death, as many of us have. 1:279.

When the pioneers came into these valleys we knew nearly all the families which composed the settlements in Upper and Lower California. 10:189.

The most of the people called Latter-day Saints have been taken from the rural and manufacturing districts of this and the old countries, and they belong to the poorest of the poor. Many of them, I may say the great majority, never had anything around them to make life very desirable; they have been acquainted with poverty and wretchedness, hence it cannot be expected that they should manifest that refinement and culture prevalent among the rich. Many and many a man here, who is now able to ride in his wagon and perhaps in his carriage, for years before he started for Zion never saw daylight. His days were spent in the coal mines, and his daily toil would commence before light in the morning and continue until after dark at night. Now what can be expected from a community so many of whose members have been brought up like this; or if not just like this, still under circumstances of poverty and privation? Certainly not what we might expect from those reared under more favorable circumstances. But I will tell you what we have in our mind's eye with regard to these very people, and what we are trying to make of them. We take the poorest we can find on earth who will receive the truth, and we are trying to make ladies and gentlemen of them. We are trying to educate them, to school their children, and to so train them that they may be able to gather around them the comforts of life, that they may pass their lives as the human family should do—that their days, weeks, and months may be pleasant to them. We prove that this is our design, for the result, to some extent, is already before us. 14:103.

Talk about these rich valleys, why there is not another people on the earth that could have come here and lived. We prayed over the land, and dedicated it and the water, air and everything pertaining to them unto the Lord, and the smiles of heaven rested on the land and it became productive, and today yields us the best of grain, fruit and vegetables. 12:288.

There never has been a land, from the days of Adam until now, that has been blessed more than this land has been blessed by our Father in Heaven; and it will still be blessed more and more, if we are faithful and humble, and thankful to God for the wheat and the corn, the oats, the fruit, the vegetables, the cattle and everything he bestows upon us, and try to use them for he building up of his Kingdom on the earth. 10:35.

You inquire if we shall stay in these mountains. I answer yes, as long as we please to do the will of God, our Father in Heaven. If we are pleased to turn away from the holy commandments of the Lord Jesus Christ, as ancient Israel did, every man turning to his own way, we shall be scattered and peeled, driven before our enemies and persecuted, until we learn to remember the Lord our God and are willing to walk in his ways. 11:274.

Many may inquire, "How long shall we stay here?" We shall stay here just as long as we ought to. "Shall we be driven, when we go?" If we will so live as to be satisfied with ourselves, and will not drive ourselves from our homes, we shall never be driven from them. Seek for the best wisdom you can obtain, learn how to apply your labor, build good houses, make fine farms, set out apple, pear, and other fruit trees that will flourish here, also the mountain currant and raspberry bushes, plant strawberry beds, and build up and adorn a beautiful city. The question now arises—"Do you think it best for us to live in cities?" Lay out your cities, but not so large that you cannot readily raise the whole city, should an enemy come upon you. 8:288.

I do not know that I have prayed for rain since I have been in these valleys until this year, during which I believe that I have prayed two or three times for rain, and then with a faint heart, for there is plenty of water flowing down these canyons in crystal streams as pure as the breezes of Zion, and it is our business to use them. 3:331.

When water is brought to the termination of the canal, which we can accomplish in a few days, I presume that the reservoirs on the line of the work and those portions which are excavated in full view contain water enough to allow the people to irrigate when necessary, and thus do away with the practice of watering only two hours a week on a city lot, and much of that to be done in the night. And that is not all, for by the time the water is fairly on a lot it is taken by the next person whose right it is to use it. And lots which have had thousands of dollars expended on them, and which would yield more than a thousand dollars' worth of fruit and vegetables, could they be properly irrigated, are only allowed a small stream of water for two hours once a week, and at the same time an adjoining lot planted with corn, the hills six feet apart and one stalk in a hill, comparatively speaking, the balance of the ground being covered with weeds, is allotted the same time and amount of water as the one on which the fruit trees and other choice vegetation are worth thousands of dollars.

There ought to be a reformation in the distribution of the water. The man who will not raise five dollars' worth of produce on his lot, has the same water privilege as the man who could raise a thousand dollars' worth. For instance, brother Staines gets the water for two hours in a week, and what are his fruit trees worth? He could make his thousand dollars a year from them, if he were disposed to sell the fruit instead of giving it away, could he have a fair portion of water. I have a lot just below him well cultivated in fruit trees, a nursery, and choice vegetables, I also can only have the water on my lot for two hours in a week; when lots nearby with but little on them except weeds, get the same water privilege, and that too in the day time, while we have to use it in the night. Water masters ought to look to this matter, until they have arranged a more just distribution. 3:329.

The river Jordan will be brought out and made to flow through a substantial canal to Great Salt Lake City. When this is done, it will not only serve as a means of irrigating, but it will form a means of transportation from the south end of Utah Lake to Great Salt Lake City. 11:116.

As soon as that is completed from Big Cottonwood to this city, we expect to make a canal on the west side of Jordan, and take its water along the east base of the west mountains, as there is more farming land on the west side of that river than on the east. When that work is accomplished we shall continue our exertions, until Provo river runs to this city. We intend to bring it around the point of the mountain to Little Cottonwood, from that to Big Cottonwood, and lead its waters upon all the land from Provo canyon to this city, for there is more water runs in that stream alone than would be needed for that purpose. 3:329.

Until the Latter-day Saints came here, not a person among all the mountaineers and those who had traveled here, so far as we could learn, believed that an ear of corn would ripen in these valleys. We know that corn and wheat produce abundantly here, and we know that we have an excellent region wherein to raise cattle, horses, and every other kind of domestic animal that we need. We also knew this when we came here thirteen years ago this summer. Bridger said to me, "Mr. Young, I would give a thousand dollars, if I knew that an ear of corn could be ripened in these mountains. I have been here twenty years, and have tried it in vain, over and over again." I told him if he would wait a year or two we would show him what could be done. A man named Wells, living with Miles Goodyear, where now is Ogden City, had a few beans growing, and carried water from the river in a pail to irrigate them. 8:288.

INDEX

K

L

M

N

O